ROBERT LOUIS STEVENSON

ROBERT LOUIS STEVENSON

A Biography

CLAIRE HARMAN

HarperCollins*Publishers*

HarperCollins*Publishers*
77–85 Fulham Palace Road,
Hammersmith, London w6 8jb

www.harpercollins.co.uk

Published by HarperCollins*Publishers* 2005

2

A catalogue record for this book
is available from the British Library

ISBN 0 00 711321 8

Set in PostScript Linotype Sabon with Bulmer display by
Rowland Phototypesetting Ltd, Bury St Edmunds, Suffolk

Printed and bound in Great Britain by
Clays Ltd, St Ives plc

To
Paul Strohm,
dear companion

Contents

Illustrations

Margaret Stevenson and young Smout, still in petticoats, 1854. *(Reproduced courtesy of the Writers Museum, Edinburgh)*

Thomas Stevenson and RLS, aged about seven. *(Reproduced courtesy of the Writers Museum, Edinburgh)*

Skerryvore lighthouse, designed and built by RLS's uncle Alan. *(Photograph © Jean Guichard)*

The Old Town of Edinburgh in the mid-nineteenth century. *(Photograph by G.W. Wilson, 1866. Mansell Collection)*

RLS aged fifteen. *(Reproduced courtesy of Lady Dunpark)*

17 Heriot Row, Edinburgh, the Stevensons' home from 1857.

The Stevenson family on holiday, around 1867. *(Reproduced courtesy of the Writers Museum, Edinburgh)*

Professor Henry Charles Fleeming Jenkin, RLS's friend and mentor during the early 1870s.

RLS, advocate, in 1875. *(Reproduced courtesy of the Writers Museum, Edinburgh)*

Sidney Colvin.

Charles Baxter.

William Ernest Henley. *(Photograph © Hulton Archive/Getty Images)*

Edmund Gosse, painted by John Singer Sargent. *(Reproduced courtesy of the National Portrait Gallery, London)*

Fanny Sitwell.

Fanny Osbourne in her youth. *(Reproduced courtesy of the Beinecke Rare Book and Manuscript Library, Yale University)*

Bob Stevenson with fellow artists at Grez-sur-Loing in the mid- to late 1870s.

A trans-continental emigrant train in the 1880s, similar to the one RLS describes in *Across the Plains*. *(Reproduced courtesy of Mary Evans Picture Library)*

Jules Simoneau and Jules Tavernier in Monterey. *(Reproduced courtesy of the Writers Museum, Edinburgh)*

RLS in 1880, aged twenty-nine. *(Reproduced courtesy of the Writers Museum, Edinburgh)*

Fanny Osbourne in 1880, just before her marriage to RLS. *(Reproduced courtesy of the Writers Museum, Edinburgh)*

Joe Strong's tidied-up vision of RLS and Fanny in the miners' dormitory at Silverado, used as frontispiece for *The Silverado Squatters. (Reproduced courtesy of the British Museum, London)*

The map of Treasure Island which appeared in the first edition of the book. *(Reproduced courtesy of the British Museum, London)*

RLS's 'edenic' home in Hyères, 'La Solitude'. *(Reproduced courtesy of the Writers Museum, Edinburgh)*

Robert Louis Stevenson and his Wife, by John Singer Sargent. *(Reproduced courtesy of the Bridgeman Art Library, London)*

Lloyd Osbourne aged about twenty. *(Reproduced courtesy of the Writers Museum, Edinburgh)*

The actor Richard Mansfield as Jekyll/Hyde, a publicity picture for the first American dramatisation in 1887. *(Reproduced courtesy of the Library of Congress)*

Henry James in 1886, drawn by John Singer Sargent.

RLS photographed by Sir Percy Shelley, 1886 or '87.

LLoyd, Fanny and RLS on the porch of Baker's Cottage at Saranac Lake, New York, during the winter of 1887–88. *(Reproduced courtesy of the Writers Museum, Edinburgh)*

RLS playing his flageolet in bed. *(Reproduced courtesy of the Writers Museum, Edinburgh)*

The elegant and expensive yacht *Casco,* on which RLS made his first Pacific cruise. *(Reproduced courtesy of the Writers Museum, Edinburgh)*

RLS balanced on the bowsprit of the schooner *Equator. (Reproduced courtesy of the Writers Museum, Edinburgh)*

Lloyd, Fanny, RLS and Margaret Stevenson entertaining David Kalakaua, King of Hawaii, on board the *Casco,* 1890. *(Reproduced courtesy of the Writers Museum, Edinburgh)*

Tembinok, the cross-dressing poet-king of Apemama. *(Reproduced courtesy of the British Library, London)*

Mataafa Iosefo, the chief whose claim to power in Samoa was vigorously supported by RLS.

Nan Tok', Fanny Stevenson, Nan Takauti and RLS on the Gilbert Islands. *(Reproduced courtesy of the Writers Museum, Edinburgh)*

RLS and Fanny on the balcony of the original building at Vailima.

RLS on his horse Jack at Vailima, c.1891. *(Reproduced courtesy of the British Library, London)*

The finished house at Vailima.

The household at Vailima in May 1892. *(Reproduced courtesy of the Writers Museum, Edinburgh)*

Belle, RLS and Fanny playing cards, c.1892.

Fanny aged fifty-three in Sydney, March 1893. *(Reproduced courtesy of the Writers Museum, Edinburgh)*

4 December 1894. Sosimo guards the body of RLS, lying in state in the hall at Vailima. *(Reproduced courtesy of the Writers Museum, Edinburgh)*

Acknowledgements

I would like to thank the following for their help with my research: the librarians and staff of the Bodleian Library; the British Library; the London Library; the Beinecke Rare Book and Manuscript Library, Yale University; New York Public Library; the National Library of Scotland; the Bancroft Library, University of California at Berkeley; les Archives de l'Assistance Publique-Hôpitaux de Paris; the Pacific Room of Apia Library, Upolu, Western Samoa; the Stevenson-Osbourne archive at the Robert Louis Stevenson Silverado Museum, St Helena, Napa, California; the Robert Louis Stevenson Museum at Saranac Lake, New York; the Writers' Museum, Lady Stair's House, Edinburgh; the Stevenson Museum at Villa Vailima, Upolu, Western Samoa; and the National University of Samoa. Anyone involved in Stevenson research has reason to be grateful for the website maintained by Richard Dury on behalf of the Association of Stevenson Scholars, an invaluable resource.

I am indebted to many people for help with specific queries, ideas, leads, suggestions and practical assistance during the writing of this book: Stuart Airlie, Scott Ashley, Mark Bostridge, Kate Clanchy, Aisling Foster, Lyndall Gordon, Siamon Gordon, Elaine Greig, Richard Holmes, Nicola Ireland, Andrew Kelly, Patrick McGuinness, Robyn Marsack, Agnès Masson, Ernest Mehew, Barry Menikoff, Andrew Nash, Nicholas Rankin, Julia Reid, Graham Robb, Karen Steele, Roger Swearingen, Belinda Thomson and Jenny Uglow. Mike Delahunt provided hot drinks and helpful guidance on a freezing January day at Baker's Cottage, Devon Jersild drove me there; while at the other end of my travels Gatoloai Tili Afamasaga, Mata'ino Te'o and Juliana Tevaga all helped me to a better understanding of Stevenson's years in Samoa. In Edinburgh Isabel Schmidt and Alison Harman have been kind hosts, as have Belinda and Richard Thomson and John and Felicitas Macfie, current owners of 17 Heriot Row.

At HarperCollins, I would like to thank Richard Johnson and

Robert Lacey for their friendly support and deft editorial skills and Holley Miles for her work on the illustrations. I am especially grateful to the trustees and administrators of the Leverhulme Trust for their award of an emeritus grant for travel expenses related to my research and to the Arts Council for a Writers' Award in 2003.

Claire Harman
AUGUST 2004

Preface

Robert Louis Stevenson has always been a popular author but never a canonical one. *The Strange Case of Dr Jekyll and Mr Hyde*, *Treasure Island*, *Kidnapped*, *A Child's Garden of Verses* – four very different popular classics – have not appeared on syllabuses of nineteenth-century literature until very recently. The critical consensus up to the last twenty years or so seems to have been that Stevenson's works were not quite 'literary' enough to study.

This has been an odd fate for a man who was thought to be, by his contemporaries in the 1870s, the star of his generation, an English stylist of giddying promise, an Elia for the *fin-de-siècle*. In his hands, the personal essay seemed to be coming to perfection in an arresting combination of high polish and novel directness, while aphorisms poured from his young mouth straight into the dictionaries of quotations. His influential friends in the world of letters, William Ernest Henley, Sidney Colvin, Leslie Stephen, Henry James and Edmund Gosse, all waited eagerly for the masterpiece. Would he excel as an essayist? a playwright? a poet? a historical novelist to equal Sir Walter Scott? His rivals watched him carefully too, none more so than Thomas Hardy, Stevenson's fellow heir-in-waiting to George Meredith in the 1880s, and Joseph Conrad, keen to distance himself, after Stevenson's death, from a writer he feared had influenced him too much.

Stevenson's impatience with his friends was clear when, after the publication of *Dr Jekyll and Mr Hyde*, they began to lament his decline into mass popularity. Making money was of more immediate importance to the invalid author than the production of 'damned masterpieces', however much he would have liked to fuse the two if possible. Though he looked like a dilettante, a flimsy 'Ariel' (as Henley and Colvin both described him), Stevenson was a highly professional writer and produced hundreds of works: essays, poems and articles, melodramas, polemical pamphlets and some thirty full-length books, among which were works as diverse as *New Arabian Nights*, *The Ebb-Tide*, *Prince Otto* and *In the South Seas*. None of these is read much any more, but then neither are his most celebrated books: *Dr Jekyll and Mr Hyde* and *Treasure Island* are so well-known that they hardly require to be read at all. We all understand what 'Jekyll-and-Hyde' signifies, and Long John Silver is more real to most people than any historical buccaneer. So in some senses, Stevenson's neglect has come at him from more than one direction.

We think of writers' careers in terms of what they publish; they think of what they have written, or intended to write. For a variety of reasons, Stevenson made a great many beginnings and relatively few ends. The extent of his unfinished works only began to be clear with the publication of Roger Swearingen's *Guide to the Prose Writings of Robert Louis Stevenson* in 1980, and was dramatically confirmed by the wealth of new evidence presented in the eight-volume Yale edition of *The Letters of Robert Louis Stevenson*, published in 1994–95, the most substantial and re-vealing addition to the Stevenson canon since the author's death. Stevenson emerged from the new *Letters* not just as an outstanding practitioner of the form but as a man of penetrating intelligence and strong feelings, with a wide range of interests, a volatile atten-tion span, powerful ambition to succeed and a constant, pressing desire to earn money. He appeared more quirkily humorous than before, but also more vulnerable, for this most eloquent of writers turns out to have been a slave to writer's block, strangely fixated on his second-rate works and casual about his best ones, always anxious that his chosen profession was neither very admirable (unlike his engineer family's) nor very sustainable.

The sense of urgency about establishing himself as a writer that Stevenson felt and his friends shared was sharpened by their con-cept of him as doomed to die young. From infancy, Stevenson's health had been poor, his physique underdeveloped, his ailments (watched over with undue care by hypochondriac parents) legion. No wonder he became convinced of his own short lease on life, and perturbed at the thought of 'outliving' it into maturity, even old age. The effects on his writing were transparent: if difficulties presented themselves, he was tempted – felt almost licensed – to bail out. Hence his biography of Hazlitt, his history of the Act of Union, biography of Viscount Dundee and novel about the Peninsular War are just four of dozens of unfinished *magna opera*, and many of his published works blazon their own incompleteness and uncertainty with a brilliant insouciance. And while he liked to think he could have achieved much more in good health, the truth is probably the reverse. Just as Coleridge's person from Porlock relieved the poet from the drudgery of having to finish 'Kubla Khan', chronic illness provided Stevenson with a constantly available excuse not to polish or even complete many of his works, leaving him free to do what he enjoyed most, which was to start something new.

What illness, or combination of illnesses, he suffered from becomes less clear as we discover more about Stevenson's life. He was brought up in the fear and expectation of developing tuberculosis, and his chest ailments all pointed to that diagnosis, although on the occasions when tests were carried out (and Stevenson had access to the very best medical attention money could buy) they never proved positive. The blood-spitting that began when he was thirty certainly indicated consumption, but he might also have been suffering from hypertension, cardiac disease, syphilis, or a combination of all of those. The cause of his death, aged forty-four, was recorded as a cerebral haemorrhage.

The fact that some things become less knowable about a subject the more data accrues around them is of utmost importance to any biographer. Order – the existing order, the existing story – will break down to some extent and the edges of the familiar portrait blur. This is the point at which it becomes possible to see glimpses of the messiness and complexity of real life poking through.

Stevenson provides a willing accomplice to this process: he was unusually greedy of experience and open to the widest possible interpretation of personality. Duality, the theme of his most famous work, is present in almost all his writing: *The Master of Ballantrae*, 'Markheim', *Deacon Brodie, Catriona*; he even introduced the theme into a topographical study of Edinburgh. He was a bilingual writer, too, in Scots and English, and 'double-handed', ambidextrous. Doubleness is central to his very theory of composition, as set out in his essay 'A Chapter on Dreams', where he claims that the inventive side of his writing was beyond his conscious control. He was fascinated by the uneven surface of 'the self', its endless ability to surprise the conscious man. In a letter of 1892 to F.W.H. Myers, one of the founders of the Society for Psychical Research (of which Stevenson was a member), Stevenson recalled various times in his life as an invalid when high fever had made him aware of having 'two consciousnesses'. He characterised these as *Myself* and *the other fellow*; the latter irrational and absurd, the former, his right mind, painfully aware of its temporary subordination. It wasn't the conflict between them that interested him so much as his awareness of their co-existence, at once scientific and poetic. More than any other nineteenth-century writer he might have said, along with his admired Walt Whitman, 'I am large, I contain multitudes'.

Stevenson was an ironist and iconoclast, an admirer of Herbert Spencer, Darwin, Thoreau and Whitman and an influential thinker in his own right, much more than is recognised. His essays addressed the urgent scientific, moral and aesthetic questions of the day and his novels and stories dramatised them. He was one of the least 'Victorian' of all Victorian writers. As a young man, he longed to emulate the style and substance of the three-decker novel, but in fact he became part of the movement which supplanted that model, a prototype modern man of letters. His interest in psychology anticipated the concerns of the next century, his confessional tone was tuned to it, even the forms he liked best – those of short story and novella – have been more popular in our own day than in his. Writers as diverse as Graham Greene, Cesare Pavese, Italo Calvino, Vladimir Nabokov and Jorge Luis Borges have revered him as a master (it is said that Borges kept his collection of Stevenson's works separate from all others on his bookshelves), and generations of readers have delighted in his wonderful powers of invention. It is this multitudinous character, inconsistent, original and constantly surprising, whom I wish to present.

1

BARON BROADNOSE

Born 1850 at Edinburgh. Pure Scotch blood; descended from
the Scotch Lighthouse Engineers, three generations. Himself
educated for the family profession . . . But the marrow of the
family was worked out, and he declined into the man of letters.

Robert Louis Stevenson, 'Autobiographical Note'[1]

IN 1884 OR THEREABOUTS, Robert Louis Stevenson purchased
a copy of a slim booklet by the scientist Francis Galton (grandson
of Erasmus Darwin and inventor of the term 'eugenics'), that pur-
ported to help members of the public forecast the mental and
physical faculties of their children by arranging in tabular form as
much data as could be gathered about their ancestors. No clear
way of making deductions from this process was indicated; Galton
seemed merely to be suggesting that the *Record of Family Faculties*
would serve as a sort of life album for future perusal. In fact his
design was more 'to further the science of heredity' than to
enlighten individuals about their genes, for Galton was offering a
prize of £500 to whichever reader compiled 'the best extracts'
from the point of view of 'completeness', 'character of evidence',
'cleanness' and 'conciseness', to be sent, with accompanying docu-
mentation if possible, to his London address.

Robert Louis Stevenson did not oblige the insatiable statistician
by posting off his copy of the booklet, and only filled in two pages
of information, one for each of his parents. Like so many of his
own books, this was one he couldn't quite finish. But Galton's
introductory remarks, full of provocative assumptions about race,

personality, inherited and acquired behaviour, touched subjects of perennial fascination to the scientist-turned-literary man. 'We do not yet know whether any given group of different faculties which may converge by inheritance upon the same family will blend, neutralise, or intensify one another,' Galton had written, 'nor whether they will be metamorphosed and issue in some new form.' The year in which the project was advertised, 1883, was a time when Stevenson himself thought he was going to be a father, an eventuality he had tried to avoid on the grounds of his poor health. But whether or not Stevenson bought Galton's book in order to predict his expected child's chances in the lottery of family attributes, the author's words certainly resonated for himself.

Robert Louis Stevenson characterised his paternal ancestors as 'a family of engineers', which they were for the two generations preceding his own, but in the seventeenth century they had been farmers and maltsters near Glasgow, 'following honest trades [. . .], playing the character parts in the Waverley Novels with propriety, if without distinction', as Stevenson wrote satirically.[2] In the mid-eighteenth century two Stevenson brothers, working in partnership as traders between Glasgow and the West Indies, both died suddenly from tropical fever within six weeks of each other while in pursuit of an agent who had cheated them. Jean, the twenty-three-year-old widow of the younger brother, was left almost destitute by his death, as her father also died in the same month and she had an infant son to support. She moved from Glasgow to Edinburgh with her child, married a man called Hogg, then in the early 1790s met and married her third husband, Thomas Smith, 'merchant burgess', ship-owner, ironmonger and underwriter.

Smith was the founder of the 'family of engineers', or rather, the step-family, since it was his new wife's teenaged son Robert Stevenson, not his own son, James Smith, who was grafted onto his thriving enterprise as heir. Thomas Smith seems to have been a man of enormous industry and ingenuity, setting up a business in lamps and oils, running something called the Greenside Company's Works in Edinburgh (a kind of super-smithy) and inventing a new system of oil lamps for lighthouses to replace the old coal-lit beacons like that on the Isle of May. The lights of 'lights' remained a source of fascination in the step-branch of the family: Robert Stevenson experimented with revolving devices, his son Thomas developed both holophotal and condensing lights, and Robert Louis Stevenson's one and only contribution to the Royal Scottish Society of Arts was a paper on a proposed new device to make lighthouse lights flash. But there was another reminder of this heritage, closer to home. One of Thomas Smith's lamp-making projects was the design of the street lighting in Edinburgh's New Town at the end of the eighteenth century. His parabolic reflector system quadrupled the power of oil-lit lamps and focused their beams, a revolutionary innovation that must have made the elegant Georgian streets look even more modern and sleek, even more of a contrast to the dark, narrow closes and wynds of the Old Town. And it was the successor to one of these lamps, just outside 17 Heriot Row, that Robert Louis Stevenson celebrated many years later in his poem about Leerie the Lamp-Lighter from *A Child's Garden of Verses*:

> *For we are very lucky, with a lamp before the door,*
> *And Leerie stops to light it as he lights so many more;*
> *And O! before you hurry by with ladder and with light,*
> *O Leerie, see a little child and nod to him tonight!*[3]

But the original lighter of the lamps had been the poet's ingenious forebear.*

Thomas Smith's involvement in lighthouse-building began in 1787, just prior to his marriage to Jean Stevenson, when he was

---

* I am grateful to John Macfie for telling me an interesting fact about the real lamplighter on Heriot Row in the 1850s: he was a piece-worker, and therefore habitually rushed his work. So the 'hurrying by' of the poem is more realism than romance.

appointed engineer to the new Board of Northern Lighthouses, a
post his stepson and three grandsons would hold after him. Until
this time, the Scottish coastline had been one of the most dangerous
in the world, so jagged and treacherous that mariners used to steer
well clear of it, keeping north of Orkney and Shetland and west
of the Hebrides. There were no maps or charts of the coastline
before the late sixteenth century, and the first lighthouse, built in
1636 on the Isle of May in the Firth of Forth, was one of only a
handful in existence before the Industrial Revolution. The Spanish
Armada, forced to go north when the English blockaded the
Channel in 1588, lost half its vessels around the Scottish coast
because of its perilousness, and the stormy Atlantic waters continued to claim lives for centuries after.

Little was done about the protection of ships around Scotland
until a series of violent storms in the early 1780s led to public
protests and the setting up of the Northern Lighthouse Board by
an Act of Parliament in 1786, with a mandate to oversee a programme of lighthouse construction. Thomas Smith, whose parabolic reflectors had impressed the Board, was appointed its first
chief engineer and sent south to pick up technical expertise from
an English lighthouse-builder.* Smith needed all the help he could
get; the Board had commissioned him to build four lighthouses,
and he was totally inexperienced. He faced innumerable difficulties, from the very design of the structures to the organisation
of labour and transport of materials to some of the bleakest spots
around the coast. But the former lamp-maker rose to the challenge
and through extraordinary persistence and hard work produced
his first lights, at Kinnaird Head beyond Fraserburgh, Eilean Glas
off Harris, North Ronaldsay and the Mull of Kintyre. None of
them is elegant or ambitious in design, but the fact that they got
built at all is quite remarkable.

Smith's stepson Robert Stevenson was a keen assistant in the

* It is not known who Smith learned from, but it could have been John Smeaton, who
built the third Eddystone light in the 1750s, and whose work was very influential on the
whole Smith/Stevenson family.

works. Jean Stevenson had intended her son for the Church, but engineering and surveying were far more to his taste and he was apprenticed to his stepfather in 1791. He proved fiercely motiv-ated; all summer he was a director of works (superintending the construction of Little Cumbrae light on the Firth of Clyde when he was still only nineteen), while in the winters he studied mathe-matics and sciences at the Andersonian Institute and Edinburgh University. In *Records of a Family of Engineers*, Robert Louis Stevenson wrote with sympathetic admiration of his grandfather's relish for the life:

> The seas into which his labours carried the new engineer were still scarce charted, the coasts still dark; his way on shore was often far beyond the convenience of any road, the isles in which he must sojourn were still partly savage. He must toss much in boats; he must often adventure on horseback by the dubious bridle-track through unfrequented wildernesses; he must sometimes plant his lighthouse in the very camp of wreckers; and he was continually enforced to the vicissitudes of outdoor life. The joy of my grandfather in this career was strong as the love of woman.[4]

The step-relationship between young Robert Stevenson and Thomas Smith was close and admiring, and it makes one wonder where Smith's natural son, James, fitted in – if at all. Thomas Smith was twice a widower before his marriage to Jean Stevenson and had five children by the first wife (only a daughter, Jane, and the son James survived infancy) and one daughter, Mary-Anne, by the second. Little information remains about James except that he left home to found his own ironmongery business, but whether this was the result of some rift with his father is not clear. Certainly to the outside world Robert Stevenson must have looked like Smith's favourite, possibly only, son. The bond between them became even more complicated when Robert married his stepsister Jane in 1799. As Robert's namesake wrote years later, 'The marriage of a man of twenty-seven and a girl of twenty, who have lived for twelve years as brother and sister, is difficult to conceive'[5] – but it was legal. The union was a sort of mirror-image of the parents': in temperament and disposition Jane resembled her pious stepmother as much as Robert did his stepfather, who was now not just parent, employer and teacher, but also father-in-law.

Smith's business, which built not only lighthouses but roads, bridges and harbours, set an intimidating example of industry and efficiency that Robert Stevenson was happy to match, or outdo. He became a full partner in 1800, the year after his marriage, and the next year went south to see for himself some of the English lighthouses and get ideas for the improvement of the firm's designs, especially from John Smeaton's handsome pharos at Eddystone. Stevenson's additions to Thomas Smith's work included adding silvered reflectors to the lights, experimenting with different oils and types of burner (he opted for a variant on the new Argand lamps that had glass chimneys above the flame, and which became standard in Victorian domestic interiors). He also tried to get the reflectors to revolve so that the lights seemed to flash (to make the lighthouse beacons easily distinguishable from lights on shore or at sea).

His ingenuity was great, and so was his ambition; in fact Stevenson turned out to be a ruthlessly single-minded man and greedy of fame. In the early years of the new century he became absorbed by the challenge of building a light on the Bell Rock, the notoriously dangerous reef in the North Sea twelve miles southeast of Arbroath, on the northern approach to the Firth of Forth. It was formerly called Inchcape Rock, but was renamed to commemorate the warning-bell which had been put there in the fourteenth century by the safety-conscious Abbot of Arbroath. At high tide the perilous outcrop, 1,400 feet at its widest, was submerged twelve feet, a death-trap to passing ships. Public pressure on the Board to build a lighthouse had met with little success, even after the loss of the warship York with all hands in the gales of 1799. The cost of the lighthouse programme had finally caught up with the Commissioners, and in any case they considered the Bell Rock simply too dangerous and difficult a location to build on. Their objections were music to the ears of young Stevenson, who relished the chance to overcome the obstacles involved; he surveyed the site independently and conducted a long campaign of letters to the Board, making the vaunting claim that his projected Bell Rock lighthouse was 'a work which cannot be reduced to the common maxims of the arts and which in some measure stands unconnected to any other branch of business'.[6]

Stevenson's lobbying seemed to have paid off when a Bill authorising construction of a lighthouse on the Bell Rock was passed in 1806, but it was not his design that the NLB chose, nor him as chief engineer: that honour went to John Rennie. Stevenson's pride was given an extra knock by his appointment as Rennie's assistant, but instead of making a loud protest he decided to get his own way by subtler means. Over the years it took to build the lighthouse, during which Stevenson was always on site and Rennie rarely, he took over the project bit by bit, and by the time it was finished, in February 1811, he had not only done almost all the work of the chief engineer but had amassed most of the credit too. God-like, he named various parts of the reef after himself, his father-in-law, the head workmen and – strategically – the Commissioners of the Board, and he encouraged the general perception of the project as entirely his own by publishing an *Account of the Bell Rock Lighthouse Including the Details of the Erection and Peculiar Structure of that Edifice*, a stirring record of the technical and human difficulties which had been overcome, in which Rennie was scarcely mentioned. The public and the newspapers were fascinated by the story, and delighted with the lighthouse that so thoroughly revolutionised the safety of the lanes into the Firth. Stevenson was suddenly famous and could be seen round Edinburgh proudly sporting the gold medal sent him by the King of Denmark for his services to seafarers.

Rennie, understandably, was piqued by Stevenson's machinations and considered him dishonest, or at best self-deluding. His assistant engineer had a history of stealing credit, Rennie complained to a friend, and 'has assumed the merit of applying coloured glass to lighthouses, of which Huddart was the actual inventor, and I have no doubt that he will assume the whole merit of planning and erecting the Bell Rock Lighthouse, if he has not already done so'.[7] That was exactly what Stevenson did, and to this day he is credited with the design, which was nothing to do with him. No shadow of guilt or self-doubt troubled the assistant engineer; the carrying-through of a plan was, to him, far more difficult and important than merely generating it. It was an attitude inherited by his son Thomas, who displayed similar confidence in his own viewpoint and who was also accused of professional plagiarism when he 'stepped in and brought to [. . .] perfection' (his son's generous phrase)[8] a revolving light designed by the French inventor Leonor Fresnel. This makes it look as if the family ethos was one of raw self-interest, but the case was rather subtler than that. The Stevensons were old-fashioned, and refused to regis-ter for patent any of their lighthouse inventions, on the grounds that as government appointees 'they regarded their original work as something due already to the nation'.[9] They made a distinction between what was owed to the Northern Lighthouse Board (ser-vice) and what was right for the family business (maximum profit), and willingly gave up exclusive rights in their own inventions in order to be able to cash in on other people's unexploited ideas. This family trait would work out interestingly in Robert Louis Stevenson, whose flexible attitude to matters of intellectual prop-erty led to the most traumatic quarrel of his life, and who remained high-minded about copyright right up to the moment when he wrote a bestseller.

Of all the engineering works that the Stevenson family were involved in, the Bell Rock lighthouse was the most impressive, firing the public imagination with its combination of romantic endeavour and futuristic technology. It already had a celebrator in the Poet Laureate Robert Southey, whose ballad 'The Inchcape Rock', published in 1803, commemorated the story of the Abbot and the bell in thrumming lines:

When the rock was hid by the surge's swell,
The mariners heard the warning bell;
And then they knew the perilous rock,
And blessed the Abbot of Aberbrothok.

Walter Scott also took a keen interest in the Bell Rock, which he visited in 1814. The NLB Commissioners had invited him on a tour of the lighthouses conducted by 'the celebrated engineer' (Scott's phrase) Robert Stevenson. The party went all round the coast, from the Isle of May in the Firth to the Inner Hebrides, calling in at Bell Rock (where Scott wrote some verses in the visitors' book) and getting out, with difficulty, to survey a jagged reef off Tiree called Skerry Vohr which Stevenson was trying to persuade the Commissioners to build a light on. The novelist was gathering material for his next book, *The Pirate*, and worked on his notes with an application which impressed Robert Stevenson, who had not at this date read any of Scott's works. '[Scott] was the most industrious occupier of time,' Stevenson recorded in his journal,

> he wrote much upon deck – often when his seat on the camp stool was by no means steady. He sometimes introduced Rob Roy's exploits in conversation so fully that when I read the Book many parts of it were like a second reading to me.[10]

The description is oddly prophetic of another industrious writer who composed much upon deck and was able to talk of his fictional creations as if they were real, Robert Stevenson's grandson. But it was Scott's work ethic, not his genius, that won Robert Stevenson's approval; he clearly thought artists in general to be rather a waste of space. Two generations later, Robert Louis Stevenson judged himself by the same rigid family standards, which venerated professionalism, inventiveness, hard work and money-making and thought little of self-expression and art. He came to feel that he was a very inadequate heir to these active men, a mere 'slinger of ink', sunk in comparative idleness. When he was writing his *Records of a Family of Engineers* in the last year of his life,

Stevenson burst out in a letter to his friend Will Low, 'I ought to have been able to build lighthouses and write *David Balfours* too.'[11] A poem Stevenson wrote in the 1880s (when, incidentally, he was living in a house named after his uncle's most famous lighthouse and surrounded by lighthouse memorabilia) expresses the same feeling of having failed his inheritance:

> *Say not of me that weakly I declined*
> *The labours of my sires, and fled the sea,*
> *The towers we founded and the lamps we lit,*
> *To play at home with paper like a child.*
> *But rather say:* In the afternoon of time
> A strenuous family dusted from its hands
> The sand of granite, and beholding far
> Along the sounding coast its pyramids
> And tall memorials catch the dying sun,
> Smiled well content, and to this childish task
> Around the fire addressed its evening hours.[12]

How neatly the change in typeface separates what the poet would like to have said about himself from what he thinks will be said. And how much more striking than his engrossed images of the strenuous family and their colossal achievements is his bitter description of himself left 'playing at home with paper like a child'.

The paternal line dominates Robert Louis Stevenson's family history, for 'the celebrated engineer' made it one of the most respectable names in Edinburgh at the beginning of the nineteenth century. Robert and his sister-wife Jean had thirteen children, only five of whom survived infancy: one girl (Jane) and four sons, three of whom followed their father into the family business, with greater or lesser enthusiasm, and the youngest of whom, Thomas, became the father of our subject.* They lived in the large house that Thomas Smith had built in 1803 in Baxter Place, fronting

---

* What happened to the fourth brother, Robert, is a complete mystery. He was born in 1808, died in 1851, didn't marry officially and doesn't figure anywhere in the extensive family papers.

onto busy Leith Street, with a long garden at the back running
to the bottom of the Calton Hill. The Stevenson children played
in the cellars or the orchard, and hung around their father's office or
the specially-built workshops, where there was always 'a coming
and going of odd, out-of-the-way characters, skippers, lightkeepers,
masons, and foremen of all sorts'.[13] Though the Stevensons were
not known for keeping a lavish table (Jean Stevenson, a strict
Calvinist, made a habit of choosing both her butcher and her cook
on religious grounds), the house was always open to employees of
the Northern Lighthouse Board. Robert Stevenson was a paternal-
istic boss, minutely concerned with all aspects of the men's lives:
their wives' confinements, their children's schooling, the welfare
of the sick and the conduct of prayers. 'My grandfather was much
of a martinet,' Stevenson reported,

> with his powerful voice, sanguine countenance, and eccentric
> and original locutions, he was well qualified to inspire a
> salutory terror in the service [. . .] In that service he was king
> to his finger-tips. All should go his way, from the principal
> lightkeeper's coat to the assistant's fender, from the gravel in
> the garden walks to the bad smell in the kitchen, or the
> oil-spots on the storeroom floor.[14]

Oddly enough, with this Jove for a father, young Thomas
Stevenson managed for years to evade discovery that he was doing
very little schoolwork. Being the youngest of many children, seventeen years his sister Jane's junior, perhaps he just adopted the
tactic of keeping his head down at home. He wasn't a stupid boy
(although he never mastered mathematics, which was a considerable handicap in his professional life), but early on developed a
strong aversion to book-learning. This amounted to an obsession
in later life, when he would stop schoolboys on the street and
advise them to learn only what seemed to them good. 'There seems
to have been nothing more rooted in him than his contempt for
all the ends, processes, and ministers of education,' his son was to
claim; 'he bravely encouraged me to neglect my lessons, and never
so much as asked me my place in school. What a boy should learn

in school he used to say is "to sit on his bum". It could scarcely be better put.'[15]

Thomas's hatred and fear of school were due to the teachers' constant use of the cane, and he was to say that the sufferings he endured there were worse than any he experienced in later life. His survival strategy was based on maintaining a low profile, as this spirited incident, related by his son, shows:

> He never seems to have worked for any class that he attended; and in Piper's took a place about half-way between the first and last of a hundred and eighty boys. Yet his friends were among the duxes. He tells most admirably how he once on a chance question got to the top of the class among all his friends; and how they kept him there for several days by liberal prompting and other obvious devices, until at last he himself wearied of the fierce light that beat upon the upper benches. 'It won't do,' he said. 'Goodbye.'[16]

Thomas, like his son, was a dreamy, quirky child with a strong vein of the perverse: 'there was always a remarkable inconsequence, an unconscious spice of the true Satanic, rebel nature, in the boy. Whatever he played with was the reverse of what he was formally supposed to be engaged in learning. As soon as he went, for instance, to a class of chemistry, there were no more experiments made by him. The thing then ceased to be a pleasure, and became an irking drudgery.'[17] It was not the temperament to mould easily to Robert Stevenson's expectations. Thomas worked for a short time in a printing office and toyed with the idea of becoming a bookseller or publisher – a practical slant to his deeper ambition, which was to be a writer. But his father was furious at this notion and before he was out of his teens Thomas had succumbed to the family fate of engineering, joining his two older brothers.

Alan, the eldest of the boys, had also needed some coercion to become an engineer. He was the scholar and polymath of the family, and wanted to study Classics and enter the Church. He turned out to be an outstanding engineer, making important improvements in optics and designing and building several lights, including the family's most beautiful lighthouse, Skerry Vohr, on that dismal Atlantic reef surveyed by his father and Scott in 1814. Skerry Vohr proved a challenge as great as Bell Rock, though Alan was not the man to brag about it. He took over when his father retired from the post of chief engineer in 1842, but found the burden of work intolerable and in 1852, when he was forty-five, suffered a 'sudden shattering of his nervous system' which forced him 'to withdraw absolutely from his profession and the world'. The few remarks about this collapse in an anonymous but highly sympathetic obituary notice indicate a family tragedy of large proportions:

> What a trial this must have been to one of his keen, intrepid temper, his high enthusiasm, and his delight in the full exercise of his powers, no one but himself and those who never left him for these long dreary years can ever tell – when his mind, his will, his affections survived, as it were, the organ through which they were wont to act – like one whose harp is all unstrung, and who has the misery to know it can do his bidding no more.[18]

The collapse happened when Alan had been married only six years and had four tiny children, two of whom, Katherine and the brilliant, mercurial Bob, were to be Robert Louis Stevenson's close friends in adult life. All through their childhoods their father was a nervous invalid, who beguiled his 'great sufferings' by reading, learning languages, committing Homer to memory, and making a verse translation of the hymns of Synesius. 'During many an hour the employment helped to soothe my pain,' Alan wrote pathetically in the prologue to his privately printed translation. It was a startling example of how violently a sensitive nature could be shipwrecked by mental breakdown.

Thomas Stevenson was not as brilliant as his brother Alan, nor as versatile as his brother David, with whom he ended up running the family business. With his robust, serious, four-square face and figure, he looked every inch the Victorian paterfamilias, but there was instability at the centre of his character too: volatile, charming and puzzling, a straight-faced joker, he must have been a difficult man to have as father. In his obituary tribute, remarkable for its air of objectivity, his son characterised him as 'a man of a some-what antique strain':

> with a blended sternness and softness that was wholly Scottish and at first somewhat bewildering; with a profound essential melancholy of disposition and (what often accompanies it) the most humorous geniality in company; shrewd and child-ish; passionately attached, passionately prejudiced; a man of many extremes, many faults of temper, and no very stable foothold for himself among life's troubles.[19]

Thomas was a staunch Tory and devout churchgoer, with a strong belief in ultimate salvation – not through any merits of his own, but through God's infinite mercy. There was not a shred of com-placency in his view of himself. In the speech he wrote to be read at his own funeral, he expressed the hope that he would not be 'disowned by Him when the last trumpet shall sound', a character-istically negative construction, and among the Bible verses to be read he chose 'Who can bring a clean thing out of an unclean? Not one.'[20] Over a lifetime's constant service to the Kirk, he never accepted any sort of lay office, on grounds of a seemingly inex-pungeable 'unworthiness'.

Melancholic by nature, Thomas Stevenson's awareness of his own sins seems morbid; like his son's creation Dr Henry Jekyll, he had perhaps an over-fine conscience about his shortcomings, shown in the story as a mark of extreme moral vanity: 'many a man would have even blazoned such irregularities as I was guilty of'.[21] Sex seems to have been the focus of Thomas's neuroses, as he held views so strong about the protection of women as to amount to a blanket condemnation of men. He believed, for instance, that any woman who wanted a divorce should be granted one automatically, whereas no man should ever have one. He also, intriguingly, set up a Magdalen Mission in Edinburgh for 'fallen women', which he supported financially all his adult life. Was this a gesture of general philanthropy or some private effort at atonement for real

or imagined crimes against women – his own, or those of his sex
in general? Thomas's interpretation of chivalry did not lie anywhere on the usual axis between protectiveness towards women
and the will to dominate them, but had a neurotic, slightly maso-
chistic edge. It was taken on almost wholesale by his son.

In the autumn of 1847 this rather troubled man, then twenty-
nine years old, was on a train to Glasgow when he met a young
woman travelling with her uncle and aunt and got into conversation. Margaret Isabella Balfour was eighteen, cheerful, unaffec-
ted and a daughter of the manse. Thomas must have been looking
out for a wife, for their first meeting was followed promptly by a
brief formal courtship and a proposal; not the behaviour of an
indecisive lover. On the brink of being thirty, Thomas was old
enough to have had a considerable history of dealings with women,
or a long-drawn-out history of wanting to have dealings with them.

Margaret came from genteel, Lowland stock and was the
youngest surviving child of a family of thirteen, nine of whom had
outlived infancy. Among her forebears were the Lairds of Pilrig
and, possibly, the John Balfour who in 1656 was one of the
religious zealots who murdered Archbishop Sharp. That notorious
incident in the history of the 'Covenanters' (which became such
an obsessive interest of her son Louis) formed part of Scott's *Tale
of Old Mortality* in which John Balfour appears as 'Balfour of
Burley'; so when Stevenson said that his father's family played 'the
character parts in the Waverley Novels' he might have added that
his mother's family appeared in the leading roles.

Margaret was good-looking (though not a beauty), intelligent
and lively. She was known as an indefatigable optimist, 'a determined looker at the bright side of things', as Sidney Colvin
described her, 'better skilled, perhaps, to shut her eyes to troubles
or differences among those she loved than to understand, compose,
or heal them'.[22] She had none of the accomplishments, such as
musical or artistic ability, that were valued as bargaining counters
in the marriage market (in worldly society at least), but her plain-
ness of manner was in itself a recommendation to the God-fearing

Thomas Stevenson. His surviving letters to his young bride-to-be show the tenderness and teasing tone of a man who really wanted to get married, addressing her as 'My dearest Mag' and indulgently calling her 'child'. Margaret must have drawn attention to his behaviour around children (clearly a matter of some concern), for he writes to reassure her, 'Don't think my love that because I am strict or inclined to be strict with children that I like them less than other people. [. . .] I have the family failing of taking strong views and expressing those views strongly.'[23] He ends the letter 'Your ever affectionate and devoted lover', an intensity that deepened after the marriage, when he wrote home frequently from his work trips, pining to be reunited with 'my own dear wife'.[24] Thomas remained extremely protective and anxious about his young bride, strenuously encouraging the idea of her frailty and poor health. Their daughter-in-law Fanny's judgement when she met them in 1880 was that Margaret – then well into middle age – was 'adored by her husband, who spoils her like a baby'.[25]

Thomas and Margaret were married about a year after they first met, on a date in August deliberately chosen to coincide with the anniversary of her father's ordination (he, naturally, performed the ceremony). Margaret proved a most devoted wife to Thomas Stevenson, subservient to his wishes and interests, protective of his well-being, mainstay of his morale. Her chief talent, Louis declared, in one of his very few analytical remarks about his mother, was for organisation, and she was good at identifying and diverting possible starting points of domestic tension. This presumably came of years dealing with her husband's sporadic dips into melancholia, and was a technique that her son would emulate closely in his dealings with an equally volatile spouse.

Although she became, in later life, a remarkably enthusiastic and adventurous traveller, tolerant of discomforts and extreme temperatures, game for anything, Margaret Stevenson spent her youth half in and half out of a sort of vaporous decline. She was encouraged in this first by a valetudinarian father, himself a sufferer from weak lungs, then by her hypochondriac husband.

All through her son's childhood, she varied between high spirits and sickliness: her chest was weak, her heart; she must rest, she must take the waters. She was only twenty-one when the baby was born, but stayed in bed most mornings and was unable to play or go out with him when she was up. Most of the active side of mothering was left to the child's nurses, yet there were welcome, if perplexing, surges of energy: one of Stevenson's earliest memories was of his mother rushing him up the stairs at their house in Inverleith Terrace to see his grandfather, as excitable and skittish as a girl.

In the summer of 1850, when Margaret was pregnant for the first and only time, old Robert Stevenson died. He had been ill for some months, but had been looking forward to his annual inspection tour of the lighthouses. When his sons tried to convince him that no more travelling was possible, the old man seemed to acquiesce, but on the day of departure 'was found in his room, furtively packing a portmanteau'.[26] Thomas Stevenson was deeply affected by the pathos of his father's decline and death and when his first child was born four months later, on 13 November, had no hesitation in naming the baby for him.

The little boy's name was in fact an amalgamation of both grandfathers', one inside the other: Robert Lewis Balfour Stevenson. The names were in strong demand in the family: Alan Stevenson had also called his first son Robert (the little boy was known as Bob), and there was a veritable epidemic of Lewis Balfours on the other side of the family; two born in 1850 (the same year as RLS), another called Lewis Henry two years earlier, Lewis ('Noona') in 1842, Lewis Charles in 1851. Despite that, Thomas and Margaret stuck with 'Lewis' for the baby's everyday name. Or 'Smout', or 'Lou', or 'Signor Sprucki', or 'Baron Broadnose': Thomas Stevenson was a great coiner of comical aliases.

Margaret, who was weakened and possibly traumatised by the experience of childbirth, was not put through that hazard again: there were no more children. This in a family that showed typical Victorian fecundity – little Lewis had *fifty-four* first cousins – must have marked out the Stevenson household as a trifle eccentric. It wasn't easy to limit a family to one child; to avoid conception successfully during a marriage that lasted another thirty-seven years must have required strict regulation of both partners' sexual appetites. But Thomas Stevenson was not the man to put anything before his young wife's well-being, and a challenge of this sort suited his self-mortifying temperament. However they solved the contraception issue, the couple remained conspicuously devoted and dependent, and fussed contentedly about each other's health.

The baby made a delicate third member of this hypochondriac household. He seemed healthy enough to begin with, but an attack of croup in his third year was so alarming that ever after his parents lived in fear of another chest infection carrying him off. Both Thomas Stevenson and his wife came from large families with a high incidence of infant mortality: between them they had twelve live siblings and twelve dead ones. Consumption was a threat – Margaret had developed a patch of 'fibroid pneumonia' after the baby's birth – and incipient tuberculosis seemed an increasingly plausible explanation for the child's uneven, rickety growth and extreme thinness.[27] So whether from genuine danger, or from excessive solicitude, the child spent long stretches of time confined to bed. The catalogue of his ailments that appears in his mother's diary is truly astonishing: in his first nine years, apart from numerous chills and colds, the boy had scarlatina, bronchitis, gastric fever, whooping cough, chickenpox and scarlet fever. But the persistent cough was what worried everyone most. It seems likely that the croup had damaged his lungs or that he suffered (among other possible things) from asthma, since his health often worsened in the damp, cold winters of smoggy Auld Reekie. The sound of his cough starting up was heard in the household with dread.

The Stevensons' first home in Edinburgh was the one Thomas had prepared for his bride and where the baby was born, 8 Howard Place, on the northern fringes of the New Town, by the Botanic Garden. They moved in 1853 to 1 Inverleith Terrace, a larger property just around the corner. In the baby's first years, Thomas and Margaret had a run of bad luck with nurses (or weren't very good at choosing them): two left unbidden and the third took the infant Smoutie to a bar and left him wrapped in a shawl on the counter while she soaked up a few gins. But the fourth hire produced a family servant of the most reassuring type: sober, single and religious to a fault. Alison Cunningham was a weaver's daughter from Fife, thirty years old when she came to the household (Margaret Stevenson was twenty-three that year) and an experienced nurse. 'Cummy' was given free rein with the toddler, and became a pivotal figure in the household.

Cummy was the type of servant who derived the keenest gratification from being indispensable, and turned down more than one suitor, it is said, to stay in the Stevensons' service for twenty years. Her devotion to Lewis, intensified by his vulnerability and the emerging realisation that he was to be the Stevensons' only child, went hand in hand with an equally powerful intention to mould the boy to her pattern. She could delight the child with her songs and dances and was selfless in the devotion of her time to his care (no trips to the bar for her, or even the usual nurse's expedient of meeting with friends in the park). Her genuine interest in his company fed the child's already pronounced egotism and her relation to him was – oddly enough – more that of companion than nanny, as Stevenson's later description of her as 'my first Wife' would seem to corroborate.

In 1857 this compact household moved from Inverleith Terrace, which had proved damp and uncongenial, to a splendid house on Heriot Row in the heart of the elegant New Town, overlooking Queen Street Gardens from the south. Beyond the gardens, whose trees were only half-mature at this date, were the tall fronts of the houses on Queen Street and in the distance, beyond the great metal river of the railway line, the smoky wynds and tenements of the Old Town climbed towards the Castle. This was the view from Lou's day and night nurseries on the top floor; Cummy's room was at the back of the house on the same floor, with views, in clear weather, of the Firth and, distantly, the coast of Fife, her home. There was a wide landing, with other bedrooms and storerooms off, and then the grand spiral staircase running down the core of the house and lit from above by a large glazed cupola. As a student, Stevenson was to be grateful for the fact that the stairs were made of stone and made little or no sound when he crept past his parents' bedroom on the first floor late at night.

Thomas and Margaret's bedroom looked out to the back of the property and had a bathroom leading off it; at the front on the same level was the elegant drawing room, with its fireplace and recesses and twelve-foot-high windows looking out on the genteel greenery of the Gardens. Down the stairs again was the ground floor, with its high-ceilinged, panelled dining room and wide entrance hall. The kitchens and sculleries were in the basement, accessible to tradesmen by the area steps. Heriot Row was a truly substantial home, exuding an aura of wealth well-spent. Nobody seeing it could have the least doubt that the only son of the house was a privileged child.

Robert Louis Stevenson's many autobiographical essays and memoirs leave vividly contrasting impressions of his childhood. On the one hand, it contained the idyllic pleasures described in essays such as 'The Manse' and 'Child's Play' and poems such as 'My Kingdom' and 'Foreign Lands', on the other it was a time of chronic ill-health and piquant terrors. There is a temptation, given the subject's own obsessive recourse to images and tropes of duality, and his 'clinching' creation of the Jekyll–Hyde poles, to see his life in terms of strong contrasts. But Stevenson was unusual – in those last days before Freud – in recognising not just the co-existence of states of mind (in childhood particularly), but their inextricability. The author of A Child's Garden of Verses was to say of his own earliest memories, 'I cannot allow that those halcyon-days or that time of "angel infancy" have ever existed for me. Rather, I was born, more or less, what I am now – Robert Louis Stevenson, and not any other, or better person.'[28] The 'good' and 'bad' parts of his childhood could no more be pulled apart than could the child and adult self. In its puzzling variability and dizzying plunges into dark and light, life was all of a piece.

Looking back on his childhood when he was twenty-nine, Stevenson concluded that he had been 'lovingly, but not always wisely treated' by his parents.[29] In fact, there were aspects of his upbringing that seem not only ill-advised, but even dangerous. It is a minor mystery, for instance, how the frail little boy survived the custom of the time to seal up a nursery 'almost hermetically'[30] so that it was always draught-free (i.e. airless), or how he ever slept, given Cummy's treatment for insomnia, which was to give the fretful child a soothing drink of strong coffee in the middle of the night. Fanny Stevenson retrospectively blamed her husband's 'feverish excitement' as a child on the powerful drugs he was given during bouts of gastric fever, and the regular use of antimonial wine, which Margaret Stevenson's doctor brother George later believed had ruined the boy's constitution. These remedies were held to be sovereign by the parents, and if the child seemed over-wrought they would sooner remove his toys or send his playmates away to calm him, than lower the doses of strong or inappropriate medicine.

Even his parents' happy marriage was problematic, for, as Stevenson was to say memorably in his essay 'Virginibus Puerisque', 'the children of lovers are orphans'. Margaret gave over much of the childcare to Cummy, not thinking any harm could come of it, the nanny being such a religious body. But the strength of Cummy's religious views (possibly a source of mild amusement to her employers) made hers a very troubling influence. Cummy was a devout member of the Free Church, and far more stringent in her interpretation of doctrine than Lou's Church of Scotland parents. The theatre was the mouth of hell, cards were 'the Devil's Books' and novels (meaning romances) paved the road to perdition. She filled the little boy's head with stories of the Martyrs of Religion, of the Covenanters and the Presbyters and the blood-drenched religious fundamentalists of the previous two centuries, stories that were rendered, confusingly enough, in highly dramatic style. (Stevenson later told Cummy mischievously that her declamations had sparked his own obsessive interest in the drama.) The Bible and the Shorter Catechism were to Lou what Mother Goose might have been to a luckier child, visits to the Covenanters' graves in Greyfriars churchyard were the substitute for playing in the park, and though there was opportunity to read adventure stories, *Cassell's Family Paper* and (clandestinely) bound copies of *Punch* downstairs, Cummy's regime of spiritual education was based around Low Church tract-writers and theologians, 'Brainerd, M'Cheyne, and Mrs Winslow, and a whole crowd of dismal and morbid devotees', as Stevenson recalled about twenty years later.

Cummy had mutually respectful relations with her employers and was trusted implicitly, but her religious brainwashing of her charge clearly subverted their authority over him. She was a simple woman who undoubtedly meant no harm, but her anxieties about the religious liberalism of the household were always clear. The Stevensons gave dinner parties and were known to drink wine; Mrs Stevenson had been flagrantly evasive of the ban on Sunday recreation by sewing a little pack onto the back of Lou's doll so that his game could pass as 'Pilgrim's Progress'. One of Stevenson's early memories was of his nurse 'comforting' him at night by pressing him to her in a ferment of prayer for the souls of his parents, who had broken the Sabbath by playing a game of whist after dinner. The scene sounds ludicrous now, but to the child spelled eternal damnation for his mother and father. He was wound up to such a pitch that he sometimes thought none of them would be saved, for even Cummy had lapses: he remembers them both straining to make out the contents in the printer's window of serial stories she herself had cut short on the grounds of them threatening to turn out to be 'regular novels'.

Dread of judgement, midnight coffee and a predisposition to overheated dreaming and daydreaming made much of the sick little boy's life a misery. He speaks of fevers that seemed to make the room swell and shrink, and 'terrible long nights, that I lay awake, troubled continually with a hacking, exhausting cough, and praying for sleep or morning from the bottom of my shaken little body'.[31] He had a recurring nightmare of standing before the Great White Throne and being asked to recite some form of words, on which salvation or damnation depended; 'his tongue stuck, his memory was blank, hell gaped for him',[32] for the idea of eternal punishment had been 'seared', as he said, into his infant conscious-ness. When his night-horrors were particularly bad, Cummy would call for Thomas Stevenson, who would try to calm his son by sitting by the bed, or outside the bedroom door, feigning conver-sations with imaginary coachmen or inn-keepers. But, as the adult Louis recalled, 'it was long, after one of these paroxysms, before I could bear to be left alone'.[33]

Though in time the severity of his nightmares lessened, Stevenson continued to dream vividly and with disturbing convic-tion of reality, so that he was unable to distinguish whether his conscious or subconscious was in control. By the time he was a student his dreams produced the impression in him, nightmarish in itself, of leading a double life, at which point he began to fear for his reason. He learned in time to control his night-terrors, more or less (partly by the use of drugs), but if he hadn't been terrified by hellfire rantings as a child, this habit of feverish dreaming and neurotic invention, that was to prove important to his writing, might possibly never have set in.

Stevenson avoided much reference in his published works to his 'Covenanting childhood', but left some strong words about it in manuscript (some of which were published in posthumous collections or used by his first biographer). There is a controlled savagery in these fragments about the adults who infected his young mind with 'high-strung religious ecstasies and terrors':

I would not only lie awake to weep for Jesus, which I have done many a time, but I would fear to trust myself to slumber lest I was not accepted and should slip, ere I awoke, into eternal ruin. I remember repeatedly [. . .] waking from a dream of Hell, clinging to the horizontal bar of the bed,

with my knees and chin together, my soul shaken, my body
convulsed with agony. It is not a pleasant subject. I piped and
snivelled over the Bible, with an earnestness that had been
talked into me. I would say nothing without adding 'If I am
spared,' as though to disarm fate by a show of submission;
and some of this feeling still remains upon me in my thirtieth
year.[34]

Of the 'morbid devotees' whose works were his constant diet, the
adult Stevenson had this to say: 'for a child, their utterances are
truly poisonous. The life of Brainerd, for instance, my mother had
the sense to forbid, when we [he and Cummy] were some way
through it. God help the poor little hearts who are thus early
plunged among the breakers of the spirit!'[35]

He makes it – for politeness' sake – sound as if he was not one
of those 'poor little hearts' himself, but the accusation of negligence
against his parents and Cummy is unmistakable – especially against
his mother for knowing better than Cummy, but being inattentive.
Colvin's description of Margaret Stevenson as 'shutting her eyes to
troubles' seems pertinent here. The child's precocious utterances,
recorded faithfully in her diary notes, clearly struck the young
mother as amusing and a source of pride, but to less sentimental
readers they brim with complex fears. Little Lou worried constantly about the quality and quantity of his prayers, whether his
family were good or bad in the Lord's eyes, and whether he would
be sufficiently adept at harp-playing during an eternity in heaven
– and all this before the age of six. Adding to his discomfort was
a strong rational streak and a quick intellect. His mother relates
that when she told him of 'the naughty woman pouring the oint-
ment upon Christ' he asked why God had made the woman so
naughty,[36] and, hearing it confirmed that Christ had died to save
him, concluded, 'Well, then, doesn't that look very much as if I
were saved already?'[37] These exchanges, engaging so adroitly with
Calvinist theology, were not intended as cute additions to the Baby
Album. The child must have been puzzled why they only elicited
fond smiles.

In the years following Stevenson's death, a minor cult grew up around the figure of his old nurse, fuelled mostly by his emotional dedication to her of *A Child's Garden of Verses*, and a passage in his fragmentary memoir in which Cummy is singled out for her tender care of him when he was sick:

> She was more patient than I can suppose of an angel; hours together she would help console me in my paroxysms; and I remember with particular distinctness, how she would lift me out of bed, and take me, rolled in blankets, to the window, whence I might look forth into the blue night starred with street-lamps, and see where the gas still burned behind the windows of other sickrooms.[38]

But in all honesty, it hardly constitutes excess of attention or devotion to attend to a chronically sick child at night. 'My second mother [. . .] angel of my infant life'; the epithets are cloyingly excessive, and one can't help wondering if Stevenson's retrospective praise of his nurse was a desperate attempt to accentuate the positive. His fond memories of his father soothing him with nonsense-stories are also in the context of the child on the other side of the door being too terrified to sleep. And the same Cummy who was ready to calm the child with cuddles and blankets was just as likely to wake him up and assault him with prayers. It was, to say the least, a confusing world.

The boy learned to read quite late (aged six), but was lazy about reading on his own and preferred to get Cummy to do it for him. He liked to be attended to as much as possible, especially by women. He had been composing his own stories some time before this, using his mother and aunt Jane Balfour as amanuenses, and his first recorded work was a history of Moses, which won him the prize of 'The Happy Sunday Book of Painted Pictures' in an informal competition among the cousins. The text is illustrated with some wonderful drawings by Lewis of the Israelites, all wearing mid-Victorian chimneypot hats, with pipes in their mouths, gathering in the manna or crossing the Red Sea.[39] He was good at drawing, in a speedy, impressionistic style: one blotchy ink picture of 'A steamer bound for Londonderry' has written on it in Thomas Stevenson's hand: 'Note. This steamer may be *bound for* London-derry but I fear she will never reach it.'[40]

Religion entered everything and dominated play; when he was aged two and a half, Lou's favourite game was 'making a church', which he did by putting a chair and stool together to form a pulpit and conducting his own solitary services in the character of both minister and congregation. At 'an astoundingly tender age'[41] he voiced strong antipathy to a theological iconoclast then attending the Edinburgh Kirk assembly. His sayings, many of them parroted from his parents or nurse (such as Cummy's constant refrain of 'If I'm spared'), were noted and preserved by his mother with the utmost care. At home, this little 'dictator' strove to be the centre of attention, and he later remembered his young self unflatteringly: 'I was as much an egotist as I have ever been; I had a feverish desire of consideration.'[42] To other children he was a bit of a liability; being an only child, he didn't know how to handle rivals and expected to dominate play. As so often with children who insist on taking the lead, he had a markedly sadistic streak too, devising a ritual involving whacks on the hand with a cane when he and his cousins were bartering items for their 'museums'. If the 'buyer' flinched during the transaction, the whole procedure had to start again.[43]

Among the flocks of Balfour and Stevenson cousins with whom he played at Colinton Manse (his grandfather Balfour's house), or Cramond (his uncle George Balfour's house), or the Royal Crescent (Uncle David Stevenson's house), or Heriot Row, Louis remained an essentially lonely figure. But school was worse, and schoolwork a great trouble. Fortunately for him, he had minimal exposure to it; the combination of his father's views on pedagogy and his parents' shared hypochondria ensured he was often at home, 'too delicate to go to school', as Margaret records.[44] That was Mr Henderson's in India Street, his first school. It didn't last long.

Perhaps Louis recited in his father's hearing the unofficial school song:

> Here we suffer grief and pain
> Under Mr Hendie's cane.
> If you don't obey his laws
> He will punish with his tawse.[45]

At age ten, he went to the Edinburgh Academy for a while (contemporary with Andrew Lang, the future folklorist, although they had nothing to do with each other at this age). There was a brief attempt at a private tutor from England, but that didn't work out either. In the interstices of these arrangements months at a time would be spent having informal lessons with Cummy, or simply being cosseted in bed, surrounded by picture books and toy soldiers and with a little shawl pinned round his shoulders. Indulged so thoroughly over the years, he could have become an appallingly spoilt brat.

His closest friend in childhood was his cousin Bob, three years his senior, a tall, dreamy boy 'more unfitted for the world [. . .] than an angel fresh from heaven'.[46] Bob spent the whole winter of 1856 with his aunt and uncle at Heriot Row, possibly because of his father Alan's mental breakdown. Louis was delighted; he had been praying for a brother or sister for years. 'We lived together in a purely visionary state,' he wrote in 'Memoirs of Himself'; the two boys invented countries to rule over, with maps and histories and lead-soldier armies, they coloured in the figures for the pasteboard theatre – Skelt's Juvenile Drama – that had been the inspired gift on Lewis's sixth birthday from his aunt Jane Warden, they talked and daydreamed. 'This visit of Bob's was altogether a great holiday in my life,' Louis recalled later.[47]

The acute sensibility that made his nights a torment also afforded the child intense pleasures. He loved going to his grandfather Balfour's house, Colinton Manse, in a quiet village southwest of Edinburgh, where there was a large garden and other children of the family to play with, and his charming, devoted aunt

Jane Balfour on call. His happiness there was 'more akin to that of an animal than of a man', he thought later:

> The sense of sunshine, of green leaves, and of the singing birds, seems never to have been so strong in me as in that place. The deodar upon the lawn, the laurel thickets, the mills, the river, the church bell, the sight of people ploughing, the Indian curiosities with which my uncles had stocked the house, the sharp contrast between this place and the city where I spent the other portion of my time, all these took hold of me, and still remain upon my memory, with a peculiar sparkle and sensuous excitement.[48]

The garden was divided up into sections by a large beech hedge and adjoined the church and churchyard. This fascinated and horrified the child, a connoisseur of graves, who imagined 'spunkies' dancing among the tombstones at night and the glinting eye of a dead man looking at him through a chink in the retaining wall. The paper mill just upstream from the manse and the snuff mill next to it made a constant sound of industry, which was as much a part of the place's charm for the child as the birdsong and running water. Stevenson recalled 'the smell of water all around', and admitted 'it is difficult to suppose it was healthful', an opinion stoutly shared by his wife Fanny, who wrote in her preface to *A Child's Garden of Verses* rather crushingly that 'in any other part of the world [the situation] would suggest malaria'.[49]

Aunt Jane lived at the manse with her widower father and was Margaret Stevenson's only unmarried sibling, older by thirteen years and by far the more motherly of the two sisters. She had been 'a wit and a beauty' when young, 'a wilful empress' whose social and marriage prospects were reversed after some accident left her sight and hearing permanently damaged. She used to say that it was a riding fall that had effected the change, but that was accepted in the family as a euphemism, and the cause was probably a disease such as scarlet fever or typhus. She proved an invaluable matriarch, as Louis recalled with affection: 'all the children of the family came home to her to be nursed, to be educated, to be mothered [. . .] there must sometimes have been half a score of us children about the Manse; and all were born a second time from Aunt Jane's tenderness'.[50] Stevenson had a charming, intensely sensual memory of sitting on the stairs at Colinton when he was a small boy and being passed over, rather than passed by, his aunt descending precipitately in her full-skirted dress:

> I heard a quick rustling behind: next moment I was enveloped in darkness; and the moment after, as the reef might see the wave rushing on past it towards the beach, I saw my aunt below rushing downwards.[51]

Aunt Jane's good spirits and kindness compensated for grandfather Balfour's withdrawn and intimidating manner. The Reverend Lewis Balfour was a man of few words, and those mostly broad Scotch, which to his grandson Louis was almost a foreign language. Scotch had been thoroughly displaced in middle-class life by English by the 1850s, but Balfour was of the old school, and only spoke English in the pulpit as a concession to his bourgeois parishioners. Louis guessed that his sermons were 'pretty dry', for the minister was an unemotional and unapproachable man. His grandson regarded him with a certain discomfort, and recalled vividly his last sight of the old gentleman at Colinton in 1860, when the boy was nine and his dying grandfather eighty-three:

> He was pale and his eyes were, to me, somewhat appallingly blood-shot. He had a dose of Gregory's mixture administered and then a barley-sugar drop to take the taste away; but when my aunt wanted to give one of the drops to me, the rigid old man interfered. No Gregory's mixture, no barley sugar, said he. I feel with a pang, that it is better he is dead for my sake; if he still see me, it is out of a clearer place than any earthly situation, whence he may make allowances and consider both sides. But had he lived in the flesh, he would have suffered perhaps as much from what I think my virtues as from what I acknowledge to be my faults.[52]

Colinton was a place of leisure and licence, where Lewis could root through the library unhindered. The child was particularly drawn to the four volumes of Joanna Baillie's melodramas, since Cummy had always enticingly denounced plays.[53] These he approached with such furtiveness that he didn't so much read them as just let a few wicked words flash into his consciousness before shutting the book up quickly. Murders and murderers, a decapitation, a dark forest, a stormy night; the child took away these strong ideas and spun them together when he was alone into stories probably much more sensational and alarming than Miss Baillie's originals. He was fond of frightening himself: at home, he used to go at night into the dark drawing room 'with a little wax taper in my hand ... a white towel over my head, intoning the dirge from *Ivanhoe,* till the sound of my voice and the sight of my face in the mirror drove me, in terror, to the gas-lit lobby'.[54]

The stolen pleasures of the Colinton library linked directly with his sanctioned obsession, Skelt's Juvenile Drama. Skelt produced dozens of different printed cutouts for use in children's toy theatres, 'a penny plain and twopence coloured', which Lewis bought in quantity at the stationer's on Antigua Street. He loved them, not so much because of the potent, transient joy of buying and colouring in a new set of characters or scenes – 'when all was painted, it is needless to deny it, all was spoiled' – but on account of the playbooks, with their stirring up of the sense of adventure and romance, the exoticism of the scenes and situations, the heart-stopping allure of the characters, highwaymen, smugglers and pirates:

> What am I? What are life, art, letters, the world, but what my Skelt has made them? He stamped himself upon my immaturity. The world was plain before I knew him, a poor penny world; but soon it was all coloured with romance. [...] Indeed, out of this cut-and-dry, dull, swaggering, obtrusive and infantile art, I seem to have learned the very spirit of my life's enjoyment; met there the shadows of the characters I was to read about and love in a late future; got the romance of *Der Freischütz* long ere I was to hear of Weber or the mighty Formes; acquired a gallery of scenes and characters with which, in the silent theatre of the brain, I might enact all novels and romances[.][55]

*   *   *

The Stevensons and their queer little son, with his unexpressive face and out-of-proportion head, made a close-knit, self-protective trio. Their shared hypochondria became a great comfort to them. When Thomas developed some unspecified complaint and was ordered to take the waters at Homburg in 1862, the family went with him. The next year it was Margaret's turn to be chief invalid and the destination was the South of France, where they stayed three months, returning through Italy on a splendidly leisurely tour and home via the Alps and the Rhine. All this time Lewis had been off school, but when Margaret was advised to return south for the winter of 1863–64, the Stevenson parents realised that if the boy was ever going to get an education they would have to leave him out of the next health tour. Thomas enrolled him at Burlington Lodge Academy in Isleworth, Surrey, chosen because three Balfour cousins were day boys there, looked after at weekends by the obliging Aunt Jane from her brother's rented house nearby. It was a well-intentioned scheme, but not a particularly good one. Lewis could only feel the separation from his parents more keenly in a boarding school so far from home (and in a foreign country), however many little Balfours were on hand.

The twelve-year-old's letters during his first and only term in Isleworth are full of characteristic touches: his stoicism, his dis-tractibility (several times stopping mid-sentence), his mixed interest in and fear of other children. 'I am getting on very well, but my cheif amusement is when I am in bed then I think of home and the holidays,' he wrote to his 'dear Parients' in September.[56] As the weeks went by, there were signs of education going on – bits of Latin and French, along with devil-may-care touches of sophisti-cation – but the dreaded time was approaching when both parents would leave the country without him, which they did on 6 November. On the eve of his thirteenth birthday the following week, Lewis wrote his mother a letter in demi-French to thank her for the huge cake she had sent him, which, he noted, weighed twelve and a half pounds and cost seventeen shillings. There had been some trouble during the fireworks on Guy Fawkes' Night when some bad boys ('les polissons') 'entrent dans notre champ et nos feux d'artifice et handkercheifs disappeared quickly but we charged them out of the feild. Je suis presque driven mad par un bruit terrible tous les garcons kik up comme grand un bruit qu'il est possible.' Writing to his parents this first time truly alone, with only a monstrous cake for company, seems to have been too much for the boy: he ends his letter abruptly and to the point: 'My dear papa you told me to tell you whenever I was miserable. I do not feel well and I wish to get home. Do take me with you.'[57]

Lewis must have guessed the effect this simple appeal would have: Thomas Stevenson wrote back quickly to comfort the boy with the promise of fetching him out at Christmas, and Lewis's subsequent letters are crowingly cheerful, looking forward to the prospect of joining them in Menton. When Lewis left Spring Grove at the end of term (the last boy to be picked up, his father being so late that he almost gave up hope) it was for good: he stayed in France until his mother finally left for home in May the next year. Menton was lovely: months of lounging in sunshine, reading, being fussed over by his mother and Cummy (brought out to attend him), being carried up and down the hotel stairs by two waiters when he was feeling weak. The party came back via Rome, Naples, Florence, Venice and the Rhine: a great improvement on Isleworth and the company of *les polissons*.

Cummy's diary of this trip, written at the request of (and addressed to) her friend Cashie, nurse to David Stevenson's children, gives a vivid glimpse of the woman with whom Lewis had spent so much of his time. Cummy had not travelled abroad before, and was appalled at how lost the world was to 'the Great Adversary'. In London, the sight of barges on the Thames on a Sunday made her lament, 'God's Holy Day is dishonoured!',[58] whereas France, with its sinister-looking priests and perpetual feeling of carnival, was even worse, a land 'where the man of sin reigns'.[59] She was shy of eating with or associating with Catholics and felt that contact with heathens was in some way eroding her capacity to reach out 'in deep, heart-felt love to Jesus'.[60] She therefore relished her minor ailments and frustrations as signs of interest from the deity, as this entry, on recovering from a slight sore throat, illustrates:

> O how good is my Gracious Heavenly Father to His back-sliding, erring child! He knows I need the rod, but O how gently does He apply it! May I be enabled to see that it is all in love when He sends affliction![61]

Cummy was not wholly consistent, of course, and proved suscep-tible to certain temptations. In Paris, she wrote to Cashie, she had been intrigued by the sight of some specially white and creamy-looking mashed potatoes, of which she sneaked tiny portions whenever the waiter's back was turned. Although they were French and possibly the work of the Devil, she had to admit, 'I never tasted anything so good.'[62]

One good thing had come of Lewis's time at Spring Grove; he had been able to indulge a growing mania for writing. 'The School Boys Magazine' ran to just one issue and all four stories were by the editor, but at least he had the possibility of an audience among his schoolfellows and cousins. An opera libretto followed the next year, with the promising title 'The Baneful Potato', and a very early version of his melodrama *Deacon Brodie* was also written at this period, telling the gripping tale of the real-life Deacon of the Wrights who in the 1780s had carried on a notorious double life: respectable alderman by day, thief by night. The Stevensons owned a piece of furniture made by Brodie that stood in Lewis's bedroom, a tangible reminder of the criminal's duality. The idea of being an author intrigued the boy, though when one of his heroes, the famous adventure writer R.M. Ballantyne, visited the house of David Stevenson while researching his novel *The Lighthouse* (about the Bell Rock) and was introduced to the family, Lewis was so awestruck that he couldn't say a thing.

Stevenson's relations with his father were never anything other than intense, complex and troubling. Thomas Stevenson had on the one hand unusual sympathy with the child, colluding instantly with his attempts to avoid school, while at the same time being in thrall to the strictest ideas of what it was to be a responsible parent. Lewis was on the whole frightened of being accountable to him, for the response was predictable. Years later he wrote to the mother of a new godson of his this heartfelt advice: 'let me beg a special grace for this little person: let me ask you not to expect from him a very rigid adherence to the truth, as we peddling elders understand it. This is a point on which I feel keenly that we often go wrong. I was myself repeatedly thrashed for lying when Heaven knows, I had no more design to lie than I had, or was capable of having, a design to tell the truth. I did but talk like a parrot.'[63]

Lewis became artful enough to know when to keep his mouth shut, as an incident which he related to Edmund Gosse in 1886 illustrates. When he was about twelve years old, he was so gripped by the romance and mystery of an empty house with a 'To Let' sign on it that he broke in by climbing through a rear window. Elated by his burgling skills, the boy then took his shoes off and prowled round, but once in the bedroom, thought he could hear someone approaching. Panic overcame him and he scuttled under the bed with his heart pounding. 'All the exaltation of spirit faded away. He saw himself captured, led away handcuffed,' and worst of all in his vision of retribution, he saw himself exposed to his parents (on their way into church) and cast off by them forever. This was such an alarming image that he lay under the bed sobbing uncontrollably for some time before realising that no one was in fact coming to get him, so he crept out and went home 'in an abject state of depression'. He was incapable of explaining to his parents what had happened, and their concern redoubled his guilty feelings, sending him into hysterics. During the evening, as he lay recuperating, he heard someone say 'He has been working at his books a great deal too much,' and the next day he was sent for a holiday in the countryside.[64]

More education was ventured sporadically, the last being at a private day-school in Edinburgh for backward and delicate children. Mr Thomson's establishment in Frederick Street, which admitted girls as well as boys and whose regime did not include homework, was the softest possible cushion upon which to place young Lewis. As far as his father was concerned, the boy's eventual career was never in doubt; he would join the family firm. Therefore formal schooling was of minor importance: the greater part of his training would be got by observation and example in an apprenticeship. To this end, Thomas took his son on the annual lighthouse tour one year, and attempted to share his own knowledge of engineering and surveying whenever opportunity allowed. There is a touching memory of this in *Records of a Family of Engineers*:

> My father would pass hours on the beach, brooding over the waves, counting them, noting their least deflection, noting where they broke. On Tweedside, or by Lyne and Manor, we have spent together whole afternoons; to me, at the time, extremely wearisome; to him, as I now am sorry to think, extremely mortifying. The river was to me a pretty and various spectacle; I could not see – I could not be made to see – it otherwise. To my father it was a chequer-board of lively forces, which he traced from pool to shallow with minute appreciation and enduring interest. [. . .] '[S]uppose you were to blast that boulder, what would happen? Follow it – use the eyes that God has given you: can you not see that a great deal of land would be reclaimed upon this side?' It was to me like school in holidays; but to him, until I had worn him out with my invincible triviality, a delight.[65]

Thomas Stevenson had seen a painting at the Royal Scottish Academy exhibition titled *Portrait of Jamie* by James Falk, depicting an adolescent boy posed with a microscope. He wrote to Falk asking if a similar portrait could be made of his son and was told that the artist didn't do much in that line, but would take a look at the boy and see if he thought he could paint him. Falk was surprised to get a reply saying that Mr Stevenson had been back to look at the 'Jamie' portrait again and had changed his mind, feeling his son was 'too stupid looking to make a picture like that'.[66] The incident stuck in Falk's mind and thirty years later he offered it to Stevenson's cousin Graham Balfour as a biographical curiosity (Balfour didn't use it): the father's turn of phrase was so odd and unsentimental. Odder still is the thought of Thomas Stevenson veering so completely between two different images of his son, one minute picturing him as a budding scientist, the next as too stupid-looking to be scrutinised.

2

VELVET COAT

Facts bearing on precocity or on the slow development of the
mental powers, deserve mention.

Francis Galton, *Record of Family Faculties*

WHEN BOB WENT UP to Sidney Sussex College, Cambridge, in
the autumn of 1866, fifteen-year-old Lewis was eager for details,
and more than a little jealous: 'Do Cambridge students indulge in
a private magazine: if so, full particulars?'[1] He himself was still at
Mr Thomson's school and bound on a different course, taking
classes in practical mechanics and being given extra maths lessons
in order to matriculate at Edinburgh University the next year as a
student of engineering. Thomas Stevenson must have realised by
this time that even if Lewis went through the hoops of getting a
degree in sciences, he was temperamentally unsuited to become an
engineer. Still they stuck to the known path, the father no doubt
rationalising that his own reluctance to join the family firm years
before had been proved wrong. His working life had been immensely useful and productive (not least of money), and his early
leanings towards authorship had not been entirely abandoned.
Had not his book on lighthouse illumination and his article on
'Harbours' for the *Encyclopaedia Britannica* been composed in
hours of leisure, the proper place for letters?

Robert Louis Stevenson's first publication, a privately-printed
sixteen-page monograph called 'The Pentland Rising: A Page of
History', fell entirely in the gentleman-amateur tradition that his

father favoured. It would not have escaped a man like Thomas Stevenson, so keenly aware of the energy potential in a wave and the importance of building a structure of exactly the right size and shape to harness or withstand it, that the intellectual energy Lewis expended on his feverish recreation might be redirected towards some serious and worthy project. The boy's interest in the Covenanters had been expressed in some highly inappropriate forms up to this point; he had started a romance based on the life of David Hackston of Rathillet, one of the fanatics who had murdered Archbishop Sharp, and in 1867–68 began a five-act tragedy on another Covenanting subject, 'The Sweet Singer'. A work of a historical or overtly religious nature would have been far more suitable, and it was in such a direction that Thomas and Margaret Stevenson now steered their son, offering to pay for the production of one hundred copies of a short history to coincide exactly with the two hundredth anniversary of the Covenanters' defeat at Rullion Green on 28 November 1666. Getting the boy's name into print, in a controlled and circumscribed way, was clearly a kind of reward and encouragement, but also an inoculation against becoming 'literary'.

Lewis must have been happy with the arrangement, for he took care to make his account of the Rising as serious and scholarly as possible, with an impressive list of references (including Wodrow, Crookshank, Kirkton, Defoe, Bishop Burnet) and a stirring, sermon-like conclusion. Still it didn't much resemble a conventional history. The facts were there, but re-imagined by the fifteen-year-old into gripping narrative:

> The wind howled fiercely over the moorland; a close, thick, wetting rain descended. Chilled to the bone, worn out with long fatigue, sinking to the knees in mire, onward they marched to destruction. One by one the weary peasants fell off from their ranks to sleep, and die in the rain-soaked moor, or to seek some house by the wayside wherein to hide till daybreak. One by one at first, then in gradually increasing numbers, till at last at every shelter that was seen, whole

troops left the waning squadrons, and rushed to hide themselves from the ferocity of the tempest. To right and left
nought could be descried but the broad expanse of the moor,
and the figures of their fellow-rebels, seen dimly through the
murky night, plodding onwards through the sinking moss.
Those who kept together – a miserable few – often halted to
rest themselves, and to allow their lagging comrades to over-
take them. Then onward they went again, still hoping for
assistance, reinforcement, and supplies; onward again,
through the wind, and the rain, and the darkness – onward
to their defeat at Pentland, and their scaffold at Edinburgh.[2]

Stevenson's later description of his apprenticeship as 'playing the
sedulous ape' to a host of better writers seems needlessly self-
mocking when one sees how expert and stylish he was already at
the age of fifteen. The prose is very deliberately crafted, with
cadences one could almost score, and there is something visionary
about his imagination, as if he had personally witnessed the bullets
dropping away from Dalzell's thick buff coat and falling into his
boots, seen the flames rising from a Covenanter's grave on the
moor and creeping round the house of his murderer. The boy's
engagement with his subject is so intense as to be almost disturbing.
Just after relating the execution of the captured martyrs, he makes
an emotional authorial interjection: perhaps it was as well that
Hugh McKail's dying speech to his comrades was drowned out by
drums and the jeers of the crowd; these sounds, he wrote, 'might,
when the mortal fight was over, when the river of death was
passed, add tenfold sweetness to the hymning of the angels, tenfold
peacefulness to the shores which they had reached'. Lewis seems
to have been as fervently pious in his mid-teens as in childhood.

It's hard to imagine how such a performance could have failed
to please the boy's father, but according to a letter in the Balfour
archive, the pamphlet was no sooner in type than Thomas
Stevenson began to worry about potential criticism of it (from
what quarter it is impossible to guess). He had criticised the first
drafts himself, as Aunt Jane recalled, who had been at Heriot
Row while Lewis was making alterations to the text 'to please his

Father': '[Lewis] had made a story of it, and, by so doing, had spoiled it, in Tom's opinion – It was printed soon after, just a small number of copies all of which Tom bought in, soon after.'[3] So the little book's literary qualities were its downfall; they 'spoiled' 'A Page of History' to the extent that it couldn't even be circulated among the aunts, family friends and co-religionists who would have been its natural audience. It must have been hard for the young author to see his first work stillborn. Nor was it the only time Thomas Stevenson pulled this trick, paying for his son's work to be printed, then censoring it. His solicitude for Lewis has the tinge of monomania, and tallies with what a family friend, Maude Parry, told Sidney Colvin about the relationship after the writer's death: 'Stevenson told us that his father had nagged him to an almost inconceivable extent. He thought it the most difficult of all relationships.'[4]

The following year Thomas Stevenson took out a lease on a house right in the heart of Covenanting country, the hamlet of Swanston on the edge of the Pentlands, only a few miles outside Edinburgh. The 'cottage' they rented there (in fact a spacious villa, almost as big as Colinton Manse) became their holiday home for the next thirteen years and a winter retreat for Lewis when he was a student. The battlefield of Rullion Green was within walking distance, as was the picturesque ruin of Glencorse Church, and Lewis, now old enough to be left to his own devices, spent days at a time walking the hills, writing and reading – especially adventure stories, caches of which the shepherd John Tod's son later recalled having found in the whin bushes above the cottage.[5] He was a keen, hardy walker and was able to make a long foot-study of the Pentlands in the years during which Swanston was the family's second home. This was to become his favourite persona over the next decade or more, the romantic solitary walker, free from responsibility and respectability, watching, listening, picking acquaintance with strangers on the road, falling in with whatever adventures presented themselves.

To true Pentlanders, Lewis Stevenson would have appeared

little more than a rich townie weekending on Allermuir, an English-speaking Unionist among terse mutterers of Lallans. No doubt some choice phrases of that dialect were shouted in his direction on the occasion, early in the Stevensons' tenancy, when the boy barged through a field of sheep and lambs with his Skye terrier Coolin, infuriating the shepherd.[6] Times had changed so rapidly in Scotland that in his late teens Stevenson knew no one of his own generation (certainly not of his class) whose primary language was Scots. 'Real' Scotsmen, like Robert Young, the gardener at Swanston, or John Tod the shepherd, or his late Grandfather Balfour, were distant, older figures who presented the paradox of being at once admirable and impossible to emulate. And with the language many temperamental traits and 'accents of the mind' were disappearing too, or seemed tantalisingly out of reach, as Stevenson's loving description of shepherd Tod in his 1887 essay 'Pastoral' indicates:

> That dread voice of his that shook the hills when he was angry, fell in ordinary talk very pleasantly upon the ear, with a kind of honied, friendly whine, not far off singing, that was eminently Scottish. He laughed not very often, and when he did, with a sudden loud haw-haw, hearty but somehow joyless, like an echo from a rock. His face was permanently set and coloured; ruddy and stiff with weathering; more like a picture than a face [...] He spoke in the richest dialect of Scots I ever heard; the words in themselves were a pleasure and often a surprise to me, so that I often came back from one of our patrols with new acquisitions; and this vocabulary he would handle like a master, stalking a little before me, 'beard on shoulder', the plaid hanging loosely about him, the yellow staff clapped under his arm, and guiding me uphill by that devious, tactical ascent which seems peculiar to men of his trade. I might count him with the best of talkers; only that talking Scotch and talking English seem incomparable acts. He touched on nothing at least, but he adorned it; when he narrated, the scene was before you; when he spoke (as he did mostly) of his own antique business, the thing took on a colour of romance and curiosity that was surprising.[7]

The 'romance and curiosity' of Scotsness haunted Stevenson all his life; he never tired of it. But the fact that his own culture could be romantic and curious to him he knew to be an unfortunate state of affairs. His writing about Scotland is therefore strongly melancholic and valedictory, quite unlike the language-revival movements of the following century which sought to resuscitate the culture by creating synthetic Scots. Within 150 years, the literary language waxed, waned and then reappeared again in the form of a sort of composite ghost of itself in the 'Scottish Renaissance' of the mid-twentieth century (pioneered by the poet Hugh MacDiarmid). But in the 1860s and '70s, the language seemed beyond revival, and what Burns had used both naturally and daringly, Stevenson could only lament and pastiche, writing of his later attempts at Scots vernacular verse, 'if it be not pure, what matters it?'[8]

Nevertheless, what Stevenson says of John Tod's quintessentially Scots trait of 'adorning' his talk and making it startlingly vivid is egregiously true of Stevenson himself; 'when he narrated, the scene was before you'. The irony is, of course, that Stevenson became known as a superlative *English* stylist because he was so alert to the power of his unknown native tongue. And as for the 'romance and curiosity' of Scotland, Stevenson's version of it in novels such as *Kidnapped, Catriona, The Master of Ballantrae* and *Weir of Hermiston* did almost as much to promote and perpetuate the Scottish myth in the twentieth century as his great forerunner Walter Scott had done in the nineteenth.

In the autumn of 1867, the bullet had to be bitten and an engineering degree begun. The contrast between Lewis's technical education at Edinburgh and Bob's 'semi-scenic life' in Cambridge, with its gentlemanly atmosphere of ancient quadrangles and cultured conversation, could hardly have been stronger. As the bell rang them in to lectures from the city streets or pubs, all classes of raw Scots youth shuffled together on the 'greasy benches', as Stevenson recalled vividly in 'The Foreigner at Home':

The first muster of a college class in Scotland is a scene of
curious and painful interest; so many lads, fresh from the
heather, hang round the stove in cloddish embarrassment,
ruffled by the presence of their smarter comrades, and afraid
of the sound of their own rustic voices.[9]

No proctors, privileges or grand ceremonials here. When the
classes broke up, many of the students had to hurry home to get
back to work in the fields in order to earn their next winter's
college fees. It must have been an eye-opener to Lewis, whose
school life (such as it was) had been spent wholly among middle-
class children, and though he approved of the 'healthy democratic
atmosphere' of the university, and admired those of the staff who
strove to put the parish boys at ease, he made no close friends
among his fellow engineering students, indeed felt increasingly
isolated and lonely.

Around this time (1868–69) Stevenson changed his name from
Lewis to the Frenchified 'Louis'. It is said that the impetus behind
the change was Thomas Stevenson's sudden and overpowering
dislike of an Edinburgh radical and dissenter called David Lewis,
who embodied, in the engineer's view, 'everything dangerous in
Church and State'.[10] But as the pronunciation remained identical,
Lewis – or Louis as we must now call him – may have intended it
more as a joke than as a gesture of political solidarity, and it
took a while to stick.* 1868 was also the year in which Thomas
Stevenson published an essay in the *Church of Scotland Home
and Foreign Missionary Record* (later produced as a pamphlet by
Blackwood's) on 'The Immutable Laws of Nature in Relation to
God's Providence'. This short work is notable for several reasons:
for its slightly simple-minded grappling with the evolutionary
controversies of the day and for its ardent struggle to develop a
response to them consistent with Church doctrine. The author
argues, for example, that a falling stone falls from two causes,
'first, proximately, in virtue of the law of gravitation; but second,

---

* W.E. Henley, who didn't meet RLS until six years after this change, always attempted
to use the earlier spelling, though this might have been as much affectation as anything.

primarily, by the supreme will of God, who has called the law of gravitation into existence' (one can catch the author's pleasure in coining that 'second, primarily'). And if man 'has been raised from the gorilla, as is hinted at by the new school of naturalists, how comes it to pass that the dog, although resembling man so little physically, should be so much more than the gorilla akin to him in all his nobler feelings and affections?' The style of argument gives one an idea of what Louis was up against when he and his father began to discourse ardently at the dinner table on matters of religion and science, for the youth had been reading Darwin, and Herbert Spencer, whose works his father would never countenance. But there is another passage in Thomas's booklet of even greater relevance, one which may well have come to haunt his son:

> Men of literature and science may therefore well pause ere they lift their pen to write a word which tends to shake the faith of others [. . .] How terrible will it be to such an author, when toiling all alone through the dark valley of the shadow of death, should conscience remind him, when thus entering the dark portals of the tomb, of the pernicious legacy which he has left to mankind![11]

Publication fascinated the young student of engineering, who had secretly become fixated on the consumption and production of literature. 'I had already my own private determination to be an author,' he wrote in 'The Education of an Engineer'.[12] But the acquisition of technique, that seemed to him all-important, was difficult. Three of the four stories in his juvenile 'School Boys Magazine' had ended on a cliffhanger with the words 'To Be Continued'. The pleasure in writing the *beginnings* of stories (natural enough in an apprentice) and a revulsion from the work involved in finishing them would remain the most marked characteristics of Stevenson's creative life.

To be continued . . . by whom? One solution to the problem was to share the burden with a collaborator. In the spring of 1868, while he was also trying to write his 'covenanting novel', Louis wrote to Bob, 'Don't you think you and I might collaborate a bit this summer. Something dramatic, blank verse and Swinburne choruses.'[13] Just the idea of collaboration then set him off in the same letter on a long sketch of two possible plays, the second of which, a tragedy about the Duke of Monmouth, got so elaborate as to put off any potential helper from the start:

> Scene, a palace chamber. Without famine and revolt and an enemy investing the plains. A. found making love to B. Enter Prince who overhears. P. and A. quarrel, P. being also in love with B. Swords are drawn but D., who resembles A. very closely separates them. Exit P., cursing and muttering

– and so forth. 'Write me your opinion of the thing and I will write the first scene which nothing can alter. I'll then send it to you for alteration, amendment and addition, and we can parcel out the rest of the thing or alter it,' he wrote humorously, acknowledging how tenacious he was likely to be of all his own ideas. What he really wanted was not a co-author, but a goad – or at the very least an enthusiastic audience. No wonder Bob didn't jump at the offer, and apart from friendly encouragement contributed nothing to 'Monmouth: A Tragedy'. But the object was achieved: the play was one of the few projects of the scores started during his teens that Louis managed to complete.

In his demanding, self-imposed and self-policed apprenticeship, Louis tried on a dizzying variety of literary styles, as he recalled satirically many years later:

> *Cain*, an epic, was (save the mark!) an imitation of *Sordello*: *Robin Hood*, a tale in verse, took an eclectic middle course among the fields of Keats, Chaucer and Morris: in *Monmouth*, a tragedy, I reclined on the bosom of Mr. Swinburne; in my innumerable gouty-footed lyrics, I followed many masters; in the first draft of *The King's Pardon*, a tragedy, I was on the trail of no lesser man than John Webster; in the second draft of the same piece, with staggering versatility, I had shifted my allegiance to Congreve [. . .] Even at the age of thirteen I had tried to do justice to the inhabitants of the famous city of Peebles in the style of the *Book of Snobs*.[14]

'Nobody had ever such pains to learn a trade as I had; but I slogged at it, day in, day out; and I frankly believe (thanks to my dire industry) I have done more with smaller gifts than almost any man of letters in the world,' Stevenson wrote modestly.[15] What he needed no time to learn, however, was *what* to write about: his subject was always, somehow, himself.

> Whenever I read a book or passage that particularly pleased me, in which a thing was said or an effect rendered with propriety, in which there was either some conspicuous force or some happy distinction in the style, I must sit down at once and set myself to ape that quality. I was unsuccessful, and I knew it; and tried again, and was again unsuccessful and always unsuccessful; but at least in these vain bouts, I got some practice in rhythm, in harmony, in construction and the co-ordination of parts. I have thus played the sedulous ape to Hazlitt, to Lamb, to Wordsworth, to Sir Thomas Browne, to Defoe, to Hawthorne, to Montaigne, to Baudelaire and to Obermann.[16]

Study, practice, impersonation; 'that, like it or not, is the way to learn to write'. One can hear in these heartening words a rallying cry for millions of would-be writers, and it may be no coincidence that much of the worst prose of the coming generation was written in imitation of Stevenson. Anyone can do it, he seems to be saying; all you need is persistence and humility. What is easy to miss (because the expression is so original) is that anyone who can coin a phrase such as 'playing the sedulous ape' to describe his debt to other authors owes nothing to anyone. The term passed straight into common parlance, and the essay itself, as Balfour averred a mere fourteen years after its first appearance in an American periodical, quickly 'became classical'.

To be continued . . . It wasn't simply a matter of by whom, but when? For three consecutive summers, Louis was obliged to attend engineering works in his capacity as apprentice to the family firm.

Instead of travelling, as Bob was doing, to Paris or Fontainebleau, he found himself stuck for weeks in a series of inaccessible locations on the Scottish coast, with no company but that of the men on the works, and no entertainments other than tobacco, drink and letters from his mother. The men must have found him an odd specimen, a skinny teenager with no real interest in or aptitude for engineering, quite unlike his father and uncle, the firm's obsessively dedicated partners. When there was an accident at the works in Anstruther, where Louis had been sent in July 1868 to observe the construction of a breakwater, the seventeen-year-old found himself in the middle of a minor uproar. Writing to his father about the incident, he reported how a little girl had pointed him out on the street, saying, 'There's the man that has the charge o't!', an identification that must have rung strangely in everyone's ears.

Louis spent most of his time in Anstruther loitering on the quay, vaguely recording the progress of the works, or biting his pencil over calculations. 'All afternoon in the office trying to strike the average time of building the edge work,' he wrote home at the end of his first week. 'I see that it is impossible. [My computation] is utterly untrustworthy, looks far wrong and could not be compared with any other decision.'[17] In the evenings, Louis retreated to his lodgings at the house of a local carpenter, and tried to make up the lost time: 'As soon as dinner was despatched,' he recorded twenty years later, 'in a chamber scented with dry rose-leaves, [I] drew in my chair to the table and proceeded to pour forth literature, at such a speed, and with such intimations of early death and immortality, as I now look back upon with wonder.'[18] Believing himself to be doomed to die young, and doomed, what's more, to spend what little time he had hanging around windswept harbour works, he felt compelled to sit up long into the night, 'toiling to leave a memory behind me'.[19]

The scent of dead rose-leaves, the intimations of mortality and the burden of his unwritten masterpieces weighed heavily. The works were weighty too; the sonorously-named 'Voces Fidelium' was to be a dramatic monologue in verse, presumably on a religious theme; 'Monmouth: A Tragedy' was still in progress, as was the novel about the Covenanter, Hackston. He had come a long way from 'The Baneful Potato'. But it was difficult to keep up a secret nocturnal career of writing, that must at times have reminded him of Deacon Brodie's double life. The nights were warm that July in Anstruther, the rose-leaves and bowls of mignonette overpowering, and the window had to be kept open. Thus moths flew in continually and scorched themselves on the candles, dropping onto 'Voces Fidelium' in a manner so disgusting that the author was driven to blow out the lights and go to bed, seething with rage and frustration. Immortality was deferred yet again.

After an evening watching a wretchedly bad performance by strolling players at Anstruther Town Hall, Louis got into a dispute with a fellow engineering apprentice about the troupe's pathetic actor-manager. His companion felt that the man would be better employed as an ordinary labourer, but Stevenson disagreed ardently, saying the player must be happier 'starving as an actor, with such artistic work as he had to do'. The parallel with his own life and frustrated ambition was all too clear, and Louis left the scruffy hall 'as sad as I have been for ever so long'.[20] By the end of the month he was writing home in unusually forcible terms:

> I am utterly sick of this grey, grim, sea-beaten hole. I have a little cold in my head which makes my eyes sore; and you can't tell how utterly sick I am and how anxious to get back among trees and flowers and something less meaningless than this bleak fertility.[21]

But his parents chose to interpret this repugnance as temporary and specific, a symptom of 'the distressing malady of being seventeen years old',[22] and Louis was packed off again the next month to spend six weeks in the 'bleak, God forsaken bay' of Wick, a fishing port only ten miles away from the most northerly point on the Scottish mainland, John o' Groats. Anstruther had been a mere forty miles from home, across the Firth from North Berwick, where the Stevensons had taken many family holidays; Wick was a much more serious exile, far beyond the reach of the railway system, cold, bare and implacably foreign. In the herring season, the town was full of men from the Outer Hebrides, mostly Gaelic speakers, while the mainlanders spoke mostly Scots-English and both communities were heavily influenced by their common Norse ancestry. Louis listened to a wayside preacher in total incomprehension of all but one word, 'Powl' (the apostle), and was incapable of conversing with one of the Highland workmen at the harbour works. 'What is still worse,' he wrote home to his mother, 'I find the people here about – that is to say the Highlanders, not the northmen – don't understand *me*.'[23]

The firm had been commissioned to build a new breakwater in Wick harbour and work was well advanced, despite the permanently bad sea conditions, which led eventually to the abandonment of the whole project in 1874.* In 1868, however, the scene was full of men and industry; wooden scaffolding was in place all along the unfinished stonework, and there was a platform of planks at the end on which stood the cranking equipment for the divers' air supply. The masons' hammers chimed continually, the air-mills turned, and every now and again a diver's helmet would surface from the choppy water and a man dressed bizarrely in a huge helmet and diving suit hoist himself up the sea-ladder.

Here was something to capture young Louis's imagination, and despite his father's strong reservations (and insistence that a doctor's opinion be sought in advance), he was eventually allowed to go diving under the strict supervision of one Bob Bain. Stevenson recalled the experience as the best part of his whole engineering career. Wearing woollen underclothes, a nightcap and many layers of insulating material, with a twenty-pound lead weight on each foot, weights hanging back and front and bolted into a helmet that felt as if it would crush him, Louis went down the ladder:

* Storms in the winters of 1868, 1871 and 1872 destroyed large parts of the breakwater. The failure of the project was later described by RLS as 'the chief disaster of my father's life'.[24]

Looking up, I saw a low, green heaven mottled with vanishing
bells of white; looking around, except for the weedy spokes
and shafts of the ladder, nothing but a green gloaming, somewhat opaque but very restful and delicious. Thirty rounds
lower, I stepped off on the *pierres perdues* of the foundation;
a dumb helmeted figure took me by the hand, and made a
gesture (as I read it) of encouragement; and looking in at the
creature's window, I beheld the face of Bain.[25]

Encouraged to try jumping up onto a six-foot-high stone, Louis
gave a small push and was amazed to find himself soaring even
higher than the projected ledge: 'Even when the strong arm of Bob
had checked my shoulders, my heels continued their ascent; so that
I blew out sideways like an autumn leaf, and must be hauled in
hand over hand, as sailors haul in the slack of a sail, and propped
upon my feet again like an intoxicated sparrow.'[26]

The weightlessness, silence and dreamlike seclusion made
diving memorable and delightful, but Wick was otherwise short
on delights. The countryside was flat and treeless, exposed for
miles at a time, and Louis would shelter from the biting wind in
small rock crevices, listening to the seabirds and repeating over
and over to himself the lines of the French poet Pierre-Jean de
Béranger, '*mon coeur est un luth suspendu/sitôt qu'on le touche,
il résonne*'.[27] Wick was a place of storms and shipwrecks, and one
morning Louis was woken by the landlady of the New Harbour
Hotel with news that a ship had come ashore near the new pier.
The sea was too high to get near the works to assess the possible
damage, but Louis reported back to his father the scene from the
cope:

> Some wood has come ashore, and the roadway seems carried
> away. There is something fishy at the far end where the cross
> wall is building; but till we are able to get along, all specu-
> lation is vain. [...]

So far, this could just pass for a technical report, but he goes on:

> The thunder at the wall when it first struck – the rush along
> ever growing higher – the great jet of snow-white spray some

forty feet above you – and the 'noise of many waters', the roar, the hiss, the 'shrieking' among the shingle as it fell head over heels at your feet. I watched if it threw the big stones at the wall: but it never moved them.[28]

It is hardly the language of a technocrat; even Burns managed to be less poetical than this in his work as a surveyor.

Evenings in the New Harbour Hotel Louis again spent alone with his 'private determination'. He finished 'Monmouth', and dedicated it, with professional seriousness, to Bob; he was also experimenting with prose sketches and metrical narratives, one based on the biblical story of Jeroboam and Ahijah, another on Chaucer's Pardoner's Tale. He wrote of his literary projects to Bob in a series of agitated letters, revealing the depth of his desires:

> Strange how my mind runs on this idea. Becoming great, becoming great, becoming great. A heart burned out with the lust of this world's approbation: a hideous disease to have, even though shielded, as it is in my case, with a certain imperturbable something – self-consciousness or common sense, I cannot tell which, – that would prevent me poisoning myself like Chatterton or drinking like Burns on the failure of my ambitious hopes.[29]

Bob was irritatingly slow to respond, but when he did, expressed similar doubts about his ability to succeed as an artist, which was his own secret intention. The two of them were in a ferment of fears and ambition, but Bob's was at once the easier and the more hopeless case: no one was forcing him to join the family firm (the example of his father's breakdown must have allowed that), but he was self-confessedly indolent and depressive. Louis's neuroses went the other way, towards overwork, having to live two lives in tandem if he wanted to be a writer at all. Nor did Louis need to drum up suicidal tendencies in order to be recognised as a full-blown romantic genius; death by natural causes seemed likely to get there first.

*   *   *

The most marked characteristic of Stevenson's years as a student of engineering was loneliness. He seems to have made no lasting friendships at all at the university, or in the pubs and streets of the Old Town where he was most often found loitering instead of attending class. He was intimidated by the diligence of the plough-boys and earnest burghers' sons who were his fellow students in natural philosophy or the dreaded mathematics. One of these students, it turned out, had only one shirt to his name and was forced to stay away from class on the days when it was being washed. Stevenson was ashamed to reflect that he needed no reason at all to stay away, but did so 'as often as he dared'. He joined the University Speculative Society in March 1869, but didn't make much of an impression there at first among the confident young future advocates and doctors who made up most of its member-ship. 'The Spec' was an exclusive debating club limited to thirty members, who met by candlelight and in full evening dress in a series of comfortable rooms in South Bridge. 'A candid fellow-member' (presumably Walter Simpson, brother of the lady who recorded this) said of the newly-recruited young engineer, 'I cannot remember that Stevenson was ever anything as a speaker. He was nervous and ineffective, and had no power of debate; but his papers were successful.'[30] His happier days at the Spec were still to come.

Thomas and Margaret Stevenson had bought their son a set of barbells to develop his chest, but no amount of callisthenics could perform that miracle; the boy didn't have an ounce of either muscle or fat. As his body grew taller and thinner, it made his head look unusually large by comparison, and his eyes, that had always been wide-set and interestingly misaligned, began to look more than ever like those of an intelligent hare. In view of how quickly his health improved in warm, dry places, it was unfortunate, to say the least, that Stevenson lived so many years in one of the 'vilest climates known to man', in the damp and cold and dark of Auld Reekie. He used to hang over the bridge by Waverley station, watching the trains taking luckier people away from his native city, and remembered with piquant dislike 'the solo of the gas burner in the little front room; a knickering, flighty, fleering and yet spectral cackle. I mind it above all on winter afternoons, late, when the window was blue and spotted with rare raindrops, and looking out, the cold evening was seen blue all over, with the lamps of Queen's and Frederick's Street dotting it with yellow and flaring eastward in the squalls. Heavens, how unhappy I have been in such circumstances.'[31]

Louis's isolation made it difficult for him to fight back fits of morbid melancholy. 'My daily life is one repression from beginning to end, and my letters to you are the safety valve,' he told Bob bluntly, just after his eighteenth birthday. He managed to be tormented with scruples, mostly about his waste or abuse of the opportunities his parents had provided him with, and attempted once to leave home on the principle that he might 'free himself from the responsibility of this wealth that was not his'.[32] To minimise his parents' total expenditure he came to the eccentric conclusion that so long as he doubted a full return to health, he would live very sparsely in 'an upper room', but when he perceived an improvement he would go back to being pampered and paid for, in order to make the quickest exit from dependence.

His plans for self-improvement all turned on renunciation of his true desires, and in these moods his single-minded pursuit of authorship struck him as not merely a feeble self-indulgence but actively wrong. Perhaps, as he wrote to Bob on a particularly gloomy day, 'to do good by writing [. . .] one must write little':[33]

> I am entering on a profession which must engross the strength
> of my powers and to which I shall try to devote my energies.
> What I should prefer would be to search dying people in lowly
> places of the town and help them; but I *cannot trust myself*
> in such places. I told you my weak point before and you will
> understand me.[34]

The pious young man was imagining himself as some sort of Jesus of the streets – and yet, he was too unworthy for that. Sunday school teaching was perhaps the only option open to him, he mused – but no, that also required a purer spirit.

The dark talk of not being trustworthy in 'lowly places of the town' refers (not without a tinge of pride) to Louis's rapid escalation of worldly knowledge during his student years. He later said that his childhood piety had gone hand in hand with its correlate, 'precocious depravity',[35] which ranged from trying to summon up the Devil to solemn, secret experiments in blasphemy. Writing about his childhood at the age of twenty-two, Stevenson was in no mood to dismiss these traits, but saw them as consistent with his adult behaviour: 'I find that same morbid bias, [. . .] the same small cowardice and small vanity, ever ready to lead me into petty falsehood.'[36] He saw 'a parallel case' between his own early years and those of the Covenanter Walter Pringle of Greenknow, whose memoirs had been one of Cummy's permitted texts. This is an extraordinary thing to say. Pringle's *Memoirs* are stuffed with the harshest language: he describes his youth as 'years of darkness, deadness, and sinfulness' when he committed 'abominations' and 'slept about the brink of the bottomless pit',[37] all in the context of later conversion, in other words, all in a priggish context. Stevenson could certainly be priggish too: the Covenanting childhood left deep divisions in his mind between good and evil, heaven and the pit, and 'something of the Shorter Catechist' hung about him, as W.E. Henley was to observe, even in his most apparently easy-going, atheistic days.

Just as in childhood Stevenson had found himself drawn fascinatedly towards the wickedness that his puritan upbringing taught him to revile, so in the freedom of adulthood and the long hours of college truancy he quickly became a habitué of some of Edinburgh's most disreputable dives. 'The underworld of the Edinburgh of 1870 had its sharp and clear geographical limits,' one historian of the town has written. 'It began in certain streets within a space of scarcely more than a few yards, and ended as abruptly.'[38] What could have been more grimly satisfying to the young moralist than the ease with which he could traverse these boundaries?

Many years later, Stevenson told his cousin Graham Balfour

that he felt his rather shabby forms of youthful dissipation were linked to the short allowance he was kept on:

> You know I very easily might have gone to the devil: I don't understand why I didn't. Even when I was almost grown up I was kept so short of money that I had to make the most of every penny. The result was that I had my dissipation all the same but I had it in the worst possible surroundings.[39]

His 'headquarters' at this time, he told Balfour, was an old pub frequented by sailors, criminals and 'the lowest order of prostitutes – threepenny whores', where he used to go and write. Eve Simpson, rather missing the point, protested later that Stevenson had no need to behave like a poor man; he had 'all his bills paid', an allowance, 'and his own study in a very hospitable home'.[40] But the dingy old pub clearly pleased him, with its interesting human traffic: '[the girls] were really singularly decent creatures, not a bit worse than anybody else'.[41]

And he made an interesting figure himself, affecting a 'scruffy, mountebankish appearance' and cultivating notoriety among the neighbours in the New Town by his 'shabby dress and dank locks'.[42] 'Hauf a laddie, hauf a lassie, hauf a yellow yite!' boys called after him on the street, not visibly ruffling the young man at all.[43] A poem of 1870 celebrates the effect his clothes and demeanour had on the average Edinburgh bourgeois:

> I walk the streets smoking my pipe
> And I love the dallying shop-girl
> That leans with rounded stern to look at the fashions;
> And I hate the bustling citizen,
> The eager and hurrying man of affairs I hate,
> Because he bears his intolerance writ on his face
> And every movement and word of him tells me how much
>   he hates me.[44]

Perhaps Stevenson was trying to become a Scottish *symboliste*; he habitually, at this date, made marginal comments on his own poetry in French: 'pas mal' or 'atroce'. The choice of free verse for this and the whole series of poems that he wrote in 1870 seems very bold and challenging, especially as Stevenson became known later as a rather conventional poet (when he was thought of in that role at all). None of these early verses – written when he was most serious about verse – was published in his lifetime, however.

The 'bustling citizen' most offended by Louis's eccentricities of behaviour and dress was, of course, his father. Thomas Stevenson was always begging his son to go to the tailor, but when Louis finally succumbed and had a garment made, he chose a dandyish black velvet smoking jacket. He wore this constantly, so it soon lost whatever smartness it had: it was totemic, marking perfectly his difference from the waistcoated and tailed bourgeois of Edinburgh. It declared that although young Stevenson was sometimes confusable with a privileged brat from the New Town, his real *milieu* was the Left Bank, his true home among artists, connoisseurs, *flâneurs*.* And in the sanded back-kitchen of the Green Elephant, the Gay Japanee or the Twinkling Eye, 'Velvet Coat' became his nickname; the boy of genius, perhaps even the *poète maudit*.

For a person brought up in such fear for his soul, Stevenson displayed a remarkable fund of basic common sense about sex. Despite their piety, neither of his parents was a prude, and his father's generous opinions about fallen women predisposed the son to think well of this class of female. Stevenson lost his virginity to one of them while still in his teens, and probably had relations with many more, as this fragment from his 1880 autobiographical notes makes clear:

> And now, since I am upon this chapter, I must tell the story of Mary H –. She was a robust, great-haunched, blue-eyed young woman, of admirable temper and, if you will let me say so of a prostitute, extraordinary modesty. Every now and again she would go to work; once, I remember, for some months in a factory down Leith Walk, from which I often met her returning; but when she was not upon the streets, she did

---

* RLS reminisced so warmly about his original velvet jacket once he was married that his wife got him a replacement made of velveteen, renewed serially thereafter.[45]

not choose to be recognised. She was perfectly self-respecting. I had certainly small fatuity at the period; for it never occurred to me that she thought of me except in the way of business, though I now remember her attempts to waken my jealousy which, being very simple, I took at the time for gospel. Years and years after all this was over and gone, when I was walking sick and sorry and alone, I met Mary somewhat carefully dressed; and we recognised each other with a joy that was, I daresay, a surprise to both. I spent three or four hours with her in a public-house parlour; she was going to emigrate in a few days to America; we had much to talk about; and she cried bitterly, and so did I. We found in that interview that we had been dear friends without knowing it; I can still hear her recalling the past in her sober, Scotch voice, and I can still feel her good honest loving hand as we said goodbye.[46]

His respectful, even loving, manner must have endeared him to the tarts of the Old Town and encouraged him to develop what was already strong – a romantic sensuousness. He was clearly rather sentimental about women, although he had no neuroses about his dealings with them. But bringing his sexual experience to bear in his writing was another matter altogether.

Prostitutes weren't the only kind of women that Stevenson associated with; he had plenty of pretty and spirited girl-cousins (there is more than a touch of gallantry in his letters to his cousin Henrietta Traqair), and liked to practise his charm on friends' sisters. A 'lady with whom my heart was [. . .] somewhat engaged' dominated his thoughts in the winter of 1870,[47] and if his poems of the time reflect actual experiences, she may have been the girl with whom he played footsie at church ('You looked so tempting in the pew'[48]), or the one with whom he skated on Duddingston Loch:

> You leaned to me, I leaned to you,
>   Our course was smooth as flight –
> We steered – a heel-touch to the left,
>   A heel-touch to the right.
>
> We swung our way through flying men,
>   Your hand lay fast in mine,

We saw the shifting crowd dispart,
The level ice-reach shine.

I swear by yon swan-travelled lake,
By yon calm hill above,
I swear had we been drowned that day
We had been drowned in love.[49]

Stevenson later admitted to having considered marrying one of the Mackenzie girls (who were neighbours of his engineering professor, Fleeming Jenkin), or Eve, the sister of his friend Walter Simpson, among whose possessions was a lock of the author's hair. But on the whole he was little attracted to ladylike girls, for reasons suggested by this passage in his 1882 essay, 'Talk and Talkers':

> The drawing-room is, indeed, an artificial place; it is so by our choice and for our sins. The subjection of women; the ideal imposed upon them from the cradle, and worn, like a hair-shirt, with so much constancy; their motherly, superior tenderness to man's vanity and self-importance; their managing arts – the arts of a civilised slave among good-natured barbarians – are all painful ingredients and all help to falsify relations.[50]

In the wake of his later fame, many colourful stories of ran-stan laddishness grew up around Stevenson, mostly revealing an undercurrent of regret that he failed to marry a Scotswoman and died childless.* In 1925, Sidney Colvin was disgusted at the claim in a book (called, baldly, *Robert Louis Stevenson, My Father*) that Louis had an illegitimate son by the daughter of the blacksmith at Swanston. But while doubting there was any truth in the Swanston claim, even Colvin had to admit 'we all knew [. . .] that Louis as a youngster was a loose fish in regard to women'.[51]

Loose fish is better than cold fish (the accusation often aimed

---

* There was a long-running myth that a mysterious lassie called 'Kate Drummond' was the love of the young RLS's life, and the mistaking of one of RLS's names for Mrs Sitwell – 'Claire' – also led to confusion until J.C. Furnas showed that she and Mrs Sitwell were one and the same.

at Colvin himself), and however uninhibited Louis was about sex, he retained high notions about chivalry and 'what is honorable in sentiment, what is essential in gratitude, or what is tolerable by other men'[52] in regard to women. This did not include political rights, however. When there were student disturbances in Edinburgh late in 1870 over the admission of women to medical classes, Stevenson wrote to his cousin Maud that he had little sympathy with the 'studentesses' who had been hissed at and jostled: 'Miss Jex-Blake [the lead campaigner] is playing for the esteem of posterity. *Soit.* I give her posterity; but I won't marry either her or her fellows. Let posterity marry them, if posterity likes – I won't.'[53] He was to revise his views about New Women somewhat in the coming years.

Stevenson was often subject to fits of morbid melancholy during these years, and wrote to Bob of aimless days looking for distractions, trying to buy hashish, thinking about getting drunk, or hanging round Greyfriars churchyard for hours at a time 'in the depths of wretchedness',[54] reading Baudelaire, who, he told Bob, 'would have corrupted St Paul'. The exquisitely self-tormenting notion struck him that he might have already used himself up, that his imagination was, in the potent word of the time, 'spent'. Alone in an inn at Dunoon in the spring of 1870, he wrote a notebook entry which explicitly links this idea of 'over-worked imagination' with the addictive effects of drug-taking:

> He who indulges habitually in the intoxicating pleasures of imagination, for the very reason that he reaps a greater pleasure than others, must resign himself to a keener pain, a more intolerable and utter prostration. It is quite possible, and even comparatively easy, so to enfold oneself in pleasant fancies, that the realities of life may seem but as the white snow-shower in the street that only gives a relish to the swept hearth and lively fire within. By such means I have forgotten hunger, I have sometimes eased pain, and I have invariably changed into the most pleasant hours of the day those very vacant and idle seasons which would otherwise have hung most heavily upon my hand. But all this is attained by the undue

prominence of purely imaginative joys, and consequently the
weakening and almost the destruction of reality. This is buying at too great a price. There are seasons when the imagination becomes somehow tranced and surfeited, as it is with me
this morning; and then upon what can one fall back? The
very faculty that we have fostered and trusted has failed us in
the hour of trial; and we have so blunted and enfeebled our
appetite for the others that they are subjectively dead to us.
[. . .] Do not suppose I am exaggerating when I talk about
all pleasures seeming stale. To me, at least, the edge of almost
everything is put on by imagination; and even nature, in these
days when the fancy is drugged and useless, wants half the
charm it has in better moments. [. . .] I am vacant, unprofitable: a leaf on a river with no volition and no aim: a mental
drunkard the morning after an intellectual debauch. Yes, I
have a more subtle opium in my own mind than any apothecary's drug; but it has a sting of its own, and leaves one as
flat and helpless as the other.[55]

Stale, flat, unprofitable: these seem familiar words from a young
man intrigued by his own existential dilemmas, and there is more
than a touch of speech-making about them, from the expository
first sentence to the anticipation of a listener's responses – 'Do not
suppose I am exaggerating when I talk . . .', 'Yes, I have a more
subtle opium . . .' For a diary entry it is wonderfully oratorical.
Perhaps Stevenson was right to fear losing touch with his imaginative powers, but not through lack of ideas so much as from a surfeit
of style.

Stevenson later served up accounts of his youth (in his autobiographical essays) in a manner so inherently witty and objectified
that the real pain of it is diluted, but there is a passage in his
'Chapter on Dreams' which is revealing about how divided a life
he was living at this time. The dream examples in the essay are
written in the third person (with the revelation at the end that all
the examples are in fact from the writer's own experience), but the
trick seems, if anything, to make the piece more confessional.
While 'the dreamer' was a student, Stevenson explains, he began
to dream in sequence, 'and thus to live a double life – one of the

day, one of the night – one that he had every reason to believe was the true one, another that he had no means of proving to be false':

> [. . .] In his dream-life, he passed a long day in the surgical theatre, his heart in his mouth, his teeth on edge, seeing monstrous malformations and the abhorred dexterity of surgeons. In a heavy, rainy, foggy evening he came forth into the South Bridge, turned up the High Street, and entered the door of a tall *land*, at the top of which he supposed himself to lodge. All night long, in his wet clothes, he climbed the stairs, stair after stair in endless series, and at every second flight a flaring lamp with a reflector. All night long, he brushed by single persons passing downward – beggarly women of the street, great, weary, muddy labourers, poor scarecrows of men, pale parodies of women – but all drowsy and weary like himself, and all single, and all brushing against him as they passed. In the end, out of a northern window, he would see day beginning to whiten over the Firth, give up the ascent, turn to descend, and in a breath be back again upon the streets, in his wet clothes, in the wet, haggard dawn, trudging to another day of monstrosities and operations.[56]

Two things are immediately striking about this vivid account: one, that it anticipates so much of Stevenson's most famous story, *The Strange Case of Dr Jekyll and Mr Hyde* – from the medical context, with its 'monstrous malformations' to the dismal cityscapes and degrading double-life; the other is the reappearance on every second flight of that endless upward staircase of a flaring 'lamp with a reflector', presumably stamped with the maker's mark, 'Stevenson and Sons'.

Stevenson implies that these nightmares 'came true' in as much as they hung so heavily on him during the day that he never seemed able to recover before it was time to resubmit to them. The account ends bathetically with the information that everything cleared up once he consulted 'a certain doctor' and was given 'a simple draught' (shades of Jekyll again), but what hangs in the reader's mind, like the nightmare itself, is what Stevenson admits just before this, that the experience left 'a great black blot upon his memory' and eventually made him begin to doubt his own sanity.

In June 1869, Thomas Stevenson took his son with him on the annual tour of inspection aboard the lighthouse steamer *Pharos*, calling at Orkney, Lewis and Skye. There was plenty to fascinate Louis, but of a romantic, not a technical, nature. At Lerwick he heard all about tobacco and brandy smuggling, and at Fair Isle saw the inlet in which the flagship of the Armada had been wrecked: 'strange to think of the great old ship, with its gilded castle of a stern, its scroll-work and emblazoning and with a Duke of Spain on board, beating her brains out on the iron bound coast'.[57] Not much survives apart from lists of his projected writings from this date, but they show another novel, sketches, stories and rough plans for at least eleven plays (listed in the notebook he took to P.G. Tait's natural philosophy lectures, the only course he attended with any regularity). But the impression that his engineering experiences (or rather, the long observation of the sea and the Scottish coast they afforded) made on him fuelled his lifetime's writing. It lies behind many of the autobiographical essays of the 1870s ('The Coast of Fife', 'Rosa Quo Locarum', 'Memoirs of an Islet', 'On the Enjoyment of Unpleasant Places', 'The Education of an Engineer'), short stories such as 'The Merry Men', 'Thrawn Janet', 'The Pavilion on the Links', and the novels *Treasure Island*, *Kidnapped* and *The Master of Ballantrae*.

By the summer of 1870, when Louis was sent on his third consecutive engineering placement, he had begun to enjoy the trips much more. For one thing, there was plenty of sea travel, which he loved, and public steamers allowed him to charm and flirt with new acquaintances in a holiday manner. On the way to the tiny islet of Earraid, which the firm was using as a base for the construction of Dhu Heartach lighthouse, he met the Cumbrian artist Sam Bough, a lawyer from Sheffield, and a pretty and spirited baronet's daughter called Amy Sinclair: 'My social successes of the last few days [. . .] are enough to turn anyone's head,' he wrote home to his mother.[58] The party stopped at Skye and boarded the *Clansman* returning from Lewis, where their high spirits and monopolisation of the captain's table were observed by a shy young tourist called Edmund Gosse, son of the naturalist P.H. Gosse, whose struggles to square fundamentalist religious views with the emerging 'new science' mirrored very closely those of Thomas Stevenson. Years afterwards, Gosse recorded his initial impressions of the young man who 'for some mysterious reason' arrested his attention: 'tall, preternaturally lean, with longish hair, and as restless and questing as a spaniel'.[59] Gosse watched the youth on deck as the sun set, 'the advance with hand on hip, the sidewise bending of the head to listen'. When the boat stopped unexpectedly a little while later, Gosse saw that they had come up an inlet and that there were lanterns glinting on the shore:

> As I leaned over the bulwarks, Stevenson was at my side, and he explained to me that we had come up this loch to take away to Glasgow a large party of emigrants driven from their homes in the interests of a deer-forest. As he spoke, a black mass became visible entering the vessel. Then, as we slipped off shore, the fact of their hopeless exile came home to these poor fugitives, and suddenly, through the absolute silence, there rose from them a wild keening and wailing, reverberated by the cliffs of the loch, and at that strange place and hour infinitely poignant. When I came on deck next morning, my unnamed friend was gone. He had put off with the engineers to visit some remote lighthouse of the Hebrides.[60]

What they were witnessing in the half-darkness was a latter-day form of Highland 'clearance', strongly similar to the notorious forced evictions of the eighteenth century. Stevenson does not mention Gosse at all or this incident in his letters home (which were too taken up with Miss Amy Sinclair), but it must surely be the inspiration for the scene in Chapter 16 of *Kidnapped* – written sixteen years later – when David Balfour sees an emigrant ship setting off from Loch Aline:

the exiles leaned over the bulwarks, weeping and reaching
out their hands to my fellow-passengers, among whom they
counted some near friends. [. . .] the chief singer in our boat
struck into a melancholy air, which was presently taken up
both by the emigrants and their friends upon the beach, so
that it sounded on all sides like a lament for the dying. I saw
the tears run down the cheeks of the men and women in the
boat, even as they bent at the oars.[61]

Earraid itself, where Stevenson was headed on the *Clansman*,
figured prominently in *Kidnapped* as the isle of Aros, on which
David Balfour believes himself to be stranded. It was his first view
of Earraid, isolated and empty except for one cotter's hut, that
Stevenson reproduced in the novel; when the firm was there in
1870, the islet had been transformed into a bustling work-station,
with sheds, a pier, a railway, a quarry, bothies for the workmen,
an iron hut for the chief engineer and a platform on which parts
of the lighthouse were preconstructed. The reef where the lighthouse was to be built, fifteen miles away, was watched through a
spyglass, and when the water was low, the engineers would put
out for it in a convoy of tenders and stone-lighters. The scene on
Dhu Heartach was another one of industrial despoliation: 'the tall
iron barrack on its spider legs, and the truncated tower, and the
cranes waving their arms, and the smoke of the engine-fire rising
in the mid-sea'.[62]

Stevenson's letters home to his parents from Earraid were typically charming, affectionate and frank. He sought to be a good
son, and bore his parents' feelings in mind to an extraordinary
degree, perhaps too much for his own good. He did not share all
their values by any means, found many of their strictures infuriating or risible, deceived them to the usual degree in such cases, yet
felt what amounts to a profound sympathy for their predicament
qua parents and never ceased to respect and love them. 'It is the
particular cross of parents that when the child grows up and
becomes himself instead of that pale ideal they had preconceived,
they must accuse their own harshness or indulgence for this natural

result,' he wrote in an uncollected essay.[63] 'They have all been like the duck and hatched swan's eggs, or the other way about; yet they tell themselves with miserable penitence that the blame lies with them; and had they sat more closely, the swan would have been a duck, and home-keeping, in spite of all.'[64] Thus he continued – for the time being – to be a staunch religionist (writing to the approved Church of Scotland paper on subjects such as foreign missions), a good Tory (he was treasurer of the University Conservative Club in 1870) and a passable student of engineering. But it couldn't last long, and didn't.

The winter of 1870–71 saw Stevenson's first real opportunity to associate with other would-be writers, and the effect was galvanising. Three law students in the Speculative Society, James Walter Ferrier, Robert Glasgow Brown and George Ormond, approached Stevenson to join them in editing a new periodical, the *Edinburgh University Magazine*. They had already found a publisher (the local booksellers), and were going to share the expenses and the profits. Of course, the likelihood of there being profits was nil and the magazine only ran for four issues, but in those four Stevenson published six articles and edited one whole number on his own. Being recognised as a fellow writer was 'the most unspeakable advance', he said later: 'it was my first draught of consideration; it reconciled me to myself and to my fellow-men'.[65]

Ferrier, the golden youth of this group, was to become one of Stevenson's best friends. Witty, wealthy and devastatingly handsome, he seemed destined for great things and was the first of these ambitious young writers to publish a book, a novel called *Mottiscliffe: An Autumn Story*. Robert Glasgow Brown also had early literary success, founding a weekly magazine called *London* in 1877, to which Stevenson and most of their group contributed. Louis's best friend, however, was a young lawyer whom he had known socially through attending the same Edinburgh church, St Stephen's. Charles Baxter was two years older than Louis and had graduated from the university in 1871, entering his father's chambers as an apprentice. Temperamentally the two young men had much in common: Baxter was idle, sentimental, and ready for any sort of practical joking. He was the ideal drinking companion and had a droll turn of phrase that was a perfect foil for Louis's high spirits and semi-hysterical flights of fancy. An anecdote that Baxter told of his first visit to Swanston makes it easy to see what Louis valued in this amiable youth:

> That night, late, in his bedroom, after reading to me (I think) 'The Devil on Crammond Sands', he flung himself back on his bed in a kind of agony exclaiming, 'Good God, will anyone ever publish me!' To soothe him, I (quite insincerely) assured him that of course someone would, for I had seen worse stuff in print myself.[66]

Baxter was put up for the Spec by Stevenson and became Secretary (he was always good with procedure, as befitted his profession). But their happiest times were spent on the streets of Edinburgh, engaged in jokes against fogeys such as the ill-tempered wine merchant Brash, whom Stevenson made the hero of a set of ribald verses, or talking to each other in ludicrously broad Scots, in the character of two old Edinburgh lawyers, Johnson and Thomson. Spontaneous jokes were their speciality, like the time they followed six men carrying a wrapped sheet of glass down George Street, as if they were chief mourners, hats off and heads bowed. As Louis wrote in one of his 'Brasheana' poems, 'Let us be fools, my friend, let us be drunken,/Let us be angry and extremely silly.'[67]

    In the spring of 1871 Louis was called on to give a paper to the Royal Scottish Society of Arts, and made a fair effort at pleasing both the examining committee and his father. One of the examiners was his professor of engineering, Fleeming Jenkin, whose early dealings with the student had not been promising. Stevenson had applied to him for one of the necessary certificates of attendance at the end of the first year, only to be told that as far as the professor was aware, his attendance had been nil. 'It is quite useless for *you* to come to me, Mr Stevenson,' Jenkin had said. 'There may be doubtful cases; there is no doubt about yours. You have simply *not* attended my class.'[68] The frankness of this impressed the truant, and Jenkin turned out to be one of the few older men towards whom Louis showed admiration and respect.

'On a New Form of Intermittent Light' is very short for a paper – ten pages of large writing, the last sentences of which have been written in a different ink and possibly a different hand: 'It must however, be noted, that none of these last methods are applicable to cases where more than one radiant is employed: for these cases either my grandfather's or Mr Wilson's contrivance must be resorted to'[69] – an anxious note, which suggests Thomas Stevenson looking over his boy's first contribution to science. The substance of Louis's proposal is that a revolving hemispherical mirror could be used in conjunction with a fixed mirror to make lighthouse lights flash. The 'revolving' part of this idea was ingenious, though from his very rudimentary diagrams it is clear that the student had given little thought to the technical and logistical difficulties. Nevertheless, Jenkin and his colleagues judged the paper 'specially noteworthy' and later in the year awarded this latest scion of the Stevenson family a silver medal for his trouble.*

Thomas Stevenson was, presumably, not so impressed by his son's performance, for it was only about ten days later that he chose an evening walk as the occasion to grill Louis on his intentions. The conversation was painful and upsetting for both, for the youth, 'tightly cross-questioned',[71] confessed that he cared for nothing but literature. Thomas had at last to swallow the fact that the experiment had gone on long enough, and had been a failure. Louis had spent four years studying at the university, three summers on the works, he had worked in a carpenter's shop, a foundry and a timberyard, and still couldn't tell one kind of wood from another or make the most basic calculations. They were flogging a dead horse.

* David Stevenson junior had a much curter judgement of the paper when approached by Graham Balfour for his professional opinion many years later, saying there were 'several objections' to his dilettante cousin's notion.[70]

An alternative career on 'the devious and barren paths of literature', as Thomas described it,[72] was out of the question, however. If the boy was going to abandon the family business, he had at least to train for a similarly dignified and worthy profession. He would have to study for the Bar. 'Tom wonderfully resigned', his wife noted in her diary on hearing the news, but though he had to accept the defeat as well as he could, Thomas Stevenson never got over the bitter disappointment of this day, and was still complaining about it in the last years of his life.

So Stevenson, after almost four years, was released from the yoke of engineering. He was going back to the university in the autumn to begin all over again as a student of law. Which was not to say he had any intention of becoming a lawyer.

3

THE CARELESS INFIDEL

Was early life laborious? Why and how? [. . .] The 'how' will distinguish various forms of mental fret and exhaustion from one another and from muscular fatigue.

Francis Galton, *Record of Family Faculties*

THE CHANGE TO reading for the Bar did not improve Stevenson's study habits. As Charles Guthrie recalled, 'We did not look for Louis at law lectures, except when the weather was bad.'[1] A notebook that survives from his law studies is peppered with caricatures and doodles, and the few notes there are on Roman citizenship segue with comical readiness into a much more engaging daydream containing lines of a later poem:

> People could appear as <u>Cognitas,</u> on whom full [?forms] had been conferred in a form of words before the magistrate. Odonot let me sleep, kind God or let me dream of her. There is summer ~~of the~~ time of hearts When insolvent, gent imprisoned to make friends dub up.
>
> > *O thou, still young at heart,*
> > *Still quick to see and feel,*
> > *Thou whose old arm takes yet the better part*
> > *An arm of steel.*[2]

Around the university, Stevenson and Baxter made a comical duo in manner and appearance: Baxter was tall, fair and square-built 'with what seemed to be an aggressively confident deportment', as one fellow student, John Geddie, recalled;[3] 'one was somehow

reminded of a slim and graceful spaniel with a big bull-dog, jowled
and "pop-eyed", trotting in its wake'.[4] The pair would sit together
near the exit of the lecture hall, poised for escape, or stage stunts
in class guaranteed to disquiet the lecturer, coming in late, sitting
down for as long as it took for the class to resume, staring about
them 'with a serious and faintly speculative air', then getting up
again and leaving.

Louis's most regular appearances were at meetings of the Spec
on Tuesday evenings, and he was often found loafing in the
society's library and rooms the rest of the week. Stevenson loved
its exclusivity and gentlemen's club comforts, but also the fact that
no one took it too seriously. Guthrie remembers him 'always in
high spirits and always good-tempered, more often standing than
sitting (and, when sitting, on any part of the chair except the seat),
chaffing and being chaffed, capping one good story with another'.[5]
Stevenson was prepared to talk casually about any subject under
the sun, it seemed (apart from the law), but the papers which he
read to the Spec still harped on religious themes. The influence of
the Covenanting prosecution on the Scotch mind, John Knox,
Paradise Lost, the relation (or lack of it, we can guess) of Christ's
teaching to modern Christianity: these were the topics upon which
Stevenson held forth to his fellow would-be advocates. The little
minister vein was still running strong in him, though it would have
been hard to ascertain his attitude to the Church from his
behaviour in public. One minute he would be mocking and provocative, as when, in Baxter's company, he mischievously interrupted three ministers sitting down to dinner at a hotel and forced a
long, elaborate grace on them; the next he would be in deadly
earnest, stopping a group of colliers on a Sunday to harangue them
for Sabbath-breaking.

Stevenson was fortunate to have found a mentor and surrogate
father at this time in Fleeming Jenkin, the professor whose painful
duty it had been to oversee his engineering studies. Jenkin had
recognised something in the truant (remarkably enough), and drew
him into his circle of friends. The Jenkin coterie was the most lively

and entertaining in Edinburgh, 'a haven, an oasis in a desert of convention and prejudice', as one of Jenkin's colleagues, Alfred Ewing, put it.[6] Jenkin was only sixteen years Louis's senior and had arrived at Edinburgh University from London in 1868 with his wife Anne, a striking and talented woman, with whom he organised elaborate private theatricals every year in their house on Great Stuart Street. The repertoire was eclectic – Shakespeare, Sheridan, Aeschylus, Charles Reade – and each play had five performances, preceded by weeks of strenuous rehearsal, directed and stage managed by Fleeming. Jenkin's ingenuity was enormous; he researched and designed costumes, went to the lengths of learning beard-making 'from an ancient Jew',[7] and engineered the wall between the dining room and the children's playroom to pivot back on hinges to form a stage, so that the dining room became an auditorium. Louis, a favourite of both the professor and his charismatic wife, was soon part of the company (as was Charles Baxter), and took part in several productions.

Jenkin was as unlike Thomas Stevenson as two men in the same profession and the same Church could be; he was an intellectual, an inventor and a teacher as well as a marvellously versatile electrical engineer, responsible for laying miles of cable under the sea and doing the preliminary work on modes of electrical transportation (which he called 'telpherage'). He had run an engineering business in London and built his own steam yacht for touring the coast with his wife and children.[8] Ten years after Stevenson first met him, Fleeming developed a passionate interest in Edison's new phonograph, which had not yet been manufactured or even exhibited outside the United States. With only a report in *The Times* to go on, he was able to replicate two versions of a machine like Edison's, which he showed at a fund-raising bazaar for the university cricket club. Mrs Jenkin was established in one booth, charging two and six for a view and trial of the new marvel, Jenkin and his friend Ewing were in another, taking turns to lecture every half hour. A farmer visiting the bazaar and trying his voice on the phonograph prepared for the ordeal by rolling up his sleeves. His address to the machine was short and eulogistic: 'What a wonderrrful instrrrument y'arrre!', but when the recording was played back to him, he turned and fled at the sound of his own voice, exclaiming 'It's no canny!'[9] When Louis got the chance to play with the amazing gadget, he and his friend W.B. Hole recorded 'various shades of Scotch accent' onto its tremulous tin-foil 'with unscientific laughter'.[10]

Louis's enthusiasm for the 'new science' of the evolutionists may well have been inspired by Jenkin, a keen follower of current controversies, who had a little-known but highly significant corre-spondence with Charles Darwin following the publication of the first edition of *On the Origin of Species*. Jenkin made the point to Darwin that his theory implied not a concentration or winnowing effect in the inheritance of characteristics, but a dilution or blend-ing – quite the opposite of what Darwin was seeking to prove. This anomaly exercised the scientist for decades and was partly answered in later editions of his work. Jenkin had made another of his brilliant coups.

No doubt the unspoken rivalry between Jenkin and Thomas Stevenson (present in Louis's mind, if nowhere else) worked itself into the contentions between father and son over what was becom-ing known as the Higher Criticism (though Thomas Stevenson would never have called it that). It is highly unlikely that Thomas Stevenson had read the works of Charles Darwin or Herbert Spencer when he attacked evolutionary theory in his stolid little pamphlet, but his son had read them and found Spencer in particu-lar a revelation: 'no more persuasive rabbi exists'.[11] In an incident recalled by Archibald Bisset, Louis held forth once about Spencer's *Theory of Evolution* on a walk to Cramond with his father and the tutor:

> At length his father said, 'I think, Louis, you've got Evo-lution on the brain. I wish you would define what the word means.' 'Well, here it is verbatim. Evolution is a continuous change from indefinite incoherent homogeneity to definite coherent heterogeneity of structure and function through suc-

cessive differentiations and integrations.' 'I think,' said his father, with a merry twinkle in his eyes, 'your friend Mr Herbert Spencer must be a very skilful writer of polysyllabic nonsense.'[12]

Louis had plenty of other 'friends', including Spinoza, part of whose *Tractatus Theologico-Politicus* he had read in a pamphlet picked up at a bookstall.[13] These were some of the 'unsettling works' which he later said 'loosened his views of life and led him into many perplexities'.[14] One of the most unsettling works of all was the New Testament, especially the gospel of Saint Matthew, which demonstrated to the young man that what was called Christianity had little to do with Christ's teaching. 'What he taught [...] was not a code of rules, but a ruling spirit; not truths, but a spirit of truth [...] What he showed us was an attitude of mind,' Stevenson wrote in 'Lay Morals'; the ethics of Christians, he said satirically, were far nearer those of Benjamin Franklin than Christ.

Another 'gospel' he was deeply affected by was that of Walt Whitman, whose poetry was treated with either caution or derision by the majority of the reading public in the 1870s. Stevenson had discovered *Leaves of Grass* soon after its publication in 1867, and kept a copy hidden at the tobacconist's shop that was his equivalent of a *poste restante*. While he acknowledged Whitman's want of 'literary tact' – the quality Stevenson himself had spent years trying to perfect – Stevenson admired, even venerated, the poet's philosophy and hugely ambitious design. He later described Whitman as 'a teacher who at a crucial moment of his youthful life had helped him to discover the right line of conduct',[15] and echoes of the electric bard can be heard all through the essays of the 1870s and eighties that gained Stevenson his reputation as an 'aggressive optimist':

> Life is a business we are all apt to mismanage, either living recklessly from day to day, or suffering ourselves to be gulled out of our moments by the inanities of custom. [...] It is the duty of the poet to induce [...] moments of clear sight. He is the declared enemy of all living by reflex action, of all

that is done betwixt sleep and waking, of all the pleasureless pleasurings and imaginary duties in which we coin away our hearts and fritter invaluable years.[16]

Stevenson was looking for a new definition of 'the spiritual' as he began to detach himself from the established Church, and he became one of the first members of the Psychological Society of Edinburgh, precursor of the Spiritualist Society, made up mostly of medical men, artists and university students. Bob was also a member (later vice-president), Stevenson himself was secretary briefly, and in 1873 he planned an article on spiritualism, probably to read to the Spec.[17] When he told his parents later that he had not come lightly to his views about religion, he hardly did justice to the rigour he had applied during these years to questions of belief and ethics. It turned out to be a lifetime's preoccupation, and at no point did he warrant his father's intemperate description of him as merely 'a careless infidel'.

The atmosphere at Heriot Row struck some observers as rather lax: both Thomas Stevenson and his son were loud, domineering talkers, and Louis shocked one set of visitors by 'contradicting his father flatly before every one at table'.[18] At a dinner party in the early 1870s, Flora Masson, daughter of Jenkin's friend Professor David Masson, remembered being placed between the father and son and being amazed (and perhaps a little wearied) at how they took exactly opposing views on every subject. Louis's talk that evening was 'almost incessant' (it was clearly one of his hyperactive days): 'I felt quite dazed at the amount of intellection he expended on each subject, however trivial in itself,' she wrote. 'The father's face at certain times was a study; an indescribable mixture of vexation, fatherly pride and admiration, and sheer bewilderment at his son's brilliant flippancies and the quick young thrusts of his wit and criticism.'[19]

Flora was a fellow member of the Jenkins' theatrical group, but remembered meeting Louis first (in the early 1870s) on a skating expedition with the professor and his family to Duddingston Loch, just to the south of Arthur's Seat. She noted how the

Jenkins always stayed in a couple, while Louis skated alone, 'a slender, dark figure with a muffler about his neck; [. . .] disappearing and reappearing like a melancholy minnow among the tall reeds that fringe the Loch'.[20] Perhaps he was auditioning for *Hamlet*. At the Jenkins' theatricals Stevenson never managed to bag a major role. One year he was the prompt, another a bit player in *Taming of the Shrew*, another time he played the part of the dandy Sir Charles Pomander in Charles Reade and Thomas Taylor's sentimental comedy *Masks and Faces* with 'a gay insolence which made his representation [. . .] most convincing'.[21] The highlight of his acting career came in 1875 as Orsino in *Twelfth Night*, but though the Heriot Row servants were mightily impressed with his appearance, and Margaret Stevenson glowed with maternal pride, the actor himself knew that in the process of being allotted a role of substance 'one more illusion' had been lost.[22]

Even though he wasn't able to command it through acting ability, Stevenson was always likely to make a bid to arrest attention at the Jenkin plays. One time when he was in charge of the curtain, he mischievously raised it while two members of the cast were larking around on stage just after finishing a particularly intense tragic scene. Though some of the audience laughed, Stevenson didn't escape a sharp reprimand from Jenkin. Flora, an intelligent young woman who later wrote novels and became the friend of both Browning and Florence Nightingale, seems to have escaped Stevenson's notice even though she was put in his way so regularly by their mutual friends. But she was watching him, and remarked how he liked to keep his costume on as long as possible after a performance (preferably right through supper). She also remembered once seeing him walk up and down the Jenkins' drawing room, watching himself in a mirror 'in a dreamy, detached way', 'as if he were acting to himself being an actor'.[23]

His parents' watchfulness grew more intense as Louis grew up and their hold over him loosened. His health became the language in which the family communicated, and was fussed over continually; uncle George Balfour, Mrs Stevenson's distinguished doctor-brother, was always being sought for out-of-hours opinions, and several times prescribed his nephew short breaks at the Bridge of Allan or Swanston. 'Rest' was the favoured cure, though from what malady is hard to tell, apart from the perennial threat of 'weakness'. Louis was very susceptible to catching viruses, and was always appallingly thin; today his appearance would suggest an immune deficiency syndrome. But when he was well, he bubbled over with vitality; his bright-eyed look, ready wit and endless appetite for talk were all legend. The collapses, when they came, were as often to do with depressed spirits as anything else.

Nevertheless, levels of fearfulness ran high in the household, and on hearing that her son wished to spend the summer of 1872 in Germany improving his knowledge of the language, Margaret Stevenson went into hysterics, saying she might never see him again. The plan was duly modified, and when Louis set out for Frankfurt that July in the company of Walter Simpson, it was for a three-week holiday, made over into another invalid tour by a rendezvous with his parents afterwards at Baden-Baden. Margaret's fears seem to have been much more to do with Louis becoming independent than becoming ill.

This tightening of parental concern may have been a response to the new friendships that Louis was enjoying, mostly with lively law students like Baxter, and people in the Jenkin circle, from which his parents were excluded. Added to this was the return to Edinburgh from Cambridge of Bob Stevenson in the summer of 1871. Bob's aimless brilliance and energy were a tonic to his younger cousin, who immediately drew him into the group of friends – Louis, Baxter, Simpson and Ferrier – who together formed a society called 'LJR'. The initials stood for 'Liberty – Justice – Reverence', fervent discussion of which – over many rounds of drinks in Advocates' Close – was one of their *raisons d'être*. (A manuscript note by Stevenson links 'LJR' with 'Whitman: humanity: [. . .] love of mankind: sense of inequality: justification of art:

decline of religion'.) More often, though, the members of LJR were to be found planning elaborate practical jokes, and devised a term, 'Jink', to describe their activities: 'as a rule of conduct, Jink consisted in doing the most absurd acts for the sake of their absurdity and the consequent laughter'.[24] They invented a character called John Libbel in whose name they carried out fake correspondences with prominent Edinburgh citizens, and for whom they printed calling cards: 'I have spent whole days going from lodging-house to lodging-house inquiring anxiously, "If Mr Libbel had come yet?"', Stevenson related, 'and when the servant or a landlady had told us "No", assuring her that he would come soon, and leaving a mysterious message.'[25] On another occasion, they started a rumour that Libbel had inherited a fortune and that they were agents of the estate. 'Libbelism' was really a form of subversive performance art, and 'Jink' a kind of Dadaism *avant la lettre*, set in 1870s Edinburgh. Stevenson's own remarks corroborate this, with their echo of 'art for art's sake': 'we were disinterested, we required none of the encouragement of success, we pursued our joke, our mystification, our *blague* for its own sake'.

Once, to their amazement, Louis and Bob were caught out by a jeweller in whose shop they had been attempting to act out 'some piece of vaulting absurdity'.[26] The shopman's eyes lit up when he realised what was going on: '"I know who you are," he cried; "you're the two Stevensons."' The man said that his colleague would be vexed; he'd been dying to see them in action. Would the young men come back later for tea? And thus, bested by one of their own victims and astonished that their real names were known to anyone, the cousins beat a hasty retreat. Just as Libbelism anticipates some of the fantastic plots of Stevenson's *New Arabian Nights*, so this scene in the jeweller's is like a comic version of his story 'Markheim'. 'Jink' was an imaginative release in more ways than one.

At this date, Bob was living at home in the Portobello district of Edinburgh with his widowed mother and sisters and studying at the city's School of Art. He was going to be an artist, and had been travelling in France for the past few summers with other painter-friends. He had always been a hero-figure to Louis, and now seemed more fortunate than ever: of the two youths, Bob was by far the more attractive, with his fine tall figure and well-grown moustaches (Louis's weedy lip-hair was the butt of jokes for years). Women all fell for him at a glance, and men loved him for his exuberant erudition and excitable character. The word 'genius' was often applied, especially with regard to his talk, though Louis's characterisation of it perhaps better suggests the description 'manic': 'the strange scale of language, flying from Shakespeare to Kant, and from Kant to Major Dyngwell [. . .] the sudden, sweeping generalisations, the absurd irrelevant particularities, the wit, wisdom, folly, humour, eloquence and bathos, each startling in its kind, and yet all luminous in the admired disorder of their combination'.[27] But this sort of wild verbal exhibitionism had another charm for Louis; as he said in the same essay, 'there are always two to a talk, giving and taking, comparing experience and according conclusions. Talk is fluid, tentative, continually "in further search and progress".'[28] In other words, impromptu, collaborative, and always *To be continued*.

Thomas and Margaret Stevenson had less reason to delight in their nephew's return to Edinburgh. With his flagrant pursuit of something that hardly had a name yet – *la vie bohème* – his art studies, his affectations of dress and his insolent wordiness, Bob must have looked like the least appropriate companion possible for their son. The parents didn't know, of course, about the long drinking sessions in Advocates' Close, the excesses of Libbelism or the long walks on which Louis and Bob behaved like a couple of mad tramps, singing and dancing on the moonlit roads out of sheer high spirits. They also, presumably, hadn't heard the story which went about a few years later, that Bob had divided his patrimony into ten equal parts and was going to allot himself one part a year for a decade, at the end of which he would commit suicide.[29] But they knew enough to be worried, and when Thomas Stevenson, snooping among his son's papers, came upon the comically-intended 'constitution' of the LJR – beginning 'Ignore everything that our parents have taught us' – he was thrown into a state of angry panic. This was presumably before the evening (31 January 1873) when Thomas decided to challenge his son with some straight questions about his beliefs.

The timing of the interview was unfortunate. Louis had been ill for weeks with diphtheria, and was freshly impressed with the fragility of life and a sense of *carpe diem*. In the spirit of honest dealing, he decided not to temporise as usual but to answer his father's questions as truthfully as he could, saying to Thomas's face that he no longer believed in the established Church or the Christian religion. 'If I had foreseen the real Hell of everything since,' he wrote miserably to Baxter after this spontaneous out-burst, 'I think I should have lied as I have done so often before.'[30] For what began as an attempt at family openness turned into as traumatic an act of 'coming out' as can be imagined: a thunderbolt to the bewildered parents, to whom confirmation of Louis's athe-ism was of course much more than a devastating personal rebuke or act of filial aggression; to believers like them, it meant the eternal damnation of their only child's soul, and the possible contami-nation of other souls. The chagrin they felt when he abandoned the family profession was nothing to him turning his back on salvation. 'And now!' Louis continued in his outpouring to Baxter,

> they are both ill, both silent, both as down in the mouth as if – I can find no simile. You may fancy how happy it is for me. If it were not too late, I think I could almost find it in my heart to retract; but it is too late; and again, am I to live my whole life as one falsehood? Of course, it is rougher than Hell upon my father; but can I help it? They don't see either that my game is not the light-hearted scoffer; that I am not (as they call me) a careless infidel: I believe as much as they do, only generally in the inverse ratio: I am, I think, as honest as they can be in what I hold.
>
> [. . .] Now, what is to take place? What a damned curse I am to my parents! As my father said, 'You have rendered my whole life a failure.' As my mother said, 'This is the

heaviest affliction that has ever befallen me.' And, O Lord, what a pleasant thing it is to have just damned the happiness of (probably) the only two people who care a damn about you in the world.[31]

The household became eerily quiet, like 'a house in which somebody is still waiting burial'. His parents went into a state of hushed emergency, Margaret pathetically suggesting that her son join the minister's youth classes, Thomas locked in his study, reading up Bishop Butler's *Analogy of Religion* in order to rejoin the fray. 'What am I to do?' Stevenson wrote despairingly to his friend. 'If all that I hold true and most desire to spread, is to be such death and worse than death, in the eyes of my father and mother, what the *devil* am I to do?'[32]

The fallout from Louis's confession continued for months, his father's anger and his mother's distress erupting uncontrollably all through the spring and summer of 1873. Margaret wept at church, Thomas was full of dark threats and despairing glances, and condemned his son's attempts at cheerfulness as 'heartless levity'.[33] When Bob went off to Antwerp to study art in the spring, Louis felt his misery at home even more sharply, and by the summer was almost prostrated by illness. This was one area where the youth could still count on a sympathetic response from his parents. They agreed that he should have a holiday, somewhere quiet in the countryside, with friendly, trustworthy people. Their choice was Cockfield Rectory in Suffolk, the home of Margaret's niece Maud and her husband, Professor Churchill Babington.

Frances Sitwell was lying on a sofa near a window at her friend Maud Babington's home when she saw a young man approach up the drive. He was wearing a straw hat and velvet jacket, carried a knapsack and looked hot, having just walked from Bury St Edmunds, a good eight miles away. 'Here is your cousin,' she remarked to Maud, who went out through the french window to meet him. The young man – very boyish, and with a strong Scottish accent – seemed shy to begin with, and jumped at the chance to go and visit the moat in the company of Mrs Sitwell's ten-year-old son, Bertie. But by the end of the day, when he and she began to talk seriously to each other, 'an instantaneous understanding' sprang up between them,[34] and strong mutual attraction. 'Laughter, and tears, too, followed hard upon each other till late into the night,' Mrs Sitwell wrote, 'and his talk was like nothing I had ever heard before, though I knew some of our best talkers and writers.'[35]

Frances Sitwell was thirty-four when she met Stevenson, and had been married since the age of sixteen to the Reverend Albert Sitwell, sometime private secretary to the Bishop of London and vicar of Minster, in Kent, since 1869. They had met in Ireland, where both grew up, and spent the earliest part of their marriage in India; Frances had also lived in Australia. The marriage was not a success, at least not from Mrs Sitwell's point of view. No one seems to have had a good word to say for her husband, 'a man of unfortunate temperament and uncongenial habits', according to E.V. Lucas.[36] The euphemism hints at cruelty and vice (was Sitwell an adulterer? a drinker?), but all we can be sure of is that by the time the couple moved to Minster with their two little boys, Frederick and Bertie, Frances was finding it necessary to spend long periods of time away from home visiting friends, of whom Maud Babington was the closest. Like Louis, she was an exile at Cockfield from an intolerable home life.

When Stevenson met her in the summer of 1873, Mrs Sitwell was mourning the death of her elder son only three months before, aged twelve. The tragedy seems to have catalysed her thoughts about a permanent separation from her husband, though she knew it would be difficult to effect one without Sitwell's agreement. She and her surviving son were tied to 'the Vicar' indefinitely unless she could become financially independent, which meant finding a job, a very daunting prospect for a woman of her social standing at the time.

One thing she didn't consider, and which speaks volumes about her character, was to throw herself into the arms of one or other of her many admirers. They were, on the whole, adorers rather than suitors, in whom she inspired devotion that verged on idolisation. 'Divining intuition like hers was genius. Vitality like hers was genius,' one of them wrote; another, 'she was the soul of honour, discretion and sympathy', 'waiting for her smile is the most delightful of anticipations, and when it comes it is always dearer than you remembered, and irradiates all who are in her company with happiness'.[37] Over the years she nurtured a string of needy young men, including Stevenson, Sidney Colvin, Cotter Morrison, Stephen Phillips and latterly Joseph Conrad, all of whom left ardent tributes to her virtues: a 'good angel', 'a priceless counsellor'; a 'deity'.[38] But above and beyond the superlatives, a genuinely extraordinary character emerges: not a wit, a beauty or a coquette, but a woman of quiet, tender and very ardent feelings, who retained a childlike capacity for simple pleasures and the subtlest appreciation of sophisticated ones. Colvin remembers her clapping her hands for joy and 'leaping in her chair' at the anticipation of a gift or treat, and described her sympathy thus: 'She cools and soothes your secret smart before ever you can name it; she divines and shares your hidden joy, or shames your fretfulness with loving laughter; she unravels the perplexities of your conscience, and finds out something better in you than you knew of; she fills you not only with generous resolutions but with power to persist in what you have resolved.'[39] It was this paragon with whom Stevenson spent the month of August 1873. Sibylline, sensitive, brave, tender, distressed, bereaved, abused: he would have fallen in love with a tenth of her.

Mrs Sitwell, as we have seen, was delighted by the young Scot and within three days of his arrival at Cockfield had written to her friend Sidney Colvin to urge him to hurry if he wanted to meet 'a brilliant and to my mind unmistakable young genius'[40] who had 'captivated the whole household'[41] at Cockfield. Colvin had been a friend of hers (how good a friend I will discuss presently) since the late 1860s. They probably met through the Babingtons: Churchill Babington was made Professor of Archaeology at Cambridge during Colvin's time there as an undergraduate. Mrs Sitwell intuited that Colvin and Stevenson would find each other interesting, but she also realised that Colvin, with his influential London literary connections, could be of use to her excitable new friend, who made no bones about the fact that the law was a bore and that he lived only for writing.

Sidney Colvin was only five years Stevenson's senior, but had the air of a much older, more sedate person. Tall and thin, with papery dry skin, a rather ponderous manner and a speech impediment, he did not seem readily appealing. On graduating from Cambridge in 1867 he began a career as an art critic and literary commentator, writing for the *Pall Mall Gazette*, the *Globe* and the *Fortnightly Review*, three of the most prestigious periodicals of the day. In 1871 he became the *Portfolio*'s main art critic and had already published a short book; he was a member of the Savile Club (as was Fleeming Jenkin) and a friend of Burne-Jones and Rossetti (whose work he promoted avidly), and when Stevenson met him in 1873 he had just been appointed Slade Professor of Fine Arts at Cambridge. A young man so well-placed in the world might well have adopted a superior air with Maud Babington's scruffy student cousin, but Colvin's manner was always respectful, courteous and hesitant – he was a very English Englishman, and though not charming himself, highly appreciative of charm. It is hard to say who was more pleased when the train pulled in at Cockfield on 6 August, the 'young genius' from Edinburgh, excited to be meeting the sage of the *Fortnightly Review*, or Colvin himself:

> If you want to realise the kind of effect [Stevenson] made, at least in the early years when I knew him best, imagine this attenuated but extraordinarily vivid and vital presence, with something about it that at first sight struck you as freakish, rare, fantastic, a touch of the elfin and unearthly, an Ariel. [...] he comprised within himself, and would flash on you in the course of a single afternoon, all the different ages and half the different characters of man, the unfaded freshness of a child, the ardent outlook and adventurous day-dreams of a boy, the steadfast courage of manhood, the quick sympathetic

tenderness of a woman, and already, as early as the mid-twenties of his life, an almost uncanny share of the ripe life-wisdom of old age.[42]

The weeks at Cockfield passed in simple pleasure trips and long lounging days. Louis was already a favourite with Maud and Professor Babington (who called him 'Stivvy'), and was a welcome companion to Bertie Sitwell, with whom he played at toy theatres and piggyback rides. The party visited Lavenham and Melford, and Louis was so ardent a helper at the school picnic that he blistered his hand slicing bread for the sandwiches. Colvin came and went, having discussed at length possible essay and book projects that Stevenson could put forward to the publisher Alexander Macmillan, and Stevenson was so excited at the prospect that he was already composing a piece on 'Roads' as he walked the lanes around Cockfield. 'Roads' seems a very apt subject for this pivotal moment in Stevenson's career, when at last there appeared to be some alternative to the path he had been set on by his parents. Soothed by Mrs Sitwell and sponsored by Colvin, Stevenson was on the brink of enjoying the literary life he craved.

'Roads' wasn't the only piece of writing Stevenson began at Cockfield; there was also an epistolary novel, or perhaps the resuscitation of an earlier attempt at a novel under the encouragement of Mrs Sitwell. Nothing remains of it now, but the heroine's name was Claire and the project seems to have been closely tied to Louis's burgeoning feelings for Mrs Sitwell herself, framed around an imagined or anticipated correspondence with her.[43] This may explain why the novel faltered pretty quickly after Louis and Mrs Sitwell were separated and began their real correspondence, which was to form such an important part of his output in the coming years. At the end of September, Louis was writing to Mrs Sitwell, 'Of course I have not been going on with Claire. I have been out of heart for that; and besides it is difficult to act before the reality. Footlights will not do with the sun; the stage moon and the real, lucid moon of one's dark life, look strangely on each other.'[44]

The record of the five weeks that Stevenson spent in Suffolk that summer is sparse but from the flood of correspondence that began as soon as he was separated from Mrs Sitwell at the end of August it becomes clear that he had in that time fallen deeply in love. In those first few days at Cockfield he must have felt that he had at last met the perfect woman, the endlessly sympathetic and eager listener he had craved all his life. Mrs Sitwell loved his high spirits, laughed at his jokes, but also encouraged his confidence, and understood immediately and without judging them his mood swings and volatile spirits. Her melting eyes seemed to see into his soul, her rendition of Bizet's 'Chant d'Amour' in the long summer evenings left him swooning. In their walks around the village and during the long days in the Rectory gardens, Mrs Sitwell had confided her marital unhappiness and he the painful rift with his parents; she stroked his hair as he sat with his head on her lap; they were fellows in suffering and in sympathy. And Louis seems to have hoped and expected that they would become more than that. His early letters call her 'my poor darling', 'my own dearest friend', and refer to the complete candour and trust that they have shared as 'all that has been between us'.[45] In the early days, at least, he must have believed that once 'that incubus' Albert Sitwell was out of the way, and once he, Louis, had become a self-supporting writer, he would be free to pursue this love of a lifetime.

Mrs Sitwell's feelings for Stevenson are very much harder to divine, as in later years she asked for all her side of their correspondence to be destroyed, and he obliged. The only surviving remarks about him by her are in a very short contribution to a collection of reminiscences called *I Can Remember Robert Louis Stevenson*, first published in 1922. There she describes them becoming 'fast friends' for life on first acquaintance, and briefly describes how she introduced him to Sidney Colvin. By the time this little article appeared, Stevenson's letters (edited by Colvin) had been in print for a couple of decades, and it was no news to the reading public that he had been in thrall to his 'Madonna', as he later called her, in the early 1870s, nor that she had later – much later – married the editor of the letters.

Even with the evidence of Stevenson's powerful feelings towards her, and the reciprocity implied by some chance remarks in his letters, even given the fact that she withheld (not surprisingly) some letters 'too sacred and intimate to print' from the Colvin editions,[46] it seems unlikely that Frances Sitwell was in love with Stevenson in the erotic sense at this or any other time. Her relation to him seems consistently to have been that of an inordinately affectionate woman rather than a woman of passion. She reciprocated his feelings in intensity but not in kind, perhaps not correcting his romantic hopes or assumptions at first because she didn't quite understand or admit them. From what Colvin says in a tribute to his by-then wife (published, anonymously, in 1908), Mrs Sitwell might be described as serially naïve or disingenuous about her sexual attractiveness:

> In the fearlessness of her purity she can afford the frankness of her affections, and shows how every fascination of her sex may in the most open freedom be the most honorably secure. Yet in a world of men and women, such an one cannot walk without kindling once and again a dangerous flame before she is aware. As in her nature there is no room for vanity, she never foresees these masculine combustions, but has a wonderful art and gentleness in allaying them, and is accustomed to convert the claims and cravings of passion into the lifelong loyalty of grateful and contented friendship.[47]

'Masculine combustions' covers a lot of Stevenson's behaviour around Mrs Sitwell, but none of Colvin's, which perhaps explains why he won the lady in the end. Nothing about Colvin was combustible. It took nine years from the death of Albert Sitwell in 1894 for him to get round to marrying the widow, who was by then sixty-four years old. The reason for the delay was given as Colvin's financial straits – he had an elderly mother to support – but this seems thin, or at the very least coldly prudent. For as E.V. Lucas remarked, by the turn of the century 'all London knew' that Colvin and Mrs Sitwell were a couple: they were constant companions though they lived apart.[48] How this arrangement was cheaper or more convenient than getting married is hard to figure. The answer to the long nuptial delay seems much more likely to be Colvin not wanting to upset his mother, who died in 1902.

It is necessary to look so far ahead, into the next century, to get some idea of the network of relationships that developed between Stevenson, Mrs Sitwell and Colvin in the 1870s. The triangular pattern usually suggests strife and rivalry, but at Cockfield Stevenson met two friends who were separately very important to him and whose relationship with each other was strengthened, possibly cemented, by their mutual concern for him. What were Colvin's relations with Mrs Sitwell in the 1870s? It is hard to tell, but I would guess that their liaison was not sexual to begin with (perhaps not ever), but an ardent friendship of the kind Mrs Sitwell also enjoyed with Stevenson. Colvin was less trouble than the young Scot, a gentle and undemanding devotee. He was her frequent companion in London and they spent time together privately (a risky business in the 1870s), including a holiday to Brittany in 1876, which Colvin wrote up lyrically in an article for the *Cornhill*.[49] By 1884, when Colvin got his job at the British Museum and with it the Museum residence where Mrs Sitwell always appeared as hostess, it seems safe to assume that they were lovers. They could have been lovers any time from meeting in the late 1860s, of course, though somehow the whole affair seems more slow-burning than that, more discreet, rarefied and tentative. Also more honest: nothing was signalled to Stevenson when he began his doomed onslaught of devotion late in 1873, and if Colvin was already having an affair with Mrs Sitwell then, one might have expected him to stand guard carefully over all new 'masculine combustions' near his mistress, even if she was incapable of recognising them herself.[50] Either way, Colvin's selflessness in doing all he could to further Stevenson's career is remarkable. For there was never a shadow of jealousy or pique in his dealings with the younger man, despite the fact – which must have been obvious to Colvin the minute he saw them together at the Rectory – that

Louis was a serious rival for Mrs Sitwell's attentions, not to say a potential monopoliser of them.

Nevertheless, there are a few intriguing scraps of evidence which could be made to argue the contrary. One is a letter which Bob Stevenson wrote to Louis on 6 February 1874, having met Colvin for the first time. He and Colvin had spoken, at cross purposes, about Stevenson's situation, provoking this confidence from the professor:

> He said [. . .] that he had been much grieved to observe the effect that certain emotions you had gone thro' lately had had upon you. He said it was a first class thing for you to do and that he knew no other man who was so game for being on the spot as you and that whatever you had lost you had gained in him such a friend for life as it is difficult to gain. I thought he was not supposed to be cognizant of what had gone on at all. I am mystified first by you, more by him.[51]

Colvin was acknowledging an extreme act of generosity on Stevenson's part – one that would deserve his never-ending fidelity in return (which he gave). What could this have been other than ceding to 'the first-comer', as Louis elsewhere calls Colvin, his love-interest in Mrs Sitwell? But in February 1874 whatever Stevenson might have 'lost' was not obvious from his letters or his demeanour (although he clearly did try hard to sublimate his feelings for Mrs Sitwell later that and the following year). This could (just) be because his 'loss' occurred *before* the letters to Mrs Sitwell begin, i.e. during the month at Cockfield in 1873. Stevenson himself referred in his first letters to her of 'all that has passed between us', and here is Bob talking of how he thought Colvin ignorant of 'what had gone on'. Mrs Sitwell herself became oddly jealous when a rival for Louis's attention appeared on the scene in the spring of 1874: her possessiveness then seems suggestive.

Then there is the ambiguous evidence of a letter from Graham Balfour to his wife Rhoda on the day in 1899 when he was appointed by Robert Louis Stevenson's estate to write the official biography of the author. Fired up with excitement at the prospect of writing Stevenson's life, and perhaps to test the extent to which he was going to be trusted, Balfour asked the widow, Fanny Stevenson, 'straight out about F. Sitwell':

> and she says Yes. F.S. used to tell people whom she knew well, as she wished not to be on false pretences. But I fancy the fat is nearly in that fire.
> Tamaitai [Fanny Stevenson] is rather bitter.[52]

The answer was *Yes*, but what was the question? It could only have been 'Are Colvin and Mrs Sitwell lovers?' if Graham Balfour was really out of the loop, for E.V. Lucas says that 'all London knew' about the relationship by this date, and the elderly-looking couple were discreet, hugely respectable and beyond the reach of harmful gossip, Albert Sitwell being five years dead. If the question was 'Were Colvin and Mrs Sitwell lovers back in the 1870s?' – which would explain the phrase 'F.S. used to tell people whom she knew well, as she wished not to be on false pretences' – what is this fat that is nearly in the fire? The exposure of Mrs Sitwell's long-term adultery? No one was likely to do that, certainly not a biographer (and cousin) of Robert Louis Stevenson, to whom both Colvin and Mrs Sitwell had been devoted. And what was 'Tamaitai' 'rather bitter' about?*

But what if the question was 'Were Stevenson and Mrs Sitwell ever lovers?' Apart from Mrs Sitwell herself, and Colvin, only Fanny Stevenson could have been expected to know the answer to that one, and it seems a more pressing question for Balfour to ask at this point of maximum favour with the widow than whether or not an obvious couple were a couple. The question cannot be

---

* Fanny Stevenson's feelings towards Colvin were, by this date, not 'bitter' so much as implacably antagonistic. Her letters to Graham Balfour during the period when he was writing Stevenson's biography (1899–1901) are full of scorn for Colvin's method and accusations of conspiracy against Colvin and RLS's old friends. She refers to Fanny Sitwell as 'a pigface' and anticipates 'heartrending wails' from the couple over the loss of control of the biography. Fanny Sitwell had written to Fanny Stevenson, the latter notes sarcastically, asking her to suppress ' "Youthful things that *he* [RLS] would have burned if he were here" '.[53]

confidently resolved one way or the other, but it does leave open
some intriguing possibilities.

The end of August came; it was time to go home, but Stevenson
strung out his departure from Cockfield by staying a few days on
the way back to Edinburgh at Colvin's cottage in Norwood, with
a visit to the Sitwells' house in Chepstow Place in Bayswater. There
he met '*le chapelain*', Mrs Sitwell's problematic husband, and was
able to observe secretly the marriage he had begun to know very
well from one side.* When they sat together under a tree in Suffolk,
or walked around Kensington Gardens on their last day in London,
the gentle, tender looks of Mrs Sitwell were a balm to Louis's
heart. His first letter to her, written when he got back to Heriot
Row, shows an intimacy that had been requited fully in spirit, if
not in deed:

> I am very tired, dear, and somewhat depressed after all that
> has happened. Do you know, I think yesterday and the day
> before were the two happiest days of my life. It seems strange
> that I should prefer them to what has gone before; and yet
> after all, perhaps not. O God, I feel very hollow and strange
> just now. I had to go out to get supper and the streets were
> wonderfully cool and dark, with all sorts of curious illumina-
> tions at odd corners from the lamps; and I could not help
> fancying as I went along all sorts of foolish things – chansons
> – about showing all these places to you, Claire, some other
> night; which is not to be. Dear, I would not have missed last
> month for eternity.[55]

Louis's new, dizzying intimacy with Mrs Sitwell in some senses
precipitated the upheavals that were to take place in the Stevenson
household that year, as he had for the first time someone – some

* I am assuming RLS *did* meet Albert Sitwell at this time because his letter of 1 September
sends greetings to Bertie and instructs FJS to 'say what is necessary, if you like, or if you
think anything necessary, to the Curate of Cumberworth and the Vicar of Roost'.[54] There
would have been no necessity for greetings of any kind had RLS not been introduced to
him.

woman – in whom to confide everything, and more. There seems to have been no limit to Mrs Sitwell's capacity for confidences, and the resulting flood of emotion from her young correspondent makes remarkable reading. The letters are highly stylised, self-indulgent monologues, in which passages of elaborate description are punctuated with long rhapsodies about his feelings. Perhaps, having been anticipated in his stillborn fiction, 'Claire', Stevenson had trouble establishing a non-rhetorical tone. Set beside his letters to Baxter, which are full of salty jokes, raucous verses and long vernacular rambles in the character of Tam Johnson (ancient drunken venial Writer to the Signet), those to Mrs Sitwell seem the work of another person altogether. Their humourlessness is striking. Chagrined that there was no quick response to one letter, he wrote on 27 September:

> I have a fear that something must have happened, and so I write frankly and fully, because I fear I may never write to you again; but O my dear, you know – you see – you must feel, in what perfect faith and absolute submission I am writing. You must feel that I shall still feel as I have felt and will work as well *for* you and *towards* you, without any recognition, as I could work with all recognition. Remember always that you are my Faith. And now, my dearest, beautiful friend, good night to you. I shall never feel otherwise to you, than now I do when I write myself
>   Your faithfullest friend R.L.S.[56]

So much fear, and so much feeling. Pages and pages went off every day to his 'friend in London' (which is all he told Baxter of the connection[57]), and every day he itched to get down to the Spec, where Mrs Sitwell was sending her replies so as not to arouse enquiry at Heriot Row. Stevenson was rather fascinated by the spectacle of himself in love, and at times asked Mrs Sitwell for copies of his letters to be sent back, for him to work into possibly saleable prose. And in the constant exercise of sensibility, he made some interesting discoveries, such as this reason for not being able 'to bring before you, what went before me':

There are little local sentiments, little abstruse connexions among things, that no one can ever impart. There is a pervading impression left of life in every place in one's memory, that one can best parallel out of things physical, by calling it a *perfume*. Well, this perfume of Edinburgh, of my early life there, and thoughts, and friends – went tonight suddenly to my head, at the mere roll of an organ three streets away. And it went off newly, to leave in my heart the strange impression of two pages of a letter I had received this afternoon, which had about them a colour, a perfume, a long thrill of sensation – which brought a rush of sunsets, and moonlight, and primroses, and a little fresh sentiment of springtime into my heart, that I shall not readily forget.[58]

Love had brought out the aesthete in Stevenson with a vengeance, for what is this reminiscent of more than Proust and his madeleine? – except that Proust was still an infant.

While Louis was enjoying his Suffolk idyll, a dramatic scene had been played out in Edinburgh around the deathbed of one of his same-name cousins, Lewis Balfour, son of Margaret Stevenson's elder brother Lewis. The dying thirty-year-old had decided that this was the right moment to tell his uncle Thomas Stevenson his opinion of Bob Stevenson: a filthy atheist, he believed, a 'blight', and 'mildew', whose pernicious influence on Louis had led the younger man astray.[59] Thomas Stevenson latched onto this at once, for it played straight to his own desire to find a scapegoat for his son's heretical opinions, and by the time Louis returned home from Suffolk, Bob had become the new *persona non grata* and Louis himself was almost exonerated. His parents were suddenly relieved and pleasant again; all that was necessary was to keep the wicked Bob out of their way.

This state of affairs clearly couldn't last long, and when Thomas Stevenson met his nephew on the street just a few days later, he let fly with sonorous condemnations. Bob responded spiritedly, as Louis wrote later to Mrs Sitwell, 'that he didn't know where I had found out that the Christian religion was not true, but that he hadn't told me. [...] I think from that point, the conversation went off into emotion and never touched shore again.'[60] The hurt generated by this public row was enormous; Bob had had to bear the brunt of his uncle's wrath (an intimidating spectacle, as he was now ready to concede), and Louis heard, second-hand, many painful things, including his father's opinion that he had ceased to care for his parents and that they in turn were ceasing to care for him. Margaret Stevenson, on hearing of the interview, went into hysterics again and Louis was left to reflect miserably that 'even the calm of our daily life is all glossing; there is a sort of tremor through it all and a whole world of repressed bitterness'.[61]

A shred of good came out of this explosive day: because his father's rage had been directed against Bob instead of himself, Louis was better able to judge how violent and threatening it really was: 'There is now, at least, one person in the world who knows what I have had to face,' he wrote to Mrs Sitwell that evening, '– damn me for facing it, as I sometimes think, in weak moments – and what a tempest of emotions my father can raise when he is really excited.'[62] Margaret Stevenson, who always hated any kind of confrontation, seems to have been finding her husband's behaviour alarming too. Her loyalty to Tom was such that she usually sided with him regardless; thus her only way of communicating to Louis that she felt he had been ill-treated was by paying him small compensatory attentions. In the month following his return home, mother and son had a pleasant lunch together in Glasgow while Thomas was at a business meeting, and she gave him a kiss spontaneously one day. The fact that Stevenson noted these things gratefully is an indication of how withheld his mother must have been normally.

The truth is that both Louis and his mother were cowed by Thomas Stevenson's rages, which were always accompanied by dramatic gestures (falling to his knees, for instance) and overemphatic language. He was known as a melancholic man, but at times the family must have feared for his sanity too, especially with the example of his elder brother Alan before them. David

Stevenson, Thomas's other brother and senior partner in the firm, was also subject to mood swings that made him difficult to work with sometimes, and in the 1880s was to suffer a mental collapse similar to Alan's. So with the threat of over-straining his father's temper, and having done – as he was constantly reminded – so much damage already, Louis was keen to placate whenever he could, acquiescing to Thomas's bizarre (and aggressive) demand that he write to the papers on the subject of Presbyterian Union – the last thing on Louis's mind at the time – and trying his best to 'make him nearly happy'.[63] His attempts were usually failures, and one time went spectacularly wrong. On an evening when his mother was away, Louis thought his father might be interested to hear some passages from a paper he had given at the Spec on the Duke of Argyll, but even in such diluted form the articulation of Louis's views on free will were too much for Thomas, who said he was being tested too far. He then launched into renewed recrimi-nations, as Louis, shaky and upset, reported to Mrs Sitwell later that night:

> He said tonight, 'He wished he had never married', and I could only echo what he said. 'A poor end', he said, 'for all my tenderness.' And what was there to answer? 'I have made all my life to suit you – I have worked for you and gone out of my way for you – and the end of it is that I find you in opposition to the Lord Jesus Christ – I find everything gone – I would ten times sooner have seen you lying in your grave than that you should be shaking the faith of other young men and bringing such ruin on other houses, as you have brought already upon this'.[64]

There were more scenes of this sort, and 'half threats of turning me out', along with some flashes of extraordinary peevishness and pique on the part of the father towards the son. Stevenson told Mrs Sitwell in early October of an incident when his mother (hear-ing, Louis imagined, of the row that had taken place in her absence) had given him a little present which Thomas then coveted. 'I was going to give it up to him, but she would not allow me,' Louis wrote. What an odd family scene this conjures up: the father sulk-ing over his wife's little gesture of kindness, the son scrambling to mollify his feelings. 'It is always a pic-nic on a volcano,' he con-cluded sadly.[65]

The strain of living in 'our ruined, miserable house' was telling on Louis. His spirits were very low, his health consequently poor, and he reported to Mrs Sitwell on 16 September 1873 that he weighed a mere eight stone six (118 pounds). This was a man who was about five foot ten high and almost twenty-three years old. Bob was appalled at what was happening to his cousin, and advised him strongly to leave home. But Louis couldn't do this cleanly, partly because of his own dependence on his parents for money, partly because of their astonishing dependence on him. When Louis suggested that he should transfer to an English university (perhaps he argued that the climate would be better for him) he met with point-blank refusal: 'I must be kept, don't you see, from persons of my own way of thinking.'[66]

Edinburgh was beginning to look like a prison. Bob was leaving in October for Antwerp; 'Roads', for all Colvin's sponsorship, had been rejected by the *Saturday Review*. Colvin had arranged the necessary forms of admission to the English Bar on Louis's behalf, but as the date for the preliminary examinations in London drew nearer, Stevenson began to fear he would miss that chance too, as he was too ill in the preceding week to go anywhere (and, pre-dictably, had done no preparation for the exam at all). He got away on 24 October by telling his parents he wanted a change and was going to Carlisle, from where he went on to London.

From this point, events moved rapidly: he went straight to Mrs Sitwell at Chepstow Place, who took one look at him and insisted that he be seen by a specialist in lung diseases. The doctor, Andrew Clark, insisted that he should think neither of sitting the law exam nor of returning to Edinburgh but go immediately to the South of France to convalesce. It was not his lungs that were the problem (though the lungs were 'delicate and just in the state when disease might very easily set in'[67]), but his nerves, which were 'quite broken down'.

Clark's diagnosis was so adamant that one wonders if Mrs Sitwell primed him on the patient's situation, for when Thomas and Margaret Stevenson hurried down to London to consult him themselves, he seemed to have understood the source of Louis's nervous collapse very well and renewed his insistence that the patient have a complete change of scene and travel *alone*. The parents were upset at this wresting of the initiative from their hands, but couldn't question the opinion of such an eminent and expensive doctor, and arrangements were made immediately for Louis to spend the winter in Menton. 'Clark', Louis wrote to Mrs Sitwell from the hotel where his parents had taken him, 'is a trump.'[68]

Thus, in the first week of November 1873, Stevenson found himself on a train out of Paris, heading for the lemon groves and white villas of the south coast of France.

4

AH WELLESS

The mental powers, like the bodily ones, must be measured by achievement; relatively as in competition with others, or absolutely by the amount and quality of intellectual work actually accomplished.

Francis Galton, *Record of Family Faculties*

'BY A CURIOUS IRONY OF FATE, the places to which we are sent when health deserts us are often singularly beautiful,' Stevenson wrote in the essay that came out of his exile to the Riviera in 1873, 'Ordered South': 'I daresay the sick man is not very inconsolable when he receives sentence of banishment, and is inclined to regard his ill-health as not the least fortunate accident of his life.' Stevenson was certainly not inconsolable; at least, not until it began to dawn on him quite what his illness signified. Clark's diagnosis of 'nothing organically wrong whatever'[1] sounded like the all-clear, but in some ways his troubles were only just beginning.

For although he danced for joy in the sunshine on his arrival in Menton, Stevenson soon began to feel oppressed and oddly incapacitated. Instead of being free to bask in warmth, to read and write, he felt that his faculties had become blunted and stupid, 'like an enthusiast leading about with him a stolid, indifferent tourist'.[2] After the fantastic flights of sensibility he had indulged in the first rush of intimacy with Mrs Sitwell, he now felt that he was played out, nervously exhausted – perhaps irreversibly 'spent'. Unlike the other invalids he met in and around the Hôtel du

Pavillon – who included a number of middle-class British consumptives, the Dewars, the Napiers and a charming family called
Dowson – Stevenson's symptoms were not of incipient tuberculosis
but of depression. In the sanatorium atmosphere of Menton, his
condition deteriorated rapidly into a profound enervation and melancholia. A game of billiards, or even reading a novel, became
exhausting to him, and after a short walk he needed a day to
recover. He had to leave a concert early because the sound of the
brass was intolerable. Stevenson describes this nervous condition
in 'Ordered South':

> The happiness of [a sensitive person] comes to depend greatly
> upon those fine shades of sensation that heighten and harmon-
> ise the coarser elements of beauty. And thus a degree of
> nervous prostration, that to other men would be hardly dis-
> agreeable, is enough to overthrow for him the whole fabric
> of his life, to take, except at rare moments, the edge off his
> pleasures, and to meet him wherever he goes with failure, and
> the sense of want, and disenchantment of the world and life.[3]

'The whole fabric of his life' did indeed seem threatened. Writing
was out of the question, but worse than that, pleasure seemed out
of the question too: he felt himself facing not the approach of
death but a slow withdrawal from life. In 'Ordered South' he
argues that this sort of withdrawal helps make death acceptable
to the sick man; is, in effect, a means to 'persuade us from a place
we have no further pleasure in'. But the very decadence of this line
of thought was another of his symptoms. Sometimes Stevenson
struggled against it, apologising to Mrs Sitwell for 'the deformity
of my hypochondriasis' and 'the sickly vanities [. . .] of a person
who does not think himself well'.[4] But by December he had
embraced the idea of becoming a chronic invalid, writing to Baxter:
'I do somewhat portend that I may not recover at all, or at best
that I shall be long about it. My system does seem extraordinarily
played out.'[5]

Stevenson was smoking opium frequently during his months in
Menton, and his drug experiences were among the most entertain-

ing he had there. Writing to Mrs Sitwell of the first time he felt the full effect of the drug, he reported 'a day of extraordinary happiness; and when I went to bed there was something almost terrifying in the pleasures that besieged me in the darkness. Wonderful tremors filled me; my head swam in the most delirious but enjoyable manner; and the bed softly oscillated with me, like a boat in a very gentle ripple.'[6] He was under the influence of the drug when he wrote one his most rapturous letters to Mrs Sitwell on 7 December, sending her a single violet the scent of which had afforded him 'a princely festival of pleasure': 'No one need tell me that the phrase is exaggerated, if I say that this violet *sings*; it sings with the same voice as the March blackbird; and the same adorable tremor goes through one's soul at the hearing of it.'[7] This was not published in Colvin's selection of Stevenson's letters that appeared in the 1890s, or it might have been read with interest by Ernest Dowson, the archetypal poet of the Nineties School, whose work owes so much to Stevenson's own. It was he, aged five, who had picked the violets on a walk with his father and Stevenson in the olive yards of Menton and presented them to the strange long-haired Scotsman.

Stevenson's sense of removal from life was increased by missing a milestone in his own career, his first appearance in print. 'Roads', rejected by the *Saturday Review*, had been accepted by the *Portfolio* and appeared in the issue of 4 December 1873. Margaret Stevenson had bought up dozens of copies and was sending them out as Christmas presents to friends, presumably with a note to explain the author's pseudonym, 'L.S. Stoneven'. No one could visit Heriot Row without her springing up to read from the article, though she and Louis's father had, as usual, a number of criticisms of its style.[8] Compared with the compact brilliance of some of Stevenson's essays of the next few years (such as 'John Knox and his Relations to Women' or his pieces on Burns and Whitman), 'Roads' seems a wispy and wordy debut. He isn't really saying much when he remarks that *sehnsucht* – 'the passion for what is ever beyond' – 'is livingly expressed in that white riband of possible travel that severs the uneven country; not a ploughman following his plough up the shining furrow, not the blue smoke of any cottage in a hollow, but is brought to us with a sense of nearness and attainability by this wavering line of junction'.[9] Nevertheless, when he eventually saw the piece in print four months after publication, he thought it represented a peak of artistic achievement that he would never regain or surpass. But this had less to do with 'Roads's intrinsic merits than with the fact that it was brimful of optimism, having been conceived and written in Cockfield, 'when my life was in flower'.[10]

Colvin came to the Riviera for several weeks that winter (he too had fragile health) and met Stevenson in Monaco, cheering the invalid enormously. They stayed in Monte Carlo until Colvin witnessed a man shooting himself at the gaming tables, after which they decided to retreat to Menton, and spent the days talking, writing and sitting in public gardens by the sea, like a couple of prematurely aged men. Mrs Sitwell's situation was a matter of vital concern to both of them (and doubtless Colvin brought with him the latest news of her struggle to separate from 'the Vicar'), but it is highly unlikely that they spoke explicitly about their feelings for her. Stevenson's references in letters to Colvin are always reserved and respectful – he calls his idol 'Mrs Sitwell'[11] – and in letters to her, he treats Colvin as one with superior claims to her attention. Part of Colvin's charm for Stevenson was the incongruity between his manner and the depth of his feelings; 'he burns with a mild, steady cold flame of exaggeration towards all whom he likes and regards', Louis described it once to Bob. 'He is a person in whom you must *believe* like a person of the Trinity, but with whom little relation in the human sense is possible.'[12]* Colvin's very presence in the South of France, and his generous sponsorship of Stevenson's career, were proofs of his earnest goodwill towards the young Scot. Their friendship had none of that bantering intimacy that marked Stevenson's relationships with Bob or Charles

---

* Writing to Tati Salmon, high chief of the Tahitian Tevas, in 1889, to prepare him for meeting Colvin, Stevenson advised, 'if you find him at first sight anyway dry it is a question of manner and you will soon see how very noble and kind a nature lies behind'.[13]

Baxter; in fact, it contained no intimacy at all 'in the human sense'. However, it proved much stronger and more durable than any other friendship, and far outlasted Stevenson's relationship with Mrs Sitwell, though nothing of the sort would have seemed possible to either young man as they sat side by side on a bench by the sea, writing separate letters to their distant 'Madonna'.

Soon after Colvin's departure from Menton, Stevenson found himself happily distracted by the company of a group of Russians living in a nearby villa who dined daily at his hotel. These were a pair of sisters, Nadia Zassetsky and Sophie Garschine (the latter an invalid), and two little girls, Pelagie, aged eight, and two-year-old Nelitchka, both daughters of Madame Zassetsky (a mother of ten), though Pelagie had been adopted by her aunt. The women were some ten or fifteen years older than Stevenson, according to Colvin's guess, and both 'brilliantly accomplished and cultivated',[14] with a fascinatingly forthright and colourful turn of phrase (in French) which was unlike anything Stevenson had experienced from female company before. After an initial frostiness towards them, when he believed, correctly, that Madame Garschine was trying to seduce him, Stevenson gave himself over to their charm and novelty, and was soon spending all his time with these exotic, sexy, bored, clever women.

A great part of his delight with the Russians, news of which stuffed his letters back to England, was centred on the toddler Nelitchka, who could say words in six languages and had already learned how to catch and hold the attention of an interested stranger. She at first called Stevenson '*polisson*' for staring at her at table, then '*Mädchen*' on account of his long hair, but soon was bringing him a flower every morning and chattering away confidingly in her polyglot babble. This played right to Stevenson's partiality; the winning little Russian was halfway to breaking his heart. 'A quand, les noces?' Madame Zassetsky asked mischievously as she watched Nelitchka feeding Louis bread.[15] 'Nellie', her sister and friend performed a tarantella for him and allowed him to join in their games; he in turn wrote them verses, sent them little presents and laughed endlessly at their locutions. 'Children are certainly too good to be true,' he wrote to Fanny Sitwell; and to his mother, rather mysteriously, 'kids are what is the matter with me'.[16] Was that an oblique rebuke to her for not having provided a sibling-playmate, or did Stevenson mean he was restless to start a family of his own? He was twenty-three at the time, a likely age for such feelings to set in. Colvin was struck the same year by Stevenson's 'radiant countenance' as he watched some little girls playing with a skipping rope under the window of Colvin's house at Hampstead: 'Had I ever seen anything so beauti-ful and wonderful?' he reports Stevenson asking him. 'Nothing in the whole wide world had ever made him half so happy before.'[17]

It seems Mrs Sitwell was wounded by Louis's sudden enthusi-asm for the two Russian women, who – as he reported daily in his letters – insisted on sitting up close to him, teasing him about his clothes, reading his palm and confiding secrets of their unhappy marriages. Madame Garschine in particular was making headway, as Stevenson's inflammatory accounts made clear. He cannot have been altogether displeased when Mrs Sitwell wrote something (destroyed now, with all her other letters) that provoked this reply:

> O my dear, don't misunderstand me; let me hear soon to tell me that you don't doubt me: I wanted to let you know really how the thing stood and perhaps I am wrong, perhaps doing that is impossible in such cases. At least, dear, believe me you have been as much in my heart these three days as ever you have been, and the thought of you troubles my breathing with the sweetest trouble. I am only happy in the thought of you, my dear – this other woman is interesting to me as a hill might be, or a book, or a picture – but you have all my heart [?my darling] . . .[18]

However mild a complaint Mrs Sitwell had sent, the fact that she sent one at all is striking. To do so is not the action of a woman trying to keep an inappropriate or unwanted suitor at arm's length, but of a woman needing reassurance that she is still the focus of his attention. Perhaps Mrs Sitwell, who had just taken the decisive

step of applying for a secretarial job at a college for working
women in Queen Square in London and who was at last breaking free of her marriage, was really in two minds about Louis
Stevenson at this date.

It is no great surprise that after a few weeks at the Hôtel Mirabeau
in the company of his charming Russian friends, Stevenson was
happy to report himself 'enormously better in the head'. Colvin
visited again and the two began to consider – or Stevenson began
to consider, and Colvin began to agree – collaborating on a
'spectacle-play' on the subject of Herostratus. After months of
inactivity, Stevenson was beginning to write again. There was
'Ordered South' ready to be sent out to *Macmillan's Magazine*
(who published it in May), and the idea for a book on 'Four Great
Scotsmen', to contain pieces about Burns, Knox, Scott and Hume.
Like the spectacle-play, nothing came of this (apart from the essays
on Burns and Knox that appeared eventually in *Virginibus Puerisque*), but Colvin's interest was vitally encouraging to the young
man who so desperately needed to find an independent income if
he was ever to escape from his parents and 'a job in an office'.

Louis had passed almost six months in the South of France, at
considerable expense to his father, and as the spring arrived in
Scotland, he was expected home. The prospect obviously filled him
with dread. As departure neared, he began desperately to posit
alternative schemes: perhaps he could remove to Göttingen, and
carry on law studies there? His parents were prepared to consider
this (Louis must have sold hard the idea of becoming 'a good
specialist in the law' under the tutelage of a 'swell professor' – a
person who happened to be one of Madame Garschine's relations),
but it was all pie in the sky. The young dandy of the Riviera had
not given a thought to law for almost a year, and had more chance
of becoming 'a good specialist' in nursery nursing than in jurispru-
dence. Faced with his parents' approval, he decided that the scheme
was impossible. By this time he was in Paris, desperately stalling,

and wanting to go with Bob to the artists' colony that had formed at Barbizon, near Fontainebleau. His nervous symptoms had come back with a vengeance (Paris is much nearer Edinburgh than is Menton): he caught a cold, and on 11 April 1874 he wrote to Mrs Sitwell, 'I see clearly enough that I must give up the game for the present: this morning I am so ill that I can see nothing for it than to crawl very cautiously home.'[19]

'The game', clearly, was against his parents. 'You know, I was doing what they didn't want,' he complained to Mrs Sitwell from Paris, 'but I put myself out of my own way to make it less unpleasant for them; and surely when one is nearly twenty-four years of age one should be allowed to do a bit of what one wants without their quarrelling with me.'[20] The peevishness of this is notable; Stevenson knew better than anyone how much his own self-interest contributed to keeping the 'game' going: 'Going home not very well is an astonishing good hold for me,' he remarked cynically. 'I shall simply be a prince.'[21] There was another factor too: he had hoped, during the long rest-cure at Menton, to make enough progress as an author to prove to his parents that writing could be a viable profession. But he had achieved so little there that he would have to resume law studies; indeed, studying would be seriously strenuous now, with so much ground to catch up. The prospect was appalling. What he really wanted to do, as he told Mrs Sitwell from Paris, was to live permanently in a country inn with a garden, near to friends but alone, and 'to settle down there for good, among books and papers'.[22] His favourite mood, he had to admit, had become 'holy terror for all action and inaction equally – a sort of shuddering revulsion from the necessary responsibilities of life'.[23] This was not 'wanting to be a writer' any more: this was *accidie*.

When Andrew Lang, the folklorist, was introduced to Stevenson in Menton, he thought him 'more like a lass than a lad, with a rather long, smooth, oval face, brown hair that is worn at greater length than is common, large lucid eyes [. . .] "Here", I thought, "is one of your aesthetic young men." '[24] 'Aesthetic young men' were beginning to seem the curse of the age, an effeminate crew full of subversive notions. But when Stevenson arrived back in Heriot Row in April 1874, looking every inch the fop in his swirling blue cloak and new Tyrolean hat, his parents swallowed down any disquiet they may have felt and welcomed the lost lamb with genuine delight. This was an enormous relief to Louis, who had been dreading a reprise of the previous autumn, and he fell in with their cheerful mood immediately.

The fear of losing their son, either to sickness or travel or marriage, had jolted Thomas and Margaret Stevenson, and it seems that while Louis was in Menton they began to repent their harshness of the previous year. They were now determined to keep him with them at any cost. His mother was suspicious of this 'Mrs Sitwell' who was spoken of so rapturously, and must have been quizzing her sisters and intimates about her, for she told Louis that Aunt Jane had once met Mrs Sitwell and thought she had very pretty small feet. (Needless to say, Aunt Jane's observations of the separated wife are unlikely to have been limited to the lady's extremities.) By the time the Stevensons were introduced to Louis's married friend in London in the autumn, Margaret's misgivings were so strong that she snubbed her. She suspected that Clark's opinion was merely 'a put-up thing' between them, and that if illness didn't carry her son off first, Frances Sitwell would.[25]

In the summer of 1874 the ecclesiastical procedure towards the Sitwells' formal separation was well advanced (and came through in July); Frances's job at the Queen Square college was to start in July also, and she was moving to Brunswick Row, just around the corner from her new workplace. When Stevenson went down to London for a protracted stay in June, he was in a confident mood, seemingly expecting to be able to take a much more prominent role in his Madonna's future. What happened there is unclear, but there seems to have been an 'emotional crisis', as Mehew puts it,[26] or even an 'explosion'.[27]

Mrs Sitwell had certainly reached a critical juncture in her life, necessitating a sort of spring-cleaning of her priorities. Louis understood nothing of the practical difficulties she faced in splitting up a home and family, protecting her surviving son, Bertie, securing employment, and launching into a new life alone, with little money. His habit of moralising on these occasions must have been very irritating, even to the sweet-natured, long-suffering matron. Did she become exasperated with his constant demands on her attention? Or was she provoked to tell him point-blank that his passion for her was too intense and/or inappropriately aimed? The available evidence (contained in some distressed notes from Stevenson written at Colvin's house at Hampstead) certainly suggests Louis had overstepped a limit and been reprimanded:

> Looking back upon some of my past in continuation of my humour of the last two or three days, I am filled with shame. [...] Try to forget utterly the R.L.S. you have known in the past: he is no more, he is dead: I shall try now to be strong and helpful, to be a good friend to you and no longer another limp dead-heavy burthen on your weary arms.[28]

Another letter reconstructs a strange scene between them the previous evening:

> You did not know I was ill last night myself; but I was; and when I hid my eyes it was that I might not see your face grow great before me, as things do when one is feverish. The terrible sculptured impassivity of a face one loves, when it is seen thus exaggerated, frightens and pains one strangely.[29]

This is neurotic, but also very intimate; the clearest glimpse we get of Stevenson's feverishly unbalanced love for his 'Madonna'. But at this moment in her life Mrs Sitwell did not need a sick youth in hysterics; she needed a quiet and efficient helper. Colvin, for example. Was this the moment when Stevenson began, reluctantly, to accept that the person she really loved and intended to share her new life with was his hesitant, lisping friend?

Stevenson's trip to London had been planned as a sort of informal induction into the city's literary life. He joined the Savile Club (proposed by the ever-helpful Colvin – a founder member of the club – and seconded by Fleeming Jenkin and Andrew Lang) and he met Leslie Stephen, for whose *Cornhill Magazine* he was writing an essay on Victor Hugo. Edmund Gosse was a member of the Savile and cultivated the friendship of the new arrival, whom he remembered having met on board the *Clansman* eight years earlier. 'Louis pervaded the club,' he wrote later; 'he was its most affable and chatty member; and he lifted it, by the ingenuity of his incessant dialectic, to the level of a sort of humorous Academe.'[30] In a suit of blue sea-cloth, a black shirt and 'a wisp of yellow carpet that did duty for a neck-tie',[31] Stevenson must have stood out emphatically against the leather club chairs. Henry James, who met him that summer, was certainly rather cool about the 'shirt-collarless Bohemian' he had been introduced to by Lang at lunch.

Though Stevenson himself records this summer as a time of depression and inertia, Gosse was impressed by his vitality – '[he was] simply bubbling with quips and jests' and displayed 'the silliness of an inspired schoolboy'. 'I cannot, for the life of me, recall any of his jokes; and written down in cold blood, they might not be funny if I did. They were not wit so much as humanity, the many-sided outlook upon life.'[32] Gosse left a vivid portrait of how Stevenson rarely sat or stood in conventional manner, but threw his legs over the arms of chairs, perched against bookshelves or sofa ends, or sat on the floor: '[he] would spend half an evening while passionately discussing some great question of morality or literature, leaping sideways in a seated posture to the length of [the] shelf, and then back again'. 'In these years especially [. . .] he gave the impression of something transitory and unreal, sometimes almost inhuman.'[33]

Colvin was trying to set up a deal with the *Portfolio* for a series of essays by 'Ah welless', as he called him,[34] that could be worked into a book later. Stevenson might have been expected to jump at this opportunity, but had reached such a low ebb that the amount of work Colvin was suggesting – an essay a month, or even an essay a quarter – seemed impossible. 'Never, please, let yourself imagine that I am fertile,'[35] he told him, adding rather preciously that he couldn't write to a deadline but had to let his works 'fall from me [...] as they ripen'.[36] This was the man who in time became a veritable word-mill: at this moment in 1874 he was indistinguishable from a dilettante.

Not that Stevenson didn't relish the *idea* of being published. Thinking over Colvin's suggestion, he began to imagine:

> Twelve or twenty such Essays, some of them purely ethical and expository, put together in a little book with narrow print in each page, antique, vine leaves about, and the following title.
>
>
>
> XII (or XX) ESSAYS ON THE
> ENJOYMENT OF THE WORLD:
> BY ROBERT LOUIS STEVENSON
> (a motto in italics)
> Publisher
> Place and date
>
>
> Of course the page is here foreshortened but you know the class of old book I have in my head. I smack my lips; would it not be nice![37]

The attention to peripherals is characteristic, so is the desire to eke out the minimum number of words into a book by expedients such as wide margins and decorations. In 'My First Book', published in 1894, Stevenson would write of the 'veneration' with which he used to regard the average three-volume novel of the time 'as a feat – not possibly of literature – but at least of physical and moral endurance'.[38]

Stevenson loved to run ahead and gloat over possible future achievements. The only problem was that having done the gloating, he often found he had exhausted his enthusiasm for a project. His notebooks and letters are full of lists of chapters for books he never so much as planned out or wrote a line of. The lists, the naming, the brave idea of a title page, were often enough in themselves – or enough to convince himself that further work would be wasted. In his *Prose Writings of Robert Louis Stevenson*, Roger Swearingen lists 393 items, only twenty-seven of which are published, principal works. Even granted that many of the pieces listed are essays and stories which were gathered up into collections later, there are still scores of unfinished essays, unstarted stories, grand schemes, false starts: enough to have furnished two or three doppelgänger careers. With a little push this way or that, Stevenson might not have been known as the author of *Treasure Island* and *Dr Jekyll and Mr Hyde* but as the playwright of *The King's Rubies*, or the biographer of Viscount Dundee.

1874 was one of the years rich in these byways. Stevenson had already picked up and set down the 'Four Great Scotsmen' book, and in the autumn was thinking of a work of fantasy to be called 'The Seaboard of Bohemia'. Since he links this to Shakespeare's *A Winter's Tale*, which was the model behind *Prince Otto*, 'The Seaboard' could have been an early intimation of that 1885 novel, which was also about Bohemia and had a character strongly based on Mesdames Garschine and Zassetsky. He was also thinking of putting together a first collection of short stories, utilising some of his 1868–69 'Covenanting Story Book'. The contents list he sent Colvin is almost comically upbeat; only three of the twelve titles were 'all ready'; the rest either 'want a few pages' (i.e. only *have* a few pages?), need 'copying', 're-organization' or are blatantly 'in gremio'.[39] 'In gremio' is where they stayed. Not one, apart from 'The Two Falconers of Cairnstane' – which was probably the original of 'An Old Song' – was ever published in the author's lifetime.

Also not published in his lifetime, but begun in the summer of 1874, was one of Stevenson's most original and most little-read books, *Fables*. He had been reviewing Edward Bulwer Lytton's *Fables in Song*, which, he felt, lacked 'the incredible element, the point of audacity with which the fabulist was wont to mock at his readers'.[40] This was exactly what Stevenson transmitted in his own experiments with the form, three of which Colvin dates from this year: 'The House of Eld', 'The Touchstone' and 'The Song of the Morrow'. The first of these is a satire on religious practice, clearly derived from Stevenson's situation vis-à-vis Presbyterian

Edinburgh. 'The Song of the Morrow' is a surreal, circular story about the longing for special knowledge (which of course the heroine does not achieve); 'though power is less than weakness, power shall you have; and though the thought is colder than winter, yet shall you think it to an end'.[41] Jorge Luis Borges, an ardent admirer of Stevenson, was particularly fond of these tales (of his own *Parables* he once said, 'I owe that to Kafka and also to a quite forgotten book, to the fables posthumously published of Robert Louis Stevenson'[42]), and it is easy to see how the collection as a whole fits in with Borges's witty expositions of the self-conscious artificiality of fiction. 'The Touchstone', a story of two brothers seeking by very different means the hand of the same princess, manages to merge the fantastic or 'audacious' with a startling sort of realism about human nature, the very 'tenderness of rough truths' that Stevenson had found wanting in Lord Lytton.[43] It is fascinating to think that these very early and highly original fictions lay in a drawer for more than twenty years while Stevenson laboured to perfect duds such as *Deacon Brodie* or *Prince Otto*.

And on what was Stevenson pinning his ambitions in 1874? Not any sort of fiction, but – bizarrely enough – ecclesiastical pamphleteering. 'An Appeal to the Clergy of the Church of Scotland'[44] was an extraordinary departure, a response to the abolition in August 1874 of the practice of Crown and other patronage in the Church of Scotland. Patronage was the issue behind the 'Disruption' of the 1840s which led to the forming of the Free Kirk; Stevenson's suggestion after its abolition was that ministers of the established Church should begin to contribute money to the support of returning Free Church ministers to compensate the latter for the years during which they had been cut off from comfortable benefices. His idea was in fact rather ridiculous (and implied that he expected Free Kirk ministers to *want* to rejoin the established Church in significant numbers), but he was convinced that he would at least 'have done good service in unveiling a sham and struck another death-blow at the existence of superannuated religion'.[45] The writing was terrible – 'Observe, I speak only of those . . .'[46] 'And the position, as I say, is one of difficulty' – and if he hadn't written so solemnly about this pamphlet in his letters, one would be tempted to think 'An Appeal' a joke thought up by Stevenson and Baxter during a wet afternoon at the Spec. But the mischievous RLS who had lived for Jink and jollity was, at this point in his life, almost eclipsed. When his twelve-page pamphlet was published (anonymously) in the spring of 1875, a copy was sent to every member of the Church's General Assembly. 'I think I am going to make a figure in Scotch ecclesiastical politics,' Stevenson wrote absurdly to Frances Sitwell, though Colvin remarked later that the pamphlet received 'no attention what-ever',[47] and a commentator in the 1920s called 'An Appeal' 'some-what gratuitous, if not impertinent'.[48]

When the new term began at Edinburgh University in the autumn, Stevenson was condemned to study again. It was his last year as a student, and his least indolent one, spurred on by a huge bribe from his parents. On passing for the Bar, he was to receive from them a thousand pounds – the equivalent of about £50,000 today. Compared with his allowance of £84 a year (newly raised to that sum, and considered by Stevenson 'very comfortable'[49]), the pros-pect was one of real comfort and independence just around the corner. His parents of course expected him to practise the law once he qualified; they probably saw the thousand pounds (an advance on his patrimony) as a necessary amount for Louis to set himself up as an advocate. Louis on the other hand envisaged a future of personal leisure and earnest philanthropy. The only drawback was that he would have to spend much of the coming academic year locked in the 'barren embraces' of law books.[50]

Money continued to be the language most often spoken in Heriot Row. Thomas Stevenson was ill towards the end of 1874, with distressing indications that he might be subject to 'some of the family ailments'.[51] 'My father is so really *mad* – I know no other word for it – that we have no pleasant time here,' Stevenson wrote to Mrs Sitwell, relating how Thomas had railed about his wife in front of Louis and the servants. The older man's mind was running on grievances, and speaking of inheritance, he cited circumstances which 'superseded the call of blood; for instance did he think he had a son who thought as Tyndall [the materialist scientist] thought; he could not leave his money to him; he was not possessor of it, to so great an extent; he only held it in trust for the views in which he believed'.[52] Thomas's declaration expressed, his son felt, 'the sense of his whole life', and in response he promised solemnly 'never to use a farthing of his money unless I am a Christian'. But Stevenson couldn't stop going on from this spontaneous, nobly meant act of self-disinheritance to be pompous about it in his letter (which, by relating the incident, was already obliquely self-congratulatory), saying, 'for me it will, of course, supersede the terms of any will written in ignorance, doubt or misapprehension [of my lack of belief]'.[53] Skirting over the uncomfortable fact that he seems to have forgotten this resolution by the time his father died, or felt it was covered by his mitigation 'I shall not let myself starve, of course',[54] the interview provides another example of how very much alike Louis and Thomas were in their principled pig-headedness and strong, rash speeches.

Stevenson was also heading for rhetorical meltdown with Mrs Sitwell. In the years he was in thrall to her, he gave her many different names, clearly a symptom of confusion about their relationship. First there was 'Claire', then 'Madame', 'Madonna', 'Maud' (from Tennyson's poem, not Mrs Babington), and 'Mother'; there was even a brief spell of 'Lady Superintendent' when Mrs Sitwell first took up that post at the College for Working Women. In Menton, Stevenson started to call her 'Consuelo', after the heroine of George Sand's *Mademoiselle Merquem*: 'Consuelo. Consolation of my spirit. Consolation.'[55] In the book, Consuelo escapes an unhappy marriage and is free to marry the young man she really loves, but in real life the plot threatened to work out rather differently, and Stevenson was hard-pressed to know how to re-imagine his relationship with his newly-independent beloved. His confusion was obvious when he signed one letter, at Christmas 1874, 'ever your faithful friend and son and priest', having spoken of her as his 'deity', whose shrine he would tend forever. Wild though this is, Mrs Sitwell must have liked it, for she marked the letter 'Keep this very safe for me.'[56]

Once Stevenson began to develop the mother–son metaphor in his letters to Mrs Sitwell, the results were astonishing:

> And so, my beautiful and good and O surely not quite *un*happy, mother of election, so you must be brave for my sake, and let me think of you with happiness and not with pain. Day by day, you become more to me; and day by day, I must acknowledge to myself how dependent I am on you for all that is good and beautiful in my poor life. This is the consolation I have given you always; and I now know no other: think of how I cling to you, Madonna, my mother; think of how you must be to me throughout life the mother's breasts to suckle me, and be brave, dear, and be for me a brave mother; if I am to be a son, you must be a mother; and surely I am a son in more than ordinary sense, begotten of the sweet soul and beautiful body of you, and taught all that ever I knew pure or holy or of good report, by the contact of your sweet soul and lovely body [. . .] I long to be with you most ardently, and I long to put my arms about your neck and kiss you, and then sit down with my head on your knees, and have a long talk, and feel you smoothing my hair.[57]

He seems desperate in these months to reach an *unchangeable* state with his tormentingly lovely and devoted friend, writing to her of the 'perpetual treasure' of her heart and his belief that 'you will never change to me any more; I believe it is safe'.[58] 'Surely between you and me, all that there is, is *restful* – is it not?' he asked nervously in January 1875, half-hoping for the answer No. Electing her as 'Mother' might have been expected to help free the relationship from the vicissitudes of sexual longing, except that Stevenson was the first to admit that 'it is not a bit like what I feel for my mother *here*'.[59] He got much nearer to articulating his ideal when he rhapsodised to her about a photograph of the Parthenon pediment sculpture known as the Three Fates, in front of which he had shed tears with her on his last visit to London. The statue evoked for him 'a great mythical woman, living alone among inaccessible mountain tops or in some lost Island in the pagan seas; [. . .] think dear, if one could love a woman like that once, see her once grow pale with passion, and once wring your lips out upon hers, would it not be a small thing to die?'[60] It is an oddly aggressive fantasy, and, directed at a woman he once hoped to possess, tinged with vindictiveness.

Sadly, there was no great mythical woman around to turn Stevenson's attention away from Frances Sitwell, love for whom was turning into festering misery. 'You are all the women in the world to me,' he told her in February, while admitting to Bob, 'I have dropped out of my service to the second rates.'[61] He still haunted howffs such as the Gay Japanee, but only to drink or take opium. All that winter he was seedy and in a 'curiously impressionable state', rather like the morbid melancholia of his early student days. A crippled girl 'with that curious voice [. . .] of sexless and ageless deformity', two lost children being walked to the police station by an officer, the trains curving out of Waverley station seen from high on the North Bridge; all these everyday things affected him queerly, 'took hold of' him, as he described it to Mrs Sitwell. 'I don't like being so sensitive in town, though,' he said, 'the impressions are more often painful than agreeable.'[62] He was turning into the Caillebotte of Edinburgh – or perhaps its de Nerval. A prose poem that he wrote that year contains this vividly neurasthenic paragraph:

The dresses of harlots swayed and swished upon the pavement. Pale faces leaped out of the crowd as they went by the lights, and passed away like a dream in the general dream of the pallid and populous streets. The coarse brass band filled the air with a rough and ready melody; and the fall of alternate feet, and the turn of shoulders and swish of dresses, fell into time with it strangely. Face after face went by; swinging dress

after dress brushed on the even stones; out of face after face
the eyes stood forth with a sordid animal invitation.[63]

This was the preoccupied, unhappy young man whom Leslie
Stephen took with him to Edinburgh Royal Infirmary one day in
February 1875. Stephen was in the city to give two lectures on the
Alps and had decided to pay a visit not only to 'Colvin's friend',
but to another young contributor to the *Cornhill* who was at that
time a long-term patient at the Infirmary. William Ernest Henley,
a twenty-six-year-old would-be writer suffering from necrosis of
the bone, had arrived in Edinburgh eighteen months earlier. He
had already had his left leg amputated below the knee (as a result
of tuberculosis), and had been told the second foot was beyond
cure, but Henley had heard of the pioneering work of the Edinburgh surgeon Joseph Lister, and came north in 1873 to be treated
by him. Lister's controversial belief was that antiseptics could be
used to prevent as well as treat putrefaction, and under his care,
with several operations and whole years of bed rest, Henley's
condition was gradually stabilising.

Stephen had been touched by the pathos of Henley's situation
and decided to take Stevenson along with him on his second visit
to the gloomy old hospital in the hope that 'Colvin's friend' might
be able to lend Henley books and visit him. It was a judicious
move: Stevenson was deeply impressed by Henley and wrote
enthusiastically to Mrs Sitwell about the 'bit of a poet' he had just
met:

> It was very sad to see him there, in a little room with two
> beds, and a couple of sick children in the other bed; a girl
> came in to visit the children and played dominoes on the
> counterpane with them; the gas flared and crackled, the fire
> burned in a dull economical way; Stephen and I sat on a
> couple of chairs and the poor fellow sat up in his bed, with
> his hair and his beard all tangled, and talked as cheerfully as
> if he had been in a King's Palace, or the great King's Palace
> of the blue air. He has taught himself two languages since he
> has been lying there. I shall try to be of use to him.[64]

Henley's intellectual energy, his enormous pleasure in talk and company, were evident from the first, as was his spirited response to his dire predicament and his tormentingly long stay in the hospital. Here was someone whom Louis could help, someone much worse off than himself, seriously ill, and without family or money. But the taint of patronage, which coloured the whole relationship, is also there from the start, with that rather priggish 'I shall try to be of use to him.' Stevenson's second mention of Henley in his letters is to 'my poet', to Bob he called him 'a poor ass in the infirmary',[65] and only a year later he was describing Henley to a woman he wanted to impress as his 'pensioner in the hospital'.

The 'poor ass' had been writing some remarkable poems while laid up. Henley became famous later for poems that addressed the nation's hunger for moral uplift, providing it with a classic text, 'Invictus', whose strongly accented rhythms and bracing sentiments have burned themselves into the popular imagination in the same way that Kipling's 'If –' began to do two decades later:

> It matters not how strait the gate
> How charged with punishments the scroll,
> I am the master of my fate
> I am the captain of my soul.

'Invictus' was written in 1875 (and Stevenson must have been one of its first readers, for he was already quoting from it that year[66]), but the 'In Hospital' sequence, written at approximately the same time, was very different. 'In Hospital' included free-verse portraits of Dr Lister, the nurses, the house-surgeon, the 'scrubber' and others, and impressionistic poems such as 'Waiting' and 'Interior'. The dismal experience of being a long-term patient in a dark backroom, where the dripping cistern is the only indication of time passing, is perfectly conveyed in 'Pastoral', 'Nocturne' and 'Vigil':

> Lived on one's back,
> In the long hours of repose
> Life is a practical nightmare
> Hideous asleep or awake.[67]

For the 1870s, when they were written, these poems were truly
innovative, though by the time they were published in book form
in 1888 Henley had given up writing in this vein.

One of the sequence, a sonnet called 'Apparition', is Henley's
often-quoted portrait of Stevenson that begins 'Thin-legged! thin-
chested! slight unspeakably', and ends:

> A deal of Ariel, just a streak of Puck,
> Much Antony, of Hamlet most of all,
> And something of the Shorter Catechist.[68]

But another of Henley's poems about Stevenson, not ever published as far as I know, gives a rather more intimate portrait of

> An Ariel quick through all his veins
> With sex and temperament and style;
> All eloquence and balls and brains;
> Heroic and also infantile.

The affectionately bantering tone carries right through the poem
to 'Wise, passionate, swaggering, puerile' in the last stanza. The
forthright, critical spirit that Henley displays here was the very
thing that attracted Stevenson to him. Opinionated, quarrelsome,
with his huge laugh and super-sized vitality, Henley was like a
sharper and more inventive Baxter, a boon companion whose restless intelligence was a match for Stevenson's own.

The friendship was cemented by Stevenson's inspired plan to
take Henley out of hospital on a couple of occasions in a carriage
(probably the swanky Stevenson barouche, of which Thomas was
very proud). To a passer-by it must have been peculiar to see the
stick-thin, boyish Stevenson carrying a burly, bearded one-legged
man down the long staircase of the Infirmary and staggering out
to where the vehicle waited. They drove out of the city to see the
new spring greenery and the cherry blossom, stopping on bridges
'to let him enjoy the great cry of green that goes up to Heaven out
of the river beds':

> he asked (more than once) 'What noise is that?' – 'The water.'
> – 'O' almost incredulously; and then quite a long while after:

'Do you know the noise of the water astonished me very much.'[69]

Henley remembered these drives all his life with intense happiness, and celebrated them in the last poem of his 'In Hospital' sequence, 'Discharged':

> *Carry me out*
> *Into the wind and the sunshine,*
> *Into the beautiful world.*
>
> *O, the wonder, the spell of the streets!*
> *The stature and strength of the horses,*
> *The rustle and echo of footfalls,*
> *The flat roar and rattle of wheels!*
> *A swift tram floats huge on us . . .*
> *It's a dream?*
> *The smell of the mud in my nostrils*
> *Blows brave – like a breath of the sea!*
> *[. . .] These are the streets . . .*
> *Each is an avenue leading*
> *Whither I will!*
>
> *Free . . . !*
> *Dizzy, hysterical, faint,*
> *I sit, and the carriage rolls on with me*
> *Into the wonderful world.*

Henley went to live in digs in Portobello when he was finally discharged that spring, and Stevenson helped get him work on the research staff of the *Encyclopaedia Britannica*, the eighth edition of which was being published in Edinburgh, and for which Stevenson had been commissioned to write articles on Burns and Béranger. Henley was in love with a woman called Anna Boyle, whom he had met when she was visiting her brother in the bed next to his at the Infirmary. Henley wanted to establish some income in order to marry (which he and Anna did three years later), though it was almost impossible to earn a living wage on the sort of hack-work he got. Stevenson came to admire enormously his determination and hard work, and Henley became the new focus of the old LJR group, a confidant of Stevenson, Baxter, Ferrier and Bob, whom he renamed the Four Musketeers.

Meeting Henley had been the one bright spot in an otherwise miserable winter for Stevenson. Although there are no references in his letters or his mother's diary notes to the lung problem he is thought to have suffered from at this stage of his life, his nervous troubles – triggered by the bleak conspiracy of broken heart and enforced study – were evident again. 'My vitality is low in every way,' he wrote to Mrs Sitwell at the end of February 1875, 'although I am not at all ill – all I want is a little warmth, a little sun, a little of the life I have when I am by you.'[70] He got his wish soon after, for in early March, as his mother recorded, 'Louis quite breaks down and is giddy.'[71] Uncle George ordered him off for a holiday, and the patient sprang back to life at the news, crowing to Mrs Sitwell the same day: 'Victory! Victory! Victory!' He met Bob in Paris and together they went on to Barbizon, the artists' colony Bob had been visiting for some seven years.

Barbizon had become a centre for the *plein air* school, precursors of the Impressionists, in the previous decade. When Louis arrived the first time, Jean-François Millet, the central figure in the group, had just died and the shutters of his house were closed up. The artists who gathered there in the summer were mostly French, British and a few Americans, including a fellow student with Bob at the *atelier* of Carolus-Duran,* Will Low, who was to become Stevenson's lifelong friend. They lodged at Siron's Inn, evoked in Louis's subsequent essay for the *Cornhill*:

> To the door [. . .] half a dozen, or maybe half a score, of people have brought out chairs, and now sit sunning themselves, and waiting the omnibus from Melun. If you go on into the court you will find as many more, some in the billiardroom over absinthe and a match of corks, some without over a last cigar and a vermouth. The doves coo and flutter from

---

* Charles Durand, called Carolus-Duran, was a portrait artist and founder of the Société des Beaux Arts.

the dovecote; Hortense is drawing water from the well; and as all the rooms open into the court, you can see the white-capped cook over the furnace in the kitchen, and some idle painter, who has stored his canvases and washed his brushes, jangling a waltz on the crazy, tongue-tied piano in the salle-à-manger.[72]

While the others painted, or discussed pigments with the salesman from Fontainebleau, Louis spent whole days on his own walking and reading in the forest, which was so close to the village that the last houses on the street were already among the trees. In the evenings at Siron's there would be couples dancing by candlelight to the music of the rickety piano, and 'so much eating goes forward, so much drinking, so much jabbering in French and English, that it would do your heart good merely to peep and listen at the door'.[73] The company was as quirky as Louis could have wanted: young men in tattered frock-coats and fezes, in striped stockings (like Bob's) or extravagant hats, covered in paint, or wax, or wine stains. Walter Simpson's younger brother Willie was there, with his bull terrier Taureau, to whom he used to feed saucers of absinthe, vermouth, coffee and champagne, and an American youth who 'always wore expensive rings so as to have the extreme enjoyment of pawning them'.[74] There was also Hiram Bloomer, a genuinely poor and shabby little man who was once refused admission to the Luxembourg Gallery on account of his raggedness. Louis fell in gratefully with this society: they were all big drinkers, voluble talkers and despisers of bourgeois life.

When Barbizon threatened to be attracting too many lady water-colourists that summer, Bob began to look for an even quieter venue, fixing on the tiny village of Grez-sur-Loing on the other side of the Fontainebleau forest. Grez was entirely rural: the one roughly-cobbled street was flanked with deep smelly ditches and littered with hay from passing loads. There was a lichened church and a row of grey stone houses, but the main draw was the commodious old stone inn at the end of the street, run by Monsieur and Madame Chevillon and their buxom daughter. The old archway opened into a low wide hall, and behind the inn a lovely garden sloped down to the Loing, with a ruined castle and old bridge downriver, ideal for landscapes. Soon Bob and his friends were in semi-permanent residence at Chevillons', and the irregular stone flags of the courtyard were strewn with cigarette stubs and dead match stalks.[75]

The Latin Quarter of Paris was Bob's other *milieu*, and his rooms in the rue Racine were permanently available to Louis as a bolt-hole during this period. Louis sited his narrator Loudon Dodd in 'an ungainly, ill-smelling hotel' in the same street in his 1892 novel *The Wrecker*, in which he evoked the magnetic attraction of the *vie bohème* to rebellious young men of the time:

> I dined, I say, at a poor restaurant and lived in a poor hotel; and this was not from need, but sentiment. My father gave me a profuse allowance, and I might have lived (had I chosen) in the Quartier de l'Étoile and driven to my studies daily. Had I done so, the glamour must have fled: I should still have been but Loudon Dodd; whereas now I was a Latin Quarter student, Murger's successor, living in flesh and blood the life of one of those romances I had loved to read, and re-read, and to dream over, among the woods of Muskegon.[76]

Louis and Bob had perfected some fine bohemian traits. One was to travel without any baggage at all except perhaps a toothbrush. Ridding oneself of material attachments was a sign of spiritual maturity, they said: a portmanteau was no better than a massive shackle. Unfortunately, travelling without linen proved expensive, as a new shirt had to be bought every couple of days and an almost-new one thrown away, and lack of a comb meant paying a barber. But it was worth it to the 'two mad Stevensons' for a day or two, for the humour of the thing, and its anecdotal value. Someone like Bloomer wouldn't have been able to keep it up at all.

The contrast when Louis got back to Edinburgh was painful, and he was instantly plunged into 'the most cold, desolate recollections of my past life here'.[77] 'I was glad to try and think of the forest, and warm my hands at the thought of it.' He had plans to go south again as soon as his exams were over, telling his mother, 'I shall go in for a year for health before all things. Try and be as much as possible a year in the open air.'[78] Still, no one in these years recollected Stevenson as an invalid. Alfred Ewing described him as enjoying 'excellent health' in 1877 and 1878;[79] Lord Dunedin said that ill-health was 'not yet upon him, and he was very cheerful and lively',[80] and Will Low thought his new acquaintance at Barbizon 'apparently as robust as any of us'.[81] But the 'health' card was still the only reliable one to play at home. In the summer of 1875, Stevenson seems to have been planning to use it and his promised thousand pounds to get well away from his parents, Edinburgh and any possibility of becoming an advocate.

Despite the months of studying, the Bar exams proved traumatic. Louis only discovered the existence of French grammar the day before he was to be examined in the subject, but was allowed to pass, as his spoken French was excellent: 'the examiner devised some special form of report',[82] Graham Balfour believed. One fellow student later claimed that Stevenson only passed his exams because he had 'been told, or had somehow got to know' the questions in advance,[83] but the scholar himself recalled a subtler technique. Asked by the Professor of Moral Philosophy a question on one of the textbooks, Louis said he didn't understand the phraseology. When told it came from the textbook, he replied, 'Yes, but you couldn't expect me to read so poor a book as that.' The professor, fortunately, found this amusing and 'laughed like a hunchback'.

So, miraculously, Stevenson passed advocate on 14 July 1875. The family drove in from Swanston in the barouche to get the results, and came away in triumph, Louis insisting on sitting up on the folded cover of the carriage, with his feet on the seat between his parents. 'He kept waving his hat,' his cousin Etta Balfour recalled, 'and calling out to people he passed, whether known or unknown, just like a man gone quite mad.'[84]

The history of Stevenson's career at the Bar was short, as he intended it to be. After a second trip to Barbizon in the summer

of 1875 with Walter Simpson and Bob, followed by a walking tour
with Simpson, a stay in Paris and a holiday in Wiesbaden with his
parents, he had to come back to Edinburgh and go through the
motions of being a lawyer. What had happened to the thousand
pounds is a mystery, as he complains all winter of not having any
cash: perhaps it had been invested for him. His days took on a
strange somnolent quality, as he described to Colvin:

> I idle finely. I read Boswell's Life of Johnson, Martin's History
> of France, Allen Ramsay, Olivier Basselin, all sorts of rubbish
> a propos of Burns, Comines, Juvenal des Ursins etc.; I walk
> about the Parliament House five forenoons a week, in wig
> and gown; I have either a five or six mile walk, or an hour or
> two hard skating on the rink, every afternoon, without fail;
> and – well, this is not so good perhaps but it is a part of my
> system – I sit up late at night and sometimes wet my whistle.[85]

Promenading at the Parliament House was the standard way for
young advocates to pick up briefs, but Stevenson was only ever
offered two, both of which, according to his cousin Etta, he refused, 'much to his father's sorrow'.[86] He only appeared in court
once, and that was under farcical circumstances. He had received
a brief to perform the formality of 'reviving' a certain case the next
day; this involved merely turning up to hear the case mentioned,
and no special knowledge was necessary. He expected the court to
be empty, but when he arrived found it packed with his friends,
who had got wind of the reluctant advocate's maiden appearance
(one can guess via Baxter, who was a practising Writer to the
Signet by then) and came 'to see how he would acquit himself'.[87]
Unfortunately, the judge that morning happened to be one whom
Stevenson had seen the evening before going into a dive and to
whom he had mischievously given the 'Bar Salute'. This was a piece
of effrontery (and potentially embarrassing knowledge) which his
lordship was unlikely to forgive; on top of this, the court was full
of grinning youths clearly up to some lark. Instead of passing
quickly through the formal procedure, the judge asked who
Stevenson was, and proceeded to quiz him on the case, about

which of course the young man knew nothing whatever. Hamming desperately for some minutes, Stevenson eventually caught sight of the solicitor, who had been keeping 'well out of the way', and referred the judge to him for all further facts. And thus, in a welter of suppressed laughter and mugging to the gallery, he began and ended his legal career. Thomas and Margaret Stevenson had a doorplate fixed to 17 Heriot Row that bore the inscription 'R.L. Stevenson, Advocate',[88] and years later, sightseers would be shown the empty document box in the corridor of the Parliament House that was similarly marked. In the meantime, 'RLS' the writer was already far away.

5

STENNIS *FRÈRE*

In the summer of 1876 an American woman travelling in Europe with her children, Mrs Samuel Osbourne, wrote home to a friend in California that she was thinking of going on from Paris to Grez-sur-Loing near Barbizon to study 'with one of two very fine painters of landscape. My only objection to them is that they are amateurs and rich Englishmen with titles,' she told him. 'One is Lord something that sounds like Simpson.'[1] That was Willie Simpson, brother of Sir Walter Simpson, Bart. The other 'rich Englishman' was Bob Stevenson.

Mrs Osbourne, born Fanny Vandegrift in 1840, was not a typical tourist. She had come to Europe the previous autumn to study art and get away from her husband, Sam, to whom she had been married for eighteen trouble-filled years. It was a bold move, but not well planned. When she and her three children, Belle (seventeen), Sam (seven) and four-year-old Hervey, arrived in Antwerp, with a view to Belle and her mother both studying at the Antwerp Academy of Fine Arts, they discovered that the school did not admit women. By this point, Fanny had rather burned her boats, not to mention spent a lot of her money. But rather than turn the party around to retrace their steps the six thousand miles or so back to Oakland, California, she went on to Paris and enrolled herself and her daughter at the Atelier des Dames in Montmartre. It was there that she heard about the informal colony of artists that gathered every summer at Barbizon and began the last part of her journey towards meeting her second husband.

The extraordinary Fanny Vandegrift was originally from

Indianapolis, the eldest child of the six surviving to a lumber merchant called Jacob Vandegrift and his wife Esther. She was a quick-witted, self-contained girl with a fiery temperament kept so closely under control that she often appeared 'cold and undemonstrative', according to her sister-in-law Cynthia.[2] Tiny in stature and not conventionally pretty by the standards of the day, with a dark complexion, arresting black eyes and dark curly hair, Fanny exuded a sexual aura that many men found irresistible. She was married young, at seventeen, to a handsome and charming twenty-year-old clerk called Samuel Osbourne, then private secretary to the State Governor of Indiana. The couple settled in Indianapolis, where, a speedy thirty-eight weeks after the wedding, their daughter Belle was born.

Sam joined the Yankee 46th Indiana Regiment when the Civil War broke out in 1861, but left after six months without having seen action and enlisted instead with the local guard, the Indiana Legion. He never stuck at anything for long. In 1863 he volunteered to accompany his tubercular brother-in-law George Marshall to California in search of a healthier climate, but when poor Marshall (a friend and former admirer of Fanny) died en route in Panama, Osbourne didn't return home but went on alone to the west coast. From there he wrote back to his bemused and anxious young wife that he was hearing such things about the fortunes to be made from silver prospecting that he intended to go on to a mining camp at Austin, Nevada, to try his luck.

The wildest days of the Gold Rush had been and gone by 1864, but the west was still buzzing with rumours about undiscovered hoards of precious metal, and 'silver fever' was well under way. The Nevada veins, Osbourne reported back to Fanny, were producing millions of dollars' worth of silver and gold and secretly funding, among other things, the Union Army's campaign against the Confederates. Prospectors who came down to San Francisco sported diamond buttons in their waistcoats, built houses of white marble and bathed in champagne. It seemed that money was there for the picking, as this contemporary news report implies:

The other day an assay of mere *croppings* yielded exceeding *four thousand dollars to the ton*. A week or so ago an assay of just such surface developments made returns of *seven thousand* dollars to the ton. Our mountains are full of rambling prospectors. Each day and almost every hour reveals new and more startling evidences of the profuse and intensified wealth of our favored county. The metal is not silver alone. There are distinct ledges of auriferous ore.[3]

Convinced that he too could make a killing, Osbourne urged Fanny to follow him out to Austin, and she, young and greedy and longing for adventure, promptly agreed.

Fanny's decision to make the long and difficult journey from Indianapolis to Austin on her own with a small child followed the most frequently recurring pattern of behaviour in her life, which was to make quick, dramatic choices and deal with the consequences later. The journey was a daunting one in 1864; with no Union Pacific railroad yet built, the only way to travel the two thousand or so miles west from Indianapolis to Austin was either by overland coach (which was rough and perilous and considered very dangerous for a lone female) or to go east to New York, take a steamer to Panama, cross the isthmus by rail, catch another steamer to San Francisco and then go on by stagecoach to Nevada, a round trip of approximately six thousand miles. Fanny's parents were naturally concerned about their daughter's plunge into the unknown. Neighbouring Illinois was at that date the furthest frontier west of the 'National Road', and the 'wildness' of the far west was legendary. Among the things Jacob Vandegrift gave his daughter before she left (along with a shareholder's rail pass that turned out to be invalid) was a pocket derringer pistol.

Evidence of what exactly happened on their journey is sparse, though Fanny's latest biographer, Alexandra Lapierre, believes that she and Belle were stuck for several days in Aspinwall, the fetid Panamanian port where the New York steamer landed, famed for its malarial climate, discomforts and diseases. Some delay to the train which was to take hundreds of passengers across to

Panama City meant that Fanny was in danger of running out of money (and missing the next boat to San Francisco), hence – it is said – she persuaded a fellow traveller from Indiana to help her acquire some mules. According to Lapierre, she and this man, a Mr Hill, then crossed the isthmus on foot, following the course of the railroad, caught the steamer *Moses Taylor* in Panama City and sailed through the Golden Gate on 20 June 1864. The narrative is enhanced by a secret rendezvous at a cemetery and a steamy episode in which Fanny holds off at gunpoint a railroad official who thinks she will sell her body for a seat on the delayed train. If true in these details,[4] the story of Fanny's journey would rival any sensational novel, but they do sound like elaborations, or at the very least, tales made crisper in the retelling. Belle Osbourne's hazy memories of crossing Panama with her mother were of a train journey through 'a strange hot jungle',[5] no mules or epic trekking (though she might have been remembering the return in 1868), and Fanny herself was almost completely silent on the subject. She did not publicise the fact that her journey on the New York steamer was conducted first class (courtesy of the captain, who found her lone predicament too great a challenge to chivalry), nor that the railroad journey from Indianapolis was paid for by a collection got up among the other passengers when Jacob Vandegrift's pass failed to work any magic with the guard. This is not to suggest that Fanny did not display enormous bravery and resourcefulness in her attempts to rejoin Sam in California – bravery and resourcefulness were her trademarks – but that she liked to cultivate mystery and drama around herself. She had a history of doing genuinely extraordinary things *and* feeling the need to exaggerate them.

Sam Osbourne was not at the dock in San Francisco to meet his wife and daughter, having been called back to Austin to deal with a threat to his claim. Unknown to Fanny, he had borrowed money to buy a third share in a mine, a nugget from which was shown to her by the friend Sam had commissioned to guide her and Belle out to Austin. 'It looks like the most ordinary stone,'

Fanny wrote home to her parents, 'and you would never suspect that with this bit of quartz Sam is going to settle us in Paradise!'[6] It was with high expectations that they set out by road on the Pony Express route into the Sierras, which Belle recalled years later: 'I remember being in a huge, rocking, bouncing, crowded stagecoach, wedged in between my mother and the window. From there I caught startling glimpses of high mountains and deep precipices.'[7]

What they met with at the scruffy encampment above the Reese River was an astonishingly primitive and ugly collection of shacks, cabins, piles of mining equipment, gravel and rubble, and a chaotic assemblage of drifters, ruffians and desperados. Austin's supposedly exceptional silver vein had only been discovered two years before, and the town had grown up rapidly around it. However, after a year, cannier investors began to suspect that they had been deceived, and the town emptied out again, from a high-point population of four thousand to a few hundreds by the time Sam Osbourne arrived, in the last wave of hopeful prospectors. But Osbourne was a gambler and an optimist; though he was borrowing money all over the place (even from his newly-widowed sister-in-law Josephine Marshall) he was personally convinced of an imminent huge find. Fanny must have been convinced of it too, for she put up uncomplainingly with the most rough and ready living conditions and expended enormous energy and ingenuity on making their cabin as habitable as possible. She made furniture from scrap, turned old dresses into curtains, tried to grow herbs and vegetables in the dry, alkaline dust patch she grandly called her kitchen garden and cooked as well as she could on a sagebrush fire with the very limited supplies that were available. Without yeast for bread, she used soda, and had to improvise a hot drink with bran that went under the name 'coffee'. Soap was also home-made, from lard, and clothes were washed with it in the yellow trickle that passed along the bed of Reese River in high summer. Austin was no place for the fastidious.

It was also no place for women, except perhaps the dozen or

so prostitutes at the brothel. Fanny was one of only fifty-seven females in the camp, Belle one of the few children. Such society as they saw was mostly men like Sam who had had some education but had not been successful in life, perhaps never would be. They congregated at the Osbournes' cabin, playing cards, talking, drinking, picking fights: there was nothing else to do. Breaking into the monotony of these long, boozy evenings were heart-stopping alarms when it seemed that the local Piute natives might be about to attack. Stories abounded of their brutality, though Fanny's experience indicates that they were more guarded than aggressive towards the marauding white miners. The Indians used to come into the camp and watch her through the cabin window, and Fanny, to her credit, tried to carry on with her chores unperturbed, only stopping to pass cups of bran 'coffee' to the silent, tattooed visitors.

It was at Austin that Fanny began smoking roll-ups, a habit that she kept for life, and practising her shooting skills on a home-made rifle range. Belle enjoyed the freedom of almost constant play, and had a picturesque memory of being lowered down the shaft of her father's mine in a bucket: 'on the brim of my little cap, stuck into a lump of clay, was a lighted candle. [. . .] The bucket was held by a rope over a windlass, and my father lowered me by turning a crank.'[8] But the unhappy fact was that Sam's venture was not 'panning out' as hoped, despite the numbers of men working on it. As Alexandra Lapierre has pointed out, the prospectors had failed to understand the economics of mining:

> If they ever did reach the rock containing the mineral, they
> would need to extract it and convey thousands of tons of rock
> to the refining equipment in order to obtain a few grams of
> silver. If you consider that simply separating mineral from
> dross was costing the miners a hundred dollars per ton, their
> ingots were certainly light-years away.[9]

Sam shared his claim with his best friend in Austin, a young Welsh-man called John Lloyd, and by March 1865 both men had tired of the drudgery of digging holes in the ground. It began to look as if nothing that glittered was auriferous ore. Leaving their debts and most of their makeshift possessions behind, they decided to move on to Virginia City on the slopes of Mount Davidson, 120 miles due west over the Shoshone and Stillwater Mountains. Virginia City had sprung up a few years before on the ground above the fabled Comstock Lode, and was already known as 'the "livest" town, for its age and population, that America had ever produced'.[10] Samuel Clemens, who under his pseudonym Mark Twain was to write the classic account of the mining boom of the 1860s, *Roughing It*, was at the time city editor for the Virginia *Daily Territorial Enterprise*, and described the atmosphere thus:

> Money was as plenty as dust; every individual considered himself wealthy, and a melancholy countenance was nowhere to be seen. There were military companies, fire companies, brass bands, banks, hotels, theatres, 'hurdy-gurdy houses', wide-open gambling palaces, political pow-wows, civic pro- cessions, street fights, murders, inquests, riots, a whisky mill every fifteen steps, a Board of Aldermen [. . .] and some talk of building a church.[11]

Sam bought shares in a mine (with yet more borrowed cash) and, in an access of sense, also got a job as a court clerk. Fanny must have been nagging him about their bills, for their situation was so tight that she too had to work, doing bits of dressmaking and babysitting. This was far from the paradisal dream that she had entertained a year or two before; Sam was still borrowing from Jacob Vandegrift, and teetering on the verge of admitting the scale of his failures: 'Most people in your fix would have blown a youngster up sky high who had filched a thousand dollars of their money into the sea,' he wrote to his father-in-law. 'You can bet high, however, that I will see this money refunded, or I will remain here till Doomsday, trying to get it back.'[12]

Virginia City was the place for betting high; sprawling, lawless and dangerous, it was full of drunks, criminals and professional card-sharps: 'Gambling went on night and day,' Fanny's sister said later, 'and the killing of men over the games still happened often enough.'[13] There were 18,000 people living in the city in the mid-1860s, and an even larger shadow-town of mine tunnels and caverns underneath. The streets were packed with freight teams, buggies and wagons. The ones that were going out to the open pits and tunnels of the mines were full of blasting powder, picks, drills, gads and shovels; the ones coming back were loaded with rocks.

It was in Virginia City that the Osbournes' marriage began to come unstuck. Fanny's loyalty had already been stretched by the hardships she and Belle had endured, and she was growing weary of seeing debts mount up and hearing the same promises endlessly repeated. She might have tolerated all this even longer, but for the discovery that Sam kept a mistress (his many casual infidelities before this, and his use of whores, she had probably guessed at too). They quarrelled violently and soon after, probably to get away from his angry wife, Sam set out on yet another prospecting adventure, this time to Montana with a friend called Samuel Orr. Months went by without a word from them, and when the winter set in, and along with it a sudden depression in the mineral market known as the 'panic of December 1865', Fanny felt too vulnerable in Virginia City and moved to San Francisco in company with John Lloyd.

It is said that almost as soon as she arrived at her hotel in San Francisco, Fanny got news that Sam Osbourne's party had been attacked on the road to Montana months before and all were presumed dead. This story seems like an obvious fabrication, a polite cover for the separation from Sam, which looked as if it was going to be permanent, one way or the other. John Lloyd was almost certainly in love with his friend's wife, and promptly suggested that the new 'widow' and her daughter should come and live in the same boarding house as him near the old shot tower. Fanny was almost certainly in love with Lloyd too; she went into mourning for Sam, but didn't go home to Indiana, as an unsupported female might have been expected to do, choosing instead to scrape a living as a seamstress in a dressmaker's shop so that she could remain on the west coast. Since she loved her parents and hadn't seen them for two years, her choice of staying in San Francisco indicates that she saw her sudden reversal of status as only temporary. Either she believed that Sam was not dead and would come back, or she was having an affair with John Lloyd, or both.

Belle's memories of the winter in the boarding house are of being devotedly attended to by Lloyd, who took her on excursions and bought her a dolls' tea set. He was studying in the evenings to be a lawyer's clerk (and later became a very successful banker), and was her mother's constant consort. So they were all in for a shock when, some time the following year, Sam Osbourne rolled into town and came to reclaim his family. Belle was delighted, for she adored her handsome father (she would later say, 'I cannot remember ever hearing a cross word from my father'[14]), but the feelings of his 'widow' are not recorded. Osbourne re-established the little family in a rented house on 5th Street and things went back to something like normal for a while. Lloyd was relegated to the position of Sunday visitor, though Fanny's letters home are notably fuller of affectionate remarks about him than about the errant husband who had so incontinently risen from the dead.

In April 1868 Fanny gave birth to a son, christened Samuel Lloyd Osbourne. If this child hadn't grown up to look very much like Sam, it might seem reasonable to question his paternity, for even before his birth his parents' marriage was under intense strain again.* When the couple had another huge row just after the baby's birth, Fanny decided to go back to her parents, taking the children with her on the tortuous route back via Panama. They stayed in Indiana for a year; then, at Sam's request, made another attempt to mend the marriage, returning to the Bay Area in June

---

* There is a puzzling reference in a letter from Anna Rearden Baeck to Anne Roller Issler in the Silverado collection (dated 27 December 1968), where she claims that Fanny Osbourne 'was almost obsessed by her barrenness with her young husband'. Margaret Mackay had implied the same in *The Violent Friend*, to support her suggestion that the baby boy was John Lloyd's son, though on what authority is unclear. Baeck was the daughter of Fanny's confidant Timothy Rearden.

1869, on the brand-new transcontinental railroad. Sam moved them to a pretty prefabricated wooden cottage in East Oakland where they spent six apparently contented years. Fanny kept house for Sam, created a garden, sewed, painted, cooked. She became a super-efficient, unsmiling domestic goddess.

But the attempted idyll didn't last, and by the time Fanny's third child, a little boy called Hervey, was born in 1871, Sam was openly living with a mistress in San Francisco, near the courthouse where he now worked as a stenographer. Divorce was not on the cards, but as Sam only came home at weekends, the separation was pretty thorough and, to a woman of Fanny's proud dispo-sition, very wounding. She responded by cultivating greater and greater independence and developing her own circle of friends from among her husband's associates. Sam Osbourne had become something of a social kingpin in San Francisco, and together with John Lloyd and a young lawyer called Timothy Rearden had founded the Bohemian Club (which in time became the most suc-cessful thing of its kind on the west coast). Members included the writer Bret Harte, the musician Oscar Weil and the poet Charles Warren Stoddard, whom Fanny got to know well. It was Timothy Rearden, though, who became her main ally, and she flirted with him shamelessly, enjoying the *frisson* of her frequent lone visits to his bachelor rooms in the city. In the copious correspondence that has survived of their relationship, Fanny's tone is almost constantly provocative: 'I suppose writing this note is another impropriety – Do you suppose Mrs Grundy went to heaven when she died? If so let me go to – the other place';[15] 'I liked the warmth and the brightness and the sound of your voice, especially when you called me "child". You sounded so old and kind then. I think you want to box my ears now. You were not truly kind, I know, only old, and you happened to have that kind of a voice.'[16] Some biographers have assumed that the two were lovers, but from what Fanny says in one letter to Rearden in November 1875, I would guess that he was homosexual, or would have liked to be: 'give me your promise that what occurred at the [Turkish] baths should never happen again', Fanny wrote. 'Could you do that? Would you? [. . .] I can hardly believe you falling back for a moment, after all these years, into the old ways.'[17] Perhaps they were lovers (Rearden married later in life), or perhaps just intimate, risqué, confidential friends.

Another member of the Bohemian Club who, with his wife Dora, got to know Fanny well was an artist called Virgil Williams. He had founded and ran San Francisco's first fine art college, the School of Design, with premises next door to those of the Bohemian Club above the California Market (then situated on the corner of Market and Pine).* Through Williams and his wife Fanny began to think she too might have a future in the arts, or at least in *la vie bohème*, and in 1874 she enrolled herself and sixteen-year-old Belle at the school as part-time students.

Fanny's relationship with her teenaged daughter had become one of strangely complicit rivalry. Fanny was only thirty-four in 1874 but looked even younger, while Belle looked older than her age. With their very similar figures and gypsy colouring, the two women were often mistaken for sisters and both played up to the coquette potential of the situation. They were, after all, both on the lookout for lovers at the same time, and attracted (or were attracted to) the same kind of man, a fact that led to many complicated situations over the next thirty or forty years. Belle had huge dark eyes and an ardent, confident manner; she was not exactly pretty, but sexy and flirtatious. At the age of only fourteen she was followed to the theatre by a young man who had been drawing her portrait clandestinely on the ferry over to San Francisco, an art student called Joe Strong (of whom more later); at sixteen, she was proposed to by a man who had met her only once, the first of many smitten suitors. Fanny had the same sultry beauty as her daughter, with the added allure of maturity and experience, and a slightly tragic, mysterious air. She had plenty of advice for Belle on voice, dress and body language and some favourite techniques for entrancing men: one was acting vulnerable – 'she had only

---

* Williams had been in Austin at the same time as the Osbournes back in the 1860s, though there is no record of them having met then.

to look helpless and bewildered, and gallant strangers leaped to her assistance', Belle recalled[18] – another, her speciality, was to fix the victim with a stare, as Robert Louis Stevenson was about to find out. Her regard, he said later, 'was like the sighting of a pistol'.

The undated photograph of Fanny in her bohemian velvet-trimmed jacket and cravat, which is the most attractive image of her to have survived, I guess to have been taken around this time, or a bit earlier, as it seems considerably less matronly than the photo taken in 1880 on the occasion of her second marriage. It is the only picture of her in which she seems to be almost smiling; her figure is trim and she looks touchingly young and untroubled, with her hair pinned up haphazardly and no jewellery or adorn-ments. It seems to fit with the period in the early 1870s when Fanny was reinventing herself as an artist and an independent spirit, years before the idea of the 'new woman' was born. She was almost certainly engaged in other flirtations, possibly affairs, at this time. Going to and from the School of Design with her mother, Fanny dressed in a skirt with a slight bustle, a tight-fitting basque, 'leg-of-mutton' sleeves and a blue velvet toque, Belle began to notice 'the attention my mother attracted and [...] how very pretty she was'.[19] She cut quite a figure at the college with her determined attitude and thirst for self-improvement, winning a silver medal for drawing in her first year. 'This did not seem to have much effect on her at the time,' Belle wrote many years later, 'but after her death I found, squeezed in her jewellery box, a little leather disk at the bottom of a black box, the medal she had taken everywhere, even to the end.'

Her mother's next move left Belle 'the most surprised person in the world'.[20] Only a year after starting at the San Francisco art school, Fanny made the wild decision to leave for a year in Europe with all three children and the boys' governess, a dumpy young woman called Kate Moss. The excuse was to carry on her and Belle's art studies in Antwerp, but the reason was yet another flare-up in her slowly disintegrating marriage. Sam objected

strongly to the plan, but didn't prevent her going; indeed he probably couldn't have prevented her, Fanny was worked up to such a
pitch of hysterical excitement. All her adult life, Fanny suffered
from what she called 'brain fevers', and she certainly seemed to be
in the grip of one of them when she wrote this description to Dora
Williams of her dash from Indianapolis to New York City: 'We
plunged over embankments into foaming torrents, at the risk of
being swept away and drowned, half a dozen times [. . .] The
story of my ride went before me [. . .] and each conductor passed
my party over his road, introducing me to the next as the lady who
drove over the Vandalia road.'[21] Typically, Fanny makes it sound as
if she had driven not just the road but the coach itself, and the ride
becomes *hers* alone, no mention of the children, Miss Kate, or the
other passengers. But at this moment in her life, she was intoxicated
by the drama of her own story and gave little thought to anyone
else. Symbolically enough, the floods they went through on the
way to New York were destroying bridges behind them.

Fanny heard the midnight chimes from Antwerp cathedral with
tears in her eyes as their ship sailed into port in October 1875: 'I
was sentimental enough to imagine it a welcome to the old world,
and to accept it as a good omen,' she wrote to Mrs Williams.[22] But
she knew nothing about Belgium, could speak neither Flemish nor
French, and had arrived to take up a course at an institution which
didn't admit women. The wonder is that the party spent three
months in the city, with nothing to do, very little money and the
frail four-year-old Hervey ill almost all the time. Though her letters
to Rearden are full of silly swaggering about her own and Belle's
attractiveness and the behaviour of men towards them, Fanny was
clearly feeling lonely and intimidated. She was sorry and surprised
to hear that Sam was missing his family badly, and, for a rare
moment, began to think she might have made a mistake:

> I didn't know I should miss [Sam] as I do. It was pitiful to
> hear my little Hervy [sic] in his delirium calling and calling
> for his father; it made me feel as if I had no right to have him
> so far away.[23]

Hervey's condition got worse, 'Antwerp fever' was raging, and so in November Fanny decided to move the bedraggled family on to Paris, spiritual home of would-be artists. They took rooms on the rue de Naples, and Belle and Fanny enrolled in the Atelier des Dames off the boulevard des Italiens, an all-women school run by a Monsieur Julien, where Belle was delighted to find herself in the same class as Louisa May Alcott's sister, May, the original of Amy in *Little Women*. Fanny attended class infrequently, being required to nurse her youngest child. They were living on a shoestring: 'Our furniture is of the most primitive character, mostly made by myself,' Fanny wrote to Dora Williams,[24] again managing to salvage some grounds for self-congratulation from a disastrous situation. But with the unexpected doctors' bills on top of everything else, the little money promised by Sam was never going to be enough, even had he been the sort of man to send regular, predictable payments. Samuel Junior remembered Paris as somewhere where he felt hungry all the time and pressed his face against the windows of patisseries in agonies of desire. If it hadn't meant another mouth to feed, Fanny might almost have been grateful for the company of Miss Kate, whom she had tried to ditch in New York. The governess, clearly worried about the children, and perhaps under separate instructions from their father, had got herself onto the boat in steerage.

Fanny was clearly culpable in what happened next. The nature of Hervey's illness was unclear (the Antwerp doctors suspected 'scrofulous consumption') and he had been given some odd treatments, including having his sides painted with 'some drug so powerful that everyone in the room is almost blinded by it', drinking fresh ox-blood and taking quinine by the tablespoon. By February 1876 – *five months* after she first began to report him ill – Hervey was still sick, but Fanny made Rearden promise not to breathe a word of it to Sam. At the slightest sign of a respite, she convinced herself that the child was improving, though Belle said (albeit with hindsight) 'we knew he was going to die long before the end came'. Fanny's denial meant that she left it far too late to inform her husband of the situation, and by the time Sam Osbourne arrived in Paris, summoned by cablegram halfway across the world, Hervey was almost dead. Fanny's grief-stricken description of the boy's last days is more like a hallucination than a memory:

> I did not dare leave him because every few hours he bled in a new place. I shall never forget the smell of blood. He would say, 'Blood, mama, get the things; wait till I am ready.' [. . .] Everyone ran from the room when he said blood; his father stayed once until he saw the probe, and then he too turned pale and ran away. None could see what my boy could bear. Through all his sufferings he never lost his mind. I only wish he had been unconscious. When in the most violent convulsions, his bones snapping in and out of joint like the crack of a whip, and covered with blood, he lay back in my arms, looking into my eyes and listening to my words through it all. [. . .] he could hardly hear, the rush of blood having torn one drum entirely away and perforating the other, but no-one can conceive what agony it was to me, and so it went on day after day, such terrible days! His bones had cut through the skin and lay bare, and yet there was no word of complaint through it all.[25]

Sam didn't stay long in Paris after the funeral. Rather than drawing him and his wife back together again, Hervey's death marked the beginning of the end of their marriage. Though Sam might have insisted on his wife's return to the States at this point, he didn't. Both bereaved parents were too numb for recriminations. They followed the little white coffin to its plot in Saint-Germain cemetery on 8 April 1876 and parted soon after, Sam back to his job and his mistress, Fanny to her continued 'studies'.*

The summer dragged on in Paris for the subdued remnant of the Osbourne family. Belle was making some progress in her art classes, it was thought, but Fanny was too miserably affected by

---

* Fanny later made great play of how her boy had only been allowed 'a pauper's grave', but this was inaccurate. Sam Osbourne bought a ten-year 'concession' on a grave plot for his son, intending to renew it, or possibly move the remains at a later date.

her child's death to take part properly. 'Brain fever' seemed to threaten again, and a complete change of air was recommended, not least because little Sam was also looking ill. From this time onwards, Fanny became (understandably) extremely neurotic about the state of her remaining son's health.

The Hôtel Chevillon at Grez-sur-Loing (where Fanny and Sam may have visited briefly just after Hervey's death) had been suggested as a quiet, congenial place in the country, frequented by painters, mostly Irish, English and American, and it was there that Fanny took the children for a couple of months to convalesce and perhaps get some informal painting lessons. Belle was charmed when she first saw the old stone building from the high seat of the diligence, and loved the vine-covered arbour and the garden that sloped down to the Loing. They seemed to have the place to themselves to begin with, with only an American, Mr Palmer, quietly dabbling with watercolours in the garden, until the dramatic arrival of Bob Stevenson, looking, typically, like 'a sort of gentleman gypsy'. Both Belle and Fanny were entranced by the charismatic Scot; Fanny wrote to Rearden swooningly about his 'wonderful grace and figure', his talent, charm, musicality, ability to speak 'all languages' and perform 'any sort of feats of strength'. The attraction seems to have been mutual, for Bob was soon instigating adventures with Mrs Osbourne such as rowing her into deep water in a canoe and deliberately capsizing it as a 'hardening-off exercise'. Fanny couldn't swim, so plenty of rescuing must have been required; also, as Belle recalled, her mother looked particularly fetching in her long-sleeved bathing costume with a scarlet kerchief tied round the waist, 'her tiny feet in red espadrilles'.[26] She and Bob dripped back to the hotel together and compared their bare legs for sunburn.

Then the other members of the group of friends began to arrive one at a time: Walter Simpson, his brother Willie, and the Irish painter Frank O'Meara, another student of Carolus-Duran. The ebullient and charming O'Meara, still only twenty, homed in quickly on Belle and was soon melting her heart with his rendition of 'The Harp that Once through Tara's Halls'. The two American women, whom Bob had feared might spoil the atmosphere at Grez, were turning out to be welcome additions to the company. They were permanently available for forest walks or river escapades or, if it rained, sessions of verse-writing or charades. Fanny became known (she was quick to relate) as 'the beautiful American' and 'the Sultana', and though she continued to present herself as an 'artist' – and completed one perfectly competent oil painting of Grez's old bridge – her studies soon became less important to her than cultivating the role of model and muse to the group of excitable bohemians. 'They paint me, making me very beautiful,' she wrote goadingly to Rearden, 'and make up sketches of my mouth, and the back of my head, and my nose, and model my arms in clay.'

Still to arrive in this erotically-charged artistic holiday camp was Louis Stevenson, the other 'mad Scotsman' of whom the Osbournes had been warned. He had spent a miserable summer in Edinburgh, battling with depression and some mysterious 'trouble' that sent him to take refuge at Henley's digs for a while (indicating that it was something to do with money: his parents were away from home at the time).[27] He wrote despondently to Frances Sitwell (to whom letters were becoming less and less frequent), 'there are times when people's lives stand still. If you were to ask a squirrel in a mechanical cage, for his autobiography, it would not be very gay.'[28] He didn't expect her to like his latest essay for the *Cornhill*, a witty meditation on marriage called 'Virginibus Puerisque'. Perhaps the theme was on his mind because Baxter, Henley and Simpson were all courting (and all married in the following two years), and Bob was always falling in love: 'In one way or another, life forces men apart and breaks up the goodly fellowships for ever,' he wrote. 'The very flexibility and ease which make men's friendships so agreeable while they endure, make them the easier to destroy and forget.'[29] The essay depicts marriage as comfortable, highly desirable (as long as both parties were 'versed in the niceties of the heart, and born with a faculty for willing compromise'[30]), but neither heroic nor romantic. Here was the perverse, witty vein that began to mark out Stevenson's writing: 'Marriage is a step so grave and decisive that it attracts light-headed, variable men by its very awfulness'; 'even if we take matrimony at its lowest, even if we regard it as no more than a sort of friendship recognised by the police, there must be degrees in the freedom and sympathy realised, and some principle to guide simple folk in their selection'; 'marriage is like life in this – that it is a field of battle, and not a bed of roses'.[31] Leslie Stephen must have been rubbing his hands with pleasure over having secured this new Elia for the *Cornhill*.

Louis was getting impatient to have a book published, and in 1876 hit on the idea of using his summer holiday to generate the material for a long travel essay. Walter Simpson, with whom he had already been on several walking tours and a sailing holiday in the Inner Hebrides, was the chosen companion. They set off from Antwerp at the end of August in two canoes, the *Cigarette* (Simpson's) and the *Arethusa*, paddled some thirty miles down the Willebroek Canal to Brussels, went by rail from Brussels to Maubeuge, then got back on water and canoed the Rivers Sambre and Oise to Pontoise in the Val d'Oise. The projected journey was to continue all the way to the Mediterranean, via the Saône and Rhône, more than double the distance they actually covered. Stevenson planned to complete the second leg the following year, but that never happened.*

Stevenson didn't write *An Inland Voyage* until the winter of 1877, by which time his motives had become nicely mixed. What he intended as 'an easy book', riding on the novelty of the itinerary, turned into an impromptu prospectus of the author's personality, philosophy and literary style. This was somewhat the result of *force majeure*, for the journey turned out to be short on incident (the episode where Stevenson loses his canoe to a fallen tree but 'sticks to his paddle' is the dramatic high point) and, as the author

---

* The second stage of their journey was almost exactly replicated forty years later in the Allies' retreat from Mons, during which, John Charteris notes in his biography of Earl Haig, the British commander read *An Inland Voyage* as escape literature.

was comically ready to admit, the whole enterprise struck many observers as pointless or absurd. Innkeepers and bargees shook their heads at the idea of travelling the waterways for pleasure, and one 'malicious' old man near Landrecies told the traveller to '"Get into a train, my little young man, [. . .] and go you away home to your parents."'[32]

The book dramatises this very desire to escape not just from home and parents but from the wider world of respectability, responsibility and 'attendance at an office'. Of course a canoe holiday with a baronet was in itself profoundly bourgeois, but 'protest against offices and the mercantile spirit' runs through the narrative like a lively undercurrent, and it is taken as read that 'the gipsily-inclined among men' are always going to get the best out of life. The narrator's heart goes out to the puppeteers at Précy, the travelling merchant and his wife, strollers and bagmen, and he is never so pleased as when he and Simpson are mistaken for peddlers in Pont-sur-Sambre on account of their scruffiness and sent to get lodgings with a butcher. They are ejected from an inn again, more violently, in La Fère, prompting the author to remark that 'once get under the wheels, and you wish society were at the devil'.[33] It's impossible to take any of this too seriously. Stevenson had once been held in a cell for six hours in Châtillon-sur-Loing while the police inspected his papers, but earlier attempts at getting himself arrested in London for looking like a beggar had not met with any success, as Colvin (who was fascinated with his friend's taste for slumming) testified: 'One and all saw through him, and refused to take him seriously as a member of the criminal classes.'[34]

The contretemps at La Fère had a good outcome, as the two canoeists ended up at an *auberge* full of military reservists, where they were able to witness the tenderness of the landlord and his wife to each other. This is the sort of 'travel' Stevenson really wants to write about: not tourist sites, but sights of ordinary life, hardships, rebuffs, oddity, humour, moments of human sympathy. The gliding progress of the *Cigarette* and the *Arethusa* alongside the towns and farms, wherries and wharves of the Low Countries and France thus becomes an elegant exercise in social voyeurism. The two companions are always *moving on*, past the camp of shabby soldiers, past the boating club, past the girls' boarding school:

> there were the girls about the garden; and here were we on the river; and there was more than one handkerchief waved as we went by. It caused quite a stir in my heart; and yet how we would have wearied and despised each other, these girls and I, if we had been introduced at a croquet party![35]

Another set of girls at Origny, calling out 'Come back again!', inspire this Heraclitean moment: 'There is a headlong, forthright tide, that bears away man with his fancies like straw, and runs fast in time and space. It is full of curves like this, your winding river of the Oise; and lingers and returns in pleasant pastorals; and yet, rightly thought upon, never returns at all.'[36] But the most striking passage in the book is not one that strains like this to moralise, but the analysis (in the chapter 'Changed Times') of the 'apotheosis of stupidity' that the author achieves by hours of uninterrupted paddling: 'the great wheels of intelligence turned idly in the head, like fly-wheels, grinding no grist. I have gone on for half an hour at a time, counting my strokes and forgetting the hundreds.'[37] This happily bovine state of mind, he realises, is 'about as near Nirvana as would be convenient in practical life':

> There was less *me* and more *not me* than I was accustomed to expect. I looked upon somebody else, who managed the paddling; I was aware of somebody else's feet against the stretcher; my own body seemed to have no more intimate relation to me than the canoe, or the river, or the river banks. Nor this alone: something inside my mind, a part of my brain, a province of my proper being, had thrown off allegiance and set up for itself, or perhaps for the somebody else who did the paddling. I had dwindled into quite a little thing in a corner of myself. I was isolated in my own skull. Thoughts presented themselves unbidden; they were not my thoughts, they were plainly someone else's[.][38]

This was 'the great exploit of our voyage', he reckons, and 'the farthest piece of travel accomplished': 'when ideas came and went like motes in a sunbeam; when trees and church spires along the bank surged up from time to time into my notice [...] when a piece of mud on the deck was sometimes an intolerable eyesore, and sometimes quite a companion for me, and the object of pleased consideration'. As in 'On the Enjoyment of Unpleasant Places' and 'Ordered South', his state of consciousness becomes the subject, the direction of travel even more 'inland' than he perhaps anticipated. His Emersonian identification of *me* and *not me* ('what philosophers call [...] *ego* and *non ego*') has its birth on the Oise in this ecstatic stupor, but was to find other expression in 'Markheim', *Deacon Brodie* and *Jekyll and Hyde*.

With the publication of essays such as 'Virginibus Puerisque', its sequel 'On Falling in Love', 'An Apology for Idlers' and *An Inland Voyage*, the word 'charming' began to be applied more and more frequently to Stevenson's writing. The charm seemed to inhere in the writer's youthfulness, optimism, wit and apparently boundless taste for self-revelation, which flattered the reader into a sense of intimacy. Stevenson wasn't yet perceived as a chronic invalid, which made him into something of a sentimental hero later: if anything, in 1878 he might have seemed to the general reader to be some kind of exercise enthusiast.

The literary world seemed primed and willing to fall in love with him. This was only partly because so many reviewers for the periodicals were his personal friends, and puffed each other's works shamelessly. Henley larded his review of *An Inland Voyage* with superlatives,* and Colvin wrote pages for the *Athenaeum*. The elegance of *An Inland Voyage* stunned P.G. Hammerton, writing in the *Academy*, who wondered 'how many people there are in England who know that Robert Louis Stevenson is, in his own way (and he is wise enough to write simply in his own way), one of the

---

* Though it is unsigned, the piece, in *London* for 25 May 1878, bears all the hallmarks of Henley's prose, and he was, as editor of the magazine at the time, known to be writing almost the whole review section single-handed.

most perfect writers living, one of the very few who may yet do something classical?'[39] Hammerton's pleasure at the advent of a new stylist, grounded in the classic English essayists yet deviating from them 'charmingly', found many seconders, not least an Oxford literary society which (as Bob reported to his cousin later) chose *An Inland Voyage* as 'the best specimen of the writing of English this century',[40] or the Eton schoolmaster who set his pupils part of the text to be translated into Latin elegiacs. For someone whose writing had been regarded for years as a kind of aberration, this was an almost indigestible reverse.

By the winter of 1877, when *An Inland Voyage* was written, there was one reader in particular whom Stevenson was keen to impress, and that was Fanny Osbourne. He first met her at Grez at the end of September or early October 1876, having finished the canoe trip with Simpson just a week or two before.[41] It seems that everyone was gathered at the long *table d'hôte* after supper at Chevillons' Inn one evening when a noise was heard outside and next thing, Louis was seen vaulting dramatically through the inn's half-door, causing 'an uproar of delight' among the company.[42] He had arrived alone on foot, and paused outside the window for several minutes to scrutinise the group, especially the two Americans, the only women present, who were obviously quite at home. At least part of this is likely to be true, as 'the day I looked through the window' is among the love-anniversaries Stevenson later wished to keep (if only he could have remembered the date). The story of their meeting became heavily mythologised later by Fanny's two children, Belle and Sam, who were both in Grez at the time. Sam was especially keen to record 'the peculiar sense of power that seemed to radiate from [Stevenson]', as if it was an angel who had landed at the table, and not just another bohemian Scot. But it's not at all certain that Sam was actually present at Louis's arrival; he left two very different accounts (the introduction to the Vailima edition, which is quoted, and *An Intimate Portrait*, which has Louis arriving by canoe, in what appears to be daylight).

Stevenson was immediately interested in 'the beautiful American', as well he might have been. He had already heard about her from Bob, first as a threat to the pleasures of Grez, then as an enhancement of them. He would also have heard the tragic story of how her little boy had died in Paris earlier that year, so reminiscent of Fanny Sitwell's loss three years earlier. Here was another bereaved matron with an absentee husband – though there the resemblance stopped, rather abruptly. Mrs Sitwell had never exuded such seething sexuality; *her* eyes had always been 'gentle', 'soft' and shining with the anticipation of sympathetic tears. The short, exotic goddess who was sitting smoking a hand-rolled cigarette at the table at Chevillons' looked about as gentle as a howitzer, and probably lost no time in fixing the newcomer with that 'sighting of a pistol' look she kept for special occasions.

A waspish portrait of Fanny at Grez by a female 'friend' evokes her presence there vividly:

> Near one end of the table, her flowing hair surmounted with the rakish little cap of a *vivandière*, her black eyes peeping out from a fringe of not very neat curls, sits the Queen of Bohemia. She is not so young as one might think, knowing only her rank and state. There are hundreds of silver threads in her hair; and further down the table sits her daughter, the princess royal, grown to womanhood. Fairy in size, like a hummingbird in movement and in purpose of life, her Majesty seems, to the not too clear-sighted observer, in spite of her thirty-eight years, scarcely more than a girl. [. . .] Her Majesty is smoking a cigarette between the soup and the roast. Her Majesty is generally smoking a cigarette when she is not sleeping, and when dining usually has her little feet upon the rungs of her neighbour's chair, while she tells strange stories of wild life among the Nevada mines, where she never saw a flower for eight years; where feverish brandy and champagne were cheaper than cool water and sweet milk; where Colonel Starbottle was her devoted admirer and Jack Hamlin told his love[.][43]

Many of the things that men found irresistible about Fanny Osbourne are catalogued critically here: her maturity, her self-possession, her worldliness, the thrilling combination of femininity and being 'one of the boys', with those tiny bare feet resting on the next chair as she smoked and talked. It conjures up exactly Fanny's self-confident manner in front of men, her assured, devastatingly focused techniques of sexual enticement. The author of the sketch was an American called Margaret Berthe Wright who was studying with Belle and Fanny at the Atelier des Dames and who for a while lived in the same building as they did in Paris. She must have hated the Osbournes by the time she wrote this article in the winter of 1877. After remarking on Fanny's monotonous drawling voice (heard rather too often, it is implied) and 'the faint shadow of the cachuca and cracovina in the free motions of her arms above her head', Wright goes on to say that though the foolishly romantic British gents in residence at Grez may have been taken in by the performance, a fellow American matron could see straight through it:

> In the highly civilised old world she may seem a lost princess, a stray daughter of the Incas, come only to shabby queenhood in Bohemia by right of her uncivilised blood and her royal birth. Before New World eyes, looking from nearer into barbarism, there is none of the glamour which sees romance and poetry in simply dusky skins, wild, free motions and turbulent lives, so that real, unromantic barrenness and poverty of nature is as visible to them in a deposed daughter of the Incas or Mexican dancer as in the pale factory girl who toils and spins and knows nothing else.[44]

But Stevenson was hooked. Here perhaps was a version of that 'great mythical woman' he had fantasised about to Mrs Sitwell, or one of the 'Powerful Matrons' in Whitman's *Leaves of Grass*: 'They are tann'd in the face by shining suns and blowing winds, /Their flesh has the old divine suppleness and strength.' Over the next few days he took every opportunity to get to know Mrs Osbourne, sitting with her by the stove and talking for hours on end in a possibly very exaggerated vein, if her reports back to Timothy Rearden in the following months are anything to go by. Bob had 'spent a large fortune at the rate of eight thousand pounds a year', she told Rearden, taken holy orders to please his mother and was now 'dying from the effects of dissipation'. Louis, 'between over-education and dissipation has ruined his health, and is dying of consumption'. He was 'the heir to an immense fortune which he will never live to inherit. His father and mother, cousins, are both threatened with insanity, and I am quite sure the son is.'[45] Holy orders? Immense fortune? *Cousins?* Fanny was a chronic embellisher, but surely much of this had its origin in Bob and Louis's incontinent romanticising, or perhaps Louis's alone. As the only non-painter in a group of artists, the skinniest and weediest among half a dozen fine young men, he was sore put to impress Mrs Osbourne, especially as her own stories of the far west were so exotic. Added to that, he was calling himself a writer, but had no book to show for it. It was Bob who still commanded Fanny Osbourne's attention, with his artistic talent, athleticism, charm and 'perfect figure'. He was like a hero out of a Ouida novel, she said to Rearden.[46]

Fanny wasn't the only 'beautiful American' at Grez; there was of course another siren present, Belle, who got even more attention than her mother. The dusky seventeen-year-old was in her element, the object of both O'Meara's and Bob's fervent gallantry, and Louis's admiration: 'Belle is frank and simple and not at all like an American miss. She looks like a Russian,' he wrote.[47] Meanwhile, Louis doted on Belle's mother, and Belle's mother doted on Bob. A *Midsummer Night's Dream* situation seemed in danger of erupting, and Bob and Louis were obviously in cahoots when Stennis *aîné* (as Bob was called *chez* Chevillon) took Fanny out on a walk one day in order to praise his cousin to the skies, explaining that Louis was by far the superior man to cultivate. Fanny Osbourne took in the meaning of this immediately, and, aided by Bob's tactful manoeuvrings, was able to transfer her interest to Stennis *frère* with no visible dints to her pride.

Louis went back to Edinburgh in high spirits, believing his feelings were at least partly requited, and wrote his essay 'On Falling in Love'. In it he describes the 'ideal story' as

> that of two people who go into love step for step, with a fluttered consciousness, like a pair of children venturing together into a dark room. From the first moment they see each other, with a pang of curiosity, through stage after stage of growing pleasure and embarrassment, they can read the expression of their own trouble in each other's eyes. There is here no declaration properly so called; the feeling is so plainly shared, that as soon as the man knows what it is in his own heart, he is sure of what it is in the woman's.[48]

Did he think this was his own case? It is likely that he and Fanny became lovers at Grez or during the week they were both in Paris on his way home, since on his next recorded meeting with her, in January 1877, he went straight to her lodgings in the rue de Douay and stayed there. There was probably at least one more unrecorded meeting between October and January; it would be hard otherwise to explain the rollercoaster agitation Stevenson experienced during those months. Stuck at Heriot Row in the autumn and early winter (while Fanny was in Paris, seeing all the Barbizonians frequently), Louis became deeply despondent, writing to Mrs Sitwell of his 'sad misfortune', and pleading with his former deity not to withdraw her friendship 'just now, when I know so well that I am making daily another tie about my heart only that it may be broken in its turn (or alas! not broken after all; for I find I have no talent for forgetfulness)'.[49]

There are indications that Louis may have dashed to Paris in November or December, for at the end of that month Fanny wrote to Rearden in rather disingenuous terms (knowing that anything she told him could get back to her husband) about the two 'mad Scotsmen' she had got to know, and how Bob Stevenson had thanked her for not laughing at his cousin 'whose fainting and hysterics and weeping were caused by ill-health'. 'He was right about his cousin,' she told Rearden casually, 'whom I like very much, and who is the wittiest man I ever met; only I do wish he wouldn't burst into tears in such an unexpected way; it is so embarrassing.'[50] Louis was disturbing company, 'sometimes, I imagine, not altogether safe', Fanny related in another letter, recalling an incident when they had been in a cab together in Paris. Stevenson had begun laughing and couldn't stop: '[he] asked me to bend his fingers back. I didn't like to do it, so he laughed harder and harder and told me that I had better[,] for if I didn't he would bend my fingers back and break every bone in them.' When Stevenson proceeded to try this, Fanny bit him hard on the hand, drawing blood, at which he 'immediately came to his senses and begged pardon, but I couldn't use my hands for more than a day afterwards'.[51] This vampiric scene (which seems to have found its way into Stevenson's story 'Olalla' years later) borders on the morbid. What with the threats and the biting, the blood and the generally hysterical tone, it didn't bode well for the relationship, though Stevenson may well have been impressed with the direct and effective manner of Fanny's response to his outburst.

By January 1877, when he managed to get to Paris on the excuse of having some 'dramas of his' translated into French,[52] Stevenson had calmed down considerably. In the congenial atmosphere of the Latin Quarter, he could live with his mistress openly and cause little scandal. What Belle and eight-year-old Sam thought about the arrangement is not known. In their copious memoirs of Stevenson, both children maintained with increasing ardour the fiction that he and their mother stayed chaste until their marriage in 1880.

Meanwhile, Stevenson was sending vignettes of his new life back to Henley and Brown at *London*; 'A Studio of Ladies' describes the zealous atmosphere among the lady amateurs of Julien's, while 'A Ball at Mr Elsinare's' has portraits of his friends under thinly disguised names: Willie Simpson (MacIntyre), O'Meara (O'Shaughnessy), Bloomer (Smiler) and Belle Osbourne (Belle Bird), 'a Californian girl, [who] has spent her childhood among Bret Harte's stories, petted by miners, and gamblers, and trappers, and ranch-men, and all the *dramatis personae* of the new romance'.[53] On the evening of the dance, the studio (which had previously been occupied by George Du Maurier and became the setting for his novel *Trilby*) was decorated with Chinese lanterns and bronze lamps strung from the rafters, and the paraphernalia of the working day was propped against the walls: an iron bedstead, a skull, dozens of casts on the shelves. Louis didn't dance, but relished being able to make this appearance with Fanny in front of so many of his friends. To his mother, he described the evening circumspectly: 'One of the matrons was a very beautiful woman indeed; I played old fogy and had a deal of talk with her, which pleased me.'[54]

The matron was still married, however, and in the spring of 1877 Sam Osbourne was coming over to France to see his wife and family and, presumably, go through the motions of another reconciliation. Fanny's feelings about this are hard to fathom; she seems to have been determined to stay in Europe (despite the enormous expense), but was not altogether dead to Sam's charm. Back in Edinburgh in the spring, Stevenson waited out the season in agonies of jealousy. 'The man with the linstock is expected in May; it makes me sick to write it. But I'm quite insane,' he wrote to Baxter, 'and when the mountain does not come to Mahomet, Mahomet will to the mountain.'[55]

Was it under Fanny's influence that Stevenson began to write so much fiction in 1877? 'An Old Song' was rewritten that winter, and he also wrote 'A Lodging for the Night', which dramatises an incident from the life of the poet and criminal François Villon, about whom Stevenson had just written an essay for the *Cornhill*. Leslie Stephen was sardonic about the prospect of Stevenson publishing a book of essays: 'he said he didn't imagine I was rich enough for such an amusement',[56] and making money was always an issue with Stevenson, if only as a way of gauging his success. It is easy to imagine Fanny, herself a notable raconteur, encouraging

Louis to think of a more popular and lucrative market for his skills. The opening of his Villon story, describing a snowy night in fifteenth-century Paris, shows him leaping fully-armed into the form:

> The whole city was sheeted up. An army might have marched from end to end and not a footfall given the alarm. If there were any belated birds in heaven, they saw the island like a large white patch, and the bridges like slim white spars, on the black ground of the river. High up overhead the snow settled among the tracery of the cathedral towers. Many a niche was drifted full; many a statue wore a long white bonnet on its grotesque or sainted head. The gargoyles had been transformed into great false noses, drooping towards the point. The crockets were like upright pillows swollen on one side. In the intervals of the wind, there was a dull sound of dripping about the precincts of the church.[57]

A couple of months later, he had started a novel called 'The Hair Trunk; or, The Ideal Commonwealth', a tale of some young bohemians founding a new society in – of all places – Samoa (Stevenson had once met a customs inspector whose stories of Samoa intrigued him[58]). Henley thought it capitally amusing, but having seen Henley weep over a mere few pages, Stevenson got no farther. A Saratoga trunk found its way into the second of Stevenson's *New Arabian Nights* stories, written the following year (and into *The Wrong Box* in 1889), and from the list of projected scenes – 'burglary, marine fight, life on desert island on W. Coast of Scotland, sloops etc' – *Kidnapped* owes quite a bit to this early novel too.

'The Sire de Malétroit's Door', another hauntingly atmospheric story, was written this year, and 'Will o' the Mill'. Fiction seemed more and more a viable path to take, even though (or especially because) Stevenson's parents thought he could 'never write a story'.[59] By August he was writing to Mrs Sitwell that he was bubbling with ideas for stories and that 'vividness and not style, is now my line; [. . .] occupation is the great thing; so that a man should have his life in his own pocket, and never be thrown out of work by anything'.[60]

Sam Osbourne's visit to his wife was cut short by a stock market alarm in California, and as soon as the American was safely back on the Atlantic in mid-June, Stevenson began making his way to join Fanny at Grez. The interval of separation had been long and traumatic, and in some ways it must have felt like having to start the relationship all over again. What the outcome was to be was still uncertain: Louis must have been hoping that divorce was imminent, but clearly Fanny had done little if anything to advance that over the spring. She and Belle were about to start yet another year – their third – of art studies, all at Sam's expense. It would not have been beyond Mrs Osbourne's wiles to have counted on finishing up at Julien's before severing her ties with the affable adulterer.

Stevenson, on the other hand, was impatient to commit himself, and ready – in theory at least – to take over responsibility for the whole Osbourne family. By the autumn, he was speaking of the group as 'us' and 'we', and beginning to fret in a fatherly way over the antics of Belle and her suitors, two of whom, gossip had it, had threatened to fight a duel over her.* He stayed in France for months on end that year, despite his parents' agitated pleas, and only came back to London, and that in a panicky rush, because Fanny became convinced that he needed emergency treatment for an eye infection. It is the first example of a pattern that was to become absolutely standard. Every deviation from full health became liable to be treated by Fanny as a medical emergency, accompanied by telegrams and mad midnight dashes and the enlistment of every friend's help. Perhaps very understandably, given her failure to act in time to save her youngest child, Fanny was never again going to leave an illness to chance.

---

* One of these must have been O'Meara. It seems unlikely that the other was Bob; he was fascinated by Belle, and half-prepared to marry her, but he was not hot-headed about her, as a letter to RLS of 11 January 1879 shows.

It was in this way that Stevenson was able to introduce his mistress to his London friends, although perhaps the circumstances were not the most auspicious: he with his eye infected, and she laid up after an accident to her foot. When she met Colvin and Mrs Sitwell, it must have been immediately clear to her that there would be no true common ground between them, however kind and attentive the couple were. Mrs Sitwell put Fanny up at Brunswick Row and she and Colvin tenderly sympathised over the foot, but Fanny was quite quelled by their refinement and wrote to Rearden, 'I was with very curious people in London, the leaders of the Purists [. . .] It seemed most incongruous to have the solemn Mr Colvin a professor at Cambridge, and the stately, beautiful Mrs Sitwell sit by me and talk in the most correct English about the progress of literature and the arts.'[61] She also met Leslie Stephen on this visit – another 'purist' if ever there was one – and Henley. They all made her feel uncomfortable, as indeed she did them. How odd it must have been to see the boyish, mercurial Stevenson excitedly introducing this short, dark-skinned American adventuress, who pronounced his name 'Lou-us' and whose build *and character* reminded Colvin powerfully of Napoleon Bonaparte. 'The eyes were full of sex and mystery,' he said in more flattering vein, 'as they changed from fire or fun to gloom or tenderness; and it was from between a fine set of small teeth that there came the clear metallic accents of her intensely human and often quaintly individual speech.'[62]

Filial duty demanded that Stevenson return home for a while, and so the yo-yoing of the lovers together and apart continued. Fanny went back to Paris, and Stevenson, moping in his study at Heriot Row, began a series of articles which was published the following year as *Edinburgh: Picturesque Notes*. Their sardonic tone makes them seem as if written by a disgruntled foreign traveller, which is pretty much what Stevenson had become. No wonder the little book provoked complaints from offended burghers:

To none but those who have themselves suffered the thing in the body, can the gloom and depression of our Edinburgh

winter be brought home. For some constitutions there is
something almost physically disgusting in the bleak ugliness
of easterly weather; the wind wearies, the sickly sky depresses
them; and they turn back from their walk to avoid the aspect
of the unrefulgent sun going down among perturbed and
pallid mists. The days are so short that a man does much of
his business, and certainly all his pleasure, by the haggard
glare of gas lamps. The roads are as heavy as a fallow. People
go by, so drenched and draggle-tailed that I have often wondered how they found the heart to undress.[63]

Stevenson was surprised that anyone should object to this view of
his native town, and protested that he would say a lot worse if
asked to write about Glasgow. He loved Edinburgh, 'this great
city of Zeus', as an ideal, but the time had come to renounce the
north, the cold, the dark, the old life of parents and dependence
and 'no dear head upon the pillow', as he complained to Henley.[64]
When a telegram came from Paris with an alarming message about
little Sam Osbourne's health, he was off like a shot in the middle
of the night.

Thomas and Margaret Stevenson must have been deeply suspicious of their son's behaviour, but as he was now twenty-seven
years old, they could hardly expect to keep him on a tight leash as
before. Ever since falling in love with Fanny, Louis had been getting
on much better with his parents, and frequently expressed his
feelings for them in touchingly affectionate terms. Back in Paris
with his mistress in February 1878, he decided to come clean and
called his father over to explain his 'new complications'. Thomas
behaved admirably, seemed to accept the situation and didn't make
any threats about money (as feared), though how Louis presented
the matter is not clear. Thomas's liberal views on divorce for any
woman but no man would have predisposed him to sympathise
with his son's lover, whom he did not, of course, meet. The incident
marked the high point of Louis's intimacy with his father: or the
only point of it, perhaps. From a café on the boulevard Saint
Michel a week or so later, Louis wrote him an extraordinary letter
which ended:

I hope I have taken a step towards more friendly – no, not that (that could scarcely be) – but more intimate, relations with you. But don't expect too much of me. I am a narrow and a sad person. Try to take me as I am.[65]

All through the beginning of 1878, Stevenson dodged to and from Paris, in states of variable nervous excitement and disorder. The relationship with Fanny was proving far from idyllic; 'one day I find her in heaven, the next in hell', he wrote to Mrs Sitwell in February, and to Henley at around the same time, 'I think almost every sort of calamity has been down on me [. . .] I am so tired, so tired; physically weary, but morally dead weary. I never have a day, but I have a kick or a dig.'[66] A blackmailer had been sending anonymous letters, presumably threatening to expose his affair with Fanny to Sam Osbourne (jeopardising her chances of ever getting a 'favourable' divorce). Was this Margaret Berthe Wright, who would have been fully aware of the comings and goings in the rue Douay? Her acid article about the bohemians of Grez was published that spring.

The agitations of his personal life somewhat overshadowed the pleasure Stevenson had anticipated for so many years when his first book, *An Inland Voyage*, was published in May. Among the chorus of admirers was George Meredith, the sage of Box Hill, whom Stevenson had met that spring while staying with his mother at nearby Burford. Stevenson considered Meredith 'the only man of genius of my acquaintance', and the living novelist he would have most wished to emulate. He idolised *The Egoist* when it was published in 1880, read it eight or nine times, and seems to have borrowed the concept of 'An Arabian Entertainment' (the subtitle of Meredith's 1855 fantasy *The Shaving of Shagpat*) for his own *New Arabian Nights*. So when Meredith wrote, 'I hope you will feel that we expect much of you,'[67] Stevenson must have considered it the most welcome form of literary benediction.

It was in Burford, and with Meredith's views on fiction ringing in his ears,[68] that Stevenson wrote the first two stories of his highly influential *New Arabian Nights*. The sensational idea behind the first story, 'The Suicide Club', grew out of one of Bob Stevenson's extravagant fantasies of luxurious death,[69] and much of Bob's character and behaviour is plundered for the creation of 'The Young Man with the Cream Tarts' who is spending his last afternoon before joining the club giving away money and indulging ludicrous jests. Bob also pervades the character of Prince Florizel of Bohemia, the fantasy royal whose restless need for excitement involves him in the Club's gruesome activities. Florizel is living in London incognito and has a taste – like the Stevenson cousins – for transgressing his true social status. He also has a remarkable ability to adopt disguises, and wealth huge enough to finance almost any conceivable stunt, such as the hiring of a London mansion for a stunningly lavish party one night, which the subsequent night is mysteriously dark and empty again. The magician aspect of Florizel, his underemployed hyper-intelligence and fascination with the darker aspects of human nature, even his sardonic tolerance of his sidekick's stolidness, all anticipate Arthur Conan Doyle's creation fifteen years later of Sherlock Holmes, another denizen of that 'fairy London' which, according to Jorge Luis Borges, Stevenson invented here.

The stories, published in instalments in *London* that summer, earned Stevenson little money or praise. He had been writing professionally for almost five years, and was still far from being able to support himself. He was in Paris for much of June, being paid by Fleeming Jenkin to act as secretary while Jenkin was a juror at that year's International Exhibition. But neither then nor in Grez later that summer was he able to deflect Fanny Osbourne from the decision she had reached. After three years of avoiding such action at all costs, Fanny was going back to her husband. 'I don't know why my mother decided to return to California, she never told me, but suddenly we were leaving,' Belle wrote later.[70] Fanny's motives are mysterious: perhaps there had been a quarrel with Louis (though there is no record of one); perhaps Sam was making demands for her return (again, there is no record of such, and his previous demands had all been ignored). The 'official' reason, unconvincing from every point of view, was expressed elliptically by Graham Balfour in his *Life of Robert Louis Stevenson*. Writing under Fanny's eye – and partly, in matters of her biography, under her direction – Balfour says that she 'was not free to follow her inclination' at this point. 'Though the step of seeking a divorce was open to her, yet the interests and feelings of others had to be considered, and for the present all idea of union [with Stevenson] was impossible.'[71]

A possible explanation for Fanny's behaviour which has not been suggested before is that she might have been pregnant in the summer of 1878. Under those circumstances, she would have needed, for appearances' sake, to reunite with Sam, if briefly. As I will discuss later, there are clues to this in the material thought to refer exclusively to a pregnancy 'scare' Fanny experienced in 1883, and it makes sense of many otherwise inexplicable actions in the coming months. But whatever the cause of her abrupt removal, Stevenson clearly felt not simply abandoned by his mistress in the short term, but to all intents and purposes permanently rejected. None of *his* interests or feelings seemed to be being considered at all, and it must have been a very broken-hearted and embittered man whom young Sam watched from the departing train at Euston on 15 August 1878, 'a diminishing figure in a brown ulster'[72] walking away down the platform, who never turned back.

6

THE AMATEUR EMIGRANT

In America [...] the mental fidget, social worry, business anxiety, and other conditions that characterise modern civilisation, are even more pressing than with us.

Francis Galton, *Record of Family Faculties*

A WEEK AFTER the Osbournes left England, Stevenson was on his way south to the Cévennes. He was in a state of collapse and wanted only to be alone. Weeks went by at Monastier, fifteen miles south of Le Puy, in a fog of depression; 'I am so ill and so tired that I can scarce finish these words,' he wrote to Baxter. He found little to charm him in the mountainside town, avoided contact with his fellow residents at the inn, and spent lacklustre hours sketching or practising with a revolver – both activities associated with Fanny. He was finishing his articles on Edinburgh and writing more of the *New Arabian Nights*, but it took enormous effort. 'I find it damned hard work to keep up a good countenance in this world nowadays, harder than anyone knows,' he wrote to Baxter ruefully. 'I hope you may never have cause to feel one half as sad as I feel.'[1] He had every reason to be envious of his old friend, who had been married a year and whose wife Grace was about to give birth to their first child.

Stevenson soon sickened of Monastier and decided to take a walking tour south through the highlands of the Cévennes. With the success of *An Inland Voyage*, he knew he would be able to make a book out of such a journey, one way or another, and had thought of a title before setting off. He wanted to walk alone and camp under the stars, not in a tent (too bothersome) but close to the ground in some sort of waterproof sleeping-bag. This primitive desire necessitated sophisticated preparations, for no such bag existed and he had to go to Le Puy and have one custom-made: a long sausage of cart-cloth lined with sheep's wool, with envelope-flaps at either end. This could be used as a huge sack for his provisions and equipment during the day, and at night he could crawl inside it to sleep. The cart-cloth was green, and the thick fleecy lining blue, so even in a contrivance for sleeping rough he had managed to introduce a dandyish element, and it was hideously expensive: eighty-five francs.

He approached the trip as if it was to be a trial of his survival skills, and took care assembling his kit: spirit lamp, lantern, candles, a leather flask, an egg-whisk, a jack-knife and a revolver, two sets of warm clothes, a pilot coat, a 'knitted spencer', a railway rug and plenty of books, of course. Then there were edibles: tinned sausage, chocolate, bottles of Beaujolais, bread and a cold leg of mutton. Saddled with this lot – well, *he* wasn't going to be saddled: a donkey must be found for the portage. After a deal of haggling and some amusing displays of resistance on the part of the vendor, 'Monsieur Steams', as the locals called Stevenson, became the owner of a small grey she-ass, price sixty-five francs plus a glass of brandy. She was 'not much bigger than a dog, the colour of a mouse, with a kindly eye and a determined under-jaw'.[2] He named her Modestine.

In the published version of his journey through the Cévennes, it was Stevenson's relations with Modestine that became the subject, rather than the walking tour itself. Walking, at an ordinary pace, was out of the question where the mouse-coloured tyrant was involved. Her rate of progress 'was something as much slower than a walk as a walk is slower than a run; it kept me hanging on each foot for an incredible length of time; in five minutes it exhausted the spirit and set up a fever in all the muscles of the leg'.[3] Precariously loaded with a new pack-saddle, the sleeping-sack full of chattels, and an open basket containing bottles and the mutton,

Modestine was trembling under the strain before they had even got out of sight of Monastier, and the two of them made such a spectacle that a passing peasant felt bound to instruct Stevenson in the use of a switch and the 'true cry or Masonic word of donkey-drivers, "Proot!"'[4] Under this new regime, Modestine moved along quite nicely for a while, but then reverted to her snail's pace, punctuated by long intervals of wayside grazing. Stevenson, to his own distress, was forced to resort to 'incessant belabouring' with the switch to get Modestine and his baggage anywhere near the first night's planned bivouac at the lake of Bouchet. 'I think I never heard of anyone in as mean a situation,' he wrote. 'The sound of my own blows sickened me.'[5]

Stevenson tended to speak lightly of his travel books, but he brought sophistication to a form that had few notable practitioners (except Heine and Sterne, both of whom he venerated). *An Inland Voyage* turned out to be about a frame of mind, and *Travels with a Donkey* a cautionary tale of how much effort and artifice were involved if the middle-class Victorian wished to get 'back to nature'. Sleeping out '*à la belle étoile*' seemed to be the hardest thing in the world to the novice tramp, who had to put in at an *auberge* the first night when Modestine failed to reach Bouchet. The romantic and the realist battled in Stevenson, for he couldn't resist describing the desolation he felt at being soaked by rain, or lost, or benighted, or faced (as often) with truculent Cévennois villagers indulging heartily in *schadenfreude*. This was far from the nobility of Thoreau's Walden or the unquenchable optimism felt in Whitman's 'Song of the Road'; Stevenson recorded his impressions as truthfully as he could, and enjoyed the incongruities that emerged. Thus he can write about his uncouth solitary eating habits, his embarrassment at sharing a dormitory at the inn in Bouchet, or the brutalising process that turns him into Modestine's frenzied scourge, with the same exactitude he applies to his description of falling asleep outdoors on a windy night, where 'my last waking effort was to listen and distinguish, and my last conscious state was one of wonder at the foreign clamour in my ears'.[6]

To Bob, when the book was finished, he admitted frankly that 'lots of it is mere protestations to F., most of which I think you will understand'.[7] The uncertainty of his future with her is *on the book's mind*, from the author's awareness that his snug, nestlike sleeping-bag 'at a pinch [. . .] might serve for two' to his gladness at getting away from the Cistercian monastery in the hills of Gevaudan, 'free to wander, free to hope, and free to love'.[8] His confusion at the *auberge* in Bouchet-Saint-Nicholas at being so near someone else's semi-naked wife is surely made worse because the situation reminds him of his new position relative to the reunited Osbournes: 'a pair keep each other in countenance; it is the single gentleman who has to blush'.[9] Even the donkey disturbs him, with her meek toleration of his thrashings and her willingness to be mounted by any stray male (Modestine was on heat and bleeding). This was hardly the female companion he dreamed about at two o'clock in the morning, exulting in the peace and solitude of the pine woods of Lozère:

> I wished a companion to lie near me in the starlight, silent and not moving, but ever within touch. For there is a fellow-ship more quiet even than solitude, and which, rightly under-stood, is solitude made perfect.[10]

As Richard Holmes has pointed out in the best of all the 'in-the-steps-of-Stevenson' books, *Footsteps*, the notebook entry from which this passage of *Travels with a Donkey* is derived is a lot more explicit, and constitutes 'in effect, a proposal of marriage to Fanny Osbourne':[11]

> The woman whom a man has learned to love wholly, in and out, with utter comprehension, is no longer another person in the troublous sense. What there is of exacting in other companionship has disappeared; there is no need to speak; a look or a word stand for such a world of feeling.[12]

But that fervent statement was written on the road, while Stevenson's head was ringing with regrets and hopes and idealisation of Fanny. 'To travel hopefully is a better thing than to arrive,' he had written in his essay 'El Dorado' earlier that summer. At the end of his journey, when he rushed to Alais by diligence to get the first word from his mistress since their parting, he was crestfallen by whatever news – or lack of news – her letters contained. In plangent messages to Henley and Colvin he spoke of 'defeat' and being 'accurst'. Modestine was sold for thirty-five francs, the sleeping-sack disposed of. He made his way northward, to Lyons, then Paris, then London, where he took refuge with Henley. 'What will become of me? God knows [...] I feel as if I had all the world upon my shoulders.'[13]

Stevenson avoided Edinburgh until Christmas, spending the rest of the year mostly with the Henleys on the Uxbridge Road in Shepherd's Bush, and with a visit to Colvin at Trinity College, Cambridge. His cousin Katherine de Mattos, whom Henley had got to know through Bob and Louis,* was separating from her husband of only four years, and Louis, being one of her trustees, saw a good deal of both her and Bob that winter. His depression over Fanny Osbourne was therefore fully on show to all his friends, and they were all avid gossips. This witnessing of Louis's distress in the winter of 1878–79, and long fireside chats about his state of mind and heart, must help explain the otherwise puzzling degree of animosity that his friends displayed later towards his wife.

No one other than Louis in this circle of friends had any money; Bob had spent up years before, Katherine was newly thrown on her own resources and Henley was always dancing a jig on the edge of bankruptcy. Louis proved a loyal friend to them all, especially Katherine, whose position won his ready sympathy, and to whom he gave access to his funds. To expedite this, he had Baxter sell 'the Debenture' (presumably where some or all of his patrimonial thousand had gone) and keep the proceeds in a deposit account. He was already paying Henley a small monthly retainer, ostensibly so that he could act as literary agent, and sent £20 to the address

---

* And for whom Henley harboured warm feelings – see his poem to her of this year, and a love poem, 'Love blows as the wind blows [...] Love blows into the heart'.[14]

of Fanny's brother Jacob Vandegrift (presumably for Fanny) at a time when he had received only £30 in total for the publication of his Cévennes book (and when £20 was the cost of a first-class passage from New York to England). The 1875 windfall must have dwindled considerably by this time, and the biggest chunk of it – £400 – had gone to the least likely candidate, Colvin. He had been the victim of a robbery in 1878 when some valuable prints he had on loan from a dealer were driven off by an opportunistic cabby outside the Savile. The cabby and an accomplice were caught, but the prints were never recovered and Colvin rashly offered to take financial responsibility for the loss – an astronomical £1,540. Stevenson immediately and unconditionally offered him £400, possibly the most spectacular example of a lifetime's habit of generosity.

Gestures such as this, however, were not always interpreted at their best. Colvin was an exception – he had the highest view of Stevenson's motives – but Henley often seemed to harbour a low-level resentment about his own position relative to Louis's. To someone like Henley, Stevenson must have seemed utterly privileged, with his deposit accounts and debentures, free board at home, run of 'a country house' at Swanston, use of a barouche and constant holidays. And the more Louis strove to share with his friends, the more a taint of 'rich kid' hung about him, despite the obvious fact that he was often strapped for cash himself. Edmund Gosse remembers him at this time as trying to obtain a third-class ticket to Edinburgh by offering the ticket clerk a first edition of Swinburne's *The Queen Mother; Rosamund*.[15]

Louis's intimacy with Henley developed rapidly in Fanny's absence, and somewhat at her expense. Perhaps due to his lameness and need to keep his friends within reach, Henley became very possessive of Stevenson, and keen to bind him to him professionally (as well as wanting him to come and live in London). He had read Louis's 'hugger-mugger melodrama' of Deacon Brodie, written back in the 1860s, and persuaded his friend to collaborate on a rewriting of it. No sooner had Henley got this idea in his head than he was fired up and could talk of nothing else: *Deacon Brodie* would catapult them both to national fame (for Henry Irving would not be able to resist the part) and, of course, it would make them rich.

Stevenson was entirely in the mood to lose himself in such a project, and Henley's enthusiasm was contagious, as a joint letter the two budding dramatists wrote to Colvin shows. They were staying together at Swanston, 'finishing' the play, and one can imagine them on a bitter January afternoon in 1879, sitting by a brisk fire in that comfortable house on the edge of the Pentlands, with a whisky bottle open and a whole luxurious evening of self-congratulation ahead. Act Three was done, Stevenson told Colvin:

> And the last tableau is the most passionate thing in the English drama since the Elizabethans. It is, by God. We send it off to copy this afternoon so you'll get it soon.
> Yours ever R.L.S.
>
> *[Henley continues]*
>
> He's quite right, Colvin. It's an admirable thing. The third Act is what a good third Act should be. We neither of us slept last night after having completed it; and small wonder. God bless you. George the Dook is a sweet creature. It's quite the most path breaking and epoch marking work ever produced.
> God bless you. It will put Irving out of conceit of his hamlet which is d--d bad, and only fit to be spelt with a small h. As for George Smith and Leslie, we shall want two good actors for them. Kyrle Bellew we have and know – but who, oh Colvin, Who is to play Leslie?[16]

Anyone suspecting Henley of irony in his references to *Deacon Brodie* being path-breaking and epoch-marking would be wrong: he always talked hyperbolically. The affectations of phrase and spelling are entirely characteristic too: in the next letter to Colvin from Swanston he asks, 'Think you it were worth gold? Publisher's gold?'[17] Henley was in some ways *in character* all the time, someone blustering and affable from a novel by Fielding, perhaps – or from a novel by Robert Louis Stevenson, that had yet to be written, *Treasure Island*'s Long John Silver.

The company of Henley and the excitement he generated around the idea of collaboration were valuable distractions for the 'miserable widower' in the winter of 1878–79, but did nothing to further his career as a writer. Goodness knows why either man thought the composition of a melodrama worth even a moment's effort when they were both capable of breaking paths and marking epochs elsewhere, Henley as a poet and Stevenson as a fiction-writer. During the year he was separated from Fanny, Stevenson finished and published *Edinburgh: Picturesque Notes* and *Travels with a Donkey in the Cévennes* and wrote the stories 'Providence and the Guitar', 'The Story of a Lie' and his remarkable mystery tale 'The Pavilion on the Links'. He also began a work (possibly based on his old Spec essay about modern Christianity[18]) called 'Lay Morals', the title of which made Bob Stevenson guffaw when he heard it. 'Lay Morals' is a densely-wrought essay and was not published in Stevenson's lifetime, but in the middle of his dis-cussion of the soul comes this passage, part of the long cogitation of which *The Strange Case of Dr Jekyll and Mr Hyde* is also part:

> It follows that man is twofold at least; that he is not a rounded and autonomous empire; but that in the same body with him there dwell other powers tributary but independent.[19]

Henley wasn't the only new collaborator; Stevenson was planning to write a book of true murder stories with Edmund Gosse, to which end they had already visited 'the scene of one famous mur-der' together.[20] Nothing came of it, but the project is an interesting further example of Stevenson's readiness, almost compulsion, to meld creatively with his closest friends. The cementing of each of his most important relationships was accompanied by an attempt at literary collaboration: Bob (with 'Monmouth: A Tragedy'), Colvin (the 'spectacle-play' in Menton), Mrs Sitwell (the epistolary novel), Fanny Osbourne (a 'sensation novel' called 'What was on the Slate' planned in 1879), Henley (*Deacon Brodie* and the other plays) and now Gosse. Even his juvenile habit of dictation to his aunt and mother and later habit of dictating to an amanuensis could be seen as forms of collaboration, especially in the way they satisfy Stevenson's impatience to get a response from an audience, to get the sort of 'fix' that would help him retain interest in his own work. Sharing the graft of writing *and* sharing the responsibility for what is produced appealed strongly to him, as he confessed obliquely in his later essay 'A Chapter on Dreams'. There was undoubtedly an erotic element in these collaborations too; to collaborate the parties need to be in contact, often in the same room, sharing ideas, exclusively accessible to each other. With someone like Gosse, who was one of many men enchanted by Stevenson, literary collaboration was a way perhaps of enjoying a strong homoerotic *frisson* in a safely non-sexual way.

Stevenson was often at the Gosses' house that summer, a 'romantic-looking gentleman', as Philip Gosse, then six years old, recalled: 'he used to wear over his shoulders a red silk shawl borrowed from my mother, as he sat on our balcony, and [...] we children eagerly leant up against him while he told us wonderful stories. Such stories! All of the sea, wrecks, mutinies and pirates. Tales of blood-curdling adventures . . . It was on these occasions that our nurse would say, with a vexatious sigh, "Whenever that there Mr Stevenson comes here, I never get you children to sleep." '[21] The elder Gosse was just as spellbound: 'I take you for my emblem in life,' he wrote to Stevenson in July 1879, 'you, the General Exhilarator.'[22] Stevenson responded to this bemusedly, for he could see nothing enviable in his own situation: 'I envy you your wife, your home, your child – I was going to say your cat. There would be cats in my home, too, if I could but get it! not for me but for the person who should share it with me. I may seem to you "the impersonation of life", Weg; but my life is the impersonation of waiting, and that's a poor creature.'[23]

At this point, the waiting had gone on almost a year. There had been several shafts of hope; in February 1879, Stevenson had heard that Fanny had retreated from Oakland to Monterey and was separated from Sam but had access to the children. Colvin had seen Fanny's letter and wrote to Henley in terms that show how conspiratorial the friends already felt against Mrs Osbourne. The letter, he said, was 'quite sane' by comparison with others, but still dealt in 'wild storms, intercepted flights, and the Lord knows what more'. Louis had sent a telegram in reply, possibly offering to go out to join her in California, but not committing himself to anything. Or so Colvin believed. 'He won't go suddenly or without telling people. – Which is as much as we can hope at present.'[24]

Stevenson fell ill that spring and attributed it directly to the fact that letters from Fanny did not come for several weeks. But this seems to have been a worse illness than a depressive collapse, or at least it had many curious symptoms, including a swollen testicle and 'irritation of the spermatic cord', as well as 'weakness, languor, loss of appetite' and an inability to walk.[25] Four months after the first attack he was suffering from an acute skin rash that made him scratch from dawn to dusk and took about six months to recover from. Was Stevenson syphilitic? The similarities between his symptoms and those of the second stage of syphilis cannot be overlooked: the rash, the enervation, the glandular swelling are all typical. Stevenson may have thought so himself, as the letter of his to Henley in August that year that describes his 'unparalleled skin irritation' contains about six more words heavily scored out, which in the opinion of the editors of the *Letters to Charles Baxter* read 'very similar to syphilis'.* Syphilis was a very prevalent disease in the late nineteenth century, and known as 'the great imitator' because so many of its symptoms are indistinguishable from those of other diseases, a characteristic that made it easier to conceal too (though there is a congenital form, most syphilis is sexually transmitted). Nor is syphilis the only plausible diagnosis of Stevenson's condition in the 1870s; a current web page written by George Addis MD suggests that his reliance on 'blue pills', a

* Ferguson and Waingrow are unaccountably confident of this reading, but the scoring over the manuscript is very thorough. Someone wanted the words entirely obliterated.[26]

common remedy for stomach ailments, could have given him mercury poisoning – the pills were composed of mercury chloride.[27]

Concerned, as always, with their son's health, Thomas and Margaret Stevenson took him off to the Shandon Hydropathic Establishment at Gairloch for an up-to-the-minute water cure, but this seems to have made the patient rather worse than better. He never felt so lonely, Stevenson was ashamed to admit, as when he spent too much time with his parents.[28] 'I want – I want – I want a holiday; I want to be happy; I want the moon, or the sun, or something,' he wrote to Colvin in April;[29] 'I want the object of my affections badly, anyway; and a big forest; and fine breathing, sweating, sunny walks; and all the trees crying aloud in a summer's wind; and a camp under the stars.'[30] But the summer dragged on with only sporadic news from Fanny, none of it very encouraging. He went to visit Meredith again at Box Hill, and Bob at his new haunt of Cernay-la-Ville, and spent many afternoons in the Savile Club engaged in 'rather foolish jesting', as Gosse described it later.[31] But everything was conducted in a spirit of *ennui*, as he wrote to Gosse: 'I have fallen altogether into a hollow-eyed, yawning way of life, like the parties in Burne-Jones's pictures.'[32]

Another spa-visit with his parents was coming up at the end of July, but Louis met them at the railway station only to say he had been 'called away on business' to London. The choice of this moment to slip away from them must have been strategic: with Thomas and Margaret safely out of the way in Cumberland, Louis was free to put into effect a plan which had been simmering for a long time, to set off for America and try to sort out the situation with Fanny once and for all. There is a tradition that his precipitate departure was triggered by a telegram from California, but the truth seems to have been rather less romantic than that, and though he understood Fanny to be ill, rushing to nurse her does not appear to have been his primary motivation. 'I must try to get her to do one of two things,' he wrote to Bob the day before he sailed from Glasgow, sounding remarkably level-headed. It was his own misery he wished to curtail, and the endless passive waiting: 'Man I was sick, sick, sick of this last year.'[33] To Colvin and Henley he said that he was only going to go as far as New York, which made Henley think the trip could not do much harm, ill-advised though it was to chase even halfway to California to please Mrs Samuel Osbourne. None of his friends liked the scheme, even though Stevenson kept saying that he could at least get another travel book out of it – which was the excuse he offered to his parents, too, when he finally got round to letting them know what he had done.

So from Edinburgh he went to London to make the arrangements, then travelled back north to Greenock, and on 7 August 1879 set sail down the Clyde in the steamship *Devonia*. 'I have never been so much detached from life,' he wrote to Colvin on departure. 'I can say honestly I have at this moment neither a regret, a hope, a fear or an inclination; except a mild one for a bottle of good wine.'[34] Suddenly and fairly arbitrarily, Stevenson had made the pivotal decision of his life.

He had considered travelling steerage, for the cheapness and the picturesque experience, but stumped up another two guineas for a second-class berth, with slightly better food and a table where he could write during the ten-day sea passage. The steerage sections of the big iron steamship were just a thin partition away from his bunk and wonky table, near enough for the kind of impressions Louis sought to record; too near indeed to block out the sounds of people vomiting, children crying, drunks shouting and the constant banging and clattering of life lived in confinement. From the start it must have been clear to him that even if he was going to be able to shape this experience into a book, it would not be of the light, 'charming' variety. The air, even in second-berth, was fetid; in steerage it was 'atrocious [...] each respiration tasted in the throat like some horrible kind of cheese; and the squalid aspect of the place was aggravated by so many people worming themselves into their clothes in the twilight of the bunks'.[35] Stevenson was

obviously disgusted at this first real contact with everyday working-class squalor. His frequenting of Edinburgh howffs, attempts
at being mistaken for a tramp and Latin Quarter scruffiness all
showed up in this context for what they really were, middle-class
slumming.

Class was constantly on his mind during the ten days aboard
the *Devonia*, but in confused ways. In *The Amateur Emigrant*, the
book of his travels which was not published in full until after his
death, he records an incident when some ladies and a gentleman
from first class came through steerage one day as sightseers, 'picking their way with little gracious titters of indulgence'. Stevenson's
indignation at their behaviour sounds very stagy: 'It was astonishing what insults these people managed to convey by their presence.
They seemed to throw their clothes in our faces.'[36] Who was this
'we' all of a sudden? Stevenson's identification with steerage was
snobbism too, but inverted, which is perhaps why he was sensitive
on this point (and kept the ladies in mind, I would guess, in
the characterisation of the prison visitors in *St Ives*). They were
class-tourists, but he was a class-impostor, travelling rough to
make a book of its novelty, a fact which would have offended
many of his fellow passengers had it been widely known. A blacksmith had spotted the fraud early on, but said nothing, and perhaps
the most telling action of the whole voyage was Stevenson asking
this man for his opinion of how he was doing at hiding his origins.
It was a glance in the mirror, an opportunity of praise, which he
simply couldn't resist. The man's politic reply was 'pretty well
[. . .] on the whole'.[37]

The intention of writing about travel both across the Atlantic
and into another social stratum therefore tripped itself up pretty
early on, and despite the promise of the title, *The Amateur Emigrant* is one of Stevenson's least successful books. He could find
little to elaborate, little to moralise over, in his observation of the
very mixed group in the bowels of the *Devonia*. Scots, Irish and
some English, they were on the whole a downtrodden, drunken
crowd, too preoccupied and too seasick to want to make acquaint-

Above Margaret
Stevenson and young
Smout, still in petticoats,
1854.

Right Thomas Stevenson
and RLS, aged about
seven. The boy's vacant
look gives some idea why
his father later backed
out of commissioning an
expensive portrait in oils.

Above Skerryvore lighthouse, designed and built by RLS's uncle Alan.

Left The Old Town of Edinburgh in the mid-nineteenth century, a view from Princes Street with Waverley Station in the foreground.

Below RLS aged fifteen, author of 'The Pentland Rising'.

Bottom left 17 Heriot Row, Edinburgh (left), the Stevensons' home from 1857.

A family group on holiday, around 1867; Thomas and Margaret Stevenson in the middle, Coolin the terrier, RLS, and the redoubtable Cummy to his left.

Above Professor Henry Charles Fleeming Jenkin, electrical engineer, inventor, amateur dramatist and RLS's friend and mentor during the troubled early 1870s.

Right RLS, advocate, in 1875. Wearing the wig and robes for this photograph was the high point of his legal career.

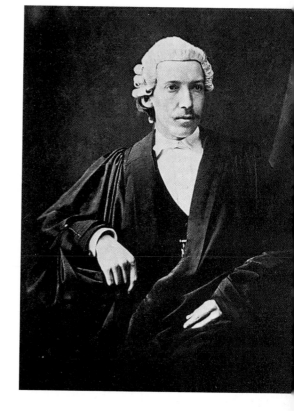

Sidney Colvin.

Charles Baxter in later life.

William Ernest Henley.

Edmund Gosse, painted by John
Singer Sargent.

Above RLS's 'Madonna', the sibylline Fanny Sitwell.

Left Fanny Osbourne in her youth, sporting the style of a would-be Left Bank artist.

'Gentleman gypsy' Bob Stevenson, in dashing striped stockings, with fellow artists by the old bridge at Grez-sur-Loing in the mid- to late 1870s. Frank O'Meara, with pipe and stick, stands to his left. The man in the bowler hat standing at Bob's far right is W.E. Henley's brother Antony.

A trans-continental emigrant train in the 1880s, similar to the one RLS describes in *Across the Plains*: 'as I passed to and fro, stepping across the prostrate, and caught now a snore, now a gasp, now a half-formed word, it gave me a measure of the worthlessness of rest in that unresting vehicle'.

Above Jules Simoneau and Jules Tavernier outside Simoneau's peeling and ramshackle hostelry in Monterey, RLS's haunt in the autumn of 1879.

Below left RLS in 1880, aged twenty-nine.

Below Fanny Osbourne in 1880, just before her marriage to RLS, looking the picture of bourgeois respectability. The studio portrait was made to send to her new parents-in-law.

Right Joe Strong's tidied-up vision of RLS and Fanny in the miners' dormitory at Silverado, used as frontispiece for *The Silverado Squatters*.

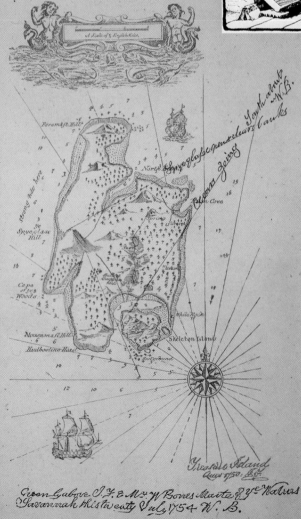

Above RLS's 'edenic' home in Hyères 'La Solitude'.

Left The map of Treasure Island which appeared in the first edition of the book. Thomas Stevenson had it drawn up by draftsmen in his office when the original, painted by RLS at Braemar, was lost by the publishers. The similarity of the island's shape to that of a disembodied Scotland was perhaps the work of Stevenson's subconscious.

ance with a Scottish *littérateur*. Even the children proved hard to befriend, and his famous charm seemed in small demand. No one, for instance, thought his idea of sleeping on deck for the fresher air was a good one, or wished to copy it.

Steerage represented (roughly) a class, but not a condition. Talking to a day-labourer from Tyneside, Stevenson discovered that the man was not an emigrant, as he had rather sweepingly assumed, but a pleasure-tripper, and was saving money on the steerage ticket in order to be able to travel home grandly in the saloon. He seemed mild and prosperous, so Stevenson was surprised and disturbed to hear him denounce the Lords, the Church and the army and argue for the redistribution of capital. These ideas were 'growing "like a seed"', the Geordie claimed, sentiments which Stevenson found 'unusually ominous and grave'.[38] He must have imagined that the well-off working classes were all Tories, like himself, only a little more bourgeois. The *Devonia* experience, it is worth noting, did absolutely nothing to alter his political views.

During the whole voyage Stevenson had been plagued by two ailments, constipation and the itch, and by the time the boat docked in New York on 17 August, he was physically exhausted. He had lost a stone in weight (where from it is hard to imagine) and needed to recruit his strength, but as soon as he arrived he rushed to look for messages at the post office. He found one from Fanny, speaking of 'inflammation of the brain'. So there was no recuperation in New York, and after one noisy and uncomfortable night at an Irish boarding house on West Street and a day of being soaked to the skin on the worst streets of the Battery, he set off immediately to begin crossing the continent. Notes were dispatched to Britain, including one to Colvin containing 'The Story of a Lie', written on board ship. Stevenson's treatment of his parents, and their likely response to his flitting, was obviously on his mind when he wrote this tale, notable for its portrait of the hero's intemperate old father 'buckrammed with immortal anger', towards whom his son has painfully mixed feelings. 'You do not know what it is to be treated with daily want of comprehension and daily small injustices, through childhood and boyhood and manhood, until you despair of a hearing, until the thing rides you like a nightmare, until you almost hate the sight of the man you love, and who's your father after all,' Dick tells his beloved, Esther, adding, somewhat paradoxically, 'My father is the best man I know in all this world; he is worth a hundred of me, only he doesn't understand me, and he can't be made to.'[39]

On the afternoon of 18 August, after a distressing ferry-ride to Jersey with hundreds of other wet, bedraggled third-class passengers, the amateur emigrant boarded a train for Pittsburgh. The vast, raw continent was by this date traversable by anyone with £12 and twelve days to spare. Engineers in frock-coats and stove-pipe hats – men just like Thomas Stevenson, ironically enough – had opened up a long clear path to the west, which as he rode the trains of the Pennsylvania and the Chicago and the Union Pacific railroads, Louis felt to be 'the one typical achievement of the age in which we live, as if it brought together into one plot all the ends of the world and all the degrees of social rank'.[40] From Pittsburgh, he went on to Chicago, and had reached Council Bluffs, Iowa, by the Friday of the first week. The train cars were too uncomfortable to write in, so Stevenson spent the time composing verses in his head instead, including one in which every stanza ends with the line 'Behind the Susquehanna and along the Delaware', a railway-inspired rhythm if ever there was one. After the fetor of the *Devonia*, the open air seemed wonderfully sweet, and riding in the cars crowded but tolerable. Still, he was the gent among the groundlings, with his railway rug and his six-volume *Bancroft's History of the United States*, surprised to find that no one wanted to share the use of his clothes-brush and horrified, at the Jersey station, to see grown people and children scramble for four oranges which he had thrown under a carriage, considering them too dry to eat.

My dear Henley, I am sitting on the top of the cars with a mill party from Missouri going west for his health. Desolate flat prairie upon all hands. Here and there a herd of cattle, a yellow butterfly or two; a patch of wild sunflowers; a wooden house or two; then a wooden church alone in miles of waste; then a windmill to pump water. When we stop, which we do often, for emigrants and freight travel together, the kine first, the men after, the whole plain is heard singing with cicadae.[41]

Stevenson wondered if this letter would be legible, for his perch on top of the wagon was both perilous and dirty. But he was in excellent spirits and convinced he was doing the right thing, as he told Henley, 'I know no one will think so; and don't care.'[42] He could see the track straight before him and straight back as far as the horizon in each direction. It was mesmerising, 'a world almost without a feature; an empty sky, an empty earth', he wrote in *Across the Plains*:

[...] on either hand the green plain ran till it touched the skirts of heaven. Along the track innumerable wild sun-flowers, no bigger than a crown-piece, bloomed in a continu-ous flower-bed; grazing beasts were seen upon the prairie at all degrees of distance and diminution; and now and again we might perceive a few dots beside the railroad which grew more and more distinct as we drew nearer till they turned into wooden cabins, and then dwindled and dwindled in our wake until they melted into their surroundings, and we were once more alone upon the billiard-board.[43]

Up to Council Bluffs, he had been riding in 'mixed trains', but there he transferred to the Union Pacific to cross Nebraska, Wyoming and part of Utah. This is what he calls 'the emigrant train', much larger, slower and more crowded than the others, with passengers segregated by gender and race (the Chinese were all put in one carriage) and the baggage riding behind in several enormous wagons. The passenger cars were long wooden boxes 'like a flat-roofed Noah's ark', with a stove at one end and a close-stool at the other, a passage down the middle and benches on both sides. These benches had reversible backs and could be made into rough-and-ready sleeping pallets by the insertion of boards and straw-filled cushions. Sleeping was difficult under any circumstances, and day-to-day life reduced to the basics of scrambling for the limited food at stations and negotiating with fellow passengers to share essentials such as washbasins and soap.

Stevenson's sense of isolation was borne home at every point on the journey. A drunk who got on at Creston, Iowa, was adroitly thrown off by the conductor just after the train began pulling out of the next station. The drunk recovered himself and shook his bundle aggressively at the conductor, while his other hand reached for his gun. Stevenson was electrified by the sudden sense of danger, but the conductor was facing down the ejected man with one hand on his hip, and all the other passengers were laughing. 'They were speaking English all about me,' Stevenson wrote in *Across the Plains*, 'but I knew I was in a foreign land.'[44] His other feelings of 'foreignness' were essentially to do with class again; even more than on the sea-voyage, Stevenson's rail experiences left him bewildered and disgusted by his fellow travellers. They seemed debased by their situation, incurious about each other except on the meanest and most external level, incapable of charity, and quick to find cheap humour in other people's misfortune or humiliation. Their general hatred of the Chinese was 'of all stupid ill-feelings [. . .] the most stupid and the worst',[45] and the derision poured on displaced native Americans loathsome to witness. 'I saw no wild or independent Indian,' Stevenson wrote in his chapter 'Despised Races', 'but now and again at way stations, a husband and wife and a few children, disgracefully dressed out with the sweepings of civilisation, came forth and stared upon the emigrants. The silent stoicism of their conduct, and the pathetic degradation of their appearance, would have touched any thinking creature, but my fellow-passengers danced and jested round them with a truly Cockney baseness. I was ashamed for the thing we call civilisation.'[46]

At Ogden, Utah, he changed to the Central Pacific railroad and entered the last phase of the journey. Many of the passengers here were emigrating to California from places in the States, Stevenson realised, that had been immigrant destinations for the Scots and

Irish on the *Devonia*. The push westward seemed overwhelming: 'Hunger, you would have thought, came out of the east like the sun.'[47] Perhaps there was no El Dorado anywhere, and 'the whole round world had been prospected and condemned'. It was impossible not to have noticed that emigrants were also streaming *away* from California, and on one occasion passengers from an eastbound train ran onto the platform calling out 'Come back!', like emissaries from Heriot Row. These were not cheering omens as the train crossed the Sierras and made its way down towards sea level and the glittering blue vistas of San Francisco Bay, Stevenson's last stop before going on south to Monterey.

Monterey in 1879 was still a predominantly Mexican town, in population if not ownership, and Spanish was the everyday tongue. The sixteenth-century Carmel Mission had long been a ruin, and the old Pacific capital now consisted of barely more than three main streets, paved with sea sand and pitted with hoofmarks and cart tracks. Most of the houses were built of adobe, with red tile roofs and wrought-iron balconies, and had thick white walls that kept them cool and slightly damp. Along the main thoroughfare, Alvarado Street, there were more modern brick and wood buildings and a wooden sidewalk to keep pedestrians out of the ruts and channels left behind after the heavy winter rain, and at a few street corners some old Spanish cannons had been stuck vertically in the ground to serve as hitching posts for horses. The style of riding, as Stevenson noted, was 'true Vaquero [. . .] men always at the hand-gallop up hill and down dale, and round the sharpest corner',[48] and the horses were almost all decked out in elaborate Mexican saddles. But it was not a rich or genteel town. A photograph survives, taken at about the time Stevenson was there, in which the main street of Monterey very strongly resembles the set of a spaghetti western.

Fanny Osbourne had moved there in the spring of 1879 with her children and twenty-four-year-old sister Nellie Vandegrift, to a two-storey adobe house on Alvarado Street, with whitewashed walls and a large garden full of fruit trees and roses. The writer Charles Warren Stoddard, who was a member of the Bohemian Club and a friend of Sam Osbourne, had recommended the place to his San Francisco artist friends as having ideal light, coastal landscape and picturesque subjects, and this was undoubtedly why Fanny chose to go there too. In Monterey she and Belle could continue some semblance of 'art studies', and mix with bohemian types, three of whom, all friends of Stoddard, were Monterey regulars: Jules Tavernier, Julian Rix (who would entertain Oscar Wilde on his visit to San Francisco in 1882) and Joe Strong, the young man who had followed Belle to the theatre all those years ago and with whom she was again involved. Sam Osbourne approved of the Monterey scheme and wholly funded it; he visited the family at weekends and holidays, and bought each member of the household a horse or pony. Belle was happy because she was able to carry on her flirtation with Joe Strong, and young Sam seems to have felt more secure in Monterey than he had for some time. However Fanny had presented it to Stevenson, the arrangement seems to have been a sincere attempt (on Sam's part at least) at finding a *modus vivendi* for the whole family rather than a definite step towards divorce.

Stevenson wasn't so naïve or romantic as to expect a hero's welcome at the end of his three-week journey to Monterey, and he didn't get one. On arrival in town, he stopped off at a saloon before going to Fanny's house to steel himself for the interview, and heard from the barman several pieces of news about the Osbourne women, including that the barman himself, Alfredo Sanchez, was engaged to marry Nellie Vandegrift. No talk, however general, about Mrs Osbourne could have sounded cheering to Stevenson under the circumstances. He left his luggage at the saloon and went on to the house on foot.

The vision he presented on the threshold of Casa Bonifacio was an alarming one, as described later by Sam junior, then eleven years old: 'His clothes, no longer picturesque but merely shabby, hung loosely on his shrunken body, and there was about him an indescribable lessening of his alertness and self-confidence.' Until that moment, Sam believed, 'I had never thought of him as being in ill-health. On the contrary, in vigor and vitality he had always seemed among the foremost of those young men at Grez; and though he did not excel in any of the sports he had shared in them exuberantly. Now he looked ill, even to my childish gaze.'[49] Fanny might well have been at a loss to know what to do with this wraithlike lover, returned like a ghost in a ballad. His physical condition was not the least dismaying thing: he was penniless, prospectless, cut off from the family she had always understood to be fabulously rich, and by his very presence was forcing the issue of the divorce and her whole future. The reunion was not jubilant, as Belle testified many years later: 'Louis's conduct [...] was not that of a romantic lover who had followed a sweetheart halfway round the world. Although he was gay and full of banter, he was almost coldly casual toward my mother – and [her attitude was] not much different toward him, except for her constant care in providing his preferences in food.'[50] Stevenson went off to find cheap lodgings in town (Fanny feared scandal if he stayed with her), and sent a few short letters back to Britain. 'All is in the wind; things might turn well or might not,' he told Colvin, and to Baxter he wrote, 'Things are damn complicated, and I have had the art to complicate 'em more since my arrival. However I hope for the best.'[51]

'The best' for Stevenson was marriage, but Fanny kept stalling about that, and the divorce that would have to precede it. Odd reasons were given for delay, such as the marriages of 'the girls': Nellie Vandegrift to Alfredo Sanchez and Belle to a wealthy Southerner whom Fanny had found for her. Fanny's concern for the proprieties at this juncture seems rather ludicrous, but she had become very anxious about how she and her family were going to be provided for, and a great deal of that depended on not flouting convention so much that she became *persona non grata*. On her own, she could only sink into semi-penury, and marriage to Stevenson (if he continued to be alienated from his parents) would mean much the same. Sam's beneficence would clearly last only as long as it suited him, and all the most expensive years of rearing Sam junior were still ahead. Belle's involvement with Joe Strong was another potential liability, as Joe hadn't a penny and was unlikely to earn much as an artist. The arranged marriage Fanny was trying to set up for her daughter (without the girl's consent) would at least have settled one member of the family comfortably, with likely benefits for the rest of them too. In the days before the married women's property laws, all these considerations had to come into play.

Her own situation was almost certainly more complicated than we know. When she was sure that Louis was on his way to her, Fanny had written to Timothy Rearden with feigned casualness to tell him that her 'literary friend from Scotland' had accepted 'an engagement to come to America and lecture; which I think great nonsense and have written to tell him so'.[52] The elaborate lying here indicates the intensity of Fanny's desire for secrecy; it also implies a lack of commitment to Stevenson. Her troubled relationship with Sam Osbourne was never going to improve, but divorce was a serious step, and permanent separation may have appealed to her more at this point, especially if Sam was willing to support her. And there was someone else still in the background of the picture at this critical moment: John Lloyd, her former lover. All through the first months of her European odyssey, Lloyd had been for Fanny 'the one friend I have in the world', and though she is unlikely to have seen him at all between 1875 and 1878, relations of some sort must have been re-established on her return to the States, for he reappeared in the role of jealous ex in 1881, writing her an extensive criticism of everything to do with Louis Stevenson, from his clothes to his accent. This means not only that Lloyd and Stevenson met in California in 1879–80, but that Lloyd considered him a rival. By 1881, although Fanny was married to Louis, Lloyd was convinced she was dissatisfied with her choice and was trying to ingratiate himself with her again (which implies that they were still in fairly regular correspondence). Her dismissal of this in an

1881 letter to Rearden is ardent – 'O the vanity of man!' – but as she was habitually disingenuous in her letters to Rearden (and knew he associated with Lloyd as well as with Sam), the tone of this can almost be guaranteed false.[53]

Stevenson most likely knew about Fanny's former relations with Lloyd, and once in Monterey may have guessed or been told that the two were still in touch. He also knew that Sam Osbourne was visiting his wife regularly, and was due in town any day. Stevenson chose not to skulk in Monterey during the conjugal visit, but to save money and some vestiges of pride by going camping in the hills on his own. The situation was threatening to become intolerable, as his remarks to Baxter in a scrambled note on 9 September indicate: 'My news is nil. I know nothing. I go out camping, that is all I know; today I leave, and shall likely be three weeks in camp; I shall send you a letter from there with more guts than this and now say good-bye to you, having had the itch and a broken heart.'[54]

So within days of his arrival in Monterey, Stevenson was setting out up the Carmel Valley, with a spring wagon and two horses, heading for the Santa Lucia mountains. His deep demoralisation is evident from the fact that he set off without adequate provisions or much idea of where he was going, and on the first evening decided to leave most of his traps at a farm run by an Englishman named Berwick, and go on with just one horse. It was a malign reprise of his walk through the Cévennes with Modestine; no care-fully-constructed pack of clothes and books and bottles, no pilot coat, no waterproof wool-lined bed. As he wandered aimlessly through the pines and cypresses and fog-streaked hillsides above Monterey, going in the wrong direction from the woman he loved and had travelled six thousand miles to see (and who was entertaining her husband), the whole enterprise took on a despairing quality. The expedition turned, in effect, into an attempt at suicide, a deliberate exposure of himself to the elements and to fate. Dazed and ill, he had got no further than eighteen miles south of Monterey when he descended into a fever: 'Two nights I lay out under a tree, in a sort of stupor, doing nothing but fetch water for myself and horse, light a fire and make coffee, and all night awake hearing the goat bells ringing and the tree frogs singing when each new noise was enough to set me mad.'[55] Only the accident of a goat rancher passing that way saved him from probable death. The man took one look at the skeletal apparition under the trees and pronounced him 'real sick'.[56]

'I am lying in an upper chamber nearly naked with flies crawling all over me and a clinking of goat bells in my ears,' Stevenson wrote to Baxter from the ranch on San Clemente Creek where his rescuer had taken him, 'the goats are coming home and it will soon be time to eat. The old bear hunter is doubtless now infusing tea; and Tom the Indian will come in with his gun in a few minutes.'[57] It was a rough but tranquil refuge, and Stevenson spent a fortnight there being tended by the bear hunter, Anson Smith, who was a captain from the old Mexican war, and his ranch-partner Jonathan Wright, both 'true frontiersmen'.[58] In return for his board among the bugs and straw, he gave lessons to the two little girls of the household in the mornings, and in the afternoons began making a draft of his emigrant book. He couldn't move far, couldn't even sit up much of the time, but comforted himself with the thought that he was at least able to write in this extremity. Perhaps the poem that he had begun to write on the train, 'Requiem', was going round in his head at this time, with its odd premonition of dying under a wide and starry sky, and the image of the hunter coming home at night:

> Under the wide and starry sky,
> Dig the grave and let me lie.
> Glad did I live and gladly die,
> And I laid me down with a will.
>
> This be the verse you grave for me:
> Here he lies where he longed to be;
> Home is the sailor, home from sea,
> And the hunter home from the hill.[59]

His experience in the Santa Lucia foothills had shaken him, as he tried to explain to Gosse:

> I do not know if I am the same man I was in Europe, perhaps I can hardly claim acquaintance with you. My head went round and looks another way now; for when I found myself over here in a new land, and all the past uprooted with one tug, and I neither glad nor sorry, I got my last lesson about mankind [. . .] There is a wonderful callousness in human nature, which enables us to live.[60]

Towards the end of September, when he was well enough to return to Monterey, Louis hobbled back to the Casa Bonifacio. His long unexplained absence must have thrown Fanny into a panic, and perhaps the sight of her tenacious lover plucked from the jaws of death impressed her with the necessity to act, for by mid-October they had evolved a plan: Fanny would return to the Bay Area (mostly for appearances' sake) and seek a 'private', i.e. consensual, divorce from Sam, during which time Louis would stay in Monterey, out of range of gossip. The temporising was not entirely over, but the all-important decision to divorce had been made at last. Belle was in no doubt that marriage to 'this penniless foreigner' would follow quickly: 'Maybe my mother saw in this contrast to my father the security from infidelity that had wrecked their marriage. At any rate she was happy when he was near.'[61]

Thus Stevenson found himself alone again in Monterey, but in a more hopeful frame of mind, lodging in the French Hotel, a cheap and bare rooming house on the edges of the old Spanish town. His days took on a simple routine: in the mornings he would go to the post office to check for mail, then call at the drugstore for a newspaper, then go to breakfast in the little whitewashed backroom at Simoneau's restaurant, the hub of his life in Monterey. Jules Simoneau was a fifty-eight-year-old expatriate Frenchman 'who had been most things from a man in business to a navvy, and kept his spirit and his kind heart through all'.[62] Photographs show a white-bearded, big-nosed, well-built man in working clothes, hands lodged in his belt, with a striking resemblance (though Stevenson is unlikely to have known it) to Walt Whitman. Stevenson left some vivid vignettes of the old Gaul 'rattling among the dishes, now clearing a semi-military chest with a "hroum-hroum", a drumming of his fists, and a snatch of music'. 'Papa Simoneau [was] always in his waist-coat and shirt sleeves, upright as a boy, with a rough, trooper-like smartness, vaunting his dishes if they were good, himself the first to condemn if they were unsuccessful; now red hot in discussion, now playing his flute with antique graces, now shamelessly hurrying off the other boarders that he might sit down to chess with me.'[63]

The clientèle that was ousted for chess was a little band of regulars who became Stevenson's only company during his last months in Monterey, a rough and ready gaggle of French-, Portuguese- and Italian-speakers. There was a captain of whalers, some fishermen, the local baker and barber (or 'tonsorial artist' as he advertised himself in the Monterey Californian) and two Ligurians. 'The sound of our talk was a little like Babel,' Stevenson recalled. 'But whatever tongue might be the speaker's fancy for the moment, the oaths that shone among his sentences were always English.'[64] These men were moved by the Scotsman's penury to donate $2 between them per week to the editor of the local paper in order to pay for Stevenson to be employed as a part-time contributor (he never found out about this act of extreme kindness). But it was Simoneau himself who was the pick of the company, the friend for whom Stevenson retained deep affection and respect all his life, and to whom he subsequently sent all his published works, though they never met again. The scruffy yard at the back of the restaurant became one of Stevenson's haunts, where he sat soaking up the sun among the empties from the restaurant and the broken tiles that had fallen off the crumbling adobe outhouse, while Simoneau's hens picked through the dust. He said later that he modelled the vegetation of Treasure Island on the Monterey coastline, and perhaps he picked up more for the book than that, for who is Simoneau like so much as the 'sea-cook' Silver, with his rough kindliness and his rattling among the pans, and who more like the pirates of the Spy-Glass inn or the Admiral Benbow than the scruffy male clientèle of Simoneau's restaurant, Monterey?

At the end of September, before Fanny left for Oakland, Stevenson had not yet written to New York to have his post forwarded, so had no news at all, not even from Baxter, custodian of his California address. But as the months went by, and Louis's own letters from the transcontinental journey, and from Monterey, and then from death's door at San Clemente, began to filter through to his friends, concern naturally grew among them. Henley had foreboded that the worst that could happen was if Louis was 'induced to go to Monterey, and there get mixed up once more in the miserable life of alarms and lies and intrigues that he led in Paris'.[65] Once he knew that 'the worst' was in train, Henley urged Colvin to get Louis back at any cost, 'married or unmarried – je m'en fiche'. 'He has gone too far to retract,' he wrote perceptively, 'he has acted and gushed and excited himself too nearly into the heroic spirit to be asked to forbear his point. All we can hope to do is to make him get through his work quickly and come back quickly.'[66]

Meanwhile Stevenson's parents had been going wild with worry ever since getting home from Cumberland to an empty house. Louis had written to attempt to explain his clandestine actions (one note was sent via Baxter, and his father's letters to Colvin and Baxter imply that there were others), but his letters must have been too upsetting for them to keep, for none survives from this period, right through to July 1880. In desperation, Thomas Stevenson had appealed first to Baxter, then Colvin, to help get his son back, offering to send money for an immediate return first-class, if, as suspected, Louis had been travelling 'on the cheap'.[67] Little could he have guessed the austerities of second-berth and steerage.

By November, Thomas Stevenson was better apprised of the situation with regard to Mrs Osbourne, and steadfastly opposed to Louis's plan to marry. His calm acceptance of Louis's confidence in Paris the previous year had obviously been in expectation that his son would not pursue a married woman further. Now he was appealing to Colvin in heart-wrenching terms: 'For God's sake use your influence. Is it fair that we should be half murdered by his conduct? I am unable to write more about this sinful mad business [. . .] Our case is painful beyond expression.'[68] Thomas does not seem to have realised that divorce and marriage were even possibilities (so little had Louis told him about the situation or his hopes); as far as he was concerned, his son was bent on open adultery, a prospect that made him talk hysterically of having to slink away from Edinburgh and move 'somewhere in England where he is not known'.[69] 'I don't know whether father or son is nearer lunacy,' Henley remarked when he heard this. 'There isn't much to choose.'[70]

Thomas's next tactic was a desperate one: he got the family doctor (presumably Uncle George) to send Louis a telegram saying that he, Thomas, was critically ill and required Louis's immediate return. 'We shall see what answer that brings,' he wrote to Colvin darkly. The bluff did not work, but precipitated instead the very crisis Thomas sought to prevent, for as Stevenson told Henley, going home at this stage was simply not an option: '[My father] would be better or dead ere I got there anyway; and I won't desert my wife.'[71] And thus, in the absence of the bride, and addressing a congregation some six thousand miles distant, Stevenson plighted his troth.

The same letter to Henley tells how Fanny had also been grievously ill and 'nearly died' in Oakland. Louis hadn't witnessed this, of course, and Fanny's dramatic illness, like the inflammation of the brain or even 'cancer' she had suffered in Monterey,[72] is likely to have had the same causes as Thomas Stevenson's in Edinburgh, that is, stress and hypochondria.

Henley's impression that Mrs Osbourne was always surrounded by 'alarms and lies and intrigues' was certainly true of this period, though they were not always of her making. Back in Monterey that summer, she had told Joe Strong of her plans to marry Belle to money. She obviously thought Joe an unsuitable son-in-law and may have suspected that he and Belle were already lovers. Far from discouraging the suitor, the news galvanised him into action, and he rushed to San Francisco to consult with Sam Osbourne, his friend and ally. Sam, affable as ever, gave his blessing to the match, and before the end of the day Joe was back in Monterey with a marriage licence. He took Belle for a walk on the beach during which he persuaded her to marry him immediately, which they did in a cottage by the shore.

That was on 9 August in Monterey, according to the official records, so Belle's story of her mother finding out 'the next day' and storming to exact revenge on them in San Francisco is obviously misremembered or distorted. Fanny doesn't seem to have known about the marriage until about 17 November, which is the date on which the *Monterey Californian* reported 'Joe Strong, the artist' as having been married in San Francisco.[73] It was probably close to the date at which the storming took place too (and coincides with Fanny's near-death illness reported by Louis to Henley). Fanny was furious not just with the runaways, but with Sam Osbourne for siding with them so thoroughly and conspiring to keep her in the dark. Sam had found an apartment for the couple on New Montgomery Avenue, took them to dinner on arrival and filled Belle's purse with twenty-dollar gold pieces. However irresponsible, it was the kind of loving gesture Fanny was absolutely incapable of making towards her daughter, relations with whom began to cool.

Colvin and Henley were appalled at the sort of company their friend had fallen in with and everything to do with the uncivilised backwater he was living in. Colvin sent on news of RLS from Joe Strong with the spelling mistakes pointedly preserved – 'The climet seems to agree well with him – his spirits are equel to his health' – and shuddered over the coarseness of the *Monterey Californian*. Neither he nor Henley had a good word to say about the few pieces of writing Stevenson managed to finish. This was not reasonable, as 'The Story of a Lie' and 'The Pavilion on the Links' both found publishers (and the latter story is one of Stevenson's best), but the

London friends were dead set against 'California and California things'.[74] When parts of *The Amateur Emigrant* began to appear, Colvin expressed the view to Baxter that it was not just bad, but probably unsaleable, 'quite below his mark',[75] for which Colvin entirely blamed Louis's circumstances: 'I don't believe [this cloud upon his talents] will go as long as he lives away from his equals and has his mind full of nothing but this infernal business. And then, if his work is no good, how is he to live? Of course there is always the chance of his settling to some cadging second-rate literary work out there, and if I am not mistaken Mrs O. would not at all object to that result.'[76] 'Mrs O.' was certainly not getting a good press back in England. One wonders what 'Mrs S.', Fanny Sitwell, thought about these angst-filled exchanges, all of which Colvin is bound to have shared with her.

Stevenson, when he heard them, dealt with criticisms of his new work as robustly as could be expected of a man whose livelihood was being held in the balance. *The Amateur Emigrant* was not meant to be compared with his earlier travel books; it 'sought to be prosaic' in keeping with the subject. And though Henley disliked 'The Pavilion on the Links', writing more plays in collaboration with him was not an attractive alternative. (Henley, probably in order to expedite funds, was going ahead with the printing of *Deacon Brodie*.) Perhaps Louis had been wrong to confess that he was at times 'terribly frightened about my work which seems to advance too slowly'.[77] And the new novella he had started, to be called 'Arizona Breckonridge, or A Vendetta in the West', was, he had to admit, 'about as bad as Ouida and not so good'.

Rolled in two camp blankets on the floor of his unfurnished room at the French Hotel, Stevenson must have wondered how long this abeyance of life would continue. He had pleurisy, which, in such a mild climate, alarmed him, and lay three days with no human contact but the sound of Simoneau's voice under his window at daybreak as he passed down the street, calling out '*Stevenson – comment ça va?*'[78] Later he confessed that he had been near starvation at this time, and was convinced he had consumption 'since I have always been threatened with that'.[79] At the same time, he was again the target of an anonymous letter-writer, this time one from Scotland, accusing him of having fathered the newborn baby of a servant at the Jenkins' house in Edinburgh. Though this was not impossible, Stevenson's response indicates no guilt whatever towards the girl, which seems enough to prove his innocence, as he was the least callous of men and intensely interested in the idea of having a child of his own.* But perhaps worst of all his worries at the time was that he was ceasing to believe that Fanny's divorce would ever happen.

Days passed just sitting in the sun, or on long walks in the 'haunting presence of the ocean':

> A great faint sound of breakers follows you high up into the inland cañons; the roar of water dwells in the clean, empty rooms of Monterey as in a shell upon the chimney; go where you will, you have but to pause and listen to hear the voice of the Pacific. You pass out of the town to the south-west, and mount the hill among pine-woods. Glade, thicket and grove surround you. You follow winding sandy tracks that lead nowither. You see a deer; a multitude of quail arises. But the sound of the sea still follows you as you advance, like that of wind among the trees, only harsher and stranger to the ear; and when at length you gain the summit, out breaks on every hand and with freshened vigour that same unending, distant, whispering rumble of the ocean[.][81]

A fisherman remembered Stevenson lying on the beach for hours at a time, 'the thinnest man I ever saw'. He wore 'one of the old kind of overcoats with a cape on it over the shoulders' (an ulster), and when asked his occupation made the rather mysterious reply, 'I sling ink.'[82] Stevenson's detached mood led to at least two near-

---

* The child, born on 5 October 1879 and christened Robert, would have been conceived (if the pregnancy went to term) around 28 December 1878, when Stevenson was certainly resident in Edinburgh. He obviously knew the girl – called, confusingly enough, Margaret Stevenson – and referred to her in a letter to Henley as 'an enchanting young lady whom you have seen'. Whether they had sexual relations is unknown, but he must have at least flirted with her, or there would have been no grounds for threats. Furnas is inclined to dismiss the subject as gossip.[80]

disasters: one with a revolver in which six charges got stuck, and another when he decided to test his theory that it was the 'Spanish moss' typical of the area that caused most fires by striking a match and setting light to one of its straggling ends: 'The tree went off simply like a rocket; in three seconds it was a roaring pillar of fire.' Fortunately he ran off fast enough to avoid detection, knowing that 'had anyone observed the result of my experiment my neck was literally not worth a pinch of snuff'.[83]

On 12 December, to his delighted surprise, Fanny's divorce came through at last and signalled Stevenson's prompt removal from Monterey. Sam Osbourne had agreed to support his ex-wife and family in the interval between the divorce and her remarriage (which Fanny was keen to defer as long as possible), but almost immediately he lost his job as a reporter at the District Court, and so the burden of maintaining the household in East Oakland – Fanny, Nellie, the cats, the dogs, the horses and, when he was home from boarding school, Sam junior – fell to the broken-down Scotsman. So Stevenson moved to a room at 608 Bush Street, San Francisco, within sight of his obligations in Oakland across the Bay, and replicated the frugal habits of Monterey under the kind and watchful eye of an Irish landlady called Mary Carson. He described his daily routine in the city in a letter to Colvin of January 1880:

> Any time between eight and half past nine in the morning, a slender gentleman in an ulster, with a volume buttoned into the breast of it, may be observed leaving No.608 Bush and descending Powell with an active step. The gentleman is R.L.S.; the volume relates to Benjamin Franklin, on whom he meditates one of his charming essays. He descends Powell, crosses Market, and descends in Sixth on a Branch of the original Pine Street Coffee House; no less[.][84]

Back in his room, he would be 'engaged darkly with an inkbottle' for some hours, then go out to Donnadieu's on Bush Street, where he could dine for fifty cents. Next would come a walk: twice or thrice a week this would be to the 'debarkadery' of the Oakland ferry to rendezvous with Fanny; more often it was a solitary climb up Telegraph Hill, so steep that the street was grass-covered (the horses couldn't manage it) and there were cleats fitted into the pavements to help foot-passengers up and down. Then more writing, and a return to the Pine Street coffee shop, 'where he once more imbrues himself to the worth of five pence in coffee and roll'. He had learned the art of eking out the butter so that it lasted exactly as long as the roll: it was the art of his current life in a nutshell.

Stevenson was bleakly amused when the landlady's little girl chanted 'Dere's de author' every time he went in or out of Bush Street, for 'the Being in question is, at least, poor enough to belong to that honorable craft'.[85] The Benjamin Franklin essay he mentioned to Colvin, like the essay on William Penn he planned, came to nothing, but he did complete an article on Thoreau for the *Cornhill*, that distant and venerable organ. The choice of exclusively American subjects could not have cheered Colvin or Henley; it seemed as if Louis was actually defecting to the Yankees for good, and he had started introducing Americanisms into his letters (as Ferrier noticed scornfully[86]). Stevenson was clearly concerned enough about losing the ability to write in a 'Cornhill' vein to hope that his Thoreau essay 'may set me up again in style, which is the great point'.[87] But his letters at this time are also full of hints that he wanted to take a new direction: 'my sympathies and interests are changed. There shall be no more books of travel for me. I care for nothing but the moral and the dramatic, not a jot for the picturesque or the beautiful, other than about people.'[88] To his Savile Club friend John Meiklejohn he confessed, 'it is not Shakespeare we take to, when we are in a hot corner; nor, certainly, George Eliot – no, nor even Balzac. It is Charles Reade, or old Dumas, or the Arabian Nights, or the best of Walter Scott; it is stories we want, not the high poetic function which represents the world [. . .] We want incident, interest, action: to the devil with your philosophy.'[89] With hindsight, this looks like a manifesto, for Reade, Dumas, the *Arabian Nights* and Scott could be said to stand godparents to several of the works to come: *Treasure Island*, *Kidnapped*, *New Arabian Nights*, *The Master of Ballantrae*.

In a sketch of San Francisco, Stevenson included a striking passage about the networks of cellars beneath the street, 'alive with mystery; opium dens, where the smokers lie one above another, shelf above shelf, close-packed and grovelling in deadly stupor'; but it is unlikely he had first-hand knowledge of them, or of the 'unknown vices and cruelties' said to go on there.[90] At a pinch, the city reminded him of Edinburgh, with its seaward face and adjacent mountain, Tamalpais, like a gilded Arthur's Seat. But San Francisco was far more exotic, with 'whiffs of alien speech, sailors singing on shipboard, Chinese coolies toiling on the shore, crowds bawling all day in the street before the Stock Exchange – one brief impression follows and obliterates another'.[91] These were the memories he drew on ten years later when writing *The Wrecker*.

Donnadieu's was not Simoneau's, and Stevenson had little company during his months in San Francisco. To indulge the luxury of talking about his beloved, he called frequently on Fanny's friend from the School of Art, Dora Williams, who lived on Geary Street with her husband Virgil. Dora was struck by Stevenson's ardent manner and habit of walking rapidly up and down the room as he spoke, but he must have seemed an odd match for her friend, with his extreme thinness, bad teeth and scruffy clothes. When Virgil Williams came home, his first impression was that 'some tramp had got in'.[92] Dora was an invalid, and thought Stevenson rather morbidly concerned with her state of health and that of the Carsons' little boy Robbie, who was feared to be dying and with whom Stevenson sat up night after night. 'O never any family for me,' he wrote to Colvin after witnessing the little boy's agonies. Thomas Stevenson was furious when he heard that his son had been 'acting nurse' at what was thought to be a deathbed, but Louis's fixation on the boy was strong. It was during these weeks, surrounded by intimations of mortality, that Stevenson began writing the fragmentary 'Memoirs of Himself' that dwell so much on his own youthful fragility.

Back in Scotland, the *Glasgow Herald* had somehow got hold of the story that Stevenson (clearly famous enough already to be a gossip-item) was 'lying seriously ill in the United States' and that latest accounts were 'very alarming'.[93] Thomas and Margaret were deluged with calls from concerned friends and onlookers, much to their distress. All they wanted was for Louis to come home, otherwise there was nothing ahead but 'destruction to himself as well as to all of us', as Thomas boomed at Colvin; 'I lay all this at the door of Herbert Spencer.'[94]

It was Colvin who relayed to the parents the fact that Mrs Osbourne had got a divorce, information which changed Thomas's mood miraculously. He now fixed on persuading Louis to leave a good long interval before marrying, and continued to ply him with advice and money (but not so much, at this point, as to fund a new life abroad). In mid-March they heard that Louis had moved from foggy, damp San Francisco to a hotel in Oakland, and then, at a dinner in Edinburgh, Thomas Stevenson heard from Baxter, probably accidentally, that Louis had been acutely ill and had had a haemorrhage – the first time that dread word appears in his history. Telegrams and letters flew to and from California: Louis had been moved to a 'friend's' house (Fanny's cottage) and was being attended by a doctor who 'said he could save him, though it would be with the greatest difficulty'.[95] Margaret was all for starting off at once to tend her boy (she didn't know that 'my dearest boy' was how Fanny Osbourne now referred to him too[96]), but the journey would have killed Thomas, they were told.

Very few letters survive from this unhappy month, but it is likely that Louis only went to the Oakland hotel because he was already seriously ill, and once he started spitting blood, was moved to the cottage, when both he and Fanny thought he was dying. The first visit of what he came to call 'Bluidy Jack' was highly significant, a confirmation of what he had 'always been threatened with', and in that sense something of a welcome development, for now he knew – or thought he knew – what he was up against, and, as he had said back in 1874 on his way home from Menton,

'It is curious how in some ways real pain is better than simple prostration and uneasiness.'[97]

There were no tests for tuberculosis at the time, so diagnosis was solely a matter of a doctor's opinion; and Stevenson was to encounter many opinionated doctors in the coming years. The research that led to the discovery of the tubercule bacillus (by the German pathologist Robert Koch), demonstrating that the primary cause of the disease was a bug you could pick up from anyone, was not published until two years later. Up till that time, TB was thought to be caused by a cocktail of 'hereditary disposition, unfavourable climate, sedentary indoor life, defective ventilation, deficiency of light and "depressing emotions"', all of which had figured large in Stevenson's existence. As he lay coughing and feverish in Oakland, he believed his congenital doom had come upon him. The fact that none of his forebears had had more than 'threats' of consumption did nothing to assuage this feeling that the disease he had contracted was fate as well as possibly fatal.

Louis stayed at the East Oakland cottage all through the crisis and for two months' convalescence. He got slowly stronger, and began to plan more projects: a play called 'The Forest State, The Greenwood State', a 'nihilist' play with Henley, 'A House Divided', and a counterblast to Henry James's book on Nathaniel Hawthorne, published the previous year. The domesticity of Fanny and her sister, the pretty garden of the cottage and the cheerful company of the pets all raised his spirits enormously, and in mid-April came conciliatory letters from home and a telegram from his father: 'Count on 250 pounds annually'. Now it became possible to plan the marriage as soon as possible, to carry through Fanny's understandable desire to get Louis's teeth pliered out and replaced by false ones, and to begin thinking of a future home; 'a ranch among the pine trees', Stevenson daydreamed, 'far from man [. . .] in the virgin forest'.[98]

On 19 May, Louis and Fanny went across to the city on the ferry and made their way to the house of a Presbyterian minister, William Scott, on Post Street. There the twenty-nine-year-old groom and the forty-year-old 'widow' (as she described herself on the marriage certificate) pledged themselves to each other with two silver rings, gold having been thought too extravagant. The only witnesses were Dora Willams, the minister's wife and the house-hold cat.

> It was not my bliss that I was interested in when I was married; it was a sort of marriage *in extremis*; and if I am where I am, it is thanks to the care of that lady, who married me when I was a mere complication of cough and bones, much fitter for an emblem of mortality than a bridegroom.[99]

7

THE PROFESSIONAL SICKIST

Our ignorance is specially great in hereditary maladies, where
much alarm undoubtedly exists which inquiry will dispel.

Francis Galton, *Record of Family Faculties*

BY THE TIME Thomas and Margaret Stevenson heard that their
son was married, he and his bride were already living halfway up
a mountain in northern California, squatting like gypsies in a
disused mining shack. It was quite a deviation from their plan to
buy a ranch among virgin forests. At the Springs Hotel in Calistoga, where the couple had gone on the recommendation of the
Williamses for the altitude and dry climate, Louis and Fanny were
told of an abandoned mining village called Silverado, on the slopes
of the mountain that dominates the valley, Mount St Helena. Silverado was empty, lonely, 2800 feet above sea level, and free. They
needed no further persuasion to give it a trial.

Having said he would do no more books of travel, Stevenson
was already planning the next one: 'It will contain our adventures
for the summer, so far as these are worth narrating; and I have
already a few pages of diary which should make up bright.'[1] Desperation jumps out of the phrase, and very likely powered the
decision to settle in Silverado for adventure's sake, for when the
Calistoga storekeeper took them up to where the old encampment
used to stand, its unsuitability was immediately obvious. The place
was a dump, knee deep in rubble and poison oak, 'a world of
lumber, old wood, old iron; a blacksmith's forge on one side, half

buried in the leaves of dwarf madronas; and on the other, an old brown wooden house'.[2] The dream of the forest ranch dissolved instantly, but the chance of getting material for a quirky book presented itself.

The storekeeper who had driven them up the mountain and the tollhouse keeper, Rufe Hanson, who was to be their nearest neighbour, must both have marvelled at the eccentricity of the couple who came back a day or two later with an eleven-year-old boy, a dog, and a cart full of trunks and boxes. They set to work to make the old mine habitable, sweeping out the deep litter of dust, stones, sticks and newspapers in the former assayer's office, installing a stove and covering the doorless portals in thick cloth. A plank was set against the threshold to allow access to the floor above, in which there were eighteen wooden bunk beds in tiers. Here they settled to sleep on the first night on heaps of straw, for all the world like animals in a broken-down byre. It was an odd return for Fanny to be living once again in a silver-miners' camp, with the ghosts of Sam Osbourne and John Lloyd ever likely to appear around a corner. It was a strange development in the life of young Sam, too, taken from his boarding school to this perch in the high forest, where he lay in straw listening to the wind and the cries of none-too-distant coyotes, with his mother and her new husband in the next bunk. None of his impressions of Silverado found their way into his otherwise garrulous memoir, *An Intimate Portrait of R.L.S.*

A former claim-owner said of Silverado that it housed over a thousand inhabitants at the peak of its use in the 1860s, but it is difficult to see how any very sizable settlement could have fitted on the site, a rocky platform approximately an acre in size, with a precipitous path down one side to where the old tollhouse used to stand, and a much longer, circuitous track that used to be access-ible by horse and cart on the other. In the very few years between it being deserted and the Stevensons' arrival, all the buildings except the assayer's office and the forge had been knocked down or removed. The tunnel of the mine remained (Stevenson used it as a wine-cellar), and the railtrack that led from it to the chutes, along with a quantity of old winding gear and so much rubble that the newlywed squatters had to lay down planks and use the old wagon-rails in order to pick their way from the 'house' to the spring. Going for a walk was virtually out of the question, 'the foot sank and slid, the boots were cut to pieces, among sharp, uneven, rolling stones',[3] so they stayed mostly on the platform, with its sunny aspect and wide views of the Napa valley far below.* It was here that Stevenson would lie naked taking his sunbaths, or sit by himself in the early morning, eating his breakfast of coffee and porridge and reading out-of-date *Cornhills*.

Their sojourn on the mountain was in two sections, the first lasting only six days. That was the point at which Fanny and Sam both came down with 'mild diphtheria' and had to be removed to a cottage in Calistoga. Stevenson's two accounts of this, to his parents and to Fanny Sitwell (a rare letter to her at this date), vary interestingly; to Mrs Sitwell, he says the diphtheria was 'slight, Sam's especially, but Fanny has been pretty sick and a little light-headed for forty-eight hours'; to his parents, he says that had they not been so prompt leaving Silverado 'we might all have been dead, for though Sam was not very bad, and Fanny only had a slight case, yet he was pretty weak, and she was nearly three days more or less out of her head and quite unable to take any nourishment'.[4] 'We might all have been dead' and 'out of her head' were part of the new heightened language with regard to health. From the date of Louis's first blood-spitting in Oakland, the couple were on permanent red alert, hysterically sensitive to each other's mortality.

The second stay at Silverado, a few weeks later, was undertaken in a more organised spirit. Joe Strong, Belle and Nellie Vandegrift (who had gone to live with the Strongs on her sister's marriage) were all summoned from San Francisco; not only would they be good company and helpful in further emergencies, Joe was to make

---

* These views have now been obscured by tree-growth, as has all sign of the old silver mine. It is in fact a far more sylvan scene today than it was in 1880, and forms part of the 'Robert Louis Stevenson Trail'.

some drawings of the Silverado site for Louis's proposed book. Belle's reminiscences of the visit were of a charming outdoor bivouac, with campfires, delicious meals cooked by her mother, plenty of talk and drink. No one disturbed them, and they could do what they liked. Fanny recalled seeing her husband sitting on a rock one day wearing a nightgown, a shawl and her mushroom hat back-to-front, with the feather over his nose.

By the end of July the party had to break up: the claim on the mine lapsed while they were squatting there, and Rufe Hanson 'jumped' it (in an absurd transaction described by Stevenson in his book) for the sake of the scrap metal on the site and the water rights. Not that this forced the squatters to leave, but they had had enough anyway, and knew that none of their makeshift shelters would withstand the merest shower when the weather changed. Stevenson was also, somewhat to his surprise, suddenly very homesick for Scotland; 'I suppose from perversity,' he wrote to his parents,

> because it is for once really rather a difficult thing to get home; and also because I want to see both of you after so long an absence – the longest we have ever had – and all the more because you have both been kinder to me this time than, it seems to me, all the sum of your former kindnesses would amount to. I have a very big heart when I think of it all; and I will say this: if you can love my wife, it will, I believe, make me love both her and you the better.[5]

He and Fanny determined to make the journey back to Britain as soon as he was well enough, staying in the meantime with Belle and Joe in San Francisco. Their longer-term plans were vague; to Fanny's brother (still put out over the divorce and remarriage) Louis expressed the intention of coming back to California the next spring, but in fact they weren't to set foot on North American soil again for another seven years. Thomas Stevenson offered to pay for everyone's passage home first-class (Sam included), so the journey itself would be a luxurious respite from the shabbiness and discomforts of the preceding year. Louis was in excellent spirits at the thought of seeing 'my dear old country and my dear old people' again. Fanny, too, was relieved and happy. Belle recalled hearing a strange sound one day as she entered the hall of the Montgomery Avenue apartment: 'with a catch at my heart, I realised it was the first time I had ever heard my mother laugh'.[6]

They set out from San Francisco on 29 July 1880, back across the plains by train to New York, where they boarded the liner *City of Chester*, reaching Liverpool on 17 August. The night before their arrival, Colvin decided, on a whim, to go and meet them off the boat, boarded the night mail for Liverpool, and was on the dock the next morning. He did not realise that Thomas and Margaret Stevenson were going to Liverpool too, so had an opportunity to observe the new family's responses to each other. 'The old folks put a most brave and most kind face on it indeed,' he reported back to Henley; Sam was 'not a bad boy' and 'distinguished himself [...] by devouring the most enormous luncheon that ever descended a mortal gullet'. Louis himself was harder to assess:

> In the face looking better than I expected, and improved by his new teeth; but weak and easily fluttered, and so small you never saw, you could put your thumb and finger round his thigh. On the whole he didn't seem to me a bit like a dying man in spite of everything. [...] When I had him alone talking in the smoking room it was quite exactly like old times; and it is clear enough that he likes his new estate so far all right, and is at peace in it; but whether you and I will ever get reconciled to the little determined brown face and white teeth and grizzling (for that's what it's up to) grizzling hair, which we are to see beside him in the future – that is another matter.[7]

The grizzling hair and the bride's age seem to have bothered Colvin unduly, given the fact that his own beloved Mrs Sitwell had reached exactly the same time of life. Of the two Mrs Stevensons, Colvin thought Louis's mother much the 'fresher'. Margaret was indeed only eleven years older than Fanny, and had had many reservations about the match. 'Doubtless she is not the daughter-in-law that I have always pictured to myself,' she told one of her cousins.[8] But this was before the two women had met. The brave faces that she and her husband put on the whole situation quickly relaxed into genuine warmth towards Fanny, whose self-contained, somewhat solemn, *maternal* manner was easy to accommodate, and whose watchful solicitude over Louis's health so closely matched their own. Stevenson's uncle George Balfour agreed, chuckling at his nephew, 'I too married a besom and have never regretted it.'[9]

First at a spa in Strathpeffer, then at Heriot Row, everyone in the party was to be spoiled. 'Wedding clothes' were bought, enough for several weddings, holidays planned and presents made. Fanny was pleased to be 'dressed properly and like a lady' for once,[10] even if she also had to indulge her mother-in-law 'trying her own things upon me from jewellery to caps, just as a child plays with dolls'.[11] Fanny tried to do the same to Louis, having discovered that his home wardrobes were packed with 'every manner of garment that a man could possibly wear under any circumstances, and some too gorgeous to wear at all', but found that he got bored after a while. Presumably the unworn glories were the result of his parents' repeated attempts over the years to make him resemble a gentleman. Fanny felt – entirely erroneously – that Louis's 'tramp days' were over.[12] He felt that they were like the couple in Tennyson's 'The Lord of Burleigh': 'She married a beggar with no seat to his trousers; presto, behold, a gentleman with an elaborate wardrobe, herself arrayed in the most elaborate toilettes, and the world a kind of modified and painfully respectable Kermesse.'[13]

Coming home in 1880 had a sharp significance for Stevenson, for in his exile he had discovered himself to be a Scot. What began as acute homesickness in California expressed itself rhapsodically once he got to Strathpeffer in 1880: 'Near here is a valley; birch woods, heather and a stream; I have lain down and died; no country, no place, was ever for a moment so delightful to my soul. And I have been a Scotchman all my life, and denied my native land!'[14] A great more denying was going to go on, of course, because the ambient temperature of his Eden was rarely high enough for comfort, but the more obvious it became that he was unlikely to be able to live there permanently, the stronger Stevenson's sentiments about Scotland became. The most interesting chapter in *The Silverado Squatters*, which he wrote in 1882, is that called 'The Scot Abroad', in which he emphasises the irrational and irresistible elements of these feelings:

> When I am at home, I feel a man from Glasgow to be something like a rival, a man from Barra to be half a foreigner. Yet let us meet in some far country, and, whether we hail from the braes of Manor or the braes of Mar, some ready-made affection joins us on the instant. It is not race. Look at us. One is Norse, one Celtic, and another Saxon. It is not community of tongue. We have it not among ourselves; and we have it almost to perfection, with English, or Irish, or American. It is no tie of faith, for we detest each other's errors. And yet somewhere, deep down in the heart of each one of us, something yearns for the old land, and the old kindly people.
>
> Of all the mysteries of the human heart, this is perhaps the most inscrutable. There is no special loveliness in that grey country, with its rainy, sea-bent archipelago; its fields of dark mountains; its unsightly places, black with coal; its treeless, sour, unfriendly-looking cornlands; its quaint, grey, castled city, where the bells clash of a Sunday, and the wind squalls, and the salt showers fly and beat. I do not even know if I desire to live there; but let me hear, in some far land, a kindred voice sing out, 'O, why left I my hame?' and it seems at once as if no beauty under the kind heavens, and no society of the wise and good, can repay me for my absence from my country. [...] There are no stars so lovely as Edinburgh street lamps. When I forget thee, Auld Reekie, may my right hand forget its cunning![15]

Only a few weeks after arriving back in Scotland, Stevenson began planning an ambitious book on the history of the Act of Union between England and Scotland in 1707, encouraged by John

Tulloch, editor of *Fraser's Magazine* and Professor of Theology at St Andrews. Stevenson's great Scots stories 'Thrawn Janet' and 'The Merry Men' belong to the following year, and *Kidnapped*, *The Master of Ballantrae*, *Catriona* and *Weir of Hermiston* to the coming decade. In a sense, he only became a writer of Scotland after this point in his life, when he gave up the idea of residing there.

The return home also, inevitably, necessitated a stocktaking of Louis's immediate and long-term prospects. He had been writing professionally for seven years by this time, but his income was still far too low to support a wife and stepchild even if he had not been ill. The alarming attack of blood-spitting in California meant that full-time work was out of the question until he could be cured or his condition stabilise, and it seems that Thomas and Margaret Stevenson resigned themselves (with very good grace) to paying for whatever was necessary to put their boy right. Both George Balfour and Andrew Clark recommended 'the Alpine cure' for Louis, under the care of the lung specialist Dr Karl Ruedi at Davos in the extreme east of Switzerland. This was the most expensive and thoroughgoing treatment available to consumptives at the time, in a location, 5,200 feet above sea level and surrounded by pine forests, thought to have the purest and driest air of any health resort in the world. Perhaps the family consulted the Davos guide-book for that year, which described the benefits of the cure thus:

> The effects of a residence at Davos cannot be overrated. The hollow chest fills out, narrow shoulders expand, the pale cheek or hectic bloom is replaced by the clear brown and red of robust health, and a year or two in this valley not only rescues the doomed from an early grave, but gives them the strength and vitality necessary for a career in life.[16]

Davos was also known as a centre for nervous invalids, which may have influenced Clark and Balfour's unanimous recommendation. The 1880 guidebook goes on to emphasise the importance of repairing *backbone* as much as lungs:

Davos demands qualities the very opposite of the resigned sentimentalism in which too frequently the phthisical youth or maiden was encouraged. Here is no place for weak and despairing resignation; here you are not pusillanimously helped to die, but are required to enter into a hard struggle for life.[17]

So in late October, Louis and Fanny, Sam and Watty Woggs, the Skye terrier puppy given to them by Walter Simpson, set off slowly across the Continent to winter in the high Alps. The journey was long and demoralising, especially for Fanny, who may well have begun to wonder what she had let herself in for. In London for a fortnight, she found the fogs made her ill and the constant visits of Louis's friends gave her headaches. But of course, everyone wanted to see Louis: it was his first contact with London literary society in fifteen months. At Henley's house in Shepherd's Bush and at the Grosvenor Hotel (where the invalid and his entourage were staying in great style), Fanny became more and more irritated with the 'fiends slightly disguised as friends', as she described them intemperately to her mother-in-law: 'If we do not get away from London I shall become an embittered woman. It is not good for the mind, or the body either, to sit smiling until I feel like a hypocritical Cheshire cat, at Louis's friends, talking stiff nothings with one and another in order to let Louis have a chance with the one he cares the most for, and all the time furtively watching the clock, and thirsting for their life's blood because they stay so late.'[18] Fanny was never one for understatement.

The couple's fecklessness is evident in the way that, given access to money (Thomas Stevenson's), neither of them had the least idea how to manage it, and they ran up such a huge bill at the Grosvenor Hotel that the generous sum allotted for the entire journey to Davos was gone in a twinkling. To complete the journey, Stevenson had to borrow from Colvin (against the 1878 loan, which Colvin had been paying back in small instalments), and write home for more. His new status as confirmed invalid had encouraged a regression into all the worst habits of dependence, and his winter at Davos was marked by lethargy and a degree of indolence not directly attributable to his physical condition, which became 'unquestionably better' there.[19] Henley wrote a devastatingly forthright critique to Baxter of this change in his friend (in an attempt to mollify Baxter's growing impatience with Louis's business incompetence), saying he was 'not morally so strong' as he used to be: 'His illness and his adventures together – and perhaps his marriage; I know not – seem, from what I can gather, to have a little sapped and weakened, and set up a process of degeneration in, his moral fibre. Thus, he has terrible fits of remorse and repentance; but he is lavish and thriftless all the same.'[20]

Baxter already loathed Fanny Stevenson, that much is clear. She was the subject of intense gossip between the group: Mrs Jenkin and Anna Henley, Katherine de Mattos and Grace Baxter all had strong opinions about the 'schoolgirl of forty' – in Henley's rude phrase – whose lack of interest in pleasing them was obviously going to prise Louis away from his old friends. Henley took on the role of mediator, but he loved intrigue too much not to stir up more of it, and his reprimands to Baxter contain a winking complicity that did not bode well for the future:

> Be as kind and as nice to Mrs Louis as ever you can. I have seen much of her, and I have modified a good deal. I like her some, and I can't help pitying her much. My wife's feeling is the same. So don't let's have any more of your abominable Baxterisms, my boy, or I shall lecture you.
>
> I fear it's a mistake, but if it be one it's an irreparable; and we must strive with all our hearts and minds – with our hearts especially – to make the best of it.[21]

Davos in 1880 was just beginning to burgeon from the small village it had been before the first tubercular patients came there in the mid-1860s to the super-sanatorium it resembled by the turn of the century, Mecca of the sick, the phthisical and winter-sporters alike. A post road had been built over the Fluela Pass in 1868, and slowly a few hotels began to appear among the scatter of houses, shops and churches. There was a Curhaus, but no sanatoria under direct medical supervision yet, and the invalids who had come in search of health lived in hotels and boarding houses. There was no railway, no electric light and only one road between Davos-Platz at one end of the valley and Davos-Dorf at the other, providing a rather dull but level walk for the 'lungers'. The clientèle were mostly German and English, and it was to the sizeable 'English' hotel, the Belvedere, that the Stevensons went on 4 November 1880, having trailed through the valley of the Prattigau from Landquart to Davos by diligence. It was nine days before Louis's thirtieth birthday.

Dr Ruedi's diagnosis, after a series of thoroughgoing medical examinations, was that Stevenson had 'chronic pneumonia, infiltration and a bronchitic tendency; also spleen enlarged'.[22] Louis reported home, 'I feel better, but variable. I see from this doctor's report, that I have more actual disease than I supposed; but there seems little doubt of my recovery.'[23] The wording indicates that Stevenson was undecided what to think about this most authoritative (and expensive) medical opinion of his life to date. Ruedi had effectively given him the opportunity to lay aside the label 'consumptive', but Stevenson was minded to hang on to it. He seems to have begun to 'enjoy his symptoms' in much the same way as the fictional Hans Castorp does in Thomas Mann's classic novel of psychosoma, set in Davos, The Magic Mountain. Though the Davos that Mann satirised was a generation after Stevenson's (the novel was written in 1927 but refers to the period around 1912), the consumptive mindset was essentially the same, with its resignation to fate and loss of will. By the middle of his first stay in the resort, Stevenson began to think it not worthwhile moving away for the summer, became fixated on his own fragility and the deaths of the young, and exhibited a perverse pride in the continuation of bad symptoms – all traits mirrored by Castorp in the novel.

TB was known as a disease of contrasts: pallor and flush, hyperactivity and languor; 'oxymorons of behaviour', as Susan Sontag has put it.[24] To a highly suggestible man like Stevenson, of course, knowledge of the symptoms might to some extent have predisposed him to get them. In Davos, he began to think of himself as a 'professional sickist', though other people seemed to feel he was not enough of one, that he was resistant to what Davos could do for him. W.G. Lockett, a later resident at Davos who compiled reminiscences of Stevenson's stay, recognised that 'the difference in mental reaction to a place like this is immense'.[25] Stevenson's mental reaction was, as ever, to resist conforming. A contributor to the Davos *Courier* in 1889 remembered him as resembling 'a great deal of the Shelley type, in his loose boyish figure, and restless radiant eyes, with a tincture in manner and conversation of French bohemianism'.[26] It wasn't the last time he would be compared with Shelley, but the context is interesting. The cult of TB, to which Stevenson contributed hugely (whether or not he actually had the disease), was essentially romantic, with the perception of the person dying (young) as a romantic personality. Conversely, the *cure* sought to crush that spirit of romantic individualism, imposing a high degree of conformity and co-operation. Dr Ruedi's patients were expected to take the air and sun at prescribed intervals, submit to set periods of immobility and consume barrowloads of food. Milk was to be drunk in quantity, and the local Valtelline wine that was high in tannin. Cigarettes were banned altogether – a horrific prospect for the chain-smoking Stevenson, who was limited to three pipes per day, one after each meal. Certain though it is that he did not keep to this regime, his consumption of nicotine was reduced, which no doubt contributed to his generally low spirits and feelings of self-pity all that winter.

The consumptive community at the Hotel Belvedere induced the same sense of claustrophobia and revulsion that Stevenson had already encountered at the Strathpeffer spa:

> *They had at first a human air*
> *In coats and flannel underwear.*
> *They rose and walked upon their feet*
> *And filled their bellies full of meat.*
> *They wiped their lips when they had done,*
> *But they were ogres every one.*

Each issuing from his secret bower,
I marked them in the morning hour.
By limp and totter, list and droop,
I singled each one from the group.
I knew them all as they went by –
I knew them by their Blasted Eye![27]

To Bob, he described his fellow residents as 'a whole crew of kind of gone-up, damp fireworks in the human form',[28] from whom there was little escape, either in the hotel or on the strictly circumscribed invalid walks outside. Davos soon began to look like a malign snowy fortress, where, as Louis wrote, 'the mountains are about you like a trap'.[29]

Fanny was not a very cheery companion; she felt ill most of the time at Davos, had little interest in seeking out friends, and few intellectual resources. She too had been examined by Ruedi and told, to her horror, that she was overweight and should diet. Louis was profoundly amused by this, as he already referred to her as a 'butterball' and 'the fat one'. The comical situation developed in which, like Jack Spratt and his wife, Fanny was put on a reducing diet while Stevenson was being stuffed full of calories and denied nicotine. Neither patient responded well, as Fanny wrote to her parents-in-law: 'If I see Louis rolling a cigarette I say, "O *very well*! smoke your cigarette and break the doctor's orders, and I shall do so too; I shall dine upon bread and butter today!" If I lay my hand accidentally upon a bit of bread Louis cries out, "Another cigarette for me!"'[30]

Communal entertainments at the Belvedere included concerts, balls and some rather deadly *tableaux vivants*. There were also amateur theatricals, which Stevenson spurned to join in, and a charity bazaar for which Fanny (driven by boredom) painted some pictures of dogs' heads, including that of the redoubtable Woggs. Unsurprisingly, Stevenson soon resorted to mild mischief-making; several residents remembered an occasion when he got up to recite Tennyson's 'Lucknow' in such an exaggerated style that one woman had to be removed from the room in hysterics. Others thought his performance 'stagey'. Stevenson struck them (he would have been delighted to hear) as 'a rather odd, exotic, theatrical kind of man; a man framed somewhat on the model of Du Maurier's aesthetes. His personality had a tinge of that picturesqueness and Bohemianism which seldom fail to sharply impinge upon the prejudices of a true-born Briton.'[31] In other words, he was a damn queer fellow.

But he wasn't entirely alone. Davos housed one very notable man of letters, whose contributions to the *Pall Mall Gazette* and the *Fortnightly* Stevenson knew well, and to whom he had a letter of introduction from Gosse. John Addington Symonds had arrived in the Alps in 1877 en route for Egypt, but found the climate so restorative that he made Davos his permanent home and was having a house built there for himself, his wife and four daughters. Symonds was an extremely cultured and sophisticated man, a first-class scholar and student of the Italian Renaissance, whom Stevenson recognised immediately as more than a match for himself. 'His various and exotic knowledge, complete although unready sympathies, and fine, full, discriminative flow of language, fit him out to be the best of talkers', Stevenson wrote in his sketch 'Talk and Talkers', though 'he does not always, perhaps not often, frankly surrender himself in conversation'.[32] Indeed there was much withheld in Symonds, as Stevenson came to appreciate over the months they spent in close companionship in the intellectual wasteland of Davos.

Symonds saw 'a great acquisition' in Stevenson, whom he judged 'really clever, and curious in matters of style'.[33] But this view modified, and in February 1881 Symonds was writing to the same friend (Horatio Brown), 'I have apprehensions about [Stevenson's] power of intellectual last. The more I see of him, the less I find of solid mental stuff. He wants years of study in tough subjects.'[34] Stevenson was never going to achieve 'intellectual last', especially not at Davos, where his neuroses were all in full bloom. Symonds must have found it trying to hear so many projects talked up one week and totally forgotten the next, as the uncertain flame of Stevenson's inspiration flared and tapered. The scatter-gun research techniques Stevenson was applying to his book on the Act of Union must have caused the double-first from Balliol to raise an eyebrow, if only to himself, and Stevenson's pretensions to academic honours (of which more later) must have struck him as quite absurd, for they were.

But the two became friends, and Symonds was solicitously watchful over Stevenson's mental and physical health, in which he saw many parallels to his own case. Before his own breakdown in 1877, and the beginning of his cure at Davos, Symonds had been 'feverish and fretful' over his work.[35] He recommended to Stevenson to try reviewing, to keep his hand in and 'save his brain'. 'He and, it appears, Leslie Stephen fear a little some eclipse,' Stevenson told Colvin. 'I am not without sharing the fear. I know my own languor as no one else does; it is a dead down-draught; a heavy fardel.'[36] Symonds thought that Stevenson never rested enough to effect Ruedi's cure (so was *temperamentally* doomed not to recover), and the witness of Horatio Brown, Symonds's friend and a frequent visitor to Davos, confirms this: 'I feel pretty sure that [Stevenson] never did any systematic open-air cure, or systematic anything. He had a far from invalid life, except when he broke down and retired to bed.'[37]

But the most interesting parallels between the two cases occur at a different level. Symonds, as all readers of his famous *Memoirs* know, was a closet homosexual hugely troubled by the degree to which his 'condition' could be considered pathological. He had read widely among theorists of behaviour and disagreed with most of them, including Krafft-Ebing; he corresponded with Whitman about the 'Calamus' section of *Leaves of Grass*, provoking an astonishing disavowal from the poet that it had anything to do with 'morbid inferences',[38] and later in his life he initiated a collaboration with Havelock Ellis that led to the publication of Ellis's *Sexual Inversion*, the first volume of the groundbreaking *Studies in the Psychology of Sex*, published in 1897, four years after Symonds's death. In that volume, Symonds wrote up his own sexual history anonymously as 'Case XVIII', in which he describes 'A' as having suffered from neurasthenia in his late teens, with insomnia, 'obscure cerebral discomfort [...] inability to concentrate attention, and dejection'. 'A' put his neurosis down to suppression of his homosexual temperament; the more he tried to divert his mind from it, the worse his symptoms became. At twenty-four A married, in an attempt to 'normalise', and the next year 'chronic disease of the lungs declared itself'. His invalidism increased all through his twenties until he reached the decision to give up any sort of marital relations and begin to 'indulge his inborn homosexual instincts'. The effect on A's health was dramatic: 'he rapidly recovered [...] the neurotic disturbances subsided; the phthisis – which had progressed as far as profuse haemorrhage and formation of cavity – was arrested'.[39]

Symonds's was a sexual case history, but its similarity to Stevenson's medical history is notable: Stevenson also suffered from chronic nervous disorders in his late teens and early twenties, had recently married and had begun to display tubercular symptoms. This is not to make the facile suggestion that Stevenson was *therefore* harbouring a 'demon' such as Symonds described, ravishing his imagination 'with "the love of the impossible"'.[40] Stevenson, it should be said at this point, seems never to have had any homosexual experiences whatever. However, his affect was almost entirely 'gay'. The reasons behind this, and the effect it had on other people, would deserve consideration even if this eccentric, boyish bohemian had not gone on to write *The Strange Case of Dr Jekyll and Mr Hyde*.

Stevenson's personal manner and habits of dress had long constituted a standing challenge to bourgeois assumptions, social *and* sexual: what better way to rile fogeys than to go around looking almost like a caricature of the limp-wrested 'Uranian' of popular myth? But on a day-to-day basis, of course, dressing and behaving like a 'yellow yite' was just as likely to confuse and embarrass homosexual men as to irritate homophobes. When Stevenson turned up at Davos, the initial signals received by Symonds must have seemed as glaring as the light from Bell Rock or Skerryvore: a wispy, boyish 'Shelleyan', married to a greying nurse-wife whom the staff at one Davos hotel mistook for his mother,* expressing ardent admiration of Walt Whitman (whose name, according to Graham Robb, was 'probably the commonest key to further intimacy' among homosexuals at the time[42]) and carrying a *letter of introduction* from Edmund Gosse!

But Symonds must have processed the available information about Stevenson very fast, for no trace of secret knowledge or special understanding enters the documented relations of the two men, and there was, presumably, no physical attraction between them, as Symonds was almost exclusively interested in more muscular specimens. But the list of sexually ambiguous and gay men who *did* find Stevenson almost mesmerisingly attractive is long, including Gosse, Andrew Lang and, later, Henry James. Added to this could be a subsidiary list of men who seemed to be responding to homosexual signals in Stevenson's work, such as Mark-André Raffalovitch, later the author of *Uranisme et unisexualité* (1896) and a friend of Aubrey Beardsley and Wilde, who in 1882, when he was still a teenager, sent Stevenson an essay in homage and thanks for *Familiar Studies in Men and Books*, the volume that contained Stevenson's paeans to Whitman, Thoreau and Poe. Symonds described Raffalovitch as being 'of the "tribe" of Walt Whitman', and Raffalovitch had every reason – from his works – to believe the same of Stevenson. The two men met in Paris in 1882, when Raffalovitch invited Stevenson to his home for lunch. After that, he didn't pursue the acquaintance further.

Sometimes these signals were emphasised by observers to the point of caricature. It is hard to tell from this description of Stevenson by the journalist and critic William Archer (in 1885)

---

* Lockett relates the story, told to him by the patrons of the hotel. When the Stevensons went to look over rooms at the pension Bergadler, Louis ('a gentleman') stayed downstairs while Fanny ('a stout lady') went upstairs. When Stevenson showed signs of impatience, the landlord 'assured him that his mother was just coming down'.[41]

whether Archer was trying to make sense of the author's 'limpness' and sensitivity, or make fun of it:

> He now sits at the foot of the table rolling a limp cigarette in his long, limp fingers, and talking eagerly all the while, with just enough trace of Scottish intonation to remind one that he is the author of 'Thrawn Janet' and the creator of Alan Breck Stewart. He has still the air and manner of a young man, for illness has neither tamed his mind nor aged his body. It has left its mark, however, in the pallor of his long oval face, with its wide-set eyes, straight nose, and thin-lipped, sensitive mouth, scarcely shaded by a light moustache, the jest and scorn of his more ribald intimates.[43]

'Boyish' is one of the epithets most often used to describe the emaciated, excitable, irreverent Scot, and this apparent youthfulness gave his brilliance a permanently precocious air, while his apparent frailty made people – men and women alike – yearn to protect him. There was, of course, an element of this in his relations with Henley and Baxter and Colvin too, all of whom felt peculiarly possessive about his friendship and jealous of the intimacy he had found in marriage. Henley always played up the 'older brother' aspect of his feelings for Louis, and they referred to each other constantly as 'Dear Lad' and 'My Boy'.

According to Andrew Lang, Stevenson 'possessed, more than any man I ever met, the power of making other men fall in love with him'.[44] Harry Moors, the American trader whom Stevenson met on arrival in Samoa in 1889, was certainly susceptible to this 'power': '[Stevenson] was not a handsome man, and yet there was something irresistibly attractive about him. The genius that was in him seemed to shine out of his face. I was struck at once by his keen, inquiring eyes, brown in colour they were strangely bright, and seemed to penetrate you like the eyes of a mesmerist.'[45] This magician-like aspect was also remarked by Horatio Brown, Symonds's friend, who recalled long talks with Stevenson at Davos 'all through snowy afternoons, when we drank old Valtelline wine and smoked, and eventually I got the impression that there was nothing of him in the room but his bright eyes moving about, and his voice'.[46]

But perhaps this mesmeric, magus power over other men arose from a desire in Stevenson himself, not necessarily a conscious one. Stevenson could have been in much deeper denial than someone like Symonds, with his forthright image of 'the wolf leaping out' when he saw a homosexual graffito,[47] or Gosse, who spoke of his true self being 'buried alive', while 'this corpse [. . .] is obliged to bustle around and make an appearance every time the feast of life is spread'.[48] *The Strange Case of Dr Jekyll and Mr Hyde* dramatises both men's dilemmas very accurately, and no wonder Symonds responded to the book's publication in 1886 with shock, writing to Stevenson that 'viewed as an allegory, it touches one too closely'.[49] But Symonds was clearly also shocked by how *self-revealing* Stevenson had been in his 'strange case'-history. He would have been more so to learn that the story came to Stevenson in a dream, the medium of self-revelation that was just beginning to be used by Charcot and Freud to penetrate a patient's underlying anxieties and desires. In the late 1880s, when *Jekyll* was published, Symonds was recording his own dreams for use by researchers into sexual inversion.

What Stevenson actually 'understood' about Symonds's inclinations, or Gosse's, or, later, those of Henry James (or Charles Stoddard's, or F.H.W. Myers's, or Mark-André Raffalovitch's . . .), is unclear, but the fact that he never expressed surprise, disgust or puzzlement about any other man's sexuality indicates that he was broad-minded, imaginative and perhaps experienced enough not to count this as an area of justifiable commentary. He can't have been unaware of the homoerotic forcefield he generated, that 'power of making other men fall in love with him'. One has to assume that he rather enjoyed it. Stevenson was a man with an insatiable appetite for attention and affection.

But at times, he seems not to have 'got the message' about Symonds at all, or to be unwilling to acknowledge it. His remarks about Catherine Symonds are interesting; in Davos, he thought he had discovered the cause of her unhappy demeanour in her having an inferior intellect to her husband's. 'As you begin to find Mrs Symonds entirely out, you begin to think better of both,' he wrote to Colvin in 1882. 'You see that Symonds is to be pitied in his marriage.'[50] The idea that her unhappiness could have had any other cause doesn't seem to have crossed his mind.

Throughout the first winter at Davos, Stevenson was planning – not writing – his *magnum opus* on the Act of Union, to be called 'Scotland and the Union: The Transformation of the Scottish Highlands'. Of all his non-works, this was the most elaborately researched and imagined; letters poured from Davos to Heriot Row with lists of necessary books, either to be purchased by Thomas Stevenson or borrowed from the Advocates' Library (that connection coming in useful at last). 'This book can be ready in a year,' he told his father, completely unrealistically, 'and will pay as I go on.' Perhaps that is why he thought it justifiable that no expense should be spared. 'It will be solid and popular both, a vast stirring book to think of. Do look out for me. *All biographies of Highlanders* might be tried. All Highland trials. Hurray!!'[51]

In the meantime, he was collecting the essays for his long-awaited first collection, *Virginibus Puerisque*. It was published, towards the end of his first winter at Davos, by C. Kegan Paul, who had also published *An Inland Voyage* and *Travels with a Donkey*. 'The vile Paul', as he was usually referred to in Stevenson's letters, had paid almost nothing for these books, and Stevenson was too little a man of business to have done anything but complain to friends about it. For his 1882 collection of essays, *Familiar Studies of Men and Books*, Stevenson went to Chatto and Windus, who paid £100, but who also expected to get the rights to the earlier works. When Paul held on to these, Thomas Stevenson had to pay him off (with *more* than £100) to clear Louis's obligations, including the withdrawal of *The Amateur Emigrant* in the autumn of 1880, when it was already in proof. This must have been a relief to the father, who not only thought the emigrant book 'the worst thing you have done' and 'entirely unworthy', but was professionally involved with the owners of the *Devonia*. It is interesting to think what a realistic turn Stevenson's writing might have taken had this book appeared in 1881. But Louis had to wait until after his father's death to tackle contemporary, realistic subjects.

Stevenson wrote very little during his first Davos winter. Tobogganing was the only new activity that gave him any pleasure, but he tended to indulge in it to the point of exhaustion. War games, that had been such a feature of his childhood, were again his obsession, and he found a willing accomplice in Sam, with whom he would spend whole days moving regiments of lead soldiers across an imaginary terrain, to be shot at by the opposition using either pellets from a spring-pistol, or a double sleeve-link for heavy artillery. Food and munitions were represented by printers' 'M's from the miniature press which had been bought for Sam just before his mother's remarriage (presumably by Stevenson, as a gesture of stepfatherly kindness). On this elaborate machine, Sam printed notepaper and small samples of poetry written by his stepfather, under the imprint of The Davos Press.*

Stevenson had wisely not forced his attention on his stepson in the early days of his relationship with Fanny, possibly expecting Sam Osbourne to have insisted on maintaining contact with his surviving son. But the move from California shifted the structure of the family: in a way, Belle had become Sam's child now, and Sam junior was theirs. Little by little, Stevenson took on an elder-brotherly role towards the boy (who hero-worshipped him from the start), expending vast ingenuity on the games they played and seldom descending into seriousness. That could be left to tutors, at Davos (where there were plenty of unemployed, consumptive clerics on hand) or later in Yorkshire, where Sam was sent to get some basic education.

---

* The machine, and copious amounts of type, are now in the Writer's Museum, Edinburgh.

Louis and Fanny were not intending to have any children of their own, as is clear from a letter that Fanny wrote to Dora Williams from Davos in December 1880 on hearing that Belle was expecting her first child in April:

> I know that Belle is quite set up about the new baby; poor soul, she will soon be set down again. The baby too, I fear. I am glad that I am too far away to have it left at my door in a basket. But what is distance? I have a moral conviction borne in upon my soul that that baby is mine, and will be mine to keep and to hold forever. – And I *don't want* a baby.
> [. . .] It would amuse Louis just as much as it would Joe to have a picturesque little being in spotless white to call him father, and he could pretty well count upon bringing it up and educating it properly, and not cast it loose upon the world, but he does not dare take the risk of perpetuating his own ill health, it is too cruel.[52]

Ill-health, 'bad genes', money, advancing age; these were all rock-solid reasons for Fanny and Louis to remain childless. But they hardly applied (except 'money') to the younger couple, and no wonder Belle was not happy with her mother's grudging response to her news. Fanny melds the issue of Belle's fertility with her own, affects to have a 'moral conviction' that the baby is hers, and seeks to underscore the difference between herself and her 'foolish' daughter in the contraception stakes. All of this, and the harsh tone of her comments, seems intensely inappropriate.

Surprisingly, Louis was no more sympathetic than his wife at the thought of becoming 'grandpapa', and referred to Belle's pregnancy as 'a vulgar error'.[53] What had happened to his former delight in small children? Clearly he still had residual longings for 'a picturesque little being in spotless white' of his own, but had come to a decision with Fanny not to risk it. As if to remind him of the days when 'kids are what is wrong with me', and to emphasise the tragedy of congenital illness, an odd scene was about to be played out at Davos. A telegram arrived in January 1881 from Frances Sitwell, asking Louis to book rooms at the Belvedere for

herself and her son Bertie, now eighteen and just out of Marl-
borough, who had been taken ill suddenly and ordered to the Alps.
'Imagine the shock,' Fanny wrote to her parents-in-law, 'when the
carriage drove up and two men lifted out a ghastly dying boy':
Bertie Sitwell was in a galloping consumption.[54]

Over the next two and a half months, Bertie underwent Ruedi's
treatment and struggled to get better. A toboggan was bought for
him, and an elaborate toy theatre, but soon it was clear that his
chances of survival were slim. Colvin came out to Davos in February to support the poor boy and his mother, with whom Louis and
Fanny were deeply sympathetic, but rather distant. This was in
part because of the appalling painfulness of the current situation
– Louis said to Colvin, 'I alternate between a stiff disregard, and
a kind of horror'[55] – and in part a sort of emotional gridlock about
the past. Stevenson seems to have actively avoided Mrs Sitwell in
the week when Fanny was away in Paris, seeing a doctor. How
different this silence was from the torrent of words that used to
flow between them only seven or eight years before, and how odd
that the man who seemingly could not write to 'Madonna' less
than once a day in the past found it impossible to write to her at
all in the months following Bertie's death in April. As he admitted
to Colvin a few weeks before the boy died, 'I feel a great deal, that
I either cannot or will not say, as you well know. It has helped to
make me more conscious of the wolverine on my own shoulders;
and that also makes me a poor judge and a poor adviser.'[56] This
frankly acknowledges the difficulty Stevenson had in coping with
anyone else's death: his own was such an overwhelming preoccupation. The poem he wrote in Bertie's memory ('In Memoriam
F.A.S.'), really an address to Frances Sitwell rather than the dead
Francis Albert, peddles a morbid optimism, which, while highly
conventional for the day (and often reverted to by Stevenson when
having to address bereaved parents), seems unlikely to have comforted Mrs Sitwell much as she left her only surviving child in the
teeming Davos graveyard:

Yet, O stricken heart, remember, O remember
How of human days he lived the better part.
April came to bloom and never dim December
Breathed its killing chills upon the head or heart.

Doomed to know not Winter, only Spring, a being
Trod the flowery April blithely for a while,
Took his fill of music, joy of thought and seeing,
Came and stayed and went, nor ever ceased to smile.[57]

But the drafts from which the poem emerged contain long passages of a much more personal nature, that go back to the mother–son and 'deity' imagery that suffused Louis's correspondence with Mrs Sitwell in 1874 and '75:

So he a while in our contested state,
A while abode, not longer – for his Sun –
Mother we say, no tenderer name we know –
With whose diviner glow
His early days had shone,
Now to withdraw her radiance had begun.
Or lest a wrong I say, not she withdrew,
But the loud stream of men day after day
And great dust columns of the common way
Between them grew and grew:
And he and she for evermore might yearn,
But to the spring the rivulets not return
Nor to the bosom comes the child again.[58]

No wonder Stevenson rejected all this for the pat rhyming quatrains of the final poem. The son in question here is ostensibly Bertie Sitwell, but more that other 'son', who had been separated from the 'mother of his heart' and who could never return to her bosom, the poet.

Louis had agreed to follow Ruedi's instructions and stay the whole year round at Davos, although the idea of being tied to one place so long went completely against his grain. 'It tells on my old gypsy nature,' he wrote to Colvin,

> like a violin hung up, I begin to lose what music there was in me; and with the music, I do not know what besides, or do not know what to call it, but something radically part of life, a rhythm, perhaps, in one's old and so brutally overridden nerves, or perhaps a kind of variety of blood that the heart has come to look for.[59]

His indolence was such that he sometimes couldn't even be bothered to write whole sentences, as in this expressive note to Baxter:

> [W]ish I were a bird; seductive Rutherfords; fifteen minutes talk, return, wish I were bird. Breathless style; unwillingness to write; wish were bird; sincerely yours R.L.S.
> It had better be explained that I am neither drunk nor mad; but only hideously lazy.[60]

Perhaps it was Bertie Sitwell's death, perhaps Fanny's illness (which seemed to get worse in Davos), that propelled them, at short notice as usual and completely against doctor's orders, away from the Magic Mountain at the end of April 1881. They went briefly to Barbizon, then Paris, perhaps hoping to revive some of the excitement of their early days together, which seemed to have been obliterated by worry and sickness since their marriage, now almost a year old. But Barbizon was empty of the old friends and talk and companionship, and Paris they found 'putrid' and 'pestilential'. They headed for Scotland and a summer in the Highlands.

Henley saw the couple on their way through London, and was shocked at the 'very curious state' Louis was in. It wasn't his physical health – Henley sent Louis to his own doctor, Zebulon Mennell, who pronounced Stevenson's lungs to be all right – but his highly nervous condition. 'He is more the Spoiled Child than it is possible to say,' Henley reported to Baxter, warning him not to bring up the thorny issue of money when they met (which was difficult, as Baxter was in charge of Stevenson's accounts). 'He is curiously excitable and unstrung; emotion is always excessive with him; and any provocation to sentiment ought steadily to be avoided.'[61]

In their rented cottage in Pitlochry, however, Louis settled down to write as he hadn't for years, producing three very different stories, ostensibly all intended for the same collection of 'crawlers': the supernatural 'Thrawn Janet' (written in Scots), 'The Body Snatcher' and 'The Merry Men'. Of these, only 'The Body Snatcher' was a conventional horror story, so much so in fact that Stevenson never sought to include it in any of his collections. He took great pride in the other two stories, especially 'Thrawn Janet', one of his few extended forays into Scots prose. It has the characteristics of a ballad or a story in the oral tradition: compactness, simple characterisation and rapidly unfolding narrative.

> By this time the foot was comin' through the passage for the door; he could hear a hand skirt alang the wa', as if the fearsome thing was feelin' for its way. The saughs tossed an' maned thegither, a long sigh cam' ower the hills, the flame o' the can'le was blawn aboot; an' there stood the corp of Thrawn Janet, wi' her grogram goun an' her black mutch, wi' the heid aye upon the shouther, an' the girn still upon the face o't – leevin', ye wad hae said – deid, as Mr Soulis weel kenned – upon the threshold o' the manse.[62]

The early editions of Stevenson's stories in Scots did not have accompanying glossaries, implying a wider knowledge of the dialect than anyone would assume today. There is Scots in 'The Merry Men' too, in Gordon Darnaway's speeches, used as an intrinsic part of the characterisation. The story, described by the author as 'a fantastic sonata about the sea and wrecks', is set on a fictional islet called Eilean Aros (based on Eirread). In common with *Kidnapped*, written five years later, it features an orphaned nephew at the mercy of a mad uncle, ships, shipwrecks and the location, but 'The Merry Men' is more contemplative and poetical, with its return to 'sad sea-feelings' and 'the horror of the charnel ocean'.

The title refers to the breakers which 'sing' during storms and seem to leap about in a frenzy of excitement. The narrator's uncle, Darnaway, has been infected by their malign spirit by long contemplation of the sea, for he enjoys the shipwrecks which the Merry Men cause and lives off the things he can scavenge from them. The story has a supernatural ending; Darnaway dies being chased into the water by a nameless, featureless 'black man' (a traditional Scots representation of the devil), akin to the running black man in 'Thrawn Janet' and the black doppelgänger in 'The Tale of Tod Lapraik' (in *Catriona*). But the true source of horror is the sea itself, as Darnaway reveals in a sudden outburst:

> 'Eh, sirs, if ye had gane doon wi' the puir lads in the *Christ-Anna*, ye would ken by now the mercy of the seas. If ye had sailed it for as lang as me, ye would hate the thocht of it as I do. If ye had but used the een God gave ye, ye would hae learned the wickedness o' that fause, saut, cauld, bullering creature, an' of a' that's in it by the Lord's permission: labsters an' partans, an' sic-like, howking in the deid; muckle, gutsy, blawing whales; an' fish – the hale clan o' them – cauld-wamed, blind-ee'd uncanny ferlies. Oh sirs,' he cried, 'the horror – the horror o' the sea!'[63]

Stevenson had still not written more than a few notes for his history of the Act of Union, but in the summer of 1881 he hatched an ambition to establish himself as a historian. He had heard that the chair of History and Constitutional Law at Edinburgh University was about to fall vacant, and decided, madly, to put himself forward for the job. It appealed to him, not surprisingly, because of the stipend of £250 a year and what he conceived as a light workload, which he for some reason thought he could perform in the summer months, leaving the rest of the year for travel. It wasn't a *blague* (though it would have made a good one); he was completely in earnest, and his foolish, fond family all supported the idea.

But they couldn't influence the board of electors, and Stevenson had to begin begging for letters of recommendation from his friends and his few academic acquaintances. Among those he approached were Colvin, Gosse, Churchill Babington, three St Andrews professors, Leslie Stephen, Symonds, Charles Guthrie and – of all people – the retiring incumbent, Aeneas Mackay. This was the very man whose lectures on constitutional law Stevenson had failed to attend back in the early 1870s, and who, when asked by Graham Balfour for his reminiscences of the author, was unable to describe him as anything other than 'a truant pupil'.[64] Mackay must have written a stiff note to Stevenson at the time of his application, for a sprightly response has survived in which Stevenson says, 'You are not the only one who has regretted my absence from your lectures; but you were to me, then, only a part of a mangle through which I was being slowly and unwillingly dragged – part of a course which I had not chosen, part, in a word, of an organized boredom.'[65] Comically frank though this is, it was hardly politic, and shows in what naïve spirit this extraordinary venture was undertaken.

The more letters he wrote, though, the more Stevenson convinced himself that the chair would suit him very well. The small matter of his total lack of qualifications didn't stop him instructing Colvin to state 'all you can in favour of me and, with your best art, turning the difficulty of my never having done anything in history, strictly speaking'.[66] Quite a difficulty to turn! Symonds's testimonial letter shows signs of the struggle, evincing 'frequent conversations' as evidence of Stevenson's historical learning and the expression of a belief that his friend had a suitably arresting *manner* to lecture successfully to undergraduates. Lang was also of the opinion that Stevenson would win 'the affections of any class of young men with whom he might be thrown'. This manner was practised on the unfortunate Sam during the autumn months, with the aspirant professor walking up and down 'sonorously addressing the class'. Stevenson of course loved to hold forth, and thought the 'lectures' went very well, but Sam admitted later that he took in nothing from them but 'the word "gentlemen," and some sanguinary details of medieval life'.[67] Needless to say, Stevenson did not get the job.

One of the lesser absurdities about applying for the Edinburgh chair had been the idea of living in Scotland, even for the summer months. 'Here I am in my native land,' Louis wrote to Gosse from Edinburgh, 'being gently blown and hailed upon, and sitting nearer and nearer to the fire.'[68] That was June – mid-summer. By August, he had developed a heavy cold and began spitting blood again. The Pitlochry party (which had included Margaret Stevenson) moved to Braemar and were joined by Thomas Stevenson, Cummy and Sam Osbourne, on holiday from his tutor in Maldon. Their cottage was in the vicinity of Balmoral, where Queen Victoria was in residence, and she could be seen in her carriage emerging from the castle gate every day, come rain or shine. As it mostly came rain, Her Britannic Majesty proved to be made of sterner stuff than Stevenson, who lay in bed or on a sofa most of the time, playing chess with his father or Sam. When Gosse, who was invited up for a visit, asked what clothes to bring, Stevenson replied, 'If you had an uncle who was a sea-captain and went to the North Pole, you had better bring his outfit.'[69]

When Gosse arrived, on 26 August, he was impressed with the co-existence of so many strong personalities within such a small space, writing home to his wife, 'This is a most entertaining household. All the persons in it are full of character and force: they use fearful language towards one another and no quarrel ensues.'[70] Cummy was delighted with the new arrival, and praised his reading of the Bible at family prayers by turning to Louis and saying, 'He's the only one of your fine friends who can do justice to the Word of God!'[71] Gosse went on walks in the rain with Thomas Stevenson and was charmed by the old man's 'excellent sound talk' and resemblance to his own father, Philip Henry Gosse, another sensitive, tyrannical fundamentalist. It would be another twenty-six years until Gosse wrote the memoir for which he is famous, *Father and Son*, that struck such a chord with survivors of the Victorian family romance, and in which Robert Louis Stevenson would have recognised many familiar situations.

In the days before Gosse's arrival, kept indoors by the heavy rain, Louis had been trying to entertain Sam with paints and paper. A map emerged from his watery doodlings, which 'took my fancy beyond expression', as he recalled in the essay 'My First Book'. Under the map, he wrote the words 'Treasure Island': 'The next thing I knew, I had some paper before me and was writing out a list of chapters.'

The Sea Cook
Or Treasure Island:
A Story for Boys.

'If this don't fetch the kids, why, they have gone rotten since my day,' he wrote excitedly to Henley. 'Will you be surprised to learn that it is about Buccaneers, that it begins in the Admiral Benbow public house on [the] Devon Coast, that it's all about a map and a treasure and a mutiny and a derelict ship and a current and a fine old Squire Trelawny (the real Tre,* purged of literature and sin, to suit the infant mind) and a doctor and another doctor, and a Sea Cook with one leg, and a sea song with the chorus "Yo-ho-ho and a bottle of Rum".'[72]

By the next day three chapters had already been written, those incomparable scenes at the Admiral Benbow with Billy Bones's arrival and Blind Pew tap-tapping up the road to deliver the Black Spot. Louis was reading the story aloud to his family at Braemar, chapter by chapter, and buoyed by their enthusiastic response, kept the pace up briskly. 'No women in the story,' he told Henley. 'Sam's orders; and who so blythe to obey? It's awful fun boy's stories [. . .] No writing, just drive along as the words come and the pen will scratch! The only stiff thing is to get it ended; that I don't see, but I look to a volcano.'[73]

So the classic adventure story (never just 'a story for boys') took shape. Thomas Stevenson suggested the apple-barrel incident, and supplied his son with a detailed list of the contents of Billy Bones's sea-chest; Sam was the essential child-audience and Fanny

---

* In other words, Shelley's friend Edward Trelawney, whom Colvin knew.

a keen critic of the narrative. None of them thought of it as more than a passing entertainment until a visitor to Braemar, the writer and journalist Alexander Japp (with whom Stevenson had been in correspondence about Thoreau), suggested it might appeal to his friend James Henderson, editor of a children's paper called *Young Folks*. Japp waxed so strong about it, and guessed at such generous remuneration (perhaps £100), that he was allowed to take away a copy of the existing chapters and an outline of the rest of the plot to show Henderson. The £100 proved illusory, but by the end of September *Young Folks* had offered to publish the story in instalments at the rate of twelve shillings and sixpence a column, Stevenson retaining copyright on the whole. As *Young Folks* was not a prestigious publication (none of the family had even heard of it before), Stevenson took the precaution of adopting a pseudonym, 'Captain George North', to protect his literary credit.

There then arose the slight problem of 'the whole'. After fifteen chapters and several large doses of praise, Stevenson had run out of steam. Then he fell ill again and work stopped altogether. At Uncle George's insistence, silence was imposed on him to save his lungs and a pine-oil respirator bought to help his breathing. 'It has a snout like a pig's,' Fanny wrote to Dora Williams, 'with comical valves on each side that flap in and out as he breathes.'[74] He had to wear this monstrous contraption day and night, and was the subject of ribald commentary in the lanes of Braemar. The Highlands had proven as bad for his health as ever, and there seemed nothing for it but a return to Davos for the winter.

At this point, 'The Sea-Cook', like so many other of Stevenson's works, might never have been finished. The author had reached Chapter 16 and was entirely stuck. 'My mouth was empty; there was not one more word of *Treasure Island* in my bosom,' he wrote later. '[I was] a good deal pleased with what I had done, and more appalled than I can depict to you in words at what remained for me to do.'[75] Something of his predicament can perhaps be detected in the story itself, as young Jim Hawkins, in the most reflective chapter of the book, circles round and round, not able to steer Ben

Gunn's flimsy coracle towards the shore. Providentially, *Young Folks* was starting to publish the chapters it already possessed, in the certainty that the rest was on its way. This forced Stevenson's hand, as did the fan mail that was already starting to come through from readers of the early chapters, and, whipped along by the necessity not to disappoint them or himself, 'Captain George' set to again in Davos and finished the story in time, overcoming his difficulty at the beginning of Chapter 16 by changing narrator from Jim to Dr Livesey. It then only took a couple more weeks to get to the glorious moment when he could write 'The End': astonishingly enough, *Treasure Island* was the first full-length narrative Stevenson had ever completed.

The plot was pure romance: a boy, a treasure map, pirates, a deserted island, loyalties tested and betrayed, a frantic chase to find gold. In some ways it was utterly conventional, not to say derivative; besides debts to Ballantyne, Defoe and Johnson (the historian of buccaneering), Stevenson later admitted that much of the Billy Bones story must have been an unconscious borrowing from Washington Irving. 'The stockade, I am told is from *Masterman Ready*,' he wrote in 'My First Book'. 'It may be, I care not a jot. These useful writers had fulfilled the poet's saying: departing, they had left behind them "Footprints on the sands of time;/Footprints that perhaps another –" and I was the other!'[76] He knew that for all its baggage of familiarity, his pirate tale was 'as original as sin'; Silver's parrot on his shoulder, the pirate song, Ben Gunn, the mad marooned sailor on the island, became, in Stevenson's hands, startlingly new.

The enduring appeal of the book resides as much in its psychological realism as in the gripping plot. The development of Jim Hawkins from gullible child to resourceful and active young man (who goes through a shocking rite of passage when forced to kill the mutinous pirate Israel Hands) gives the story weight and significance. Stevenson follows through in imagination, making us share the aftermath of the crisis once Hands's body has fallen from the mast of the *Hispaniola*:

Owing to the cant of the vessel, the masts hung far out over the water, and from my perch on the cross-trees I had nothing below me but the surface of the bay. Hands, who was not so. far up, was, in consequence, nearer to the ship, and fell between me and the bulwarks. He rose once to the surface in a lather of foam and blood, and then sank again for good. As the water settled I could see him lying huddled together on the clean, bright sand in the shadow of the vessel's sides. A fish or two whipped past his body. Sometimes, by the quivering of the water, he appeared to move a little, as if he were trying to rise. But he was dead enough, for all that, being both shot and drowned, and was food for fish in the very place where he had designed my slaughter.[77]

There is no sentimentality in the book at all; the adult world Jim is about to join is a place of unbridled greed and self-interest (Dr Livesey being the only exception), and the former crimes of the pirates, though never made explicit, show in their brutal manners and powerful fear of each other. Even Silver's parrot, survivor of many buccaneer generations and named after the wicked old Captain Flint whom all the pirates dreaded, uses language 'passing belief for wickedness', for, as Silver remarks, 'You can't touch pitch and not be mucked.'

The creation of Long John Silver was in itself one of Stevenson's finest achievements, a fictional character far more real to most people now than any historical pirate:

His left leg was cut off close by the hip, and under the left shoulder he carried a crutch, which he managed with wonderful dexterity, hopping about upon it like a bird. He was very tall and strong, with a face as big as a ham – plain and pale, but intelligent and smiling. Indeed, he seemed in the most cheerful spirits, whistling as he moved about among the tables, with a merry word or a slap on the shoulder for the more favoured of his guests.[78]

Silver's benign, even charming, exterior and fatherly solicitude for Jim Hawkins, and his abrupt changes of demeanour from willing servant to bloodthirsty gang-leader, provide a constantly shifting background against which Jim has to learn to evaluate character, a trope Stevenson was to use in many other novels. 'I thought I knew what a buccaneer was like,' Jim says, reflecting on Silver's misleading appearance, 'a very different creature, according to me, from this clean and pleasant-tempered landlord.'[79] The unlikely friendship between the two is at the heart of the book, and proof of Jim's growing judgement, as well as of Silver's core qualities of courage and geniality, is that the two retain a grudging but genuine admiration for each other at the end, despite discovering how little they actually have in common.

The serialisation in *Young Folks* gave 'Captain George North' quite a following among its juvenile subscribers, but of course had very little impact on the public at large. Some of Stevenson's friends who were sent the cuttings of 'Treasure Island; or The Mutiny of the Hispaniola' were delighted by it (especially Henley), but the story didn't appear in book form for another two years, not through lack of interest from publishers, but from the author's lack of enterprise. 1883 is therefore the date at which it (and Stevenson himself, to some extent) took off. A reviewer in the *Spectator*, writing five years later, said, 'Boys who have lived since "Treasure Island" was published, are boys who have a right to look back on all previous boyhoods with compassion.'[80] And by the time Stevenson was asked to write an essay about it in 1894 for a volume called *My First Book* (regardless of the fact that it was nothing like his *first* book), he could refer to *Treasure Island* with a slightly bemused air as a tale 'that seems to have given much pleasure'.[81]

8

UXORIOUS BILLY

By the end of October 1881, Louis was back in Davos, 'on my Patmos, or rather Pisgah, with five months of snow before me'.[1] The Belvedere and its English 'crock-company' was spurned; this time he, Fanny and Sam were renting a chalet midway along the upper part of Davos valley, with a view southwards to the Tinzenhorn. There was room for the printing press and its accessories, for the wood-engraving tools that Stevenson had bought to entertain himself with, for Fanny's paints and for the six hundred lead soldiers Sam had accumulated. In the large attic, they set up a permanent war game site, complete with 'mountains, towns, rivers, "good" and "bad" roads, bridges, morasses etc.', as Sam remembered it.[2] These games could last for weeks, and became very complex; Stevenson even went as far as writing war reports for two separate imaginary newspapers, the Glendarule *Times* and the Yallobally *Record*. It was intensely playful play, and, like everything Stevenson did in this vein, less a return to childish things than a continuation and sophistication of pleasures he had never put away. For his *kriegspiel* with Sam, he was studying Hamley's *Operations of War*, the authority on martial strategy since 1800, and it can't be entirely coincidental that during this winter he began to plan a biography of the Duke of Wellington.

Before that, Stevenson had become extremely excited about the prospect of writing a biography of Hazlitt, a commission from the publisher George Bentley. Despite months of research, and a huge admiration for the author of *Table-Talk, Principles of Human*

Action and the *Essays*, despite also the opportunity to earn money, this was another false start. Graham Balfour was among the commentators who believed that Stevenson took a disgust against his hero on reading the *Liber Amoris*, with its stark revelations of Hazlitt's sexual susceptibilities, but Gosse disagreed strongly with this surmise. Stevenson was not the man to be shocked by Hazlitt's confessional memoir, Gosse wrote to Augustine Birrell in 1902: 'He would see the vulgarity, and, what is worse, the slight insanity of it all. But the processes of desire are so mysterious, and Stevenson so fully realised that, in the case of an artist, it is what art he deposits, not what desire he takes in, which is of interest, and he was, moreover, so devoid of the least touch of cant, that I rather resent your words on this subject.'[3]

Stevenson had a productive winter at the Chalet am Stein. He finished 'Treasure Island' for *Young Folks*, wrote *The Silverado Squatters* for his new publisher, Chatto and Windus (it was published in 1883), composed two long essays on 'Talk and Talkers' for the *Cornhill*, and collected his 'Suicide Club' stories and other short fiction as a two-volume *New Arabian Nights*, published by Chatto in 1882. 'Who says I am written out,' he wrote to Henley, '– damn their beards! I spill more ink than half the crawling slovens.'[4]

'Talk and Talkers', intended as a celebration of Louis's friendships with Henley, Bob, Jenkin, Simpson, Gosse and Symonds (who all appear under disguised names), caused a certain amount of dissent among his circle back in Britain, some of whom had trouble identifying themselves, few of whom seemed pleased with their portraits. Henley in particular became agitated – 'savage' was his word – at the omission of Ferrier and Colvin from the group (although Stevenson had explained that he tried and failed with the latter), and to Baxter lamented the inclusion of Gosse, 'who has led the poor dear young man astray'.[5] Baxter was the last person to take this calmly; his former intimacy with Stevenson seemed to have worn very thin. Their experience had diverged sharply (Baxter lost a daughter in 1881), and letters like this from the married invalid of Davos only emphasised the irretrievability of the past:

> Ah! what would I not give to steal this evening with you through the big, echoing, college archway and away south under the street lamps, and to dear Brash's, now defunct! But the old time is dead also; never, never, to revive. It was a sad time, too, but so gay and so hopeful, and we had such sport with all our low spirits, and all our distresses, that it looks like a lamplit, vicious fairy land behind me. O for ten Edinburgh minutes – sixpence between us, and the ever glorious Lothian Road, or dear mysterious Leith Walk! But here, a sheer hulk, lies poor Tom Bowling; – here in this strange place, whose very strangeness would have been heaven to him then; – and aspires – yes, C.B. with tears – after the past.
> [...] I swear by the eternal sky
> Johnson – nor Thomson – ne'er shall die!
> Yet I fancy they are dead too; dead like Brash.[6]

There had been many changes in the group; Ferrier was dying of drink in Edinburgh, Henley had finally begun to earn a decent wage as the editor of *Cassell's Magazine of Art* (a post arranged for him by Colvin), and Bob was teaching a class at Cambridge (another Colvin arrangement). Bob had married, secretly, in 1881, a dentist's daughter called Louisa Purland, who lived with her sister and earned her own living (which was just as well, as Bob was almost penniless). The couple were not living together, only taking holidays occasionally; 'a curious arrangement', as Louis explained to his mother, 'but not altogether a bad one'.[7] But Louisa, like Simpson's wife Anne, was to prove ultimately unfriendly towards Louis and Fanny, and a divisive influence.

Louis's own marriage was as puzzling and divisive, if not more so, in his friends' eyes, and Henley can't have been pleased that the second 'Talk and Talkers' essay concluded with this passage about the unmatchable intimacy of marriage, one of many ardent tributes by Stevenson to his wife:

Marriage is one long conversation, chequered by disputes. The disputes are valueless; they but ingrain the difference; the heroic heart of woman prompting her at once to nail her colours to the mast. But in the intervals, almost unconsciously and with no desire to shine, the whole material of life is turned over and over, ideas are struck out and shared, the two persons more and more adapt their notions one to suit the other, and in process of time, without sound of trumpet, they conduct each other into new worlds of thought.[8]

Fanny's ailments during the second winter in Davos were legion; stomach disorder, 'brain-fever', heart trouble, sore throat – she was hardly well for a week. In December, she was sent to Bern for treatment and told she may have had a gall bladder infection, or ulceration of the bowels, perhaps even cancer again, while Fanny herself believed (confusingly) that she had malaria. 'I wish to God I or anybody knew what was the matter with my wife,' Stevenson wrote to Gosse,[9] a cry he had made often enough about himself. A Swiss nurse was hired to look after her, and four or five months' convalescence recommended. The irony was that Louis's health seemed to improve (on the whole) in Davos, even though he hated the place.

The Swiss nurse didn't last long, nor the domestic servants who were hired that winter at the Chalet am Stein. The Stevensons were clearly not very good employers, or posed too much of a challenge to the average skivvy, with their shouting matches and chaotic habits: 'their housekeeping was amusing and original', as Symonds's wife Catherine put it.[10] During bouts of illness, the household went into meltdown. Horatio Brown, who liked to spend afternoons with Stevenson at the chalet, smoking, drinking and talking, was greeted one time by this alarming sight: '[Stevenson] was lying, ghastly, in bed – purple cheek-bones, bloodless lips – fever all over him – without appetite – and all about him utterly forlorn. Woggs squealing, Mrs Stevenson doing her best to make things comfortable.'[11]

It was Fanny's lingering illness that made them leave Davos in

April 1882 for London, and the rest of the summer was spent at a number of locations in England and Scotland, with many short separations that bore home to Louis his dependence on his wife: 'Marriage does soften a person up,' he wrote to her in October. Anticipating their reunion at Kingussie in the summer, he drew her a picture of 'The fat and the lean' near a railway station, 'the lean' rushing so fast to meet 'the fat' that his hat has fallen off. With it were these charmingly inconsequential verses:

> *With thoughts reverential and stilly*
> *This long correspondence I close;*
> *The union of you and your Billy*
> *Now pledges my pen to repose.*
>
> *On paper as white as a lily,*
> *In writing as sable as crows,*
> *The thoughts of Uxorious Billy*
> *Were daily sent forward in prose.*
>
> *The postman, industrious gillie,*
> *Has laboured, but now may repose;*
> *For you and Uxorious Billy*
> *On Saturday part from their woes.*

But don't come if tired, dear. Your loving husband Louis

> *In this emblem, please to view*
> *Uxorious Billy far from you.*

Gosse was right to point out how well Stevenson understood the paradoxical 'processes of desire'. It did not, however, make it

easy to write about them, or, specifically, to write about sex, as
Stevenson was to find out with the composition of *Prince Otto* in
1883. The introductory passages of 'The Story of a Lie', written
on board the *Devonia* as he made his way to California, are a
gloss on the subject, with his feelings for Fanny clearly in mind:

> All comprehension is creation; the woman I love is somewhat
> of my handiwork; and the great lover, like the great painter,
> is he that can so embellish his subject as to make her more
> than human, whilst yet by a cunning art he has so based his
> apotheosis on the nature of the case that the woman can
> go on being a true woman, and give her character free
> play and show littleness or cherish spite, or be greedy of
> common pleasures, and he continue to worship without
> incongruity. To love a character is only the heroic way of
> understanding it.[12]

On dismissing Stevenson from Davos in the spring, Dr Ruedi had
pronounced his lungs 'splendid',[13] but made it clear that the only
way to prevent a relapse was for him to live in the South of France,
or a similarly warm and sunny climate, within fifteen miles of the
sea. Andrew Clark seconded this opinion, warning Stevenson in
September that he should be 'very careful' about where he chose
to winter, if he did not return to Davos. In London for the consul-
tation, there seemed no point going back to chilly Edinburgh, so
Louis set off at once for France. As Fanny was too ill to accompany
him, Bob did so, at least as far as Montpellier, where anxiety
about his own wife's health made him turn home. It was the usual
Stevenson family shuttlecock of illness and alarum.

   As a result, Stevenson was left alone in a hotel in Montpellier,
supposedly house-hunting but actually incapable of doing anything
at all. He withheld from Fanny the news that he had started haemorrhaging again, telling her humorously about his other symptoms,
a skin rash from patent plasters and a digestive disorder that made
his face scarlet for two hours after every meal. 'I shall be missed
here, if only as a piece of colour,'[14] he wrote, adding in a postscript
how much he longed to see her, his constant refrain that year. Laid

up in a hotel bedroom, lonely, ill, friendless, and condemned to a new regime of '*silence et repos*' by the local doctor, Stevenson wrote to Fanny, 'I have neither pluck nor patience and I must own I have wearied awful for you. But you will never understand that bit of my character. I don't want you when I'm ill; at least, it's only one half of me that wants you, and I don't like to think of you coming back and not finding me better than when we parted.' This forthright statement shows his impatience with always being 'the patient'. He had never yet been truly healthy for his wife, and it sickened him. Fanny on the other hand showed no symptoms of dissatisfaction with the situation. She was so focused on the business of being married to an invalid that it was impossible to imagine what she would do if he ever got well.

Fanny got out to Marseilles in mid-October and found a spacious villa for rent in a valley called Saint Marcel five miles out of town. It was a hasty and bad decision. The house at Saint Marcel was in poor repair, dirty, run-down and infested with fleas, and as the Stevensons had no spare cash at all Fanny had to appeal immediately to Margaret Stevenson for the money to fix it up. She clumsily overdid the style of these letters, writing of their circumstances in tones of deepest gloom and foreboding, and dressing her lamentations in vapour-thin cheeriness. The Stevenson parents were never going to refuse their son money (even though the family business was going through a rough patch), so these performances were unnecessary, and Fanny might have held her fire had she known just how often the same appeal would need to be made in the following couple of years.

The unavoidable truth was that Louis had no current or prospective income to speak of, being too ill even to get out of the house, never mind to work. 'A very little wood-cutting, the newspapers, and a note about every two days to write, completely exhausts my surplus energy,' he wrote to his mother on his thirty-second birthday. He should have been in the prime of life. The news that an actor-manager called Crichton had bought provincial rights on *Deacon Brodie* for a year excited Stevenson enormously, but promised very little actual money (5 per cent of gross profits between the two authors). But he and Henley were so grateful for the opportunity to get the play staged that payment seemed somewhat beside the point.

'I have scratched down hints as to costume,' Stevenson wrote to Henley in mid-December, when the production was already well in preparation in Bradford. 'O how I envy you! how – how – how. And yet not envy – but if only I could be there, too! – what a Tremendous Lesson I shall lose.'[15] Stevenson's exclusion from this long-awaited reward accentuated the fact that *Deacon Brodie* had really become more Henley's play than their joint project. Without Henley's determination to rewrite it in 1878–79, the manuscript would have remained among Stevenson's abandoned juvenilia. No doubt it would have been better off there, but once conceived, the idea of the melodrama had overpowered both men. The time and effort invested in the play then became the justification for spending yet more time 'perfecting' it; predictably, it got worse and worse.

Stevenson had tired of the project first, having much more on his mind in the winter of 1879–80 than the Deacon of the Wrights, and Henley's decision to go it alone while his friend was pursuing Mrs Osbourne in California had more than a little reproachfulness in it, as if the play was a child of their union whom Stevenson had flippantly abandoned. Henley's determination to bring it up to scratch alone must also have been motivated by his desire to prove himself the better writer, or at the very least senior partner in the firm of Henley and Stevenson. His investment in the play was high, and no sooner had he got his version of it printed in 1880 than he started again revising the script, not once, but twice that year. It was always, it seemed, to be a work in progress, even after publication. And now the news of the Yorkshire production struck both authors not as an end to their struggles but as an opportunity to get hints for yet more revisions, a 'Tremendous Lesson' from which they and their troublesome text could benefit.

Henley was of course in Bradford for the first of *Deacon*

Brodie's three performances at Pullan's Theatre of Varieties, and wrote his co-dramatist a full account of everything that went wrong. To his anxious eye, it was 'most ineptly done [. . .] there never was such a hodgepodge of blundering since time began'.[16] Owing to the Christmas panto, the cast was under-rehearsed and distracted, there were no scenery or props, the stage management was terrible and the noise of carpentry backstage was audible throughout. To any other observer, the most obvious evidence of carpentry would have been on stage rather than off, but Henley was convinced that the play itself had held up well: 'The play, dear lad, is a veritable play. It stood the strain superbly. The action moved from point to point with a vigour that surprised me.'[17]

Stevenson immediately began to have ideas for more melo-dramas, including one based on *Great Expectations*, or perhaps – he couldn't decide – on Dumas's *Richard Arlington*. He referred to the hero as 'Piparlington' and urged Henley to give it thought. Stevenson's donation of great ideas to Henley at this time seems particularly frivolous, as he was in no position to do any work himself. Saint Marcel disagreed with him profoundly, a 'depressing well-bucket of a house, where sciatica and sleeplessness abide'.[18] He moved out to a hotel in Nice on New Year's Day 1883, leaving his wife and Sam, on holiday from his Bournemouth crammer, to wind up the establishment as best they could.

The following weeks saw a series of alarms that show Fanny wrought to an extremely high pitch of nervous tension. Louis's earliest telegrams and letters from Nice for some reason went astray and, not having heard from him, Fanny presumed that he had collapsed, or even died, on the journey. Leaving Woggs behind, but grabbing Sam, her silver box and a loaded revolver, she set off to find the corpse, stopping everywhere en route to Nice, informing the police, telegramming hotels, and generally behaving like a tragic heroine. Sweeping into the Grand Hotel in Nice, she found her husband sitting placidly in bed, reading. 'You should have seen the arrival!' he wrote later to his parents. 'Captain Kidd [i.e. Sam] as respectable as paint – with the wild woman, and the treasure,

and the impending fatal weapon!'[19] The Stevenson parents masked
their scorn of this histrionic episode by referring to 'Cassandra's'
journey as 'a most farcical romance', but others were not so ready
to laugh. Colvin, who had been planning to visit the Stevensons
that month, was beginning to run out of patience with 'that maniac
partner', as he now referred to Fanny, whose reports of Louis's
frailty always appeared exaggerated. News of her latest escapade
infuriated him, as he wrote to Baxter:

> I suppose we must simply put down three parts of it to nerves
> and the love of harrowing her own and other people's feelings
> [...] I have given up going now but shall do so in March
> [...] My advice is that they should stay in a hotel, not at
> Nice, but some quieter place (which incidentally would save
> him from her housekeeping) until I or some practical person
> can go and manage for them about a new house.[20]

Clearly Colvin did not consider Fanny in the least bit 'a practical
person' – the very thing she prided herself on. He was, to a great
extent, right, too. For all her frontier skills and cultivation of
earth-goddess feminine mystique, Fanny was more often the cause
or amplifier of crises than their resolver. In stark contrast to Louis's
habitual optimism, she never took anything lightly; as soon as
there was a setback in her husband's health (as so often) she
prepared for the start of Act Five. One night in Saint Marcel, as
she related to Symonds, she was woken by Louis asking so urgently
for a light to be lit, in such a low whisper, that she thought he was
dying. 'Imagine my relief when I held up the candle, to see him all
right, whispering "There are burglars in the house". My "Oh, is
that all," mystified and then amused him greatly.'[21]

Not that anyone who saw Louis at this period would have
blamed his wife for her anxious solicitude. His weight in mid-
January 1883, measured by the doctor at Nice, was down to seven
stone eleven and a half (109½ pounds), less than at any time in
his adult life. He was a mere wisp. And confusingly, no one was
any nearer to a firm diagnosis of what really ailed him. '[I] now
beg, with open mouth, to know what's wrong with me,' he told

his parents. 'I have no idea. No more the doctor seems to have. I begin to suspect nerves; but do nerves produce expectoration and blood in large quantities? Question. There seem to be ghastly finger posts, like so many gallowses, pointing Davos-wards.'[22]

Neither he nor Fanny was in any doubt that a return to Davos or a similar spa would turn Stevenson once and for all into a permanent invalid, or 'a Symonds person', as Fanny put it.[23] But Stevenson was so emaciated and feeble that winter that there seemed few alternatives; they even thought desperately of asking sixty-one-year-old Cummy to come and look after him. It was as if the adult Louis had somehow gone into reverse; was becoming smaller, relapsing into a state of infantile dependency and needing his nanny. Nice itself reminded him of his visit there in 1863 with his parents and Cummy, and the contrast between the relatively robust child he had been then and the incapacitated adult he had become must have added to his already depressed and helpless feelings. Almost every letter home included a request for money and smelled of defeat, for the prospect of getting a suitable house in France, of being fit enough to work again or able to afford anything, was receding rapidly. 'We did think we had at last got to a place where we should be able to live on a fixed sum and feel like people,' he wrote sadly to his parents.

The only work he was able to complete in this half year was the one which reconstructed with such uncanny verisimilitude the pleasures, fears and fancies of his 'first' childhood, *A Child's Garden of Verses*, called at this stage 'Penny Whistles'. He wrote to Cummy of his intention to dedicate the book to her, 'in place of a great many things that I might have said and that I ought to have done to prove that I am not altogether unconscious of the great debt of gratitude I owe you'.[24] She was, he said, 'the only person who will really understand it'. It is likely, in the service of openness, that Stevenson sent a copy of this letter to his mother, for she wrote soon after, objecting to his choice of dedicatee and obviously miffed at the imputation of her own inferiority. She suggested that it might be more appropriate to dedicate the verses to Aunt Jane, but stopped short of pointing out that the most suitable candidate of all would be herself. 'I stick to what I said about Cummy,' her son replied; 'she has had the most trouble and the least thanks. Ecco! As for Auntie, she is my aunt, and she is a lady, and I am often decently civil to her, and I don't think I ever insulted her: four advantages that could not be alleged for Cummy.'[25] In mollification, he added two short poems to the 'envoys' at the back of the collection, 'To My Mother' and 'To Auntie', but the dedicatory verse 'To Alison Cunningham. From Her Boy' so far outdid these in feeling and intensity that the envoys seemed even more like dutiful squibs by comparison:

> For the long nights you lay awake
> And watched for my unworthy sake:
> For your most comfortable hand
> That led me through the uneven land:
> For all the story books you read:
> For all the pains you comforted:
> For all you pitied, all you bore,
> In sad and happy days of yore: –
> My second mother, my first wife,
> The angel of my infant life –
> From the sick child, now well and old,
> Take, nurse, the little book you hold!

'Well and old' was certainly a polite lie, and there was no acknowledgement of Cummy's other legacy, of terrifying 'night thoughts', very evident in sinister poems such as 'Shadow March', with its image of Night staring through the window, 'the breath of the Bogie' in the speaker's hair and the inexorable march of shadows towards the bed. But the emotionalism of the dedication – *mother, wife, angel* – is even more striking than its whitewashing, especially since Stevenson had tended to neglect his old nurse in adult life, relying on news being relayed to her through Heriot Row. The evocation of his childhood in the poems had stirred Stevenson up considerably; indeed it could be said that no one was more affected by the sweetly melancholic spell they cast than the author himself.

Stevenson certainly didn't think of his collection of 'nursery verses' as a potential money-spinner (unlike the wretched *Brodie*), but it eventually became one of his three all-time bestsellers and a classic. Stevenson was self-conscious about his talent as a poet, restricting himself on the whole to comic and casual forms, but the many brilliant examples of impromptu verse in his letters and notebooks show he kept a remarkable skill supple and flexible all his life. *A Child's Garden*, though his first book of verse, therefore has the fluency of long practice. Its novelty was that it was the first piece of juvenile literature that seriously attempted to reproduce childish sensibilities and concerns. Children loved it – still do – because the poems are short, direct, funny, brilliantly cadenced (perhaps children appreciate this best of all) and not mawkish; adults read it for the same pleasures, plus the ironic commentary on adult life which the naïve point of view allowed. Examples of poems in the latter category include 'Happy Thought' and 'System', in which a complacent narrator guesses that a dirty child who lacks 'lots of toys and things to eat [. . .] is a naughty child, I'm sure –/Or else his dear papa is poor'; in the first category are the classics 'Windy Nights', 'My Shadow', 'The Lamp-Lighter', 'Foreign Lands', 'From a Railway Carriage', poems so embedded now in the collective literary unconscious as to be seldom associated with an author at all:

> Faster than fairies, faster than witches,
> Bridges and houses, hedges and ditches;
> And charging along like troops in a battle,
> All through the meadows the horses and cattle:
> All of the sights of the hill and the plain
> Fly as thick as driving rain;
> And ever again, in the wink of an eye,
> Painted stations whistle by.[26]

The 'sick child' whom Stevenson recalls in the dedication is a powerful presence in the book, if a veiled one. Only 'The Land of Counterpane' specifically refers to a time 'When I was sick and lay a-bed' (and even then makes it sound like a rare and rich experience), but the figure of the isolated, sleepless or fearful child, a paradigm of sickness, is everywhere. It is as if Stevenson was looking for a way to express the continued sense of apartness and anxiety that his chronic ill-health perpetuated. Childhood was not, in that important respect, a distant, unreachable country for Stevenson, but one whose worst aspects he had never managed to escape.

The arresting melancholy of the book comes from this sense of shadow and ghostly presences, an unstated lament about illness, past and present. The circumstances under which he finished the book were extraordinary. He had been working on the poems since the summer of 1881, thought them almost ready to publish by the spring of 1883, but then was motivated to write another twenty-two poems, considerably enlarging the book. During the last stages, in Hyères, he was almost shut down by illness; forbidden to speak, with his right arm bound close to his body because of lung haemorrhaging, he was being kept in a darkened room on account of an attack of ophthalmia which Fanny feared would leave him permanently blind. In this tormenting time, he asked for paper to be pinned to a board so that he could complete 'Penny Whistles' in bed, writing left-handed, as he had so often had to do in the past. A more bizarre parody of 'The Land of Counterpane' could hardly be imagined:

> *I was the giant great and still*
> *That sits upon the pillow-hill,*
> *And sees before him, dale and plain,*
> *The pleasant land of counterpane.*[27]

The pun in the last word seems intentional from the adult author, now critically ill, bound and gagged in the dark. In other respects, his determination to finish the book can be seen as marking one of Stevenson's finest hours, the triumph of imagination over circumstances, art over life.

* * *

The house where Stevenson endured that miserable illness was also one he would look back on, rather puzzlingly, as the happiest of all his homes. He and Fanny moved to 'La Solitude' in Hyères-les-Palmiers in February 1883, drawn by the resort's growing popularity with consumptives, who clustered in the town's many new spa hotels. Not that Louis intended to mix with invalids if he could help it; 'La Solitude', a queer little house on the sloping rue de la Pierre Glissante, was to live up to its name. In appearance, it was like a joke of Davos, a miniature Swiss chalet that had started life as a show-house in the Paris Exposition of 1878. The Stevensons' landlord had gone to considerable trouble to have it reconstructed on his Mediterranean slope, but the effect was slightly ludicrous. The rooms were tiny and few; two up, two down, with a kitchen built into the hill at the back, and the narrow balcony on the first floor was flush with the street (fortunately not a very busy one). The Stevensons were delighted with it and hoped to stay 'some years'. There were views to the sea and of the hills beyond Toulon, but the property's greatest asset was its garden, with steep, winding paths and lots of mature trees. 'By day, this garden fades into nothing, overpowered by its surroundings and the luminous distance,' Stevenson wrote to Will Low, 'but at night and when the moon is out, that garden, the arbour, the flight of stairs that mount the artificial hillock, the plumed blue gum trees that hang trembling, become the very skirts of Paradise.'[28]

The move to Hyères marked a welcome if undramatic temporary improvement in Stevenson's health, but his situation overall was bad. He had produced very little work in the preceding eight months and had spent a fortune on hotel bills, travelling costs and medical care; now he had news from home that his father's business was under severe strain, mismanaged by Uncle David, who had begun to suffer from mental hallucinations (the dreaded 'hereditary madness'). Worse, Thomas Stevenson had been advised by his doctors to retire; the unavoidable consequence would be a drying up of the parental money well.

The prospect of having to start supporting himself properly,

even, indeed, of having to support his parents before long, shook
Stevenson into manic action. During the spring and summer of
1883, as well as *A Child's Garden of Verses*, he wrote or finished
several magazine articles, including another about Grez and –
Woggs in mind – 'The Character of Dogs'; he solicited and got
(through Henley's agency) a publisher for *Treasure Island*, un-
touched since its magazine serialisation almost two years before,
and he wrote a whole new adventure story for *Young Folks* called
The Black Arrow. He also took up the rudimentary 'The Forest
State, The Greenwood State' (the melodrama he began in California) and worked slavishly all through the summer of 1883 to
make it into his first novel for adults, *Prince Otto*, and began, with
Fanny as collaborator, a sequel to *New Arabian Nights*. His main
hope for money was still, however, play-writing. 'The theatre is
the gold mine,' he wrote confidently to his mother. Fanny thought
so too, urging Henley to seek 'outcroppings that you and Louis
may work to your very great advantage',[29] an unfortunate image
perhaps, given her conspicuously unsuccessful experience of prospecting in Nevada.

Oddly enough, Stevenson never seemed to consider writing a
play on his own, however often he and Henley disagreed about
subjects and treatment (and despite the fact that Henley wrote lots
of plays without a collaborator). Henley rejected the 'Piparlington'
plan quickly and was unimpressed by Stevenson's other suggestions that summer, that they should dramatise 'The Merry Men',
Prince Otto (unfinished as a novel, but ready to morph back at
any moment into a play), or, wildly, a contemporary news story
about two American-Irishmen, Gallagher and Norman, who had
been apprehended on the way from Birmingham to London with
a trunk full of dynamite. Without encouragement for this idea,
Stevenson's initial frenzy of excitement soon fizzled out. There was
no need even to wait for Henley's thumbs-down; Stevenson himself
knew from the start it was 'rot', even in the heat of seeing the
whole thing leap up in his imagination: 'Grand part for Shiel Barry,
the man with the dynamite; making that portmanteau *live*; children

playing about it and so on. [...] Damn it, we should make it hum. With a few Irish words. It would be rot, but would it not live?'[30] So many of Stevenson's plans and projections ended this way, at their conception, with a sort of blowing of a fuse when the material couldn't quite contain the author's enthusiasm.

Stevenson was always 'deep in schemes'[31] and unable to choose between them. Starting, stopping, writing lists of chapter headings: it looks like skittishness, but was probably a necessary device to avoid being without something to work on. When he was ill, anything that involved research, such as his projected biography of Hazlitt, had to be put aside completely, and the times when he was physically able to work on what remained – fiction – were so unpredictable and few that further hindrances became intolerable, as he wrote to Gosse, over whose rival career, income and output he kept watch jealously: 'I have to tinker at my things in little sittings; and the rent or the butcher or something is always calling me off to rattle up a pot-boiler. And then comes a back-set of my health and I have to twiddle my fingers and play patience [...] Treasure your strength, and may you never learn by experience the profound ennui and irritation of the shelved artist.'[32]

Stevenson was particularly frustrated when he wrote that letter (in September 1883) because he had ambitions for *Prince Otto* which he was beginning to suspect were unattainable. In his essay 'My First Book', written in 1893, Stevenson expressed his inhibitions about writing a full-length novel, speaking of it as an 'ideal' which, despite ten or twelve attempts, he couldn't realise. He describes his failure in physical terms, as if the 'little books and little essays and short stories' for which he got 'patted on the back'[33] were as much as his childishly slight self could produce. The stamina required to write a novel awed him: 'For so long a time the slant is to continue unchanged, the vein to keep running; for so long a time you must hold at command the same quality of style; for so long a time your puppets are to be always vital, always consistent, always vigorous. I remember I used to look, in those days, upon every three-volume novel with a sort of veneration, as a feat – not possibly of literature – but at least of physical and moral endurance and the courage of Ajax.'[34] Although he is writing here of the composition of 'The Sea-Cook', these remarks are very applicable to *Prince Otto*, his first novel for adults. We have his wife's word for it, and the evidence of Stevenson's letters, that he laboured over *Prince Otto* more than any other book. To Henley he sent anxious calculations of how far he had got, using 'Cornhill pages' as units, as if the production of a novel was primarily a matter of filling up a predetermined space. 'Quite a novel, by God,' he wrote, when he reached 160 of these 'Cornhills', having adjusted the figures (upwards of course) on the grounds that he thought his handwriting had got smaller over time. Such were the stratagems he needed to urge himself onwards.

It is possible that Stevenson's anxiety about breaking into novel-writing for adults made him avoid things he found easy or natural. From the start, he was defensive, describing the work-in-progress as 'a semi-reasonable and sentimental Arabian Night: that is to say, the unreality is there and the classic pomp. But the people are more developed, though they all talk like books – none of your colloquial wash; and the action, if there had ever been such a State of Grünewald might have taken place.'[35] 'The whole thing,' he added later, 'is not a romance, nor yet a comedy, nor yet a romantic comedy; but a kind of preparation of some of the elements of all three in a glass jar.'[36] In fact, the mix was even odder than that: 'The Forest State, The Greenwood State' had been a tragedy in blank verse.

Prince Otto has seldom been reprinted and is regarded with something like embarrassment by Stevenson's apologists. He seems to be labouring in it to find out what he was best at – fine writing, dramatic action, creation of character, fantasy. The hero is a dreamy dilettante, ruler of a Ruritanian principality called Grünewald, on the point of revolution due to his poor management. At the start of the story his young wife, Seraphina, has taken over government of the state, guided by the machiavellian Baron Gondremark, who is thought to be her lover. Gondremark, whose real mistress is the Countess von Rosen, is plotting to have Otto abducted so that he will be free to pursue expansionist ambitions against the neighbouring states, with a view to forming a republic. When Otto learns of this, he condemns himself for his weakness and decides to abandon the throne and go into hiding. Seraphina's formerly harsh attitude to her husband is melted by this voluntary sacrifice of power (not, as one might expect, hardened by his cowardice) and she recants her allegiance with Gondremark, stabbing the Baron in a moment of anger and setting off a revolution against the palace when the Grünewalders think him dead.

This summary implies more excitement and drama than the book actually delivers. Its genesis as a 'melo' makes it markedly stagy, with heavy reliance on reported action and enclosed, interior scenes, absurd passages of philosophical repartee and pensive soliloquising. The action is stiff and unlikely, even the settings are dull – library, palace gardens, ladies' and gentlemen's apartments – and surprisingly domestic for a story about a coup d'état, especially coming from a man so obsessively interested in war games and military history. These choices seem perverse and puzzling.

An essential part of the book, and the thing that was to mark it off from 'stories for boys', was sex, mostly in the shape of the Countess von Rosen, 'a jolly, elderly – how shall I say? – fuckstress', as Stevenson wrote excitedly to Henley.[37] Fanny was more than ready to act as special adviser here; though Stevenson said he was thinking of Madame Zassetsky when he began this story in 1879, by 1883 he was adding many elements from his wife's behaviour too. The low number of female characters in Stevenson's novels and stories has often led commentators to accuse him of misogyny or narrowness, but his experience with Prince Otto shows that it was not misogyny that discouraged him from writing about women, but the difficulty he found in representing them realistically, which he was to encounter again and again. The Countess is a seasoned coquette with a powerful instinct for body language, at one point crossing her legs and flashing a view of 'smooth black stocking and snowy petticoat' – the author's favourites – and knocking Otto out with a kiss: 'when their lips encountered, [he] was dumbfounded by the sudden convulsion of his being'.[38] The Countess's beauty is described as 'flash[ing] like a weapon full on the beholder'; '[she] always had a dagger in reserve', 'She met Otto with the dart of tender gaiety', all reminiscent of Stevenson's early remarks about Fanny's regard being like 'the sighting of a pistol'. But Stevenson's marriage turned out less of a help than a hindrance in the depiction of a strong, sexy, mature woman, since it provided a constant study, but of a rather unusual specimen. Critical distance from such a character was impossible, it being – in all but name – a portrait of his wife.

The other strong woman in *Otto*, Princess Seraphina, turns out to be more convincing, despite being set up as a 'puppet'. She is intelligent and questing, 'a woman of affairs' who has transgressed gender stereotypes by developing 'manlike ambitions'. Somewhat to the author's surprise, it seems, Seraphina becomes the moral focus of this deeply moralistic book and is the heroine of the only scene to break out of comic-opera mode, the one dealing with her flight through the forest:

> presently the whole wood rocked and began to run along with her. [. . .] She strangled and fled before her fears. And yet in the last fortress, reason, blown upon by these gusts of terror, still shone with a troubled light. She knew, yet she could not act upon her knowledge; she knew that she must stop, and yet she still ran.[39]

Though Seraphina is described in sexually insulting ways as 'a chit', 'a mincing doll' and 'wooden', it is the Countess who ends up looking hollow. In the scene where the two women confront each other (the most worked-on scene in Stevenson's whole career to date) we get this piece of pure nonsense: ' "O you immature fool!", the Countess cried, rising to her feet, and pointing at the Princess the closed fan that now began to tremble in her hand. "O wooden doll!" '[40] Stevenson was careful to record that this chapter had needed rewriting nine or ten times and that the penultimate draft was by Fanny, to whom he had turned for help in despair. According to Fanny they 'fought the path' of the Countess 'inch by inch', though how much of the final version Fanny can be held responsible for is unclear, possibly on purpose.

Prince Otto is most interesting now for the gender anarchy it portrays. Otto describes himself as 'a plexus of weaknesses, an impotent Prince'[41] who prefers 'the warm atmosphere of women and flattery and idle chatter'[42] to any other. Yet he is ruled by notions of honour and feels 'almost dangerous' as he broods on his humiliation by the macho Baron Gondremark, pacing his apartment 'like a leopard' one minute, only to transform himself in an instant (in yet another 'split personality' moment) into a dandy again, 'curled and scented and adorned'.[43] He is an object of scorn or pity throughout, except latterly to his wife, whose permanent retirement with him to her parents' house is surely the ultimate in emasculation (it is part of *Prince Otto*'s stiltedness that this is meant to recall the ending of another Bohemian romance, *The Winter's Tale*). Seraphina is the one with 'manlike ambitions', bravery and physical endurance. Even the sexy Countess is gender ambiguous: when she embraces Otto (and causes that 'sudden convulsion of his being') she is, after all, in drag, disguised as her own 'brother'.

Fanny Stevenson claimed that the character of Otto began as a portrait of Bob, 'but fell insensibly into what my husband conceived himself',[44] which makes Otto's pronounced effeminacy all the more interesting:

> He is not ill-looking; he has hair of a ruddy gold, which naturally curls, and his eyes are dark, a combination which I always regard as the mark of some congenital deficiency, physical or moral; his features are irregular but pleasing; the nose perhaps a little short, and the mouth a little womanish. His address is excellent, and he can express himself with point. But to pierce below these externals is to come on a vacuity of any sterling quality, a deliquescence of the moral

nature, a frivolity and inconsequence of purpose that mark
the nearly perfect fruit of a decadent age.[45]

There is a sort of decadence in the writing here as well as in the
conception, a self-indulgence in private joking of this sort, a purple
vein. *Prince Otto* shows Stevenson in the vanguard of the 'decadent
age' he didn't live to see in perfect fruit at the *fin de siècle*; the
elegant stylist who was also author of bracing boys' stories and
who was here sending himself up in the character of a dilettante
incapable of mastering his own domain.

Fanny's approval of *Prince Otto* (at the time of its writing; by
1906 she was calling it 'fantastic and artificial to a degree'[46]) struck
Stevenson as 'fatal', since they seldom agreed about the quality of
his work. He felt remarkably anxious about the book, not sure
whether it was the work of genius he wanted it to be. To his
mother he wrote that *Otto* was 'hitherto, my best' – a remarkable
statement from the author of *Virginibus Puerisque*, *New Arabian
Nights* and *Treasure Island* – juxtaposed with the hope that it
represented 'just a first step on another road: where I mean to
leave a mark'.[47]

But the style was far too ornate for most tastes. Henley was
unsure how to praise it, and wrote an offensive letter trying to,
while Gosse felt he had to make his objections clear: 'Forgive me
for saying that it is not worthy of you. It is a wilful and monstrous
sacrifice on the altar of George Meredith, whose errors you should
be the last to imitate and exaggerate.'[48] The critics were on the
whole puzzled and sales were unimpressive. One reviewer likened
the novel to 'a Gilbert comedy' (nothing could have been better
guaranteed to infuriate the author), others thought it was a children's story (this despite the rather heavy-handed introduction of
'adult' themes), but the general sense of bemusement was expressed by the reviewer in *Academy*: 'We all expected that "Prince
Otto" was to prove the *magnum opus*. Well, we were wrong.'[49]
Was Stevenson doomed to be the author of 'little essays' and adventures for boys? He had set out to write a volume of substance, but
was distressed to find how difficult that was. And his failure to

write about sex was chastening. He returned to his former position of keeping women characters to a minimum, and as for 'fuck-stresses', avoiding them altogether.

In defence of his labour over *Prince Otto*, Stevenson wrote to Colvin, 'The big effort, instead of being the masterpiece, may be the blotted copy, the gymnastic exercise. This no man can tell; only the brutal and licentious public, snouting in Mudie's wash trough, can return a dubious answer.'[50] Up to this point, true popularity in the mass market, symbolised by Mudie, the immensely influential circulating library, had seemed remote to Stevenson. *The Black Arrow*, his other adventure story for *Young Folks*, set during the Wars of the Roses, was written in two months flat in 1883, all, the author attested, for the sake of a quick return. Yet the real money-maker was just sitting in a drawer, waiting to be published. Why Stevenson didn't think of *Treasure Island* immediately when casting round for income is hard to understand. Perhaps the brief period of revision with a view to publication in 1882, when Thomas Stevenson suggested inserting 'a long passage [. . .] of a religious character',[51] had killed off his interest. It was only when Henley threw the clippings on the desk of a colleague at Cassell's that a serious gesture towards publication was made. 'There's a book for you!' Henley exclaimed, then clumped out of the office on his wooden leg, more like John Silver than ever. It was the best favour he ever did Stevenson in their long and troubled friendship.

Stevenson had been paid £34.7s.6d altogether for the serialisation of 'The Sea-Cook' in *Young Folks*, and seemed to think that that represented the greater part of anything he could ever earn on the story. Calculating his total income over the previous five years in April 1883 (£655), he noted that almost two thirds of that had come from magazine publication. Magazine publication was still the focus of his ambitions, which must have made 'The Sea-Cook' seem to him like a failure, since it hadn't made *Young Folks'* circulation rise at all (unlike the serialisation of *The Black Arrow*, which sent sales through the roof). Stevenson wrote to Henley that he had 'no idea' what the book might be worth: £50 would be 'a deal more than I deserved'. When Cassell's offered twice that, with a royalty of £20 per thousand copies sold, Stevenson was astounded and overjoyed: 'A hundred pounds, all alive, oh!' he wrote to his parents ecstatically. 'A hundred jingling, tingling, golden, minted quid. Is not this wonderful?'[52]

The rush of writing activity and multiplicity of schemes in 1883 was not purely to do with amassing money for his family's immediate needs. Some time during that period Fanny thought she was pregnant. The only remaining evidence of this is in a letter from Stevenson to Walter Simpson at the end of the year – a Christmas letter to the old friend he least frequently contacted:

> I must tell you a joke. A month or two ago, there was an alarm: it looked like family. Prostration: I saw myself financially ruined, I saw the child born sickly etc. Then, said I, I must look this thing on the good side; proceeded to do so studiously; and with such a result that when the alarm passed off – I was inconsolable![53]

Looking at Stevenson's letters of that year in the light of this revelation, one can guess that the suspected pregnancy happened around May or early June, when there are many exclamations on the 'sub-celestial' life he and Fanny were leading at La Solitude, revitalised schemes for future writing, attempts to master account-keeping at last, more references than usual to Fanny being 'out of sorts' and 'sick', and cryptic utterances about fate, such as this to Gosse:

> The devil has always an imp or two in every house; and my imps are getting lively. The good lady, the dear kind lady, the sweet, excellent lady, Nemesis, whom alone I adore, has fixed her wooden eye upon me. I fall prone; spare me, Mother Nemesis![54]

But having brought himself round to the idea of fatherhood, the pang Stevenson felt when the pregnancy turned out to be a false alarm must have been all the sharper. After all, dismenhorrea, the classic first sign of pregnancy, is also symptomatic of menopause; at forty-three Fanny may have been having irregular periods and certainly would have been less fertile than before. Rationally, neither she nor Louis wanted a baby at all, as her letter to Dora Williams from Davos on news of Belle's first pregnancy showed. But not having the choice was another matter.

Belle's son Austin was by now almost two years old, and the family was living in Honolulu (under the patronage of a business-man who had commissioned Joe to do some paintings). In the autumn of 1883, Belle was pregnant again and gave birth the next spring to another little boy, whom she named Hervey. Fanny's scornfulness and oddity about this second pregnancy are again remarkable. 'Belle I hear is going to have another baby and her dog is dead,' Fanny wrote to Dora Williams from Hyères. 'I'm not going to have another baby and my dog is not dead.'[55] The next surviving letter to Dora Williams mentions that Belle 'has presented the world with another little Strong. Her generosity in that respect doesn't fill me with elation';[56] again a rather sour note from a new grandmother. Though Joe and Belle were a feckless couple, Fanny's forebodings about the birth of Austin had proved false. Her odd remarks then about her 'moral conviction [. . .] that the new baby is mine',[57] like her rudeness about the second child, suggest confused feelings of rivalry towards her daughter. In this case, her sarcasm was ill-placed. Little Hervey died in infancy of pneumonia.

As for Louis, though he reported Fanny's suspected pregnancy to Simpson as a 'joke', it was of course nothing of the sort. When circumstances seemed to be overtaking them and it 'looked like family', Stevenson found in himself (yet again) a surprisingly deep well of feeling about fatherhood. This is surely behind his extra solicitude for his parents during that year, his concern for Sam's future, his taking up (or at least, trying on for size) the role of head of the family, as well as the preoccupations evident in *A*

Child's Garden and essays such as 'A Penny Plain and Twopence Coloured', with its marvellous evocation of the joys of play.

It may also be behind his problematic poem 'God gave to me a child in part', which first appeared in print after the author's death.

> God gave to me a child in part
> Yet wholly gave the father's heart: –
> Child of my soul, O whither now,
> Unborn, unmothered, goest thou?

> [. . .] My voice may reach you, O my dear –
> A father's voice perhaps the child may hear;
> And pitying, you may turn your view
> On that poor father whom you never knew.

> Alas! alone he sits, who then,
> Immortal among mortal men
> Sat hand in hand with love, and all day through
> With your dear mother, wondered over you.[58]

The reasons why this poem is problematic are that there is no date to its composition and the manuscript fragments from which it derives include other lines such as 'When they told me you were dead//Forgive me, bright and laughing lad/Forgive me if my soul was glad,' which suggest (in a fictional form, of course) the poet having fathered a viable child who died.[59] An 'alarm' that 'passes off' (such as Fanny's in 1883) is not the same as a miscarriage or stillbirth, and while of course the poem could be entirely imaginative, these seem odd subjects to choose for that purpose. The fragments also include the lines 'Where art thou gone? And where is she?/Alas!/She too has left me, O my child,/As you I left.'[60] At this point – if one is taking the liberty of reading this as autobiography – the puzzle gets more complicated, for of course Fanny Stevenson had not 'gone' anywhere in 1883, so this would refer to some other woman, some other pregnancy, or child.

There is a note in the Yale manuscript, prepared for the Bibliophile Society of Boston (by an unnamed hand), which estimates the date of the draft poem as the early 1870s. But there is another possibility, of course: that the poem, which seems to compound two events, could be about Fanny being pregnant (not just thinking she might be) *at a different time*. And the time when she was 'gone' (the only woman to abandon Stevenson in the true sense) was when she left Paris for California in 1878. If she had been expecting Stevenson's child then, it would explain her desire to return abruptly to her husband, her rural seclusion in Monterey, her lover's agonised waiting for news. It is an intriguing possibility.

Whether or not it reprised an earlier, similar event, the realisation that he and Fanny were not going to have a child in 1883 made Stevenson reassess what was left, and face the fact that from now on his whole posterity was going to be in his work. It was an unfortunate time to be judging himself this way: the potboilers outnumbered the rest by far, and there seemed no end in sight to a life of hack-writing, impeded by bouts of sickness. It was a low point, a muted mid-life crisis, from which Stevenson could not begin to imagine the successes of the coming years, the productivity and mastery he would enjoy, the fame, money and – most marvellous of all – the escape from invalidism. To Will Low he wrote of his position in terms of resignation: 'I am now a person with an established ill-health – a wife – a dog possessed with an evil, a Gadarene spirit – a chalet on a hill, looking out over the Mediterranean – a certain reputation – and very obscure finances':

> nearly three years ago that fatal Thirty struck; and yet the great work is not yet done – not yet even conceived. But so, as one goes on, the wood seems to thicken, the footpath to narrow and the House Beautiful on the hill's summit to draw further and further away. We learn indeed to use our means; but only to learn, along with it, the paralysing knowledge that these means are only applicable to two or three poor, commonplace motives. Eight years ago, if I could have slung ink as I can now, I should have thought myself well on the road after Shakespeare; and now – I find I have only got a pair of walking shoes and not yet begun to travel.[61]

Having tottered back into half-health, there was no budging from the South of France. Friends who wanted to see Stevenson had to come to him, and stay at one of the local hotels, La Solitude being far too small even to entertain guests for dinner in comfort; all the dishes had to be lowered in front of the diners over their heads. Colvin had already visited in the spring of 1883; Henley and Baxter planned a trip to Hyères later that year. Stevenson longed to see them: his only company, apart from Fanny and the local girl, Valentine Roch, whom they had hired as a maid, was an English apothecary called Powell and his wife, and the local wine merchant. His need to see old friends gained piquancy after the death in September 1883 of Walter Ferrier, aged thirty-two. The news hit Stevenson 'like a thunderclap': though Ferrier was a chronic alcoholic, he had not been expected to die before the officially precarious consumptive. Stevenson had spent his life preparing to face his own death, but not anyone else's: 'I never could have believed how much I would mind this,' he wrote to Henley.[62] To Gosse, who hadn't known Ferrier, he wrote how the death of an old friend had 'shelved' his powers: 'I stare upon the paper, not write.'[63]

Regret for neglecting the friendship haunted him, and so did the man. Alone in La Solitude, Stevenson felt he could hear Ferrier's laughter again and sense his presence, with his customary strength of sensory recall: 'I see his coral waistcoat studs that he wore the first time he dined in my house; I see his attitude, leaning back a little, already with something of a portly air, and laughing internally. How I admired him! And now in the West Kirk.'[64] The 'awful smash and humiliation' of Ferrier's descent could not obliterate in Stevenson's mind his friend's essential goodness, but the co-existence of these things in the one person troubled him deeply: 'if anything looked liker irony than this fitting of a man out with these rich qualities and faculties to be wrecked and aborted from the very stocks, I do not know the name of it', he wrote to Henley.

The name of it, yet unknown, was surely Henry Jekyll. Of all the many possible elements contributing to his fictional 'Strange

ROBERT LOUIS STEVENSON

Case' of divided self, two years from composition, Stevenson's response to Ferrier's tragic end has escaped remark, but does seem significant. His recollection of his last interview with Ferrier, before leaving for America in 1879, has the same sorrowful hopeless tone of Jekyll's friends' testimonies: 'I waited hours for him, and at last he came. "My God," I said, "you have had too much again." He did not deny it, as he did in the old days. He said "Yes", with a terrible simplicity.'[65] Ferrier drunk (having taken, like Jekyll, a transforming 'potion') was the 'lunatic brother' of the 'good true Ferrier': 'The curse was on him. Even his friends did not know him but by fits. I have passed hours with him when he was so wise, good, and sweet, that I never knew the like of it in any other.'[66] These restitutions are like the episodes of heightened virtue that characterise Jekyll's decline, yet there were also times, like his collapse in 1883, when Ferrier seemed lost, as morally and intellectually 'wild and blind'[67] as the unequivocally evil Edward Hyde. Ferrier's distraught mother had as good as blamed Stevenson's influence for the change, writing to him early in 1883 that her son 'now exists among the number of those degraded ones whose society on earth is shunned by the moral and virtuous among mankind'.[68] Yet Stevenson himself considered Ferrier to have been 'the nobler being' of the two of them, 'the best gentleman, in all kinder senses, that I ever knew'.[69]

In the weeks following Ferrier's death, Stevenson returned to writing a story called 'The Travelling Companion' that he had started in 1881 and put by. All that is known about this tale, destroyed by the author after the publication of *Jekyll and Hyde* on the grounds that it had been superseded, is that it dealt with the theme of the double life and was a shocker (intended for the collection of horrid tales that was to include 'The Merry Men' and 'Thrawn Janet'). The fact that he went back to work on it at this juncture shows his preoccupations flowing in and out of various channels, trying as usual to line up idea and mood and vehicle. In many ways it is astonishing that *Jekyll and Hyde* ever got written at all, its themes were such a constant preoccupation.

Despite Fanny's confusing mixture of pleadings and warnings, Henley and Baxter's long-anticipated visit went ahead in January 1884 and was a great success, for the men at least, who soon decamped on a trip to Menton and Nice. La Solitude was simply too cramped to cope with such boisterous company – or the men wanted to get out of range of Cassandra, whose powers of foresight required things to go as badly as possible. When the party broke up in Nice, Stevenson had a severe collapse and Fanny had to go to his rescue again. She wrote assuring Baxter that their taxing visit had not been to blame, 'though it now seems, as I said it would, like a dream'.[70] But as the situation worsened, with a local doctor taking one look at the shuddering, vomiting, skeletal Stevenson and pronouncing him almost dead, Fanny's letters and telegrams took on high colouring. 'I feel like a mother with her baby,' she wrote pointedly to his mother. 'I watched every breath Louis drew all night.' She complained to Baxter both that the Stevensons seemed indifferent to their son's mortal danger – 'I find it quite impossible to make anyone understand how very ill Louis has been'[71] – and that they were 'too wild' and volatile to be kept informed of his condition.[72] Her hysterical responses and mania to control the situation must have made her a very agitating presence. When a professional nurse was hired to take over breath-watching duty, Stevenson's remarks were interesting: 'I have had a nurse for two days now: a strange experience. Everything is done for me. I am much recovered.'[73]

Fanny, angry with Henley and Baxter for bringing on – as she saw it – this latest collapse, had imperiously summoned Walter Simpson to Nice to help her nurse Louis and was appalled when he declined to come. It was not the first indication that the friends' patience was wearing thin: Colvin had given notice a year before to Baxter that he wasn't going to be frightened by Fanny again: 'and she may cry Wolf till she is hoarse. I expect [Louis] has been pretty baddish, but nothing approaching what she gave me to understand.'[74] This battle over the quantification of Stevenson's illness obscured the fact that he was much more than 'baddish' in the first months of 1884: he confided to his mother that it had been 'chuck farthing for my life',[75] and to Bob that he had been in constant pain and extremely depressed: 'when Pain draws a lingering fiddle-bow, and all the nerves begin to sing, I am conscious of an almost irresistible temptation to join in, alto: L'Invitation à la Boo-Hoo'.[76] Those closest to him seemed obsessed with charting his distance from death: Stevenson himself was naturally more concerned with what was happening to his life, and the prognosis was poor: the doctor in Nice had told him to regard himself as an old man, stay as immobile as possible and give up drink.

> Of that lean, feverish, voluble and whiskeyfied young Scot, who once sparked through France and Britain, bent on art and the pleasures of the flesh, there now remains no quality but the strong language. That, at least, I shall take gravewards: my last word, it's like, will be an execration; the hired nurse, the weeping widow and the anxious medical attendant, shall be embraced in one all-round and comprehensive detonation, and at a breath the Temper that was known as R.L.S. will flit from its discarded tenement.[77]

The humour of this detracts (as it was meant to) from the real and intense distress of Stevenson's situation. He was not able to work, although Prince Otto was tantalisingly near completion. He was in pain, an object of pity, a burden to his parents, possibly a bore to his friends. Most of the time he was ostentatiously stoical, but his underlying mood was black. On one occasion, feverish, he grabbed Fanny and shook her 'like a terrier shaking a rat'. Some previously unpublished notes in the Yale archives exist from this period, scribbled messages from times when Stevenson was forbidden to talk, which convey some of the 'suppressed wrath' he felt at being confined to bed, constantly dependent on others, their fussiness and impositions on his attention. The one-way transcription is hauntingly suggestive of the long hours in the sickroom:

> O how I did suffer from rheumatism last night.
> red hot veins; and in the knee, knives cutting and bombs going off

It *occupies* my knee.

I only touched the pla *[sic]* to remind you I had recently had
some sandwiches
lift me up straighter
then why make me unhappy
what o'clock?

It just does seem too hard
What I want is for you to do what you want and to go
about your own affairs, and you wont understand me.
that woman'll be the death of me
du vin et de l'*eau*

Why did you come?
I can now never ring again

I didn't ring
You bring yellow stuff and a smoke and sit and tell me
stories
I believe it to be partheno-genesis on Bob's part
I have to pass the evening still
Pour out the Rhine wine
Will you read to me?
Voice bad? Nothing happened last night

Only two hours now. You are tired.
Time for you to cut and run for your denner *[sic]*
What is the fat one up to?[78]

There is also a note in French to the doctor describing his symptoms: the blood he had been spitting was '*bien caillé*' (clotted), his
kidneys very painful and he had only pissed twice in thirty-six
hours. This wreck was only to get worse, however: when the local
corporation dumped a mound of putrid refuse on the road from
La Solitude into Hyères, Stevenson developed ophthalmia and had
to stay in the dark wearing bandages or goggles – another bizarre
invalid accessory, like the Braemar pig's snout. Fanny was convinced that he was at risk of permanent blindness and it was in

the shadow of this threat that he sat in bed with the board and paper over his knees, finishing *A Child's Garden*, no doubt desperate to find distraction from his dismal circumstances. Any time he had a respite, he made the most of it, and was out dancing round a bonfire in the garden in April with Fanny and Valentine to celebrate the news that a journalist he hated (but didn't know personally) had been convicted of criminal libel. That led to a chill, and the worst haemorrhage of his life. Fanny was so frightened by the quantity of blood he coughed that her hand shook hopelessly over the ergotine bottle. The patient dosed himself, then wrote on a piece of paper, still preserved, 'Don't be frightened. If this is death, it is an easy one.' The selfless kindness of this is astonishing, though, confusingly for Fanny, she could never quite tell at this date which way the invalid's temper would jump.

News of this dangerous attack shook Stevenson's London friends into action. Henley called Baxter and Bob together to discuss what they could do and they decided to send Dr Mennell over to Hyères to take charge of the treatment – nominally at their expense, though it was Thomas Stevenson, predictably, who ended up paying the bill. Mennell stayed about a week, established that his patient's case was not hopeless and left Fanny a set of instructions for various possible emergencies. His prognosis was that several small arteries in the lung had ruptured and that Stevenson should for the time being have no excitement or disturbance of any kind. The patient would be very frail in the short term but not necessarily forever: 'I see no reason why he should not live for some years to come and even get much stronger than he is now,' the doctor wrote to Baxter.

On Mennell's advice, Louis was to return to the spa at Royat, but Thomas and Margaret Stevenson had to be dissuaded from joining him there for fear of overtaxing his strength (which was nil: Fanny had to lift him in and out of bed at this period). Walter Ferrier's sister, Elizabeth ('Coggie'), who had been with them for weeks already in Hyères, was to accompany them, and Valentine Roch. It was a terrible period for Fanny, harrowed by worry, long wakeful nights and her husband's alarming switches of temper, as she described to Baxter and Henley: 'He is very unlike himself, very irritable and angry [. . .] He is in a very curious state [. . .] and takes everything seriously and as an insult.'[79] He improved a little in his weeks at Royat, but there was to be no return to Hyères. An outbreak of cholera there persuaded Fanny that it would be too much of a risk to go back, but their decision to go on to London in July instead of making for another resort such as Nice or Menton was surprising. It may have been influenced by the fact that Henley had arranged for *Deacon Brodie* to be performed at the Prince's Theatre that month, starring (if that's quite the right word) his younger brother Teddy. Though Stevenson by now thought the play 'dam bad', he realised its importance to Henley: 'It is about Henley, not *Brodie*, that I care,' he wrote to Colvin on the eve of his return to England.[80] In London, there would be a chance to see the friends and colleagues who had expressed such acute anxiety about his health, as well as to have medical consultations. Like all Stevenson's arrangements, things didn't turn out as planned. Their chattels were abandoned in the South of France for almost a year, until Fanny could get over to fetch them and shut up the quaint little hillside chalet, with its birds and trees, picturesque ruins and sweeping views, 'Eden and Beulah and the Delectable Mountains and Eldorado', as Stevenson had once described it,[81] all rolled into one.

9

A WEEVIL IN A BISCUIT

Minor ailments. A knowledge of these gives considerable help towards understanding the 'constitution' of a person, and it is a matter of great interest to learn the connection between the family tendency to minor and to graver maladies. The former may be outlets and safety valves to prevent the occurrence of the latter.

Francis Galton, *Record of Family Faculties*

WHEN THE CURTAIN WENT UP on the matinée performance of *Deacon Brodie* on 2 July 1884, the audience was full of Stevenson's friends and admirers: Henley, of course, Colvin, Gosse, Leslie Stephen, Robert Browning and Henry James, a friend of Colvin and of Gosse. Fanny was there too, and Stevenson's parents, but he himself, having rushed in from France the previous day, was too exhausted to attend. He spent the evening alone at his hotel, a potent absence that was guaranteed to quicken his friends' sympathies and concern.

The audience at the Prince's Theatre was enthusiastic and the few reviews polite, but this was more to honour the authors than the play itself, which no one liked much, apart from Henley. The curtain call at the end of the performance rather went to the big man's head and he was soon predicting huge success, but Colvin, as always, was quick with cold water and wrote to him, 'I thought I felt [the public's] pulse too, and that by the play as a whole they were disappointed, baffled, and thrown out. [...] the Deacon is, as you have written him, morally unintelligible, unconvincing, and

non-existent, neither can any amount of brilliant speeches or effective acting make him otherwise.'[1] But Henley's confidence was
robust enough to withstand even such forthright criticism, and he
went down to Richmond, where the Stevenson entourage had
settled temporarily, full of plans for more collaborations. His vitality was tonic to Stevenson, and his enthusiasm infectious. Within
weeks they were working on two more plays, *Beau Austin* and
Admiral Guinea.

The question of where Louis was going to live next was urgent.
George Balfour was in town, and Dr Mennell, both of whom
gave good reports of his health and strongly implied that Fanny
must have been exaggerating his symptoms. There was no reason
why he shouldn't live in England, they said. Fanny took exception
to this (either from the slur on her judgement or the prospect of
having to stay in Britain, or both) and insisted on another opinion.
Her specialist said exactly the opposite: both lungs were seriously
affected and Stevenson should repair to the Alps again for the
winter. This inability to get consistent or definitive diagnoses kept
the prospect of recovery forever at bay, as the patient remarked
tetchily a few months later: 'the doctors all seem agreed in
saying that my complaint is quite unknown and will allow of
no prognosis'.[2] Duty rather than doctors finally swayed the couple
towards wintering on the south coast, as Thomas Stevenson's visible decline made Louis anxious to be as near home as he could
manage. England would do for a while; there were the joint projects with Henley to sustain him and some sense of literary life.
There was Sam, too, cramming for university at a tutor's in
Bournemouth. On a trip down to see him, Fanny and Louis decided
to make their base there, first in lodgings, then at their first real
home.

Bournemouth was a popular destination for invalids, being
sheltered, relatively warm (for Britain) and only a couple of hours'
train ride from the capital, but Stevenson's health didn't improve
at all during his three years in the town, and he later described his
existence there as like that of 'a weevil in a biscuit'.[3] His first six

months were spent coughing, first from his lung haemorrhage, then from the complications of a protracted 'flu which Fanny blamed on her mother-in-law or Henley, depending on whom she was more annoyed with at the time. Stevenson's description of his symptoms is pitiful: the morphine he had been prescribed for the cough made him vomit, he couldn't eat, had 'a smart fever, with shivers and aches of the beastliest; and am fit for nothing but sleep. Now, I sweat all the time, day and night. The cough is from the throat, which is in a state of fine congestion; uvula much elongated; sores all over; larynx and pharynx both involved; lung not very bad; liver, all things considered, wonderful, but Robert Louis Stevenson in a devil of a decayed state.'[4]

The morphine didn't just affect his stomach. Quite often in the letters of this period he seems to be on automatic pilot, distracted or mentally disconnected, as in this ending of a letter to Colvin:

[Drawing of a hat]

A HAT

[Drawing of a house]

A SMALL HOUSE IN THE MOUNTAINS OF ETRURIA.
THE DOOR IS ON THE OTHER SIDE.
AND CAN ONLY BE SHOWN IN ANOTHER PICTURE.

[Drawing of a door]

DOOR OF THE HOUSE[5]

In September, Stevenson complained of being 'full of the vilest drugs', 'stupid' and 'Mind gone'; the lethargy and inability to concentrate which morphine caused were quite unlike the giddying highs and happy, warm feelings he had previously got from opium, cocaine and hashish. By November he was writing to Henley, 'I am not sure that my incapacity to work is wholly due to illness; I believe the morphine I have been taking for my bray, may have a hand in it. It moderates the bray; but I think sews up the donkey.'[6] Worst of all, morphine gave him nightmares of a particularly vivid and terrifying nature. His waking hours were spent in a daze and his nights in restlessness or horror.

Not surprisingly, the work he attempted to do under these circumstances was sometimes pretty poor. In 1893 he recalled the 'waves of faintness and nausea' through which he had composed one of the plays with Henley. Henley himself was stubbornly insensitive to his friend's weakness, or decided that he knew best what would distract him from it. He made frequent visits to Bournemouth throughout the autumn of 1884 to cheer the invalid along with their new projects and even tried to invite himself for Christmas Day so they could carry on 'making changes in ye *Beau*'.[7] They were both still persuaded that the theatre could earn them serious money: the reception of *Deacon Brodie* seemed promising, and they were flattered when the actor-producer H. Beerbohm Tree suggested they adapt a French melodrama for him, *L'Auberge des Andrêts* by Frédéric Dumont (called *Macaire* in the English version). Beerbohm Tree pulled out of the project about a year later and *Macaire* was never produced, but the play – unpromisingly subtitled 'A Melodramatic Farce' – is interesting for its close family resemblance to all Stevenson's other double-life narratives. The character of Macaire was not new to Stevenson; he had been one of the heroes of Skelt's Juvenile Drama, mentioned by name in Stevenson's homage to Skelt, 'A Penny Plain and Twopence Coloured', but in his and Henley's adult play Macaire's speeches about his delight in deception could come straight from the mouth of Edward Hyde, or Long John Silver, or Deacon Brodie, or – with a more ironic inflection – that of Markheim, the conscience-stricken murderer in a story Stevenson wrote during that first Bournemouth winter: 'Blessings on that frontier line! The criminal hops across, and lo! The reputable man. [...] What is crime? discovery. Virtue? opportunity.'[8] It's a vivid illustration of the way things came round again and again in Stevenson's imagination, and almost got trapped there: *Macaire* adapted Dumont, repeated Skelt, but also anticipated *Dr Jekyll and Mr Hyde*, reprised *Deacon Brodie* and *Treasure Island*, ventriloquised 'Markheim'.

Skelt was the least useful of all Stevenson's returning obsessions. The antique ghost flapped fatuously round the new plays that Stevenson and Henley were rattling off that autumn, which read now more like sickroom pastimes than works of art, full of stock characters and low-grade melodrama. Henley thought they signified 'hope for the British Drama yet',[9] but when Beerbohm Tree came down to Bournemouth to hear parts of *Macaire* read aloud, he found it so hard to keep awake that he had to keep prodding his leg with a hatpin he had taken from Fanny's dressing room.[10] *Beau Austin*, a short piece set in the Regency period on the theme of husband-making, was no better. A noble-hearted heiress called Dorothy is forced into company again with her seducer, the worldly and callous Beau Austin, when she visits Tunbridge Wells. Through the protests of her admirer Fenwick and her brother Anthony, Austin is made to see the error of his ways (this happens instantly) and proposes to his spurned mistress. But though she is 'ruined' (and secretly still loves Austin) Dorothy is a woman of principle, and refuses him. This cements Austin's admiration ('she is fit to be a queen!'[11]) and after a skirmish with Anthony, he makes a public declaration of his guilt and his love for Dorothy in front of the Duke of York and other representatives of high society (all of whom remain speechless, as well they might). For some reason, Dorothy now finds him acceptable, and the play ends quickly with her saying, 'My hero! Take me!'

Admiral Guinea is almost as bad a play, but more interesting in terms of what was going on – or not – in Stevenson's mind. Its reusing of several elements from *Treasure Island* shows not just a paucity of invention but a strange despoiling or defacing of what Stevenson had already achieved in that book. Captain John Gaunt, a reformed slaver (formerly known as 'Admiral Guinea'), is faced with the prospect of his only daughter wanting to marry a man who is very like himself when young, a privateer. He withholds permission to the match, sending the youth (Kit) off on a drinking binge during which he is persuaded by a disaffected old comrade of Gaunt, David Pew, to rob the captain's sea-chest, which they suppose full of treasure. The attempted burglary is interrupted and Kit is set up by Pew to take the blame, a hanging matter. The captain's treasure turns out to be mementoes of his dead wife, a pious woman who wasted away in spiritual distress following an incident at sea when Gaunt caused the deaths of over two hundred slaves. Her example led to Gaunt's reform, and her daughter's pleadings similarly move him to release Kit and agree to the marriage.

The references to *Treasure Island* are clumsily insistent: the play is set in Barnstaple, partly at the Admiral Benbow inn; Pew is the same blind blackguard as in the novel, though much more coarsely characterised; Pew's tap-tapping with his stick announces his approach; a sea-chest is raided, a shanty sung, Flint the pirate and the *Walrus* are invoked. The indulgence of reprising such details indicates that Henley and Stevenson thought this little playlet could really be put on a level with the increasingly famous novel; indeed, *Treasure Island* being 'a story for boys' and *Admiral Guinea* 'hope for the British Drama', they possibly considered it superior. Or at least, perhaps Henley did. The following year, looking back through *Admiral Guinea*, Stevenson had nothing but harsh words to say of it:

> God man, it is a low, black dirty, blackguard, ragged piece: vomitable in many parts – simply vomitable. Pew is in places, a reproach to both art and man. [. . .] I believe in playing dark with second and third-rate work. Do not let us *gober* [overvalue] ourselves – and above all, not *gober* dam potboilers.[12]

Stevenson's growing displeasure with *Admiral Guinea* was partly due to his father's strong criticism of the play. When he read it in the autumn of 1884, Thomas Stevenson, depressed and ill, wrote back to his son that it was 'far too much for me. The combination or at least proximity of Nonconformist pious slang with the crawling obscenity of Pew is to me past all endurance and I must say that I cannot agree to pay for propagating such a production unless it can be altered [. . .] my intense solicitude for your fame compels me thus to write.'[13] Clearly, Thomas had been called upon to foot the printer's bill again (*Admiral Guinea*, like *Beau Austin*, was privately produced), and felt he had a right as well as a responsibility to voice his objections, as he had done so often before. A modern reader might puzzle over his cavilling, for the play is very moralistic and the anxious, God-fearing, guilt-ridden, Bible-reading main character is very like Thomas Stevenson himself. Perhaps it was that resemblance more than the nonconformist slang that stuck in the old man's craw.

The persistence of Stevenson and Henley in writing plays is more remarkable than their persistent failure. They could hardly have done other than fail, with so little knowledge of, interest in or sympathy with what was going on in contemporary British theatre. Stevenson never witnessed a performance of one of his own plays – not a rehearsal even – and seemed queerly unconcerned about the fact. Indeed there is a sense in which he seems to have been deliberately *avoiding* his own plays, as if seeing them would spoil the entertainment he derived from them in his head. Lecturing on 'Stevenson as a Dramatist' in 1903, the playwright Arthur Wing Pinero could hardly restrain his scorn of Stevenson's presumption: 'he was deliberately using outworn models, and doing it, too, in a sportive, half-disdainful spirit'.[14] Stevenson had dramatic but no theatrical talent, Pinero concluded, and lacked the application to acquire it. So the plays drowned in fine writing, the authors aiming at 'absolute beauty of words, such beauty as Ruskin or Pater or Newman might achieve in an eloquent passage, not the beauty of dramatic fitness to the character and the situation'.[15]

'Stevenson, I think, came soonest out of the spell,' Lloyd Osbourne wrote later of the partnership with Henley, 'was the first to rub his eyes and recover his common sense.'[16] Towards the end of the first year in England, Stevenson's interest in the plays was waning, but by then he was writing *Kidnapped* and *Dr Jekyll*, and Henley was writing – nothing much. The balance had shifted between them over the years, as Henley remarked to Baxter: 'Louis has grown faster than I have.'[17]

And of course there was another obstacle to the partnership flourishing: 'the Bedlamite', as Henley called Fanny: 'I love her,' he protested unconvincingly to Baxter, 'but I won't collaborate with her *and* her husband, and I begin to feel that the one means both.'[18] Fanny was always outwardly friendly towards Henley for her husband's sake, but her relations with the blustering, noisy poet were stiffening considerably on closer acquaintance. Henley visited too often, stayed too long, over-excited Louis and drank all the whisky. Fanny expressed enthusiasm for the new plays and even tried to contribute ideas to them, but her prime concern became to limit Henley's monopoly of her husband's attention, monitor his behaviour around the invalid and stand guard over their *tête-à-têtes*. Henley, unsurprisingly, was scornful of her posing as guard dog to his old friend, and was, by implication, critical of Louis for tolerating it.

Fanny was beginning to have confidence in her own writing, and perhaps had real ambitions for it. *Prince Otto* had made her feel indispensable, and Louis was planning a sequel to *New Arabian Nights* to which she was contributing not just ideas but whole chapters, specifically the Mormon story, 'The Destroying Angel' and 'The Fair Cuban', which features human sacrifice and voodoo. She was writing stories for separate publication too (although they didn't always get accepted, even when covered by letters from her husband). According to Fanny, the whole idea of *The Dynamiter* was her work, derived from stories that she made up to entertain Louis when he was bedridden in Hyères, which they later thought of making into a linked collection. They share the title page, but Fanny never claimed responsibility for the final draft, which seems to have been mostly Stevenson's doing, warts and all, and in his accounts of the hard work he did on the book through the early winter of 1884 he always refers to 'my', rather than 'our', 'Arabs'. In fact it followed the pattern typical of Stevenson's collaborations, with the collaborator providing plot-lines and situations that he could work on, but he retaining overall control of the final version.

More New Arabian Nights: The Dynamiter is, like its prede-cessor, a combination of realism and camp. We are back in the 'fairy London' of the earlier book, but instead of it being the backdrop to the individualised psychodramas of the Suicide Club, the city now plays a more causative role, presenting a rich, menac-ing sea of possibilities. This is a modern cosmopolis, noisy and bustling ('London roars like the noise of battle; four million desti-nies are here concentred'[19]), which depersonalises its inhabitants and – in Stevenson's vision – seems to feed off the process:

> as he advanced into the labyrinth of the south-west, his ear was gradually mastered by the silence. Street after street looked down upon his solitary figure, house after house echoed upon his passage with a ghostly jar, shop after shop displayed its shuttered front and its commercial legend; and meanwhile he steered his course, under day's effulgent dome and through this encampment of diurnal sleepers, lonely as a ship.[20]

Here we get a glimpse of the sinister city in which Stevenson locates Dr Jekyll, the London, too, of Sherlock Holmes, Dorian Gray, Conrad's *The Secret Agent*. It is also the 'dreadful city' of the *fin de siècle*, that obsessed and oppressed the poets Arthur Symons, Lionel Johnson and Ernest Dowson. In *The Dynamiter*, London both consumes and conceals people: the three idle young men who set out at the beginning of the book to seize every opportunity of adventure (and perhaps get the reward for tracking down a wanted man) are lured into company where class and motives have been rendered indecipherable, into buildings which are abandoned, or become prisons, or are in danger of being blown up. The structure lacks the cohesiveness of the Suicide Club stories (and Fanny Stevenson's contributions are gripping but, literally, outlandish, with their distracting removal of the narrative to a Mormon settlement in the American far west and a Caribbean swamp), but the book was also surprisingly topical and politically partisan, drawing together a number of rather disconnected narratives under a frame story about terrorists. The Fenians about whom Stevenson had wanted to write a play in 1883 had not gone to waste: here is M'Guire on his way to plant a bomb in central London, released into a kind of ecstasy as the device ticks down:

> It seemed as if a sudden, genial heat were spread about his brain; for a second or two, he saw the world as red as blood; and thereafter entered into a complete possession of himself, with an incredible cheerfulness of spirits, prompting him to sing and chuckle as he walked. And yet this mirth seemed to belong to things external; and within, like a black and leaden-heavy kernel, he was conscious of the weight upon his soul.[21]

The bomb outrages of the early 1880s, perpetrated by campaigners for Home Rule for Ireland, had appalled the staunch Unionist Stevenson, who despised the cowardliness of the acts. He satirises the bombers freely in this story, showing their complacency about taking 'generous stipends' from supporters and their beastly attempts to give a bomb to a little girl in the street. But Stevenson also recognises and exploits the dramatic potential of the situation. The 'genial heat' of M'Guire's bloody vision becomes cold panic when he realises that he hasn't got enough change to discharge the cab in which the bomb has been left. The extraordinariness of his mission has made him overlook this essential detail, and he is forced to borrow the sum from Mr Godall the cigar merchant (Prince Florizel from the earlier stories, in disguise), who happens to be passing. Godall is wordy; precious seconds pass, and – disastrously – the sharp-eyed cabbie makes M'Guire remove the bag from the taxi. The desperate bomber, knowing that the device is about to explode, has to rush towards the Embankment and throw the bag into the river, an action so energetic that he falls in after it and drowns.

The bag in question is a Gladstone bag – no mistaking there whom Stevenson held culpable for succouring the terrorists. But the most explicit political statement in the book is its dedication to two members of the Metropolitan Police, William Cole and Thomas Cox, both seriously injured while removing an explosive device from Westminster Hall in January 1885 (between Stevenson finishing the book and its printing). Two days later, General Gordon was killed at Khartoum after a ten-month siege, causing a huge public outcry against the Whig government for not having sent relief forces earlier. Stevenson mentions Gordon's 'tragic enterprise' in his address to Cole and Cox in *The Dynamiter*; privately he was deeply shaken by the 'ineffable shame' to the nation that both incidents exposed. On hearing of Gordon's death, Gladstone was reputed to have said, 'It is the man's own temerity,' a remark that infuriated Stevenson, who wrote to Symonds:

> *Voilà le Bourgeois! le voilà nu!* But why should I blame Glad-
> stone, when I too am a Bourgeois? when I have held my
> peace? Why did I hold my peace? Because I am a sceptic: i.e.
> a Bourgeois. We believe in nothing, Symonds: you don't, and
> I don't; and these are two reasons, out of a handful of mil-
> lions, why England stands before the world dripping with
> blood and daubed with dishonour. I will first try to take the
> beam out of my own eye; trusting that even private effort
> somehow betters and braces the general atmosphere. See, for
> example, if England has shown (I put it hypothetically) one
> spark of manly sensibility, they have been shamed into it by
> the spectacle of Gordon. Impotent and small and (if you like)
> spiteful as it is, the mere fact of people taking their names off
> the Gordon Memorial Committee rather than sit thereon with
> Gladstone, is the first glimmer of a sense of responsibility that
> I have observed.[22]

Gladstone had been an avid reader of *Treasure Island*, apparently unable to put the book down, so it's not unlikely that he read *The*

Dynamiter too when it was published just over a year later. He certainly read *Dr Jekyll and Mr Hyde* in 1886 ('while forming a ministry' according to F.H.W. Myers, whose sister-in-law had given the Prime Minister the book[23]) and admired that. Perhaps he was too much 'a man of fog, evasions [. . .] and a general deliquescence of the spine' – as Stevenson described him to Colvin[24] – to get riled by the virulent anti-Fenianism of Stevenson's stories – if he perceived it fully.

The decline of Thomas Stevenson into almost permanent ill-health, depression and senility darkened the years in Bournemouth profoundly. Parents and child were seeing more of each other than for years, so dissimulation was difficult, and though Louis played down his symptoms as much as he could so as not to distress his father, at times it must have seemed that they were proceeding towards the grave pretty much apace. Thinking it would cheer and stimulate him (and show how much he was respected professionally), Louis encouraged his father to stand for election as president of the Royal Society of Edinburgh in 1884, which, under duress, Thomas did, and won. But just about the only person not to be pleased by this result was Thomas himself, who said it made him 'sadly perplexed' and reckoned that it was seniority, not ability, that had secured the appointment. This response, while realistically admitting what everyone else denied – i.e. that Thomas was no longer capable of performing the duties of the president – displays a sort of ill grace which was conspicuously absent from Louis's repertoire of behaviour and which he may have studied to avoid.

The Stevenson parents were in no doubt of Fanny's dislike of England and eagerness to get abroad again, perhaps to America, and it was partly as a bribe to her – or reward for her patience thus far – that early in 1885 they offered to buy her a house in Bournemouth and furnish it. This was too good to refuse, and in April Louis and Fanny moved into a yellow-brick villa on Alum Chine Road, about a mile's walk from the sea along the shady, pine-wooded gully of the Chine in an area that was still mostly heathland. The house had grounds of about an acre, with a pigeon house, a stable and coach house they never used, and a kitchen garden where Fanny grew corn, tomatoes, raspberries and salad leaves (a much better diet than most British people could dream of at that date, even if it must have been a struggle to get the tomatoes to ripen to anything approaching Californian standards). Towards the end of the garden the ground dropped away into a steep heather-covered slope with rhododendrons and a thin stream at the bottom, like a genteel version of the platform at Silverado. Stevenson liked to sun himself at the top of this bank, which faced the trees of the Chine, with the sea just out of sight beyond. In fact, though the house was called 'Sea View', the sea was only visible in a chink from one upper window. They renamed it 'Skerryvore' in honour of Alan Stevenson's *chef d'oeuvre*, and Louis hung a ship's bell from a wreck at the lighthouse at the back of the house under a little wooden canopy: an odd memento, when you think about it.

The house itself cost an enormous £1700, and £500 more was spent on the furnishings. Thomas Stevenson took his daughter-in-law on a shopping spree in London, clearly hoping that he could pin the couple down with possessions. There were old oak boxes and yellow damask throws in the drawing room, with a carved figure of St Cecilia and two Japanese vases on the mantel which were a present from Katherine de Mattos. 'Skerryvore will not look much like other people's houses,' Fanny wrote to her mother-in-law, 'but it will please me so much more than if it did.'[25] Louis got carried away in a curiosity shop and bought a chest decorated with eighteenth-century prints and a convex mirror which he thought 'sublime', adding comically, 'no picture can be so decorative and so cheerful'.[26] Over the fireplace in the 'Blue Room' hung Turner's engraving of the Bell Rock Lighthouse, with two Piranesi etchings opposite; and as the months went by the walls filled up, with photographs of Henley and Colvin, with landscapes, portraits, 'a small armoury of buccaneering weapons'[27] in tribute to

Treasure Island, and a two-foot-high plaster group by Auguste Rodin called *Le Printemps*, a gift from the artist, whose Paris studio the Stevensons had visited in 1886.* The style of the interior was sparse by high-Victorian standards, but as neither Louis nor Fanny was used to accumulating things, it amused and amazed them to look round their suburban home. Fanny recounted her husband coming downstairs one day and saying, 'This room is so beautiful that it positively gives me a qualm.'[29] And with the mirror reflecting at maximum azimuth their newly-acquired goods and the satisfied smiles of his wife, Stevenson was able to report 'my mind shows symptoms, I think, of reawakening'.[30]

It was during this first year in Bournemouth that the best and most evocative portrait of Stevenson was painted, by John Singer Sargent, who had already done one painting of him the previous December and who was later commissioned to do another by some wealthy American admirers of the writer. 'I was very much impressed by him,' Sargent wrote later to Henry James, 'he seemed to me the most intense creature I had ever met.'[31] The 1885 portrait shows Stevenson and Fanny in the dining room at 'Skerryvore', he in motion, to the left of the frame, she seated and half out of the picture to the right, with a dark doorway just off-centre between them, open and showing the muted light from an outside door at the end of a shadowy hallway. Louis's face and hands reflect some light from behind the observer's view; there is also a concentrated shimmering effect from the exotic costume in which Fanny appears (the theatricality of which is striking) and some reflected light off two prints on the wall, again half out of the frame, but the rest of the picture is very dark. 'Sargent was down again and painted a portrait of me walking about in my own dining room, in my own velveteen jacket and twisting, as I go my own moustache,' Stevenson reported to Will Low:

---

* Fanny had been shocked on that occasion by 'the brutal coarseness of Rodin's work [...] he and Louis had, continually, to stand between me and the works lest I should see them'.[28] Rodin was a friend of Henley, and made a striking head of the poet in bronze, copies of which are in the National Portrait Galleries of Scotland and England.

At one corner a glimpse of my wife in an Indian dress and seated in a chair that was once my grandfather's [...] adds a touch of poesy and comicality. It is, I think, excellent; but it is too eccentric to be exhibited. I am at one extreme corner; my wife, in this wild dress and looking like a ghost, is at the extreme other end; between us an open door exhibits my palatial entrance hall and part of my respected staircase. All this is touched in lovely, with that witty touch of Sargent's; but of course it looks damn queer as a whole.[32]

Stevenson wasn't the only person to think it queer (he described it to Sargent as resembling a 'caged maniac lecturing about the foreign specimen in the corner'[33]). When the picture was framed and varnished, Sargent sent it round to Colvin's 'to know whether he considers it interesting or obnoxious'. Sargent had been disappointed when the first friend he showed it to judged the composition 'paradoxical': 'It ought not to be in the least,' the painter wrote to Stevenson, 'so perhaps it is unlucky that I did not cut it down to a single figure like this [here he sketched Louis standing alone]: we will see.'[34] Fortunately Sargent left the canvas as it was. The unconventional arrangement of the figures gives the effect of a viewfinder having moved out of its original alignment, as the eye of the beholder follows the movements of the pacing figure. The effect is of restless motion, 'caged' indeed in this domestic prison (the claustrophobic dimensions and darkness of which are obvious), with Fanny in her finery at the original centre of the group and Louis going back and forth in front of her like a nervy pendulum.

The chair in which Fanny appears in the picture had belonged to Louis's grandfather, but was renamed at about this time 'Henry James's chair' in honour of the novelist, with whom Stevenson had struck up a mutually admiring friendship. They had met six years before in London, when James's impression had been of 'a shirt-collarless Bohemian and a great deal (in an inoffensive way) of a poseur',[35] and Stevenson had dismissed James as 'a mere club fizzle'. But neither writer had read the other's works at that date.

By 1884, James was happy to pay Stevenson a compliment in an essay called 'The Art of Fiction', saying that *Treasure Island* 'succeeded wonderfully in what it attempts'. This was part of James's reply to issues raised earlier in the year by Walter Besant (later founder of the Society of Authors), who said that novel-writing should have a 'conscious moral purpose', also that writers shouldn't stray beyond what they knew first-hand. James counter-argued that the novel should not have a conscious moral purpose at all but should 'trace the implication of things' and deal with 'all life, all feeling, all observation, all vision'. The novel should 'compete with life' and recreate reality, as painting did; 'as the picture is reality, so the novel is history'. It was probably this part of James's article that Stevenson thought 'dreadful nonsense' when he read the piece in *Longman's Magazine* in September,[36] as he addresses the analogy in his reply published three months later in the same magazine. Stevenson's essay, 'A Humble Remonstrance', contends that the novel is never a 'transcript of life', but a signifi-cant, and essentially artful, simplification of some aspect of it; the very difference of fiction from reality constitutes both 'the method and the meaning of the work':

> Our art is occupied, and bound to be occupied, not so much in making stories true as in making them typical; not so much in capturing the lineaments of each fact, as in mar-shalling all of them towards a common end. For the welter of impressions, all forcible but all discrete, which life presents, it substitutes a certain artificial series of impressions, all indeed most feebly represented, but all aiming to the same effect.[37]

As with all subjects that were near to his heart, Stevenson couldn't help getting carried away with the force of his own argument, restating it with escalating eloquence:

> Life is monstrous, infinite, illogical, abrupt and poignant; a work of art, in comparison, is neat, finite, self-contained, rational, flowing and emasculate. Life imposes by brute energy, like inarticulate thunder; art catches the ear, among

the far louder noises of experience, like an air artificially made by a discreet musician.[38]

Questions of literary craft were rarely raised in public at that date, and Stevenson relished the chance to air his views. But James responded to the brilliance of the article rather than to its argument. He wrote immediately to Stevenson promising 'not words of discussion, dissent, retort or remonstrance, but of hearty sympathy, charged with the assurance of my enjoyment of everything you write. It's a luxury, in this immoral age, to encounter some one who *does* write – who is really acquainted with that lovely art.'[39] This sort of thing was always happening. Stevenson would speak his mind, and be rewarded by compliments to his 'lovely art' and 'the native *gaiety* of all that you write', as James went on to say. His reply to James's letter was very friendly, but insisted on taking the debate further:

> Seriously, from the dearth of information and thoughtful interest in the art of literature, those who try to practise it with any deliberate purpose run the risk of finding no fit audience. People suppose that it is 'the stuff' that interests them; they think, for instance, that the prodigious fine thoughts and sentiments in Shakespeare impress by their own weight, not understanding that the unpolished diamond is but a stone. They think that striking situations, or good dialogue, are got by studying life; they will not rise to understand that they are prepared by deliberate artifice and set off by painful suppressions. Now, I want the whole thing well ventilated, for my own education and the public's, and I beg you to look as quick as you can, to follow me up with every circumstance of defeat where we differ, and [...] to emphasise the points where we agree.[40]

'James is to make a rejoinder,' Stevenson told Henley in March, anticipating the chance to write another himself. He was disappointed with the small space he had been allotted for the first article and had grand schemes to follow them both with a 'Treatise of the Art of Literature', 'a small, arid book that shall some day appear'.[41] But it didn't, despite Stevenson spending his Christmas holiday in bed writing a piece 'On Some Technical Elements in Style'. James was much more interested in cultivating the Scotsman's friendship than immediately engaging his views on a theory of writing. The irony is that James is always hauled out as a kind of sponsor to Stevenson's literary credibility, proof that Stevenson could engage the serious attention of serious writers among his contemporaries, that he was not just a romancer and pale *belle lettrist*. But here we have evidence that James to some extent sidelined or neutralised Stevenson's seriousness and, wittingly or not, encouraged him to stick to '*gaiety*'.

Circumstances helped cement the friendship, for James's invalid sister Alice was moved to Bournemouth early in 1885 for her health, and by the spring James had decided to take rooms in the town to make visiting her easier (and to work on his novel *The Bostonians*). He called at Skerryvore as soon as he could, and after an initial misunderstanding with Valentine at the door (she mistook him for a tradesman) found his host very friendly, clever and wonderfully animated; 'an interesting, charming creature [...] more or less dying here', he wrote to William Dean Howells.[42] Soon James was visiting every evening, sitting in 'his' chair, being plied with drink and conversation. He was bearded at that date, forty-one years old, and bore, Fanny thought, a strong resemblance to another frequent visitor to Bournemouth, the Prince of Wales (who had set up his glamorous mistress, Lillie Langtry, in a house very close to Alum Chine Road). She described James comically to her mother-in-law as 'a gentle, amiable, soothing, sleepy sort, fat and dimpled',[43] but was pleased and proud to have such a distinguished fellow countryman their particular friend; James had better manners and a less *English* snobbism than many of Louis's acquaintances, and made none of those invidious bachelor-days comparisons that underlay all Henley's talk. Fanny made an American meal in his honour on 19 May, the couple's fifth wedding anniversary, at which he was the only guest, and James responded by buying them another mirror, about which Stevenson wrote 'The Mirror Speaks':

Long I none but dealers saw;
Till before my silent eye
One that sees came passing by.
Now with an outlandish grace,
To the sparkling fire I face
In the blue room at Skerryvore;
Where I wait until the door
Open, and the Prince of Men,
Henry James, shall come again.

'Prince of Men' is a powerful compliment, and James paid plenty in return, especially after Stevenson was dead, when he seemed virtually inconsolable. The strength of James's feelings then – not particularly easy to have guessed from his behaviour towards Stevenson during his lifetime – is very evident in a letter to Gosse of 17 December 1894:

> I meant to write to you tonight on another matter – but of what can one think, or utter or dream, save of this ghastly extinction of the beloved R.L.S.? It is too miserable for cold words – it's an absolute desolation. It makes me cold and sick – and with the absolute, almost alarmed sense, of the visible, material quenching of an indispensable light.[44]

The dynamics of the Stevenson marriage fascinated Henry James. While he delighted in the brilliant company of the husband, privately he had a low opinion of the wife, a 'poor, barbarous and merely instinctive lady',[45] as he described her later, whose association with Stevenson had raised her up a little, but only temporarily. Alice James was even harsher, and wrote in her diary five years later that Fanny looked like 'an appendage to a hand organ' (i.e. a monkey), compounding the idea of 'primitiveness' with the remark that Mrs Stevenson's powerful egotism produced 'the strangest feeling of being in the presence of an unclothed being'.[46] No wonder the Stevensons' later removal to Samoa was so easy to caricature as a form of 'going native': in the eyes of polite society Fanny was halfway there already.

Stevenson himself shared much of this view of Fanny as 'primitive' and 'instinctive', though to him those were not terms of abuse. He often classified her as 'other' – indeed, that was the essence of her attraction for him – addressing her jokily in letters ('Dear weird woman', 'My dear fellow', 'Dear Dutchwoman') and describing her as 'the foreign specimen' in Sargent's portrait. But sometimes there was a sharper edge to his characterisation of his wife. To Henley and to his parents (interesting choices) he satirised her as a powerful machine called 'the Vandegrifter' that he ran the risk of getting caught in daily. In one letter he describes having 'got my little finger into a steam press called the Vandegrifter (patent) and my whole body and soul had to go through after it. I came out as limp as a lady's novel, but the Vandegrifter suffered in the process, and is fairly knocked about.'[47] The unsentimentality of this is a kind of compliment, but not much of one, especially when written for Henley's eyes. In a letter to James about the same time, he served up this description of one of his and Fanny's quarrels:

> [My wife] is a woman (as you know) not without art: the art of extracting the gloom of the eclipse from sunshine; and she has recently laboured in this field not without success or (as we used to say) not without a blessing. It is strange: 'we fell out my wife and I' the other night; she tackled me savagely for being a canary-bird; I replied (bleatingly) protesting that there was no use turning life into King Lear; presently it was discovered that there were two dead combatants upon the field, each slain by an arrow of the truth, and we tenderly carried off each other's corpses. Here is a little comedy for Henry James to write! The beauty was each thought the other quite unscathed at first. But we had dealt shrewd stabs.[48]

This is a fellow novelist's observation rather than a husband's. That '(as you know)' is a particularly conspiratorial touch, for the likelihood of the two men having spoken openly about Fanny's quirks of temperament was nil; but this was Stevenson's way of indicating that he had seen James watching the situation – and had been doing so himself.

*　　*　　*

In 'A Humble Remonstrance', written in November 1884, Stevenson had spoken of how fiction 'substitutes a certain artificial series of impressions' for 'the welter of impressions, all forcible but all discrete, which life presents'. At exactly the same time, he was working on a story which was one of the most ambitious of his career and which conveys just that 'welter of impressions' that he suggested was unachievable. 'Markheim' is the story of a murder and its immediate aftermath, a 'shocker' thought up and written quickly for the 1884 Christmas number of the *Pall Mall Gazette*. It turned out too short, so was held back, allowing Stevenson time to revise it extensively for Unwin's Christmas annual the following year (Stevenson's 1881 story 'The Body Snatcher', full of gruesome gothic, was sent as substitute to *Pall Mall*). The story begins in a pawnshop on Christmas Day, with a nervous young man, Markheim, purporting to want to buy something. The dealer who runs the shop is sarcastic, having only known Markheim hitherto as a supplier of stolen goods, and he becomes impatient when his increasingly excitable customer seems to be wasting time with talk of charity and love, saying, 'I in love! I never had the time, nor have I the time to-day for all this nonsense.' This seals the dealer's fate, allowing Markheim to carry through his real purpose, which is to murder and rob him: 'the long, skewer-like dagger flashed and fell. The dealer struggled like a hen, striking his temple on the shelf, and then tumbled on the floor in a heap.'[49] In the aftermath of the crime, Markheim is almost in a trance:

> Time had some score of small voices in that shop, some stately and slow as was becoming to their great age; others garrulous and hurried. All these told out the seconds in an intricate chorus of tickings. Then the passage of a lad's feet, heavily running on the pavement, broke in upon these smaller voices and startled Markheim into the consciousness of his surroundings. He looked about him awfully. The candle stood on the counter, its flame solemnly wagging in a draught; and by that inconsiderable movement, the whole room was filled with noiseless bustle and kept heaving like a sea: the tall

shadows nodding, the gross blots of darkness swelling and dwindling as with respiration, the faces of the portraits and the china gods changing and wavering like images in water. The inner door stood ajar, and peered into that leaguer of shadows with a long slit of daylight like a pointing finger.[50]

Convinced that someone must have heard the murder being committed, Markheim's imagination torments him with visions of imminent discovery, and he comes to feel that there is a presence in the building: 'now it was a faceless thing, and yet had eyes to see with; and again it was a shadow of himself; and yet again [he] beheld the image of the dead dealer, reinspired with cunning and hatred'. His worst fears are confirmed when he is upstairs searching for the dealer's cash and hears a step, then sees the door handle turn. What follows is a great coup of suspense writing, as unguessable as it is bizarre:

> What to expect he knew not, whether the dead man walking, or the official ministers of human justice, or some chance witness blindly stumbling in to consign him to the gallows. But when a face was thrust into the aperture, glanced round the room, looked at him, nodded and smiled as if in friendly recognition, and then withdrew again, and the door closed behind it, his fear broke loose from his control in a hoarse cry. At the sound of this the visitant returned.
> 'Did you call me?' he asked, pleasantly[.][51]

This creature has 'a strange air of the common-place' yet also seems 'not of the earth and not of God'.[52] Markheim thinks he bears 'a likeness to himself', and is surprised to find how much the thing knows about Markheim's innermost thoughts, as well as knowing what is happening elsewhere – for instance that the dealer's servant is on her way home and will soon discover the murder. Convinced that this is an agent of evil and that he, being an 'unwilling sinner', wants nothing to do with his help, Markheim tries to defend his actions, only to be told that they are of little interest to the creature: 'the bad man is dear to me; not the bad act, whose fruits, if we could follow them far enough down the hurtling cataract of the ages, might yet be found more blessed than those of the rarest virtues'.[53] Is the creature Markheim's conscience, or his soul? his doppelgänger, or a supernatural tempter? The great subtlety of the story lies in its withholding of an answer to these questions. Markheim is so struck by the creature's evidence of predestination that he decides the only way to prove his own wish to be good is to give himself up; 'from that, to your galling disappointment, you shall see that I can draw both energy and courage'.[54] Far from being galled, the creature is transformed: his features (always described in watery, shifting terms) 'began to undergo a wonderful and lovely change; they brightened and softened with a tender triumph; and, even as they brightened, faded and dislimned'.

'Markheim' is an extraordinary story for two reasons: one, because it replicates so much from the murder scene in *Crime and Punishment*, the other because it is so original. The history of Stevenson's admiration for Dostoievsky's great book is not very widely known; the first English translation, in 1886, post-dates 'Markheim', but Stevenson seems to have read the novel in a French version of 1884, a copy of which was handed on to him by Henry James, 'only partially cut' as Henley claimed later.[55]* The fact that 'the Master' couldn't finish *Crime and Punishment* seems to illustrate the very differences in attitude to fiction that Stevenson had wanted to debate with him earlier, and certainly the 'reality' that Dostoievsky represented was not the kind James would ever choose to recreate. But Stevenson was simply bowled

---

* The similarities between 'Markheim' and Dostoievsky's novel are so strong that it seems impossible Stevenson could have written his story without knowledge of the other, but evidence is sparse. The first draft of 'Markheim', written in November 1884, differs very little from the final version and predates by five months the beginning of Stevenson's friendship with Henry James. Perhaps the French copy of *Le Crime et le châtiment* that James is said to have handed on to Stevenson was not the first version Stevenson had read. He had read an English translation of Dostoievsky's *Insulted and Injured* before this, possibly as early as 1881 (when a review of it appeared alongside one of 'Virginibus Puerisque' in the same periodical). Roger Swearingen has drawn my attention to this, and to the possibility that Stevenson and Dostoievsky might have been responding to some common other source; he suggests E.T.A. Hoffmann, whom both writers admired.

over by the novel: 'it is not reading a book, it is having a brain fever, to read it',[56] he wrote to Henley, and to Symonds:

It was like having an illness. James did not care for it because the character of Raskolnikoff was not objective; and at that I divined a great gulf between us and, on further reflection, the existence of a certain impotence in many minds of today, which prevents them from living *in* a book or a character, and keeps them standing afar off, spectators of a puppet show. To such I suppose the book may seem empty in the centre; to others it is a room, a house of life, into which they themselves enter, and are tortured or purified.[57]

In the only two letters where he mentions Dostoievsky's novel, Stevenson never links 'Markheim' with it, but the similarities are striking, as a scholar called Edgar C. Knowlton pointed out as early as 1916. Knowlton compared passages from the two works in parallel columns and came up with evidence of a kind of imaginative shadowing; the nervousness of the murderers (both essentially 'good' characters who have targeted people they think vicious), the suspicions of the victims, the brutality and suddenness of the crimes, the anxieties of both murderers that the corpses might come back to life, the torment of hearing others approach, the ringing at the door of unscheduled visitors, the removal of keys from the bodies, the 'reflective condition' that overtakes both criminals. Here are the two murder scenes, Dostoievsky's first (in David McDuff's translation):

As she attempted to untie the ribbon she turned towards the window in search of more light [. . .] and for a few seconds she moved right away and stood with her back to him. He undid his coat and freed the axe from its loop, but did not take it right out [. . .] 'Why on earth has he wrapped it up like this?' the old woman exclaimed in annoyance, and she moved a little way towards him.

There was not another second to be lost. He took the axe right out, swung it up in both hands, barely conscious of what he was doing.[58]

And this is the build-up to Stevenson's murder scene:

The dealer stooped once more, this time to replace the glass upon the shelf, his thin blond hair falling over his eyes as he did so. Markheim moved a little nearer, with one hand in the pocket of his greatcoat; he drew himself up and filled his lungs; at the same time many different emotions were depicted together on his face – terror, horror, and resolve, fascination and a physical repulsion; and through a haggard lift of his upper lip his teeth looked out.

'This may perhaps suit' observed the dealer: and then, as he began to re-arise, Markheim bounded from behind upon his victim.[59]

But from this very close emulation of Dostoievsky's story, 'Markheim' develops in an ingenious way. The intervention of the supernatural (yet 'common-place') 'creature', his subtle arguments about predestination and the nature of evil and Markheim's refusal to compound his crime (seen here as a form of stubbornness as much as anything) are all entirely Stevenson's own inventions. 'Markheim' represents a feverish kind of homage to the power of Dostoievsky's narrative gifts as much as to his actual tale, an acknowledgement of how affecting the experience of reading him had been.

G.K. Chesterton described Stevenson's years in Bournemouth as a 'revolt into respectability',[60] but the 'revolt' didn't last long, or go far. The emaciated Scot cut an odd figure stalking about on the West Cliff in the latest of his black velvet jackets, long lank hair blowing (it was kept long at this date, Fanny later claimed, for warmth), and his wife was no better, with her determined face 'marked by unmistakable strength of character', as William Archer put it, nervously, 'hair of an unglossy black, and her complexion darker than one would expect in a woman of Dutch-American race'.[61] They stuck out like a sore thumb on Alum Chine Road, and relished it, observing none of the social obligations of newcomers. Fanny complained to Colvin that neighbours were calling on them 'in droves', aware that the dying Mr Stevenson (so much younger-looking than his foreign wife) was 'quite literary'. Fanny's response was to play up to this: 'I murmur vaguely, "I dunno, m'sure," at which they show faint surprise, and slightly bridle.'[62]

When Adelaide Boodle, a young woman who lived nearby and who had admired 'The Treasure of Franchard' (in *New Arabian Nights*), took the initiative and called to meet the author, it took so long for anyone to answer the door that her mother burst into tears. The owners were perfectly welcoming, however (if rather inattentive), and a lopsided friendship developed in which Miss Boodle played the role of would-be disciple to both Louis and Fanny. More usefully, she played the piano too, and helped Stevenson pick out tunes with one finger on the instrument he had rented to entertain himself. Her gushing memoir of life at Skerryvore, dedicated to Stevenson's biographer-cousin and endorsed by Fanny's grandson Austin Strong, contains many ardent tributes to the author's wife, or *Sine Qua Non* as her title has it. Clearly Fanny could inspire devotion as well as dislike: Boodle doesn't just eulogise Fanny's careful nursing of Stevenson, her domestic skills and personal charisma (getting quite breathless about the Sine Qua Non's 'glorious head' and flashing eyes), but puts her literary talent almost on a par with her husband's, at one point calling Fanny the 'heroic bread-winner' for writing a short story for *Scribner's Magazine*.[63] But even Boodle has to admit that the couple could be violent towards each other, however jokily she expresses it: 'There were moments when the casual looker-on might have felt it his duty to shout for the police – hastening their steps perhaps with cries of "murder!"'[64]

A glamour was growing up around Stevenson. Evidence of his physical frailty combined with a seemingly unstoppable output of writing worked powerfully on friends and the public alike. He was a genius, he was going to die young, like a Romantic poet. Like Shelley, to be more specific. The poet's only son, Sir Percy, lived near Bournemouth at Boscombe Manor and he and his wife became friendly with the Stevensons in 1886. Lady Jane was a formidable keeper of the family flame (albeit not her family); there was a silk-lined alcove in the drawing room at Boscombe where she displayed the urn containing Shelley's heart – snatched from the funeral pyre by Trelawny – with a lamp kept perpetually burning by it. Mary Wollstonecraft's death-mask, which fascinated Stevenson, was also in their possession, and other relics, including many of Mary Shelley's papers, were housed in Lady Jane's 'Sanctum'. Though of course she had never met her husband's father, Lady Jane insisted that Stevenson was the very image of him, while to Margaret Stevenson she joked that Louis was really *her* son. Sir Percy, a keen amateur actor and photographer, took a series of photos of Stevenson that may have been indulging his wife's fancy, for the subject is dramatically draped in what looks like a cape or blanket, possibly 'in the character' of the poet. Stevenson was satirical about the supposed likeness – 'I seem but a Shelley with less oil, and no genius; though I have had the fortune to live longer and (partly) to grow up'[65] – but went along with it, so may have been more flattered than he was quite prepared to admit. Fanny was certainly gratified by the Shelleys' warmth of friendship towards them both, and could hardly have failed to be impressed by Lady Shelley's example as managing director of a writer's posthumous career.*

The Stevensons got to know the Shelleys through the elderly poet Sir Henry Taylor and his family, who lived at a villa called 'The Roost'. Taylor, author of the 1830s bestseller *Philip Van Artevelde*, had once been as famous as his friend Tennyson, now the grandest of grand old men holding court nearby at Freshwater on the Isle of Wight. Taylor died in 1886, or Stevenson might well have been introduced into the Poet Laureate's circle (he did meet Benjamin Jowett, and was invited by him to Oxford). But the

---

* Lady Shelley's possessiveness and forceful nature were remarkable. On the death of her mother-in-law in 1851, she arranged for the exhumation of William Godwin's and Mary Wollstonecraft's remains from the graveyard of St Pancras and their removal to Bournemouth, where she wanted all three bodies to be interred together. When the vicar of St Peter's objected, Lady Jane sat outside with the coffins on a carriage until he saw sense. The grave, on a rise in the churchyard overlooking a busy shopping centre, now contains the bodies of Godwin, Wollstonecraft, Mary Shelley, her son Sir Percy and Lady Jane.

beautiful Lady Taylor and her writer daughters Ida and Una remained friends with Stevenson all his life, and their circle included F.H.W. Myers, founder of the Society for Psychical Research, with whom Stevenson struck up an important correspondence later.

Owning a house seemed to attract a flood of visitors; 'Aunt Alan' Stevenson (Bob and Katherine's mother), Katherine de Mattos, Coggie Ferrier, Colvin and the Jenkins from Edinburgh all visited that year, as did Bob, who was facing a difficult juncture in his life. Now he was married and had a child, his pursuit of the artist's life was no longer feasible, and Louis, Henley and Colvin (Slade Professor of Fine Art at Cambridge at this date) were encouraging him to take up art history seriously. Bob eventually excelled in this field – his book on Velasquez is a classic – but in 1885 he was only just scraping by. He was still Stevenson's favourite company, and the only guest who could match his host's fervour for war-gaming now that sixteen-year-old Sam had outgrown it, but the difference in their fortunes made Louis feel guilty, and the burgher of Skerryvore tried to channel some of his money towards Bob by commissioning him to decorate the panels in the hall.

Skerryvore was expensive to keep up. The Stevensons had three servants: a housekeeper called Mrs Watts, her daughter Agnes, who was maidservant, and Valentine Roch, who functioned more as a lady's maid.* 'I do not live cheaply, and I question if I ever shall,' Louis wrote to his parents in December, in fine understatement. The prospect of ever earning a living seemed remote, even though Stevenson's output had increased dramatically: *A Child's Garden of Verses* and *The Dynamiter* were published in the spring of 1885, and *Prince Otto* was about to appear too. The life of the Duke of Wellington still beckoned, and then there were the plays, and ideas for plays, endlessly rolling down the production line: 'Hester Noble' and 'The King's Rubies' were just two more in

---

* When Fanny was away, Valentine slept on the floor in Stevenson's room to guard against health crises, and when word got round the neighbourhood about this it was assumed that she was his mistress.

1885 alone. Colvin and Henley in particular were understandably eager to have Stevenson live up to their long championship of his work. But no one quite appeared to know where to assign the fame they all seemed to agree he should have. Was he a story-writer, an essayist, a dramatist, a children's author, a dying poet? What could be made of such a protean writer?

10

THE DREAMER

Keenness of sensation in each of its forms is a valuable natural gift, unfortunately no means are as yet easily accessible for testing it in different persons; there are no anthropometric laboratories as yet in existence to which any one may go, and on payment of a small fee have all his faculties measured and registered.

Francis Galton, *Record of Family Faculties*

WHEN HIS FORMER MENTOR Fleeming Jenkin died suddenly of blood poisoning in June 1885, aged only fifty-three, Stevenson's reaction was almost as intense as that to Walter Ferrier's death two years earlier. He was unprepared to survive his friends; it made him feel like a cheat. As with his impulse to comfort and care for Ferrier's sister Coggie, Stevenson now showed anxious solicitude for Jenkin's widow Anne, and immediately agreed to undertake a biographical memoir of Fleeming. This was a generous promise from a man so pressed to earn money, but Stevenson's sense of gratitude to Jenkin kept him at the memoir with a fervour he could seldom maintain for other works, even though it took many months and meant laying by the novel he had just started, a gripping adventure about a Lowland boy stranded in the Highlands in the years just after the Jacobite Rebellion.

There were many visitors that summer, and excursions to London and Cambridge; too much activity for the frail author, who collapsed under the strain of an attempted holiday to Dartmoor. The holiday group, which included Sam and Katherine de Mattos, got as far as Exeter, where they had to stay put in a hotel for several weeks until Louis could be moved home. It was an alarming interval; the patient was brimful of ergotine and behaving very oddly: 'he has just given up insisting that he should be lifted into bed in a kneeling position, his face to the pillow', Fanny reported to Henley, 'and then still kneeling he was lifted bodily around, and then a third time held up in the air while he drew out his feet. I never performed a feat as difficult.'[1] The spectacle frightened Katherine, but not Fanny, who was in her element in these crises: 'Strangely enough, I am not so cast down as I was before this. Here is something tangible that I understand, at least, and when I can do something.'

The aborted holiday had started well: on their way to Devon Stevenson and Fanny had called on Thomas Hardy at his new house, 'Max Gate', just outside Dorchester. Fanny sent her mother-in-law an amusing description of the 'pale, gentle, frightened little man, that one felt an instant tenderness for, with a wife – ugly is no word for it, who said, "whatever shall we do?" I had never heard a living being say it before.' The meeting between the two writers was an odd convergence of nineteenth-century literary misfits; Hardy the backward-looking modernist (ten years Stevenson's senior, but living on till 1928); Stevenson the forward-looking traditionalist (whose early death sealed him into the Victorian age). In the summer of 1885, they were both probably eyeing each other up as to who would prove the worthiest successor to Meredith, with whom both men were friends. Stevenson was shocked, as we shall see, by the publication in 1892 of *Tess of the d'Urbervilles*, but in 1885 was a keen admirer of *Far from the Madding Crowd*, and was so taken with *The Mayor of Casterbridge* when it appeared in 1886 that he asked permission to dramatise it. It would have been an odd form of collaboration – somewhere between a homage to Hardy and hitching a ride. Hardy greeted the suggestion with touching eagerness, saying, 'I feel several inches taller at the idea,'[2] but nothing came of it.

The long wait for *Prince Otto* to go on sale hadn't diminished Stevenson's expectations for that novel, nor Fanny's (who anticipated it would create much more of a sensation than *Treasure Island* even[3]). But all the things that *Otto* represented to Stevenson in terms of craft, authority, effort and polish were about to be brushed aside by the instant success of the novella-length 'shilling shocker' he composed at a gallop in the weeks immediately preceding *Otto*'s publication. If he had been asked at the end of 1885 which he considered the best of his works, there is little doubt he would have named the Bohemian romance on which he was staking his hopes as a serious novelist. *The Strange Case of Dr Jekyll and Mr Hyde* might not even have got a mention. Stevenson did not seek to be known as a sensationalist, and had felt compromised by the way the *Pall Mall Magazine* advertised 'The Body Snatcher' at Christmas 1884, sending six sandwich-men around the streets of London (at double rates) wearing coffin-shaped boards and plaster skulls specially made by a theatre property company – until the police 'suppressed the nuisance'.[4]

The story of the composition of *Jekyll and Hyde* is that of Stevenson's most thoroughgoing collaboration of all: the collaboration of his conscious and unconscious selves. The fact that the story 'came to him in dream' was always reckoned to be of significance: by the public, for whom it augmented or validated the supernatural content of the tale; by the promoters of the Stevenson myth, for whom it proved the author's super-receptivity to inspiration; and of course by Fanny Stevenson, whose 'management' of the dream-material illustrated her own pivotal importance in the composition of her husband's works. She told the story several times, the first official version in a letter to Stevenson's biographer Graham Balfour in 1899:

> Louis wrote Jekyll and Hyde with great rapidity on the lines of his dream. In the small hours of one morning I was wakened by cries of horror from him. I, thinking he had a nightmare, waked him. He said, angrily, 'Why did you wake me? I was dreaming a fine boguey tale'. I had waked him at the first transformation scene. He had had in his mind an idea of a double life story, but it was not the same as the dream.

He asked me, as usual, to make no criticisms until the first draft was done. As he didn't like to get tired by discussing my proposed changes in his work it was the custom that I should put my criticisms in writing. In this tale I felt and still feel that he was hampered by his dream. The powder – which I thought might be changed – he couldn't eliminate because he saw it so plainly in the dream. In the original story he had Jekyll bad all through, and working for the Hyde change only for a disguise. I wrote pages of criticism, pointing out that he had here a great moral allegory that the dream was obscuring. I didn't like the opening, which was confused – again the dream – and proposed that Hyde should run over the child showing that he was an evil force without humanity. I left my paper with Louis, who was in his bedroom writing in bed. After quite a long interval his bell rang for me, and Lloyd and I went upstairs. As I entered the door Louis pointed with a long dramatic finger (you know) to a pile of ashes on the hearth of the fireplace saying that I was right and there was the tale. I nearly fainted away with misery and horror when I saw *all* was gone. He was already hard at work at the new version which was finished in a few days more. I wanted to make further objections concerning the powder but after that pile of ashes had not the courage.[5]

Sam Osbourne (called here by his later name of Lloyd), who was hanging around at Skerryvore waiting for a decision about his return to college, wrote up his own version of the story years later in *An Intimate Portrait of R.L.S.*, stressing the author's possession by quasi-mystical forces. According to Sam, Stevenson appeared one day 'very preoccupied' and announced that he must not be disturbed, as he was 'working with extraordinary success on a new story'. For three days the household maintained a reverential 'tiptoeing silence' as the work progressed, and Sam watched his stepfather through an open door (odd, under the circumstances, that this wasn't closed) 'sitting up in bed, filling page after page, and apparently never pausing for a moment'.[6] Here is the iconic description of the writer, bed-ridden, battling with chronic illness, yet pouring out the pages.

Sam's story goes on in a manner that stretches credulity, but by 1924, when he published this, all the other witnesses to the incident were dead and *Dr Jekyll and Mr Hyde* was one of the most famous stories in the world, available in dozens of languages and already filmed twenty times (including the classic 1920 John Stuart Robertson version starring John Barrymore). Sam claimed that Stevenson's initial three-day frenzy of writing ended with him reading the piece aloud to Fanny *and* Sam, being bitterly disappointed by Fanny's cool response and ready criticisms (as opposed to Sam's 'spellbound' attention) and then having an almighty row with his wife, 'so impassioned, so outraged, and [...] so painful' that the boy had to creep away, 'unable to bear it any longer'.[7] Sam later discovered his mother sitting 'pale and desolate before the fire, staring into it'; Stevenson then came down the stairs, 'burst in', shouted at Fanny again and threw his manuscript on the fire: 'Imagine my feelings – my mother's feelings – as we saw it blazing up; as we saw those precious pages wrinkling and blackening and turning into flame!'[8] But all was not lost. Though it looked like a fit of temper, Stevenson's destruction of the script – according to Sam – was actually an act of submission to his wife's judgement. The first version was mainly a 'shocker'; on reflection Stevenson thought Fanny was right to insist he bring out the story's allegorical potential. Another three days of wild scribbling followed, during which Stevenson produced the printed version; 'sixty-four thousand words in six days', Sam marvelled, 'more than ten thousand words a day [...] and on top of that copied out the whole in another two days, and had it in the post on the third!'[9] A true nine-days' wonder, except that it actually took Stevenson more like six weeks to have the manuscript ready, if his own remark to Frederick Myers in March 1886 is to be believed: 'Jekyll was conceived, written, rewritten, re-rewritten, and printed inside ten weeks.'[10]

Stevenson himself emphasised the significance of the story's dream genesis in an interview he gave to a reporter from the *New York Herald* on his arrival in America in September 1887:

I was very hard up for money, and I felt that I had to do something. I thought and thought, and tried hard to find a subject to write about. At night I dreamed the story, not precisely as it is written, for of course there are always stupidities in dreams, but practically it came to me as a gift, and what makes it appear more odd is that I am quite in the habit of dreaming stories [. . .] I go on making them while I sleep quite as hard, apparently, as when I am awake. They sometimes come to me in the form of nightmares, in so far that they make me cry out aloud. But I am never deceived by them. Even when fast asleep I know that it is I who am inventing, and when I cry out it is with gratification to know that the story is so good.

[. . .] For instance, all I dreamed about Dr Jekyll was that one man was being pressed into a cabinet, when he swallowed a drug and changed into another being. I awoke and said at once that I had found the missing link for which I had been looking so long, and before I again went to sleep almost every detail of the story, as it stands, was clear to me. Of course, writing it was another thing.[11]

A few weeks after this interview, and clearly prompted by the interest journalists had shown in the dream story, Stevenson was writing 'A Chapter on Dreams', an essay elaborating this idea of his subconscious as a story-mill. The argument was reversed, however: he no longer said that he was 'never deceived' by the provenance of his dream-work, and that 'even when fast asleep I know that it is I who am inventing'. Now, he claimed to be *always* deceived. He represented his subconscious as a separate and independent state, personifying its forces (plural, as against a single, conscious 'I') as 'the Brownies', spirit-like, anarchic and amoral: 'my Brownies are somewhat fantastic, like their stories hot and hot, full of passion and the picturesque, alive with animating incident; and they have no prejudice against the supernatural'.[12] This fanciful figure helped him dissociate himself from the eruption of imaginative 'dark forces' in *The Strange Case of Dr Jekyll and Mr Hyde*, the literary equivalent of a dramatic and violent 'return of the repressed'.

The dreams Stevenson uses as examples in his essay – presented in the third person as those of an unnamed 'dreamer' – are 'irresponsible inventions, told for the teller's pleasure, with no eye to the crass public or the thwart reviewer: tales where a thread might be dropped, or one adventure quitted for another, on fancy's least suggestion'.[13] Though he depicts the artful/artist dreamer (i.e. the writer who uses dreams as source-material) as one who harnesses the power of the subconscious in order to turn '[the] amusement of story-telling to (what is called) account', the power of *The Strange Case of Dr Jekyll and Mr Hyde* derives largely from its innovative use of the former, unimpeded, 'irresponsible' impulses. Clearly the process of slipping out of one mode of consciousness into another, less 'accountable', one was pertinent to the shaping of the Jekyll/Hyde schism.

But the main thrust of Stevenson's essay proposes that he can take neither credit nor responsibility for his creations; his conscious self has so little to do with it. It is a statement of what an ego-psychologist would now call the problem of self-appointment:

> For myself – what I call I, my conscious ego, the denizen of the pineal gland unless he has changed his residence since Descartes, the man with the conscience and the variable bank-account, the man with the hat and the boots, and the privilege of voting and not carrying his candidate at the general elections – I am sometimes tempted to suppose he is no story-teller at all, but a creature as matter of fact as any cheesemonger or any cheese, and a realist bemired up to the ears in actuality; so that, by that account, the whole of my published fiction should be the single-handed product of some Brownie, some Familiar, some unseen collaborator, whom I keep locked in a back garret, while I get all the praise and he but a share (which I cannot prevent him getting) of the pudding. I am an excellent advisor, something like Molière's servant; I pull back and I cut down; and I dress the whole in the best words and sentences that I can find and make; I hold the pen, too; and I do the sitting at the table, which is about the worst of it; and when all is done, I make up the manuscript and pay for the registration; so that, on the whole, I have some claim to share,

though not so largely as I do, in the profits of our common enterprise.[14]

The Strange Case of Dr Jekyll and Mr Hyde, the story which had sparked these odd protestations of innocence or irresponsibility, was the product, Stevenson reveals, of years worrying at the same theme: 'I had long been trying to write a story on this subject, to find a body, a vehicle, for that strong sense of man's double being which must at times come in upon and overwhelm the mind of every thinking creature.'[15] Stevenson's interest in the subconscious shaped both the use he made of his dreams (putting them 'to (what is called) account') and their preoccupations with the divided self, of which *Jekyll and Hyde* can be seen as the most cogent and 'analytical' instance. Jekyll's 'Strange Case' inevitably suggests to the modern mind the case-studies of Sigmund Freud, though Stevenson's very public display of his own 'dream-work' predates the birth of Freudian psychoanalysis by several years. The two men were possibly reading the same scientific literature, though, for Fanny's subscription to the *Lancet* put her and Louis in touch with the latest research into hysteria and 'moral insanity' which was being undertaken by Freud's teacher Jean-Martin Charcot at the Salpêtrière Hospital in Paris.* Fanny later claimed that her husband had got the germ of the Jekyll and Hyde story from 'a paper he had read in a French scientific journal on sub-consciousness'.[16] Stevenson spoke of having read an article on the case of 'Louis V' – a young Frenchman who suffered dramatic personality changes after severe shock – but said it was sent him by F.H.W. Myers *after* the publication of *Jekyll and Hyde*. 'Louis V'; 'Louis S': they both sound like patients of Dr Freud, whose own publication of 'strange cases', beginning in the 1880s, was to change so radically the understanding of identity and revolutionise the ways in which readers read and writers write. Coming in just

---

* It is even possible that Fanny (or Louis) had some experience of being treated at the Salpêtrière, a hospital for hysterics, as Stevenson refers familiarly to the great doctor in two later letters, and seems to have recommended him to Colvin, whom Henry James reports returning from 'a long regime of Charcot' in April 1889.

before this wholesale professionalisation of psychology, Stevenson's story is not just full of latent meanings, but heaving with blatant ones too.

The story is now so embedded in popular culture that it hardly exists as a work of literature. Everyone knows what 'Jekyll-and-Hyde' signifies: there is little motivation to read the book. Indeed, reading the book spoils 'the story', which we all know is about an over-vaunting scientist whose experiments in the chemical induction of personality-change unleash an increasingly bestial alter-ego who eventually destroys him. Not surprisingly, coming from an author who had virtually been adopted into the Shelley family, the story's themes are strongly reminiscent of *Frankenstein* and the Prometheus myth; there were also, as critics were ready to point out, clear echoes of Poe's artful doppelgänger story 'William Wilson' and James Hogg's *Private Memoirs and Confessions of a Justified Sinner*, with its overlapping third- and first-person narratives and its linking of the murderous, self-licensed Robert Colwan to his demonic alter-ego, Gil-Martin. But the dissimilarities between Poe and Hogg and Stevenson are revealing, too, as one reviewer of *Jekyll and Hyde* suggested:

> The double personality does not in [Stevenson's] romance take the form of a personified conscience, the doppel ganger of the sinner, a 'double' like his own double which Goethe is fabled to have seen. No; the 'separable self' in this 'strange case' [. . .], with its unlikeness to its master, with its hideous caprices, and appalling vitality, and terrible power of growth and increase, is, to our thinking, a notion as novel as it is terrific. We would welcome a spectre, a ghoul, or even a vampire gladly, rather than meet Mr Edward Hyde.[17]

The believability of the story, its familiar, smog-filled urban setting (purportedly London, but with a strong flavour of Old Town Edinburgh) and its cast of solid Victorian professional men, 'intelligent, reputable [. . .] all good judges of wine', made the gothic elements more striking. Dr Jekyll is a prosperous, philanthropic, 'smooth-faced' middle-aged man, his friend Utterson is a lawyer,

Lanyon another doctor and Utterson's godson Enfield a man-about-town. The introduction of young, classless and criminal-looking Edward Hyde into this society shatters its gentlemen's-club cosiness, and Jekyll's friends can only account for the doctor's choice of 'protégé' in terms of a hidden vice and possible black-mailing.

The story is laid out like a dossier of witness statements, with three overlapping narratives. The first is a detective story (a term not yet in use, but which this book helped form), detailing Utterson's growing suspicions about Hyde, his puzzling over the nature of the Jekyll/Hyde relationship, his urging on of the police in the search for Carew's murderer and his lone pursuit of the investigation once the police have given up. When Utterson is called in by the servants to break down Jekyll's laboratory door with an axe and discovers not his friend, as anticipated, but Hyde, writhing in his death agonies after taking poison, the story looks as if it is over, but there are more puzzles, notably Jekyll's will, and a note that suggests he is still alive, not lying murdered some-where by his psychopathic companion.

The second and third sections consist of two documents found in the laboratory. One is a letter by Lanyon telling for the first time of Jekyll's self-experimentations with 'powders' and how Lanyon once agreed to supply some of them to a friend of Jekyll, hitherto unknown to him. The reader recognises the description of Hyde immediately, but it is only now, well over halfway through the book, that Stevenson reveals the identity of the two characters.

> [Hyde] put the glass to his lips, and drank at one gulp. A cry followed; he reeled, staggered, clutched at the table and held on, staring with injected eyes, gasping with open mouth; and as I looked there came, I thought, a change – he seemed to swell – his face became suddenly black, and the features seemed to melt and alter – and the next moment I had sprung to my feet and leaped back against the wall, my arm raised to shield me from that prodigy, my mind submerged in terror.
>
> 'O God!' I screamed, and 'O God!' again and again; for there before my eyes, pale and shaken, and half fainting, and

groping before him with his hands, like a man restored from death – there stood Henry Jekyll![18]

Here, with its gestures and speeches straight out of 'melo', *Jekyll and Hyde* turns instantly into psychological horror. The last document, a long suicide note, lets us read in Jekyll's own words the exact nature of his experimentations and their consequences. Jekyll is smoothly articulate, even poetical, as he relates how the misdeeds of his youth led him to concealment and 'a profound duplicity of life'. Something of that duplicity is evident even at this confessional moment, for Jekyll's 'statement' is, unsurprisingly, a highly subjective piece of self-justification. The vague 'irregularities' which he admits to are placed in the context of such 'high views' as to render them more an indicator of his super-fine sensibilities than objectively or inherently bad. Jekyll seems to be preparing his audience (Utterson) for an aspirational reading of his self-experimentations, a Promethean interpretation, with himself cast as the doomed romantic striver-after-knowledge.

> I thus drew steadily nearer to that truth, by whose partial discovery I have been doomed to such a dreadful shipwreck: that man is not truly one, but truly two. [. . .] It was on the moral side, and in my own person, that I learned to recognise the thorough and primitive duality of man; I saw that, of the two natures that contended in the field of my consciousness, even if I could rightly be said to be either, it was only because I was radically both.[19]

There follows Jekyll's description of the first mixing and taking of 'the powders' and the subsequent transformation into Hyde, an insistently physical piece of writing:

> The most racking pains succeeded: a grinding in the bones, deadly nausea, and a horror of the spirit that cannot be exceeded at the hour of birth or death. Then these agonies began swiftly to subside, and I came to myself as if out of a great sickness. There was something strange in my sensations, something indescribably new, and from its very novelty, indescribably sweet. I felt younger, lighter, happier in body; within

> I was conscious of a heady recklessness, a current of dis-
> ordered sensual images running like a mill race in my fancy,
> a solution of the bonds of obligation, an unknown but not
> an innocent freedom of the soul.[20]

The person who emerges from this quasi-sexual, chemically-induced convulsion is Edward Hyde. When he creeps out from the laboratory, situated symbolically at the back of Jekyll's house and opening onto a different street, he is able for the first time to see himself in a mirror. Not only is he smaller than Jekyll, but, in a highly inventive detail, he is also thinner and younger, being young and undeveloped in vice: 'I was conscious of no repugnance, rather of a leap of welcome,' he says. 'This, too, was myself.' Much of the book's fascination can be summed up in that simple statement, so evocative of Whitman's similarly shocking and liberating 'I contain multitudes'. The meaning was perhaps too clear for comfort. Of Stevenson's friends, Henry James complained of the book's sensationalism, Myers sent a long list of possible revisions and refinements, and Symonds wrote, 'It is indeed a dreadful book, most dreadful because of a certain moral callousness, a want of sympathy, a shutting out of hope. [...] Most of us at some epoch of our lives have been upon the verge of developing a Mr Hyde.'[21]

Symonds may have been voicing here a worry similar to that of Jekyll's bachelor friends in the story itself: that a comfortable, if hypocritical, status quo was being threatened with exposure. Certainly the *Strange Case* is full of latent sexual meanings, and its huge cultural impact derived in part from its frank acknowledgement that there was plenty in late-Victorian life which Victorian fiction could not, or refused to, deal with. In his defence of the story in a letter to Robert Bridges in 1886, the poet Gerard Manley Hopkins expressed the shrewd opinion that the scene in *Jekyll and Hyde* where Hyde tramples over the little girl in the street 'is perhaps a convention: [Stevenson] was thinking of something unsuitable for fiction'.[22]

Many – indeed, most – modern critics have interpreted the novel as a psycho-sexual allegory. Elaine Showalter has called it

'a fable of *fin-de-siècle* homosexual panic, the discovery and resistance of the homosexual self', in which 'Jekyll's apparent infatuation with Hyde reflects the late nineteenth-century upper-middle-
class eroticisation of working-class men as the ideal homosexual
objects';[23] Wayne Koestenbaum has written that *Jekyll and Hyde*
'defines queerness as the horror that comes from not being able to
explain away an uncanny doubleness';[24] and Karl Miller, in his
Doubles: Studies in Literary History, has identified Stevenson as
the leading figure in the 'School of Duality' that 'framed a dialect,
and a dialectic, for the love that dared not speak its name – for
the vexed question of homosexuality and bisexuality'.[25] These
opinions obviously pick up on Stevenson's own 'doubleness', his
confusion and disruption of what was expected from an effemi-
nate-looking man, but there was an assumption at the time of its
first publication that the story dealt with unspeakably shameful
heterosexual practices, the scope of which was being made public
for the first time that year by Richard von Krafft-Ebing's groundbreaking work on deviant sexuality, *Psychopathia Sexualis*. The
film versions of *Jekyll and Hyde* abound in added prostitutes to
accommodate this interpretation (of course there are no prostitutes
in the book itself), and to reflect the historical fact that only two
years after the story began to cause a sensation among the reading
public on both sides of the Atlantic, the savage Whitechapel murders of 'Jack the Ripper' also began (targeting 'fallen' women and
characterised by evisceration, thereby suggesting the work of a
psychopathic moralist with a medical/anatomical background).
The novel has thereby become co-opted into the (highly mythologised) real-life Whitechapel story, which, like the mystery of
Jekyll, has never been satisfactorily resolved. At the time of the
murders, the connection with Stevenson's book seemed so close
that a stage version of *Jekyll and Hyde* was taken off at the Lyceum
as a gesture to public feeling: 'There is no taste in London just
now for horrors on the stage. There is quite sufficient to make us
shudder out of doors.'[26]

Jekyll and Hyde is about the secrets which respectability hides, and the pleasures of that deception, so it is appropriate enough that Stevenson leaves the nature of Jekyll's sins (not Hyde's) unspecified. The fragments of early draft that survive show the author muting significantly the story's sexual content: 'disgraceful pleasures' in the draft becomes the euphemism 'certain appetites', and Jekyll no longer confesses to 'a career of cruel, soulless and degrading vice' and vices that were 'at once criminal in the sight of the law and abhorrent in themselves'.[27] 'Criminal' certainly indicates that Stevenson meant 'homosexual', but it would be entirely in keeping with his views on sexual tolerance that he removed this term in order not to link any specific sexual behaviour with the psychopathic Hyde mind-set. The resulting implication that the 'certain appetites' hinted at were to do with masturbation or illicit heterosexual sex were also not what the author intended, as is evident from his response to an early stage version of the story, which made Hyde into a 'voluptuary':

> [Hyde] was not good-looking [. . .] and not, Great Gods! a mere voluptuary. There is no harm in a voluptuary; and none, with my hand on my heart and in the sight of God, none – no harm whatever – in what prurient fools call 'immorality'. The harm was in Jekyll, because he was a hypocrite – not because he was fond of women; he says so himself; but people are so filled full of folly and inverted lust, that they can think of nothing but sexuality. The Hypocrite let out the beast Hyde – who is no more sexual than another, but who is the essence of cruelty and malice, and selfishness and cowardice, and these are the diabolic in man – not this poor wish to have a woman, that they make such a cry about.[28]

So much for the author's view, trampled down in the street early on in the story's life and never revived. Film versions of the novel rely on the voluptuary as much as they do the Missing-Link make-over always allotted Hyde (notably in Rouben Mamoulian's 1931 version and Victor Fleming's remake ten years later, starring Spencer Tracy). In the book, Hyde's repulsiveness is essentially indefinable. Enfield recalls 'something wrong in his appearance,

something downright detestable [. . .] He must be deformed somewhere; he gives a strong feeling of deformity, although I couldn't
specify the point,' while Utterson can't account for the fear and
loathing he feels when looking at Hyde: 'There is something more,
if I could find a name for it. God bless me, the man seems hardly
human! Something troglodytic, shall we say? [. . .] or is it the
mere radiance of a foul soul that thus transpired through, and
transfigures, its clay continent?'[29] Hyde and Jekyll could never be
mistaken for each other, even when, as in the description of 'The
Last Night' at the laboratory, they both resort to wearing a mask
as cover, because they are not just dissimilar in stature, demeanour
and age (Jekyll is about fifty, Hyde a youth), but totally different
personae. The young Jorge Luis Borges made this point forcibly in
his review of the 1941 Victor Fleming film, which, he said, 'avoids
all surprise and mystery: in the early scenes [. . .] Spencer Tracy
fearlessly drinks the versatile potion and transforms himself into
Spencer Tracy, with a different wig and Negroid features. [. . .]
In the book, the identity of Jekyll and Hyde is a surprise: the
author saves it for the end of the ninth chapter. The allegorical
tale pretends to be a detective story; no reader guesses that Hyde
and Jekyll are the same person.'[30] Borges returned to the subject
many times, emphasising the story's lost impact: 'I don't think
anyone would have guessed that [Jekyll and Hyde were the same
man]. Have you ever suspected that Sherlock Holmes was the
Hound of the Baskervilles? Well, no, you haven't . . . Have you
ever suspected that Hamlet may be Claudius?'[31]

Longman's must have realised that they were on to a winner,
for on receipt of the manuscript they decided to make *Jekyll and
Hyde* into a small book rather than a serial for their magazine. It
was a rapid success on both sides of the Atlantic, selling 40,000
copies in six months in Great Britain and – unknown to the author
– an astonishing 250,000 legal and pirated copies in North
America. Passing through Southampton in April, Fanny heard a
vendor shouting it on the streets, 'DOCtor Jekyll! DOCtor
Jekyll!',[32] Margaret Stevenson got wind of a sermon being preached

about the book in Glasgow, and Charles Baxter heard that Queen Victoria was reading it. The story quickly became common property, as Stevenson's first biographer, Graham Balfour, wrote in 1901: 'Its success was probably due rather to the moral instincts of the public than to any conscious perception of the merits of its art. It was read by those who never read fiction, it was quoted in pulpits, and made the subject of leading articles in religious papers.'[33] It was, in other words, an instant classic.

The 'Brownies' had done so well with *Jekyll and Hyde* that Stevenson may have become a little superstitious about them. Between finishing the story and its publication in January 1886, he wrote another story derived from a dream, 'Olalla'. As Edwin M. Eigner has shown,[34] 'Olalla' owes even more to Edward Bulwer-Lytton's 'Strange Story', of which it seems to be an unwitting plagiarism. This was another sort of 'dreaming' that Stevenson was prone to (as with Washington Irving and *Treasure Island*), perhaps more truly subconscious than the ordinary, sleep-engendered sort.

'Olalla' deals explicitly – and to the modern eye rather crudely – with racial degeneration, a subject which was coming increasingly into debate through the work of contemporary gene theorists such as Francis Galton, and which had always intrigued Stevenson. In the story, an English officer is sent to convalesce from his wounds at the home of a formerly grand provincial family in Spain. His hosts are puzzling; the beautiful but impassive 'Senora' remains aloof, presumably from pride, while her half-witted, hairy, 'dusky' son Felipe shows evidence of a profound sadism and bestial lack of control. In a series of sensational incidents, culminating in a quasi-vampiric attack by the Senora (who bites his hand through to the bone), the Englishman discovers a strain of insanity in the family, but by this time he has fallen in love with the daughter of the house, the stunningly beautiful, pious, poetry-writing Olalla, whom he wishes to marry. Their early meetings are wordless and instantly, powerfully erotic. Olalla, with her perfect face and form (which Stevenson dwells on at some length, especially her breasts, which are exposed by a split-bodiced dress), ends up renouncing her feelings for the Englishman in order not to pass on and perhaps intensify the family's bad blood, an act of what could be called sui-eugenics.

Stevenson hardly ever mentioned this story without apologising for its 'not very defensible' nature, but whether he was referring to the eroticism, the vampirism or the theory is not clear. It was probably the first of these; the dishonourable treatment of women (in life) was getting to be an obsessive issue for the author, and here he was representing (in fiction) one woman as a blood-sucking degenerate and another as a sex object. And one wonders what Fanny made of this story, with its melting heroine so clearly not modelled on herself and the insane Moorish matron replicating so closely the scene in the Paris cab years before when she had bitten Louis's hand and drawn blood.

Sam, who was eighteen in 1886, had not done well in his first year at Edinburgh University, and Stevenson thought he should hold back from the exams rather than fail. After the event, Stevenson admitted that his cautious pessimism over his stepson's chances was just like his father's treatment of himself – 'my conduct has been exactly his all through'.[35] History did seem to be repeating itself; in fact, Sam's career was becoming so like a reprise of Stevenson's own as to suggest conscious copying. Not only was Sam living at Heriot Row (in Louis's old room), studying engineering, attending meetings of the 'Spec', and wearing *a velvet coat*, he was about to drop out, just as Louis had done. The rapid success of *Dr Jekyll and Mr Hyde* had impressed the boy deeply (he kept a close record of his stepfather's sales), and in the autumn following its publication he announced that he too wanted to become a writer. He was even preparing to share Louis's fate as an invalid, convinced as he was in the summer of 1886 that he ran the risk of permanent blindness. He started to practise the piano blindfold, and pleaded to have a typewriter bought for him so that he could pursue his writing vocation in the coming darkness. The threat of Sam losing his sight aroused his mother's acute anxiety (which must have been gratifying), and she whipped him from one specialist to another in the hope of a cure, but as the eye problem coincided with exam-time in Edinburgh, and was completely rectified by the acquisition of a pair of glasses, it is unlikely to have been too severe in the first place.

The winter of 1886–87 was an important period of transition for the boy. While he was in Barbados on a long holiday he got news that his father, now remarried to a Miss Paul (known dismissively by Fanny as 'Paulie') and with a second family in California, had disappeared suddenly without trace. No one ever found out what happened to Sam Osbourne Senior, though there were 'evil rumours' that he might have run off with another woman, committed suicide or been murdered. This dark turn in the family history naturally disturbed Sam, who from this point onwards decided to drop his ill-starred patronymic and be known by his middle name, Lloyd. His allegiances turned wholly towards Stevenson as the father-figure, and he strove to cement their bond with proofs of special affinity, cutting short his very long holiday in Barbados because he had had a premonition of Louis being critically ill. This sort of psychic phenomenon always went down well at home: Fanny was a great visionary herself.

Lloyd's decision to 'become a writer' was a course of action (or inaction) to which neither Louis nor Fanny could reasonably object, nor did they. Stevenson positively encouraged the boy, though his 1888 essay addressed to Lloyd, 'A Letter to a Young Gentleman who Proposes to Embrace the Career of Art', strikes many warning notes about writing as a profession: 'the temptation is almost as common as the vocation is rare', 'perpetual effort' was necessary, and 'what you may decently expect, if you have some talent and much industry, is such an income as a clerk will earn with a tenth or perhaps a twentieth of your nervous output'.[36] The difficulties which Lloyd's decision posed for the whole family were obvious: he would continue to be a dependant, possibly an expensive one, and his work would be hard to criticise or praise honestly. But the lengths to which Stevenson went to accommodate his stepson's desires and requirements show a trust in and affection for him that remained almost entirely unclouded for the rest of his life, most of which they spent sharing a home together, and during which they collaborated on three books. Lloyd had not grown up to be a particularly attractive character, and he didn't improve with age; he was lazy, not very clever, addicted to being 'kept', made two bad marriages, had children out of wedlock and wrote lots of poor or indifferent books (at one point admitting that he could get anything published because of his association with Stevenson). His conduct as co-keeper of the flame with his mother in the years following Stevenson's death was characterised by raw self-interest, his letters by speciousness and bully's stratagems. All in all, it is hard to see what his stepfather saw in him, yet Stevenson loved him and cared for him, to the point of dotage even, as he wrote to Henley in the early summer of 1887:

> I find in the contemplation of the youth Lloyd much benefit: he is [a] dam fine youth. Happy am I, to be even this much of a father! [...] Perhaps as we approach this foul time of life, young folk become necessary? 'Tis a problem. We know what form this craving wears in certain cases. But perhaps it is a genuine thing in itself: the age of paternity coming, a demand sets in. Thus perhaps my present (and crescent) infatuation for the youth Lloyd; but no, I think it is because the youth himself improves so much, and is such a dam, dam, dam fine youth.[37]

The context of this is important: Henley and his wife Anna had been married nine years and had not yet had a child (though Anna had suffered many miscarriages). Stevenson recognised frustrated paternity as a cause of sadness in his friend – and indeed when Henley's only child, Margaret, was born the following year, Henley proved the most obsessively fond father imaginable. Frustrated paternity did not play half so great a role in Stevenson's own life, but even so he derived 'much benefit' from the presence and the fact of Lloyd (Belle at this point was completely out of the picture).

The quotation has another current running in it which should not pass unremarked: the proximity of the two 'cravings', one parental, the other sexual. Perhaps, Stevenson suggests (in a trope that would become familiar in psychoanalysis), they are essentially the same. It's a rather remarkable statement, deliberating using charged words such as 'infatuation', 'craving' and 'demand' to *distinguish* his feelings from those in 'certain [paedophilic or homoerotic] cases'. And those cases themselves are, characteristically, acknowledged rather than condemned or vilified.

Stevenson's admiration for his stepson was never again so emphatically expressed but, as I have indicated, didn't diminish significantly, despite trials later. Wayne Koestenbaum is the most explicit of those commentators who have read the relationship as homoerotic, representing Stevenson's literary collaborations with Lloyd in terms of a pederastic seduction (they 'began in a game' but 'marked a darker purpose'[38]). This seems to me a wilful sensationalisation of the available evidence in the specific case of Stevenson and Lloyd, though Koestenbaum's alertness to homoerotic language and situations elsewhere in Stevenson's work and life is instructive. In the spring of 1887, with Lloyd's father vanished and Louis's father dying, the two can be seen drawing together for comfort to form a new relationship which has almost more of a sibling flavour than that of father-and-son, a pale version of the closeness Louis had felt to Bob in the days of 'the two Stevensons'.

Within weeks of *Jekyll and Hyde* being published, Stevenson's remarkable engine was at work again on the novel he had laid by the previous summer in order to write the Jenkin memoir. *Kidnapped* (an arresting and novel title) was based around a notorious incident that took place in the troubled aftermath of the 1745 Jacobite Rebellion, and which Stevenson had previously thought to include in his 'Transformation of the Highlands', the assassination of Colin Campbell, the King's collector, at Appin in 1749. This romantic subject was to make another 'story for boys' for *Young Folks Magazine*; it was also perhaps a bid to please Thomas Stevenson with a reassuringly Scottish, wholesome adventure story after all the flim-flam of *Prince Otto*, the crudeness of the Henley plays and the sensationalism of *Jekyll*. The evocation of the West Highland coastline was to be an oblique homage to the Stevenson family firm and the episode set on the islet of Earraid a specific reference to Louis's years as an apprentice engineer. All this must have mollified the ailing old man's anxieties, especially when Stevenson agreed – in theory, at any rate – to his father's predictable suggestion that the new book ought to include 'a scene of religion'.[39]

Though marketed as a children's story, *Kidnapped* was not in quite the same key as *Treasure Island* and *The Black Arrow*, as Henry James recognised when he noted in his copy: 'this coquetry of [Stevenson's] pretending he writes "for boys"'.[40] The narrator, David Balfour, a reserved, manly, Lowland, Low-Church sixteen-year-old, is very different from the prepubescent boy-heroes of the earlier stories, and has an unillusioned outlook on life. The story touches on weighty historical and cultural matters: the bungled management of the Jacobite cause in the aftermath of the '45, the hardening of attitudes in the Calvinist Lowlands and the beginning of the process which led to the hated Highland clearances. The Appin murder itself was unusual matter for a *Young Folks* yarn. But in the dedication of *Kidnapped* (to Baxter), Stevenson makes a point of 'how little I am touched by the desire of accuracy', even to the extent of changing the year of the murder from 1752 to 1751 (it's not at all clear why). Despite the high number of actual historical figures in the story, including Alan Breck Stewart, the probable assassin, Cluny Macpherson, the Jacobite chieftain, Robin Oig, son of Rob Roy and James Stewart, 'James of the

Glens', Alan's kinsman and the man who is tried and executed in his place, and his extremely clever use of all the 'true' material, Stevenson wanted to be judged here as a fiction writer rather than a historian.

The method is very like that of Sir Walter Scott, and *Kidnapped* stands comparison with the works of the master on any ground other than sheer length. The necessity of writing in instalments kept the narrative bowling along at a bracing pace in a series of superbly imagined episodes: the sinister House of Shaws where David's wicked uncle Ebenezer tries to murder the boy by sending him up a staircase leading to a steep drop, the kidnap itself, the fight in the roundhouse, David's ordeal after the shipwreck, Cluny Macpherson's terrorist-cell hide-out 'like a wasp's nest' in the mountains, the flight across the moorlands with Alan Breck, all done with sharp attention to detail, especially physical discomfort:

> I would be aroused in the gloaming, to sit up in the same puddle where I had slept, and sup cold drammach; the rain driving sharp in my face or running down my back in icy trickles; the mist enfolding us like as in a gloomy chamber – or perhaps if the wind blew, falling suddenly apart and showing us the gulf of some dark valley where the streams were crying aloud.[41]

It's a very unsentimental book; the gross Captain Hoseason and his crew (of the *Covenant* – surely a satirical choice of name) present a remarkable catalogue of vices and the character of Ransome the cabin boy a brief but arresting study in abuse:

> He swore horribly whenever he remembered, but more like a silly schoolboy than a man; and boasted of many wild and bad things that he had done, stealthy thefts, false accusations, ay, and even murder; but all with such a dearth of likelihood in the details, and such a weak and crazy swagger in the delivery, as disposed me rather to pity than to believe him. [. . .] It was the pitifullest thing in life to see this unhappy, unfriended creature staggering and dancing and talking he knew not what. Some of the men laughed, but not all; others would grow as black as thunder (thinking perhaps of their

own childhood or their own children) and bid him stop that nonsense and think what he was doing. As for me, I felt ashamed to look at him, and the poor child still comes about me in my dreams.[42]

Kidnapped is both a romance and a novel of realism, and the odd coupling of the two things is symbolised and acted out in the relationship between the volatile, charismatic Alan Breck Stewart and his cautious companion David, whose politics and temperaments are so wildly different. This is reminiscent of the Hawkins/ Silver relationship and anticipates the much darker and more destructive connection between the Durie brothers in *The Master of Ballantrae*, but it is also a fairly obvious way of separating and analysing the two different kinds of Scottishness in Stevenson himself. The 'Shorter Catechist' was always on duty in the author, but willing to be 'kidnapped' any moment by the romance of a vigorous, glamorous warrior culture. The disunity of Scotland is lamented throughout, for David is, like his creator, a 'foreigner at home', who knows no Gaelic, cannot recognise tartans and is loyal to an English King. Yet Alan, despite his pride in being a 'Hieland shentleman' of long pedigree, is so 'native' that he has had to spend years in exile, and with his lace cuffs and court mannerisms has all but turned into a Frenchman.

The vision of Scotland that the book projects is essentially tragic, for in the wide variety of Scots life it illustrates – Lowland churchmen, Highland chiefs, clansmen, fisherfolk, mariners, itinerant preachers, evicted crofters, Latin-spouting city lawyers – everyone is to a greater or lesser extent embattled or threatened. The effects of this traumatic, schismatic period in Scots history were all too plainly felt by the author, who longed to be a 'native Maker' in a language and culture which were almost too fragmentary and diverse to be usable. In the same year as he finished *Kidnapped*, Stevenson was writing the poems, in Scots and in English, which made up the collection *Underwoods*. It was a 'two-minded' book as well as a bilingual one: the first half, in English, contains highly personal poems mostly addressed to friends; the second half, in

Scots, is quite different in style and tone, full of bracing lyrics and ballads. But the dialect in which he composed these 'native' verses was, he admitted in a prefatory note, far from pure. His remarks are in response to a contemporary research project on dialect which illustrated how multifarious and localised Scots language had become.

> I am from the Lothians myself; it is there I heard the language spoken about my childhood; and it is in the drawling Lothian voice that I repeat it to myself. Let the precisians call my speech that of the Lothians. And if it be not pure, alas! what matters it? The day draws near when this illustrious and malleable tongue shall be quite forgotten; and Burns's Ayrshire, and Dr MacDonald's Aberdeen awa', and Scott's brave, metropolitan utterance will be all equally the ghosts of speech. Till then I would love to have my hour as a native Maker, and be read by my own countryfolk in our own dying language: an ambition surely of the heart rather than of the head, so restricted as it is in prospect of endurance, so parochial in bounds of space.[43]

It is a melancholy reflection, with an inbuilt irony: the writer admits the tragic fact that his native tongue is dying, and does so in the foreign tongue which is his first language, and of which he is a world-acknowledged master. What *Underwoods* illustrates very clearly is that Stevenson's pre-eminence as an English stylist relied on his access to Scots. There were things he could only express in Scots – books, stories, poems, letters he felt compelled to write in it – and he revelled in the language like a holiday, for that is what it was.

The last chapters of *Kidnapped* were churned out by Stevenson 'without interest or inspiration, almost word by word', as he wrote to George Iles in 1887.[44] It shows: the novel stops rather than ends, with a sentence that is the beginning of a new paragraph: 'The hand of Providence brought me in my drifting to the very doors of the British Linen Company's bank.' This is almost shockingly unsatisfactory. Stevenson had intended to write more, but simply

Robert Louis Stevenson and his Wife, by John Singer Sargent, painted in the drawing room at 'Skerryvore' in Bournemouth in 1885. 'I am at one extreme corner,' RLS wrote to Will Low, 'my wife, in this wild dress and looking like a ghost, is at the extreme other end; between us an open door exhibits my palatial entrance hall and a part of my respected staircase.'

Above Lloyd Osbourne aged about twenty, the 'young gentleman who proposes to embrace the career of art'.

Right The actor Richard Mansfield as Jekyll/Hyde, a publicity picture for the first American dramatisation of RLS's novel in 1887.

Henry James in 1886, drawn by John Singer Sargent.

RLS photographed by Sir Percy Shelley, 1886 or '87. The cloak and the pose were probably meant to bring out RLS's supposed likeness to the photographer's father.

Lloyd, Fanny and RLS, all in buffalo-skin coats bought in Canada, on the porch of Baker's Cottage at Saranac Lake, New York, during the winter of 1887–88. Their loyal and hardy servant Valentine Roch is on the extreme left.

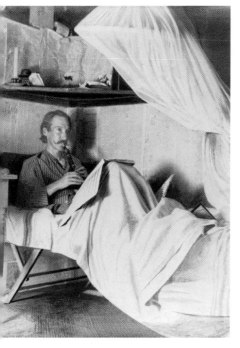

RLS playing his flageolet in bed.

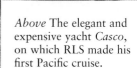

Above The elegant and expensive yacht *Casco*, on which RLS made his first Pacific cruise.

Left RLS, barefoot and having the time of his life, balanced on the bowsprit of the schooner *Equator*.

Above Lloyd, Fanny, RLS and the widowed Margaret Stevenson entertaining David Kalakaua, King of Hawaii, on board the *Casco*, 1890.

Above Tembinok, the cross-dressing poet-king of Apemama.

Left Mataafa Iosefo, the chief whose claim to power in Samoa was vigorously supported by RLS.

Gilbert Islands 'flower children': Nan Tok', Fanny Stevenson, Nan Takauti and RLS.

The original building at Vailima, which Henry Adams described as 'very like a bandstand in a German beer-garden', with the 'insane stork' and his wife on the balcony and Tin Jack and H.J. Moors seated on the steps.

A South Seas Don Quixote: RLS on his horse Jack at Vailima, *c*.1891.

The finished house at Vailima, with Lloyd Osbourne in the doorway to the new hall. Margaret Stevenson's rooms were immediately above where he is standing, Fanny's in the middle of the first floor and RLS's study at the further end.

Above The household at Vailima in May 1892. On the veranda, from left to right: Joe Strong and Cocky the parrot, Margaret Stevenson, Lloyd Osbourne, RLS, Fanny, Simi the steward; on the steps, from left to right: Auvea (plantation worker), Mary Carter the Australian maid, Elena the laundress, Arrick the pantry-boy, Talolo (chief cook), Austin Strong, Belle Strong, Lafaele the cattle-man and Tomasi, assistant cook (with the axe).

Different degrees of concentration: Belle, RLS and Fanny playing cards, c.1892.

4 December 1894. Sosimo guards the body of RLS, lying in state in the hall at Vailima, draped in the Union flag and tapa mats brought by the local chiefs as funerary gifts. Fanny offered the flag to Henley later, and was disgusted by his refusal of it.

Fanny aged fifty-three in Sydne March 1893, eerily calm and beautiful during a respite from psychotic illness.

ran out of energy, and on Colvin's advice wrote a postscript explaining that the projected later episodes would appear in a sequel. It is remarkable that *Young Folks* did not revolt at this; all the reviewers complained about it.

Baling out of *Kidnapped* was a symptom of a general malaise which affected Stevenson in Bournemouth in the year following the publication of *Jekyll and Hyde*, despite the increase in renown and income he was enjoying. He was skittish and highly strung, had short, troubling rifts with three close friends (Henley, Bob and – astonishingly – Colvin), and got neurotically overheated about matters of public morals, in particular the notorious Crawford divorce case, about which he wrote two bridling letters to *The Times*. His pleasures were those of a bored adolescent; he spent whole days preparing and conducting war games, mostly with Bob, and tested Charles Baxter's love of pranks to the limit by sending him a series of elaborate postal hoaxes. Even his 'piano-pickling' took on a neurotic intensity, to the extent that he was sometimes spending five hours a day at it straight, getting too exhausted to do anything else.

Thomas Stevenson's steady decline and changed personality may have been more profoundly disturbing to his son than Louis ever expressed outright. Meeting his parents in London in March 1886, Stevenson was shocked to recognise that his father's death was 'thoroughly begun',[45] and foolishly but filially insisted on taking care of the old man for a while. So the two invalids went together to Smedley's Hydropathic in Matlock, a state-of-the-art spa in the middle of the Derbyshire Dales, and spent just over a week being wrapped in wet flannel, having their feet soaked in mustard, their chests rubbed with chilli paste and limbs dabbed with vinegar. No wonder with this larder full of astringents on him, Stevenson quickly developed the itch. Thomas Stevenson was more agitated by the 'nonconforming atmosphere', and proved pettish and irritable. He didn't seem to enjoy his son's company much and both men missed their wives. When Louis mentioned that his mother might be able to visit, Thomas 'laughed aloud like a little child for joy'.[46] Louis tried to counter his own homesickness by studying the times of trains back to Bournemouth.

There are signs, though, that Thomas was trying to resolve his long-simmering grievances against his son. A few months after this, on another trip to London to see a specialist, he called at the Royal Institution to visit his old friend Sir James Dewar, to whom he had once complained vehemently about Louis's desertion of the family firm. Dewar had defended the youth at the time and made a good-humoured bet that in ten years Louis would earn from writing 'a bigger income than the old firm had ever commanded', at which, to Dewar's surprise, Thomas Stevenson became furious and 'repulsed all attempts at reconciliation'. His visit to Dewar in London in 1887 was to make amends for this. The old man was so feeble that he had to be lifted in and out of the cab. ' "I cudna be in London without coming to shake your hand and confess that you were richt after a' about Louis, and I was wrong," ' Dewar recalls him saying. 'The frail old frame shook with emotion, and he muttered, "I ken this is my last visit to the South." '[47]

Possibly because of his debility, Thomas Stevenson had got into an acrimonious dispute with his nephews David and Charles, who currently ran the family firm, over the distribution of the business profits. The matter turned on the fact that Thomas still received the greater part of the annual profits even though he was no longer working, which naturally had begun to agitate the nephews. The arrangement had been made when the elder David Stevenson had retired in 1883, and presupposed the whole business passing to his side of the family at Thomas's death. So the temporary, unfair overpayment of Thomas was to compensate him and his heirs for soon being cut off from any income whatever.

In the middle of this bitter and distasteful family dispute, which threatened to go to law, Stevenson found a distraction in the most impetuous plan of gallantry of his whole career. His limited ability to act out his political principles in life had always been a source of profound frustration and shame to him. He tried, sporadically and unsuccessfully, to give up worrying about it for the sake of

his health, saying he had 'died to politics' over the prosecution of
the Sudan campaign of 1883–84: 'If ever I could do anything,' he
declared then to his father, 'I suppose I ought to do it; but till that
hour comes I will not vex my soul.'[48] Well, the hour did seem to
have come in the spring of 1887, when the newspapers were full
of the plight of a family called Curtin in County Kerry, boycotted
and persecuted by Irish nationalists ever since a raid on their farm
in November 1885 during which John Curtin and one of the
marauders died. The issue was a straightforward one for the
Unionist author: the tenants who had been evicted by the British
government deserved their fate, the pro-British settlers didn't. The
parallels with the Highland clearances, over which his partisanship
swung entirely the other way, did not seem to strike him.

It was the fact that the besieged family were mostly women
that really agitated Stevenson, and that in all the months of the
boycott no one had stepped in to protect them; 'all the manhood
of England and the world stands aghast before a threat of murder',
he wrote in disgust. His wild scheme, outlined in a letter to Anne
Jenkin written one sleepless night, was to remove himself and his
household to Ireland and either join the Curtins themselves, or
rent another of the targeted farms. The likelihood of getting killed
doing this seems to have been the main draw of the plan; 'a writer
being murdered would attract attention', he wrote, adding that his
health made him particularly expendable. His letter sets out the
pros and cons in a compellingly immediate style, like thinking
aloud. Did he *talk* like this, like a hyperactive barrister who can't
decide which brief to defend?

> The Curtin women are probably highly uninteresting females.
> I haven't a doubt of it. But the Government cannot, men will
> not, protect them. If I am the only one to see this public duty,
> it is to the public and the Right I should perform it – not to
> Mesdames Curtin. Fourth Objection: I am married. 'I have
> married a wife!' I seem to have heard it before. It smells
> ancient; what was the context? [It was what the publican said
> as excuse in Luke 14:20] Fifth Objection: My wife has had a

mean life (1), loves me (2), could not bear to lose me (3). (1) I admit: I am sorry. (2) But what does she love me for? and (3) she must lose me soon or late. And after all, because we run this risk, it does not follow that we should fail. Sixth Objection: My wife wouldn't like it. No, she wouldn't. Who would? But the Curtins don't like it. And all who are to suffer if this goes on, won't like it. And if there is a great wrong, somebody must suffer. Seventh Objection: I won't like it. No, I will not; I have thought it through, and I will not. But what of that? And both she and I may like it more than we suppose. We shall lose friends, all comforts, all society: so has everybody who has ever done anything; but we shall have some excitement, and that's a fine thing, and we shall be trying to do the right, and that's not to be despised.[49]

Fanny expressed her opinion of the scheme forthrightly: it was madness from every point of view, she didn't want any part of it, yet would of course go along if Louis really felt there was no alternative. This was astute, as well as heartfelt, for she must have guessed that he would not be able to follow through. Lloyd remembered his mother being 'much more calm than the circumstances warranted' at the time, though he himself felt far from calm, being the only able-bodied male of the proposed party, and designated 'chief martyr in this Irish fantasy'.[50] He later thought that Stevenson's plan to help the Curtins was an obvious example of 'practical Tolstoyism'. His stepfather, he said, was at the time 'steeped, not only in Tolstoy, but in all Russian literature'.[51]*

Stevenson was more likely to have been thinking of the Curtin boycott as a chance to be like General Gordon, besieged, holding the fort, dying in action rather than facing 'inglorious death by disease'. He had somehow acquired a relic of the hero, a cigarette paper on which Gordon had written in Arabic his 'last message' from Khartoum. It is a request for information about troop locations, and still exists in the Yale archive. Stevenson treasured the tiny scrap of paper and, according to his mother, 'took it with him wherever he lived'.[52]

---

* This may well be true, though Tolstoy is not mentioned once in Stevenson's letters.

Events overtook Stevenson, but not before he had tried to arrange a meeting with the Chief Secretary for Ireland, Arthur Balfour (with whom he could claim a distant blood tie, and whose brother, Eustace, was a fellow member of the Savile Club). He hoped to see the minister on his way through London to France, where he and Fanny were going for a holiday. But on 4 May news came that Thomas Stevenson was critically ill, so the couple set off at once for Edinburgh, arriving two days before the old man died. He didn't recognise his son during that time, as Louis recalled in his bleak poem 'The Last Sight':

> Once more I saw him. In the lofty room,
> Where oft with lights and company his tongue
> Was trump to honest laughter, sate attired
> A something in his likeness. 'Look!' said one,
> Unkindly kind, 'look up, it is your boy!'
> And the dread changeling gazed on me in vain.[53]

Louis arranged the funeral, which was a remarkably elaborate affair involving over a hundred invited guests and a procession of forty or fifty carriages, the largest private funeral anyone could remember in Edinburgh. It started from Heriot Row, where Louis, Bob and Lloyd received the guests, and went on to the New Calton Burying Ground on the other side of the town. The weather was bad, even though it was May, and Louis, who had been struggling with a cold all week, ran out of energy halfway through the proceedings and was unable to attend the interment, leaving Bob to act as chief mourner in his place. Poor Margaret Stevenson must have been wondering how long it would be till the next funeral.

Thomas Stevenson left his estate tied up in such a way that his wife had a life rent on the residue, to be passed on to Louis at her death. This was not a very helpful arrangement, given Louis's uncertain hold on life, and though he was entitled to £3000 from the estate's capital, his father's death did not leave him as well off as many of his friends and family imagined. The people who benefited significantly from Thomas Stevenson's careful custodianship of money from his share of the business, from his own father and from his uncle Robert – who had made him sole heir in 1851 to £4500 – were Fanny Stevenson and her children, but they had to wait another ten years.

Margaret Stevenson had every intention of sharing her resources with her son, and sharing her widowhood with him, too. Her brother George had examined Louis while he was in Edinburgh and recommended Colorado as a good place for him to winter, so Margaret generously offered to pay for the whole family's removal there that August, including herself, Lloyd and Valentine. She was already thinking of selling up Heriot Row and going to live with Louis and Fanny permanently, a prospect which Fanny did not blench at, though it can't have struck her as ideal.

It was clear that Scotland was out of the question as a home for Louis; just a few weeks in windswept Edinburgh had almost finished him off. He left the city on the last day of May 1887 and headed back to Bournemouth, mercifully unaware that he was taking his leave of his native country for good. Flora Masson saw the open cab pass on its way along Princes Street to the station, piled with untidily-packed luggage. A man stood up and waved his hat to get her attention, and she recognised Stevenson, calling, 'Goodbye! Goodbye!'[54]

Thomas Stevenson's valet, a man called John Cruikshank, came with them from Edinburgh, an unlooked-for kind of inheritance. He spent a few weeks opening the door at Skerryvore, but the arrangement was doomed not to last long. 'We have a butler: by God! He doesn't buttle, but the point of the thing is the style. When Fanny gardens, he stands over her and looks genteel,' Stevenson wrote comically to Colvin.[55] But Cruikshank fell in with 'bad companions' in Bournemouth and by July had been asked to leave, no doubt to mutual relief. The Stevensons must have been puzzling employers for a gentleman's gentleman; their scruffy clothes, disarming manners and unconcern for the proprieties probably struck Cruikshank as insulting. His brief sojourn in their household marks the high-water mark of Stevenson's 'revolt into respectability', a process inherently farcical, as evident the evening in June 1887 when the Stevensons attempted to impress an American millionaire by inviting him down to Bournemouth for dinner. Charles Fairchild was John Singer Sargent's friend and patron, and had commissioned Sargent's first portrait of Stevenson in 1884 as a present for his wife, who, like Fairchild, was an ardent fan of the writer. When Sargent said that Fairchild wanted to meet them, the Stevensons could hardly refuse, especially as he seemed to want to bankroll their coming trip to the States. But on the afternoon of the dinner, the cat Ginger stole the fish from the cellar and Valentine forgot the cream for the white soup. Cruikshank had bungled the purchase of the wine, so they had only one bottle of indifferent hock to serve to the millionaire, and as the nation had ground to a halt that day for Queen Victoria's Golden Jubilee, none of these deficiencies was remediable. Worst of all, on the same train as Fairchild from London was a surprise visitor, Teddy Henley, whom Fanny had to welcome in with a fixed smile. The soup was inedible, the leg of lamb Valentine had bought much too small, and all they could put together for dessert was 'some hastily improvised custard in very small cups', as Fanny recalled in an agonised, humorous letter to her mother-in-law: 'Fortunately, your cheese was still to the fore, and it was pathetic to hear both Mr Fairchild and Teddy praise the cheese which they ate until for shame's sake they had to leave off [. . .] I believe Valentine and John wept together in the pantry.'[56]

Despite the dinner, Fairchild stuck to his purpose. He proposed to arrange (and, presumably, pay for) all their travel from New York westwards, as well as accommodation when they got to Colorado. In the east, they were to stay at the Fairchilds' home in Newport, Rhode Island, where, he promised, they would be safe from society and newshounds alike, for, as Fairchild knew better than the Stevensons themselves at this date, *Jekyll and Hyde* had turned its author into very hot property in America. Anywhere other than under the protection of powerful friends such as himself, he told Fanny, 'our lives will be hunted out of us, as the people were all Louis mad'.

Right up to the last minute, Stevenson had wanted nothing but to get away, but taking his leave of the servants he was overcome by emotion and wept copiously. 'It had suddenly come upon him that he loved Skerryvore, Westbourne, Bournemouth, even the Poole Road with an almost morbid sentimentality,' Fanny wrote to Adelaide Boodle.[57] To Colvin, with whom he had had a mis-understanding, all the more disturbing because such things were rare between them, Louis wrote emotionally on the eve of departure:

> Here I am in this dismantled house hoping to leave tomorrow, yet still in doubt; this time of my life is at an end: if it leaves bitterness in your mind, what kind of a time has it been?
>
> The last day – the last evening – in the old house – with a sad, but God knows, nowise a bitter heart; I wish I could say with hope.[58]

11

BELOW ZERO

Nearly every individual is notable for some peculiarity of mind
or disposition, and in some few persons the sanguine, melancholy, nervous or lymphatic temperament is well marked. All
such peculiarities should be noted as they are strongly hereditary. Moreover the study of them is peculiarly attractive.

Francis Galton, *Record of Family Faculties*

THE LAST VIEW of the Old World, when it came, was hurried.
The Stevenson party, which consisted of Louis, Fanny, Margaret
Stevenson, Lloyd and the indispensable Valentine Roch, stayed two
nights at a hotel in Finsbury while friends came and went, saying
goodbye and bringing presents. Gosse ran around town trying to
get Stevenson a copy of Hardy's new novel, *The Woodlanders*, to
read on the journey; Henry James turned up with a case of champagne; William Archer fetched a lawyer so that a last-minute codi-
cil could be added to his friend's will. Aunt Alan, Coggie Ferrier,
even Cummy, turned up to say goodbye, and the London friends
were of course in attendance: Henley, Katherine de Mattos and
Colvin, pained and saddened by his recent rift. Colvin stayed the
last night in the same hotel, protectively close to Louis, and accompanied him to the docks the next day: 'Leaving the ship's side as
she weighed anchor, and waving farewell to the party from the
boat which landed me,' he wrote with sorrow some years later, 'I
little knew what was the truth, that I was looking on the face of
my friend for the last time.'[1]

Stevenson himself was far from gloomy, in fact his spirits

picked up almost as soon as they got under way. After years of being virtually housebound at Skerryvore, he suddenly found himself 'really enjoying my life; there is nothing like being at sea, after all. And O why have I allowed myself to rot so long on land?'[2] He needed all his good cheer to overcome the peculiar conditions of the voyage. Fanny had made the booking on the *Ludgate Hill* – a ship of 'one of the less frequented lines'[3] – on the recommendation of Colvin's brother. They expected it to be more private and spacious than usual, and from London to Le Havre the Stevenson party did indeed seem to have the boat to themselves. But once across the Channel it became clear why: the *Ludgate Hill* was picking up a consignment of apes, cows and over a hundred horses. They had booked themselves onto a floating zoo.

The smell of course was atrocious, and the 'dreadfully human'[4] cries of the confined animals inescapable day or night. Fanny, who was a bad sailor anyway, often prostrated in her cabin with sickness, must have found the two-and-a-half-week journey across the Atlantic hellish, especially since both Louis and his mother were being determinedly upbeat about everything. Margaret Stevenson, whose letters to her sister Jane provide a valuable extra record of these years, reported that the ship was dirty and uncomfortable even before the animals were loaded, 'but we agreed to make the best of things and look upon it as an "adventure"'.[5] Louis frisked about the boat, administering Henry James's champagne to the sick and declaring that the pervasive stink of ordure was 'gran' for the health', while the iron vessel rolled so much mid-ocean that the fittings came loose in the bedroom. 'O it was lovely,' he wrote to Colvin on reaching shore, 'a thousandfold pleasanter than a great big Birmingham liner like a new hotel; and we liked the officers, and made friends with the quartermasters, and I (at least) made a friend of a baboon [. . .] whose embraces have pretty near cost me a coat.'[6] Mrs Stevenson meanwhile was enjoying the oddity of looking out through her porthole at a row of horses, 'and still stranger, in the saloon, to see a horse looking *in* at one of the windows'.[7]

The degree to which 'it was lovely' only struck Stevenson a few weeks after the voyage, when he became convinced that he had just spent one of the happiest times of his life.

> I could not have believed it possible; we had the beastliest weather, and many discomforts; but the mere fact of its being a tramp-ship, gave us many comforts; we could cut about with the men and officers, stay in the wheel house, discuss all manner of things, and really be a little at sea. And truly there is nothing else. I had literally forgotten what happiness was, and the full mind – full of external and physical things, not full of cares and labours and rot about a fellow's behaviour. My heart literally sang[.][8]

Here was the antidote not just to invalidism, but also to 'cares and labours and rot about a fellow's behaviour' – in other words, writing. The restlessness that habitually plagued Stevenson in his creative life was all blown away at sea, by healthy, manly, carefree activity. A conventional crossing would not have given him half so much pleasure, and from this time on he was gripped by a craving to go yacht-cruising.

Lloyd Osbourne wrote later that the crossing to America in 1887 represented Stevenson's passing from one epoch of his life to another: 'from that time until his death he became, indeed, one of the most conspicuous figures in contemporary literature'.[9] On board the *Ludgate Hill*, Stevenson had no clear idea how well *Jekyll and Hyde* was selling in the States, for he wasn't getting a cent from the pirated editions (an issue he was quick to raise with reporters later). But the first whiff of his new celebrity came even before they touched land, when the pilot of the boat guiding them into New York City Harbour turned out to be nicknamed 'Mr Hyde' by his workmates. None of Fairchild's intimations quite prepared the author for any kind of reception at the quayside, but waiting alongside his old friend Will Low were 'a dozen reporters',[10] E.L. Burlingame, the editor of *Scribner's Magazine*, and a telegram from Fairchild himself, who had sent a carriage and booked the whole Stevenson party into the Victoria, a luxury

hotel with lifts and new-fangled 'fixed-in' plumbing. More journalists turned up there the first evening hoping to see the author of
Jekyll and Hyde, who didn't yet have enough experience of celebrity to know quite how to deal with them. Everyone had read the
book, it seemed, and T.R. Sullivan's stage adaptation was about
to open in New York, starring Richard Mansfield (a very well-
known actor of the day). One reporter, from the *New York Herald*,
asked specifically about *Dr Jekyll and Mr Hyde* and *Deacon
Brodie*, a pairing (suggested by the fact that Teddy Henley's production of *Deacon Brodie* had just started its North American tour
in the city) that was to become increasingly significant over the next
few months. Stevenson was dismissive about *Brodie* ('although I
have no idea whether it will please an audience, I don't think either
Mr Henley or I are ashamed of it'[11]), but answered at length about
the dream-genesis of *Jekyll*, cementing in the public mind the idea
of himself as a wispy paranormalist and encouraging another journalist to report a supposedly 'psychic' event on the quay (a letter
from London echoing the author's vaguely-stated wish to visit
Japan). Stevenson must have been aware that he was sounding, or
could be made to sound, a bit foolish, and the flurry of attention
that greeted them at the Victoria – flowers, strangers, friends,
flunkies – was exhausting and oppressive after the freedom of the
sea voyage. He came down with a cold almost immediately and
decided to retreat to Fairchild's house in Newport, Rhode Island
the next day, leaving Fanny and his mother in the city to attend
the play and bask in the author's New World fame.

Stevenson's short visit to Rhode Island made an odd interlude:
he spent most of his time there in bed, talking excitedly and chain-
smoking. His portrait by Sargent (the one in which he is seated in
a wicker chair) had been hanging in the Fairchild mansion for a
couple of years, but had not prepared the millionaire's daughter,
Sally, for the relative uncouthness of the man himself, whom she
recalled years later with candour as 'dirty in appearance [. . .]
peculiar and shabby'. The arrival of the 'wild woman' and the rest
of the troupe a few days later was hardly reassuring: Margaret

Stevenson and Valentine were the only respectable-looking members of the party, and even so, neither of them could be exactly described as *stylish* (though Margaret, with her plentiful supply of starched white widow's caps, did at least look *clean*). By the end of the week, the Fairchilds' polite smiles must have been wearing rather thin: Stevenson filled the house with his unconventional entourage, attracted stray admirers to the door and forgot to pay his large bill at the chemist's. And no amount of celebrity could compensate Sally Fairchild for the fact that the writer 'smoked too much, and burned holes in our sheets'.[12]

Back in New York City, in a hotel on the Lower East Side, Stevenson got down to business with Edward Burlingame, who was offering an astonishing deal: twelve articles in twelve months for £60 each. Stevenson accepted the commission with amazement (and, naturally, a little trepidation), but refused an even more lucrative offer from the publisher Sam McClure, who had been commissioned by Joseph Pulitzer to bag the author for the *New York World*. The suggested £2000 a year for a weekly article was too much for Stevenson: 'They would drive even an honest man into being a mere lucre-hunter in three weeks,' he wrote to Colvin, whose eyes must have been bulging out of his smooth round head at the sums mentioned. But he did let McClure reserialise *The Black Arrow*, under the title 'The Outlaws of Tunstall Forest', and publish it as a book for the first time – getting into trouble on the way for breaking an agreement with Scribner's not to offer books elsewhere. It was a bad, unbusinesslike mistake, but Stevenson's faculties seem to have been almost fuddled by the amounts of money being offered at every turn. McClure says the writer 'blushed and looked confused' when offered $8000 for a sequel to *Kidnapped*, and said 'he didn't think any novel of his was worth as much as $8000'.[13] 'You have no idea how much is made of me here,' he told Colvin. But if anything, the London friends got an even stronger impression of Stevenson's new earning power than was yet true: the figures seemed to stick in their heads as if they had all been paid rather than just talked up, and to someone as virulently anti-American as Henley, Stevenson might as well have sold his soul to the devil as a book to McClure and twelve essays to *Scribner's*.

Was Stevenson being rather priggish about the possible dangers of being overpaid? A more practical and less scrupulous person might have taken every dollar available and shared it out with his friends. Some such thought may have crossed Henley's mind when he was told in January 1888 that Louis had just refused $5000 for a single story, preferring to rest content with his £720 from *Scribner's*. Nevertheless, Stevenson's finances looked secure for the first time ever, and the family anticipated a comfortable winter in the States. Colorado had been discounted as a possible destination by this time; now Fanny and Lloyd were scouting the Adirondacks for somewhere suitable. Their choice of Saranac Lake, 250 miles upstate from New York City, was mostly to do with the climate (mountainous, with sharply cold winters) and the vicinity of an innovative TB specialist called Edward Livingston Trudeau. Trudeau, who was himself tubercular, was pioneering an open-air cure at his new Adirondack Cottage Sanatorium and had set up the first North American laboratory devoted to researching the disease. His clinic was only three years old and had not yet begun to attract Davos-like spa-goers and all the invalid society that Stevenson so loathed; the remoteness of Saranac was also attractive: 'the country for 150 square miles is in a state of nature, without roads, and all the communication by streams and lakes and portages'.[14] In the course of being fêted in New York Stevenson had met some congenial people, including Low's friend the sculptor Augustus Saint-Gaudens,* 'but the thing at large is a bore and a fraud', he wrote to Walter Simpson once he had moved out of the city. 'I am much happier up here, where I see no one and live my own life.'[15]

---

* Saint-Gaudens made a small bas-relief medallion of the writer, later used as the model for the memorial to RLS in St Giles Cathedral, Edinburgh. It is notable for an instance of concrete Bowdlerism, as it were, with the genteel substitution of a pen for the cigarette in the author's hand, and a couch for the pillow-crowded bed of the original.

The white wooden cottage they moved to on a hillside just outside Saranac Lake belonged to a mountain guide called Andrew Baker, who shuffled his own family of wife and two daughters into the back of the property to accommodate the new tenants. It was a small place for so many people: the Stevensons' half had a sitting room with a fireplace, from which three rooms led in different directions, a small kitchen to one side, a bedroom with a view to the front (which was allotted to Margaret Stevenson) and another bedroom to the other side (for Louis and Fanny), with a room beyond that which was used as Louis's study. Lloyd slept in a room in the attic and Valentine had a space the same size as the store room on the other side of the kitchen. They still envisaged going back to Bournemouth after the winter, so had not brought many possessions with them, but Stevenson decorated the mantel-piece with two red tobacco boxes, one either end, and a whisky bottle in the middle where a more conventional household might have placed the clock. The tobacco boxes were essential: Mrs Baker later remembered Stevenson as the most extreme chain-smoker she ever knew, and the mantelpiece at the cottage still bears witness to it, with the scorch marks made by his abandoned or forgotten roll-ups visible to this day.

Saranac Lake was still mainly a trappers' and hunters' desti-nation, a remote village with a sawmill, one small hotel, no run-ning water and, as yet, no railroad (though it was about to get a narrow-gauge that winter and – to Stevenson's amazement – had a long-established bawdy-house). The seven cottages of Trudeau's rudimentary sanatorium were on a piece of land on the side of a mountain about half a mile out of town, and were run by the intrepid doctor almost single-handed, using lumberjacks and trappers to help care for the bedridden. Stevenson was attended by Trudeau but kept well away from the clinic, pre-ferring his own private version of the same 'open-air' cure in the cottage with its surrounding woods. He was very happy with the change of scene and enraptured with the bright fall colours and the romance of the landscape. The view of the river just below the cottage pleased him, and the hills, where he took solitary woodland walks, reminded him of the Highlands. He felt better than he had for years, and got to work on his *Scribner's* essays immediately.

Part of the luxury of this commission was that the essays could be on any subject he pleased; the first, his 'Chapter on Dreams', was finished in five days, and 'The Lantern-Bearers' almost as quickly. All twelve pieces were completed during his six months at Saranac and published in *Scribner's* one a month through 1888. It was the most efficient and profitable paid work he had yet done, and a release from the usual pattern of dashing from one partly-written work to another in the hope of meeting many deadlines and obligations, though he still felt 'terror' at the prospect of starting them. Nothing was going to alleviate that.

Charles Baxter, Stevenson's most sincerely solicitous friend, rejoiced in the change he perceived: 'I cannot tell you how welcome your last letter was. It smelt so of good health and spirits and was so like the olden times.'[16] It began to look as if a cure might really be possible, and at the same time there began to be cause to wonder if Stevenson was in fact tubercular at all, for when he had his sputum analysed in one of Dr Trudeau's advanced bacillus tests, it showed negative. Trudeau said later that he 'never heard any abnormal physical sounds in Stevenson's chest',[17] and, like Ruedi before him, suspected that Stevenson's was an arrested case of the disease. Later commentators, citing the facts that Stevenson survived another fifteen years after the onset of blood-spitting, died of non-pulmonary causes and never infected any other member of his household, have suggested that his ailment may have been not TB but bronchietasis, an acute condition with some shared symptoms. Recently, two American researchers have introduced yet another thesis, that Stevenson may have suffered from haemorrhagic telangiectasia, or Osler-Rendu-Weber Syndrome: 'This would explain his chronic respiratory complaints, recurrent episodes of pulmonary hemorrhage, and his death of probable cerebral hemorrhage.'[18] It would also explain his mother's and maternal grandfather's similar symptoms (including Margaret's 'apparent stroke' in 1867); Osler-Rendu-Weber Syndrome is hereditary.*

The negative result of Trudeau's sputum test may have affected Stevenson's attitude to his health, though he never remarked on it. It is notable that from this time on he started to be severely practical about his choice of where to live, and was never prostrated by illness again. Perhaps thinking of himself as consumptive had made him fatalistic; seeing that his symptoms could be improved so much by travel certainly made the idea of returning to Bournemouth in the spring tantamount to a death-wish. And at the same time, money and his mother's extraordinary adaptability (little to be guessed at from her years as an Edinburgh *bourgeoise*) made it possible to consider much wider options for the future.

Stevenson never made a friend of Edward Trudeau, though there were few enough people to associate with in Saranac Lake and the doctor must have been one of the most philanthropic and intelligent men he met in his life. The one recorded visit by Stevenson to Trudeau's laboratory, where the doctor practised vivisection as part of his research, indicates that the writer took a profound revulsion against the spirit in which the research was conducted as well as the experiments themselves. It shows a side of Stevenson's character rarely illustrated, a high-minded and possibly wrong-headed narrowness. The story goes that Stevenson found it intolerable to stay in the laboratory for long, and bolted suddenly onto the porch. When Trudeau followed, wondering if his guest had been taken ill, Stevenson made this peremptory reply: 'Your light may be very bright to you, Trudeau, but to me it smells of oil like the devil.' This condemnation of a man who, after all, was doing more for pathology than anyone else in the country at

---

* The authors note that there was a five-month gap in Margaret Stevenson's diary in the winter of 1867–68, followed by a resumption of entries in a deteriorated hand and reporting periods of impaired lucidity: 'The brain is also weak so I often talk nonsense not being able to remember the words I want.'[19]

that date, seems presumptuous to say the least, though Trudeau took no offence. His account in his autobiography is careful to exculpate them both:

> Stevenson saw no mutilated animals in my laboratory. The only things he saw were the diseased organs in bottles and cultures of the germs which had produced the disease. These were the things which turned him sick. I remember he went out just after I made this remark:
>
> 'This little scum on the tube is consumption, and the cause of more human suffering than anything else in this world. We can produce tuberculosis in the guinea-pig with it, and if we could learn to cure tuberculosis in the guinea-pig this great burden of human suffering might be lifted from the world.'
>
> Stevenson, however, saw only the diseased lungs and the disgusting scum growing on the broth, and it was these things that turned his stomach, not any suffering animals which he saw.[20]

The winter set in early and was a severe one, much harder to cope with in the exposed, flimsy Adirondack cottage than at Davos. Fanny had come back from a long trip to see her family in Indiana via Montreal, bringing full-length buffalo-skin coats, hats and boots for everyone, but there was little or no insulation in the house, and heating only in the sitting room (the open fire), one bedroom (a stove) and the kitchen (the cooker). The snow began to fall in November, cutting off Stevenson's walks, and by December the temperature had dropped so low that the ink froze in its pot overnight. This was even more of a disaster than is to be expected, as Stevenson was no longer the only author in the household. Lloyd was busy on a comic detective novel called 'The Finsbury Tontine', and Fanny had just finished a short story, 'The Nixie', which she was able to sell to *Scribner's Magazine*.

Among the visitors to Saranac before the weather got really bad were Sam McClure, armed with more publishing schemes and contracts, and the persevering Fairchilds. The millionaires had to slum it in Plattsburg and struggle up the track in a buggy only to have Mrs Fairchild refused entry to the cottage on account of having a slight head cold. This was at Fanny's insistence, of course, and the visitors had to be satisfied with an interview conducted farcically by sign language through a closed window. They were only allowed indoors the next day when both could show clean handkerchiefs, so no wonder they cut their trip short and went home. Fanny apologised after the event for seeming severe, but probably relished this exercise of power, seeing their patrons reduced to grimacing and gesticulating out in the cold.

The winter in Saranac was picturesque and uncomfortable, as Lloyd recalled: 'sleighs, snow-shoes and frozen lakes; voyageurs in quaint costumes and with French to match; red-hot stoves and steaming windows [...] consumptives in bright caps and many-hued woollens gaily tobogganing at forty below zero; buffalo coats an inch thick; snow-storms, snow-drifts, Arctic cold'.[21] As the temperature dropped to below 25 degrees at night, life in Baker's Cottage contracted. The front porch was closed up, leaving the only entrance through the kitchen. Poor Valentine in her unheated cupboard woke to find the handkerchief under her pillow frozen and Stevenson got frostbite in bed, mistaking the sensation in his ear for a rat nibbling him. 'At times it was unbelievably cold,' Lloyd wrote later, 'one was really comfortable only in bed, with a hot soapstone at one's feet.'[22] The stoves warmed up quickly, but hardly radiated at all, draughts were plentiful and piercing and, huddled round the fireplace, the family must have wondered what else they would have to endure to win Louis continuing respite from 'Bloody Jack'. Fanny had her usual bad reaction to cold high places and made as many journeys away from Saranac as she could manage; Margaret Stevenson and Lloyd also took breaks in New York and Boston. In fact, everyone but Louis found the conditions intolerable, but he was braced by them: his brain, he reckoned, was working 'with much vivacity'.

The novelty of feeling well brought a surge of creative energy, as his account of 'The Genesis of The Master of Ballantrae' records. What he describes is not so much a moment of inspiration, as a decision to be inspired:

I was walking one night in the verandah of a small house in which I lived, outside the hamlet of Saranac. It was winter; the night was very dark; the air extraordinarily clear and cold, and sweet with the purity of forests. From a good way below, the river was to be heard contending with ice and boulders: a few lights appeared, scattered unevenly among the darkness, but so far away as not to lessen the sense of isolation. For the making of a story here were fine conditions. I was besides moved with the spirit of emulation, having just finished my third or fourth perusal of [Marryat's] *The Phantom Ship*. 'Come', said I to my engine, 'let us make a tale, a story of many years and countries, of the sea and the land, savagery and civilisation; a story that shall have the same large features, and may be treated in the same summary elliptic method as the book you have been reading and admiring.' I was here brought up with a reflection exceedingly just in itself, but which as the sequel shows, I failed to profit by. I saw that Marryat, not less than Homer, Milton and Virgil, profited by the choice of a familiar and legendary subject; so that he prepared his readers on the very title-page; and this set me cudgelling my brains, if by any chance I could hit upon some similar belief to be the centre-piece of my own meditated fiction. In the course of this vain search there cropped up in my memory a singular case of a buried and resuscitated fakir, which I had been often told by an uncle of mine, then lately dead, Inspector-General John Balfour.[23]

This idea that a writer can 'meditate a fiction' in the abstract and worry about the focal point later is exactly the opposite of what 'inspiration' usually signifies, and Stevenson's admission that the process involved 'cudgelling' and striving is refreshingly frank. Yet the net result of 'how-I did-it' pieces like this – and he was keen to write them – is to evoke just that romanticised view of composition he is gainsaying: the beauties of nature, remoteness from mankind and a mystical silence engender the 'right' creative atmosphere and, though the author then says 'Come' only to his 'engine', the image is strongly evocative of a magician summoning up meinies, or Brownies.

The novel that emerged from this exercise, *The Master of Ballantrae*, was hindered rather than helped by the author's insistence on sticking with his uncle's story of the fakir, for the part of the book that has always attracted criticism is the ending, where the body of the wicked 'Master', James Durie, is exhumed and resuscitated by his Indian servant, Secundra Dass, causing the instant death from shock of the Master's tormented brother, Henry. The scene – which takes place in the Adirondacks on a moonlit winter night – is extremely picturesque, with a tableau of Secundra toiling to dig up the frozen grave: 'his blows resounded [...] as thick as sobs; and behind him, strangely deformed and ink-black upon the frosty ground, the creature's shadow repeated and parodied his swift gesticulations'.[24] But it is odd that this, the 'centre-piece' of Stevenson's plan, should seem in execution like an expedient, and Stevenson himself came to write of it as though it had been an imposition rather than his own doggedly maintained choice. In letters, he contrived to blame *Scribner's* and the demands of serial publication for rushing him on to a forced conclusion: 'I hope I shall pull off that damned ending; but it still depresses me: this is your doing, Mr Burlingame: you would have it there and then, and I fear it – I fear that ending.'[25]

Marryat may have kick-started Stevenson's engine on this occasion, but it ran on a mixture of Scott and James Hogg. Hogg provides the groundbass of demonism and murderous sibling rivalry, while Scott strongly influences the domestic scenes. The structure is particularly Scott-ish: the novel ostensibly being the land-agent Ephraim Mackellar's account of the fall of the house of Durisdeer after the Jacobite Rebellion. It is essentially (like *Jekyll and Hyde*) a dossier of evidence: letters, eye-witness accounts and extracts from other people's memoirs assembled and drawn together by Mackellar to augment his own story. In a preface set slightly in the future (1889), the papers have fallen into the hands of Mr Johnstone Thomson, an Edinburgh lawyer (an affectionate portrait of Charles Baxter), whose writer friend (Stevenson) agrees to edit them for publication. But the playful preface was dropped from the first edition, on the grounds that it was 'a little too like Scott', nor did Stevenson use the eighteenth-century legal endorsement he solicited from Baxter, though Baxter, with his usual readiness and ingenuity, had composed a perfect example by return of post.[26]

The story of the 'fraternal enemies', James Durie, the Master of Ballantrae, and his younger brother Henry (were these Christian names coincidental, or another private joke?), made yet another return to the theme of the double. Stevenson described the Master as being 'all I know of the devil'; like Edward Hyde he is completely wicked, while his brother, like Jekyll, is a mixture of virtues and vices, 'neither very bad nor very able'. The Master is notably clever, resourceful and brave, the only character, apart from Alison Graeme, who shows spirit. The book is deliberately confusing in this way, for the amoral Master should not be the hero of the story, nor his ineffectual brother Henry. Henry's patience passes for virtue, but once that has worn out he becomes as bad as his devilish brother, crazed for revenge and transformed as dramatically as Jekyll:

> There was something very daunting in his look; something to my eyes not rightly human; the face, lean, dark and aged, the mouth painful, the teeth disclosed in a perpetual rictus; the eyeball swimming clear of the lids upon a field of blood-shot white.

The tragedy is set in motion when the etiolated Durie family decides that its only hope of survival is to divide loyalties politically during the Jacobite rebellion of 1745. At the toss of a coin, one brother rides off to join Prince Charlie while the younger stays at home, allied to the English King's party (like a dark version of Kidnapped, to which the book has many links). When news reaches them that James has died at Culloden, Henry inherits the title of Master and eventually marries his brother's former fiancée, Alison Graeme. But years later, James returns to Durisdeer, demanding money and his old place, and a bitter struggle breaks out between the brothers. Henry seems to have killed James in a duel and is branded as a fratricide, but in another ghastly twist of the plot it transpires that his brother escaped wounded and resumes his persecution with new energy. It is a mark of Stevenson's skill as a romancer that the plot remains gripping at this point, if not exactly credible. The movement of the conflict to and fro has the familiar structure of a ballad or a folk-tale, and the third appearance of the Master, his third 'death' (burial alive) and subsequent resuscitation by the fakir move along like verse and antiphon.

Cashing in on the success of *Jekyll* – and clearly also a sort of rival to it – *Deacon Brodie* was on tour in the States, with Henley's rambunctious younger brother in the lead. Henley still valued the play highly and hoped to make serious money from it, but Stevenson was getting weary not just of the material – 'my poor old Deacon' – but with his own weak-mindedness in letting Henley do what he liked with the play. When Teddy and two other actors on the tour got drunk and started a fight in Philadelphia, Stevenson began to sicken of the whole thing and was rather glad than crestfallen when a theatre in New York reneged on its booking. Fanny sent pointedly critical letters from New York telling of Teddy's shameless (and, needless to say, unsuccessful) attempts to sponge off her, which in turn made Stevenson rage against him in letters to Baxter. But though the focus of his anger seemed to be the shiftless Teddy, he was clearly also impatient with his stubborn, demanding collaborator, and with himself for having tiptoed round Henley's pride and Henley's ego for so long.

The trouble over the play was a sort of warm-up for the bout to come. The row that brewed up between Stevenson and Henley in the spring of 1888 and which led to their acrimonious, permanent separation has been described as one of the most famous literary quarrels of the age, but it was hardly 'literary' at all. The trigger for it now seems extremely trivial, and must always have done, for details of the proceedings were carefully suppressed for years by all parties concerned, particularly Charles Baxter, who deposited his bundle of 'Quarrel Letters' at the National Library of Scotland under a thirty-year embargo. They chart the composition of what could be thought of as Henley and Stevenson's final collaboration: 'The Nixie: A Melodramatic Farce'.

The prologue was spoken by Samuel McClure, who travelled to London that spring, armed with letters of introduction from Stevenson. His intention was to set up a publishing link with the London literary scene, using Henley as a sort of agent (this was at Stevenson's suggestion), but when he met with Henley and his set, he was struck by the extent of their disaffection with Louis. His account, in his *Autobiography*, emphasises their peevishness; most of Stevenson's friends seemed 'very annoyed by the attention [Stevenson] had received in America. There was a note of detraction in their talk which surprised and, at first, puzzled me.' Henley was 'particularly emphatic', and complained that 'his own influence upon Stevenson's work was not sufficiently recognised'. No doubt it was especially bitter for the man who had slogged for almost a decade over *Deacon Brodie* to see the derivative *Jekyll and Hyde* – the work of a mere few days, according to the papers – shoot its author to fame and wealth. None of the 'friends' seemed pleased at Stevenson's success, and they told McClure that Louis 'was a much overrated man, and that his cousin, R.A.M. Stevenson, was the real genius of the family'.[27]

McClure's 'agency' plan came to nothing, either because he found Henley uncongenial or because he wanted to stay loyal to his new star author once the quarrel broke. If, as I think, McClure's trip to London took place some time in February, he would have been carrying back news of his business meetings when he visited Saranac Lake again on 19 March. The reservations about Henley which McClure expresses in his *Autobiography* may have been perceptible then by Stevenson; indeed it is hard to see how McClure could have completely suppressed his bemusement.*

---

* Ernest Mehew assumes that McClure's visit to London – undated in his *Autobiography* – followed his last to Saranac Lake on 19 March 1888.[28] But by 19 March 'The Nixie' was in print and Henley's fateful letter about it to RLS was already on its way across the Atlantic. It is less likely that McClure got to England quicker than RLS's response, posted on 22 or 23 March, than that the date of his trip to England was towards the end of February, at which time RLS was mentioning him in a letter to Henley (letter 2016) as 'the American Tillotson' – exactly the same description RLS gave of McClure in his (undated) letters of introduction. In that case, when McClure went to Saranac on 19 March, it would have been *after* his excursion.

Act One began when Henley saw the March 1888 issue of *Scribner's Magazine*, containing Fanny's short story, 'The Nixie', and immediately recognised an idea of Katherine de Mattos's which had been discussed one evening the previous year at his house with Louis and Fanny present. Katherine's story (which may or may not have been written already when she told the Stevensons about it – accounts differed later) was about the meeting on board a train of a young man and a girl whose feyness conceals the fact that she is an escaped lunatic. Fanny had jumped in immediately with some enthusiastic suggestions for improvements – why not make the girl turn out to be a water sprite rather than a lunatic? Katherine must have winced at this, for she withdrew into polite refusal of both the possible changes to her plot and Fanny's insistent offers of help – collaboration, even. Fanny was either genuinely unable to understand that her interference was unwelcome, or wilfully determined to press for her own version of the story (she was, after all, the great improver of *Jekyll and Hyde*), but from any point of view her behaviour was neither subtle nor sensitive. Despite some attempts by Henley to place Katherine's story over the next few months, it failed to get published, and Fanny kept on nagging to be allowed to have a go herself. Katherine's eventual concession (when she was visiting the Stevensons in Bournemouth) cannot be viewed as anything other than a collapse under pressure; Louis knew this, as he admitted to Baxter later:

> Katherine even while she consented – as she did to me with her own lips – expressed unwillingness; I told my wife so; and I asked her to go no farther. But she had taken a fancy to the idea, and when Katherine had tried her version and failed and wrote to tell us so, nothing would serve her but to act on this unwilling consent, and try hers.[29]

This astonishing admission that Fanny wrote 'The Nixie' against her husband's advice, standing, meanly, on the letter not the spirit of Katherine's caving-in, comes in the midst of so many hysterical letters by Stevenson protesting his wife's innocence that it could pass unnoticed. But there it is, in a letter to Baxter of 20 April

1888, in which he also implies that the whole ghastly quarrel with Henley that brewed up out of this small incident was actually a proxy match on behalf of the two women. He hints that Katherine habitually played on Henley's admiration in an inappropriate way; 'frankly she can do what she will with Henley'. But everything Stevenson says about the influence of Katherine on Henley is truer ten times of Fanny's influence on himself: 'remember that [his conduct] was all packed into him by an angry woman whom he admires. And what an angry woman is, we all know; and what a man is when he admires.'[30]

The publication of Fanny's story was enough to rouse the jealousy of Henley's circle, even had it been a completely original work. The fact that *Scribner's* accepted it so quickly looked like nepotism, since the magazine had invested so heavily in Fanny's husband's essays ('Beggars' appeared in the same issue). It must have rankled that Louis and Fanny seemed to be covetously withholding credit (i.e. funds) from Katherine for work that was hers, while acting like Lord and Lady Bountiful with their regular contingency payments to Bob, Katherine and Henley himself. Possibly the cousins misunderstood how tied up their uncle Thomas's estate had really been (certainly the newspapers had jumped to the conclusion that Louis inherited a fortune); Louis's pensions to them, carefully calculated to be neither too little nor too much, can only have caused embarrassment and possibly resentment. Baxter, who as agent knew exactly what Louis's financial situation was, commented wisely: 'It is a dangerous thing for a rich man as you now are, or seem to him [Henley], to give money; and I'm afraid that the recent gifts which it gave you so much pleasure to suggest, and me to carry out, may have carried a certain gall with them'.[31]

In this atmosphere of grudge and sour grapes, Fanny's treatment of Katherine seemed the final, clinching condemnation of her character. Henley's unforgivable mistake (unless he was *trying* to break with Louis, which is quite likely) was to try – again – to open Louis's eyes on the subject. This is what the quarrel was about: not plagiarism, but Henley's persistent attention to Fanny's

faults. In his letter, written on 9 March, among a great deal which
is melancholic and almost despairing about himself and his prospects, Henley inserted a short paragraph about 'The Nixie',
expressing 'considerable amazement' that the by-line did not
acknowledge Katherine at all. 'It's Katherine's, surely it's Katherine's?' he wrote.[32] The style was typical, a little blustering, a little
posturing, but the note of sly complicity was guaranteed to inflame
his correspondent and, married with the content, seemed explosively insulting to Uxorious Billy.

Enter Stevenson, in great disturbance, reading a letter. His
immediate response was to put on his most distant and formal
manner and write back 'with indescribable difficulty', asking
Henley to apply to Katherine for the facts. That would clear everything up, for Katherine knew the whole prehistory of 'The Nixie',
to defend which (it was implied) would be completely beneath his
dignity. Meanwhile he could only hint at the 'agony' that the
accusation against his wife caused him. To Baxter by the same
post he wrote bursting with bitterness and agitation:

> I fear I have come to an end with Henley; the Lord knows if
> I have not tried hard to be a friend to him, the Lord knows
> even that I have not altogether failed. There is not one of that
> crew that I have not helped in every kind of strait, with
> money, with service, and that I was not willing to have risked
> my life for; and yet the years come, and every year there is a
> fresh outburst against me and mine.
>
> [. . .] I cannot say it is anger I feel, but it is despair. My
> last reconciliation with Henley is not yet a year old; and here
> is the devil again. I am weary of it all – weary, weary, weary.
> And this letter was (so the writer said) intended to cheer me
> on a sick-bed! May God preserve me from such consolations;
> I slept but once last night, and then woke in an agony, dream-
> ing I was quarrelling with you; the miserable cold day was
> creeping in, and I remembered you were the last of my old
> friends with whom I could say I was still on the old terms.
>
> [. . .] It will probably come to a smash; and I shall have
> to get you to give the poor creature an allowance, pretending
> it comes from [. . .] anybody but me. Desert him I could not:

my life is all bound about these thorns; but whether I can continue to go on cutting my hands and my wife's hands, is quite another question. [. . .] The tale of the plays which I have gone on writing without hope, because I thought they kept him up, is of itself something; and I can say he never knew – and never shall know – that I thought these days and months a sacrifice. On the other hand, there have been, I think there still are, some warm feelings; they have never been warm enough to make him close his mouth, even where he knew he could hurt me sorely, even to the friends whom he knew I prized[.][33]

Stevenson must have spent a sleepless night indeed to have reached this pitch so soon. But clearly the desire to draw up a final account with Henley had been with him some time, since he already had a draft of it in his head. He waited for a reply in miserable suspense; the post took between ten and fourteen days each way, so it was almost a month before he heard back from Henley. In the interval he kept writing to Baxter, describing his symptoms of distress: 'I feel this business with a keenness that I cannot describe; I get on during the day well enough; only that whenever I think of it, I have palpitations. But at night! sleep is quite out of the question; and I have been obliged to take to opiates. God knows I would rather have died than have this happen.'[34] '[T]he dreadful part of a thing like this, is that it shakes your confidence in all affection, and inspires you with a strange, sick longing to creep back into yourself and care for no one.'[35]

If Louis and Henley had still been living in the same country, the matter might well have been resolved and their friendship patched up as before. But the fact that all their dealings were by letter at this date, to be waited for, then pored over, copied and circulated, discussed and dissected, doomed this argument to be irreconcilable. After Louis's initial flare-up, to which he could 'find no form of signature', his next to Henley bore the usual 'R.L.S.', and the one after that ended 'Yours affectionately', indicating a strong willingness to make up. But then another post would come, with fresh cause for offence and no sign of an apology, and more fuel would be added to the fire. When Katherine wrote that Henley 'had a perfect right to be astonished [about 'The Nixie'] but his having said so has nothing to do with me',[36] Stevenson was so disgusted at her primness that he copied the letter out to send to Baxter, who was at the same time getting post from Henley detailing his own side of the story, and his own impatience with letters from Saranac: 'The immense superiority, the sham set of "facts"; the assumption that I am necessarily guilty, the complete ignoring of the circumstance that my acquaintance with the case is probably a good deal more intimate and peculiar than his own [. . .] the directions as to conduct and action – all these things have set me wild.'[37]

Fanny must have known the contents of the offending letter from Henley before she left for California on 26 March, as Louis's reply was written four days before that. Henley had marked his letter 'Private and Confidential', but it would have been impossible for Louis to conceal it from Fanny, or mask the distress evident in the letters to Baxter which were written before her departure. By the time she got to the West Coast, where she was going to look once more into the prospect of buying a ranch, and to meet Belle for the first time in years, Fanny was in a state of impacted rage against Henley and his cronies, whom, she felt, were really endangering Louis's health, possibly his life, by the stress they were causing. She wrote to Baxter in tragic style: 'Had Henley only been satisfied with making the charge to me, I should have been bound to say nothing to Louis on account of the ill effects of such a thing upon his health. As it is, they have nearly, perhaps, quite murdered him. It is very hard for me to keep on living; I may not be able to, but must try for my dear Louis's sake. If I cannot, then I leave my curse upon the murderers and slanderers.'

The charge against her was 'horrible', 'untrue': 'How could anyone believe that I could rob my dearest friend, the one upon whom I was always seeking to heap benefits.' Fanny very likely *did* believe she had tried to help Katherine (now, for the first time, being called her 'dearest friend'), but her difficulties coping with

English snobbery and the pronounced anti-Americanism of the Henley set may have led her to misunderstand the tone of almost all their dealings. Fanny was a humourless and self-deluding woman: wrong, certainly; mad, possibly – but not bad. It is extremely unlikely that she wanted to do deliberate harm, unlike Henley, who was always spoiling for a fight.

Only a postscript to Henley's first reply has survived (possibly Stevenson destroyed the main body of the letter), but a draft in the archive at Yale,[38] in Henley's and Bob Stevenson's hands, could be a rough version of that letter, or of the one Henley told Baxter on 7 April he had torn up at Katherine's request. In it, 'Henley' (i.e. he and Bob together, and possibly Katherine too) makes some apology for causing Louis pain, but goes on to restate and reinforce the accusation against Fanny. 'Of what passed in my presence I retain the impression that Katherine showed herself extremely unwilling to discuss the question,' the draft reads, 'and resented – ironically of course as you know she does – the possibility of any interference in the matter. [. . .] Having once shown her reluctance and begged Fanny at the outset in my house to leave her and her story alone Katherine imagined that she had done enough and that she must leave the rest to Fanny's own taste. [. . . Katherine's story] was already completely written and all suggestions were earnestly deprecated.'[39] Despite the mean tone of all these letters, the point which Henley insisted on repeating seems to have been perfectly clear and valid: that Katherine had been bullied out of her intellectual property.

Meanwhile, off-stage in California, Fanny was working herself into full-blown hysterics. All winter she had complained of 'brain congestion', and had been recommended by the doctor not to so much as read a book for fear of overtaxing herself. Under the strain of the quarrel, she began to fear she might completely break down. It is hard to guess quite what the term 'brain congestion' might signify here: migraine, perhaps (though her symptoms don't seem to have been acute enough for that), menopausal headaches (Fanny turned forty-eight in 1888), altitude sickness, depression?

Her letter to Baxter seems to exhibit symptoms not merely of anger but derangement:

> Louis always said that my worst point was my devilish pride. Perhaps God means that it should be humbled. Every day I say to myself can this be *I, myself*? really I, myself? Nothing that I have said here shall I say to Louis, – unless I become quite mad, in which case nothing will make any difference. If it so happens that I must go back to perfidious Albion, I shall learn to be false. For Louis's sake I shall pretend to be their friend still – while he lives; but that in my heart I can ever forgive those who have borne false witness against me –! While they eat their bread from my hand – and oh, they will do that – I shall smile and wish it were poison that might wither their bodies as they have my heart. Please burn this letter lest it be said that I was mad when I made my will. Those who falsely (knowing it to be false) accuse me of theft, I cannot trust to be honest. They may try to rob my boy after they have murdered us. I can leave clear proof of my sanity in the clearness with which I am managing affairs.[40]

Nothing could be less clear as 'proof of sanity', as Baxter must have realised, since he kept the letter carefully with the rest.

The angry woman raged; but not at her husband. One result of this debacle was a reinforcement of the already very strong bonds between Louis and Fanny. The letters they wrote each other during this separation are notably tender and affectionate. Separately hysterical, each strove to calm the other. The knowledge of what Louis was going through on her behalf redoubled Fanny's loyalty and gratitude towards him, and the imminent ejection from his life of the friends ('fiends') whom she now freely admitted she had always hated must have gladdened her heart. The response the quarrel had aroused in Louis was infinitely reassuring to Fanny: that, merely by her being a woman and his wife, he would always defend her.

There are two other significant players who ought to be mentioned: one is Baxter (the stage manager), the other Bob (the prompt). Baxter found himself in the unenviable position of confidant to both Henley and Louis, and recipient of Fanny's ravings.

All through these bleak months of discord, his good sense, anxious care and long acquaintance with both men made the crisis tolerable for Louis, who was understandably worried that *all* his old friends might, in his absence, side against him. The crisis elicited from Baxter what amount to declarations of love; he began to address Louis as 'my dear' (to which Louis responded in kind), and in a confessional moment admitted that he had gone through a phase a few years back of thinking Louis was tired of him: 'I know now how the days of your youth and the friends that were its companions never lose their interest for you. I know the steadfast love which has seemed to me like that of a woman but for a time I doubted and was sad.'[41] Stevenson's answer acknowledged how queer – in both senses – this state of affairs was: 'It is strange when you think what a couple of heartless drunken young dogs we were, that we should be what we are today: that you should so write, and I so accept what you have written [. . .] My wife, to whom I sent on your letter, was equally affected with myself.'[42]

How Henley would have scoffed at the whole of that letter, had he read it. He, too, employed the idea of Louis as feminine, but as a denigration, moaning to Baxter apropos Stevenson's self-centredness:

> I begin to suspect that from the first I have given him too much: so much, indeed, that he has been conscious, when I myself have not, of a momentary transfer of interest from him to myself and my own immediate griefs and troubles. Such a perception as his is too feminine to be baffled; such an affection is too feminine to be endured.[43]

It was clear whom Henley blamed for the despicable softening process that had spoiled his friend: Fanny. She had emasculated Louis, and not deferred, as wives should, to their husbands' bachelor friendships. The remarks he made to Baxter about her were scornful and crude: 'Lewis has known me longer than his spouse, and he has never known me to lie or truckle or do anything that is base. He can't have slept with Fanny all these years, and not have caught her in the act of lying.' By coincidence, Henley was

about to publish his *Book of Verses* that year, containing the
twelve-year-old 'In Hospital' sequence, with an envoi addressed to
Baxter which celebrated the joint friendship of himself, Louis,
Baxter and Walter Ferrier by comparison with Dumas's Musketeers (in other words, glorifying those very days as 'heartless,
drunken young dogs' that Stevenson felt dead and gone).

Remembered now as a showdown with Henley, the quarrel
had possibly even more impact on Louis in regard to his relations
with Bob, boon companion, boyhood hero and adored 'other half'.
Bob's is a silent but potent presence throughout the whole affair,
his handwriting on archive drafts of letters from both Henley and
Katherine proof of his complicity, his very concealment behind the
others a mark of deep-seated resentments and jealousies against
his cousin. The relationship had been changing, naturally enough,
since the advent of Mrs Osbourne into their lives at Grez; her
flirtation with Bob was always going to make subsequent social
dealings with him difficult. Bob's marriage was another impediment, as his wife Louisa was said to dislike Louis (as Walter Simpson's wife did too, apparently). Louis himself didn't seem to
understand why his cousin had become 'somewhat withdrawn
from the touch of friendship'[44] by the summer of 1886, despite
their ardent reunions in war-gaming and juvenile larks at Skerryvore, but it does seem likely to have stemmed from jealousy. Family
and old friends are notoriously prone to be embarrassed, puzzled
or resentful when someone they have known in obscurity becomes
famous. To this, Bob had the added sting of having always been
the one tipped for success; his looks and health alone might have
done it, but his talents as a painter and writer always promised far
more than his weedy cousin's literary dilettantism. But here was
Louis, fought over by publishers, wallowing in dollars, heir to
family money over which Bob and Katherine had equal, if not
better, rights. No wonder if Bob was aggrieved. And no wonder
Louis had difficulty finishing his novel about 'fraternal enemies'
hounding each other to death in *The Master of Ballantrae*. The
plot was beginning to look horribly prophetic.

The quarrel, in effect, altered the whole structure of Louis's life. He had previously been a man who derived a great deal of stimulus and pleasure from having a close group of friends; from now on he continued friendships with individuals in that group, but on a totally different footing and in the context of having to share them with (i.e. risk losing them to, at any minute) new, harsh enemies. If he had gone back to Europe, those last ties with Colvin, Baxter, Gosse and James might have snapped too; as it was, the distance that helped precipitate the break with Henley made it easier to sustain friendly relations with the others. A correspondence can be continued quietly, intensely even, without the knowledge of mutual acquaintances. Letters now became of enormous importance to Stevenson, and the fact that there was always a delay built into his communications with friends from this time onwards had far-reaching effects on his letter-writing style, as we shall see.

As his old friendship structures collapsed, so the domestic ones became all-in-all. Stevenson was thrown back entirely on the family group. His feelings for Fanny intensified; he also took comfort in his mother's company. Margaret Stevenson's unreflective and optimistic nature was balm during the crisis (which she politely ignored) and her presence was now Louis's only link with the past. Mother and son were left alone at Saranac for long stretches of time and were very content together: without Thomas to domineer them and Cummy to show up Margaret's inferior mothering skills, their relationship was unimpeded for the first time in decades. During one of Fanny's many absences from Baker's Cottage, Margaret wrote to her sister that it seemed 'oddly like the old days at Heriot Row. Then, when "Papa dined out", Lou and I used to indulge in little dishes we were not allowed at other times, – particularly rabbit-pie, I remember – and so we do still. I sometimes almost forget that my baby has grown up!'[45] The revived relationship didn't seem to make Fanny feel threatened; she and 'the old lady' (a mere eleven years her senior) had little in common but a happy tolerance of each other.

Louis had proved an inspired step-parent to Lloyd, and now committed himself even further. The apprentice writer, still only nineteen years old, had been hammering away at his comic novel during the winter and showing pages of it to his stepfather for comments and advice. Louis had written to his wife in October that some of it was 'incredibly bad; and I don't know yet if he has the power to better it for the press';[46] to Symonds he described it as 'so silly, so gay, so absurd, in spots (to my partial eyes) so genuinely humorous'.[47] There was no talk at this point of collaboration, or any serious expectation that Lloyd's story could get published, but by the spring Stevenson had offered to rewrite the book. Lloyd's account of this decision, written in 1924, gives some idea of what sort of fiction-writer Stevenson was taking on:

> [A]fter a pause, he added, through the faint cloud of his cigarette smoke: 'But of course it is unequal; some of it is pretty poor; and what is almost worse is the good stuff you have wasted [. . .] Why, I could take up that book, and in one quick, easy rewriting could make it sing!'
> Our eyes met; it was all decided in that one glance.
> 'By God, why shouldn't I!' he exclaimed. 'That is, if you don't mind?'
> Mind!
> I was transported with joy. What would-be writer of nineteen would not have been? It was my vindication; the proof that I had not been living in a fool's paradise, and had indeed talent, and a future.[48]

The decision to back Lloyd's book was of course far from 'proof' of the boy's talent. If Stevenson had had any faith in his stepson's ability to become a writer, he would have left him to make his own way in the publishing world. The decision to lend his name to The Wrong Box was tantamount to issuing Lloyd with a guest pass into the world of letters and absolving him from any further effort, and the only reason to do so was to save him having to get a real job or lead a life away from home. This would settle several issues at once, and comfort Fanny, who fussed about her son continually. The family would stick together, become a sort of writing 'firm': Stevenson and stepson, perhaps. The plan worked, insofar as Lloyd never had any trouble getting anything published, and was indulged in his delusion of having literary talent until his life's end, but it did Stevenson no favours. It made the proven author look stupid to share the title page of Lloyd's scatty, chatty novel. Sam McClure told Stevenson as much when he was shown the manuscript, provoking a frosty answer, as McClure recalled in his memoirs: 'I thought it a good story for a young man to have written; but I told Stevenson that I doubted the wisdom of his putting his name to it as joint author. This annoyed him, and he afterwards wrote me that he couldn't take advice on such matters.'[49]

Stevenson had left Bournemouth expecting to return for the summers at least, but now was in no mood to do so, even without Fanny at his side swearing never to set foot again in 'perfidious Albion'. An alternative to Saranac was desperately needed, however, and Margaret Stevenson's suggestion that they should all go on an extended yacht-cruise (she offered to pay half) suddenly seemed the ideal solution to the problem. The Indian Ocean, the eastern seaboard of North America and the Greek Islands were all mooted – with a view to writing a book, as planned earlier in Hyères – but the eventual destination was chosen almost by chance. Fanny, out in California, had been scouting round for somewhere to live, and also (presumably) trying to sort out the implications of her ex-husband's disappearance. She was even thinking of buying Sam's own ranch from his unfortunate wife Paulie, who could not keep it up and whose case 'might have been mine – but for you', as she wrote to her husband.[50] Joe Strong's father, who had been a missionary in Hawaii for a number of years, highly recommended a summer cruise to 'the Gallivantings' (Fanny's joke generic name for Pacific island groups), as 'they are really pastures new, and very little is known about them', and the choice of the Pacific was clinched when she heard of a luxury schooner for hire in San Francisco which it would be possible to have complete with a captain and crew for an extensive Pacific island tour. The trip would take about seven months and would cost a fortune: £2000 – that is, about £100,000 in current money (Bob's allowance, deemed by Louis to be enough for comfort, was £10 a quarter). Fanny telegrammed the news that the boat could be ready in ten days: 'Reply immediately'. The drama of the quick decision was just what Stevenson needed to lift him soaringly out of his troubles on a wave of adrenalin. He cabled back by return, 'Blessed girl, take the yacht and expect us in ten days.'

'My dear Charles,' he wrote to Baxter,

> I have found a yacht and we are going the full pitch for seven months. If I cannot get my health back (more or less) 'tis madness; but of course, there is the hope, and I will play big. We telegraph to you today not to invest £2,000; and now I write to ask you to send same sum *quam celerrimum* to our account at Messrs John Paton & Co., 52 William Street, New York.
>
> [. . .] If this business fails to set me up, well, 2,000 is gone, and I know I can't get better. We sail from San Francisco, June 15th, for the South Seas in the yacht *Casco*.

12

ONA

THE *CASCO* WAS A luxury yacht, ninety-four feet long, seventy-four tons weight, beautifully rigged and sparred and as elegant as a swan. Her owner, a Dr Merritt of Oakland, was rightly proud of the boat and her fittings; *Casco* combined all the comforts of the high-Victorian parlour with the ability to get away from it all. Everything about her was trim, clean and rich: cushioned seats round the cockpit, velvet-covered sofas in the main cabin, brass curtain rods, crimson carpets, white and gold panelling and bevelled mirrors. Merritt was not at all sure he wanted to hire this beauty to a man as unfastidious about dress and person as Stevenson, and he insisted on vetting the whole party – especially the old lady – before agreeing to let the *Casco* go for $500 a month basic rent, with all repairs, provisioning and wages to be paid by the lessee.

Stevenson had arrived in San Francisco in a state of high excitement, but was not pleased to find his rooms at the Occidental Hotel full of flowers from admirers and the by-now-usual gaggle of newspaper reporters on his tail. He and Lloyd decamped early and lived on the *Casco* in Oakland Creek until departure, stocking up for the long voyage. There were to be eleven people on board – Fanny, Louis, Margaret, Lloyd, Valentine, the captain, four hands and a cook – and they would be continuously at sea for about a month on the first run of the journey, to Nukahiva in the Marquesas, about ten degrees south of the Equator. From there they would travel further south, to the Society Islands, then back north again in a sharp inverted triangle to Hawaii. From Hawaii, *Casco* would return to San Francisco and her anxious owner, who expressed the fear to Margaret Stevenson that the party might love the boat too much ever to come back.

As usual, Stevenson planned to cover his expenses by producing a travel book, but this time the expenses were so huge that the book had to be suitably ambitious too. It was going to be one of the first books about the South Seas to be illustrated with photographs – a brilliant idea to bring high-tech and primitivism together, almost certainly conceived for Lloyd's benefit, since it meant lots of lovely gadgets needed to be purchased: cameras, a tripod, glass plates and a typewriter. All this was loaded onto the *Casco*, along with tinned food, dried meat, champagne and tobacco for eleven. Margaret Stevenson had brought with her from Edinburgh several bandboxes full of the starched white organdie widow's caps that were her constant wear, so she would never be without a fresh one, and there were also, hidden forward, the necessary items for a burial at sea, for the captain had taken note of Stevenson's 'startling physical weakness'[1] and wanted to be prepared.

Belle had come up to San Francisco to see the party off. She had become something of an old 'island hand' from living in Honolulu for the previous six years with Joe, where they hobnobbed with the Hawaiian royal family and lived the strange life of the Pacific whites – at once trashy and exalted – that Stevenson was about to join. The fact that indolent, drunken, sparsely-talented Joe could pass as an 'official artist' in Hawaii was evidence of the credit whites had there, and of how quickly they were using it up. Joe had even been part of a Hawaiian embassy to Samoa in recent years – or perhaps it was more a spying mission – to evaluate the influence of the 'Powers', Britain, Germany, France and the United

States, who between them were busily carving up the Pacific. King Kalakaua of Hawaii, Joe's patron, was naturally concerned at the speed with which neighbouring island groups were being taken over. He liked to think of himself as the most influential ruler in the Pacific, and the leader to whom all Polynesians should look in the struggle (weak enough) against Western colonialism, but of course his own group, the Sandwich Islands, so much the nearest to America, and so much influenced by Western culture already, would be the first to go.

Joe and Belle had become sponsors of Stevenson's Pacific holiday (as he still thought of it) and were going to introduce him to Kalakaua when the *Casco* landed at Hawaii, some time the following year. Belle encouraged all the women on the voyage to revise their wardrobes drastically to cope with the tropical heat, and among the many items being stowed in the *Casco*'s mahogany cupboards were a number of voluminous *holokus* and *mumus*, the shapeless, sack-like 'missionary dresses' that were worn all over the Pacific, by whites and native women alike. It was easy to see that they had been designed by missionaries: every inch of flesh from the epiglottis to the toe was covered, and the material hung loosely from a gathered yoke above the breast. They were not as cool as the light cotton trousers and collarless shirts that men wore in the tropics, but at least they kept the sun off delicate northern skin and made the corset redundant. Margaret had some of these dresses made, but was 'putting off as long as I can' the moment when she would have to appear in them;[2] Fanny, on the other hand, saw nothing but liberation in their massy folds, and hardly wore any other kind of garment ever again.

If Merritt had been chary of his floating tenants' suitability, his chosen master of the *Casco*, Captain A.H. Otis, was more so. Otis, who disliked tourists, began the voyage in sullen withdrawal from his passengers, none of whom (*three* women!) looked as if they would be any use in an emergency, and all of whom, except the maid and perhaps the old lady, were highly-strung and talkative. The writer himself was childishly delighted with the boat, and pranced from bowsprit to helm like an intoxicated water-sprite; the writer's mother wanted to take walks along the narrowest part of the deck; the writer's wife insisted on chatting to the man at the wheel and the man at the compass, both located just by the benches in the open-air cockpit they used as a sitting room. This indiscipline aggravated the captain considerably, but he was yet too scornful of the party to use anything but sarcasm on them. 'Please don't talk to [the steersman] today, Mrs Stevenson,' he said to Fanny. 'Today I want him to steer.' And when she retaliated by asking what he would do if her mother-in-law fell overboard, Otis replied dryly, 'Put it in the log.'[3]

How much idea did Stevenson have of what awaited them in the Pacific? The physical and practical demands of life at sea for such a long, uninterrupted period were unknown to him; his Atlantic crossings had all been in steamships and liners, whereas the *Casco*, a mere ninety-foot wand of wood bobbing up and down on an ocean half the size of the globe, would need excellent seamanship, good luck and good weather in order to reach Nukahiva intact. The risks were to be borne home to them later on their three-thousand-mile voyage, but when they sailed across San Francisco Bay on 28 June 1888, and out through the Golden Gate (which had no bridge across it yet), the Stevensons were, for the most part, ignorant of any danger but sea-sickness.

Stevenson's concept of 'the South Seas' had been long forming. A visitor to Heriot Row in 1875 (during Louis's days as a law student) had first told him of the wonderful climate of the Pacific, particularly the Navigator Islands (Samoa), and how beneficial it was to sufferers from respiratory diseases. Louis became 'sick with desire to go there; beautiful places, green forever; perfect shapes of men and women, with red flowers in their hair; and nothing to do but study oratory and etiquette, sit in the sun, and pick up the fruits as they fall'.[4] This paradisal notion must have been in his mind when he located his ideal commonwealth in Samoa in the unfinished novel 'The Hair Trunk'. During his residence in San Francisco in 1879–80, Stevenson's interest in the South Seas was fed by Charles Warren Stoddard, whose bachelor digs on Nob Hill were full of Polynesian artefacts collected during his many visits to the Sandwich Islands (where he was at that moment). Stoddard had lent Stevenson Herman Melville's *Typee* and *Omoo*, works which fascinated the Scot, who was – perhaps consciously – reproducing exactly in the *Casco*'s itinerary Melville's first journey into the Pacific, to the Marquesas, Tahiti and then Hawaii.

Mark Twain had also lived in the Sandwich Islands and very probably talked about the Pacific with Stevenson – who was, after all, on his way there – when they met in New York that summer.* Then there were the encouragement and example of Joe and Belle Strong, who knew Stoddard well (he found them their house in Hawaii), and Joe's parents, former missionaries, all of whom had managed to live well in the Pacific on relatively little money. Books of history and science, such as the voyages of Captain Cook and Darwin's accounts of the Galapagos Islands (which Stevenson wanted to see), had contributed to Stevenson's preconception, as had contemporary books of leisure travel – a recent innovation – including Stoddard's own *South Sea Idylls* and *Summer Cruising in the South Seas*, with its swooning descriptions of native boys' beauty. The other strong tradition of Pacific travel writing emphasised the perils to the white man of entering the territory of 'the other', a brutal, primitive world of cannibals, black magic and bestial sex, inhospitable islands 'peopled with lascivious monkeys',[6] where civilisation would meet its doom.

As Point Reyes and Mount Tamalpais receded to specks behind them, all that the passengers on the *Casco* thought of was the exoticism of their adventure. None more so perhaps than Margaret Stevenson, fifty-nine-year-old widow and late invalid of Edin-

---

* Twain and Stevenson met in Washington Square during the week (at the end of April 1888) Stevenson spent in New York City. Twain, another writer who habitually had a multiplicity of works in progress and was subject to writer's block, was also obsessed by doubles and the idea that he had a 'dream self' that seemed to lead a separate life. *Jekyll and Hyde* had affected him profoundly. In 1910, when the writer lay dying, his last continuous speech was on this very subject, 'about "the laws of mentality", about Jekyll and Hyde and dual personality'.[5]

burgh: 'Isn't it wonderful that I am going to see all these strange, out-of-the-way places?' she wrote excitedly to her sister Jane. 'I always longed so much to see them, and I can hardly believe that all those childish longings are to come true.'[7] The early days on the boat were very pleasant for those who got over their sea-sickness quickly (Fanny didn't, but her lack of complaint about her poor sea-legs was one of her noblest sacrifices for love). 'There is upon the whole no better life,' Stevenson wrote to Colvin. 'Fine, clean emotions, a world all and always beautiful; air better than wine; interest unflagging.'[8] Louis had the 'stateroom' to himself, where he could work, and Lloyd had the other bedroom, while all three women slept in the drawing room on shelves that were hidden during the day with little lace curtains. In the mornings, Stevenson would write before breakfast, and dictate to Lloyd at the typewriter in the latter part of the morning. The women passed the time reading, playing cards, sewing and knitting, and Fanny made some attempts to improve the truly awful efforts of the cook. Other than that, there was the sea to watch and the night sky to marvel at and the sound of Louis's flageolet ('in which he was persistent', Otis remarked[9]) to try to ignore.

Otis was relieved to find that his employer, though an author, did not want to talk about his books. The captain had read only one of them, *Treasure Island*, and knew there were others that he might be challenged to remark on. The fact that this gruff bibliophobe had read *any* of Stevenson's works at all is another indication of how widespread the writer's fame had become. Gradually, Otis came to admire the thin man's unflappability; though the women all screeched when the *Casco*, going at remarkable speed, first put her rail under water, Stevenson said nothing, and he proved just as cool during the storm they approached on the tenth day out, which necessitated three days of anxious confinement below deck. It became apparent to the captain at this point that the boat was significantly undermanned; he was the only navigator on board and had to stay at the wheel without respite during bad weather. If anything happened to him, the whole

ship would be imperilled. That possibility came horribly close
when a freak squall, 'black as a black cat', as the captain later
described it, hit the *Casco* as they neared the Marquesas.[10] The
ship was knocked down so that the edge of the cabin was under
water and water was pouring in through the deadlights below that
the women had failed to close (against Otis's repeated advice, as
he was keen to point out in his reminiscences).

Towards dawn on 28 July, the magical moment arrived when
land was sighted: the distant volcanic peak of Ua-huna. 'The first
experience can never be repeated,' Stevenson wrote in *In the South
Seas*; 'the first love, the first sunrise, the first South Sea Island, are
memories apart and touched [by] a virginity of sense':[11]

> Not one soul aboard the *Casco* had set foot upon the islands,
> or knew, except by accident, one word of any of the island
> tongues; and it was with something perhaps of the same anxi-
> ous pleasure as thrilled the bosoms of discoverers that we
> drew near these problematic shores. The land heaved up in
> peaks and rising vales; it fell in cliffs and buttresses; its colour
> ran through fifty modulations in a scale of pearl and rose and
> olive; and it was crowned above by opalescent clouds.[12]

They bore along the shore, looking without success for signs of
life, and eventually reached Anaho Bay, where no sooner had they
anchored than a canoe was spotted on its way out from the shore.
On board were the local chief and a white trader called Regler,
the advance party for dozens of small boats that followed. Soon
the *Casco* was swarming with natives, 'stalwart, six-foot men in
every state of undress; some in a shirt, some in a loin-cloth, one in
a handkerchief, improperly adjusted'.[13] Here was a 'strange, and
to us, rather alarming' sight for Margaret Stevenson to report
home. 'The display of legs was something we were not accustomed
to; but as they were all tattooed in most wonderful patterns, it
really looked quite as if they were wearing open-work silk tights,'
she wrote to her sister.[14] One can imagine the whoops around the
Edinburgh tea-tables when this was read aloud to Jane's cronies.

The Marquesans had brought with them quantities of fruit and

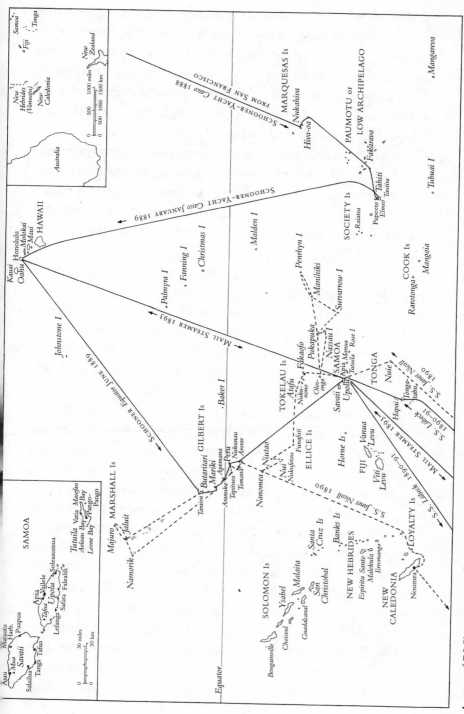

A map of RLS's cruises in the South Seas on *Casco* (1888–89), *Equator* (1889) and the *Janet Nicoll* (1890; indicated by the broken line). The routes of the *Lübeck* from Samoa to Australia and of the mail steamers by which RLS visited Sydney and Hawaii are also shown.

curios, but as trade, not gifts, and they seemed distinctly displeased when no one on *Casco* showed any sign of wanting to buy. Many of them carried knives, and their aspect seemed threatening; one in particular repelled Louis 'as something bestial, squatting on his hams in a canoe, sucking an orange and spitting it out again to alternate sides with ape-like vivacity'.[15] Louis began to feel apprehensive; the Marquesans were rumoured still to practise cannibalism. He showed them round the boat, to murmurs of amazement and appreciation. The men measured up dimensions against their fine brown arms and the women went from chair to chair, trying them all for comfort. One was so excited by the softness of the *Casco*'s red velvet that she hoisted up her skirt and rubbed her bare bottom along it 'with cries of wonder and delight'.[16]

Hours later, the boat was still full of islanders, now arranged in silent, watchful groups. Adopting a policy of pacifism, the boat party attempted to go about their ordinary business and, writing up his journal in his cabin, Louis found himself the object of steady observation: 'three brown-skinned generations, squatted cross-legged upon the floor, and regarding me in silence with embarrassing eyes.[. . .] A kind of despair came over me, to sit there helpless under all these staring orbs, and be thus blocked in my cabin by this speechless crowd: and a kind of rage to think they were beyond the reach of articulate communication, like furred animals, or folk born deaf, or the dwellers of some alien planet.'[17]

This introduction to the islanders proved deceptive, however, and the very men who intimidated Stevenson by their silence and watchfulness were, on the *Casco*'s last day at Nukahiva, bidding him an emotional and dignified farewell, plying him with gifts and calling him 'Ona' (a pidgin form of 'Owner'), their tribute to his apparent wealth and importance. In the intervening weeks, the Stevensons had got to know the small communities at Anaho and Tai-o-hae on the opposite side of the island and had begun to understand something of Marquesan manners (which, Stevenson was to admit on further knowledge of the South Seas, were the most difficult in Polynesia for Westerners to fathom quickly). They had been welcomed on shore and given a feast of delicious, novel food (breadfruit mashed with coconut, small green onions, roast pig in banana leaf). They had also seen the former ritual 'high places' where that other type of meat – 'long pig' – had been prepared, and met the last eater of it, 'such a mild and benevolent old gentleman', Margaret Stevenson wrote, 'that it is difficult to believe he was till quite recently a cannibal'.[18] This cheerful carnivore came on board the *Casco* to experiment with Lloyd's typewriter, and solemnly tapped out his name over and over.

Margaret was having the time of her life; she was delighted with the taste of coconut juice (which was just as well, as they would all be drinking a lot of it in the coming years) and the native feast spread for them at Atuona, which she ate from a banana leaf while seated on a mat. She had bathed for the first time in twenty-six years, climbed a hill 'higher than Arthur's Seat', met the ex-cannibal chief and seen Marquesan dancers climb on each other's shoulders and do 'some other strange things'.[19] Her photos of Queen Victoria (whom Margaret, in her starched organdie widow's cap, somewhat resembled) had been much admired, as had her gloves, which one chief in Atuatua quaintly called 'British tattooing'. There was something beguiling about the place; even church-going took on a lotus-eating aspect, with the natives crooning like 'nothing but a gigantic lime-tree full of bees', so lulling that Mrs Stevenson almost fell asleep. From Fakarava, she described to Jane a perfectly clear day, on which 'the little, fleecy, white clouds in the sky were exactly mirrored in the water. We could see the white coral reefs at the bottom distinctly, and the sea was a very tender green that was peculiarly beautiful. Then at night there was a superb moon, and Fanny and I sat long on the beach to enjoy it, while Louis walked up and down playing tunes on his pipes.'[20] The anniversary of her wedding day brought back thoughts of home, and her 'dear husband'. Loyalty and love for him would never have allowed her to admit how much better off both she and Louis were now that the slab stone of Tom's melancholy and inflexibility had been lifted from their shoulders.

Another time, the *Casco* entertained a Marquesan queen on board, and Fanny, stuck for a gesture of goodwill, taught her how to roll a cigarette, Mexican style (whatever that was). 'Fanny took a cigarette also to keep her company, and we all sat around and smiled and patted each other in the absence of any mutual language.'[21] Polynesian, which had at first seemed such an insuperable barrier, turned out 'easy to smatter', being already full of English borrowings. And there were plenty of interpreters on hand too, for every islet seemed to have its share of pale faces – missionaries, traders or the 'broken white folk', in Stevenson's pregnant phrase, who were to people his later fiction.

During these first weeks in the Marquesas, Stevenson was bursting with ideas and excitement at the novelty and 'incredible' interest of everything around him, which he could hardly bring himself to share with Colvin or anyone else back in Britain, for fear of spoiling the sensation when he eventually published his articles in *Scribner's*. The picturesque aspects of the South Seas, though delightful to him personally, played little part in this; he rather surprised himself by finding the political, cultural and anthropological issues far more riveting. In consequence, his non-fiction was to take on a tone very different from that of the charming, light-hearted essays and travel books with which he had first made his name in the 1870s, a change for which few people were prepared to forgive him.

But that was in the future; the only writing that Stevenson was doing at this time was in his journal. The insidious effects of white settlement, which were clear enough to any passer-through, he itemised and analysed; opium addiction and diseases such as smallpox, TB and syphilis were everywhere, the islands were depopulated, villages deserted, but there was a psychological malaise among the Marquesans too, which he was right to think had been paid little attention before. They suffered from a dispiritedness which Stevenson was to see again and again in the South Seas

(Samoa being an exception greatly influenced his eventual choice of a home there). Suicide rates were high: the Polynesian, he believed, 'falls easily into despondency; bereavement, disappointment, the fear of novel visitations, the decay or proscription of ancient pleasures, easily incline him to be sad, and sadness detaches him from life'.[22] The usual explanation for this phenomenon was that the islanders were 'childlike', weak and fanciful, but Stevenson, no doubt strongly influenced by his reading of Galton as well as Spencer and Darwin, saw them as a race in irreversible decline, their fertility extraordinarily low, their vulnerability to disease high, their capacity for strong feeling of any kind – pleasure or conflict – sapped by lack of use. For someone like himself, whose physical (and mental) frailty had prompted a lifetime of 'aggressive optimism', the apathy of these ostensibly more fortunate people than himself was shocking. He was dismayed at the shrugging fatalism of a young mother in Anaho who held out her child and said, '*Tenez* – a little baby like this; then dead. All the Kanaques die. Then no more.' 'So tranquil a despair' in the girl and her husband affected Stevenson deeply: 'the husband smilingly made his sack; and the unconscious babe struggled to reach a pot of raspberry jam, friendship's offering, which I had just brought up the den; and in a perspective of centuries I saw their case as ours, death coming in like a tide, and the day already numbered when there should be no more Beretani, and no more of any race whatever, and (what oddly touched me) no more literary works and no more readers'.[23] An appalling prospect for this childless man to contemplate, the utter oblivion of '*no more literary works and no more readers*' – truly a fate worse than death.

'Childlike' was one common way of describing Polynesians; 'apelike' was the other (as in Stevenson's impression of the Marquesan in the boat at their first landfall, with his 'bestial' consumption of the orange). Stevenson used both analogies freely in his writing about the South Seas, but was wary of both. He realised that the differences between his own culture and that of the Polynesian made judgement of their manners impossible. The chief in

Atuona, for instance, had repelled Stevenson on their first meeting with his 'indescribably raffish' air and 'low, cruel laugh, part boastful, part bashful' when the subject of cannibalism was referred to. But here was an instance where Stevenson's usual moral instincts could not be trusted. The man, Moipu, presented too many puzzles. This didn't make him any less repulsive socially, but fascinating to the novelist, as he tried to get the measure of the chief on a visit to *Casco*:

> In his appreciation of jams and pickles, in his delight in the reverberating mirrors of the dining cabin, and consequent endless repetition of Moipus and Mata-Galahis [Lloyd's ceremonial name in the Marquesas], he showed himself engagingly a child. And yet I am not sure; and what seemed childishness may have been rather courtly art. His manners struck me as beyond the mark; they were refined and caressing to the point of grossness, and when I think of the serene absent-mindedness with which he first strolled in upon our party, and then recall his running on hands and knees along the cabin sofas, pawing the velvet, dipping into the beds, and bleating commendary 'mitais' with exaggerated emphasis like some enormous over-mannered ape, I feel the more sure that both must have been calculated. And I sometimes wonder next, if Moipu were quite alone in this polite duplicity, and ask myself whether the *Casco* were quite so much admired in the Marquesas as our visitors desired us to suppose.[24]

But the thing that struck Stevenson most strongly about the Marquesans was the similarities between their situation and that of the Scottish Highlanders in the seventeenth and eighteenth centuries, his late study at Davos. Like the Highlanders, the Polynesians were persecuted and driven off their land, had customs proscribed (tattooing for the islanders, the wearing of tartan and herding of cattle for the Scots), had chiefs deposed and clans disarmed. 'The grumbling, the secret ferment, the fears and resentments, the alarms and sudden councils of Marquesan chiefs reminded me continually of the days of Lovat and Struan,' Stevenson wrote,[25] and much of the Marquesans' current demoralisation seemed to stem, like that of the old Highlanders, from the 'convulsive and transitory state' they had been thrown into by interfering, colonising powers. The parallels are illuminating as social history and also as a gloss on Stevenson's own writing, obsessed as it always had been with the nature of Scottishness. In the South Seas, he became a native 'makar', both of Polynesia (his ballads 'The Feast of Famine' and 'The Song of Rahéro' were written on this voyage) and of Scotland, writing some of his most Scots books under the shade of tropical trees: *The Master of Ballantrae* (which he had with him, unfinished, on the *Casco*), *Weir of Hermiston*, *Catriona* and his homage to his lighthouse-building forebears, *Records of a Family of Engineers*.

In September, the *Casco* travelled on south to the Paumotus in the Low Archipelago, about five hundred miles south-south-east of the Marquesas. The party spent a couple of weeks in Fakarava, then went on to Tahiti, in the nearby Society Islands. Compared with the Marquesas, Tahiti seemed relatively 'spoiled', 'a sort of halfway house between savage life and civilisation', as Margaret Stevenson described it, 'with the drawbacks of both and the advantages of neither'. The capital, Papeete, with its French colonial buildings and street lamps, its mercantile shabbiness and human flotsam of white sailors and traders and backwater diplomats, gave Stevenson his first full-scale view of the contemporary Pacific, and became the setting for the start of *The Ebb-Tide*, his most grimly realistic book. Paul Gauguin, arriving in the same place three years later as a semi-official artist for his government (somewhat like Joe Strong in Hawaii and Samoa), had retreated as quickly as possible from Papeete to a village on the south coast of the island, where he could study paradise lost and the golden body of his thirteen-year-old mistress in peace. For all his startling modernism of technique (which would have shocked Stevenson had he ever seen the pictures), Gauguin's view of the Pacific was extremely romantic, as the title of his book about it, *Noa-Noa* ('Fragrance'), indicates.

It was left to Stevenson, the 'romancer', to revise the myth of the South Seas.

Stevenson spent much longer than he had intended in and around Tahiti, for he had become ill in Fakarava and by the time they reached Papeete was worse, with threatenings of another haemorrhage. This was ominous, as he had been feeling so much better at sea and in the Marquesas, where his spirits had been as high as it was possible for them to be. Perhaps after three months' excitement and novelty, he had simply become exhausted; the results, at any rate, were alarming. Otis, called to Louis's bedside, was impressed by his *sang-froid* as, between drags on his cigarette, the lessee gave brief, precise instructions about what to do with the charter if he died.

In something of the same spirit, Stevenson sent a letter to Henley along with the flood of outbound post for England. One of his stated reasons for going on the Pacific voyage in the first place had been to get away from the nagging memory of the Nixie affair: 'folk can't write to you at sea'. Now the whole party was longing for contact with the old country. Their forwarded mail was waiting in Honolulu, months away, but at least Tahiti had a mail service going out, and Stevenson was able to send his former friend a short, kind note, beginning as in the old days, 'Dear Lad', and ending, 'Yours affectionately'. Stevenson kept on sending Henley cheerful letters from time to time during his remaining years in the South Seas, and was encouraged to think that friendly relations had been re-established. Henley accepted poems and articles from him for the *Scots Observer*, the Edinburgh-based newspaper of which he became editor in 1888, and sent news of home (the birth of his daughter the same year was an engrossing topic), but the cynicism of Henley's new feelings towards Stevenson never, mercifully, made itself clear. In private, Henley continued to carp about the quarrel, and what he believed were the 'Stevensonian' origins of a falling-off of friendship between him and Colvin, telling his new confidant, Charles Whibley, 'I don't give a damn for the whole crowd, of course.'[26] In 1889, he wrote a bleak poem about the finality of ending a friendship ('Friends ... old friends ...'[27]), and in 1891 some bitter verses about Time and Change addressed to Stevenson (and titled 'I.M. R.L.S.' for its publication later) which ended, cruelly, 'O, we that were dear, we are all-too near,/With the thick of the world between us.'[28]

Stevenson's illness in Tahiti meant the party had to find somewhere to live on shore, and after some determined negotiating by Fanny they were able to hire a horse and wagon (essential to get the invalid quickly to sea if necessary) and make for the village of Tautira, in the south-east of the island. This was a lucky choice; the Stevensons' memories of Tautira were of a paradisal setting, and the most genial and affectionate people they had yet met, particularly the sub-chief, Ori-a-Ori, a magnificently built Tahitian, 'more like a Roman Emperor in bronze than words can express',[29] who acted as their host, interpreter and guide. Nursed by Ori and his wife, and a charming local Princess, Moë (who coaxed Louis's waning appetite back to life with his first taste of raw fish in miti sauce), the patient soon began to recover. Ori's house was in the middle of the village, and from his sickbed Stevenson could watch the village children playing and the islanders going about their undemanding daily business. He was working on the manuscript of *The Master of Ballantrae* once more – in how different a place from the deep freeze of Saranac where it was begun. Months of idling and his latest brush with death left him tormentingly aware of the fix his family would be in if he died suddenly in the middle of nowhere. With this in mind, he wrote out for Lloyd instructions about how his literary estate was to be managed. The letter, carefully preserved by Lloyd (who used it as a stick with which to beat Colvin in after years), shows what Stevenson thought of his own status at this juncture. He was confident of deserving a collected edition of his works, a volume of reliquae, including letters, edited by Colvin, and a biographical sketch, also envisaged as being by Colvin.

The interval at Tautira turned out much longer than expected, for news came from the *Casco* that Otis had discovered dry rot in both masts. This necessitated taking the boat back to Papeete to be patched up (two new replacement masts were not available), and weeks of waiting. Ori's generous insistence that the Stevensons stay as long as they wanted in his house further cemented the bond between the two families, all of whom wept freely at the offer. More tears were shed when Louis and the chief both gave orations at a present-giving ceremony (though neither quite understood the other's language), and yet more when the village children processed in 'the rich one's' honour. Safe inside his wing-chair at the Savile, Colvin must have been staggered to read Fanny's account of these lachrymose occasions and how her husband had taken to wearing only a *pareu* (a cotton sarong) and a flower behind his ear. Stevenson had gone native!

Colvin cannot have been pleased to hear, either, that Stevenson's latest literary ideas were all to do with the South Seas: his book about the islands, and an oddball project, that threatened to take up vast amounts of time for little or no financial reward, the collection and translation of the poems and traditions of Tahiti. Stevenson had been drawn into this, enthusiastically, by an extraordinary Tahitian character, Tati Salmon, chief of the Tevas. Tati was half-Teva and half-Jewish and had been educated in England. 'He is trying to rescue the literature of his native land from the oblivion, into which but for him, it must fall,' Fanny explained to Colvin. Here was another analogy with the Scots: a dying language. No wonder Stevenson became engrossed with helping Tati and was thinking of coming back to Tautira the following year to spend at least six months working on the project in collaboration. For, odd though it is to remember, the Stevensons still did think of this Polynesian cruise as a holiday, and expected to be back in Bournemouth in the spring, with Miss Boodle and the Taylors and the overgrown vegetable patch overlooking the Chine. They had told Tati all about Skerryvore, and were expecting him to visit them there.

The idea that Tautira (and the whole Polynesian experience) was temporary enhanced the idyll for both Louis and Fanny, who were never so enraptured by Samoa, where they ended up living, as they were by this Tahitian backwater. Fanny loved the 'fairy story' aspects of their life there: the beauty of the people, their easy sensuality and grace. She was thrilled to exchange names, in native fashion, with the princess, went barefoot everywhere and partook of ceremonies that Margaret Stevenson probably did not entirely understand: '[Fanny] lies on a pillow in the chief's smoking-room,' she wrote to Jane, 'and can even take a whiff of a native cigarette and pass it on to the other members of the company in the approved way.'[30] Gone were the endless ailments of Davos, the hysterical alarms of Hyères. 'I could live and die in beautiful Tautira,' she told Colvin.

On Christmas Day 1888, the whole population of the village came down to the beach to see the *Casco* leave on its long journey north to Hawaii. A French *gendarme* on shore fired a salute, which the *Casco*'s Winchester answered in melancholy echo. 'I anticipate a devil of an awakening,' Stevenson wrote to Baxter, 'from a mighty pleasant dream.'[31] The passage to Honolulu almost cured the whole party of yacht-cruising; it took a month and was very rough and dangerous. Rations were short, tempers frayed, and when the sea conditions became perilous north of the equator, with a spell becalmed followed by the tail-end of a hurricane, Otis decided to make a run for it rather than risk a protracted voyage with dwindling resources. 'The yacht was soon under double-reefed fore and main sails, with the bonnet off the jib,' he told Arthur Johnstone later, 'flying from a gale that swept her like a toy across the sea.'[32] All the rest of the way, the passengers were kept below decks, the hatches were fastened and the crew lashed to their posts to save them from being knocked overboard: 'the cut of the spray on the exposed face was sharp and unpleasant', as Otis recalled. Asked years later how Stevenson had taken it, the captain replied, 'Why, man, he never turned a hair; in fact, I am convinced that he enjoyed it.'[33]

When the *Casco* flew into Honolulu harbour in late January 1889, Belle and her eight-year-old son Austin came out in a small boat to greet them. She was struck by how well Louis looked, despite his recent illness. The whole party was starving hungry and ate a huge dinner that night at the Royal Hawaiian Hotel: 'But, oh dear me, this place is so civilised!' Margaret complained to her sister. Honolulu had roads and street lamps, electric lighting and one of the world's most advanced telephone systems. The Royal Hawaiian Hotel was staggeringly large and luxurious, and the city also boasted a racecourse and an opera house. This was the work of the king, David Kalakaua, a charming, cultivated man who had travelled the world and brought back from his meetings with Queen Victoria, the Tsar and the Emperors of Germany and Japan a desire to modernise his country and a taste for court procedure and regalia. He had a white palace with landscaped grounds, splendid carriages and horses, and was only ever seen in Western-style clothes, with a dress uniform that was almost absurdly cluttered with chains, ribbons and medals. His power, however, had been considerably reduced in the previous two years by the rise of the Reform Party (backed by American business interests), and soon after Kalakaua's death in 1891 the Sandwich Islands were to fall entirely into American hands.

Once the *Casco* had dropped anchor, Kalakaua lost little time in cultivating the acquaintance of his distinguished visitor, much lauded in advance by the Strongs and Stoddard. He invited Stevenson to the palace and was in turn entertained on the yacht, where his capacity to consume champagne surprised even the bibulous Scot; Kalakaua downed five bottles in three and a half hours, rather 'too convivial' for a monarch, perhaps.[34] The king was fascinated by Stevenson's planned book on the South Seas, and probably saw political advantage in it for himself, for he often, in the five months the author spent in Hawaii, tried to persuade Stevenson to make a permanent home there. But of all places in the Pacific, Hawaii was the least attractive to any of the party.

Having arrived with little idea of what they wanted to do next – or could afford to do, rather – the Stevensons had many decisions to make. The question was not whether they were going back to

Britain, but whether the return would be almost immediate or in another year, after a further Pacific cruise. A missionary ship called the *Morning Star* was getting ready for a comprehensive tour of Micronesia, and Stevenson thought it would be an ideal opportunity to gather more material for his book – the limitations of his first tour were only just becoming clear. The proposed trip would be arduous and possibly dangerous: Margaret Stevenson, due to go home to see her ageing sister, was not going to join in. Fanny, however, was ready for anything: 'I hate the sea,' she told Colvin, 'and am afraid of it (though no one will believe that because in time of danger I do not make an outcry – nevertheless I am afraid of it, and it is not kind to me), but I love the tropic weather, and the wild people, and to see my two boys so happy.'

The new cruise would need financing, and though seven months' post waited for Stevenson in Honolulu, none of it contained any money. There was nothing with which to pay off Otis and the *Casco*, and Stevenson had to fall back on the desperate expedient of drawing on Scribner's in the hope that they would be prepared to pay $5000 for *The Wrong Box*, Lloyd's comic novel, now (almost) ready for the press. That Stevenson thought of it as Lloyd's rather than his own is evident in his insistence that the book was 'screamingly funny', a wholly uncharacteristic phrase describing a kind of writing he couldn't do himself. $5000 was far more than it was worth, to Scribner's or anyone (McClure, it might be recalled, had turned the book down in Saranac), but Stevenson was steely about it, and insisted on keeping the British rights, too. The only concession that Scribner's got for their five thousand was to put Stevenson's name first on the title page.

In moments of clear sight, Stevenson admitted that Lloyd was still an utter novice: 'Lloyd is learning to make a rude shot at story telling; he will get on,' he wrote to Colvin on 9 May 1889. 'As soon as he has done his first draft of *The Pearlfisher* [a new story, begun in Honolulu], I shall put him on to do and to elaborate all by himself short stories; there he must learn his art. But I doubt he will ever be very much of a stylist; it is, as yet, rather the root of the matter that he shows: a great knack at certain characters, some sound comedy, and an eye for the picturesque.'[35] Colvin of course did not include this letter in his edition; its tone of resignation is too damning: Lloyd 'will get on', and – with a little luck – might one day be able 'to elaborate all by himself'. The moment had passed when Lloyd's abilities might be challenged to a fair test. The tall, handsome, unintellectual twenty-year-old had given up all thought of a university degree or a regular job. And in truth, it was hardly his fault if he got the impression that his contribution to the works of RLS was invaluable, and that he was a true heir, not just to his stepfather's semi-miraculous money-making capacity, but to the genius.

Lloyd had become, in J.C. Furnas's phrase, a sort of 'kinsman-retainer', something between a son and a brother to Stevenson. On the whole, it was a satisfactory relation (remarkably much more so than most stepfather–stepson scenarios), and certainly kept Fanny happy. But to some extent, Louis's hands were tied: he had been so conspicuously dependent on his own family until well into middle age that he was in no position to object now the tables were turned. He was devising a plan for Lloyd and Joe 'to start a little money, honestly got' on the forthcoming cruise: Joe would paint island scenes onto magic lantern slides, and take photographs, while Lloyd would gather materials for a series of lectures. They could later tour together with their 'diorama' and possibly produce a book. 'It should be the making of poor Joe; for whom my affection is very lively,' Stevenson wrote to Colvin. Still, it irked him to be responsible for such a 'Skimpolian' household, as he made clear in an exasperated letter to Baxter from Honolulu: 'This family has been a sore trouble to me.' A sentence later, he was calling the same 'Skimpolians' 'truculent fools who do not know the meaning of money. It is heartbreaking; but there – the burthen is on the back.'[36]

Joe and Belle's marriage, which the Stevensons had never seen much of before, seemed to be in crisis. That Joe had huge debts, drank too much and was semi-addicted to opium cannot have struck anyone as news, depressing though it was. But for some reason, it was Belle who earned the opprobrium of her mother and stepfather, whereas she might have been expected to get their support against a feckless and dissolute husband. They thought Joe was 'a good fellow', 'likeable', even 'lovable', and the elaborate diorama plan was intended to help him recover a sense of purpose and become more 'forrit-gaun' as Stevenson described it.[37] But Belle was going to be excluded from the next cruise altogether, was being ordered, in fact, to go to Sydney with Austin and wait for the rest of the family there. Stevenson gave humane instructions to a Sydney lawyer to use his discretion if Belle needed slightly more than the £15 he was going to give her a month, but all the same, the arrangement was clearly intended as a form of punishment, or containment. One can only conclude that Belle could not be trusted in Honolulu on her own. What her misdemeanours were have been eroded from the record, but Colvin, who obliterated some remarks about the Strongs from at least one letter, must have had some reason to complain to Baxter that Belle was 'a really degrading connection' for their mutual friend.[38] And perhaps there is a clue to at least one of her weaknesses in the anecdote she tells in her memoirs of the boat trip to Australia, on which she was 'persuaded' to join a card game. She told the players that she only had one Honolulu dollar, and would only play until she lost it. 'I was still in the game when we reached Sydney,' she recalled proudly.[39]

When the *Casco* headed back to California, the Stevensons moved to a cottage on the beach at Waikiki, about three miles from the centre of Honolulu, with an outbuilding for the photographic equipment and a large garden where Ah Fu, the Chinese cook they had picked up in Tahiti, kept poultry and grew vegetables. Margaret Stevenson did not stay there long: she was booked to return to San Francisco on 10 May. Valentine Roch was also leaving the group, under some sort of cloud. Fanny, who later never had a good word to say about Valentine, despite her years of service, was convinced that she had been pilfering, but from what Stevenson said to Baxter, that it had been 'the usual tale of the maid on board the yacht',[40] it sounds as if the reason for her dismissal may have been some sexual misconduct. Perhaps Valentine was pregnant; she never went back to Europe, but settled in California with a husband called Brown. Her reminiscences of RLS, solicited by Rosaline Masson in the 1920s, have a plaintive and aggrieved air, harp on the happy days at Skerryvore and conclude that Stevenson's 'teachings' helped her 'to bear many injustices which nearly broke my heart' at their parting.[41]

Towards the end of his stay in Honolulu, Stevenson made a trip on his own, lasting twelve days, to the island of Molokai, the leper settlement made famous by the work of 'Father Damien' (Joseph de Veuster), the Belgian missionary who had devoted twenty-six years to the care of the sick there. Damien, who had died less than two months before Stevenson's arrival, had been a controversial figure in the Sandwich Islands, and the subject of gossip, but everything that Stevenson saw on Molokai convinced him that the priest had been 'superb with generosity, residual candour and fundamental good humour. [...] A man, with all the grime and paltriness of mankind; but a saint and a hero all the more for that.'[42] What was Stevenson doing on Molokai? He hardly knew himself, apart from satisfying a morbid curiosity to see the outcasts and perhaps get an interesting chapter for his book (he did write some articles about the colony for the New York Sun, but they were not included in In the South Seas). But he could no sooner have resisted the chance to visit the lepers than he could have withheld his complete attention and sympathy from patients and staff when he got there. 'Highly strung organization and temperament, quick to feel, quick to love – a very affectionate disposition,' is how the settlement doctor – clearly too busy to expand his notes – saw the visitor, whom he knew only as 'some writer'.[43] Molokai made a revealing brief episode in Stevenson's life, and shows him at his most greedy of experience. Here was the ex-Covenanter having to endure the religiose pipings of Catholic nuns, but admiring to the full their 'moral loveliness', the gloved invalid refraining from shaking hands with the lepers, yet who gave the impression to the doctor that he was considering Molokai as a place to live; the man with a 'horror of the horrible' putting himself to the test. 'I have seen sights that cannot be told, and heard stories that cannot be repeated: yet I never admired my poor race so much, nor (strange as it may seem) loved life more than in the settlement.'[44]

> Robert Louis Stevenson and party leave today by the schooner *Equator* for the Gilbert Islands. [. . .] It is to be hoped that Mr Stevenson will not fall victim to native spears; but in his present state of bodily health, perhaps the temptation to kill him may not be very strong.

Thus some wag on the staff of the *Honolulu Pacific Advertiser* noted the departure of Stevenson and his companions (Fanny, Lloyd, Joe and Ah Fu) from Hawaii on 24 June 1889. The *Equator* was both the name of the boat they had chartered and their destination, for the Gilbert Islands, about 1500 miles south-west of Hawaii, lie almost exactly 'on the line'. The *Equator* was a small trading schooner of sixty-two tons, owned by Wightman Brothers of San Francisco, and was bound initially for the firm's trading station on the atoll of Butaritari, due to go on eventually to Samoa in the Navigator Islands. Stevenson had come to an ingenious agreement with the company to pay a lump sum for a four-month cruise, with an extra fee for any unscheduled stops he might request of the captain – a congenial Scots-Irishman called Dennis Reid – and the right to stay up to three days in any of the scheduled stops. This way, he hoped to see as many islands as possible in the allotted time. After Samoa they wanted to press on to Sydney in order to be back in England, via China, Ceylon and Suez, by May or June 1890.

It was a very different berth from the *Casco*; a working ship, to begin with, with a motley crew of Americans, Hawaiians, a

Swede, a couple of Scots, a Prussian – fifteen men (as Belle observed) to one woman. There was a teenaged stowaway, a nine-year-old cabin boy and a 'colonial lad' called Sir Charles Selph (not an aristocrat but, ridiculously enough, christened 'Sir Charles' by hopeful parents). Captain Reid was a lively, humorous man, and the atmosphere on board was comradely; Stevenson's thirty-ninth birthday was celebrated by the whole crew, with speeches, champagne, merriment and impromptu musical entertainment by the family on the hurdy-gurdy, guitar and fiddle which they had brought along. No doubt the terrible flageolet also played its part. The Stevensons were coming to resemble more and more a sort of itinerant vaudeville routine.

> Rains, calms, squalls, bang – there's the foretopmast gone; rain, calms, squalls, away with the staysail; more rain, more calms, more squalls; a prodigious heavy sea all the time, and the *Equator* staggering and hovering like a swallow in a storm; and the cabin, nine feet square, crowded with wet human beings, and the rain avalanching on the deck, and the leaks dripping everywhere.[45]

So Stevenson described the voyage to Colvin. On 13 July they arrived in the Gilberts, unfrequented atolls very different from the islands they had visited in Polynesia; these were flat, featureless and constantly exposed to the glaring equatorial sun. 'Life on such islands is in many points like life on shipboard,' Stevenson remarked,[46] acknowledging perhaps a sense of disappointment with their destination. They were unprepared for what awaited them in Butaritari; the Gilberts, being so far out of the way for most traders, might have been expected to be more simple and 'unspoilt' than Tautira even, but here were one after another of the native open houses, with everyone stretched out asleep. The people looked dead – they turned out to be dead drunk: Butaritari was in the middle of a communal binge of epic proportions, nine days of revelling and mayhem. The nominal excuse for the celebration, the fourth of July, gives an indication of the influences at work in the Gilberts at the period; the reason for the drunkenness was that the local king, Tebureimoa, had, for the occasion, lifted the taboo on selling spirits to natives. This taboo was much more effective than any outsider-imposed laws, as it was broken at the risk of one's life.* When the king lifted the taboo, therefore, the rush to contravene the usual ban was overwhelming.

Hence the Butaritarans were mostly dead to the world when the *Equator*'s crew came ashore, and when Stevenson arrived at the king's house (a shed of corrugated iron, recognisable as a palace because there was a flag flying outside and a European-style privy surrounded by a tinsel curtain) there lolled his majesty Tebureimoa himself: 'He wore pyjamas which sorrowfully misbecame his bulk; his nose was hooked and cruel, his body overcome with sodden corpulence, his eye timorous and dull; he seemed at once oppressed with drowsiness and held awake by apprehension.'[47] The last of four brothers to hold the throne, this comatose monarch had, in a former life, been known as 'Mr Corpse' for his brutal suppression of enemies, but in recent years his warlike spirit had been considerably subdued 'by opium and Christianity', as Stevenson remarked.

The more they saw, that first day in the Gilberts, the more anxious the party became for their safety. Not only was everyone on the island intoxicated (and, when they began to wake up, got worse), many of the king's guards were tipsily handling firearms. One courtier performed an obscene pantomime with a woman of the court; elsewhere, Stevenson was truly shocked to see two half-naked, drunken women fighting: 'The first was uppermost, her teeth locked in her adversary's face, shaking her like a dog; the other impotently fought and scratched. For a moment we saw them wallow and grapple there like vermin; then the mob closed and shut them in. [. . .] The harm done was probably not much, yet I could have looked on death and massacre with less revolt.'[48]

---

* The European laws against the sale of alcohol all round the Pacific, which sought to 'protect' natives from the demon drink to which they seemed particularly susceptible, did not apply to whites, and no laws on drink whatever pertained in American-influenced Micronesia.

Despite these disheartening scenes, Stevenson decided not to retreat to the *Equator* for the night but to stay ashore, as planned. The revolvers were sent for from the ship, and Louis, Fanny, Lloyd and Adolf Rick, the Prussian store-manager who was acting as their liaison, all established their self-defence credentials by ostentatiously carrying out some target-practice on the public highway, picking off bottles in as swaggering a manner as they could muster. Stevenson went to bed 'agreeably excited' by this latest risk to his life, buoyed up as usual by an enormous dose of adrenalin.

During the weeks Stevenson spent in Butaritari, he never saw the king in a good light, though Tebureimoa did at least manage to sober up enough to restore the taboo on the sale of alcohol before anarchy broke out completely. He also significantly helped the Stevensons by agreeing to taboo their dwelling (which was being invaded all the time by disorderly and ill-intentioned natives). Rick's wife had effected this by telling the king that Stevenson was a friend of Queen Victoria, bidden to report on the islands. Stevenson was soon promoted in the public mind to Heir Apparent to the British throne; meanwhile, he really was 'reporting to the authorities' in the form of a letter, sent via Rick, the US commercial agent, to the Assistant Secretary of State in Washington, complaining of the lack of controls on alcohol sales. He was beginning to make a point of registering his opinions and advice on contentious matters in this part of the world so obviously ill-served by 'the Powers'. He had already written a letter to *The Times* about German intervention in Samoan affairs (which he heard all about in Honolulu), and was bravely willing to carry on being a thorn in authority's flesh all his time in the Pacific.

The Gilberts provided Stevenson with few delights but many remarkable stories, which made grimly entertaining chapters in his book. The history of the four king-brothers, for example, had many fairy-tale elements, including its cruelty. Tebureimoa's eldest brother, the first convert to Christianity in the area, had had seventeen wives, none of whom could be so much as looked at on pain of death. These queens acted as the king's oarswomen and executioners: 'they killed by the sight like basilisks; a chance view of one of those boatwomen was a crime to be wiped out with blood'.[49] The taboo on seeing them had held up the construction of the pier being built by Wightman Brothers (owners of the *Equator*), for the queens, being the slaves of their husband, had been put to work on it, meaning no one else could go near. 'Such was the ideal of wifely purity in an isle where nubile virgins went naked as in paradise.'[50]

Stevenson would certainly never have guessed, when he was straining for a glimpse of ankle on Duddingston Loch, that he would one day be cast among so much naked female flesh. His remarks on it are more surprised than prurient; he recognised the allure of the traditional *ridi*, or grass skirt, the 'enticing' looks of the women from under the bush-style Gilbertan hairdo, the charm of seeing 'silent damsels' wading in the canal, 'baring their brown thighs'. One missionary had described the region to Stevenson as 'a Paradise of naked women' for the resident whites,[51] but if that was meant as a hint to the youthful-looking husband of the pistol-packing matron, Uxorious Billy was not the man to act on it. He observed how the native women's virtue was closely guarded by themselves and their menfolk, and that the white beachcombers who tried to take advantage of an apparent erotic free-for-all often came to grief. But the traders weren't always sexual exploiters: Stevenson met some who were 'admirable to their native wives'. The women, he believed, were legitimately married to the white men, or as good as (there was a flattering and highly unlikely story that, in the absence of a Bible, one of his own works had been used for a nuptial pair to swear on). And he heard of (or met) one native bride whose certificate, 'when she proudly showed it, proved to run thus, that she was "married for one night", and her gracious partner was at liberty to "send her to hell" the next morning'.[52] This was the story that became almost word for word the starting point of Stevenson's novella 'The Beach of Falesá'. But in real life, unlike in his fiction, he thought the girl was 'none the wiser or the worse for the dastardly trick'.

382   ROBERT LOUIS STEVENSON

The camera that they took with them to the Gilbert Islands must have been a good one, for the pictures, though grainy, look quite unposed, as if the subjects did not have to stand still for long.* There are photos of hula dancers, of the girls in their *ridi* skirts, of the missionaries, of the *Equator*. But the best is of Stevenson himself, lounging on the ground in company with Fanny and a native couple called Nan Tok' and Nei Takauti. Nan Tok' was a handsome, young, subservient husband; Nei Takauti a woman 'getting old', previously married, mysteriously powerful and dominant. They were Louis and Fanny's Butaritaran counterparts, as the grouping of the photo suggests, for the wives are sitting together in the middle, holding hands (Fanny is carefully studying and copying what Nei Takauti is doing), and the two younger husbands are semi-recumbent at their sides. Stevenson looks incredibly well and handsome; *laid back* is the phrase that comes irrepressibly to mind, for, barefoot and wearing flowers in their hair, he and Fanny look more like a couple from the 1960s than the 1880s.

Had the photographs from the various Pacific voyages been used, as originally intended, as illustrations for *In the South Seas*, they would have helped readers get some foothold in the enormous variety of material Stevenson wanted to present.† His book was getting out of hand already, and he hadn't even started writing it. Two volumes minimum, he now thought. Fanny confided in Colvin her fear that Louis was going to spoil 'the most enchanting material that any one ever had in the whole world' by writing 'a sort of scientific and historical impersonal thing'.[53] This was certainly a danger for Stevenson, whose record of 'serious' non-fiction projects had been so unsuccessful, but whether Fanny was right to think that the material was such a gift that *anyone* – even she – 'could

---

* They started off with at least two cameras, but one went overboard almost as soon as they reached the Marquesas in July 1888.

† As it was, the illustrations used in the *Black and White* magazine edition (1 February 1891) were engravings of the photographs, quaintly antiquing the images of Stevenson's travels instead of presenting them in the newer, more realistic form. The picture of Nan Tok' and Nei Takauti with the Stevensons is labelled 'Arcadian life at Butaritari'.

write a book that the whole world would jump at'[54] is another matter. 'Please keep any letters of mine that contain any incidents of our wanderings,' she wrote to Colvin. 'If the worst comes to the worst, Louis can go back to my letters to refresh his memory.' And of course, not quite *anyone* could write the world-shaking book she could knock off so easily; Margaret Stevenson's letters from the voyage of the *Casco* 'are of no use', Fanny wrote categorically, 'interesting as they are'.

Late in August, the *Equator* took the Stevensons on to Apemama, one of the island capitals of the Gilberts, and left them there while the ship went off trading. The party settled down for what they expected would be a week or two, in a specially constructed enclave of charming thatched huts like birdcages on stilts. This had been provided for them (and tabooed) by the king, Tembinok, 'the last tyrant, the last erect vestige of a dead society'.[55] There was only one white resident on Apemama, and none of the 'development' (trade, drink and opium) that had wreaked such ruin already in Butaritari. Tembinok was sole ruler and sole merchant, sole husband in his 'palace of many women'. Hugely stout and shrill-voiced ('with a note like a sea-bird's'), the king made an alarming spectacle in a variety of garish costumes, including a green velvet jacket and a woman's frock, in which he looked 'ominous and weird beyond belief', as Stevenson described it.[56] But Stevenson was most impressed by the king's accomplishments, not least of which was his command of English: 'a poet, a musician, a historian or perhaps rather more a genealogist – it is strange to see him lying in his house among a lot of wives (nominal wives) writing the History of Apemema in an account book –; his description of one of his own songs, which he sang to me himself, as "about sweethearts, and trees and the sea – and no true, all-the-same lie", seems about as compendious a definition of lyric poetry as a man could ask'.[57]

By the end of October, it seemed they might be doomed to stay with Tembinok forever, for there was no sign of the *Equator*. The vegetable seeds that Fanny had planted were sprouting, but that was small comfort compared to the thought of being stranded in the Gilberts. When the schooner *J.L. Tiernan* came by, they almost took passage on it, but sent letters instead, Stevenson writing to Colvin for the first time like one who was really cut off from his former life, and intuited that he might never return:

> God knows how you are: I begin to weary dreadfully to see you. [...] I wonder what has befallen me too, that flimsy part of me that lives (or dwindles) in the public mind; and what has befallen of *The Master*, and what kind of a Box *The Wrong Box* has been found? It is odd to know nothing of all this.[58]

In fact, *The Master of Ballantrae*, published that September, had been received very well, with one or two exceptions: Symonds thought the story 'decrepit',[59] and George Moore, writing in *Hawk*, said it was 'a story of adventure with the story left out', though he knew that 'the *Spectator*, the *Saturday Review*, the whole of Bedford Park, and all the aesthetics of Clapham and Peckham Rye' would disagree with him.[60] Andrew Lang had used his review of *The Master of Ballantrae* as an opportunity to review Stevenson's whole career to date, with flattering comparisons to Addison, Scott and Zola. William Archer called it 'something very like a classic', and Margaret Oliphant saw 'sheer genius and literary force such as we have never known the like of'.[61] The book they all hated, however, was *The Wrong Box*, an 'undignified and unworthy exhibition'; Stevenson had 'deluded' the public by putting his name to it. It would 'try the faith of [Stevenson's] most ardent admirers', the *Athenaeum* said: 'To have aided in the production of a book three-fourths of which consist of tedious levity is indeed not a thing to be proud of.'[62]

Stevenson knew nothing of this when he began his next collaboration with Lloyd that autumn, but it is doubtful if it would have put him off (indeed he shrugged off all criticism of this kind when he *did* get to hear of it). Collaboration with Lloyd was much more a matter of contingency than an artistic choice, one way of lightening the 'burthen on the back'. By the time they reached

Apemama, Joe Strong had done something to put himself well and truly in the doghouse, and the 'diorama' scheme had been ditched. 'People are unco' hard to help in this world,' Stevenson wrote to Colvin. '[Joe] does no more business for, or with, me. I would rather pay him handsomely to keep hands off.'[63] Lloyd was thus promoted to top wastrel, and, his career as a lecturer in tatters, was 'unemployed' again. In Honolulu, they had heard the story of the *Wandering Minstrel*, whose crew had been found marooned on Midway Island, an isolated reef, and brought back to Hawaii. The crew's story, and that of another maroon on Midway, a suspected murderer, was full of inexplicable inconsistencies, and had intrigued Stevenson and his family. On the *Equator* they heard more about the Pacific trade in wrecked ships and, putting the two together, recognised a potential 'police-novel' theme.

Stevenson was also motivated to start a new novel in order to finance his latest, wildly exciting, plan – to buy or build a schooner of his own and live semi-permanently at sea, dipping from one island group to another, as a sort of gentleman trader. The vessel was to be a topsail schooner of ninety tons, and everything on it had been imagined in detail: the rifle racks, the library, 'the patent davits' and the name, of course, the *Northern Light*, sentimentally recalling Stevenson's forebears. The cost was expected to be about $1500, which is what Stevenson and Lloyd were going to ask for their novel, *The Wrecker*. The vision was blatantly inconsiderate of Fanny's feelings about sea-travel, but as it also included buying a small island of their own as a base, perhaps Stevenson and Lloyd were intending to leave the matriarch on shore a great deal. They could be forever setting out in the *Northern Light* to do a bit of trading, and she could keep house for them both on an atoll, gardening fork in one hand, *Lancet* in the other, her indomitable Napoleonic profile black against the westering sun. On further acquaintance with traders in the Gilberts, however, Stevenson had to admit that he would not be able to bear a life among so many unscrupulous people, and the dream of the *Northern Light* was extinguished abruptly.

The Wrecker, however, went ahead. It was a very different sort of collaboration from *The Wrong Box* – which had been essentially Lloyd's story revised by Stevenson. *The Wrecker* was jointly planned and executed; each chapter was discussed in advance, drafted by Lloyd and rewritten by Stevenson. Hence Stevenson was fed ideas by Lloyd and relieved of the drudgery of making a first draft, while retaining control over the work at all times. Lloyd got plenty out of the arrangement too, seeing his apprentice work, full of jokes and burlesque, transformed into something much more substantial, and gaining, for the duration of the composition, his stepfather's undivided attention. Much of the writing was done in Apemama, with Lloyd and Louis sitting under a cramped tent of mosquito netting together, working on different parts of the book. Here was a new kind of family firm being set up, an unexpected branch of 'Stevenson and Son'.

The book that emerged from this was not, however, a very coherent one. From the start, it was going to be a hybrid work, for Lloyd's talents were suited to the emerging detective genre and Stevenson's were not at all. In his epilogue to the book, Stevenson obliquely apologises for the mismatch by telling how the co-authors had been 'at once attracted and repelled by that very modern form of the police novel or mystery', the problem with which was 'insincerity and shallowness of tone'. 'The mind of the reader, always bent to pick up clues, receives no impression of reality or life, rather of an airless, elaborate mechanism; and the book remains enthralling, but insignificant, like a game of chess, not a work of human art.'[64] If any novel answers to such a description it is *The Wrecker*, with its puzzling switches of tone, location, intention and style. Stevenson's apologia (which sounds oddly like a pre-emptive book review) makes a bold attempt to pass this off as deliberate, claiming the authors desired to have their mystery story 'inhere in life' and reflect 'the tone of the age, its movement, the mingling of races and classes in the dollar hunt'.[65]

It was the method of composition that made *The Wrecker* haphazard. The constant need to compromise and the length of time it took to write (two years) were such that Stevenson confessed he had lost the thread of the early story, and there are many small 'continuity' mistakes which no amount of theorising can recast as art. The characters don't develop so much as morph, especially Loudon Dodd, the American artist at the centre of the main story, who seems to lack the backing of the authors until about halfway through, as if he and they are part of the culture of speculation, investment and risk which is so large an issue in the plot.

The method falls somewhere between the broad-canvas inclusiveness of Dickens (with its perils of mere sprawling) and the mystery writer's deliberate false starts and false emphases; the result is a book which demands concentration in the wrong places. It is long, twice the size of most Stevenson novels, and oddly repetitive or 'doubled'. New characters are introduced who seem duplicates of existing ones, and situations proliferate in the same way; thus Tommy Hadden and Carthew in the closing chapters repeat very closely the partnership of Dodd and Pinkerton earlier; Carthew's disappointment of his family is like Dodd's, yet both receive surprise inheritances at crucial moments; Captain Wicks is a character very like Captain Nares (for all Stevenson's professed pride in Nares as a special creation), and both are parodied in Captain Trent; boats abound, and name changes: Wicks to Kirkup (passing himself off as Trent once Trent is dead), Carthew to Dickson (and later to Goddedal), the *Dream* to the *Currency Lass* (itself stealing the name of a public house), the whole crew of the latter to the crew of the *Flying Scud*, and so on. All this gives the story an odd, circular feel, which may have been intentional (putting us off the trail) or simply a symptom of the authors' haste and confusion.

Some passages from *The Wrecker* may give an idea of how various the book is. The prologue, set in Tai-o-hae, introduces Loudon Dodd as an 'old, salted trader', a man of business, normally unscrupulous. This is the contemporary Pacific world that Stevenson was to explore in 'The Beach of Falesá', *The Ebb-Tide*

and *In the South Seas*. The next chapters, however, are entirely
burlesque, switching back several decades to Dodd's youth as an
unwilling student at the Muskegon Commercial College, his art
studies in Paris and succession of casual jobs, including acting as
co-ordinator of 'Pinkerton's Hebdomadary Picnics' around San
Francisco Bay:

> By eight o'clock, any Sunday morning, I was to be observed
> by an admiring public on the wharf. The garb and attributes
> of sacrifice consisted of a black frockcoat, rosetted, its pockets
> bulging with sweetmeats and inferior cigars, trousers of light
> blue, a silk hat like a reflector, and a varnished wand. A
> goodly steamer guarded my one flank, panting and throbbing,
> flags fluttering fore and aft of her, illustrative of the Drom-
> edary and patriotism. My other flank was covered by the
> ticket-office, strongly held by a trusty character of the Scots
> persuasion, rosetted like his superior, and smoking a cigar to
> mark the occasion festive.[66]

Stevenson-Osbourne sounds here remarkably like Mark Twain,
and at other points like a pastiche Dickens (they were aware of
the influence: in the epilogue Stevenson makes the comic admission
that the method of 'fortifying' a mystery story that he and Lloyd
imagined they had invented turned out to be 'the method of
Charles Dickens in his later work'). Lloyd's supposed knack with
accents and dialects is in evidence throughout, and must always
have made people cringe. 'Indade, and there's nothing in the house
beyont the furnicher,' says the Irish landlady, while the Sydney
down-and-out talks of the 'ryleways' and 'tryde', the German
businessman observes that 'a pig nokket of cold is good', and the
English officer chimes in with 'aw! I dawn't knaw you, do I?'

Lloyd told Graham Balfour that 'the storm was mine; so were
the fight and the murders on the *Currency Lass*; the picnics in San
Francisco, and the commercial details of Loudon's partnership.
Nares was mine and Pinkerton to a great degree, and Captain
Brown was mine throughout'.[67] Stevenson was dead by the time
Lloyd said this, so there was no risk of contradiction, but it is

notable that Lloyd has claimed for himself the best parts of the book. The storm is a remarkable piece of writing, and wholly 'Stevensonian'. Was this because Stevenson revised it thoroughly, or because Lloyd and he were exerting a palpable influence on each other's style? Nothing that Lloyd wrote in his post-RLS career approaches this:

> The wind and the wild seas, now vastly swollen, indefatigably hunted us. I stood on deck, choking with fear; I seemed to lose all power upon my limbs; my knees were as paper when she plunged into the murderous valleys; my heart collapsed when some black mountain fell in avalanche beside her counter.[68]

More extraordinary still is Lloyd's attribution to himself of 'the fight and the murders on the *Currency Lass*'. This explosively violent chapter seems at first to have no place in Stevenson's *oeuvre*; it is brutal and graphic ('a face, that of the sailor Holdorsen, appeared below the bulkheads in the cabin doorway. Carthew shattered it . . .'[69]), and dwells on the mechanics of killing a dozen or so men in cold blood with an aggressive insistence that the reader shares the experience in full. But there is something brilliant about it too: the quick succession of trigger events plummeting the situation out of normality and into horror, the inevitability and unstoppability of the consequences, and the *work* involved in the massacre, the persistence it requires. When the crew of the *Currency Lass* realise that one man remains of the witnesses, Hadden begs for him to be spared: 'One man can't hurt us [. . .] We can't go on with this. I spoke to him at dinner,' and the narrator adds, 'The sound of his supplications was perhaps audible to the unfortunate below.' Carthew, determined to finish the business, goes below but cannot bring himself to shoot:

> A sense of danger, of daring, had alone nerved Carthew to enter the forecastle; and here was the enemy crying and pleading like a frightened child. His obsequious 'Here, sir,' his horrid fluency of obtestation, made the murder tenfold more revolting.

Carthew flees, but Wicks goes down instead; the victim, thinking it is Carthew again, begins to emerge from his hiding place, and Wicks 'emptied his revolver at the voice, which broke into mouse-like whimperings and groans'.

The extra clause in that sentence is symptomatic of the whole chapter: nothing is left to the imagination. How different this is from the invisible violence of Edward Hyde, the fight in the round-house in *Kidnapped*, or the murder of Israel Hands in *Treasure Island* (a book with many echoes in *The Wrecker*). Stevenson and Osbourne separately couldn't have done this; in collaboration, and with the sole responsibility removed from either man, they turned up with a scene like nothing else in nineteenth-century fiction, a scene from a twenty-first-century gangster film.

One scene stands out biographically, and that is the confrontation between Dodd and Pinkerton following the loss of their investment in the *Flying Scud*. It is interesting for the characterisation of Mamie Pinkerton and for the depiction of the rapid breakdown of relations between two old friends once a third party – the wife of one – is involved. Mamie herself is the nearest to a portrait of Fanny Stevenson that we ever get in Stevenson's works – far more like life than the Countess von Rosen in *Prince Otto* or the Fair Cuban in *The Dynamiter*. She is a flat, conventional character until the quarrel scene, where she slowly reveals her teeth; stung by the troubles visited on her husband, she launches into a harangue against Dodd which seems to capture exactly the tone and excesses of the Vandegrifter:

> 'You think you can do what you please with James; you trust to his affection, do you not? [...] But it was perhaps an unfortunate day for you when we were married, for I at least am not blind [...] It makes me furious! His wages! a share of his wages! That would have been your pittance, that would have been your share of the *Flying Scud* [...] But we do not want your charity; thank God, I can work for my own husband!'[...]

Heaven knows to what a height she might have risen,

being, by this time, bodily whirled away in her own hurricane of words.[70]

Mamie's loyalty to her husband, and his to Dodd, and Dodd's to him, make it impossible that all three of them can know all the facts of the case; the resulting meltdown seems to replay the agonies of the break with Henley in miniature form. But, pathetically, Stevenson awards his characters the chance to acknowledge the forces at work in their disagreement (marriage, mostly), and includes a coda in which Pinkerton chases after his friend on the street to excuse his wife's anger against him: 'Don't think hard of Mamie [. . .] It's the way she's made; it's her high-toned loyalty.' Dodd's response, heavy with Brutus–Cassius overtones, is a fantasy finale to the Nixie affair, the noble utterance Stevenson craved from Henley, or Bob, and was never going to hear:

> 'It never can [blow over]', I returned, sighing: 'and don't you try to make it! Don't name me, unless it's with an oath. And get home to her right away. Good-bye, my best of friends. Good-bye and God bless you. We shall never meet again.'[71]

The voyage on the *Equator* helped change the whole basis of Stevenson's future plans for remaining in the Pacific. When his pipe-dream of the private island and the private yacht passed, his new objective became to find a place to live that had good communications with the outside world and a modicum of civilised life. This narrowed the choice down to Suva, Papeete, Honolulu or Apia, of which the last, in Samoa, was the most appealing on several counts; Samoa was one of the few independent island groups left in the region and its people were renowned for being, in Lloyd's phrase, 'attractive and uncontaminated'.[72] And when the *Equator* finally turned up at Apemama, several weeks late, it was to Samoa that it and the Stevenson party were bound.

13

TUSI TALA

The mode of life, so far as it affects growth or health, would,
if known, throw light on the effect of nurture over nature.

Francis Galton, *Record of Family Faculties*

ON 7 DECEMBER 1889, a clergyman called Clarke, working for
the London Missionary Society in Samoa, was making his way
along the main street of Apia, a long sandy track that followed
the curve of the harbour, when he came across an odd party of
Europeans, two men and a woman, apparently just landed from
the schooner in the bay. The woman wore a print gown, large gold
earrings, a straw hat with shells decorating the brim, and had a
guitar slung across her back. The younger man carried a banjo
and was wearing striped pyjamas, a slouch straw hat 'of native
make' and dark blue sun-spectacles, while the other man was
dressed in white flannels 'that had seen many better days, a white
drill yachting cap with prominent peak, a cigarette in his mouth,
and a photographic camera in his hand. Both the men were bare-
footed. [. . .] My first thought was that, probably, they were wandering players *en route* to New Zealand, compelled by their
poverty to take the cheap conveyance of a trading vessel.'[1] So the
Stevenson family appeared to a passer-by. Clarke only realised that
they were 'gentlefolk' when he met them again in the town's main
hotel, the Tivoli, the following week; he was to become Stevenson's
closest friend among the missionaries.

Another significant meeting that first day in Samoa was with

Harry Jay Moors, an American trader who had settled on the main island, Upolu, in the early 1880s. Moors boarded the *Equator* on business and recognised Stevenson immediately (presumably from newspaper articles); characteristically he lost no time in making acquaintance, and asked the newcomers back to his house. '[Stevenson] appeared to be intensely nervous, highly strung, easily excited,' Moors remembered, noticing how, once ashore, the author 'began to walk up and down [the sand] in a most lively, not to say eccentric, manner. He could not stand still. When I took him into my house, he walked about the room, plying me with questions, one after another, darting up and down.'[2] Moors supposed the whole party were unnerved by their long trip from the Gilbert Islands. He didn't yet realise that, for Stevenson, this was quite normal behaviour.

The Stevensons had arrived in Samoa at an important moment in its history. The Germans had exercised significant power in the islands since the establishment of successful copra, cocoa and banana plantations in the 1850s, and 'the German firm'* had been responsible for building Apia harbour and establishing regular steamship communications between Samoa, New Zealand, Australia and San Francisco. German interference in Samoan affairs, however, had aroused British and American objections, and after the deposition by Germany of the Samoan king, Malietoa Laupepa, in 1887, and the installation of a pro-German puppet ruler, Tupua Tamasese, all three powers sent warships to the islands. Seven were in Apia harbour when a hurricane struck in March 1889 (just a month after Stevenson had been writing to *The Times* from Hawaii about the exile of Laupepa), and the wrecks of the *Vandalia*, the *Trenton* and the *Olga*, the first two American and the last German, were still cluttering the bay when the Stevensons arrived on the *Equator* in December.

The sudden loss of the warships by act of God did what no

* Actually two firms, Godeffroy of Hamburg and its successor, the 'D.H and P.G' – Deutsche Handels-und Plantagen-Gessellschaft der Sudsee-Inseln zu Hamburg, known humorously as 'The Long-Handle Firm'.[3]

earlier diplomacy had effected, and in the summer of 1889 representatives of Germany, Britain and the United States met in Berlin to work out a plan for Samoa, eventually agreeing to grant the islands free elections. But no date was set for this reform, and in the interim the powers (Germany was by far the dominant one) decided that the former native king should be brought back from exile. Laupepa was not unpopular among his countrymen, but was in an almost impossible position: during his absence most Samoans had transferred their allegiance to Mataafa Iosefo, the man who had led a violent insurgence against Tamasese and who had the backing of some British and American residents (Moors was one). The reintroduction of the ousted king became the trigger to all the civil unrest during Stevenson's residence in Samoa. Mataafa was represented by the Germans as a 'rebel leader', but as even Laupepa supported him and the stooge Tamasese was now discarded, there was no logical reason why the elections could not take place immediately and confirm in office Mataafa, whom almost everyone (Samoan) wanted as king.

The fact that Laupepa had appealed to Britain for help ('offered to accept the supremacy of England' is how Stevenson put it[4]) *before* the 1887 crisis and had been refused had been one of the main complaints in Stevenson's letter to *The Times* from Honolulu (at which time, of course, he knew nothing of Samoa first-hand). It was clear to him then that 'encroachment on the one side [Germany's] and weakness on the other [Britain, and to a lesser extent, the US]' had conspired to create a situation for the Samoans soluble, if at all, only by revolt. When Stevenson reached Apia, full of curiosity to see what progress had been made on this issue which had gripped him from afar, he can only have been discouraged (and at the same time, of course, fired up) by the sight of the scrap-metal in the bay and the news that two days before his arrival Laupepa had been formally recognised as king.

Moors was a useful informant on this and all Samoan affairs. In fact Moors was a force to be reckoned with: his success as a trader and planter (he exported large amounts of copra) had made him wealthy and influential on Upolu, where 'everyone' owed him money on mortgage.[5] He had married a Samoan wife and had a daughter by her, and was fairly independent of the 'Beach' and its besetting vices of drink and dissipation. For a white man in the tropics, he was remarkably reliable and effective, but 'a curious being', as Stevenson told Baxter, 'not of the best character'. Stevenson was told that Moors had taken a 'great though secret' part in the recent war; in later years, he was suspected of being the motive force behind what had looked like a purely Samoan-based petition to transfer the islands to American control. The senior surviving native leader at the time (1919) was described by the German administrator as 'simply a tool of H.J. Moors'.[6]

So it was just as well that Stevenson quickly made an ally of the American. He came to rely on him (with his usual readiness to delegate business matters) for most of the duties of a banker, agent, broker and even literary adviser. Within days of their arrival, Moors had invited the writer to come and stay at his house on Beach Road, right by the sea, while Fanny, Lloyd and Ah Fu went inland, trying to find a higher and more sheltered location. Moors is the man who described Stevenson's eyes as penetrating 'like the eyes of a mesmerist' on first acquaintance, 'not a handsome man, and yet there was something irresistibly attractive about him'.[7] For his part, Stevenson's first impression of Moors had been one of 'repulsion', which he imagined was mutual, and he told Baxter that he had been 'forced' to be Moors' guest on Beach Road, 'rather against my will, for his looks, his round blue eyes etc. went against me'.[8] Quite what it was in Moors' round blue eyes that alarmed the writer must be left to the imagination: 'we both got over it', Stevenson continued, 'and grew to like each other; and it's my belief he won't cheat me'. Indeed, Moors immediately began the process of making himself indispensable to Stevenson by offering to provide him with detailed information on Samoan history for his book, and soon manoeuvred himself into the position of devoted but critical lieutenant. Critical, mostly, of Stevenson's entourage, whom Moors came to despise heartily.

The *Equator* left Apia on 10 December, without the Stevensons. They were staying on for a month or so, and would travel to Sydney via the monthly German steamer service, the *Lübeck*. The run took only nine days – an astonishingly easy connection with the 'civilised' world; it meant that post (and visitors) could be sent from Samoa to Britain in a matter of weeks rather than months, an important factor in the decision Stevenson was coming to. Joe Strong had been packed off on the *Lübeck* already; thought to be dying from cardiac disease, he was being returned to the arms of his wife and child. Stevenson felt it impossible either to desert or support the 'lovable' cormorant, but the prospect of being saddled with Belle the Widow was even more alarming. His liabilities seemed to be increasing by the minute.

So it was not very surprising (especially given the help, example and encouragement of Harry Moors) that within weeks of arriving in Upolu, Louis and Fanny decided to set up home and start a plantation in Samoa. They had found an estate for sale, four hundred acres on the slopes of Mount Vaea, entirely overgrown and virtually inaccessible except for a stony track that connected it to Apia, three miles away, but it was hoped that a house could be built and a plantation formed within the year. 'At least' fifty head of cattle were thought to roam on the estate (property of the landowner) and probably as many pigs, of the delightful, many-coloured, boar's-nose variety common to the islands. The estate had two waterfalls and several streams running through it (hence the name they gave it, 'Vailima', 'five waters') and a wonderful view of Apia harbour and the sea from its elevated position. It is unlikely that either Fanny or Louis had yet attempted to climb the mountain to the little plateau from which there is a spectacular view inland as well as north to the ocean; in fact, from what Louis says, he may not even have inspected the land he bought for $4000: it was, after all, only 'an impassable jungle' at this time. Everything was left in Moors' hands: the making of a path, the initial clearance work and a temporary cottage for the Stevensons to live in while a proper house was built. Even the money was being put up by Moors to expedite the transaction.

So Stevenson was not going home again, except on an immediate errand to pack up and sell Skerryvore. On the way to Sydney in early February 1890 he began writing his explanatory letters, to Colvin, Baxter, Lady Taylor, Miss Boodle, Anne Jenkin, giving the reasons for his decision. He loved the Pacific, he told them; the climate and the change of life had transformed him from a pallid tapeworm to a tanned, active, productive (if still very thin) man. The estate, when functioning, would provide some income and an inheritance for his many dependants; he could, most importantly, write best when free from the chronic ailments that haunted him in Europe and the States. It was more explanation than anyone needed; few of his friends can have imagined that Louis would ever be cured or comfortable at 'home' – a place he had spent most of his life away from. Yet the sense of guilt on one side and abandonment on the other was palpable; Henry James wrote to tell Stevenson of the 'long howl of horror' that had gone up among his friends. Colvin, the worst hit, seemed to take the news as a personal reproach, an indication that his role as adviser and critic was being spurned. In a frank passage in *Memories and Notes*, Colvin admits, 'I persuaded myself that from living permanently in that outlandish world and far from cultivated society both [Stevenson] and his writing must deteriorate.'[9] The thought was to colour all Colvin's subsequent dealings with his friend, as he struggled to be appreciative of the South Seas essays ('overloaded with information and the results of study') and the new 'outlandish' turn of Stevenson's fiction.

And of course Stevenson's reputation, which his friends in Britain were in a better position than him to evaluate, was affected profoundly by his removal to Samoa. To the public at large, it appeared an exciting and romantic twist in the celebrity author's life, as Gosse remarked: 'Since Byron was in Greece, nothing has appealed to the ordinary literary man as so picturesque as that you should be in the South Seas.'[10] To friends, it meant an abeyance or complete cessation of the flow of ideas, jokes and shared literary interests between him and them. Intellectual isolation was inevitable, especially when new young writers were being taken up in his place. When he got to Sydney, and looked through eight months' post, Stevenson found Lang's letters full of Rider Haggard and Henry James's of a brilliant young poet called Rudyard Kipling. Colvin, in later years, was to transfer his literary patronage from Stevenson to a new novelist called Joseph Conrad (one of the few in literary circles, incidentally, who admired Stevenson's South Seas essays[11]). In his fortieth year, Stevenson could no longer be thought of as 'young' or 'promising'; he had outgrown his resemblance to Shelley, or outlived it, rather. And by signing the deeds to Vailima, he entered a strangely unreal zone in his friends' imaginations, as if, indeed, he had done what they had been taught to expect for twenty years, and died.

If the reaction to Stevenson's arrival in New York City in 1887 had been a surprise, Sydney in 1890 was worse. The papers were full of articles, photographs and gossip about him; reporters flooded to the Union Hotel, and cards poured in from every literary and social club in the city, begging to ask 'the greatest author living' to address them, or dine, or receive honours. Belle Strong, having languished in Sydney for months in a boarding house, was delighted to have some of this glamour rub off on herself and her son, who were saluted by the doorman at the hotel, and recognised as one of the great man's 'family'.

Not that the management of the Union Hotel recognised greatness in the chaotic sprawl of people and luggage suddenly arrived in their lobby. Cedar-wood chests held together with rope, palm-leaf baskets, covered buckets made of tree trunks, rolls of tapa matting, shells and calabashes gathered into bags made of fish-net – and in the middle of all this, a short fat woman and a tall thin man, a Chinese servant and a bespectacled youth, all dressed like tinkers and shouting instructions to the staff. Their removal to the humbler Oxford Hotel must have seemed like a relief to the Union until the next day, when the identity of the party became known, and a delegation had to be sent round to apologise, to the great satisfaction of the snubbed celebrities.

With a view to Sydney being 'our metropolis' in the future, Stevenson told his mother that he was 'laying himself out' to be sociable,[12] as was Fanny, though it was a strain for both of them after the life they had got used to in the islands. Astonishingly enough, Margaret was coming to live with them in Samoa. Heriot Row was to be let and some of the furniture shipped out to the tropics; a bold move for the sixty-one-year-old widow, who was proving such an excellent traveller and good sport. Ah Fu was going home to China for a while, but intended to come back and live with them too. Stevenson gave the cook a packet of stamped, self-addressed envelopes so that he could get in touch easily if he was in any difficulty or needed money, but despite this precaution, they never saw their Chinese friend again.

The Union Club became Louis's headquarters in Sydney: it had a library and a smoking room, and offered protection from journalists. It was probably there that he read the article, reprinted in a Sydney newspaper from a religious periodical, that awakened in Stevenson what he liked to call The Old Man Virulent. The article included a letter (taken from private correspondence) from the Rev. C.M. Hyde, a senior American missionary in Hawaii, which thoroughly denigrated the work and character of the late Father Damien of Molokai. Stevenson, fresh from witnessing the legacy of the 'dead saint', saw red, and, having worked himself up into the heroic mood by asking his dumbstruck wife and step-children whether they were prepared to lose everything for this cause, proceeded to write a vitriolic response. 'I have struck as hard as I knew how,' he wrote to his mother, 'nor do I think my answer can fail to do away (in the minds of all who see it) with the effect of Hyde's incredible and really villainous production.'[13] 'Father Damien: An Open Letter to the Reverend Dr Hyde of Honolulu' gave Stevenson the long-awaited opportunity 'to feel the button off the foil and to plunge home', as he put it in a thoroughly Three Musketeers way.[14] 'I conceive you as a man quite beyond and below the reticences of civility: with what measure you mete, with that shall it be meted to you again,' he wrote, in this dramatically direct, almost Swiftian, address. He conceived Hyde lounging in his 'pleasant room' in Honolulu, 'stretching your limbs', leading family prayers in utter ignorance and scorn of the conditions under which Damien had worked, and which he, Stevenson, was of course able to characterise vividly:

> Had you been there, it is my belief that nature would have triumphed even in you; and as the boat drew but a little nearer, and you beheld the stairs crowded with abominable deformations of our common manhood, and saw yourself landing in the midst of such a population as only now and then surrounds us in the horror of a nightmare – what a haggard eye you would have rolled over your reluctant shoulder towards the house on Beretania Street! Had you gone on; had you found every fourth face a blot upon the landscape; had you visited the hospital and seen the butt-ends of human beings lying there almost unrecognisable, but still breathing, still thinking, still remembering; you would have understood that life in the lazaretto is an ordeal from which the nerves of a man's spirit shrink, even as his eye quails under the brightness of the sun; you would have felt it was (even today) a pitiful place to visit and a hell to dwell in.[15]

The 'Letter' was privately printed by the author and circulated to friends and influential people, including (if Belle Strong's list is correct) Queen Victoria, the US president (she doesn't seem sure who that was) and 'The Pope of Rome'.[16] Stevenson then sat back and waited for Hyde's libel writ and his own financial ruin, but four months later he had heard nothing, and wrote anxiously to Burlingame about the fate of his 'inflammatory squib': 'Has Hyde turned upon me, have I fallen like Danvers Carew[?]' he asked, acknowledging the coincidence of the reverend gentleman's name and that of Jekyll's nemesis. Hyde was hardly moved at all, it turned out (as one might expect), and dismissed Stevenson as 'somewhat of a crank' when interviewed about the matter by a newspaper.[17] Stevenson, on the other hand, seethed over the subject for four months, by which time he was prepared to admit that in the heat of the moment he might have been slightly unjust to Hyde (he had not, for instance, checked facts and so forth, as Hyde pointed out in his eventual published reply[18]). But at least Stevenson could feel the heat of the moment, and react to it with splendid panache. His behaviour was a little foolish, but enormously admirable.

In Sydney, Louis finished and sent to Scribner's the first ten chapters of *The Wrecker*. As if to emphasise what a piecemeal production this novel was to be, the model for one character had only just walked into the lives of Stevenson and Osbourne. This was Jack Buckland, 'Tin Jack' as he was known ('Tin' being an island version of 'Mister'), a South Sea trader and adventurer who appears in the story as Tommy Hadden, the remittance man. Stevenson admitted that the peculiarities of collaboration encouraged him to make all the minor characters in *The Wrecker* 'almost undisguised' portraits from life. 'This is not as you know my method', he told Burlingame, but 'has sprung partly from the scope of the book, partly from convenience [. . .] it is so ready a thing to say to your collaborator, "O, make him so and so!" '[19] This shockingly frank admission of creative laziness, or rather *disinclination*, would have confirmed all the worst fears of one reviewer, Margaret Oliphant, who when she read the book on publication in 1892 felt that Stevenson was cynically exploiting his own popularity to pass off inferior work.

Stevenson's two-month stop in Sydney turned out to be the end rather than the beginning of his journey to London, for during it he not only caught cold and began blood-spitting again, but also lost the inclination to go back. He was spending most of his time at the Union Club in bed, with work propped on his knees as at Hyères and Davos, 'the old business', as he wrote to Mrs Sitwell.[20] This was discouraging enough; hearing of an influenza epidemic in Britain was the last straw: he and Fanny panicked and pulled out of the onward journey, deciding instead to spend the summer at sea again in the Pacific, returning to England – perhaps – after that. He told Mrs Sitwell that though he no longer thought England would kill him – 'I seem incapable of dying' – he could not face the 'suffering, and weakness and painful disability that might ensue'. When his cough became worse and looked as if it was developing into pleurisy, the need to get him on a boat seemed as desperate as the former need to get the ergotine bottle to his lips. Fanny rushed round Sydney harbour (during a seamen's strike) trying to get berths on any kind of vessel going back into equatorial seas, and on 11 April she, Lloyd, Louis and their new friend Jack Buckland set out on the trading steamer *Janet Nicoll*, bound for Auckland and then, under sealed orders, for 'the South Seas and nothing more definite'.[21]

Within a fortnight, as Stevenson reported gleefully to Baxter, he was 'cutting about on Savage Island, and having my pockets [. . .] – and my trouser pockets – picked of tobacco by the houris of that ilk, and sitting prating with missionaries, and clambering down cliffs to get photographs like a man of iron'.[22] To Henry James he wrote on the same theme, the Pacific's miraculously beneficial effect, but went further, saying, 'I was never very fond of towns, houses, society or (it seems) civilisation. [. . .] The sea, islands, the islanders, the island life and climate, make and keep me truly happier. These last two years I have been much at sea and I have *never wearied*.'[23] That was the key to it, surely: the novelty, the difficulty, the release from wearisome things, including, perhaps, having to face his friends' disappointment back home. His illnesses did not entirely go away in the Pacific – blood-spittings recurred from time to time, fevers, collapses of energy and many ailments arising from chronic undernourishment and exhaustion – but wonderfully, miraculously, Stevenson seemed cured of his hypochondria.

The *Janet Nicoll* was a rough, workaday vessel with a crew of nine white men and about forty Polynesians. It was cramped and hot, full of rats, flies and cockroaches (some of which ate holes in the camera bellows), and rolled like a drunk; a man on Savage

Island told the passengers later that it had made him feel sick just to watch the boat from the shore. Stevenson was almost thrown out of his bunk on several occasions, and had great difficulty working, with one hand clamped on his papers and the other 'spearing the ink bottle like a flying fish'.[24] There was also a minor disaster when ten pounds of 'calcium fire' bought by Lloyd and Tin Jack as entertainments for islanders ignited a package of fireworks and set fire to their cabin. Fanny only just stopped some sailors throwing overboard a smouldering trunk containing Louis's manuscripts.

Even Louis was prepared to admit that life on the *Janet* was pretty uncomfortable, as he described humorously to McClure:

> Our clothes are falling from our bodies with filth, age, rot, and particularly from the effects of the last washing they received on the isle of Majuro in the Marshall Group where a reliable coloured man took them away and (after a due interval) brought them back thickly caked with soap but apparently quite innocent of water. The whole ship's company, owner, captain, engineer, supercargo and passengers are dressed like beggar men (and in the case of Mrs Stevenson like a beggar woman); all go with bare feet, all are in rags and many partly naked [. . .] Lloyd is spotted like the pard with the effects of coral poisoning. The ship wallows deep with barbaric trumpery collected by Mrs Stevenson, two-penny spears are triced up in the rigging; whenever the ship rolls, I look to have a shark's tooth scimitar discharged upon my dead head; and as I walk about the cabin dictating to Lloyd, my path is impeded by a Manihiki drum, vainly sprinkled on the outside with buhac powder, but supposed internally to be one clotted bolus of cockroaches.[25]

The ship's route, after its initial stop in Auckland, would have been exactly suited to researching island life, had it ever stopped more than a few hours at each place. They made thirty-three land-falls during the three-and-a-half-month trip, including Upolu (where Louis and Fanny rushed on shore to check the progress of work at Vailima) and islands to the east of Samoa as far as Penrhyn

Island. Then they went west and north to the Tokelaus and Ellices, all the way through the Gilberts (where the Stevensons saw Tembi-nok again) and on to the Marshalls. However, Stevenson put almost nothing from this trip into the 'big book' on the South Seas. His initial burst of energy and interest in that was spent. Fanny was dictating to Lloyd a diary of the whole voyage, published eventually as *The Cruise of the Janet Nichol* (she never spelled the name of the boat correctly). This was ostensibly to help Louis remember details of the journey, but was really a bid to show him how travel-writing should be done. She said as much to Colvin the following year, while lamenting the dullness of her husband's treatment of his material.[26]

The *Janet*'s voyage bore better fruit for Stevenson in his fiction; 'Tin Jack' had slipped straight into *The Wrecker*; Ben Hird, the supercargo on the *Janet* (a charming, educated man, who became co-dedicatee of *Island Nights' Entertainments*), suggested traits for Herrick and Attwater in *The Ebb-Tide*; and evidence of 'devil-work' in Apemama found its way into 'The Beach of Falesá'. Stevenson might also have noted the difficulty that Mr Henderson, owner of the *Janet*, was having finding on any chart the location of an island he had bought; the situation seems to be reversed in *The Ebb-Tide*, in which Attwater uses the uncharted, unfindable nature of his own island as a form of camouflage.

By the time they reached Noumea, Stevenson had had enough of the *Janet* and chose to stay back to rest and work while Lloyd and Fanny completed the trip to Sydney via New Caledonia. He followed a few days later in the more sedate SS *Stockton*. Back in Sydney, Stevenson was once again confined to bed at the Union Club for much of the time. He and his wife decided against any attempt to go to England that autumn and sent Lloyd alone instead to oversee the sale and shipping of goods from Skerryvore (a heavy responsibility for the twenty-two-year-old known to be 'not a man of business'). In January of the following year (1891), Lloyd was to accompany Margaret Stevenson out to Samoa. Everything tended towards the new life at Vailima, and as soon as they knew that a cottage, however makeshift, was ready for them in the grounds of their own estate, Louis and Fanny were back on the *Lübeck* and bound for Apia.

The first four months at Vailima were ones of uninterrupted exertion, a 'laborious, destitute and delightful' life, as Stevenson described it, of bush-clearing, planting, overseeing and organising. Moors had cleared about ten acres of land, but the track up from Apia was still almost impenetrable and the ground around their two-storey cottage was full of burnt tree stumps and felled trees. Neither Louis nor Fanny had any idea beforehand of the scale of the task ahead, nor the difficulties of getting half a dozen 'consistently obstructionist' Samoans to do their bidding.[27] Louis found it necessary to use 'High Words' almost constantly – it was his only crop, he joked to Baxter – and Fanny was doggedly determined not to let the native 'boys' get the better of her. Louis overheard her one day chastising a lazy worker in pidgin: 'I no pay that boy. I see him all day. He no do nothing.'[28]

The discomforts of the hut were as bad as, or worse than, Silverado. It had an iron roof and open eaves, so it both leaked and was deafeningly noisy during the rain (they had arrived just at the beginning of the rainy season). It was also very exposed to the wind, making it difficult to keep any sort of lamp burning indoors. As Samoa is only twelve degrees south of the equator, the sun sets very quickly, at about half past six every night of the year. With the lamps often unlightable because of the wind, Fanny and Louis had to sit for hours in the evenings in uncanny darkness, listening to tree frogs, the rain and the tall ironwood trees creaking and clashing around them. They had little to eat (one night they dined off an avocado, a ship's biscuit and a piece of bread between the two of them), and few entertainments. Even the flageolet was almost useless, Fanny may have rejoiced to learn, for it had gone spectacularly out of tune in the humidity.

But the place was very beautiful, and as Louis explored the

estate he found an immense variety of plants and trees, palms, giant coconut, hibiscus, 'dripping lianas and tufted with orchids; tree ferns; ferns depending with air roots from the steep banks; great arums – I had not skill enough to say if any of them were the edible kind, one of our staples here; hundreds of bananas'.[29] To the west, Mount Vaea made a spectacular rise to a height of thirteen hundred feet, all covered in forest, and to the east the ground fell away towards the valley of Vaisignano, the river that rises in the centre of the island. The estate's five waters were both useful and picturesque; one of the streams fell, down a delightful small waterfall, into a pool deep enough to bathe in, and there was a drinking-water spring which was eventually diverted to the house in pipes. Fresh prawns were discovered in the stream, and pigeons in the forest, and though the banana trees proved to be the non-fruiting kind, there were plenty of lemons and limes around the property, and orange trees by the bathing pool. Lloyd later found that the unripe oranges came in handy when all the cricket balls had been lost in the bush.

Fanny and Louis acquired two former Auckland tramcar horses as pack animals, very needful for hauling goods up from Apia: Louis also had a horse called Jack, a skittish, ugly animal, which one observer said 'would not have been owned by any self-respecting English costermonger'.[30] Trotting into Apia on this beast, wearing his yachting cap, filthy whites and riding boots, Stevenson 'almost suggested a South Sea Don Quixote', a comparison that would have delighted him. As well as horses, they kept a cat (to keep down the rats), hens, a boar and three sows, but as the hens didn't lay and both the pigs and horses were always getting out of their enclosures, and the cat threatened to be as good at keeping down chickens as rats, the smallholding often seemed more trouble than it was worth.

They had very few servants in these arduous early days on the site, only a German cook called Paul Einfürer (late of the *Lübeck*), who turned out to be a hopeless drunkard, and a Samoan overseer called Henry Simele, a local chief, keen to improve himself, who spent his evenings submitting to lessons in decimals and basic surveying (an old skill suddenly coming in useful for Stevenson). The gangs of native boys at work clearing the land and making the new building were hard to organise and had no concept of punctuality. It was the Stevensons' first encounter with *fa'a Samoa*, 'the Samoan way', which, if they had perceived it clearly, might have dissuaded them from trying to set up and run a plantation there. Fanny and Louis were obliged to put in long days of back-breaking work.

Fanny threw herself into the establishment of a vegetable garden with 'the industry of a bee or a devil', as Louis put it. Not all his remarks went down well. His ill-timed description of his wife revealing 'the soul of a peasant' rather than that of an artist (which Fanny recorded in the diary she had begun to keep) stung her to the quick, and she brooded on it for weeks. His attempts at reconciliation are also recorded: 'Louis assures me that the peasant class is a most interesting one and he admires it hugely.'[31] It was the first indication of the growing distance between husband and wife that was to become very distressing to Louis over the next couple of years.

The Stevensons certainly seemed like a strange and not particularly happy couple to two curious tourists, the historian Henry Adams and the painter and illustrator John La Farge, who made their way up the track from Apia to meet the famous writer and his wife one afternoon in October 1890. Adams was bemused by the 'squalor like a railroad navvy's board hut' and the 'pervasive atmosphere of dirt' that hung around, but that was nothing to the appearance of the feral creatures they disturbed:

> Imagine a man so thin and emaciated that he looked like a bundle of sticks in a bag, with a head and eyes morbidly intelligent and restless. He was costumed in very dirty striped cotton pyjamas, the baggy legs tucked into coarse knit woollen stockings, one of which was bright brown in colour, the other a purplish dark tone. With him was a woman who retired for a moment into the house to reappear a moment

afterwards, probably in some change of costume, but, as far
as I could see, the change could have consisted only in putting
shoes on her bare feet. She wore the usual missionary nightgown which was no cleaner than her husband's shirt and
drawers, but she omitted the stockings. Her complexion and
eyes were dark and strong, like a half-breed Mexican[.][32]

Despite the filth, Adams found his host immediately interesting.
Stevenson's restlessness and excitability struck him as they had so
many others: '[he] perches like a parrot on every available projec-
tion, jumping from one to another, and talking incessantly', and
though it was galling that the Scot had never heard of him (whereas
he knew La Farge by repute), Adams was happy to make better
acquaintance during the three months he stayed in Samoa, and left
an amusing description of the couple arriving at the American
Consul's house for a dinner: '[Stevenson] appeared first, looking
like an insane stork, very warm and very restless [. . .] Presently
Mrs Stevenson in a reddish cotton nightgown staggered up the
steps and sank into a chair, gasping, and unable to speak.' Though,
as a fellow American from a very different class and background,
Adams obviously found the 'Apache squaw' somewhat beyond
the pale, he thought Stevenson 'astonishingly agreeable, dancing
about, brandishing his long arms above his head, and looking so
attenuated in the thin flannel shirt which is his constant wear, that
I expected to see him break in sections'.[33]

The American Consul, Harold Marsh Sewell, was part of an
expanding white government class in Samoa subsequent to the
Berlin Treaty. The new Chief Justice, a Swede called Conrad Cedercrantz, arrived in Apia in December 1890, and the following year
the President of the Municipal Council, Baron Arnold Senfft von
Pilsach (a Prussian), and three Land Commissioners took up their
posts. The British Land Commissioner was Bazett Haggard,
brother of the novelist Rider Haggard, who was to become a friend
of Stevenson (though he suffered increasingly from alcoholism).
There were three existing Consuls representing the three 'powers';
altogether quite a number of foreign administrators for a small

island group supposed to be ruling itself. And though the re-establishment of Laupepa as king seemed to be working, Mataafa was all the while secretly strengthening his position for the inevitable clash of arms.

The clearing of the land around the new house at Vailima, and the endless making and remaking of paths through the bush, proved difficult; however much hacking and cutting one did, next day more greenery would spring up in the rich volcanic soil, and to leave a patch untended for a week was to lose it. Stevenson became intrigued with the 'unconcealed vitality of these vegetables, their exuberant number and strength, the attempts – I can use no other word – of lianas to enwrap and capture the intruder, the awful silence; the knowledge that all my efforts are only like the performance of an actor, the thing of a moment, and the wood will silently and swiftly heal them up with fresh effervescence'.[34] The most pernicious and interesting weed that he had to deal with was *tuitui*, 'the sensitive plant', 'a singular insidious thing, shrinking and biting like a weasel; clutching by its roots as a limpet clutches to a rock'.[35] He documented his struggles with this tenacious stinger in his long journal-letters to Colvin (subsequently *Vailima Letters*, the first of Stevenson's correspondence to be published), and in a long poem called 'The Woodman' that became a sort of rainforest version of Marvell's 'The Garden':

> *Thick round me in the teeming mud*
> *Briar and fern strove to the blood:*
> *The hooked liana in his gin*
> *Noosed his reluctant neighbours in:*
> *There the green murderer throve and spread,*
> *Upon his smothering victims fed,*
> *And wantoned on his climbing coil.*[36]

Stevenson became so preoccupied with gardening – and with the battle against 'sensitive' in particular – that he began to claim it was far more satisfying than writing books. How much so he hurried to express in words: 'I would rather do a good hour's work weeding sensitive [. . .] than write two pages of my best,' he told R.D. Blackmore; '*Nothing* is so interesting as weeding.'[37] A great part of the interest was the novelty of being able to do physical work at all. Stevenson had never before exerted himself or worked up a sweat over anything: now he spent hours in the bush every day, getting filthy, and tasting a new pleasure, 'a quiet conscience' when he stopped.[38] 'Sensitive' satisfied every need: it was exotic, poetic, 'touchy', indefatigable; it inspired botanical discoveries and led to metaphysical ones: 'I give my advice thus to a young plant: have a strong root, a weak stem, and an indigestible seed: so you will outlast the eternal city, and your progeny will clothe mountains, and the irascible planter will blaspheme in vain. The weak point of *tuitui* is that its stem is strong.'[39] But there was also 'the horror of the thing', reawakening his neurasthenic side:

> This business fascinates me like a tune or a passion; yet all the while I thrill with a strong distaste. The horror of the thing, objective and subjective, is always present to my mind; the horror of creeping things, a superstitious horror of the void and the powers about me, the horror of my own devastation and continual murders. The life of the plants comes through my fingertips, their struggles go to my heart like supplications. I feel myself blood boltered; then I look back on my cleared grass, and count myself an ally in a fair quarrel, and make stout my heart.[40]

What did Colvin make of this? With the post only leaving Samoa once a month, 'correspondence' in the usual sense between the friends was no longer possible; the intervals killed dead any give-and-take. And even when letters began their month-long journey from Apia, carefully packed and registered, they often disappeared en route. 'It seems absurd to write,' Stevenson complained to Mrs Jenkin, 'we have every reason to suppose nobody ever receives them.' But he understood that as well as frustrations, these new circumstances allowed him licence, too, and if his monologues to Colvin show self-doubt, restlessness and an extreme self-consciousness about his art, they also manifest a wonderful free-dom and inventiveness.* 'I begin to see the whole scheme of letter writing,' he said sardonically to his friend, 'you sit down every day and pour out an equable stream of twaddle.'[42] In other words, his letter-writing could become an endless riff, and that 'equable stream' a stream of consciousness. This makes his letters from this last period of his life some of the most extraordinary ever written, a one-way ticket into his mind. Stevenson did not have any idea whether his musings on 'sensitive' would amuse the real-life, flesh-and-blood Colvin; he wouldn't get a response for at least two months, and by that time it wouldn't matter. His commerce was now with abstract, rather than merely absent, friends. In a pivotal passage from his letter of 20 March 1891, Stevenson stumbles on this truth, that his 'virtual' friendship with Colvin was not only more pleasurable than the real thing, but also more real:

> Though I write so little, I pass all my hours of fieldwork in continual converse and imaginary correspondence. I scarce pull up a weed, but I invent a sentence on the matter to yourself; it does not get written; *autant en emportent ly vents*; but the intent is there, and for me (in some sort) the com-panionship. Today for instance we had a great talk. I was toiling, the sweat dripping from my nose in the hot fit after a squall of rain; methought you asked me – frankly, was I happy. Happy (said I), I was only happy once: that was at Hyères; it came to an end from a variety of reasons, decline of health, change of place, increase of money, age with his stealing steps: since then, as before then, I know not what it means. But I know pleasure still; pleasure with a thousand faces, and none perfect, a thousand tongues all broken, a thousand hands and all of them with scratching nails. High among these I place this delight of weeding out here alone by the garrulous water, under the silence of the high wood,

---

* Oscar Wilde was too irritated by the self-consciousness of these letters when he read them in print six years later to allow that Stevenson was doing something innovative. Wilde wrote to Robbie Ross from his cell in HM Prison, Reading, that he felt Stevenson 'merely extended the sphere of the artificial by taking to digging. [. . .] To chop wood with any advantage to oneself, or profit to others, one should not be able to describe the process. In point of fact the natural life is the unconscious life.'[41]

broken by incongruous sounds of birds. And take my life all through, look at it fore and back, and upside down, – though I would very fain change myself, I would not change my circumstances – unless it were to bring you here. And yet God knows perhaps this intercourse of writing serves as well; and I wonder, were you here indeed, would I commune so continually with the thought of you: I say I wonder for a form; I know, and I know I should not.[43]

Back in Britain, Lloyd was in Edinburgh, helping 'Aunt Maggie', as the Osbournes called Margaret Stevenson, prepare for her removal to Samoa. Lloyd was keen on intrigue and tale-telling, and passed on with full flourishes of significance to his mother and stepfather the news that Henley (living in Howard Place, just a few doors from Stevenson's old home) had not yet been to call on Stevenson's mother. This apparently trivial social oversight opened up for Stevenson all the bitterness of the Nixie affair. He had hoped that the bad feeling created then had dissipated, but now Henley's ill-will seemed utterly beyond question, and his lack of consideration for 'an old woman very much alone' the cruellest way to continue old grudges against himself. 'He has chosen to strike me there,' Stevenson wrote melodramatically to Baxter, 'and I am done with him for time and for eternity.'[44]

In response to the perceived snub, Louis drafted an absurdly pompous note to Henley, rewriting it next day into a coldly formal declaration that he was severing all future ties. The incident was 'not so much a death as an obituary notice', he told Colvin. 'But it leaves me practically in active relations with only one of my old friends besides yourself: Charles Baxter.'[45] The incident happened as *Beau Austin* was finally creaking its way onto the stage in London, produced by and starring no less than the man who had kept himself awake with hatpin-pricks at the Skerryvore reading, Beerbohm Tree.* Henley did not attend the first performance (on

---

* It was a stopgap, apparently; Tree had nothing else ready.[46]

3 November 1890), but Oscar Wilde, Henry James, William Archer and George Moore did. The reviews were poor – only Archer could find a word of praise for 'ye Beau' – and Henley, whose great success as the editor of the *Scots Observer* (later the *National Observer*) had diverted him from his ambitions as a playwright, seemed to have lost interest in the works altogether. Asked by Baxter what to do with the unpublished plays now that the authors were finally separated, he replied, 'I am indifferent – absolutely.'[47] But he wasn't indifferent to Stevenson: Henley remained embittered by their quarrel, anxious to monitor mutual friends such as Baxter for signs of defection to 'the enemy', and eager to vilify Stevenson in the circle of young acolytes who were coming to be known as 'The Henley Regatta' (Max Beerbohm's phrase, coined in the 1890s). Oddly enough, this didn't prevent Henley from publishing articles and poems by his former friend in the newspapers he edited (seven items in all after the Nixie affair), but it shows very poorly against Stevenson's much more generous-hearted impulses, for, predictably, within a short time of this 'final' break all Louis could think of were the things he had loved about Henley. 'What a miss I have of him,' he wrote sadly to Baxter in February 1891. 'The charm, the wit, the vigour of the man, haunt my memory; my past is all full of his big presence and his welcome, wooden footstep: let it be a past henceforward: a beloved past, without continuation.'[48]

Stevenson's detractors had plenty to get their teeth into with the publication of his *Ballads* in December 1890 and the private circulation of some of the South Sea letters (in an edition of twenty-two, to establish copyright). *Ballads* contained 'The Song of Rahéro', 'The Feast of Famine' and 'Ticonderoga', all pretty clod-hopping poems, which had served their purpose as entertainments for King Kalakaua or the crew of the *Janet*, but were never going to impress the literary men of London, as Stevenson ought to have realised. Cosmo Monkhouse took the opportunity to claim in his review that Stevenson's mastery of metre had *always* been 'imperfect and not unlikely to break down on a longer and more exacting exercise', and that the 'infelicities of expression and defects of style' in the new poems were shameful.[49] Gosse was rude about them too: in a letter to G.A. Armour he said, 'I confess we are all disappointed here. The effort to become a Polynesian Walter Scott is a little too obvious, the inspiration a little too mechanical.[...] The fact seems to be that it is very nice to *live* in Samoa, but not healthy to *write* there. Within a three-mile radius of Charing Cross is the literary atmosphere, I suspect.'[50]

The South Seas: A Record of Three Cruises, in its tiny copyright edition, had only been read by a handful of Stevenson's friends, but their response to it was so negative that Stevenson went on the defensive, claiming to Colvin that the material had never been intended as anything but '*a quarry* [...] *from which the book may be drawn*'.[51] McClure was very disappointed by the results of his long wait. In Saranac, Stevenson had contracted to write fifty-two 'letters from the South Seas' to be published serially in the New York *Sun* and collected as a book later; now McClure was faced with fifteen quasi-chapters which 'in no way fulfil the definition of the word "letter" as used in newspaper correspondence'.[52] The publisher was forced to syndicate the material at much lower rates than originally hoped, and the amount Stevenson made from it (just over £1000) was about a third of what had been promised, nowhere near enough to cover the expense of the cruises. This loss of income, as well as the sharp rebuff to his pride, finally dissuaded Stevenson from going on with the book: 'I cannot fight longer,' he told Colvin, 'really five years were wanting, when I could have made a book; but I have a family, and – perhaps I could not make the book after all, and anyway, I'll never be allowed for Fanny has strong opinions and I prefer her peace of mind to my ideas.'[53] The Samoan section of the book, which he had just begun, he completed and published in August 1892 as *A Footnote to History*, but neither that, nor *In the South Seas* (nor *Ballads*, but with much better reason), has ever yet caught the public imagination.

'I lost my chance not dying,' Stevenson wrote to Colvin, only half-jokingly; 'there seems blooming little fear of it now. [...] If only the public will continue to support me!' That they 'supported', with large sales, *Treasure Island*, *New Arabian Nights*, *Dr Jekyll and Mr Hyde*, *Kidnapped* and *A Child's Garden of Verses* was of vital importance, for the expenses of Vailima were, predictably, completely out of control. Moors estimated the cost of the first phase of building to have been about $12,400, the cost of the second phase (begun in 1891–92) $7500 and the upkeep around $6500 per annum,[54] that is, about £4000 to build and £1300 to run.

Stevenson's new fiction included 'The Bottle Imp' and 'The Beach of Falesá', two entirely different kinds of South Sea story. 'The Bottle Imp', a moral fable set in Hawaii, was begun in Honolulu in 1889 and probably finished in Apia when Stevenson first visited that year. The story reworked a familiar plot from the German folk tradition which had surfaced in Grimm ('Spiritus Familiaris') and LaMotte-Foque, as well as in popular drama (Stevenson knew a stage version from Sir Percy and Lady Shelley's library in Bournemouth): the holder of a magic bottle can have anything he wishes for, and be none the worse for it, provided he can sell the bottle afterwards at less than he originally paid. If not, he faces eternal damnation, a sort of cumulative punishment for everything done through the bottle's agency in the past. In Stevenson's version of the story, the bottle does not grant its owners' wishes in obvious ways, and has done more harm than good over the centuries. Nor can good people counteract the bottle's influence, for the Polynesian couple in 'The Bottle Imp' behave selflessly, both ready to sacrifice themselves, yet the curse of being granted their wish is inexorable. It is a very northern, Scottish story, for all its Hawaiian accoutrements.

'The Bottle Imp' was pivotal in establishing Stevenson's fame in Samoa, where he had been viewed with some puzzlement to begin with, as no one could work out the basis of his wealth and authority. One of the missionaries in Upolu asked him for a contribution that he could translate for the church magazine; thus 'The Bottle Imp' became the first work of fiction to be published in the Samoan language, which had no original printed literature at this date, only the Bible and religious tracts. The currency of the tale among the islanders raised Stevenson's prestige to a new level; he was perceived not only as rich and kingly in his strange mansion above Apia (Vailima was quite unlike any building previously erected on the island), but a sense of magic and glamour clung to him. He was given the native name 'Tusi Tala' – 'teller of tales' – and became the subject of avid and possibly satirical speculation. Stevenson told Arthur Conan Doyle (with whom he had begun to correspond after reading the early Sherlock Holmes stories) that native visitors to Vailima who had read 'The Bottle Imp' were apt to imagine it was not a fiction at all, and looking round his house and grounds would ask, 'Where is the bottle?'[55]

'Teller of tales' was far too sentimental a name for the author of 'The Beach of Falesá', the idea of which Stevenson said 'shot through me like a bullet in one of my moments of awe' while he was clearing the jungle in the early days at Vailima. What struck him then was the way the uncanniness of the forest could communicate itself to even the most rational mind. The story that came of this, and which he worked on for over a year (in the knowledge that it would never be a popular, money-making book like *Kidnapped* or *Dr Jekyll*), Stevenson was proud to recognise as 'the first realistic South Sea story; I mean with real South Sea character and details of life. Everybody else who has tried, that I have seen, got carried away by the romance, and ended in a kind of sugar candy sham epic, and the whole effect was lost – there was no etching, no human grin, consequently no conviction.'[56]

Odd though it is to hear Stevenson, the writer of romances, bragging about his success as a realist, it was precisely the case that 'Falesá' broke new ground, and not just in writing about the South Seas. All Stevenson's major works add to the genres they belong to, and it could be said that his minor works add even more (if you count 'The Beach of Falesá' as 'a minor work', which is debatable). There is a sense in which he felt free to experiment more where he guessed he would never entirely please his public, or his literary guardians, and in this respect his removal from the environs of Charing Cross proved useful. 'The Beach of Falesá' unsettles the reader from the outset by offering no absolute standards of any kind: those of the islanders are uninterpretable, and those of the whites a matter of relativity, with the narrator, a trader called John Wiltshire, the poor best of a very bad lot. Wiltshire is a brilliantly conceived creation: just decent enough for toleration, while wholly a part of the degenerate white trading community that this book so thoroughly condemns. His repugnance at the sight of Randall, formerly a functioning sea-captain, but now a fly-blown drunkard squatting on the floor of a filthy hut, sets him up as a man of discrimination, however crude, as does his realisation that he has better goods to sell on the island than any of his rivals (a fact that is proved irrelevant, as his rivals are all cheats). But Wiltshire's own shortcomings are soon (and casually) made clear, as in this conversation with Case, the trader who is showing him round Falesá:

'By the by', says Case, 'we must get you a wife.'
'That's so', said I, 'I had forgotten.'
There was a crowd of girls about us, and I pulled myself up and looked among them like a Bashaw. [...]
'That's pretty', says he.
I saw one coming on the other side alone. She had been fishing; all she wore was a chemise, and it was wetted through, and a cutty sark at that. She was young and very slender for an island maid, with a long face, a high forehead, and a sly, strange, blindish look, between a cat's and a baby's.
'Who's she?' said I. 'She'll do.'[57]

The sham marriage that follows is a masterpiece of grotesque realism, with a (nameless) Negro trader dressed with a paper collar to mimic a priest, pretending to read from 'an odd volume of a novel, and the words of his service not fit to be set down'.[58] Case completes the burlesque by making a fake certificate from a page of the ledger, which states that Uma, the bride, 'is illegally married to *Mr John Wiltshire* for one night, and Mr John Wiltshire is at liberty to send her to hell next morning'. 'A nice paper to put in a girl's hand and see her hide away like gold. A man might easily feel cheap for less,' Wiltshire comments, adding that he blames the missionaries for this state of affairs; without their interference 'I had never needed this deception, but taken all the wives I wished and left them when I pleased, with a clear conscience.'[59]

There are many equally vivid scenes in the novella – the description of the bush at night, the tabooing of Wiltshire's house, his exposure of Case's 'devil-work' (none the less potent, in the end, for being fake), the fight between the two men and its gruesome climax: 'His body kicked under me like a spring sofa [...] the blood came over my hands, I remember, hot as tea' – but it was the marriage, and in particular the wording of the certificate, that arrested the story's first readers, Clement Shorter and McClure's brother, Robert. They thought the tricking of Uma into having sex with Wiltshire 'too strong' for a family paper and insisted on changes. Stevenson refused, of course – it would have made nonsense of the whole story – and warned Colvin that 'financially it may prove a heavy disappointment'. But despite the author's objections, Shorter went ahead and made many alterations, omitting the marriage contract altogether for the magazine serialisation (it was reinstated, but still in bowdlerised form, for the book publication in 1893), saying later, 'no editor who knows his business would worry himself about the feelings of an author, however great, when he had such a point for decision'.[60]

This rather confirmed all Stevenson's worst fears about what was deemed suitable for 'that great hulking, bullering whale, the public'. 'This is a poison bad world for the romancer, this Anglo-Saxon world,' he wrote to Colvin. 'I usually get out of it by not having any women in at all; but when I remember I had "The Treasure of Franchard" refused as unfit for a family magazine, I feel despair weigh upon my wrists.'[61] Stevenson was fatalistic about this treatment, for the editors of the day were ruthless and powerful, and he was pretty much at their mercy. He seldom kept a copy of a manuscript, or had anything to check proofs against (and he was sloppy about proof-correction anyway), and only saw a copy of the mutilated 'Beach of Falesá' (in the *Illustrated London News*) when a visitor to Samoa, Lady Jersey, happened to have one with her. But he was becoming more and more aware of the conditions that constrained him as an artist. In 1892, while at the beginning of a new novel, 'The Young Chevalier', he expounded the problem to Colvin:

> I am afraid my touch is a little broad in a love story; I cannot mean one thing and write another. If I have got to kill a man, I kill him good; and if my characters have to go to bed with each other – well, I want them to go. As for women, I am no more in any fear of them: I can do a sort all right, age makes me less afraid of a petticoat; but I am a little in fear of grossness. [...]
>
> Of course Meredith can do it, and so could Shakespeare; but with all my romance, I am a realist and a prosaist, and a most fanatical lover of plain physical sensations plainly and expressly rendered: hence my perils. To do love in the same spirit as I did (for instance) D. Balfour's fatigue in the heather; my dear sir, there were grossness ready made! [...]
>
> Think how beautiful it would be not to have to mind the critics, and not even the darkest of the crowd – Sidney Colvin. I should probably amuse myself with works that would make your hair curl, if you had any left.[62]

Margaret Stevenson arrived in Sydney on the SS *Lusitania* early in 1891, staying in Melbourne with a niece for a couple of months while the new building at Vailima was rushed into a state of readiness. Margaret described to her sister Jane how delightful her room was, the best in the house, with doors onto the wide veranda and a view of the sea. Fanny had put up the ensigns from the *Casco* at one end of the room and a tapa banner with the word 'welcome' on it in Samoan; she had also hung a framed photograph of Thomas Stevenson – a touch guaranteed to please her mother-in-law. The following week, more members of the new household arrived from

Sydney: Belle, Joe, Austin, several cats and a tame cockatoo called Cocky. Belle was charmed by the singing of the natives who rowed them from the *Lübeck* to the shore, and by the fine figures of the Samoans in their *lava-lava*s, brightly-coloured lengths of cloth which the men tied round the waist and the women either at the waist or above the breast. Everything delighted Belle: the phosphorescent flashes of rotting wood on the path to the estate, the scents of ylang-ylang and woodsmoke, the bold colours of Vailima (peacock-blue wooden walls and red iron roof), and most of all the sight of 'Pineapple Cottage', the new name of the former 'navvy's hut', now reconstructed and remodelled at a slight distance from the main house, the Strongs' new home.

Austin was now ten years old, the age Lloyd had been the last summer at Grez. He was to spend most of the next three and a half years at Vailima, getting bits of lessons from various members of the family – verse from Aunt Maggie, history and basic maths from his step-grandfather, 'Uncle Louis'. He made many friends among the servants, especially Arrick, the pantry boy (a strategically important friend for any ten-year-old), and was allowed to help on the estate, even becoming 'overseer' for one brief, heady afternoon. Vailima and its enormous grounds made an ideal playground, and he recalled for Graham Balfour the excitement of seeing his first flying foxes appear over the house in the evening and 'the distant booming of the surf and the roar of the waterfall after the rains', the pack horses returning from Apia 'with their iron cages filled and creaking with thrilling looking boxes and bundles. The excitements and mysteries of every day and night', glorious mornings with 'everything sparkling and diamond clear [. . .] one could almost hear the plants growing'.[63]

The gathering together of the clan at Vailima transformed it from a scruffy nest for an insane stork to something like a commune or small village, all the more chaotic for being yet unfinished. 'I never saw such a busy place; it fairly buzzed with activity,' Belle said.[64] There were already plans to expand the house; Margaret expected to be moved from her pale-green boudoir to a suite of two rooms in the extension (as big as, if not slightly bigger than, the original building), which was going to contain a magnificent, sixty-foot-long hall on the ground floor. She and Lloyd were the main proponents of the extension (Margaret was putting down £500 towards the £1200 cost); left to himself, Louis wanted an end to building; he was indeed showing signs of restlessness with the whole enterprise and talked again of buying an island elsewhere.

Meanwhile, a separate kitchen was being erected at the back of the house and Fanny was trying to lay out a patch of recent jungle as a tennis court. The tennis court was one of many unusual features: Vailima had the only row of peas in the Pacific, and the only fireplace. The staircase, too, was new to native eyes, and one of the houseboys, asked on his first day of work to take a bucket of water up to a bedroom, put the bucket handle between his teeth and shinned up the outside post. When the family introduced him to the staircase, he found it so novel that for two or three days he did nothing but run up and down, 'chuckling and crowing in an ecstasy of joy'.[65]

Fanny's attempts at growing vegetables had been heroic, but were often frustrated. When she asked her devoted servant Lafaele to plant some vanilla seedlings for her, he put them in upside down. Having shouted at him about this, she and Belle replanted all the seedlings root-downward, only to find that overnight the repentant Samoan redid his work as a surprise for her. On another occasion, Lafaele removed all the tags from a consignment of plants from an American nursery because he had been told to be very careful about the labels. Fanny's rudimentary tropical garden was little the worse for being full of unidentifiable plants, however, and the site now – possibly containing some descendants of those early plantings – has been made into the most splendid botanical collection in the islands, the National Botanical Gardens of Samoa.

Aunt Maggie did no heavy work, of course, and had brought with her a white maidservant from Australia called Mary Carter, whom neither Fanny nor Belle liked. 'The bush is no place for fine

lady companions,' Fanny told her diary,[66] while Belle, who resented
the fact that Mary would never do anything for anyone other than
Margaret (who was paying her), thought the maid 'a great trial to
us'.[67] What Mary thought of the pyjamaed slovens of Vailima does
not require much guessing. With a true servant's regard for the
proprieties, she insisted on maintaining certain standards of respectability, and wore corsets and elaborately starched and
goffered European clothes when even her employer had given them
up. She can be seen in John Davis's famous photo of the household,
shining white, scowling and utterly encased in whalebone, a sacrifice indeed at temperatures which rarely dipped below 85 degrees.
She left as soon as her first year's contract expired.

With the arrival of the piano on 1 July 1891, the furnishing of
Vailima was complete. There is something touching in the fact that
this instrument, which no one in the family could play properly,
was transported all the way from the drawing room at Heriot Row
to Apia harbour, where it was hung from poles and carried, with
infinite pains and, no doubt, much puzzlement, by eleven native
men. It took them eight hours to get up the track – pretty remarkable, given the conditions. When it arrived, and was hauled up to
Margaret's room on the first floor, the piano was judged to be in
'tolerably good tune', though how the tin-eared Stevensons could
have recognised that is another matter. The household's unquenchable enthusiasm for music-making was now given full rein, and on
most evenings at Vailima the night air was rent with the sounds of
Lloyd's clarinet and banjo, Joe's flute, Fanny's guitar and, of
course, the trusty flageolet (recently revived with new parts
brought from London), while Belle hammered out an accompani-
ment. As Baxter wrote, when he heard about all this, 'I am glad –
very glad – that orchestra is, and is likely to remain at least 17,000
miles away.'[68]

Gosse's reference to Stevenson becoming a Polynesian Walter Scott
was more pertinent than he intended. Both writers were set upon

the treadmill in order to pay for over-ambitious building projects: Scott with the costs of Abbotsford after his publisher went bankrupt, Stevenson with Vailima now that hordes of dependants needed a roof over their heads. Stevenson made the comparison himself, in 1892, when he called Vailima 'sub-Priorsford'. He had worked out his productivity rate against that of the Waverley novelist (an impossible example to follow) and concluded that he was 'about one half the man Sir Walter was for application and driving the dull pen. Of the merit we shall not talk . . .'[69] His vastly improved health had made such productivity sustainable, and his routine became somewhat ascetic. 'I am now an old, but healthy skeleton, and degenerate much towards the machine,' he reported to Elizabeth Fairchild (last seen gesticulating through a window at Saranac):

> By six at work; stopped at half-past ten, to give a history lesson to a step-grandson; eleven, lunch; after lunch we have a musical performance till two; then to work again; bath, 4.40; dinner five; cards in the evening till eight; and then to bed – only I have no bed; only a chest with a mat and blankets – and read myself to sleep.[70]

Graham Balfour, who made the first of three long visits to Vailima in August 1892, reported even earlier wakings – 4.30 or 5.00 in the morning, when a light would be visible in the writer's room. 'This is my season,' Stevenson told Colvin,[71] proudly reporting his progress: 'The Beach of Falesá', *The Wrecker*, *A Footnote to History*, a history of Scotland and a family memoir, never completed, but published posthumously as *Records of a Family of Engineers*. In the same year, 1891, there was a novel begun about the Revolutionary Wars, called, unpromisingly, 'The Shovels of Newton French', and more novels in 1892, started like so many hares: 'Sophia Scarlet', 'The Young Chevalier', 'David Balfour' (the sequel to *Kidnapped*), *Weir of Hermiston* and a boys' story called 'The Go-Between'. But the return of health also suggested to Stevenson alternative methods of making money; he longed for writing to be a pastime again and fantasised about a real job, such as being

British Consul of Samoa. Meanwhile, he continued to hope that his plantation would become viable: 'I would rather, from soon on, be released from the obligation to write,' he told Colvin. 'In five or six years, this plantation – suppose it and us still to exist – should pretty well support us and pay wages.'[72]

Stevenson was reckoning without the absence of the Protestant work ethic, most obviously in his two managers, Joe and Lloyd. Moors left a scathing résumé of their achievements: 'as for Joe Strong, who for some time held the position of Overseer-in-Ordinary to the Vailima King – well, he might have made a very good landscape gardener, but he was too esthetic for cacao growing. And Lloyd Osbourne, who was a sort of general manager of the place, just liked to sit down and "watch things grow"; and if they didn't grow, they didn't.'[73] In his correspondence, Moors was even more blunt, confirming that Stevenson 'was indeed the Work Horse supporting with difficulty, and in a trembling way, the whole expense of a large household of idling adults – Human Sponges'.[74]

The famous photograph of the household taken by the local postmaster, John Davis, on 11 May 1892, that was to become the iconic image of the writer at the height of his fame, illustrates the extent of Louis's liabilities. The emaciated milk cow is in the centre of the group, with Stevenson's wife, glowering miserably at the camera, to his left. Margaret sits very straight ('upright and queenly' is how Austin remembered her[75]), in her *holoku* and widow's cap, while Lloyd stands behind her, specs off, arms folded, trying to look commanding. Belle and Austin are on the steps and Joe stands apart at the back with Cocky on his shoulder, looking unready and unwilling to be photographed. His scruffy yachting cap, scarf and *lava-lava* (tied, eccentrically, over trousers) are quite a contrast to shining Mary Carter and the cleanly Samoans included in the family group: Simi the steward, Talolo and Tomasi the cooks, Elena the laundress (carefully dressed and wreathed in flowers), Arrick, Lafaele and Auvea.

Joe's position at the edge of the group was prophetic of the fact that he was about to be ejected from it. Louis's opinion had turned with difficulty away from his 'loveable' son-in-law: in Sydney, it turned out, Joe had been misspending money intended for the upkeep of his wife and child. He had also kept to himself a windfall he got from some painting commissions; his meanness then and Belle's relative patience and long-suffering did much to make Stevenson transfer his sympathies to the wronged wife. Given board and lodging for his whole family in return for work on the estate at Vailima, Joe failed to reform his ways. His drinking continued (opium-taking too, one presumes), and he cheated the estate by feeding the chickens lime and pocketing the money for seed. In a dramatic night-time scene, he was discovered by Louis stealing from the storeroom, for which he had made a duplicate key. Joe's resemblance to Deacon Brodie was completed by the further discovery that he had been leading a double life, and had a Samoan 'wife' in Apia, a woman with whom he had had relations during his 1889 trip to the islands as official artist from Hawaii. Adultery was not new behaviour from Joe, of course (nor from Belle, one might hazard to guess), but the whole of Apia knew about this long before Vailima did, and divorce followed swiftly. Despite some pathetic returns to the house to plead for another free ride on the gravy train, Joe was sent packing. Louis had offered to give him the steerage fare to Sydney and second cabin to Japan, but he seems not to have grasped this chance to escape, and though Belle said he left Samoa, the next year he was painting murals for the refurbishment of the Tivoli Hotel (newly acquired by Moors and rumoured to be operating as a brothel). The year after, Joe went with Moors to Chicago to decorate the exhibit called 'Samoan Islanders' at the World's Fair. Thus Samoa was represented to the world at that great international exhibition by half a dozen dazed native women posed in modified island dress in front of some painted coconut palms, the latest work from the brush of Joseph Dwight Strong.

14

THE TAME CELEBRITY

Let now your soul in this substantial world
Some anchor strike. Be here the body moored; –
This spectacle immutably from now
The picture in your eye; and when time strikes,
And the green scene goes on the instant blind –
The ultimate helpers, where your horse today
Conveyed you dreaming, bear your body dead.

'An End of Travel'[1]

IN SAMOA, Stevenson was intrigued to think of himself as 'the farthest, I suppose, of all that ever blackened paper with English words', but his exile was impenetrable to all but a handful of visitors, and he knew he was unlikely to see his friends again. Colvin couldn't bear the thought of the long sea-voyages, Baxter was beset with money troubles (and, secretly, drink), and Henley of course considered himself 'all too near' in Edinburgh.[2] But Stevenson's fame, and his exotic isolation, were stirring other, unknown or unmet writers to make the pilgrimage to Samoa: Marcel Schwob, the French novelist with whom Stevenson had corresponded sporadically since 1882, was longing to meet his hero; J.M. Barrie, the young Scots writer whose letters charmed RLS and prompted extravagant replies, was hoping to visit in 1893, as was Arthur Conan Doyle, creator of Sherlock Holmes.

Stevenson had little idea of his own fame, and found it 'very queer' on a trip to Sydney in 1893 that so many passers-by pointed him out on the street. His image had become familiar to the public from newspapers around the world, and there were plenty of photographs to choose from, as he seems never to have refused an opportunity to sit in front of a camera. Editors ran filler stories about the author constantly: 'the gossip-columns of the news-papers pullulate with gossip about you', Gosse told him, providing some spoof examples:

> 'All our readers will rejoice to learn that the aged fictionist L.R. Stevenson has ascended the throne of Tahiti of which island he is now a native.'
> 'Mr R.L. Stevenson, who is thirty-one years of age, is still partial to periwinkles, which he eats with a silver pin, pre-sented to him by the German population of Samoa.'[3]

Journalists who made their way to Vailima were often treated negligently by Stevenson, who resented being disturbed from his work. He met a reporter from the *San Francisco Examiner* in a sleeveless undershirt and rolled-up trousers, and sat with a can of tobacco 'within easy reach' all through the interview, nonchalantly rolling a fresh smoke 'as soon as the old one gave out', while 'as he talked he gently toyed among his shapely toes with his disengaged hand'.[4] Whenever possible, reporters were handed over to Mrs Stevenson, who would show them round the newly extended house, the pride of which was the new hall on the ground floor, entirely floored and panelled in varnished Californian redwood, 'a sort of parody upon the old English oaken hall', as the British Consul, Sir Berry Cusack-Smith, spitefully put it. Here hung Sarg-ent's portrait of Louis and Fanny at Skerryvore, some of Bob's paintings, a rather bad portrait of Robert Stevenson (now at the Stevenson Museum in St Helena, California), a bust of the same, the Rodin *Printemps*, slightly damaged by its travels, and numer-ous photographs of friends such as Gosse and Colvin. There was a reproduction of the Opie portrait of Mary Wollstonecraft, which Fanny pointed out with pride to a journalist from *Woman and Home*, speaking of their closeness to Lady Shelley.[5] Both Fanny and Lloyd were keen to promote the association: Lloyd had spent time and his stepfather's money in London getting the pistols which

Sir Percy and Lady Shelley had presented to Stevenson pompously engraved with details of the gift.

The absurdity of his position was not lost on Stevenson. Meeting his cousin Graham Balfour off a boat in Apia in August 1892, Stevenson was bemused by the response of the crew and passengers to his name: champagne was popped, and the clicking of a camera 'kept time to my progress like a pair of castanets':

> The whole celebrity business was particularly characteristic; the Captain has certainly never read a word of mine; and as for the Jew with the Kodak, he had never heard of me till he came on board. There was a third admirer who sent messages in to the Captain's cabin asking if the Lion would accept a gift of Webster's *Unabridged*. I went out to him and signified a manly willingness to accept a gift of anything. He stood and bowed before me, his eyes danced with excitement. 'Mr Stevenson' he said and his voice trembled, 'Your name is very well known to me. I have been in the publishing line in Canada and I have handled many of your works for the trade.' Come, I said, here is genuine appreciation.[6]

Quite different from this was the imaginative space that Stevenson was beginning to take up in the minds of some fellow writers. His Prospero-like exile half out of this world had endowed him with a sort of magus status. Rudyard Kipling, the new literary star, in turmoil after proposing to Carrie Balestier in 1891, vowed to 'get clean away and re-sort myself' with a pilgrimage to his hero, Stevenson,[7] and when delirious in illness eight years later, raved about being in a submarine on his way to Vailima. Schwob (a consumptive) also saw Stevenson as a sort of healer, and made the journey to Samoa to share in his cure as well as his company, though he didn't arrive till after Stevenson's death (and then found the climate uncongenial). The novelist John Galsworthy too, unknown to Stevenson, had set out from England late in 1892 'to visit Robert Louis Stevenson in Samoa'. The nearest he got was Adelaide, where in March 1893 he began the return journey to Cape Town on the clipper *Torrens*. This previously unrecorded incident (unrecorded in Stevenson biography, that is) is remarkable for the fact that the first mate of the *Torrens*, with whom Galsworthy and his companion Ted Sanderson became friendly, was Merchant Seaman Joseph Conrad, soon to turn novelist and become the new favourite of Fanny Sitwell and Sidney Colvin. In view of Conrad's subsequently troubled relationship with Stevenson as a literary influence, it is strange to think of him sailing in southern waters at this time, hearing Galsworthy's regrets about not reaching Vailima and mulling over the phenomenon of 'RLS'.[8]

With the removal of Joe and guardianship of her son Austin given to Louis, Belle Strong became completely dependent on her stepfather. It became politic for her to ingratiate herself with him and the household, but her resources were limited; apart from cheerfulness and a childish delight in dressing things and people up, Belle was not much use at anything. She had none of her mother's readiness to work, indeed, she hated getting her hands dirty, and though she was a competent seamstress, could not always be making little outfits for her pets among the servants' children. They already had striped jackets to wear as a Vailima 'uniform' for special occasions, and *lava-lavas* whimsically made (at Louis's request) from Stewart tartan. Belle's name among the natives was 'Teuila', meaning 'the one who adorns things'. Like Fanny's names 'Tamaitai' ('high-born lady') and 'Aolele' ('the flying cloud'), it may not always have been respectfully applied.

When Louis began to suffer from writer's cramp in the summer of 1892, Belle came into her own as an amanuensis, a role in which she continued till the writer's death. Her spelling and punctuation were poor, so Stevenson had to proceed more slowly than he might have wished; her presence also undoubtedly affected the content of his dictation (letters mostly, but later some literary work). The sight of Belle's round hand on the envelope must have been strangely unwelcome to Colvin and the others back home, a further barrier to intimacy, and her habit of interjecting comments in the letters was an insistent reminder of her mediumship. But Stevenson was very glad of her help, and glad, as always, to have an immediate audience to perform to. For her part, Belle moved swiftly from merely secretarial duties to general maintenance; 'she runs me like a baby', he told Barrie. She chose his socks, trimmed his hair, fussed over his cufflinks and kept a pile of autographs ready to send to fans.

Though there is no evidence (or likelihood) of a sexual relationship between Belle and her stepfather, the intimacy which grew between them in this period became far more sustaining and comforting to the writer than his marriage. For relations between Louis and Fanny were under enormous strain. At first, this seemed the result of mere exhaustion, but it persisted and worsened during the period when they were moving into the new house in the second half of 1891. With Louis's health stabilising, and the excuse lost for constantly moving on, everything seemed suddenly difficult, even contentious, as if their mutual anxiety about his imminent death had been the only thing holding their marriage together. Hence Stevenson's plangent remark about being 'only ever happy once – and that was at Hyères', and his announcement to Colvin, 'I am gay no more.'⁹ The couple went on separate trips away – Louis around the Samoan islands in the spring of 1891, and Fanny to Fiji that autumn – and slept in separate rooms, Louis indulging the discomforts of the hard makeshift bed in his study and reading himself to sleep at night.

It was only in the spring of 1893 that Stevenson felt able to reveal to Colvin that for the past eighteen months his wife had been suffering from a severe psychotic illness:

> At first it only seemed a kind of set against *me*; she made every talk an argument, then a quarrel; till I fled her, and lived in a kind of isolation in my own room. [. . .] I felt so dreadfully alone then. You know about F. there's nothing you can say is *wrong*, only it ain't *right*; it ain't *she*; at first she annoyed me dreadfully; now of course, that one understands, it is more anxious and pitiful.¹⁰

Without this explicit statement to Colvin, it would be virtually impossible to detect any hint of trouble in Stevenson's letters during the period in question, such is his determination to protect his wife. His sporadic reports that she had been 'very ill' would of course have aroused no concern whatever: Fanny was always 'very ill' one way or another, and had had plenty of nervous collapses in the past, from the breakdown following Hervey's death to the 'brain-congestion' of 1879. And the symptoms of this illness – if it was distinctly different from those – could have been contained, at a pinch, in the pathology of that generous hold-all, the menopause. Fanny was withdrawn, moody, obsessive (or alternatively, shrill and alarmist); she had attacks of angina, and 'aneurism', and was more than ever 'ill to manage'.[11] Louis found this distressing and puzzling, as is clear from this letter to Anne Jenkin in May 1892:

> She has been quite sharply ill indeed, and I can't think what was wrong with her; for the rest she keeps ailing, which is a miserable thing – but she gives herself no chance, being always out fighting in her garden, with the industry of a bee or a devil, and the rest is what she knows not. I need not speak; I know little of it myself; and indeed we are an indefatigable household, up early, down late.[12]

And then he changes the subject ... His tendency was to make light of his wife's symptoms, as he did at first to Colvin (though his comparison of Fanny's to 'my father's case' betrays a fear of insanity setting in[13]), but photographs of Fanny at Vailima always show a very set jaw and furrowed brow. The servants thought her 'aitu', or uncanny, and at a siva, or traditional seated dance, the locals evoked her 'with a pantomime of terror well-fitted to call up her haunting, indefatigable and diminutive presence'.[14] Her work in the garden became manic, not pleasurable; she disrupted the rhythm of the household by being late for every meal, and she had started to find company agitating. Increasingly, Stevenson had to excuse himself from social events, or divert them away from

Vailima, to avoid potentially embarrassing scenes when Fanny was in one of these dismaying phases.

The description of himself and his wife which Stevenson sent to J.M. Barrie early in 1893 (exactly the time he was confessing his anxieties to Colvin) obliquely glosses the troubled state of affairs:

> Here follows a catalogue of my menagerie:
>   R.L.S.
>   The Tame Celebrity.
>   Native name, *Tusi Tala*
> Exceedingly lean, dark, rather ruddy – black eyes [. . .] crow's-footed, beginning to be grizzled, general appearance of a blasted boy – or blighted youth – or to borrow Carlyle on De Quincey 'Child that has been in hell'. Past eccentric – obscure and O no we never mention it – present, industrious, respectable and fatuously contented. [. . .] Hopelessly entangled in apron strings. Drinks plenty. Curses some. Temper unstable. Manners purple on an emergency, but liable to trances. [. . .]
>   Fanny V. de G. Stevenson.
>   The Weird Woman.
>   Native name, Tamaitai.
> This is what you will have to look out for, Mr Barrie. If you don't get on with her, it's a pity about your visit. She runs the show. Infinitely little, extraordinary wig of gray curls, handsome waxen face like Napoleon's, insane black eyes, boy's hands, tiny bare feet, a cigarette, wild blue native dress usually spotted with garden mould. [. . .] Hellish energy; relieved by fortnights of entire hibernation. Can make anything from a house to a row, all fine and large of their kind. [. . .] The Living Partizan: a violent friend, a brimstone enemy. [. . .] Is always either loathed or slavishly adored; indifference impossible. The natives think her uncanny and that devils serve her. Dreams dreams, and sees visions.[15]

'A violent friend, a brimstone enemy'; this brilliantly concise summation of his wife's character indicates the complexity of Stevenson's situation. In it is packed all the reciprocal ardour of their love for each other and the harsh sacrifices that Stevenson had been made to pay for it. Awe and loyalty, bemusement, pride and distaste are all there, but perhaps most striking is the critical objectivity at work, the intimidating intellectual power usually kept under such close guard with reference to his wife, or suspended altogether. This word-portrait of Fanny makes it clear that if anyone could ever have demolished her it would not have been Bob, or Katherine, or the Margaret Berthe Wrights of this world, or Henley still festering over the old quarrel, but Uxorious Billy himself.

When describing Belle to J.M. Barrie, Louis was able to be much more light-hearted (she was taking the dictation, after all), passing on the local rumour that she was Louis's illegitimate daughter by a Moorish woman. It was an idea that 'delighted' Louis and which he liked to play up, as Belle told Charles Warren Stoddard: '[Louis] introduces me as his daughter, and when he talks about the old days in Morocco he is magnificent. He tells me long tales about my mother which invariably wind up with "She was a damned fine woman!" '[16] The irony of this is transparent; physically no one could have mistaken Belle for the daughter of anyone but Fanny, in colouring and size so much her double. But by reminiscing about a dear departed 'Moorish' wife and mother, Louis and Belle were not indulging a fantasy, but stating a present truth: Fanny *had* been 'a damned fine woman' – in the past.

The physical and intellectual isolation of Stevenson's years in Samoa had many effects, from the obsessive interest he began to take in Polynesian history and politics to the systematic questioning of his own methods and achievement. The new realism in his work, possibly fuelled by the difficulty he had in 'explaining' Samoa to his distant audience, was not to find many appreciators until long after his death, and he knew he had to keep turning out stories *in his own manner*, as it were, and not just to pay the bills. Hence the sequel to *Kidnapped* (or completion of *Kidnapped*, to be more accurate), the book called 'David Balfour' by the author, published in Britain as *Catriona*. Hence also the pursuit of crowd-pleasing Scots historical themes in 'Heathercat', 'The Young Chevalier', *St Ives* and *Weir of Hermiston* – all left unfinished at his death.

The title *Catriona* was an unfortunate imposition by the publisher, as the daughter of James More Drummond is not central to Stevenson's romance (while the narrator, David Balfour, is). The love story between her and David is in fact a bit of a red herring: *Catriona* is rather a dissection of the Appin murder trial of 1752, a sort of three-dimensional fictional model of that notorious case. Perhaps Stevenson's imagination was most usefully exercised this way, in speculation about the emotional underpinnings of historical events. The romance element is not decorative or distracting, but shown to be inherent in the facts: in this respect Stevenson was perhaps Scott's only true successor. History, for him, suggested play of character and motive; it was this that made him think the Covenanting writers 'delightful' and which animated his reading of documents such as the transcripts of the trial of James of the Glens, one of the texts on the Highlands that his father sent out to Davos in 1881. Now, twelve years later and with a strangely similar model of political intrigue playing out before him day to day in Samoa, Stevenson was able to construct a story that illustrated in ingenious ways the oddities and tragedy of the case.

The Samoan struggle, and the parallels with the Highland crises of the eighteenth century it brought constantly to mind, clearly informed Stevenson's treatment of his theme, which was of a conflict that 'had the externals of a sober process of law, [but was] in its essence a clan battle between savage clans'.[17] The removal of the good man, the honest witness, from a show trial; the triumph of rhetoric over plain speech, revenge over justice – these things reflect to some extent the frustrations of watching history unfold, disastrously, in Samoa. 'It is a singular thing that I should live here in the South Seas under conditions so new and striking, and yet my imagination so continually inhabit that cold old huddle of grey hills from which we come,' Stevenson wrote to Barrie, but of course it wasn't singular at all. He was going through a sharp twist of homesickness, and *Catriona* is probably his most Scots book, most notably in the quantity and variety of Scots language used in it. David's soft Lowland dialect (the most 'English' in the book) is differently constructed from Catriona's Highland phraseology (her 'correctness' in this is part of her clan standing); both are politer than the Edinburgh lawyer Charles Stewart, whose vocabulary and dry manner the ex-advocate knew so well; Stewart in turn, though a Highlander, has nothing of Black Andie's power of vernacular, and Andie's tale, told in broad Scots, is immediately followed by a fight with a Gaelic-speaker, who claims the story for his own tradition. Stevenson in this way wittily and deftly demonstrates the problems with Scots diversity that had concerned him all his life.

Black Andie's narrative, 'The Tale of Tod Lapraik', is the story-within-a-story at the heart of the novel, a political allegory that deals again with the theme of the double. David Balfour is told the tale while he is incarcerated on the Bass Rock, but it is about the Rock, too, and a protagonist who, like Davie, would like to be elsewhere and who sells his soul in order to escape. In 'Tod Lapraik' the bogle is seen dancing for joy among the solan geese on the Bass in ways reminiscent of Hyde's glee before the mirror: 'it lowped and flang and capered and span like a teetotum, and whiles we could hear it skelloch as it span'.[18] Like 'Thrawn Janet' (which, with 'Tod Lapraik', the author ranked among his proudest achievements), the story imitates the oral tradition; the characterisation is simple, the theme supernatural and the narrative moves rapidly to a startling crisis. These are templates of what Stevenson thought story-telling should be: direct and stirring, 'not making stories true', as he had said in 'A Humble Remonstrance', 'as making them typical'.

Catriona sparked a revival of that old debate with Henry James, for when the American objected to the 'almost painful under-feeding' of the visual imagination in the novel, Stevenson responded spiritedly with a sort of battle-cry: 'War to the adjective.

[. . .] Death to the optic nerve [. . .] I *hear* people talking, and I *feel* them acting, and that seems to me to be fiction.'[19] Both the response and James's initial criticism are rather mystifying, for the vividness of Stevenson's descriptive writing in *Catriona* relies heavily, as always, on the visual, as in this passage when Davie is rowed down the Firth by his captors and the Bass Rock comes into view:

> There began to fall a greyness on the face of the sea; little dabs of pink and red, like coals of slow fire, came in the east; and at the same time the geese awakened, and began crying about the top of the Bass. It is just the one crag of rock, as everybody knows, but great enough to carve a city from. The sea was extremely little, but there went a hollow plowter round the base of it. With the growing of the dawn I could see it clearer and clearer; the straight crags painted with sea-birds' droppings like a morning frost, the sloping top of it green with grass, the clan of white geese that cried about the sides, and the black, broken buildings of the prison sitting close on the sea's edge.[20]

Light effects, colours, mass; these were all staples in Stevenson's descriptive technique. One can only conclude that in claiming to wish death on the optic nerve, he was trying to humour James, or was carried away by having elicited any sort of comment on his style from the cautious mandarin of De Vere Gardens.

David Balfour proved a resilient hero. Dropped mid-paragraph at the end of *Kidnapped* by his exhausted creator, he might have proved hard to revive, but his development in *Catriona* is one of Stevenson's major achievements, a 'full length' portrait, which the author recognised as exceeding anything by Scott: 'He never drew a full length like Davie, with his shrewdness and simplicity, and stockishness and charm. Yet, you'll see, the public won't want it; they want more Alan. Well, they can't get it. And readers of "Tess" can have no use for my David, and his innocent but real love affairs.'[21] The reference to Hardy's novel *Tess of the d'Urbervilles*, published in 1891, was a troubling one for Stevenson. He was never explicit about what upset him so much in that novel (which, he admitted, he never finished reading), but it seems to have been the inclusion, and then 'untrue' treatment, of the rape scene. It was 'as false a thing as ever I perused', he complained to Colvin in the first flush of his anger. 'If ever I do a rape, which may the almighty God forfend! You would hear a noise about my rape, and it should be a man that did it.'[22] This rather cranky objection was clearly in extenuation of the problems he had dealing with sex in 'The Beach of Falesá', about to be serialised in the *Illustrated London News* with cuts to the text of which the author was yet ignorant. When Barrie told him later in the year of similar absurd changes that the serial publishers had made to Hardy's *Tess* (making Angel Clare transport the milkmaids across a river by barrow instead of in his arms), Stevenson was somewhat mollified as a fellow sufferer at the hands of the censor, but it did nothing to change his basic revulsion at Hardy's novel. This indeed increased as he became aware slowly of Hardy's critical success in England and began to consider the implications for himself. He started sounding out his friends as if there were ranks to be drawn up, as indeed there were, though it is odd to see the co-author of *The Wrecker* leading an attack on grossness, or attempting to separate the issues of treatment and content so completely.

For though Stevenson's own method was fairly consistent (in the sort of sensual realism and 'plain physical sensations plainly and expressly rendered' he favoured), his subject-matter and manner varied too extravagantly for many readers to associate him with any kind of 'consistency'. Which was the more characteristic book, *The Wrecker* or *Treasure Island*, *Catriona* or *Island Nights' Entertainments* (which included 'The Beach of Falesá' and 'The Bottle Imp')? Was *Kidnapped* a story for children or for adults? Was *The Ebb-Tide* a story by Stevenson or Osbourne? What was left of the elegant aphorist of *Virginibus Puerisque*? When he was alive and charming, these questions seemed of importance only to his friends as they strove to see some shape evolving in this extraordinarily gifted writer's career. When he was dead, that very versatility seemed suspect, the career chaotic (as indeed it was and most are), the 'masterpiece' missing. When the new discipline of 'English Literature' emerged in the new century, Stevenson was nowhere to be seen. He had been popular, he had been a romancer, a writer for boys, a Scot.

The summer of 1892 saw the first visit to Vailima of Graham Balfour, the thirty-four-year-old son of Margaret's cousin Thomas. Handsome, modest, moustachioed and over six foot tall, Graham was as fine a specimen of Scots manhood as could have been wished. Like Louis, he had studied for the bar but never practised, and later in his career he would become a respected writer on educational issues, a director of education (for Staffordshire), a knight of the realm and his cousin's first biographer.

Balfour got on well with everyone and became the idol of the household. To Lloyd, with whom he was lodged in Pineapple Cottage, he was the ideal bachelor companion, to Belle he was someone to flirt with (though Balfour did nothing whatever to encourage her), to Margaret Stevenson he was a source of great family pride. Fanny was in awe of his good looks and Oxford degree, while Stevenson was delighted with his cousin's quiet, clever, manly company. He found in Balfour the sympathetic kinsman-helper that Lloyd had never quite managed to become. Graham understood the tone and context of Louis's talk perfectly, the literary and legal references, the dialect, the family 'accent of mind', and his presence encouraged Louis to start setting down reminiscences of his youth in Scotland. Balfour seemed the ideal custodian of this information; he would understand how to transmit it eventually to Colvin, Stevenson's designated biographer. Thus in the copious Balfour papers now housed at the National Library of Scotland are page after page in Graham's hand of notes taken at Vailima of Stevenson's table-talk and memories, long before anyone other than Colvin was being considered as the 'official' keeper of the flame.

Relatively few of Balfour's personal impressions of Vailima made their way into his 1901 biography of his cousin, though the thorough knowledge of the household he acquired over his three extended stays in 1892, '93 and '94 (amounting to fourteen months altogether) allowed him unique insight into the problems of how to present that last phase of Stevenson's life (sympathetic concealment of Fanny's illness, for instance, and of many other sensitive family issues, was essential). He was given the name 'Pelema': not a 'native' title of significance, but a pidgin version of Stevenson's frequent jokey reference to his cousin as 'that blame Balfour'.

Another 'cousin' visited Samoa in the summer of 1892 and did much to agitate the volatile situation at Vailima. Margaret Child-Villiers, wife of the Governor of New South Wales, Lord Jersey, had been invited to the islands by Bazett Haggard with her seventeen-year-old daughter Margaret and her brother, Captain Rupert Leigh, an ADC to the Governor. The dark-haired, vivacious, forty-three-year-old Countess fell in immediately with Stevenson, whose growing reputation as a controversialist in the region must have intrigued her, and he in turn was delighted with a dose of English manners, aristocratic *élan* and female charm. Within hours of meeting, Haggard was at the door of Vailima with a request from Lady Jersey to be included on a visit which Louis and Fanny had planned to make to Malie, on the southern coast of Upolu, where Mataafa had set up his rebel headquarters. Captain Leigh had already expressed a desire to come along on the jaunt, using an assumed name so as not to implicate Lord Jersey's office. Now Lady Jersey wanted to join in too, in the guise of Mr Stevenson's 'cousin'. No sooner was this irresponsible desire expressed than Stevenson was sending letters all round, to Mataafa, telling him to expect a 'Miss Amelia Balfour' who would require separate sleeping quarters, to Leigh and to 'Miss Balfour' herself (in a letter frivolously dated 1745 and referring to Mataafa as 'the king over the water'), with details of their rendezvous by the ford of Gase-Gase. 'This lark is certainly huge,' Stevenson wrote to Colvin, revelling in the escape into melodrama. On the day of the tryst, the Vailima party hid in a thicket hard by the ford: 'Thirty minutes late. Had the secret oozed out? Were they arrested? [. . .] Haggard, insane with secrecy and romance, over- took me, almost bore me down, shouting "Ride, ride!" like the hero in a ballad.'[23] No one seemed to consider that this pantomime might have detracted from the respect due to Mataafa; they were all too much on the spree. For a couple of days, Stevenson was as elated as a child playing hide and seek in the garden of Colinton Manse.

The 'wild round of gaiety' that accompanied Lady Jersey's visit included a steeplechase, dinners, the joint writing of a 'Ouida romance' about Haggard, and the opening of a girls' school in Apia where Stevenson was able to appreciate the siren's 'voice of gold'.[24]* No wonder Fanny was less than thrilled with the English visitors and left an acid account of them in her diary: 'The Jerseys have been and gone, trailing clouds of glory over the island. [. . .] They were a selfish "champagne Charley" set [. . .] Lady Jersey tall and leggy and awkward, with bold black eyes and sensual mouth; very selfish and greedy of admiration, a touch of vul- garity.'[26]

The larks with Lady Jersey may have been wonderful for letting off steam, but were ill-conceived politically and compounded Stevenson's growing reputation in diplomatic circles as a publicity- seeking nuisance. His letters to *The Times* about Samoa (there were ten of them published altogether) were too long, too particular and too bridlingly rhetorical to win much praise or even attention from his British and American literary friends, though they were noted by the Foreign and Consular Office. But again the Old Man Virul- ent felt moved to have his say, enclosing with one letter copies of extensive correspondence with Baron Pilsach, the main object of his ire. Pilsach had been left in charge of five rebel chiefs who had surrendered themselves to the Chief Justice, Conrad Cedercrantz,

---

* Fanny's voice is often described by her husband during this period as 'shrill', and the general tone at Vailima 'a Babel fit for the bottomless pit; my wife, her daughter, her grandson and my mother all shrieking at each other round the house'.[25]

on the understanding that they would be well treated during six months' incarceration. In Cedercrantz's absence, Pilsach had mined the Apia prison and threatened to blow it up at any attempt at escape or rescue. This was one of many issues Stevenson took up with zeal. Petty corruption, tax avoidance, non-payment of rent among the government administrators – most of his complaints were aimed at the Germans, whose lack of interest in Samoan self-government and continued ambition to take over the islands grew daily more alarming and infuriating to Stevenson. *The Times* continued to print his letters, though noting in one editorial that the 'very fury' of the novelist's attack 'suggests the possibility that the glowing indignation which inflames the champion may have so warped his judgement as to make him less than just to his opponents'.[27] In fact, Stevenson had no personal animus against Cedercrantz whatever, even found him charming, and was well aware of his letters' one-sidedness (also their tiresomeness, writing to Lang that they made his 'jaws yawn to re-read'[28]). Still, he stuck pig-headedly to what he saw as the task in hand, informing *The Times* in September 1892 that he would carry on troubling the editor 'with these twopenny concerns [. . .] until some step is taken by the three Powers, or until I have quite exhausted your indulgence'.[29]

Stevenson was lucky to have a powerful supporter in Lord Rosebery, then Foreign Secretary, who was a great admirer of his books. Without friends in such high places, Stevenson might well have found himself deported from Samoa as a troublemaker, for his support of Mataafa raised rumours at one point that the author was personally trying to engineer a war. Nothing put him off adding fat to the fire, however, and he went ahead quickly with *A Footnote to History: Eight Years of Trouble in Samoa*, hoping it would be in time to be of 'some service to a distracted country'. Aware that such a book might be refused by his publishers, Stevenson was prepared to bear the costs himself. 'You will I daresay be appalled to receive three (possibly four) chapters of a new book of the least attractive sort: a history of nowhere in a corner [which] very likely no one would possibly wish to read [. . .], but I wish to publish,' he wrote to Burlingame in November 1891.[30] In the end, *A Footnote* found publishers on both sides of the Atlantic (such was the draw of the author's name), and appeared in August 1892. Stevenson waited impatiently for some reaction, but as with his other forays into public invective, the effect was disappointing. The most response he got was an unwelcome one: the threat of legal action from a missionary who felt he had been libelled. Still, Stevenson had stood up robustly for his principles yet again.

To friends in England, Stevenson's interest in Samoan politics was beginning to seem an unholy bore. Colvin must have tired of having to act as an apologist on behalf of 'Tusi Tala': he wanted 'Ah welless' back, in spirit if not in body, and wrote to say so in strong terms:

> Do [any of our white affairs] interest you at all[?]. I could remark in passing that for three letters or more you have not uttered a single word about anything but your beloved blacks – or chocolates – confound them; beloved no doubt to you; to us detested, as shutting out your thoughts, or so it often seems, from the main currents of human affairs, and oh so much less interesting than any dog, cat, mouse, house, or jenny-wren of our own known and hereditary associations, loves and latitudes. [. . .] please let us have a letter or two with something besides native politics, prisons, *kava* feasts, and such things as our Cockney stomachs can ill assimilate.[31]

Stevenson replied with remarkable patience, 'Dear Colvin, please remember that my life passes among my "blacks or chocolates". [. . .] You must try to exercise a trifle of imagination, and put yourself, perhaps with an effort, into some sort of sympathy with these people, or how am I to write to you?'[32] Colvin apologised subsequently for what he knew had been an intemperate outburst, and admitted in his published *Memories and Notes* that he had become 'hypercritical about the quality and value of some of the work sent home from the Pacific', which was 'disappointingly lacking in the thrill and romance one expected of [Stevenson] in relating experiences which had realized the dream of his youth'.[33] This sense of dashed expectations was widespread among Stevenson's friends and admirers. 'I see that romantic surroundings are the worst surroundings possible for a romantic writer,' Oscar Wilde wrote. 'In Gower Street Stevenson could have written a new *Trois Mousquetaires*. In Samoa he wrote letters to *The Times* about Germans.'[34]

Graham Greene, a subsequent admirer of Stevenson, but critical of those who overvalued the 'spurious maturity' of his essays and early works, felt quite the opposite: that it was only in these last years, and faced with the challenge of the South Sea material, that Stevenson began to 'shed disguising graces'. 'If he is to survive for us,' Greene wrote, '[it will be as] the tired, disheartened writer of the last eight years, pegging desperately away at what he failed to recognise as his masterworks.'[35] The book Greene must have had in mind as an example of 'pegging away at a masterwork' was *The Ebb-Tide*, the composition of which is documented thoroughly in Stevenson's letters of 1893. Few better accounts exist of a novelist suffering the agonies of writer's block. Stevenson had returned to the novel, based on Lloyd's 'Pearl Fisher' (begun in Hawaii three years earlier), while *Catriona* was in production, putting aside another Scottish novel, *Weir of Hermiston*, to make some money from an easy job. By the time Stevenson began to work steadily on it, in February 1893, Lloyd had no further part in the writing, and the original large scheme, for a book as long as *The Wrecker*, had been abandoned. Stevenson had decided to concentrate on the character of Attwater, the refined, elusive monomaniac living on an uncharted pearl-fishing island in the South Seas, whose story takes up the whole second half of the book and was entirely the work of the one writer.

In May, Stevenson reported to Colvin that he was 'grinding singly' at the manuscript, and had reached page 82 of a projected 110 or so. 'Not much Waverley Novels about this!' he remarked, referring to the slow rate of production, only twenty-four pages in three weeks. On the sixteenth he complained that the work was like 'a crucifixion',[36] and dreaded having to finish his letter and return to 'the damned thing lying waiting for me on p.88, where I last broke down':

> I break down at every paragraph, I may observe, and lie here, and sweat, and curse over the blame thing, till I can get one sentence wrung out after another. Strange doom! after having worked so easily for so long![37]

Page 88 was to prove as inescapable as his old recurring nightmare of the everlasting stair, for he thought he had finished it on the sixteenth, but two days later was back again, and feared a relapse even further, to page 85. On 20 May he lamented only having written or revised eleven pages in nine days; then he pushed on to page 100, only to slip back, by the beginning of June, to page 93. So it went on, an ebbing tide indeed, a book which he might almost have imagined disappearing under his pen. And the difficulty was not artistry so much as 'my total inability to write', as he bravely confessed to Colvin:

> Yesterday I was a living half hour upon a single clause and have a gallery of variants that would surprise you. And this sort of trouble (which I cannot avoid) unfortunately produces nothing when done but alembication and the far-fetched.[38]

To another correspondent he wrote in a more humorous vein:

> Be it known to this fluent generation that I, R.L.S., in the forty-third year of my age and the twentieth of my pro-fessional life, wrote twenty-four pages in twenty-one days: working from six to eleven, and again in the afternoon from two to four, without fail or interruption. Such are the gifts the gods have endowed us withal; such was the facility of this prolific writer![39]

The labour of writing *The Ebb-Tide* left him incapable of deciding whether the book was 'an extraordinary work' or 'forced, violent, alembicated' (the phrases appear in the same letter[40]), whether the characters 'knocked spots' or were 'a troop of swine'.[41] In fact, all those things are true to some degree. The story begins with three white beachcombers facing utter destitution in Papeete after 'a long apprenticeship in going downward': Davis, an American sea-captain, is an alcoholic whose negligence killed seven of his former crew; Huish, an unscrupulous and degenerate cockney clerk; and Herrick, an Oxford-educated man who has sunk through various levels of failure and disgrace and is now in self-exile in the Pacific. When the chance arises to take over the charter of a schooner blighted by smallpox, the desperados take it and set out, with what they have been told is a cargo of Californian champagne, to make some money in Sydney.

Far out at sea, they discover that most of the cargo is water, not champagne, and propelled off-course by bad weather, they are in worse straits, it seems, than before. The sighting of an island which is not on the chart but of which there are rumours reported in the mariners' directory leads the men to speculate that some valuable private trade goes on there, and they approach to investigate. Thus they meet Attwater, the owner of the island, a tall, impeccably dressed Englishman, guarded and cultured, who has assumed absolute power over his native servants (all but three of whom have recently died from an outbreak of smallpox). He is an ex-missionary and ardent evangelist – 'God hears the bell!' he tells his guests, 'we sit in this verandah on a lighted stage with all heaven for spectators!'[42] – whose choice of habitation, it becomes clear, has as much to do with socio-religious experimentation as commerce. When he isolates Herrick from his shipmates, intending to win over the only member of the trio worth saving, Herrick's loyalties (if that is quite the right word) are torn between this coolly superior new acquaintance and the wretches with whom he has shared destitution, and who clearly intend to rob, blackmail or kill their host.

The stand-off ends in a tense attempt at a parley and Huish's crude attack on Attwater with a bottle of vitriol, anticipated by the pearl trader, who shoots him dead. Attwater gets his convert in the unattractive shape of Davis, and the novel ends with the ex-alcoholic pleading with Herrick to stay on the island and share the 'peace of believing'. It wasn't an ending that pleased the critics (perhaps they didn't admit its profound cynicism), though the reviews were pretty favourable, if restrained. No one recognised the birth of a new and very modern literary motif in Stevenson's invention of a hidden settlement ruled over by a maverick lone white man, the theme to be taken up in the following decade by H.G. Wells in *The Island of Dr Moreau,** Conrad in *Heart of Darkness* and *Lord Jim* and Rider Haggard in *Heart of the World*, and penetrating into popular culture as far as Superman's arch-enemy Lex Luther and some of Ian Fleming's Bond villains.

Another innovative, under-appreciated work by Stevenson from these last years of his life was the stories collected post-humously as *Fables* (which included some of the stories written in the 1870s). 'The Persons of the Tale', written some time between 1881 and 1894, is particularly remarkable, a 'postmodern' fiction created before the dawn of Modernism. In it, two of the characters from *Treasure Island*, Long John Silver and Captain Smollett, take a break between chapters thirty-two and thirty-three of the novel to smoke a pipe 'not far from the story' and discuss their relative importance to the author, as they perceive it. ' "Who am I to pipe up with my opinions?" ' Smollett says. ' "I know the Author's on the side of good; he tells me so, it runs out of his pen as he writes." ' Silver argues that though he is the villain of the story, he knows he has the author's sympathy: ' "I'm his favourite chara'ter. He does me fathoms better'n he does you – fathoms, he does. And he likes doing me. He keeps me on deck mostly all the time, crutch and all, and he leaves you measling in the hold, where nobody can't see you, nor wants to." ' Smollett replies that the author ' "has to get a story [. . .] and to have a man like the doctor (say)

---

* Wells's ghastly novel of 1896 is remarkable for another strong link with Stevenson, which may be entirely coincidental (as he could have heard the story only from hearsay by the date when *The Island of Dr Moreau* was published), and that is the incident in Dr Trudeau's laboratory on his island in Saranac Lake when Stevenson voiced repulsion at the practice of vivisection. The similarity with the scene in Moreau's laboratory, even to the names of the doctors, is peculiar.

given a proper chance, he has to put in men like you and Hands." '
They are called back into the novel by the opening of the ink bottle
and the author writing the words 'Chapter XXXIII' (the chapter
of *Treasure Island* in which Silver's authority is overturned).[43]
Fables was lucky to get published, as Fanny hated the stories. 'I
can't see that they mean anything at all,' she wrote to her mother-
in-law in November 1895. 'I wouldn't let Louis publish them when
he wrote them, and am disgusted that it should have been done
now. They were written in what I used to call one of Louis's lapses,
and are foolish and meaningless.'[44] But Charles Baxter spirited the
manuscripts away from Vailima, and negotiated magazine publication in 1895 and book publication the following year.

Early in 1893 the extension to Vailima was finished, at huge cost,
considerable inconvenience and against the wishes of the Work
Horse. Margaret Stevenson, at whose strong insistence the whole
project had been instigated, chose just this moment to go back to
Scotland for an indefinite visit. The ostensible reason was 'la
grippe', but it seems likely that she wanted a respite from having
to witness the symptoms of Fanny's deterioration. Austin Strong
had been sent away to school in California (to live with his great-
aunt Nellie Vandegrift and her husband in Monterey) and Graham
Balfour was off on his travels; the household was therefore at its
smallest when Fanny suffered her worst 'fit' yet, as Stevenson
confided to Colvin (in the one explicit letter on the subject):

> The last was a hell of a scene which lasted all night – I will
> never tell anyone what about, it could not be believed, and
> was so unlike herself or any of us – in which Belle and I held
> her for about two hours; she wanted to run away.[45]

Desperate for some remedy, Louis and Belle decided to take Fanny
to Sydney to consult a doctor, booking in to the Oxford Hotel
again in late February. Released by a sense of holiday and a seeming improvement in Fanny, Louis went on a spending spree, buying

new clothes for all of them, including a sumptuous black velvet gown for his wife, made secretly, to Belle's measurements, as a surprise. They also had their photographs taken, and those of Fanny are among the most remarkable of all images of her. Unlike the scowling, dark, rather masculine figure she usually presents in pictures from these years, in Sydney the fifty-three-year-old 'weird woman' looked suddenly beautiful again, with a steady, sleepwalking look in her eyes and an almost magical youthfulness of feature.

But it wasn't to last. 'The first few weeks were delightful,' Louis told Colvin,

> her voice quiet again – no more of that anxious shrillness about nothing, that had so long echoed in my ears. And then she got bad again. Since she has been back, also she has been kind – querulously so, but kind. And today's fit (which was the most insane she has yet had) was still only gentle and melancholy. I am broken on the wheel, or feel like it. Belle and Lloyd are both as good as gold. Belle has her faults and plenty of them; but she has been a blessed friend to me.[46]

In April, Louis wrote to his mother that they were 'all recovered or recovering', but Belle interrupted the dictation and exhorted Louis to 'tell the truth – that Fanny is not recovering'. Louis continues, 'But though it is true she seems to have taken a cast back, she is far indeed from being so dreadfully ill as she was before.' At this, Belle abandons dictation and writes in her own person, '(She lies in bed, doesn't smoke, doesn't want to eat or speak; Louis does not want to alarm you but I think you should know what a really anxious time we are going through [. . .] The doctor says there is no danger and I hope he is right, but I would like to see her take an interest in something. Belle.)'[47]

Louis kept reporting his wife 'much better' over the next few months in letters to Colvin, and indeed never complained again to him about the problem, showing himself perhaps too much his mother's son in this capacity to shut his eyes to unpleasantness. He was relieved to get a diagnosis for his wife's illness of Bright's Disease from a doctor in Honolulu: Fanny seemed relieved too –

a kidney disorder was so much easier to live with. But the likelihood of Fanny having had Bright's, which affects mostly young people and of which she had few symptoms except the sporadic stomach cramps, seems remote. Bright's Disease is also traditionally confusable with syphilis.

When Fanny resumed writing her diary in July 1893, the domestic atmosphere it recorded was as bad as before. Her continuing instability is evident in her drive to justify all her own actions and criticise all those of her husband, often described as 'in the sulks'. Contention seems the dominant note, and Louis the isolated target. When the menfolk of Vailima, on the outbreak of war in the islands, warned her and Belle to keep a low profile (for obvious reasons), she complained to her diary, 'Lloyd and Pelema are young, and of course intolerant, but it is a little surprise [sic] to find Louis with the same ideas.'[48] And when they all advised against attending a Fourth of July ball in Apia, Fanny and Belle became set on going. 'Louis in deep sulks at our attitude, Lloyd sweetly amiable, Pelema keeping out of sight,' she wrote, with a flash of the old humour, but went on to register petty complaints about Louis insisting on leaving the ball before three in the morning (so that he could work next day) and the fact that she and Belle had not dressed up as much as the other American women, who all, she notes pointedly, had elaborate new gowns for the occasion.

Once war had broken out in Samoa, it became, in Fanny's mind, a sort of extension of the marital battleground. She persisted in misinterpreting Louis's motives and loyalties in order to have something substantial to disagree with him about, pretending to find his placation of the Samoan Secretary of State sinister, and 'furious' over what she thought was a lessening of his fervour towards Mataafa. 'I intend to do everything in my power to save Mataafa,' she wrote dramatically on 17 July 1893:

> And if Louis turns his face from him by the fraction of an inch, I shall wear black in public[.] [I]f they murder him, or if he is brought in to Apia a prisoner I shall go down alone and kiss his hand as my king. Louis says this is all arrant mad

quixotism. I suppose it is; but when I look at the white men
at the head of the government and cannot make up my mind
which is the greater coward, my woman's heart burns with
shame and fury and I am ready for my madness.[49]

To some extent, as Louis knew, Fanny had *always* been like this:
self-dramatising, highly strung, over-emphatic. The thought could
not have been comforting, for she was now, to a greater or lesser
extent, deranged. Louis's description of himself to Barrie at the
end of this year as 'fatuously contented' was a deliberately misleading one. There is no doubt that though he tried to keep it secret,
the last three years of Stevenson's life were deeply unhappy.

The Samoan war, when it came, lasted only nine days. There
had been skirmishes since the spring of 1893 between Mataafa's
and Laupepa's men, but the trigger was Mataafa's raising of his
flag at Malie, declaring himself king. On 8 July, government forces
defeated him at Vailele (as it was obvious they would) and he fled
to the tiny island of Manono, just off the western end of Upolu.
Holed up there, he could easily have been beaten by Laupepa, but
before the showdown took place British and German warships
were sent to Manono and forced Mataafa to surrender. He was
then deported to the Marquesas and the chiefs who had fought
with him were put in prison in Apia.

Stevenson's support of these imprisoned chiefs, by means of
visits to them and continued agitation of the authorities about the
conditions under which they were being kept, earned him their
deep gratitude, and when they were released they offered to make
a road from Vailima in commemoration of it. The opening of 'The
Road of the Loving Heart' (suitably marked with a sign that made
the political origins of the gift quite clear) was occasion for one of
the many feasts that Stevenson and his family gave at Vailima.
Birthdays, Thanksgiving, the arrival of a British warship's crew
into Apia; almost anything could suggest one of these parties,
photographs of which show everyone seated on the floor on the
wide verandas (twelve feet deep all round) facing a rather
intimidating quantity of taro, bananas and ship's biscuits. The

most splendid party they ever gave was a ball in February 1894, to which 'all the big-wigs' on the island were invited, and which only the German Consul and Cedercrantz refused to attend. There were bowls of *kava* (the mildly hallucinogenic local root that is pounded to make the Samoan national drink), a claret cup and beer, caviar and devilled chicken, Scottisches and gavottes:

> For music the two Johnson boys and an unhanged thief and villain of a Hawaiian, with two boys who sang and played tambourine and bells, made the best band ever heard in Apia – bar men-of-wars. The floor was waxed to perfection, falls were frequent and heavy. The room shone all over with the glow of the four big lamps, and the sideboard glittered with all the silver and two lamps of its own. The front of the house shone from end to end [...] in the most lavish and resplendent manner with sixty-five coloured paper lanterns at a total cost of twelve dollars and I don't know how much for candles.[50]

Stevenson still had hopes that Vailima would become 'really a place of business',[51] and had been discussing banana yields with Graham Balfour, and the possibility of getting a tramway built from the house to the port. The cash-flow problem no longer looked like a temporary one; nor did Louis's restored vitality. He had come to think of himself, almost glumly, as indestructible, doomed 'to see it out'[52] despite persistent migraines throughout 1893, a new and thoroughly unpleasant development. The symptoms seemed so obviously connected to his intake of alcohol and tobacco that he contemplated the unthinkable – giving both up – with 'nauseating intimations that it ought to be forever', as he confided to Gosse.[53] 'Cigarettes without intermission except when coughing or kissing' is how Stevenson had described his nicotine habit to Barrie,[54] so no wonder his resolve to give up proved unsustainable. He must have reasoned that the headaches would simply have to be endured, perhaps with the aid of another strong coffee, or a glass of Merlot.

Baxter's slide into alcoholism, which Colvin had been trying

to keep from his friend, had to be confessed in 1894, as he was
intending to make the journey out to Samoa. The deaths of his
wife Grace in March 1893 and his father the following year, and
continuing business troubles, had set Baxter on a downward path,
and Colvin thought him 'completely unhinged' at their latest meeting, creating 'deplorable scenes'.[55] Baxter had put forward the idea
(obviously for his own benefit as well as Louis's – he would get a
commission as agent) to publish a limited collected edition of
Stevenson's works to date, to be sold by subscription at the highest
price possible, and to be called the Edinburgh Edition. Louis was
delighted at the prospect, especially since he was not required to
do anything (all the editing, such as it was, was done by Colvin,
and the complex negotiations with the many publishers involved
were undertaken by Baxter). The estimated profits from the venture
would be eight to ten thousand pounds – an enormous sum that
would be the saving of them all. And Baxter's hopes were amply
justified: the Edinburgh Edition sold out its subscription within
two months of being advertised and eventually realised something
near £10,000. But by then it was a memorial, not a work in
progress.[56]

The edition was dedicated to Fanny:

> *I saw rain falling and the rainbow drawn*
> *On Lammermuir. Harkening I heard again*
> *In my precipitous city beaten bells*
> *Winnow the keen sea wind. And here afar*
> *Intent on my own race and place I wrote.*

> *Take thou the writing: thine it is. For who*
> *Burnished the sword, blew on the drowsy coal,*
> *Held still the target higher, chary of praise*
> *And prodigal of censure – who but thou?*
> *So now, in the end, if this the least be good,*
> *If any deed be done, if any fire*
> *Burn in the imperfect page, the praise be thine.*[57]

*   *   *

The search for Stevenson's 'masterpiece' might have gone on for years, like the hunt for a hidden will, had he not left unfinished at his death *Weir of Hermiston*, on which his friends fell with gratitude, especially Colvin, who felt it held 'certainly the highest place' among Stevenson's works, citing 'the ripened art [. . .] the wide range of character and emotion over which he sweeps with so assured a hand, his vital poetry of vision and magic of pre-sentment'.[58] Arnold Bennett also thought *Weir* surpassed 'all Stevenson's previous achievement',[59] a dubious compliment which Stevenson would have been the first to raise an eyebrow at. But of course what his friends really valued was *Weir*'s potential, and, perhaps, an end to having to worry about the meaning of Stevenson's *oeuvre*. The line had been drawn, the author had died young and his last work naturally acquired a symbolic status beyond all the others, indicating what might have issued from that fertile brain and hard-pressed body had Stevenson been spared.

Stevenson had started the story in 1890, put it by several times, and only worked on it consistently in the last weeks of his life, having spent months beforehand slogging away at *St Ives* (also unfinished). *St Ives*, set during the Napoleonic Wars, was described by the author as 'a mere tissue of adventures', and represented all he most disliked about his own talent: 'a very little dose of inspiration, and a pretty little trick of style, long lost, improved by the most heroic industry'.[60] From the first pages of *Weir*, on the other hand, it is obvious that Stevenson was relishing both his subject and his style. The writing is pithy and sardonic; Weir discusses old capital cases with his bride-to-be, by way of love-talk; she, in a comically constructed line, is described as 'pious, anxious, tender, tearful, and incompetent'; Mrs Weir hears the local minister 'booming outside on the dogmatic ramparts [. . .] like the cannon of a beleaguered city', while Dandie Elliott is seen 'honouring the Sabbath by a sacred vacancy of mind'. Weir himself is a great character-study, based on a real-life 'hanging judge', Lord Brax-field, the last on the Scottish bench, according to Stevenson, to employ the pure Scots idiom. Weir has no affectations, not even that of judicial impartiality. He is natural to the point of grossness, continually offending his refined son by his manners and language and terrifying his meek wife, who thinks him 'the extreme, if scarcely the ideal, of his sex'. But the recondite pleasure Weir finds in his work (condemning criminals to death) is not mere sadism, as his son believes, nor does Weir lack finer feelings; he is simply impotent to express them. His stoicism about this disability is deftly portrayed by the author: 'If [Weir] failed to gain his son's friendship, or even his son's toleration, on he went up the great, bare staircase of his duty, uncheered and undepressed.'[61]

There are two prominent women characters in the book, both (in a return to the double motif) called Kirstie Elliott; one is the young woman whom Archie Weir loves, the other her aunt, a Border-country earth-goddess, emotional and strong-minded. The chapter about the elder Kirstie alone in her bedroom, 'A Nocturnal Visit', represents the first time the author had allowed any sustained attention to rest in the thoughts of a female character:

> By the faint light of her nocturnal rush, she stood before the looking-glass, carried her shapely arms above her head, and gathered up the treasures of her tresses. She was never backward to admire herself; that kind of modesty was a stranger to her nature; and she paused, struck with a pleased wonder at the sight. 'Ye daft auld wife!' she said, answering a thought that was not; and she blushed with the innocent consciousness of a child. Hastily she did up the massive and shining coils, hastily donned a wrapper, and with the rush-light in her hand, stole into the hall.[62]

The strong characterisation of the elder Kirstie, and her mature womanliness, seemed a relief to many critics who had feared that to Stevenson 'woman remained the eternal puzzle'.[63] 'It will be an eternal pity if a writer like Stevenson passes away without having once applied his marvellous gifts of vision and sympathy to the reproduction and transfiguration of every-day human life,' Israel Zangwill had written when reviewing the all-male Ebb-Tide, 'if he is content to play perpetually with wrecks and treasures and islands, and to be remembered as an exquisite artist in the abnormal.'[64] *Weir of Hermiston* gave everyone the opportunity to forget those apparent shortcomings, the 'abnormality' of his stories of blacks and chocolates, the dubious status of his collaborations, and return to an image of the author as they had first loved him: a brilliant stylist, a whirlwind of potential, a young man with a half-developed idea to be continued.

Every reader who picks up *Weir of Hermiston* knows it is an uncompleted novel, yet the end, coming as it does mid-sentence, is always a shock:

> There arose from before him the curtains of boyhood, and he saw for the first time the ambiguous face of woman as she is. In vain, he looked back over the interview; he saw not where he had offended. It seemed unprovoked, a wilful convulsion of brute nature

That is where Louis stopped work at midday on Monday, 3 December 1894. In the afternoon he gave Austin a lesson in French and later in the day (Fanny said it was about 6 p.m.) he was on the back veranda with his wife, helping her prepare the dressing for a salad. By her account in a letter to Anne Jenkin written two days later, Fanny had been having presentiments of disaster all day and Louis was 'trying to cheer me up'. 'One of the last things he did was to play a game of solitaire with cards for me to watch, thinking it would amuse me and take my mind off the terror that oppressed me.'[65] This is an odd detail, for solitaire is not a game with any spectator-value, and Fanny, an avid card-player, is as likely to have played it herself as stood and watched someone else do so. Perhaps Louis was trying to entertain her with a commentary on his game as she worked – some such benign picture of the concerned spouse is certainly what Fanny wanted to suggest. It could also have been the case that Louis was sitting out 'the terror' of his wife's dark mood by retreating into this quintessentially solitary pastime.

When it came to making the mayonnaise (Louis's special request – again it sounds as if he was trying to humour or divert his wife), he took the job of dripping the oil in, while Fanny dealt with the egg yolks. 'Suddenly he set down the bottle, knelt by the table leaning his head against it,' Fanny wrote, unable to finish her account, which Belle completed: 'He suddenly said, "What's that?" or "What a pain!" and put both hands to his head. "Do I look strange?" he asked, and then he reeled and fell backwards.'[66] The servant Sosimo ran to help, Fanny cried out for hot water to be fetched, and as they half-carried him into the big hall, Louis, according to Austin Strong, said, 'All right Fanny, I can walk.'[67] Belle had come down to see what her mother was shouting about, and found Louis unconscious in a chair, breathing heavily, his feet in the hot water, his hands being chafed to keep his circulation active. Lloyd, arriving up the garden, unaware of an emergency, was sent immediately down to Apia to fetch help, while Margaret, Fanny and Belle did their best, rubbing brandy on Louis's skin: 'We saw that he was dying,' Belle wrote, 'though each said to the other "he is surely better" or "his pulse is stronger"':

> [...] as the room darkened one by one all the Samoans on the place crept in silently and sat on the floor in a wide semi-circle around him. Some fanned him, others waited on one knee for a message and others ran down the road with lanterns to light the doctor.[68]

Lloyd found two doctors, the first to arrive the surgeon from HMS *Wallaroo*, who took Stevenson's limping pulse, but clearly felt there was no hope of revival. Seeing the writer's emaciated arms, he exclaimed, 'How can anybody write books with arms like these?'[69] Their local doctor, Bernard Funk, came next, but there was nothing to be done except fetch a bed into the hall and listen to the prayers of Aunt Maggie and her friend Clarke, the missionary. In between those, there were only fewer, fainter breaths.

Stevenson died just after eight o'clock that evening, of a cerebral haemorrhage, according to Funk's certification. There was no commotion or outcry; the family, who had lived with this death for so long, seemed numb. They laid out the body in dress trousers, a white shirt and gold studs, and two of the 'boys' put the corpse's hands together, 'interlacing the fingers with tender care'.[70] The news spread quickly, and all through the evening local chiefs and their families came to pay their respects, laying on the body the fine woven mats that were Samoans' most precious currency and saying their dignified, brief farewells: 'Tofa, Tusi Tala,' 'Alofa, Tusi Tala.'

In the tropical heat, the burial needed to take place quickly, but the place where Louis had wanted to be laid, the plateau of Mount Vaea that was visible from the house, had no path to it. Lloyd, thrust into authority, had to find some way of accessing the site and appealed to all their friends on the island to send whoever was available to help cut a path. More than forty Samoans, including some chiefs, came promptly the next day and began the seemingly impossible task of clearing the virgin jungle up the mountainside. Two paths exist today, one following approximately the line of that first, most direct one; both are very steep at points and tiring to climb in the equatorial humidity. The construction of the original path at speed on the day after Stevenson's death was a feat of love as well as industry, the latest and greatest mark of the Samoans' respect and affection for their most sympathetic sojourner.

On a 'gloomy, gusty, sodden December day' in London, Sidney Colvin entered the street after lunching at a government office in Westminster, and saw newspaper posters 'flapping dankly in the street corners, with the words "Death of R.L. Stevenson" printed large upon them'.[71] Baxter, on his way to Samoa, heard the news in Port Said. He reached Vailima almost eight weeks later. In his bags were copies of the first two volumes of the Edinburgh Edition.

POSTSCRIPTS

The memories of ladies are excellent repositories of personal
matters, dates, and other details; a family inquiry greatly interests them, and they are zealous correspondents.

Francis Galton, *Record of Family Faculties*

FANNY STAYED ON AT VAILIMA, shocked, lost, helpless, for a
couple of years. She had a large cement-slab tomb built over
Louis's grave, and bronze plaques designed for it by a San
Franciscan dilettante called Frank Gellett Burgess, with the poem
'Requiem' on one side and Ruth's speech to Naomi, in Samoan,
on the other.* Her demands to the British government to annex
Samoa so that the grave would become part of the Empire and
Louis lie in British soil were politely ignored by the authorities.

Unsuccessful, too, were Fanny's plans to start farming seriously, to go into production of the ingredients for making perfume.
By 1897, the year that Margaret Stevenson died in Edinburgh
(releasing to the heirs the rest of Thomas Stevenson's substantial
legacy), the family had decided to move back to California, where
Fanny had an imposing house built for herself on the corner of
Hyde Street and Lombard in San Francisco. She rented Vailima
out to a man called Chatfield, editor of the Samoan daily newspaper, but got into an expensive lawsuit against him over the

---

* Because it appears on Stevenson's tomb, 'Requiem' is one of very few texts by the
author easily available in Samoa. It has been set to music and taught to generations of
Samoan schoolchildren, holding a place in the island's culture something like that of
'Greensleeves' in ours.

expenses and upkeep, and it was eventually sold (minus the site around the grave) to a German merchant for the knockdown price of £1750. When the Germans annexed Samoa in 1900, Vailima became, ironically enough, the Governor's residence.

Lloyd, who married an American called Katherine Durham in 1896, brought his wife to live at Vailima for a brief period, and for an even briefer period served as American Vice Consul in Samoa. His first son, Alan, was born in 1897 and another, Louis, three years afterwards. Katherine, at first approved of by Fanny, fell out with the whole family one by one, went through a bitter divorce from Lloyd and spent years in contention over the 'truth' about RLS, publishing several books on the subject, much to her mother-in-law's annoyance.

The wealth produced by the Stevenson literary estate, of which Lloyd received more than half, allowed him to live in the manner to which he had become accustomed; he wrote several more novels over the next fifty years, married and divorced again, bought a lot of cars, went on a lot of cruises and spent his last years living on the Côte d'Azur with a Frenchwoman called Yvonne Payerne, his junior by forty years, by whom he had another son. Among his acquaintances was Somerset Maugham and among his enthusiasms the political ideology of Benito Mussolini.[1] The general effect of his post-collaboration career as a writer can be expressed mathematically: Stevenson-plus-Osbourne, minus Stevenson, is less than Osbourne.

Belle inherited land adjoining Vailima from her stepfather, who had purchased it in 1893, but became enormously rich in later life, not so much through her connection with the Stevenson estate or her own published memoirs (including *Memories of Vailima*, with Lloyd, and her autobiography, *This Life I've Loved*) but from the discovery of oil in the 1920s on land owned by her then husband, Edward Salisbury Field. 'Ned' was also an author of sorts, and had been Fanny Stevenson's protégé and secretary in the 1910s, possibly also her lover. He was forty years younger than Stevenson's widow, and twelve years younger than Belle. Another protégé of Fanny, Gellett Burgess, was also thought to have been her lover in the late 1890s, but the impassioned letters that seem to prove this (wrongly identified for years in the Bancroft Library at Berkeley) are in fact from Belle. That brings to at least four the number of men mother and daughter shared.

In 1899, Graham Balfour was called to a meeting with Fanny and Lloyd in London and asked to take over from Colvin the task of writing Stevenson's biography. Colvin had not been consulted about this, only vaguely threatened and grumbled at. The family had developed an elaborate critique of his methods and motives, the main thrust of which was that he was being too slow. But no one could have justly accused him of laziness, when within four and a half years he had not only held down his full-time job at the British Museum but overseen the publication of the Edinburgh Edition, the preparation and production of several posthumous Stevenson works, the editing of the Vailima letters and, as the archives show, prepared a good deal of background work on the biography.

Balfour was clearly aware of the fine line he would have to tread between the 'family' and Stevenson's soon-to-be-ousted mentor and friend. But the offer to write the biography was irresistible; not so much for the money (£750, of which he was to get half, the family the rest) as for the chance to write the official 'life' of his cousin, by now one of the most celebrated writers on the planet. Henry James, who described Balfour to Gosse as 'very lean & brown & excellent', watched over the progress of the book with nervous interest and wrote a long appreciative letter to the author when the *Life* finally appeared in 1901: 'The whole thing, the whole renewal of contact and revival of sight of him has greatly affected me,' James said, 'bringing back so the various wonder of him – so that one feels, as anew, *stricken*':

> The question really is, however, for the critical spirit, whether Louis's work itself doesn't *pay* somewhat for the so complete exhibition of the man and the life. You may say that the work was, or *is*, the man and the life as well; still, the books are

jealous and a certain supremacy and mystery (above all) has, as it were, gone from them. [...] he is thus as artist and creator in some degree the victim of himself.[2]

James's 'The Real Right Thing', written in the year that Graham Balfour was starting his book, features a novice biographer preparing to write the life of an author whose work he has idolised. The sense of the dead man's presence haunts both him and the writer's widow ('a strange woman, and he had never thought her agreeable'), and the more he examines the archive, the greater is his sense of wrongdoing. In the story, the biographer eventually gives up his task, an outcome James perhaps wished in Balfour's case.

Half a year after the publication of Balfour's biography, Henley published a review of it in the *Pall Mall Gazette* that he made the excuse for a full-scale onslaught on his dead friend's character and reputation. 'Not, if I can help it, shall this faultless, or very nearly faultless, monster go down to after years as the Lewis I knew. [I decline] to be concerned with this Seraph in Chocolate, this barley-sugar effigy of a real man.' The article poured scorn on Stevenson's moralisings and vanity, even his invalidism ('Are we not all stricken men?'), criticised his removal to America and the Pacific and judged him an over-strained stylist, a third- or fourth-class romancer. 'At bottom Stevenson was an excellent fellow. But he was of his essence what the French call *personnel*. He was, that is, incessantly and passionately interested in Stevenson.'[3]

James wrote to Balfour of 'the long accumulated jealousy, rancour – I mean, of invidious vanity' in Henley's review,[4] but the backlash against Stevenson had already begun. His style was being treated as a joke among the group of friends (known to James of course) around Ford Madox Ford, who recalled 'hearing Stephen Crane [...] comment upon a sentence of Robert Louis Stevenson that he was reading. The sentence was: "With interjected finger he delayed the motion of the timepiece." "By God, poor dear!" Crane exclaimed. "That man put back the clock of English fiction fifty years." '[5]

Ford's collaborator Joseph Conrad, if present, would not have laughed loud at this joke. His and Ford's first novel, *Romance* (originally called 'Seraphina', like the heroine of *Prince Otto*), had been written specifically to 'tap the audience for Stevenson, Anthony Hope and Rider Haggard',[6] but Conrad was very touchy about both the style of the novel and the fact that it took two men eight years to write it: Stevenson, he reminded Ford, produced his masterpieces much more quickly than that. The comparison stuck in Conrad's mind, as it was bound to: by 1900 he had been taken up by Colvin and Frances Sitwell, and was their new 'young man'. But the last person he wanted to be associated with was the 'conscious virtuoso' of Vailima with his (apparently) obnoxious fluency. 'I am no sort of airy R.L. Stevenson who considered his art a prostitute and the artist as no better than one,' Conrad wrote to his agent in 1902.[7] But the fact that he had read Stevenson with minute attention is obvious: *Heart of Darkness* is not just full of *The Ebb-Tide*, but usefully adapted Gordon Darnaway's speech in 'The Merry Men' about 'the horror! – the horror, the sea!'*

Colvin and Mrs Sitwell married on a dull, grey day in June 1903, at the Marylebone church where their late friend Robert Browning had married Elizabeth Barrett. Henry James was one of only four guests, all of whom had instructions to enter by a side door and wear everyday dress. On the way to the reception at the Great Grand Central Hotel Colvin requested the party to walk in ones and twos on opposite sides of the street, so as not to arouse the suspicions of passers-by. The hotel staff of the Great Grand Central, too, could in this way be kept from guessing that anything untowardly festive was going on. Circumspection still ruled this relationship. The groom was fifty-eight years old, the bride sixty-four.

---

* For further similarities between *Heart of Darkness* and 'The Merry Men' see Daniel Balderston, 'Borges's Frame of Reference: The Strange Case of Robert Louis Stevenson' (Princeton University PhD thesis, 1981), p.161n: 'It should be added that the relationship between Marlow and Kurtz, the fascination with the experience of one who has gone over the edge, is remarkably similar to the one between the nephew and the uncle [in 'The Merry Men'].'

Fanny Stevenson's house on Hyde Street survived the fire that devastated San Francisco in 1906 after the earthquake only because concerned citizens, knowing the building to contain the papers of the dead novelist, left other fire-fighting duties to protect it. Fanny died in 1914, aged seventy-four, but Henry James had long before this noted 'a darkening of her mind – as with a further receding from all that had lifted her life out of its native poverties'.[8] 'I am afraid you will find FS a relation of questionable joy,' he wrote to a friend seeking an introduction to Stevenson's widow, '– old, changed, barbaric, weary, queer. You come too late.'[9] 'It's all a strange history,' he sighed, 'and histories never end, but go on living in their consequences.'

Notes

ABBREVIATIONS

CB – Charles Baxter

FJS – Frances Jane Sitwell

FS – Fanny Stevenson (*née* Vandegrift, formerly Osbourne)

GB – Graham Balfour

HJ – Henry James

IF – Isobel Field (*née* Osbourne, formerly Strong; 'Belle')

LO – Samuel Lloyd Osbourne

MIS – Margaret Isabella Stevenson (*née* Balfour)

RAMS – Robert Alan Mowbray Stevenson

RLS – Robert Louis Stevenson

SC – Sidney Colvin

TS – Thomas Stevenson

WEH – William Ernest Henley

BL – Manuscript Collections, British Library

MS Bancroft – Stevenson-Osbourne family papers 1839–1970, Bancroft Library, University of California, Berkeley, California

MS Silverado – Manuscripts relating to Robert Louis Stevenson, Fanny Osbourne and her family in the collection of the Silverado Museum, St Helena, California

MS Yale – Robert Louis Stevenson Collection, Beinecke Rare Book and Manuscript Library, Yale University, New Haven, Connecticut

NLS – National Library of Scotland, Edinburgh

NLS Balfour – National Library of Scotland, Papers of Sir Graham Balfour

Balfour – Graham Balfour, *The Life of Robert Louis Stevenson*, 2 vols (London and New York, 1901)

Bathurst – Bella Bathurst, *The Lighthouse Stevensons* (London, 1999)

Baxter Letters – Delancey Ferguson and Marshall Waingrow (eds), *R.L.S.: Stevenson's Letters to Charles Baxter* (London and New Haven, 1956)

Collected Poems – *The Collected Poems of Robert Louis Stevenson*, ed. Roger C. Lewis (Edinburgh, 2003)

Colvin – Sidney Colvin, *Memories and Notes* (London, 1921)

Field – Isobel Strong Field, *This Life I've Loved* (London, 1937)

From Saranac – Margaret Isabella Stevenson, *From Saranac to the Marquesas and Beyond* (London, 1903)

Furnas – J.C. Furnas, *Voyage to Windward: The Life of Robert Louis Stevenson* (London, 1952)

Gosse – Edmund Gosse, *Critical Kit-Kats* (London, 1913)

Hammerton – J.A. Hammerton (ed.), *Stevensoniana: An Anecdotal Life and Appreciation of Robert Louis Stevenson* (Edinburgh, 1907)

ICR – Rosaline Masson (ed.), *I Can Remember Robert Louis Stevenson* (Edinburgh, 1925)

Letters – Bradford A. Booth and Ernest Mehew (eds), *The Letters of Robert Louis Stevenson*, 8 vols (Yale University Press, New Haven and London, 1994–95)

Lucas – E.V. Lucas, *The Colvins and their Friends* (London, 1928)

Maixner – Paul Maixner (ed.), *Robert Louis Stevenson: The Critical Heritage* (London, 1981)

'Memoirs' – 'Memoirs of Himself', Vailima Edition of the Works of Robert Louis Stevenson, vol. 26

Portrait – Lloyd Osbourne, *An Intimate Portrait of R.L.S.* (New York, 1924)

Swearingen – Roger G. Swearingen, *The Prose Writings of Robert Louis Stevenson: A Guide* (London, 1980)

Tusitala – The Tusitala Edition of the Works of Robert Louis Stevenson, 35 vols (London, 1923–24)

Vailima – The Vailima Edition of the Works of Robert Louis Stevenson, 26 vols (New York and London, 1923)

1 : BARON BROADNOSE
1 MS Yale
2 'Records of a Family of Engineers', Vailima, vol. 12, p.411
3 'The Lamplighter', *Collected Poems*, p.39
4 'Records of a Family of Engineers', Vailima, vol. 12, pp.426–7
5 Ibid., pp.432–3
6 Quoted in Bathurst, p.72
7 Ibid., pp.99–100
8 'Thomas Stevenson, Civil Engineer', Vailima, vol. 12, p.106
9 Ibid., p.107
10 Quoted in Bathurst, p.103
11 *Letters,* vol. 8, p.235
12 *Collected Poems*, p.98
13 Balfour, vol. 1, p.22
14 Ibid., p.9
15 MS Huntington, the Huntington Library, San Marino, California, quoted and partly published in ibid., p.18
16 Balfour, vol. 1, p.20
17 Ibid., p.24
18 Hammerton, p.5
19 'Thomas Stevenson, Civil Engineer', Vailima, vol. 12, p.108
20 MS Bancroft
21 Vailima, vol. 7, p.428
22 Quoted in *Letters,* vol. 1, p.31
23 TS to MIS, 21 June 1848, MS Bancroft
24 Ibid., 1 March 1850
25 FS to Dora Williams, September 1880, MS Yale
26 Balfour, vol. 1, p.8
27 J.C. Furnas suggests that this may have been due to thyroid problems, and that the 'croup' might have been diphtheria; see Furnas, p.421 n8 and 9
28 'Notes of Childhood', MS Yale, vault 805, box 2

29 'Memoirs', p.220
30 FS, in Preface to *Collected Poems,* Biographical Collection of the Works of Robert Louis Stevenson (New York, 1908), p.vi
31 'Notes of Childhood', MS Yale, vault 805, box 2
32 'A Chapter on Dreams', Vailima, vol. 12, p.234
33 'Notes of Childhood', MS Yale, vault 805, box 2
34 'Memoirs', pp.215–16
35 Ibid., p.217
36 'Stevenson's Infancy', Vailima, vol. 26, p.276
37 Ibid., p.280
38 'Memoirs', pp.209–10
39 NLS, Acc 10356
40 MS Bancroft, Robert Louis Stevenson collection of letters and papers c.1873–1949, C–H 107
41 Furnas, p.31
42 'Memoirs', p.220
43 Hammerton, p.12
44 Vailima, vol. 26, p.295
45 *ICR*, p.152
46 'Memoirs', p.218
47 Ibid.
48 Ibid., p.211
49 FS, in Preface to *Collected Poems,* Biographical Collection of the Works of Robert Louis Stevenson (New York, 1908), p.vii
50 'Memoirs', p.214
51 'Reminiscences of Colinton Manse', MS Yale, vault 805, box 2
52 'Memoirs', p.213
53 'Reminiscences of Colinton Manse', MS Yale, vault 805, box 2
54 RLS to WEH, June 1881, *Letters,* vol. 3, p.199
55 'A Penny Plain and Twopence Coloured', Vailima, vol. 12, pp.169–70

56 *Letters*, vol. 1, p.95
57 Ibid., p.98
58 *Cummy's Diary: A diary kept by Robert Louis Stevenson's nurse, Alison Cunningham, while travelling with him on the continent during 1863*, with a preface and notes by Robert T. Skinner (London, 1926), p.2
59 Ibid., p.54
60 Ibid., p.37
61 Ibid., p.60
62 Ibid., p.7
63 RLS to Emily Robertson, *Letters*, vol. 5, p.83
64 NLS Balfour, 9897, ff128–9
65 Balfour, vol. 1, p.87
66 NLS Balfour, 9895, f118

2 : VELVET COAT

1 *Letters*, vol. 1, p.111
2 *Vailima*, vol. 26, pp.47–8
3 Jane Whyte Balfour to Graham Balfour, 25 January 1900, NLS Balfour, 9895, f15
4 Maude Parry to SC, n.d., NLS Balfour, 9896
5 *ICR*, pp.34–5
6 As related by the shepherd's son; ibid., p.35
7 'Pastoral', *Memories and Portraits*, *Vailima*, vol. 12, pp.76–7
8 Note to 'Underwoods', *Collected Poems*, p.71
9 *Vailima*, vol. 12, p.19
10 Charles Guthrie, *Robert Louis Stevenson: Some Personal Recollections* (Edinburgh, 1924), p.24
11 'A Layman' (Thomas Stevenson), *The Immutable Laws of Nature in Relation to God's Providence* (Edinburgh and London, 1868), pp.12–13
12 *Vailima*, vol. 12, p.375
13 *Letters*, vol. 1, p.121
14 *Memories and Portraits*, *Vailima*, vol. 12, pp.50–1
15 *Letters*, vol. 6, p.47
16 *Vailima*, vol. 12, pp.49–50
17 *Letters*, vol. 1, p.130

18 'The Education of an Engineer', *Vailima*, vol. 12, p.376
19 Ibid.
20 *Letters*, vol. 1, p.132
21 Ibid., p.136
22 Colvin, p.108
23 *Letters*, vol. 1, p.142
24 'Thomas Stevenson, Civil Engineer', *Vailima*, vol. 12, p.105
25 'The Education of an Engineer', *Vailima*, vol. 12, pp.379, 380
26 Ibid.
27 'On the Enjoyment of Unpleasant Places', *Vailima*, vol. 24, p.340. I have Graham Robb to thank for identifying the quote from Béranger's 'Le Refus'
28 *Letters*, vol. 1, p.157
29 Ibid., p.143
30 Eve Blantyre Simpson, *Robert Louis Stevenson* (Boston and London, 1906), pp.34–5
31 *Letters*, vol. 4, pp.305–6
32 MS Yale, vault 805, box 2
33 *Letters*, vol. 1, p.166
34 Ibid.
35 'Notes of Childhood', MS Yale, vault 805, box 2
36 Ibid., p.4
37 *The Memoirs of Walter Pringle of Greenknow*, ed. W. Wood (Edinburgh, 1847), p.6
38 Moray Maclaren, *Stevenson and Edinburgh: A Centenary Study* (London, 1950), p.80
39 Quoted in *Letters*, vol. 1, p.210
40 Eve Blantyre Simpson, *Robert Louis Stevenson* (Boston and London, 1906), pp.29–31
41 *Letters*, vol. 1, p.211
42 Eve Blantyre Simpson, *Robert Louis Stevenson* (Boston and London, 1906), pp.29, 40
43 *ICR*, p.159. The second meaning of 'yellow yite' in the *Scottish National Dictionary*, vol.10 (Edinburgh, 1976), is 'a person of small stature', 'also [. . .] a general term of contempt'
44 'My brain swims empty and light', *Collected Poems*, p.260
45 NLS Balfour, 9895, f155

46 This section of RLS's fragmentary autobiography, written in 1880, is in NLS Balfour, 9897
47 'A College Magazine', Vailima, vol. 12, p.59
48 'You looked so tempting in the pew', Collected Poems, pp.243–4
49 'Duddingston', ibid., p.245
50 'Talk and Talkers', 2nd paper, Vailima, vol. 12, p.144
51 NLS Balfour, 9896
52 'Memoirs', p.223
53 Letters, vol. 1, p.208
54 Ibid., p.193
55 MS Yale; published in Tusitala, vol. 30, and in the Edinburgh Edition of the Works of Robert Louis Stevenson
56 Vailima, vol. 12, pp.235–6
57 Letters, vol. 1, p.188
58 Ibid., p.198
59 Gosse, p.276
60 Ibid., p.277
61 Kidnapped, Vailima, vol. 9, pp.170–1
62 Memories and Portraits, Vailima, vol. 12, p.98
63 It was printed posthumously as an 'unfinished treatise' in the Edinburgh Edition
64 'Reflections and Remarks on Human Life', Vailima, vol. 26, p.117
65 'A College Magazine', Vailima, vol. 12, p.58
66 Quoted in Letters, vol. 1, p.41 n3
67 Collected Poems, p.312
68 'Memoir of Fleeming Jenkin', Vailima, vol. 11, p.529
69 NLS, Acc 4534
70 D.A. Stevenson to GB, n.d., NLS Balfour, 9895, f37
71 Letters, vol. 6, p.47
72 MS Yale, box 2, vol. 4, folder D

3 : THE CARELESS INFIDEL

1 Charles Guthrie, Robert Louis Stevenson: Some Personal Recollections (Edinburgh, 1924), p.31

2 NLS, MS 9822, Law Notes, Caricatures, Drawings and Verses
3 ICR, p.100
4 Ibid., p.101
5 Charles Guthrie, Robert Louis Stevenson: Some Personal Recollections (Edinburgh, 1924), p.34
6 Sir Alfred Ewing, An Engineer's Outlook (London, n.d.), p.250
7 ICR, p.123
8 An amusing account of how this yacht, the Purgle, got into trouble on its maiden voyage is included in RLS's 'Memoir of Fleeming Jenkin', Vailima, vol. 11
9 Flora Masson recalling 'Louis Stevenson in Edinburgh', ICR, pp.135–6
10 'Memoir of Fleeming Jenkin', Vailima, vol. 11, pp.526–7
11 Literary Papers, Vailima, vol. 4, p.472
12 ICR, p.53
13 Ibid., p.52
14 'Lay Morals', Vailima, vol. 24, p.186
15 J.A. Symonds, Walt Whitman: A Study (1893), p.40
16 'Walt Whitman', Vailima, vol. 4, p.114
17 Though it was never completed; see Swearingen, p.11
18 ICR, p.58
19 Ibid., p.95
20 Flora Masson, Victorians All (Edinburgh, 1931), p.93
21 ICR, p.46
22 'Memoir of Fleeming Jenkin', Vailima, vol. 11, p.519
23 Flora Masson, Victorians All (Edinburgh, 1931), pp.100, 101
24 Balfour, vol. 1, p.109
25 Ibid., p.111
26 Ibid.
27 'Talk and Talkers', 1st paper, Vailima, vol. 12, p.121
28 Ibid., pp.112–13
29 Portrait, p.5
30 Letters, vol. 1, p.273
31 Ibid.
32 Ibid., p.274

33 Ibid., p.296

34 Colvin, p.104

35 *ICR*, p.88

36 Lucas, p.64

37 Ibid., pp.338–9

38 'HB' [Cotter Morrison] to FJS, MS Yale, vault 805, folder M; 'X' [Sidney Colvin], *Her Infinite Variety*, ed. E.V. Lucas (London, 1908), p.71; *Letters*, vol. 1, p.303

39 'X' [Sidney Colvin], *Her Infinite Variety*, ed. E.V. Lucas (London, 1908), p.71

40 *ICR*, p.88

41 Colvin, p.103

42 Ibid., p.101

43 See the very thorough investigation of the available 'Claire' material in Furnas, pp.394–9

44 *Letters*, vol. 1, p.319

45 Ibid., pp.293, 292

46 *ICR*, p.88

47 'X' [Sidney Colvin], *Her Infinite Variety*, ed. E.V. Lucas (London, 1908), pp.71–2

48 E.V. Lucas, *Reading, Writing and Remembering: A Literary Record* (London, 1932), p.61

49 'At the Land's End of France' was reproduced in the last chapter of Colvin's *Memories and Notes*

50 Ernest Mehew sees Mrs Sitwell and Colvin as a pair from the start, mutually concerned in these years for their young friend. Furnas sees the possibility of Mrs Sitwell having 'slipped into carnal congress with Louis or any other disciple' as 'most unlikely'; Furnas, p.84

51 Quoted in *Letters*, vol. 1, p.477n

52 NLS Balfour, 9894, f233

53 FS to GB, November 1899, NLS Balfour, 9894, f274

54 *Letters*, vol. 1, p.288

55 Ibid.

56 Ibid., pp.320–1

57 Ibid., p.369

58 Ibid., pp.336–7

59 Ibid., p.294

60 Ibid., p.295

61 Ibid.

62 Ibid., p.294

63 Ibid., p.312

64 Ibid.

65 Ibid., p.325

66 Ibid., p.331

67 'Notes from his Mother's Diary', Vailima, vol. 26, p.325

68 *Letters*, vol. 1, p.354

4 : AH WELLESS

1 *Letters*, vol. 1, p.352

2 'Ordered South', Vailima, vol. 2, p.104

3 Ibid., pp.110–11

4 *Letters*, vol. 1, p.375

5 Ibid., p.395

6 Ibid., p.402

7 Ibid., p.401

8 See ibid., p.422

9 Vailima, vol. 24, p.320

10 *Letters*, vol. 1, p.506

11 Ibid., p.430

12 *Letters*, vol. 2, p.317

13 *Letters*, vol. 6, p.269

14 Colvin, p.114

15 *Letters*, vol. 1, p.457

16 Ibid., pp.437, 429

17 SC, fragmentary recollections, not included in *Memories and Notes*, MS Yale, vault 805, box 2, folder G

18 *Letters*, vol. 1, pp.464–5. (The conjectural reading of two or three inked-out words is by Ernest Mehew)

19 Ibid., p.501

20 Ibid.

21 Ibid., p.504

22 Ibid.

23 *Letters*, vol. 2, p.10

24 Andrew Lang, *Adventures Among Books* (London, 1903), p.43

25 *Letters*, vol. 2, p.3

26 Ibid., p.1

27 Furnas, p.96

28 *Letters*, vol. 2, p.25

29 Ibid., p.26

30 Gosse, p.281

31 Ibid., p.282

32 Ibid., pp.279–80

33 Balfour, vol. 1, p.176

34 E.V. Lucas, *Reading, Writing and Remembering* (London, 1932), p.60

35 *Letters*, vol. 2, p.33
36 Ibid., p.32
37 Ibid., p.43
38 Vailima, vol. 5, p.xx
39 *Letters*, vol. 2, p.74
40 'On Lord Lytton's Fables in Song', Vailima, vol. 24, p.54
41 *Fables*, Vailima, vol. 25, p.249
42 Jorge Luis Borges, *Conversations*, ed. Richard Burgin (Jackson, 1998). Daniel Balderston, in his PhD thesis, 'Borges's Frame of Reference: The Strange Case of Robert Louis Stevenson' (Princeton University, 1981), records Borges's interjections during a reading of 'The Song of the Morrow', showing the great writer's delight at Stevenson's phraseology
43 Vailima, vol. 24, p.50
44 Miscellanea, Vailima, vol. 26
45 *Letters*, vol. 2, p.41
46 Vailima, vol. 26, p.104
47 *Letters*, vol. 2, p.41 n3
48 J.A. MacCulloch, *Robert Louis Stevenson and the Bridge of Allan* (1927), p.151
49 *Letters*, vol. 2, p.4
50 Ibid., p.145
51 Ibid., p.95
52 Ibid., p.97
53 Ibid., pp.97-8
54 Ibid., p.98
55 *Letters*, vol. 1, p.385
56 *Letters*, vol. 2, p.94 and n
57 Ibid., pp.96-7, 108
58 Ibid., p.104
59 Ibid., p.198
60 Ibid., pp.76-7
61 Ibid., p.124
62 Ibid., p.114
63 'A Summer Night', reprinted in Appendix to ibid., p.334
64 Ibid., p.117
65 Ibid., pp.120, 124
66 In a letter to FJS, ?8 May 1875, ibid., p.135
67 'In Hospital', *The Works of W.E. Henley* (London, 1908), vol. 1
68 Ibid.
69 *Letters*, vol. 2, p.132
70 Ibid., p.123
71 Ibid., p.123 n1
72 'Forest Notes', Vailima, vol. 24, pp.391-2
73 Ibid., pp.392-3
74 *Portrait*, p.3
75 Details from Margaret B. Wright, 'Bohemian Days', *Scribner's Monthly*, vol. 16 (May 1878), pp.121-9
76 *The Wrecker*, Chapter 2, Vailima, vol. 17, p.63
77 *Letters*, vol. 2, p.130
78 Ibid., p.125
79 *ICR*, p.114
80 Ibid., p.96
81 Ibid., p.295
82 NLS Balfour, 9897, f107
83 *ICR*, p.162
84 Ibid., p.65
85 *Letters*, vol. 2, p.166
86 *ICR*, p.65
87 Graham Balfour's notes, taken from conversations with RLS; NLS Balfour, 9897, ff109, 110
88 Eve Blantyre Simpson, *Robert Louis Stevenson* (Boston and London, 1906), p.42

5 : STENNIS *FRÈRE*

1 FS to Timothy Rearden, Paris, June 1876, MS Silverado, notebook 1, letter 32
2 Margaret Mackay, *The Violent Friend* (London, 1969), p.4
3 *Daily Territorial Enterprise*, 1862-63, quoted in Mark Twain, *Roughing It* (Mark Twain Library edition, Berkeley, 1995), p.176
4 Alexandra Lapierre, *Fanny Stevenson* (London, 1995), does not specify the sources
5 Field, p.17
6 Quoted in Alexandra Lapierre, *Fanny Stevenson* (London, 1995), p.33
7 Field, p.17
8 Ibid., p.18
9 Alexandra Lapierre, *Fanny Stevenson* (London, 1995), p.40
10 Mark Twain, *Roughing It* (Mark

Twain Library edition, Berkeley, 1995), pp.281-2

11 Ibid., p.282

12 Quoted in Alexandra Lapierre, *Fanny Stevenson* (London, 1995), p.57

13 Nellie Vandegrift Sanchez, *The Life of Mrs Robert Louis Stevenson* (1920), pp.30-1

14 Field, p.45

15 FS to Timothy Rearden, n.d., ?1864, MS Silverado, notebook 1, letter 3

16 Ibid., letter 35

17 Ibid., letter 25

18 Field, p.82

19 Ibid., p.80

20 Ibid., p.81

21 FS to Dora Williams, 25 August 1875, MS Yale, vault Stevenson, 3834

22 Ibid.

23 FS to Timothy Rearden, 31 October 1875, MS Silverado, notebook 1, letter 24

24 MS Yale, vault Stevenson, 3834

25 FS to Timothy Rearden, 18 April 1876, MS Silverado, notebook 1, letter 31

26 Field, p.104

27 Perhaps this was something like the incident in 'The Misadventures of John Nicolson' when John goes briefly on the run to escape duns. The cryptic references to RLS's 'trouble' are in *Letters*, vol. 2, pp.178 and n6, 181 and n2

28 Ibid., p.176

29 'Virginibus Puerisque', Vailima, vol. 2, p.11

30 Ibid., p.20

31 Ibid., pp.25, 16, 25

32 Vailima, vol. 1, pp.53-4

33 Ibid., p.104

34 Colvin, p.109

35 Vailima, vol. 1, p.137

36 Ibid., p.96

37 Ibid., p.131

38 Ibid., pp.131-2

39 Quoted in Maixner, p.56

40 Ibid., p.8

41 Mehew shows in *Letters*, vol. 2,

p.191 n1 that RLS was in Paris on 20 September 1876, and again in mid-October on his way back to Edinburgh (which he reached on 16 October). I am therefore guessing that RLS went from Pontoise to Paris briefly (he says in his letter he was buying books there), then on to Grez, where Simpson would have preceded him by a few days

42 *ICR*, p.173

43 Margaret B. Wright, 'Bohemian Days', *Scribner's Monthly*, vol. 16 (May 1878)

44 Ibid.

45 FS to Timothy Rearden, April 1877, MS Silverado

46 FS to Timothy Rearden, 25 July 1876, MS Silverado

47 'A Ball at Mr Elsinare's', *The Lantern-Bearers and Other Essays* (ed. Jeremy Treglown; London, 1988), p.52

48 Vailima, vol. 2, p.43

49 *Letters*, vol. 2, p.193

50 FS to Timothy Rearden, 13 December 1876, MS Silverado

51 FS to Timothy Rearden, 'p.m. Feb 1877 Paris', MS Yale

52 FS to Timothy Rearden, 13 December 1876, MS Silverado

53 *The Lantern-Bearers and Other Essays* (ed. Jeremy Treglown; London, 1988), p.52

54 *Letters*, vol. 2, p.199

55 Ibid., p.205

56 Ibid., p.208

57 Vailima, vol. 3, p.348

58 See *Letters*, vol. 2, p.145 n3

59 Ibid., p.236

60 Ibid., pp.218, 219

61 Quoted in ibid., p.225 n1

62 Colvin, p.130

63 Vailima, vol. 1, p.440

64 *Letters*, vol. 2, p.227

65 Ibid., pp.241-2

66 Ibid., pp.244, 240

67 Maixner, p.54

68 Hammerton, pp.35-6

69 Related by Birge Harrison in *ICR*, p.179

70 Field, p.111
71 Balfour, vol. 1, p.188
72 *Portrait*, p.13

6 : THE AMATEUR
EMIGRANT

1 *Letters*, vol. 2, p.268
2 Vailima, vol. 1, p.210
3 Ibid., p.216
4 Ibid., p.217
5 Ibid., p.220
6 Ibid., p.249
7 *Letters*, vol. 2, p.313
8 Vailima, vol. 1, p.277
9 Ibid., p.230
10 Ibid., pp.297–8
11 Richard Holmes, *Footsteps*
   (London, 1985), p.54
12 RLS, *The Cévennes Journal:
   Notes on a Journey Through the
   French Highlands*, ed. Gordon
   Golding et al. (Edinburgh, 1978),
   p.81
13 *Letters*, vol. 2, pp.280–1
14 'Echoes' no. xxiv, *The Works of
   W.E. Henley* (London, 1908), vol. 1
15 Gosse, p.282
16 *Letters*, vol. 2, pp.297–8
17 Ibid., p.300
18 See Malcolm Elwin, *The Strange
   Case of Robert Louis Stevenson*
   (London, 1950), p.2, and
   Swearingen, p.41
19 'Lay Morals', Vailima, vol. 24,
   p.202
20 Colvin provided this information;
   see *Letters*, vol. 2, p.314 n7
21 Philip Gosse, *My Pirate Library*
   (London, 1926), pp.9–10
22 Quoted in *Letters*, vol. 2, p.330 n6
23 Ibid., p.330
24 SC to WEH, quoted in Lucas,
   p.113
25 *Letters*, vol. 2, p.315
26 MS Yale; see *Letters*, vol. 3, p.7 n2
   and Baxter Letters, p.66 n11
27 See *www.unibg.it/rls* and follow
   'biographical links' to 'The Blue
   Pills'
28 See RLS to FS, *Letters*, vol. 2,
   p.312

29 Ibid., p.315
30 Ibid.
31 26 February 1900, quoted in ibid.,
   p.320 n2
32 Ibid., p.328
33 *Letters*, vol. 3, p.6
34 Ibid., pp.2–3
35 Vailima, vol. 2, pp.279–80
36 Ibid., p.255
37 *Scribner's Magazine*, May 1888,
   quoted in Balfour, vol. 1, pp.196–7
38 Vailima, vol. 2, pp.283–4
39 Vailima, vol. 3, pp.498–9
40 'Across the Plains', Vailima, vol. 2,
   p.372
41 *Letters*, vol. 3, p.10
42 Ibid.
43 Vailima, vol. 2, pp.364–5
44 Ibid., p.350
45 Ibid., p.283
46 Ibid., p.387
47 Ibid., p.380
48 'The Old Pacific Capital', ibid.,
   p.413
49 *Portrait*, pp.16–17
50 Elsie Noble Caldwell, *Last Witness
   for Robert Louis Stevenson*
   (Norman, Oklahoma, 1960), p.10
51 *Letters*, vol. 3, p.13
52 FS to Timothy Rearden, n.d., MS
   Silverado, notebook 1, letter 54
53 FS to Timothy Rearden, Davos,
   n.d., MS Silverado, notebook 1,
   letter 58
54 *Letters*, vol. 3, p.12
55 Ibid., p.16
56 Ibid.
57 Ibid., pp.13–14
58 Ibid., p.13
59 *Collected Poems*, p.88
60 *Letters*, vol. 3, p.16
61 Elsie Noble Caldwell, *Last Witness
   for Robert Louis Stevenson*
   (Norman, Oklahoma, 1960), p.10
62 James D. Hart (ed.), *From Scotland
   to Silverado* (Cambridge, Mass.,
   1966), pp.172–8
63 Ibid.
64 Ibid.
65 *Letters*, vol. 3, p.5
66 Ibid., p.41
67 Ibid., p.12

68 Ibid., pp.23–4
69 SC to CB, ibid., p.38
70 Ibid., p.41
71 Ibid., p.27
72 See Edward Berwick's 'Reminiscences of Robert Louis Stevenson', MS Bancroft, C-H 107
73 See Roy Nickerson, *Robert Louis Stevenson in California: A Remarkable Courtship* (San Francisco, 1982), pp.57–8
74 WEH to SC, *Letters*, vol. 3, p.41
75 Ibid., p.38
76 Ibid.
77 Ibid., p.21
78 'Simoneau's at Monterey', James D. Hart (ed.), *From Scotland to Silverado* (Cambridge, Mass., 1966)
79 *Letters*, vol. 3, pp.41, 42
80 See Furnas, Appendix, 'Controversy', p.399. See also RLS to WEH, *Letters*, vol. 3, p.55, and Mehew's footnote
81 'The Old Pacific Capital', Vailima, vol. 2, pp.403–4
82 George R. Stewart Jr, 'Glimpses of Stevenson', NLS Balfour, 9897, ff176–87
83 'The Old Pacific Capital', Vailima, vol. 2, p.410
84 *Letters*, vol. 3, p.45
85 Ibid., p.46
86 See the letter from Ferrier to his sister Elizabeth ('Coggie'), 1 June 1880, quoted in ibid., p.74
87 Ibid., p.44
88 Ibid., p.60
89 Ibid., p.61
90 'San Francisco', James D. Hart (ed.), *From Scotland to Silverado* (Cambridge, Mass., 1966)
91 Ibid.
92 'Dora Williams: reminiscence of RLS for the Century Club of San Francisco in aid of the Robert Louis Stevenson memorial' (n.d.), MS Bancroft
93 *Letters*, vol. 3, p.42
94 Ibid., p.43
95 SC, quoting to WEH part of a letter from FS; see ibid., p.71
96 Ibid.

97 *Letters*, vol. 1, p.502
98 *Letters*, vol. 3, p.76
99 RLS to P.G. Hammerton, July 1881, ibid., p.203

7 : THE PROFESSIONAL SICKIST

1 *Letters*, vol. 3, p.83
2 *The Silverado Squatters*, Vailima, vol. 2, p.489
3 Ibid., p.565
4 *Letters*, vol. 3, p.86
5 Ibid., p.87
6 Field, p.126
7 Lucas, pp.127–8
8 Quoted in Margaret Mackay, *The Violent Friend* (London, 1969), p.119
9 *Letters*, vol. 8, p.45
10 *Letters*, vol. 3, p.104n
11 Ibid., p.105
12 Ibid.
13 Ibid.
14 Ibid., p.96
15 *The Silverado Squatters*, Vailima, vol. 2, pp.471–2
16 J. Weber, *Davos* (Zürich and London, c.1880), p.28
17 Ibid., p.27
18 *Letters*, vol. 3, p.111 n2, and FSTo MIS, 13 October 1880,mS Silverado
19 *Portrait*, p.25
20 WEH to CB, 18 May 1881, *Letters*, vol. 3, p.182
21 Ibid., p.184
22 Ibid., p.118
23 Ibid., p.120
24 Susan Sontag, *Illness as Metaphor* (London, 1991), p.12
25 W.G. Lockett, *Robert Louis Stevenson at Davos* (London, 1934), pp.81–2
26 J. Weber, *Davos* (Zürich and London, c.1880), p.73
27 'On Some Ghastly Companions at a Spa', *Collected Poems*, p.327
28 *Letters*, vol. 3, p.126
29 'Davos in Winter', Vailima, vol. 24, p.467

30 *Letters*, vol. 3, p.123
31 Harold Vailings, quoted in W.G. Lockett, *Robert Louis Stevenson at Davos* (London, 1934), p.72
32 *Vailima*, vol. 12, pp.126–7
33 John Addington Symonds to H.F. Brown, 17 November 1880, Herbert M. Schueller and Robert L. Peters, *The Letters of J.A. Symonds* (Detroit, 1967–69), vol. 2, p.659
34 Ibid., p.664
35 Phyllis Grosskurth (ed.), *The Memoirs of John Addington Symonds* (London, 1984), p.260
36 *Letters*, vol. 3, p.162
37 W.G. Lockett, *Robert Louis Stevenson at Davos* (London, 1934), p.245
38 Walt Whitman to J.A. Symonds, 19 August 1890
39 All quotations in Phyllis Grosskurth (ed.), *The Memoirs of John Addington Symonds* (London, 1984), Appendix 1, p.287
40 Ibid., p.188
41 W.G. Lockett, *Robert Louis Stevenson at Davos* (London, 1934), p.50
42 Graham Robb, *Strangers: Homosexual Love in the Nineteenth Century* (London, 2003), p.144
43 Hammerton, p.77
44 Andrew Lang, *Adventures Among Books* (London, 1903), p.51
45 H.J. Moors, *With Stevenson in Samoa* (London, 1911), p.2
46 Horatio Brown to W.G. Lockett, quoted in W.G. Lockett, *Robert Louis Stevenson at Davos* (London, 1934), p.245
47 Phyllis Grosskurth (ed.), *The Memoirs of John Addington Symonds* (London, 1984), p.187
48 Quoted in Graham Robb, *Strangers: Homosexual Love in the Nineteenth Century* (London, 2003), p.128
49 Herbert M. Schueller and Robert L. Peters, *The Letters of J.A. Symonds* (Detroit, 1967–69), vol. 3, p.120
50 *Letters*, vol. 3, p.313
51 Ibid., p.131
52 FS to Dora Williams, December 1880, MS Yale, vault Stevenson, 3834
53 *Letters*, vol. 3, p.153
54 Ibid., p.151
55 Ibid., p.161
56 Ibid., pp.161–2
57 *Collected Poems*, p.93
58 MS Yale, B5980. It was published as a separate poem by the Boston Bibliophile Society and reprinted in later collections, including Janet Adam Smith's *Collected Poems*, though she admits in her notes (p.526) that she had not consulted the manuscript
59 *Letters*, vol. 3, p.161
60 Ibid., p.164
61 Ibid., pp.183–4
62 *Vailima*, vol. 11, p.171
63 Ibid., p.30
64 NLS Balfour, 9895, f76
65 *Letters*, vol. 3, pp.200–1
66 Ibid., p.197
67 *Portrait*, pp. 31, 32
68 *Letters*, vol. 3, p.186
69 Ibid., p.222
70 Quoted in Ann Thwaite, *Edmund Gosse: A Literary Landscape* (Oxford, 1985), p.217
71 Ibid.
72 *Letters*, vol. 3, p.224
73 Ibid., pp.224–5
74 FS to Dora Williams, September 1881, MS Yale, vault Stevenson, 3834
75 'My First Book', *Vailima*, vol. 5, p.xxvi
76 Ibid., p.xxiv
77 *Treasure Island*, Chapter 27, *Vailima*, vol. 5, p.239
78 Ibid., Chapter 8, p.75
79 Ibid.
80 Maixner, p.235
81 *Vailima*, vol. 5, p.xxviii

8 : UXORIOUS BILLY

1 *Letters*, vol. 3, p.242
2 *Portrait*, p.37
3 Evan Charteris (ed.), *The Life and*

Letters of Sir Edmund Gosse (London, 1931), pp.284–5

4 *Letters*, vol. 3, p.329

5 WEH to CB, 15 April 1882, quoted in ibid., p.317 n1

6 Ibid., pp.263–4

7 Ibid., p.325

8 Vailima, vol. 12, p.144

9 *Letters*, vol. 3, p.271

10 W.G. Lockett, *Robert Louis Stevenson at Davos* (London, 1934), p.102

11 Ibid., p.103

12 Vailima, vol. 3, p.470

13 *Letters*, vol. 3, p.322

14 *Letters*, vol. 4, p.2

15 Ibid., p.38

16 Damian Atkinson (ed.), *The Selected Letters of W.E. Henley* (Aldershot, 2000), pp.112–13

17 Ibid.

18 *Letters*, vol. 4, p.59

19 Ibid., p.58

20 Ibid., p.53n

21 Ibid., p.55

22 Ibid., p.46

23 Ibid., p.55

24 Ibid., p.76

25 Ibid., pp.84–5

26 'From a Railway Carriage', *Collected Poems*, p.44

27 *Collected Poems*, p.32

28 *Letters*, vol. 4, p.195

29 Ibid., p.106

30 Ibid., p.97

31 Ibid., p.162

32 Ibid., p.163

33 Vailima, vol. 5, p.xix

34 Ibid., p.xx

35 *Letters*, vol. 4, p.115

36 Ibid., p.194

37 Ibid., p.115

38 Vailima, vol. 5, p.496

39 Ibid., p.562

40 Ibid., pp.536–7

41 Ibid., p.525

42 Ibid., p.430

43 Ibid., p.458

44 Ibid., p.325

45 Ibid., p.411

46 Ibid., p.325

47 *Letters*, vol. 4, p.212

48 Evan Charteris (ed.), *The Life and Letters of Sir Edmund Gosse* (London, 1931), pp.180–1

49 Maixner, p.197

50 *Letters*, vol. 4, p.246

51 Swearingen, p.66

52 *Letters*, vol. 4, pp.119–20

53 Ibid., p.228

54 21 May 1883, ibid., p.54

55 n.d., marked 'late spring 1884, Hyères' in another hand. MS Yale, vault Stevenson, 3852 (see 3834). The conjectural dating of this manuscript letter is probably a bit late, as the next letter – also from Hyères – announces the child's birth, and the Stevensons were only there between February 1883 and June 1884

56 Hyères, n.d., 'spring 1884', MS Yale, vault Stevenson, 3852 (see 3834)

57 *Letters*, vol. 3, p.153n

58 *Collected Poems*, p.329

59 MS Yale, B6257

60 Ibid.

61 *Letters*, vol. 4, p.87

62 Ibid., p.154

63 Ibid., p.162

64 Ibid., p.157

65 Ibid., p.159

66 Ibid., p.158

67 Ibid., p.166

68 Mrs M.L. Ferrier to RLS, 4 February 1883, MS Yale, 4469

69 *Letters*, vol. 4, p.183

70 Ibid., p.238

71 Ibid., p.241

72 Ibid., p.237

73 Ibid., p.234

74 Ibid., p.53n

75 Ibid., p.240

76 Ibid., p.249

77 Ibid., pp.249–50

78 MS Yale, Stevenson notebook 59; 6536, 6504

79 *Letters*, vol. 4, pp.293–4

80 Ibid., p.309

81 Ibid., p.102

9 : A WEEVIL IN A BISCUIT

1 Lucas, p.158
2 *Letters*, vol. 5, p.80
3 *Letters*, vol. 7, p.280
4 *Letters*, vol. 5, p.27
5 Ibid., p.4
6 Ibid., p.23
7 Ibid., p.49 n8
8 Vailima, vol. 6, pp.267–8
9 *Letters*, vol. 5, p.4 n3
10 H. Pearson, *Beerbohm Tree* (London, 1956), pp.48–9
11 Vailima, vol. 6, p.181
12 *Letters*, vol. 5, p.101
13 Ibid., p.20 n2
14 Arthur Wing Pinero, *Robert Louis Stevenson: The Dramatist* (New York, 1914), p.30
15 Ibid., p.63
16 *Portrait*, p.57
17 *Letters*, vol. 5, p.4 n3
18 Ibid.
19 Vailima, vol. 7, p.29
20 Ibid., pp.30–1
21 Ibid., p.209
22 *Letters*, vol. 5, p.81
23 Maixner, p.221
24 *Letters*, vol. 4, p.245
25 FS to MIS, 29 July 1885, MS Silverado
26 *Letters*, vol. 5, p.123
27 William Archer, quoted in Hammerton, p.76
28 FS to GB, 5 January 1901, NLS Balfour, 9895, f130
29 FS to MIS, 8 October 1885, MS Silverado
30 *Letters*, vol. 5, p.123
31 Leon Edel, *The Life of Henry James* (London, 1953–72), vol. 3, p.87
32 *Letters*, vol. 5, p.137
33 John Singer Sargent to RLS, ?January 1886, MS Yale, 5427
34 Ibid.
35 HJ to T.S. Perry, 14 September 1879, Leon Edel (ed.), Henry James, *Letters* (Cambridge, Mass., 1974–84), vol. 2, p.225
36 *Letters*, vol. 5, p.9
37 Vailima, vol. 12, p.212
38 Ibid., p.213
39 Leon Edel (ed.), Henry James, *Letters* (Cambridge, Mass., 1974–84), vol. 3, p.57
40 *Letters*, vol. 5, p.42
41 Ibid., p.89
42 Quoted in Leon Edel, *The Life of Henry James* (London, 1953–72), vol.3, p.70
43 FS to MIS, April/May 1885, MS Silverado
44 Leon Edel (ed.), Henry James, *Letters* (Cambridge, Mass., 1974–84), vol. 3, p.495
45 Frank McLynn, *Robert Louis Stevenson: A Biography* (London, 1993), p.246
46 Leon Edel (ed.), *The Diary of Alice James* (New York, 1964), p.93
47 *Letters*, vol. 5, p.196
48 Ibid., p.340
49 Vailima, vol. 11, p.134
50 Ibid.
51 Ibid., p.145
52 Ibid., p.146
53 Ibid., p.150
54 Ibid., p.155
55 *Letters*, vol. 5, p.151 n5
56 Ibid., p.151
57 Ibid., p.221
58 Fyodor Dostoievsky, *Crime and Punishment* (trans. David McDuff), p.114
59 Vailima, vol. 11, pp.133–4
60 G.K. Chesterton, *Robert Louis Stevenson* (London,1927)
61 Hammerton, p.77
62 *Letters*, vol. 5, p.121
63 Adelaide Boodle, *RLS and his Sine Qua Non* (London, 1926), p.42
64 Ibid., p.11
65 *Letters*, vol. 5, p.339

10 : THE DREAMER

1 *Letters*, vol. 5, p.126
2 Richard Little Purdy and Michael Millgate (eds), *The Collected Letters of Thomas Hardy* (Oxford, 1978–88), pp.146–7
3 MS Yale, B3782
4 Hammerton, p.318

5 NLS, MS9895, 157v–158v
6 *Portrait*, p.63
7 Ibid., p.64
8 Ibid., pp.64, 65
9 Ibid., pp.66–7
10 *Letters*, vol. 5, p.216
11 Hammerton, pp.84–5
12 Vailima, vol. 12, p.249
13 Ibid., p.238
14 Ibid., pp.246–7
15 Ibid.
16 Tusitala, vol. 5, p.xvi
17 Maixner, p.200
18 Vailima, vol. 7, p.426
19 Ibid., pp.429–30
20 Ibid., p.432
21 Herbert M. Schueller and Robert L. Peters, *The Letters of J.A. Symonds* (Detroit, 1967–69), vol. 3, pp.120–1
22 C.C. Abbott (ed.), *Letters of G.M. Hopkins to Robert Bridges* (Oxford, 1955), p.236
23 Elaine Showalter, *Sexual Anarchy: Gender and Culture at the Fin de Siècle* (New York, 1990; London, 1991), pp.107, 110
24 Wayne Koestenbaum, *Double Talk: The Erotics of Male Literary Collaboration* (New York and London, 1989), p.147
25 Karl Miller, *Doubles: Studies in Literary History* (Oxford, 1985), p.216
26 Robert Mighall (ed.), *The Strange Case of Dr Jekyll and Mr Hyde and Other Tales of Terror* (London, 2002), p.160
27 Ibid., p.155
28 *Letters*, vol. 6, p.56
29 Vailima, vol. 7, p.366
30 Jorge Luis Borges, *Selected Non-Fictions*, ed. Eliot Weinberger (London, 1999), p.260
31 Daniel Balderston, 'Borges's Frame of Reference: The Strange Case of Robert Louis Stevenson' (Princeton University PhD thesis, 1981), p.332
32 MS Yale, B3828
33 Balfour, vol. 2, pp.17–18
34 In *Robert Louis Stevenson and Romantic Tradition* (Princeton, 1966)
35 *Letters*, vol. 5, p.130
36 Vailima, vol. 12, p.355
37 *Letters*, vol. 5, p.404
38 Wayne Koestenbaum, *Double Talk* (New York and London, 1989), p.145
39 *Letters*, vol. 5, p.182
40 See facsimile in Barry Menikoff's edition of *Kidnapped* (San Marino, Cal., 1999)
41 Ibid., p.216
42 Ibid., pp.46, 64
43 *Collected Poems*, pp.71–2
44 *Letters*, vol. 6, p.48
45 *Letters*, vol. 5, p.236
46 Ibid., p.246
47 MS Yale, vault Stevenson, box 2, vol 4, folder D
48 *Letters*, vol. 5, p.138
49 Ibid., p.390
50 *Portrait*, p.70
51 Ibid., pp.70, 68
52 MS Yale, vault Stevenson, box 8, folder 120
53 *Collected Poems*, p.282. The published poem represents the last six lines of a much longer, unpublished work
54 Flora Masson, *Victorians All* (Edinburgh, 1931), p.107
55 *Letters*, vol. 5, p.418
56 FS to MIS, 23 June 1887, MS Silverado, partly published in *Letters*, vol. 5, pp.428–9
57 *Letters*, vol. 5, p.445
58 Ibid., p.443

11 : BELOW ZERO

1 Tusitala, vol. 33, p.141
2 *Letters*, vol. 6, p.5
3 SC to Edmund Gosse, 17 August 1887, BL Ashley 5057
4 *From Saranac*, p.4
5 Ibid.
6 *Letters*, vol. 6, p.6
7 *From Saranac*, p.6
8 *Letters*, vol. 6, p.17
9 *Portrait*, p.77
10 W.H. Low, *A Chronicle of*

Friendships 1873-1900 (London, 1908), p.372

11 Hammerton, p.85

12 MS Bancroft, Edgar M. Kahn, 'Some Aspects of Robert Louis Stevenson' (1955), p.4

13 S.S. McClure, *My Autobiography* (London, 1914), p.188

14 *Letters*, vol. 6, p.103

15 Ibid., p.18

16 Baxter Letters, p.178

17 Elsie Noble Caldwell, *Last Witness for Robert Louis Stevenson* (Norman, Oklahoma, 1960), p.12

18 Alan E. Guttmacher and J.R. Callahan, 'Did Robert Louis Stevenson Have Hereditary Hemorrhagic Telangiectasia?', *American Journal of Medical Genetics*, 91 (2000)

19 MIS, unpublished diary, 30 January 1868, MS Yale, B 7304

20 Edward L. Trudeau, *Autobiography* (Philadelphia, 1916)

21 *Portrait*, p.74

22 Ibid., p.75

23 Vailima, vol. 14, pp.15-16

24 Ibid., pp.360-1

25 *Letters*, vol. 6, p.277

26 It is printed as a footnote in ibid., p.99

27 S.S. McClure, *My Autobiography* (London, 1914), pp.193-4

28 *Letters*, vol. 6, p.129 n1

29 Ibid., p.172

30 Ibid.

31 Baxter Letters, p.202

32 *Letters*, vol. 6, p.130

33 Ibid., pp.132-4

34 Ibid., p.147

35 Ibid., p.136

36 Ibid., p.169

37 Ibid., p.168

38 Published in ibid., pp.163-5

39 Ibid., pp.164-5

40 Ibid., p.182

41 Ibid., p.167

42 Ibid., p.176

43 Ibid., p.177

44 RLS to Will Low, April 1887, *Letters*, vol. 5, p.394

45 *From Saranac*, p.26

46 *Letters*, vol. 6, p.38

47 Ibid., p.65

48 *Portrait*, p.80

49 S.S. McClure, *My Autobiography* (London, 1914), p188

50 FS to RLS, San Francisco, 1888, MS Yale, vault Stevenson, 3744

12 : ONA

1 Arthur Johnstone, *Recollections of Robert Louis Stevenson in the Pacific* (London, 1905), p.18

2 *From Saranac*, p.53

3 Ibid., pp.67-8

4 *Letters*, vol. 2, p.145

5 Justin Kaplan, *Mr Clemens and Mark Twain* (London, 1967), p.388

6 *Letters*, vol. 6, p.206 n2

7 *From Saranac*, p.61

8 *Letters*, vol. 6, p.276

9 Arthur Johnstone, *Recollections of Robert Louis Stevenson in the Pacific* (London, 1905), p.23

10 Ibid., p.19

11 Vailima, vol. 16, p.15

12 Ibid., p.16

13 Ibid., p.19

14 *From Saranac*, p.76

15 Vailima, vol. 16, p.19

16 Ibid., p.25

17 Ibid., p.20

18 *From Saranac*, p.81

19 Ibid., p.83

20 Ibid., p.154

21 Ibid., p.115

22 Vailima, vol. 16, p.62

23 Ibid., p.44

24 Ibid., p.184

25 Ibid., p.26

26 11 January 1892, quoted in John Connell, *W.E. Henley* (London, 1949), pp.234-5

27 *The Works of W.E. Henley* (London, 1908), vol. 1, pp.181-2

28 Ibid., p.229

29 FS to SC, 4 December 1888, quoted in *Letters*, vol. 6, p.229

30 *From Saranac*, 6 November

31 *Letters*, vol. 6, p.221

32 Arthur Johnstone, *Recollections of*

Robert Louis Stevenson in the
Pacific (London, 1905), p.46
33 Ibid.
34 Letters, vol. 6, p.243
35 Ibid., p.293
36 Ibid., pp.285–6
37 Ibid., p.296
38 Ibid., p.265n
39 Field, p.231
40 Letters, vol. 6, p.249
41 ICR, p.212
42 Letters, vol. 6, p.311
43 ICR, p.222
44 Letters, vol. 6, p.311
45 Ibid., pp.334–5
46 Vailima, vol. 16, p.270
47 Ibid., pp.275–6
48 Ibid., p.312
49 Ibid., pp.279–80
50 Ibid.
51 Ibid., p.345
52 Ibid., p.347
53 Letters, vol. 6, p.303
54 Ibid.
55 Vailima, vol. 16, p.359
56 Ibid., p.368
57 Letters, vol. 6, p.329
58 Ibid.
59 Herbert M. Schueller and Robert L.
Peters, The Letters of J.A. Symonds
(Detroit, 1967–69), vol. 3, p.410
60 See Maixner, p.354
61 Ibid., p.360
62 Ibid., p.335
63 Letters, vol. 6, p.330
64 Vailima, vol. 17, pp.597–8
65 Ibid.
66 Ibid., pp.170–1
67 Balfour, vol. 2, pp.33–4
68 Vailima, vol. 17, p.297
69 Ibid., p.555
70 Ibid., pp.402–3
71 Ibid., p.405
72 Portrait, p.112

13 : TUSI TALA

1 W.E. Clarke, Reminiscences of
Robert Louis Stevenson (London
Missionary Society pamphlet, n.d.)
2 ICR, p.224
3 See Mehew's notes on both

companies in Letters, vol. 6,
pp. 251 n3 and 346 n4
4 Ibid., p.251
5 Ibid., p.381
6 J.W. Davidson, Samoa mo Samoa:
The Emergence of the Independent
State of Western Samoa
(Melbourne, 1967), p.96
7 H.J. Moors, With Stevenson in
Samoa (London, 1911), p.2
8 Letters, vol. 6, p.381
9 Colvin, p.145
10 Evan Charteris (ed.), The Life and
Letters of Sir Edmund Gosse
(London, 1931), pp.232–3
11 Colvin, p.149
12 Letters, vol. 6, p.373
13 Ibid.
14 Vailima, vol. 15, pp.481–2
15 Ibid., p.488
16 Field, p.243
17 San Francisco Examiner, 17 May
1890, quoted in Letters, vol. 6,
p.420 n3
18 Reprinted in H.W. Kent, Dr Hyde
and Mr Stevenson (Rutland, Vt,
1973), Appendix E
19 Letters, vol. 6, p.376
20 Ibid., p.409
21 Fanny Vandegrift Stevenson, The
Cruise of the Janet Nichol (London,
1915), p.2
22 Letters, vol. 6, p.388
23 Ibid., p.403
24 Ibid., p.389
25 Ibid., p.398
26 Letters, vol. 7, p.80
27 Ibid., p.15
28 Ibid., p.24
29 Ibid., p.22
30 ICR, p.265
31 Fanny and Robert Louis Stevenson,
Our Samoan Adventure, ed.
Charles Neider (London, 1956),
p.61
32 J.C. Levenson, Ernest Samuels et al.
(eds), The Letters of Henry Adams
(Cambridge, Mass. and London,
1982–88), vol. 3, pp.296–7
33 Ibid., pp.851–2
34 Letters, vol. 7, p.27
35 Ibid., p.26

36 *Collected Poems*, p.195
37 *Letters*, vol. 7, pp.18, 20
38 Ibid., p.20
39 Ibid., p.28
40 Ibid., pp.93–4
41 *The Complete Letters of Oscar Wilde*, ed. Merlin Holland and Rupert Hart-Davis, pp.789–90
42 *Letters*, vol. 7, p.24
43 Ibid., p.93
44 Ibid., p.53
45 Ibid., p.60
46 See WH to CB, 17 September 1891, Baxter Letters, p.285
47 Ibid.
48 *Letters*, vol. 7, p.88
49 Maixner, p.372
50 Gosse to G.A. Armour, 31 January 1891, Evan Charteris (ed.), *The Life and Letters of Sir Edmund Gosse* (London, 1931), p.225
51 *Letters*, vol. 7, p.115
52 S.S. McClure to RLS, early 1891, quoted in Swearingen, p.142
53 *Letters*, vol. 7, p.102
54 H.J. Moors, *With Stevenson in Samoa* (London, 1911), p.44
55 *Letters*, vol. 8, p.155
56 *Letters*, vol. 7, p.161
57 Barry Menikoff, *Robert Louis Stevenson and 'The Beach of Falesá': A Study in Victorian Publishing* (Edinburgh, 1984), p.119
58 Ibid., p.123
59 Ibid., p.124
60 Clement Shorter, *Letters to an Editor* (1914), p. iv; quoted in Swearingen, p.154
61 *Letters*, vol. 7, p.231
62 Ibid., pp.284, 311
63 Austin Strong to GB, 29 June 1925, NLS Balfour, 9896
64 Field, p.253
65 Hammerton, p.110
66 Fanny and Robert Louis Stevenson, *Our Samoan Adventure*, ed. Charles Neider (London, 1956), p.100
67 Field, p.256
68 CB to RLS, 17 September 1891, quoted in Baxter Letters, p.284 n8
69 *Letters*, vol. 7, p.246
70 Ibid., p.253
71 Ibid., p.198
72 Ibid., p.202
73 H.J. Moors, *With Stevenson in Samoa* (London, 1911), p.115
74 George L. McKay, *Some Notes on Robert Louis Stevenson, his Finances and his Agents and his Publishers* (New Haven, 1958), p.41
75 Austin Strong to GB, 29 June 1925, NLS Balfour, 9896

14 : THE TAME CELEBRITY

1 *Collected Poems*, p.199
2 *The Works of W.E. Henley* (London, 1908), vol. 1, p.229
3 Evan Charteris (ed.), *The Life and Letters of Sir Edmund Gosse* (London, 1931), p.232
4 Hammerton, p.112
5 Ibid., p.101
6 *Letters*, vol. 7, p.343
7 Quoted in Adam Nicolson, *The Hated Wife: Carrie Kipling 1862–1939* (London, 2001), p.25
8 See Frederick R. Karl, *Joseph Conrad: The Three Lives* (New York, 1979), p.322
9 *Letters*, vol. 7, pp.93, 40
10 *Letters*, vol. 8, p.40
11 *Letters*, vol. 7, p.325
12 Ibid., p.295
13 Ibid., p.345
14 Ibid., p.388
15 *Letters*, vol. 8, pp.44–5
16 Ibid., p.45 n5
17 *Catriona*, Vailima, vol. 10, p.222
18 Ibid., p.202
19 *Letters*, vol. 8, p.193
20 *Catriona*, Chapter XIV, Vailima, vol. 10, p.222
21 *Letters*, vol. 8, p.38
22 *Letters*, vol. 7, p.284
23 Ibid., pp.359–60
24 Ibid., p.365
25 Ibid., p.210
26 Fanny and Robert Louis Stevenson, *Our Samoan Adventure*, ed.

Charles Neider (London, 1956), pp.185–6

27 *Letters*, vol. 7, p.338n
28 Ibid., p.312
29 Ibid., p.382
30 Ibid., pp.195–6
31 SC to RLS, 21 March 1894, quoted in *Letters*, vol. 8, p.279n
32 Ibid., pp.281–2
33 Colvin, pp.148–9
34 Merlin Holland and Rupert Hart-Davis (eds), *The Complete Letters of Oscar Wilde* (London, 2000), p.789
35 Graham Greene, 'From Feathers to Iron', *Collected Essays* (London, 1999), p.63
36 *Letters*, vol. 8, p.68
37 Ibid.
38 Ibid., p.88
39 To S.R. Crockett, ibid., p.77
40 Ibid., pp.68, 70
41 Ibid. and Maixner, p.450
42 Vailima, vol. 18, p.150
43 Vailima, vol. 25, pp.183–7
44 MS Yale, B3809
45 *Letters*, vol. 8, p.40
46 Ibid.
47 Ibid., p.61
48 Fanny and Robert Louis Stevenson, *Our Samoan Adventure*, ed. Charles Neider (London, 1956), p.219
49 Ibid., pp.235–6. I have adjusted the punctuation of the printed version as indicated, as it does not make sense otherwise
50 *Letters*, vol. 8, p.246
51 Ibid., p.217
52 Ibid., p.340
53 Ibid., p.105
54 Ibid., p.44
55 Ibid., p.356 n2
56 For a full account of the genesis, production, reception and significance of the Edinburgh Edition, see Andrew Nash, 'The Dead Should be Protected from their Own Carelessness', *The Culture of Collected Editions* (Basingstoke, 2003), pp.111–27
57 *Collected Poems*, p.300
58 Maixner, p.468
59 Ibid., p.465
60 *Letters*, vol. 8, p.371
61 Vailima, vol. 18, p.244
62 Ibid., pp.376–7
63 Maixner, p.466
64 Ibid., p.462
65 *Letters*, vol. 8, p.408
66 Ibid., p.402
67 Ibid., p.402 n2. Austin only told Graham Balfour this story in 1910
68 Ibid.
69 13 January 1895, Margaret Isabella Stevenson, *Letters from Samoa 1891–95* (London, 1906), p.327
70 Belle Strong's account, *Letters*, vol. 8, p.403
71 Colvin, pp.147–8

POSTSCRIPTS

1 Lloyd Osbourne, 20 Letters to Isobel Field, July–December 1940, MS Bancroft
2 Leon Edel (ed.), Henry James, *Letters* (Cambridge, Mass., 1974–84), vol. 4, p.213
3 Maixner, pp.494–500
4 HJ to GB, 25 November 1901, NLS Balfour, 9895, f5203
5 Ford Madox Ford, *Memories and Impressions* (Harmondsworth, 1971), p.182
6 Frederick R. Karl, *Joseph Conrad: The Three Lives* (New York, 1979), p.438
7 Frederick R. Karl et al. (eds), *Collected Letters of Joseph Conrad* (Cambridge, 1983–2002), vol. 2, p.371
8 HJ to GB, 3 July 1902, NLS Balfour, 9895, f255
9 Leon Edel (ed.), Henry James, *Letters* (Cambridge, Mass., 1974–84), vol. 4, p.241

Select Bibliography

C.C. Abbott (ed.), *Letters of G.M. Hopkins to Robert Bridges* (Oxford, 1955)

Damian Atkinson (ed.), *The Selected Letters of W.E. Henley* (Aldershot, 2000)

Graham Balfour, *The Life of Robert Louis Stevenson* (London and New York, 1901), 2 vols

Bella Bathurst, *The Lighthouse Stevensons* (London, 1999)

Adelaide Boodle, *RLS and his Sine Qua Non* (London, 1926)

Jorge Luis Borges, *Borges on Writing* (London, 1974)

Jorge Luis Borges, *Selected Non-Fictions*, ed. Eliot Weinberger (London, 1999)

George E. Brown, *A Book of RLS* (London, 1919)

Richard Burgin (ed.), *Jorge Luis Borges: Conversations* (Jackson, 1998)

Jenni Calder, *RLS: A Life Study* (London, 1980)

Elsie Noble Caldwell, *Last Witness for Robert Louis Stevenson* (Norman, Oklahoma, 1960)

Evan Charteris (ed.), *The Life and Letters of Sir Edmund Gosse* (London, 1931)

G.K. Chesterton, *Robert Louis Stevenson* (London, 1927)

William B. Churchward, *My Consulate in Samoa* (London, 1887)

W.E. Clarke, *Reminiscences of Robert Louis Stevenson* (London Missionary Society pamphlet, n.d.)

Sidney Colvin, *Memories and Notes* (London, 1921)

Sidney Colvin, *Robert Louis Stevenson: His Work and Personality* (London, 1924)

John Connell, *W.E. Henley* (London, 1949)

David Daiches, *Robert Louis Stevenson, A Re-evaluation* (London, 1946)

J.W. Davidson, *Samoa mo Samoa: The Emergence of the Independent State of Western Samoa* (Melbourne, 1967)

484 ROBERT LOUIS STEVENSON

Davos as Health-Resort: A Handbook (1907)

A. Grove Day (ed.), *Travels in Hawaii* (Honolulu, 1973)

Leon Edel, *The Life of Henry James* (London, 1953–72), 5 vols

Leon Edel (ed.), *The Diary of Alice James* (New York, 1964)

Leon Edel (ed.), Henry James, *Letters* (Cambridge, Mass.,
    1974–84), 4 vols

Edwin M. Eigner, *Robert Louis Stevenson and Romantic Tradition*
    (Princeton, 1966)

Malcolm Elwin, *The Strange Case of Robert Louis Stevenson*
    (London, 1950)

Sir Alfred Ewing, *An Engineer's Outlook* (London, n.d.)

Delancey Ferguson and Marshall Waingrow (eds), *R.L.S.:
    Stevenson's Letters to Charles Baxter* (London and New Haven,
    1956)

Isobel Strong Field, *Memories of Vailima* (1902)

Isobel Strong Field, *This Life I've Loved* (London, 1937)

Ford Madox Ford, *Memories and Impressions* (Harmondsworth,
    1971)

J.C. Furnas, *Voyage to Windward: The Life of Robert Louis
    Stevenson* (London, 1952)

Francis Galton, *Record of Family Faculties: Consisting of Tabular
    Forms and Directions for Entering Data, with an Explanatory
    Preface* (London, 1884)

Carlo Ginzburg, *No Island is an Island: Four Glances at English
    Literature in a World Perspective* (New York, 2000)

Edmund Gosse, *Critical Kit-Kats* (London, 1913)

Graham Greene, *Collected Essays* (London, 1999)

Phyllis Grosskurth (ed.), *The Memoirs of John Addington Symonds*
    (London, 1984)

Charles Guthrie, *Robert Louis Stevenson: Some Personal
    Recollections* (Edinburgh, 1924)

J.A. Hammerton (ed.), *Stevensoniana: An Anecdotal Life and
    Appreciation of Robert Louis Stevenson* (Edinburgh, 1907)

J.R. Hammond, *A Robert Louis Stevenson Companion* (London,
    1984)

J.R. Hammond, *A Robert Louis Stevenson Chronology*
    (Basingstoke, 1997)

James D. Hart (ed.), *From Scotland to Silverado* (Cambridge, Mass.,
    1966)

The Works of W.E. Henley (London, 1908), 7 vols

[George Herbert, 13th Earl of Pembroke, and George H. Kingsley], *South Sea Bubbles by the Earl and the Doctor* (Leipzig, 1874)

Merlin Holland and Rupert Hart-Davis (eds), *The Complete Letters of Oscar Wilde* (London, 2000)

Richard Holmes, *Footsteps: Adventures of a Romantic Biographer* (London, 1985)

W.E. Houghton, *The Victorian Frame of Mind, 1830–1870* (New Haven, 1957)

Linda K. Hughes, *Strange Bedfellows: W.E. Henley and Feminist Fashion History* (Bicester, 1997)

Anne Roller Issler, *Happier for his Presence: San Francisco and Robert Louis Stevenson* (Palo Alto, 1949)

Anne Roller Issler, *Our Mountain Hermitage: Silverado and Robert Louis Stevenson* (Palo Alto, 1950)

Michael Jacobs, *The Good and Simple Life: Artist Colonies in Europe and America* (Oxford, 1985)

Henry James, 'Robert Louis Stevenson', in *Notes on Novelists* (London, 1914)

Arthur Johnstone, *Recollections of Robert Louis Stevenson in the Pacific* (London, 1905)

Frederick R. Karl, *Joseph Conrad: The Three Lives* (New York, 1979)

Frederick R. Karl et al. (eds), *Collected Letters of Joseph Conrad* (Cambridge, 1983–2002), 6 vols

H.W. Kent, *Dr Hyde and Mr Stevenson: The Life of the Reverend Charles Ewen Hyde* (Rutland, Vt, 1973)

Wayne Koestenbaum, *Double Talk: The Erotics of Male Literary Collaboration* (New York and London, 1989)

Andrew Lang, *Adventures Among Books* (London, 1903)

Alexandra Lapierre (trans. Carol Cosman), *Fanny Stevenson: Muse, Adventuress and Romantic Enigma* (London, 1995)

J.C. Levenson, Ernest Samuels et al. (eds), *The Letters of Henry Adams* (Cambridge, Mass. and London, 1982–88), 6 vols

W.G. Lockett, *Robert Louis Stevenson at Davos* (London, 1934)

W.H. Low, *A Chronicle of Friendships 1873–1900* (London, 1908)

E.V. Lucas (ed.), *Her Infinite Variety* (London, 1908)

E.V. Lucas, *The Colvins and their Friends* (London, 1928)

E.V. Lucas, *Reading, Writing and Remembering: A Literary Record* (London, 1932)

S.S. McClure, *My Autobiography* (London, 1914)

J.A. MacCulloch, *Robert Louis Stevenson and the Bridge of Allan* (1927)

Sr Martha Mary McGaw, *Stevenson in Hawaii* (Honolulu, 1950)

George L. McKay (compiler), *A Stevenson Library. Catalogue of a Collection of Writings by and about Robert Louis Stevenson Formed by Edwin J. Beinecke* (New Haven, 1951–64), 6 vols

George L. McKay, *Some Notes on Robert Louis Stevenson, his Finances and his Agents and his Publishers* (New Haven, 1958)

Margaret Mackay, *Island Boy: Robert Louis Stevenson and his Step-Grandson in Samoa* (London, 1969)

Margaret Mackay, *The Violent Friend: The Story of Mrs Robert Louis Stevenson 1840–1914* (London, 1969)

Moray McLaren, *Stevenson and Edinburgh, A Centenary Study* (London, 1950)

Frank McLynn, *Robert Louis Stevenson: A Biography* (London, 1993)

Paul Maixner (ed.), *Robert Louis Stevenson: The Critical Heritage* (London, 1981)

Flora Masson, *Victorians All* (Edinburgh, 1931)

Rosaline Masson (ed.), *I Can Remember Robert Louis Stevenson* (Edinburgh, 1925)

Barry Menikoff, *Robert Louis Stevenson and 'The Beach of Falesá': A Study in Victorian Publishing* (Edinburgh, 1984)

Barry Menikoff (ed.), *Kidnapped, or the Lad with the Silver Button* (San Marino, Cal., 1999)

Robert Mighall (ed.), *The Strange Case of Dr Jekyll and Mr Hyde and Other Tales of Terror* (London, 2002)

Karl Miller, *Doubles: Studies in Literary History* (Oxford, 1985)

D.G. Moir, *Pentland Walks: Their Literary and Historical Associations* (Edinburgh, 1977)

George Monteiro (ed.), *The Correspondence of Henry James and Henry Adams* (Baton Rouge, 1992)

H.J. Moors, *With Stevenson in Samoa* (London, 1911)

Roy Nickerson, *Robert Louis Stevenson in California: A Remarkable Courtship* (San Francisco, 1982)

Adam Nicolson, *The Hated Wife: Carrie Kipling 1862–1939* (London, 2001)

Andrew Noble (ed.), *From the Clyde to California: Robert Louis Stevenson's Emigrant Journey* (Aberdeen, 1985)

Lloyd Osbourne, *An Intimate Portrait of R.L.S.* (New York, 1924)

Hesketh Pearson, *Beerbohm Tree: His Life and Laughter* (London, 1988)

Arthur Wing Pinero, *Robert Louis Stevenson: The Dramatist*, a lecture with an introduction by Clayton Hamilton (New York, 1914)

W.F. Prideaux (revised Livingston), *A Bibliography of the Works of Robert Louis Stevenson* (London, 1918)

[Walter Pringle], *The Memoirs of Walter Pringle of Greenknow*, ed. W. Wood (Edinburgh, 1847)

Richard Little Purdy and Michael Millgate (eds), *The Collected Letters of Thomas Hardy* (Oxford, 1978–88), 5 vols

Graham Robb, *Strangers: Homosexual Love in the Nineteenth Century* (London, 2003)

Nellie Vandegrift Sanchez, *The Life of Mrs Robert Louis Stevenson* (1920)

Alan Sandison, *Robert Louis Stevenson and the Appearance of Modernism* (London, 1996)

Herbert M. Schueller and Robert L. Peters, *The Letters of J.A. Symonds* (Detroit, 1967–69), 3 vols

Marcel Schwob, *Oeuvres* (Paris, 2002)

Elaine Showalter, *Sexual Anarchy: Gender and Culture at the Fin de Siècle* (New York, 1990; London, 1991)

Eve Blantyre Simpson, *Robert Louis Stevenson* (Boston and London, 1906)

Robert T. Skinner (ed.), *Cummy's Diary: A Diary Kept by Robert Louis Stevenson's Nurse Alison Cunningham While Travelling with him on the Continent During 1863* (London, 1926)

Janet Adam Smith, *Henry James and Robert Louis Stevenson: A Record of Friendship and Criticism* (London, 1948)

Susan Sontag, *Illness as Metaphor* and *Aids and its Metaphors* (London, 1991)

Fanny Vandegrift Stevenson, *The Cruise of the Janet Nichol* (London, 1915)

Fanny and Robert Louis Stevenson, *Our Samoan Adventure*, ed. Charles Neider (London, 1956)

Margaret Isabella Stevenson, *From Saranac to the Marquesas and Beyond* (London, 1903)

Margaret Isabella Stevenson, *Letters from Samoa 1891–95* (London, 1906)

Robert Stevenson, *Account of the Bell Rock Lighthouse, Including the Details of the Erection and Peculiar Structure of that Edifice* (Edinburgh, n.d.)

Robert Louis Stevenson, Collected Works, Vailima Edition (London, 1923), 26 vols

Robert Louis Stevenson, *Collected Poems*, ed. Janet Adam Smith (London and New York, second edition 1971)

Robert Louis Stevenson, *The Lantern-Bearers and Other Essays*, ed. Jeremy Treglown (London, 1988)

Robert Louis Stevenson, *The Collected Shorter Fiction*, ed. Peter Stoneley (London, 1991)

Robert Louis Stevenson, *Essays and Poems*, ed. Claire Harman (London, 1992)

Robert Louis Stevenson, *The Complete Short Stories*, ed. Ian Bell (Edinburgh, 1993)

'A Layman' [Thomas Stevenson], *The Immutable Laws of Nature in Relation to God's Providence* (Edinburgh and London, 1868)

Thomas Stevenson, *Christianity Confirmed by Jewish and Heathen Testimony and Deductions from Physical Science* (Edinburgh, 1877)

Roger G. Swearingen, *The Prose Writings of Robert Louis Stevenson: A Guide* (London, 1980)

Robert Taylor, *Saranac: America's Magic Mountain* (Boston, 1986)

Una Taylor, *Guests and Memories: Annals of a Seaside Villa* (Oxford, 1924)

R.C. Terry (ed.), *Robert Louis Stevenson: Interviews and Recollections* (Basingstoke, 1995)

Ann Thwaite, *Edmund Gosse: A Literary Landscape* (Oxford, 1985)

Edward L.Trudeau, *Autobiography* (Philadelphia, 1916)

Mark Twain, *Roughing It* (Mark Twain Library edition, Berkeley, 1995)

Robert Mackenzie Watson, *History of Samoa* (Wellington, 1908)

Roderick Watson (ed.), *Robert Louis Stevenson, Shorter Scottish Fiction* (Edinburgh, 1995)

J. Weber, *Davos* (Zurich and London, c.1880)

Margaret B. Wright, 'Bohemian Days', *Scribner's Monthly*, vol. 16 (May 1878), pp.121–9

Articles and Essays About Stevenson

Scott Ashley, 'Primitivism, Celticism and Morbidity in the Atlantic fin de siècle', *Symbolism, Decadence and the Fin de Siècle: French and European Perspectives*, ed. P. McGuinness (Exeter, 2000)

Daniel Balderston, 'Borges's Frame of Reference: The Strange Case of Robert Louis Stevenson' (Princeton University PhD thesis, 1981)

Hilary J. Beattie, 'Father and Son: The Origins of the Strange Case of Dr Jekyll and Mr Hyde', *Psychoanalytic Study of the Child*, 56 (2001), pp.317–60

Alexander Clunas, 'Robert Louis Stevenson: Precursor of the Post-Moderns?', *Cencrastus*, 6 (1981), pp.9–11

Alan E. Guttmacher and J.R. Callahan, 'Did Robert Louis Stevenson Have Hereditary Hemorrhagic Telangiectasia?', *American Journal of Medical Genetics*, 91 (2000)

Stephen Heath, 'Psychopathia Sexualis: Stevenson's Strange Case', *Critical Quarterly*, 28 (1986), pp.93–108

Edgar C. Knowlton, 'A Russian Influence on Stevenson', *Modern Philology*, vol. XIV, no. 8 (December 1916), pp.449–54

Vladimir Nabokov, 'The Strange Case of Dr Jekyll and Mr Hyde', *Lectures on Literature*, ed. Fredson Bowers (London, 1980), pp.179–205

Andrew Nash, ' "The Dead Should be Protected from Their Own Carelessness": Collected Editions of Robert Louis Stevenson 1894–1924', *The Culture of Collected Editions* (Basingstoke, 2003), pp.111–27

Julia Reid, 'Robert Louis Stevenson and the Evolutionary Science' (St Anne's College, University of Oxford, D.Phil thesis, 2002)

Belinda Thomson, 'A Frenchman and a Scot in the South Seas', *Van Gogh Museum Journal* (2003), pp.57–70

See also the extensive reading lists, filmography and databases at www.unibg.it/rls

Index